"Some books are different—the content can't be Googled from the Internet, the authors have real-life experiences to share, the code can be used in real-world projects. This is one of those books. And it's not a simple upgrade of the 1st edition; this book has been completely refitted to present WinForms 2.0 as it should be presented."

—*Neal Myrddin, Independent Developer*

"Chris and Michael nail the soul of Windows Forms 2.0. This book provides an insightful view into the design of Windows Forms and the integration of new 2.0 features. It is just as applicable for the first-time Windows Forms programmer as the seasoned line of business developer. The What's New in 2.0 appendix is worth the price of admission alone."

—*Mike Harsh, Windows Forms Program Manager, Microsoft, Inc.*

"This book takes an amazingly broad and deep technology, and breaks it into manageable pieces that are easily consumed. You cannot survive building a complex WinForms application without this book."

—*Ryan Dorrell, Chief Technology Officer, AgileThought*

"*Windows Forms 2.0 Programming* offers something for every .NET developer. Experienced developers will appreciate the in-depth coverage of new 2.0 features, including the most comprehensive coverage of ClickOnce deployment, multithreading, and the new designer integration found anywhere. Developers new to Winforms programming will appreciate the coverage of the fundamentals all Winforms developers need to know. Whether you're an experienced WinForms developer or just beginning, you need this book."

—*Fritz Onion, cofounder of Pluralsight, author of* Essential ASP.NET, *and ASP.NET MVP*

"I don't want just a description of the WinForms widgets. I can get that online or from other books. What I want is a roadmap for pitfalls to avoid, and innovative solutions for common problems. That is where this book shines. All of us who found the first edition of this book to be an indispensible part of our reference library will appreciate this updated edition that describes WinForms 2.0."

—*Johan Ericsson, Software Engineer, Agilent Technologies*

"The books Chris Sells writes are always insightful and this newest addition is no different. This book in particular is for those who want to understand not just the flashy surface of Windows Forms 2.0, but also how it fits into the .NET environment. Readers will have this book at their desks, not stuck on their shelves, for quite a long time."

—*Yoshimatsu Fumiaki, Software Engineer based in Tokyo Japan*

"Chris and Mike have done an excellent job presenting the information you need to be successful with Windows Forms."

—*Jessica Fosler, Dev Tech Lead, Microsoft*

"This book is the 'must have' teaching and reference book for WinForms 2.0."

—*Jim Rittenhouse, Senior Software Engineer, Siemens*

Windows Forms 2.0 Programming

Microsoft .NET Development Series

John Montgomery, *Series Advisor*
Don Box, *Series Advisor*
Martin Heller, *Series Editor*

The Microsoft .NET Development Series is supported and developed by the leaders and experts of Microsoft development technologies including Microsoft architects and DevelopMentor instructors. The books in this series provide a core resource of information and understanding every developer needs in order to write effective applications and managed code. Learn from the leaders how to maximize your use of the .NET Framework and its programming languages.

Titles in the Series

Brad Abrams, *.NET Framework Standard Library Annotated Reference Volume 1: Base Class Library and Extended Numerics Library*, 0-321-15489-4

Brad Abrams and Tamara Abrams, *.NET Framework Standard Library Annotated Reference, Volume 2: Networking Library, Reflection Library, and XML Library*, 0-321-19445-4

Keith Ballinger, *.NET Web Services: Architecture and Implementation*, 0-321-11359-4

Bob Beauchemin and Dan Sullivan, *A Developer's Guide to SQL Server 2005*, 0-321-38218-8

Bob Beauchemin, Niels Berglund, Dan Sullivan, *A First Look at SQL Server 2005 for Developers*, 0-321-18059-3

Don Box with Chris Sells, *Essential .NET, Volume 1: The Common Language Runtime*, 0-201-73411-7

Keith Brown, *The .NET Developer's Guide to Windows Security*, 0-321-22835-9

Eric Carter and Eric Lippert, *Visual Studio Tools for Office: Using C# with Excel, Word, Outlook, and InfoPath*, 0-321-33488-4

Eric Carter and Eric Lippert, *Visual Studio Tools for Office: Using Visual Basic 2005 with Excel, Word, Outlook, and InfoPath*, 0-321-41175-7

Mahesh Chand, *Graphics Programming with GDI+*, 0-321-16077-0

Krzysztof Cwalina and Brad Abrams, *Framework Design Guidelines: Conventions, Idioms, and Patterns for Reusable .NET Libraries*, 0-321-24675-6

Len Fenster, *Effective Use of Microsoft Enterprise Library: Building Blocks for Creating Enterprise Applications and Services*, 0-321-33421-3

Sam Guckenheimer and Juan J. Perez, *Software Engineering with Microsoft Visual Studio Team System*, 0-321-27872-0

Anders Hejlsberg, Scott Wiltamuth, Peter Golde, *The C# Programming Language*, Second Edition, 0-321-33443-4

Alex Homer, Dave Sussman, Mark Fussell, *ADO.NET and System.Xml v. 2.0—The Beta Version*, 0-321-24712-4

Alex Homer and Dave Sussman, *ASP.NET 2.0 Illustrated*, 0-321-41834-4

Alex Homer, Dave Sussman, Rob Howard, *ASP.NET v. 2.0—The Beta Version*, 0-321-25727-8

Joe Kaplan and Ryan Dunn, *The .NET Developer's Guide to Directory Services Programming*, 0-321-35017-0

Mark Michaelis, *Essential C# 2.0*, 0-321-15077-5

James S. Miller and Susann Ragsdale, *The Common Language Infrastructure Annotated Standard*, 0-321-15493-2

Christian Nagel, *Enterprise Services with the .NET Framework: Developing Distributed Business Solutions with .NET Enterprise Services*, 0-321-24673-X

Brian Noyes, *Data Binding with Windows Forms 2.0: Programming Smart Client Data Applications with .NET*, 0-321-26892-X

Fritz Onion, *Essential ASP.NET with Examples in C#*, 0-201-76040-1

Fritz Onion, *Essential ASP.NET with Examples in Visual Basic .NET*, 0-201-76039-8

Ted Pattison and Dr. Joe Hummel, *Building Applications and Components with Visual Basic .NET*, 0-201-73495-8

Dr. Neil Roodyn, *eXtreme .NET: Introducing eXtreme Programming Techniques to .NET Developers*, 0-321-30363-6

Chris Sells and Michael Weinhardt, *Windows Forms 2.0 Programming*, 0-321-26796-6

Chris Sells, *Windows Forms Programming in C#*, 0-321-11620-8

Chris Sells and Justin Gehtland, *Windows Forms Programming in Visual Basic .NET*, 0-321-12519-3

Guy Smith-Ferrier, *.NET Internationalization: The Developer's Guide to Building Global Windows and Web Applications*, 0-321-34138-4

Paul Vick, *The Visual Basic .NET Programming Language*, 0-321-16951-4

Damien Watkins, Mark Hammond, Brad Abrams, *Programming in the .NET Environment*, 0-201-77018-0

Shawn Wildermuth, *Pragmatic ADO.NET: Data Access for the Internet World*, 0-201-74568-2

Paul Yao and David Durant, *.NET Compact Framework Programming with C#*, 0-321-17403-8

Paul Yao and David Durant, *.NET Compact Framework Programming with Visual Basic .NET*, 0-321-17404-6

For more information go to www.awprofessional.com/msdotnetseries/

Windows
Forms 2.0
Programming

Chris Sells and
Michael Weinhardt

✦✦Addison-Wesley

Upper Saddle River, NJ • Boston • Indianapolis • San Francisco
New York • Toronto • Montreal • London • Munich • Paris • Madrid
Cape Town • Sydney • Tokyo • Singapore • Mexico City

Many of the designations used by manufacturers and sellers to distinguish their products are claimed as trademarks. Where those designations appear in this book, and the publisher was aware of a trademark claim, the designations have been printed with initial capital letters or in all capitals.

The .NET logo is either a registered trademark or trademark of Microsoft Corporation in the United States and/or other countries and is used under license from Microsoft. The following articles were originally printed in *MSDN Magazine*, and are reprinted in this book with permission. ".NET Zero Deployment: Security and Versioning Models in the Windows Forms Engine Help You Create and Deploy Smart Clients" by Chris Sells, *MSDN Magazine*, July 2002. "Visual Studio .NET: Building Windows Forms Controls and Components with Rich Design-Time Features" by Michael Weinhardt and Chris Sells, *MSDN Magazine*, April 2003. "Visual Studio .NET: Building Windows Forms Controls and Components with Rich Design-Time Features, Part 2" by Michael Weinhardt and Chris Sells, *MSDN Magazine*, May 2003. ".NET Framework 2.0: Craft a Rich UI for Your .NET App with Enhanced Windows Forms Support" by Michael Weinhardt and Chris Sells, *MSDN Magazine*, May 2004. "Smart Tags: Simplify UI Development with Custom Designer Actions in Visual Studio" by Michael Weinhardt, *MSDN Magazine*, July 2005. "Draft a Rich UI: Ground Rules for Building Enhanced Windows Forms Support into Your .NET App" by Michael Weinhardt and Chris Sells, *MSDN Magazine*, May 2005.

The authors and publisher have taken care in the preparation of this book, but make no expressed or implied warranty of any kind and assume no responsibility for errors or omissions. No liability is assumed for incidental or consequential damages in connection with or arising out of the use of the information or programs contained herein.

The publisher offers excellent discounts on this book when ordered in quantity for bulk purchases or special sales, which may include electronic versions and/or custom covers and content particular to your business, training goals, marketing focus, and branding interests. For more information, please contact:

U.S. Corporate and Government Sales
(800) 382-3419
corpsales@pearsontechgroup.com

For sales outside the United States please contact:

International Sales
international@pearsoned.com

 The Safari® Enabled icon on the cover of your favorite technology book means the book is available through Safari Bookshelf. When you buy this book, you get free access to the online edition for 45 days. Safari Bookshelf is an electronic reference library that lets you easily search thousands of technical books, find code samples, download chapters, and access technical information whenever and wherever you need it.

To gain 45-day Safari Enabled access to this book:

- Go to http://www.awprofessional.com/safarienabled
- Complete the brief registration form
- Enter the coupon code FMEI-8X3G-CYPK-IXF2-62A

If you have difficulty registering on Safari Bookshelf or accessing the online edition, please e-mail customer-service@safaribooksonline.com.

Visit us on the Web: www.awprofessional.com

Library of Congress Cataloging-in-Publication Data:
Sells, Chris.
    Windows Forms 2.0 programming/Chris Sells & Michael Weinhardt.
        p. cm.
    ISBN 0-321-26796-6 (pbk. : alk. paper)
1. Microsoft .NET Framework. 2. Computer software—Development. I. Weinhardt, Michael. II. Title.

    QA76.76.M52S44 2006
    005.2'768—dc22

2006000194

ISBN 0-3212-6796-6

Text printed in the United States on recycled paper at Edwards Brothers in Ann Arbor, Michigan
Second printing, February 2009

To my wife, Melissa, and my sons John and Tom. They define the heaven that exceeds my grasp. And to my parents, who made me a reader from the beginning and who passed on the secret writer gene, much to my surprise.

—Chris Sells

To Josef and Lili, for all that I am and all that I've done. To Alex, for all that I would like to be and wish I could do.

—Michael Weinhardt

Contents

About the Authors

Chris Sells is a program manager for the Connected Systems Division. He's written several books, including *Programming Windows Presentation Foundation* (O'Reilly), *Windows Forms Programming in C#* (Addison-Wesley), and *ATL Internals* (Addison-Wesley). In his free time, Chris hosts various conferences and makes a pest of himself on Microsoft internal product team discussion lists. More information about Chris—and his various projects—is available at http://www.sellsbrothers.com.

Michael Weinhardt is a programmer/writer at Microsoft, working on the Windows Client SDK. Michael has coauthored a variety of articles with Chris, contributed to the "Wonders of Windows Forms" column at MSDN Online, reviewed several Windows technology books, and generally loves communicating the whys and wherefores of technology to his peers. Michael is sure that his parents attribute his fascination in technology to their purchase of an Amiga 1000 in the mid-80s. They would be right.

Foreword

A LONG, LONG TIME AGO when I began programming PC GUIs, there were none of these fancy framework thingies. One wrote a whole lot of C code in a case statement long enough to cut a giant's undershirt out of. I'd spent a couple weeks understanding and implementing DDE (yes, DDE) in the application we were building (and frankly, it was not the most pleasant experience) when I ran across an article in a magazine showing how this fancy thing called "Smalltalk" could do DDE in a couple of lines of code. *Wow!* I thought. *That's the way I want to program!* I've been working with and on UI frameworks pretty much ever since, which is how I ended up working on Windows Forms at Microsoft.

For V1 of Windows Forms, our goal was to produce a comprehensive UI framework that combined the ease of use of VB with the extensibility and flexibility of MFC. Along the way, we picked up additional goals, including rich design-time extensibility, GDI+ support, and support for partial trust for No Touch Deployment (NTD). I think we did a reasonable job of meeting these goals. Despite the focus on the "web stuff" when we first released, there are an enormous number of people using Windows Forms today to build all types of applications, from photo management software to applications supporting core business processes. I find seeing the interesting applications people build with Windows Forms one of the more rewarding parts of my job. However, to be honest, there are areas where we could have done better—for example, NTD had no Visual Studio support and could be complex to debug when things went wrong—so overall, I have to give V1 of Windows Forms a "shows promise" rating.

V2 of Windows Forms is about delivering on that promise. This is a major upgrade to Windows Forms. Almost every area of Windows Forms—design-time and run-time—has been improved. As Chris and Michael call out in Appendix A: What's New in Windows Forms 2.0, we have incorporated completely new features and a large number of improvements to our existing features (apparently we have 329 new types, 139 updated types, and 14,323 new members). Rather than repeat Appendix A, I'm going to call out three new features that I think illustrate how we achieved our goals for this version of Windows Forms: solve deployment, enable great-looking apps, and enhance productivity.

Deployment

I think the single most significant feature in V2 of the .NET Framework (not just Windows Forms, but the whole .NET Framework) is ClickOnce. ClickOnce delivers on the promise of No Touch Deployment to bring easy, reliable, and manageable web-based deployment to client applications. Deploying your application via the web is now simply a matter of stepping through a wizard in Visual Studio 2005.

Great-Looking Apps

Ever since I joined Microsoft, customers have asked for the ability to build applications that look like Microsoft Office "out of the box," and you can do exactly that with V2 of Windows Forms using the new menu strip, tool strip, and status strip controls—ToolStrip, MenuStrip, and StatusStrip. Not only do the strip controls support the standard Windows and Office look and feel, but they can also be customized to look like pretty much anything you fancy.

Productivity

We've added a whole set of design-time and run-time improvements that we believe will help you to be more productive. One of my favorite new designer features is SnapLines, which allows you to quickly align controls with each other as you lay out your forms. Once you've used a designer with SnapLines, you never want to go back—it's the designer equivalent of IntelliSense.

The Future

After shipping V2, our thoughts are naturally turning to the future. Predicting the future is a dangerous business—most of the predictions from when I was a kid mean we should be supporting actors in either *The Jetsons* or *1984* by now—and so I'm a little nervous about making any long-term predictions. However, I can say a few things based on where we are and what I would like to see us do. First, the .NET Framework and managed code is here to stay: It is the programming model of the present and the future. Learning to use the .NET Framework and Windows

Forms is a solid investment for the future. Second, to paraphrase Samuel Clemens terribly, "Reports of the death of client apps are greatly exaggerated." Client applications are here to stay, can now be deployed as easily as web applications, provide significant business value, and will provide more value as time progresses. Third, as part of our continued investment in Windows Forms, we will ensure that Windows Forms works well with new technologies coming down the pipe such as those in WinFX. This allows you to build applications today with the knowledge that you will be able to enhance those applications in the future using both Windows Forms and these new technologies as they become available. Finally, from a Windows Forms perspective, I believe we need to broaden what we provide into a framework and design experience that addresses the end-to-end process of building a client application. We have a great designer to help you build your UI, but you still have to write way too much code to build your whole application. I would like to see us provide a great designer-based experience for your entire application, not just your forms.

So hopefully what I've said about Windows Forms has got you at least a little curious to find out more—which is where this book comes in. The first edition of this book was a great overview of and introduction to Windows Forms. The same is true of this second edition. Whether you are learning Windows Forms for the first time or if you just want to get a handle on the new stuff we've done in V2, this book will help you. It covers all of the significant feature areas, from the basics of creating Forms, through ToolStrips and data binding to deployment with ClickOnce.

The book is a great balancing act: It neither ignores Visual Studio 2005 nor reduces itself to a simplistic "Click here then click here" walkthrough of Visual Studio 2005 features. The book not only explains the concepts and shows you how to use those concepts in code, but it also shows you how the designer helps you to be more productive by automatically generating the code for you. This leaves you with a solid understanding of both how things work and how to use Visual Studio 2005 to get things done as productively as possible. The chapters on data binding (16 and 17) are a great example of this approach. The source code examples are another great balancing act: They are neither too short to be useful nor so long as to be overwhelming. To quote Alan Cooper, they are "Goldilocks code" examples because they are "just right."

I would like to particularly highlight the chapters on data binding (Chapters 16 and 17), not just because data binding is very close to my heart, but because the book does an excellent job of explaining how data binding works and how to use it effectively. I would also like to highlight the chapters on writing design-time behavior for your controls and components (Chapters 11 and 12) because this is a subject that is often neglected. These chapters alone make this a "must read" book.

So, in summary, this book will leave you not only in a position to effectively use what we provide as part of Windows Forms but also with the understanding you need to write your own run-time and design-time extensions to what we provide.

I'd like to close with some acknowledgments and thanks. First, thanks to the entire Windows Forms team, who have worked tirelessly to build and ship what I believe is a great product. I'm very proud of what we have achieved. Second, my thanks to Michael and Chris not only for producing a book that does a great job of explaining our product and will make it easier for our customers to use, but also for their contributions to the wider Windows Forms community. Thanks to Michael for his great articles on MSDN and feedback on Windows Forms V2— particularly his feedback on the ToolStrip controls. Thanks to Chris for his seemingly boundless enthusiasm for Windows Forms, his excellent writing on Windows Forms, his deep understanding of Windows Forms, MFC, and Windows, and his polite and measured but enthusiastic and copious feedback on every aspect of the product. Both Mike and Chris have helped enormously both in promoting understanding of the product and in helping make Windows Forms as good as it is today. And finally, my thanks to our customers: Every single feature in Windows Forms V2 is based on your feedback. So to all of you who took the time to give us feedback and suggestions: Thanks! Please keep it coming!

I hope you have fun using Windows Forms.

Mark Boulter
PM Technical Lead,
Client Development Tools, Microsoft

Preface

WINDOWS 1.0 PROGRAMMERS had a straightforward life. They had almost no choices about how to do things; either there was an application programming interface (API), or there wasn't, and most of the time there wasn't. This meant that developers had to build almost everything by hand. At the time, this wasn't a problem. All Windows programmers had the same limitations, so everyone's apps more or less operated with the same limited set of functionality.

A modern Windows developer, on the other hand, is inundated with choices. The invention of the web alone gives us static Hypertext Markup Language (HTML), server-based user interface (UI) interaction via ASP.NET, and client-side UI interaction via ActiveX controls or AJAX (to name a few).[1] On the client side, we have native frameworks like Microsoft Foundation Classes (MFC), Active Template Library (ATL), and the next-generation managed framework known as the Windows Presentation Foundation (WPF is part of WinFX, the follow-on to the .NET Framework). How does a developer choose? Where does Windows Forms 2.0, the topic of this book, fit into this pantheon?

Client technologies on Windows provide a range of reach and richness in inverse proportion to each other. Reach is the ability of a user interface (UI) to work across operating systems, whereas richness is the ability for a UI to take advantage of the operating system on which it runs. So even though static HTML works almost everywhere, to the extent that your HTML uses client-side JScript, reach is diminished for browsers that don't support the scripting constructs

---

[1] AJAX stands for Asynchronous JavaScript and XML, as defined by Jesse James Garrett, "Ajax: A New Approach to Web Applications," http://www.adaptivepath.com/publications/essays/archives/000385.php (http://tinysells.com/38).

being used. Even further down the reach scale are ActiveX controls, which work only on Windows but allow full access to its richness.[2]

At the other extreme we have WPF, a completely new managed framework built on top of DirectX. WPF encompasses documents, layout, animation, 2-D, 3-D, text, and graphics primitives in a single, cohesive whole. This framework provides the richest client technology that Microsoft has ever built, and it takes maximum advantage of the platform on which it runs, including any hardware 3-D graphics acceleration that may be available. However, at the time of this writing, WPF has not yet shipped and works only under Windows XP, Windows Server 2003, and Windows Vista.[3]

Where does that leave Windows Forms 2.0? It doesn't quite offer the richness of WPF, but it's far richer than the HTML-based technologies. Windows Forms 2.0 also is much richer than Windows Forms 1.0, with greatly enhanced support for flexible layout, modern menu strip and tool strip controls, data binding, multithreading, typed resources and settings, and, most importantly, ClickOnce deployment.

With ClickOnce, for the first time, users can deploy Windows applications as easily as web applications. Even better, ClickOnce allows Windows applications to be installed locally, integrated with the Start menu, and accessed even if no network connection is available. These options are not available for users of Web applications.

So Windows Forms 2.0 is high on the richness scale, but what about the reach scale? Unlike web applications, Windows Forms requires that users' machines operate on Windows, specifically Windows 98 or later for PCs. However, it also supports other devices, such as Pocket PCs or Smartphones, via the .NET Compact Framework. This means that you can write a Windows Forms 2.0 application and run it on your Windows smartphone.

Based on this level of richness and reach, what kinds of applications should you build with Windows Forms? As it turns out, folks have used Windows Forms to build almost every kind of application, including productivity applications, utilities, enterprise tools, and more—even games. Windows Forms can be used to build smaller things, such as Microsoft's own internal human resources application (called HeadTrax), or larger things, such as most of the UI enhancements that have been built on top of Visual Studio since the 2002 edition. This range of applications can be built because of Windows Forms' range of features and tools, its reach, and, as of this version, the maturity of the implementation based on community usage and feedback.

---

[2] At one point, the Component Object Model (COM) and ActiveX were made to work across platforms, but they have long since been relegated to Windows only.

[3] WinFX (which inclues WPF) and Windows Vista are scheduled to ship in 2006.

In fact, the .NET developer community has embraced Windows Forms to a degree that defies the early .NET focus on web-based applications. Based on talking to my friends in the training industry and on the sales of the first edition of this book, I conclude that a large and growing number of developers write Windows Forms applications. It's for those developers that we've written this book.

Who Should Read This Book?

When writing this book, we wanted to provide real-world Windows Forms coverage for programmers who've programmed in .NET—and those who haven't. To that end, we briefly introduce core .NET topics as they come up. However, we don't pretend to cover the .NET Framework completely. It's too large a topic. Instead, when we think more information would be useful, we reference another work that provides the full details. In particular, you'll find that we've referenced *Essential .NET*, by Don Box, with Chris Sells, a great deal, making it a good companion to this book. In the same category, we also recommend *Advanced .NET Remoting*, by Ingo Rammer, and *Applied Microsoft .NET Framework Programming*, by Jeffrey Richter. (For more details on these books, see the Bibliography.)

One core .NET topic is of special importance to Windows Forms programmers, and we cover it in more detail in Appendix C: Delegates and Events. This coverage is particularly important if you're new to .NET, although we don't recommend diving into that topic until you've got a Windows Forms-specific frame of reference (which is provided about one-third of the way through Chapter 1: Hello, Windows Forms).

Also of particular importance to former (or soon-to-be former) MFC programmers, we've provided Appendix B: Moving from MFC, and Appendix F: Document Management. Although Windows Forms doesn't provide all the features of MFC, we've worked hard on the material and code samples in this book to plug most of the gaps.

One other note: Many years ago, one of the authors wrote his first five-day training course. The topic, Windows 95, included a few hours of coverage on the new controls: what they looked like, what their properties, methods, and events were, and how to program against them. Those hours seemed like days for everyone involved. The details of a particular control are interesting only when you're putting it to use, and when that time comes, the control-specific documentation and Visual Studio's IntelliSense help support do a marvelous job of giving you the information you need.

To that end, this book covers none of the standard controls completely. Instead, when a control is interesting in the context of the current topic—such as the DataGridView control in Chapter 17: Applied Data Binding—we cover that control appropriately. Also, to give you a list of all the components and controls and to introduce you to each one's major functionality, Appendix D: Component and Control Survey provides a list of the standard controls and components. We wouldn't think of wasting your time by attempting to be more thorough than the reference documentation that comes with the .NET Framework software development kit (SDK) and Visual Studio 2005. Instead, this book focuses on the real-world scenarios that aren't covered in detail elsewhere. Finally, to help you understand the differences between components and controls and how to build both, we've provided Chapter 9: Components and Chapter 10: Controls.

Conventions

If you've decided to take the plunge with this book, we'd like to thank you for your faith and express our hope that we live up to it. To aid you in reading the text, we want to let you in on some conventions we use.

First, there is the mode of address that we use throughout the book (except for this preface). Because Chris and Michael worked so closely and so hard on every word in this book, the use of "I" really means "both authors," whereas the use of "we" means "the authors and you." Although we sometimes use "you" directly, Michael and Chris lean toward the inclusive.

The wonderful thing about Windows Forms is how visual it is, and that's why we use a lot of figures to illustrate its features. Some of those pictures really need to be in color to make the point, so be sure to check the color pages at the center of this book for those color plates.

As useful as figures are, we both think primarily in code. Code is shown in monospace type:

```
System.Console.WriteLine("Hello, Windows Forms.");
```

Console application activation is also shown in monospace type:

```
C:\> csc.exe hello.cs
```

When a part of a code snippet or a command line activation is of particular interest, we mark it in bold and often provide a comment:

```
// Notice the use of the .NET System namespace
System.Console.WriteLine("Hello, Windows Forms.");
```

When we want to direct your attention to a piece of code more fully, we replace superfluous code with ellipses:

```
class MyForm : System.Windows.Forms.Form {
    ... // fields
    private void MyForm_Load(
        object sender, System.ComponentModel.EventArgs e) {

        MessageBox.Show("Hello from MyForm");
    }
}
```

Furthermore, to make the printed code more readable, we often drop namespaces and protection keywords when they don't provide additional information:

```
// Shortened "System.Windows.Forms.Form" base class
class MyForm : Form {
    ... // fields

    // Removed "private" specifier and "System.ComponentModel" namespace
    void MyForm_Load(object sender, EventArgs e) {
        MessageBox.Show("Hello from MyForm");
    }
}
```

When showing .NET attributes, we use their abbreviated name:

```
[Serializable] // Instead of [SerializableAttribute]
class MyCustomType {...}
```

C# lets you drop the "Attribute" suffix for convenience, but remember to append this suffix when you look up the details of the attribute class in the online documentation.

For clarity, we sometimes omit error checking from the printed code, but we try to leave it in the sample code that you'll find at our web site.

In the text, we often put a word or phrase in italics to indicate a new term that we're about to define. As an example of this kind of term and its definition, *hegemony* is a preponderant influence or authority, as well as a potent business practice.

Sometimes, we mention keyboard shortcuts because we find them convenient. The ones I mention are the default Visual Studio 2005 (VS05) key bindings for C# programmers. If you're not using those key bindings, you'll need to map the keyboard shortcuts to your own settings.

Finally, because this is the second edition of this book, we've taken care to mark new and updated types in the margins with graphics and in the code with comments. Also, for a summary of what's new in Windows Forms, check out Appendix A: What's New in Windows Forms 2.0.

Contact

The up-to-date information for this book, including the source code and the errata, are maintained at http://www.sellsbrothers.com/writing/wfbook. This site also lets you send feedback about the book, both complimentary and less so.

Michael's Acknowledgments

Writing a book is not just the application of pen to paper, nor is its creation confined to the authors. Whether they know it or not, many people have helped make this book what it is.

My parents, Josef and Lili: Without a doubt, I could not have seen this book through to the end if it weren't for the immeasurable and unquestioning love and support of my parents. They've been there for me in this way since the day I was born, which I find truly staggering. How can I thank them enough? I simply cannot. Instead, I try and do the best I can by making the most out of the life they've provided. For this reason, I put everything I had into this book.

My brother, Alex: When he applied to attend a university, he definitely met the entry requirements. However, he was told by the university that he shouldn't bother because it would be very unlikely he would complete his studies successfully. Of course, they were very wrong. When I endure some of the darker moments in writing and want to throw it all away, I think of all he has accomplished in his life. Then I very quickly realize that writing so completely pales in comparison, before pulling my head in and keeping on writing. He is a big inspiration in my life, and he helped me to stay the course on this book. I thought he should know.

My coauthor, Chris Sells: I have often written with Chris because I enjoy it so much. It's fun, it's a challenge, and it usually results in the production of something that I can really be proud of. When Chris asked me to coauthor this book, I couldn't say no. I'm still surprised by how much latitude he gave me to work with, more than a one-to-one update of the first edition, and I can't thank him enough for his faith, and for all that he has given over the years.

My friends Kym Phillpotts and Hodaka Shibata: They've been there for me for the long haul, and when I think of good mates, I instantly think of them.

"Mr. Windows Forms," Mark Boulter: Even though I've never met Mark in the physical world, he has played a huge role in fueling my passion for Windows Forms and the desire to tell its story. I'd always hoped that he would write the foreword for this book, and I am honored he did.

My safety net, Microsoft's Jessica Fosler: When I had technical and conceptual questions that often needed quick responses, Jessica always provided articulate, comprehensive, and prompt answers, for which I am very grateful. And, as if that weren't enough, Jessica made time to review our entire book, provide thorough and positive commentary, and, for good measure, threw in some great prose.

Our main reviewer, Christophe Nasarre: Christophe performed two reviews in a very limited time. It is almost scary how good he is and how much the book improved as a result of his efforts. I can honestly say that I felt comfortable about this book only after his involvement, and if I ever write another book, I'll be disappointed if he isn't available. Merci!

Our Microsoft reviewers, Sameer Bhangar, Barry Briggs, Felix Cheung, Andrew Coates, Jamie Cool, Shreeman Dash, Erick Ellis, Shawn Farkas, David Guyer, Mike Harsh, Zach Kramer, Steve Lasker, Elizabeth Maher, Chris Meyer, Mark Rideout, and Joe Stegman: All had a role in the development of Windows Forms 2.0, so it was a little nerve racking letting them review our exposition of their work. However, it was also vital because they provided extremely comprehensive technical and conceptual commentary that dramatically improved the quality of the end result.

Our user reviewers, William Bartholomew, Ron Green, Kym Phillpotts, and Fumiaki Yoshimatsu: No technology book can be released without reviews from people who will actually use the technology and will lean on our book to learn about it. From this perspective, these guys provided valuable insight that nicely juxtaposed the more technical focus provided by the Microsofties.

Betsy Hardinger, Grammar Guru Extraordinaire: Betsy, as Chris likes to call her, is a grammar geek. She loves what she does. She's incredible at what she does. She's funny. She puts Strunk and White to shame.

And, last but not least, Addison-Wesley: This is my first experience with a technical book publisher, and it was a great one. The editors pretty much let us tell the story the way we wanted, always making sure we had what we needed and never pressuring us. Thanks!

Chris's Acknowledgments

Although this book is dedicated to my family, I'd also like to acknowledge them here. I work from my home, and in completing the book I often had to spend a great deal of extra time to get the thing out the door. My wife, Melissa, is always enormously understanding when I have a deadline and gives me the space I need to meet it. Also, I tend to leave my office door open because I like my family, and often my boys, John and Tom, will come in to talk to me about their day. Even though they're only eleven and ten, respectively, they're uncharacteristically understanding when it comes to letting me focus on my work for "just another five minutes" (although woe is me if I overpromise and underdeliver to those two, I'll tell you).

Although my family gave me the space to write, this book would not be what it is without the efforts of my coauthor. Michael dedicated most of two years to this book. Michael's job was primarily to update the chapters based on the additions and changes in Windows Forms 2.0, but he did far more than that. His efforts in re-evaluating each and every part of the story and his willingness to try new ways to present information produced a far better book than the first edition. You should keep an eye out for Michael's future writings. He's definitely one of the good ones.

I also need to give special thanks to Mark Boulter for having a positive influence both on the Windows Forms technology and on my understanding of it, and also for writing our foreword. He doesn't consider himself a writer, so I literally had to call him and beg for his participation after he told me "no," but I couldn't imagine anyone else I'd want to do it.

Special attention needs to be paid to any book's reviewers. Without the reviewers, authors might think that when they've written prose that covers a topic, they're actually finished. Oh, hated reviews, which correct this assumption, and sweet reviewers, who make sure our readers aren't tortured with inaccurate or unreadable prose and uncompiling code. Our grand inquisitor was Christophe Nasarre, who flayed us so thoroughly in our first round of reviews that we asked him to be the sole reviewer in the second round. Christophe is such a wonderful reviewer that he's always busy with reviews, but he was able to squeeze us into an extremely short period while still finding things I'm embarrassed to have written in the first place. Thanks, Christophe! This book is immeasurably better because of your efforts.

We also had a dedicated team of reviewers from outside Microsoft, including Ryan Dorrell, Kym Phillpotts, Fumiaki Yoshimatsu, Ron Green, and William Bartholomew. External reviewers are particularly important because they're not steeped in the internal history of Windows Forms, and they represent our target audience. Thanks, guys!

On the other hand, this book represents not only Mike's and my work with Windows Forms, but also a large number of Microsoft employees who took the time to review our chapters in their areas of expertise and make sure we weren't missing the important things. This group includes Joe Stegman, Steve Lasker, Andrew Coates, Chris Meyer, Elizabeth Maher, David Guyer, Jessica Fosler, Sameer Bhangar, Felix Cheung, Mark Rideout, Shreeman Dash, Shawn Farkas, Erick Ellis, Mike Harsh, Jamie Cool, Zach Kramer, and Barry Briggs. Of special note are Steve Lasker, who gave us especially deep feedback on the data binding chapters on very short notice, and Jessica Fosler, who was our final authority on a huge range of topics. Michael and I tried very hard to make sure that we didn't slaughter the story of your technology; thanks for all the details we couldn't have found any other way.

I'd like to thank *MSDN Magazine, MSDN Online,* and *Windows Developer* magazine for allowing us to reuse material from articles that they originally published (as listed in the Bibliography). I'd also like to thank the readers of the first edition of this book, whose feedback on the initial pieces and the first edition helped shape the final version of this content, as well as inspired me to dig ever deeper.

Last but not least, I'd like to thank the fine folks at Addison-Wesley. In increasingly tight times, they still manage to provide me an environment where I can write what I think best. Special thanks go to Betsy Hardinger: copy editor, frustrated fiction author, kindred spirit, and hyphen mentor. In addition to turning my prose into English, she also managed to catch technical inconsistencies that hard-core developers missed. Thanks, Betsy!

These folks, along with a bunch I'm sure I've missed, have helped shape everything good that comes through in this book. The errors that remain are our own.

Chris Sells
sellsbrothers.com

Michael Weinhardt
mikedub.net

1

Hello, Windows Forms

A S EASY TO USE AS WINDOWS FORMS is, the sheer amount of functionality it provides can make it intimidating—especially when combined with the huge number of features in Visual Studio 2005 (VS05) solely for the purpose of building Windows Forms code. This chapter takes a quick look at Windows Forms, including forms, controls, application settings, resources, dialogs, drawing, printing, data binding, threading, and even deployment over the web. We also look at how the VS05 integrated development environment (IDE) facilitates Windows Forms development. The remaining chapters will stuff you full, providing the sumptuous details of these topics, but in this chapter, you'll get your first taste.

Windows Forms from Scratch

A typical Windows Forms application has at least one form. Without the form, it's just an "application," which is pretty boring. A *form* is simply a window, the unit of the Microsoft user interface we've seen since Windows 1.0.

One form in a Windows Forms application is typically the *main form*, meaning that it is either the parent or the owner of all other forms that may be shown during the lifetime of the application.[1] It's where the main menu is shown, along with the tool strip, status strip, and so on. Typically, the main form also governs the lifetime of a Windows Forms application; generally when an application starts, the main form is opened, and when the main form is closed, the application exits.

The main form of an application can be a simple message box, a dialog, a Single Document Interface (SDI) window, a Multiple Document Interface (MDI) window, or something

---

[1] The distinction between a form's "parent" and its "owner" is covered in detail in Chapter 2: Forms.

more complicated (such as the forms you're used to seeing in applications like VS05). These latter forms may include multiple child windows, tool windows, and floating tool strips.

If your application is simple, you can implement it using the staple of any windowing system, the lowly *message box:*

```
class MyFirstApp {
  static void Main() {
    System.Windows.Forms.MessageBox.Show("Hello, Windows Forms!");
  }
}
```

If you're new to C#, Main is the entry point for any C# application.[2] The Main method must be a member of a class, and hence the need for MyFirstApp. However, the .NET runtime doesn't create an instance of the MyFirstApp class when our code is loaded and executed, so our Main method must be marked *static*. In this way, you mark a method as available without requiring the instantiation of the type that exposes it.

The single line of real code in our first Windows Forms application calls the static Show method of the MessageBox class contained within the System.Windows.Forms namespace. *Namespaces* are used extensively in the .NET Framework Class Libraries (.NET Framework) to separate types such as classes, structures, and enumerations into logical groupings. This separation is necessary when you have thousands of Microsoft employees working on the .NET Framework, hundreds of third parties extending it, and millions of programmers trying to learn it. Without namespaces, you would need all kinds of wacky conventions to keep things uniquely named (as demonstrated by the existing Win32 API).

However, as necessary as namespaces are, they require a little too much typing for me, so I recommend the C# *using* statement:

```
using System.Windows.Forms; // For MessageBox

class MyFirstApp {
  static void Main() {
    MessageBox.Show("Hello, Windows Forms!");
  }
}
```

When the compiler sees that the MessageBox class is being used, it first looks in the *global namespace,* which is where all types end up that aren't contained by a namespace (for

---

[2] The entry point is the method that the Common Language Runtime (CLR) calls when an application is launched. For details, refer to Essential .NET (Addison-Wesley, 2003), by Don Box, with Chris Sells.

example, the MyFirstApp class is in the global namespace). If the compiler can't find the type in the global namespace, it looks at all the namespaces currently being used—in this case, System.Windows.Forms. If the compiler finds a type name being used that exists in two or more namespaces, it produces an error and we're forced to go back to the long notation. In practice, this is rare enough to make the short notation predominant when you type code by hand.

However, even though the MessageBox class is enormously handy for showing your users simple string information it's hard to build a real application with MessageBox. For most things, you need an instance of the Form class, located in System.Windows.Forms:

```
using System.Windows.Forms; // For Form

class MyFirstApp {
  static void Main() {
    Form form = new Form();
    form.Show(); // Not what you want to do
  }
}
```

Although this code shows the form, you'll have to be quick to see it because the Show method displays the form modelessly. If you're not steeped in user interface lore, a *modeless* form is one that's displayed while allowing other activities (called *modes*) to take place. So, control is returned to the Main method immediately after Show puts our new form on the screen, which promptly returns and exits the process, taking our nascent form with it. To show a form *modally*—that is, to not return control to the Main function until the form has closed—you could call the ShowDialog method:

```
using System.Windows.Forms;

class MyFirstApp {
  static void Main() {
    Form form = new Form();
    form.ShowDialog(); // Still not what you want to do
  }
}
```

This code would show a blank form and wait for the user to close it before returning control to the Main method, but it's not the code you generally write. Instead, to make it accessible from other parts of your application, you designate one form as the main form.

To do this, pass the main form as an argument to the Application object's static Run method, which also resides in the System.Windows.Forms namespace:

```
using System.Windows.Forms; // For Form, Application

class MyFirstApp {
  static void Main() {
    Form form = new Form();
    Application.Run(form); // This is what you want to do
  }
}
```

The Run method shows the main form. When the form is closed, Run returns, letting our Main method exit and close the process. To see this in action, you can compile your first Windows Forms application using the following command:[3]

```
C:\> csc.exe /t:winexe /r:System.Windows.Forms.dll MyFirstApp.cs
```

The csc.exe command invokes the compiler on our source file, asking it to produce a Windows application via the /t flag (where the "t" stands for "target"), pulling in the System.Windows.Forms.dll library using the /r flag (where the "r" stands for "reference").[4]

The job of the compiler is to pull together the various source code files into a .NET assembly. An *assembly* is a collection of .NET types, code, or resources (or all three). An assembly can be either an *application,* in which case it has an .exe extension, or a *library,* in which case it has a .dll extension. The only real difference between assembly types is whether the assembly has an entry point that can be called by Windows when the assembly is launched (.exe files do, and .dll files do not).

Now that the compiler has produced MyFirstApp.exe, you can execute it and see an application so boring, it's not even worth a screen shot. When you close the form, MyFirstApp.exe exits, ending your first Windows Forms experience.

To spice things up a bit, we can set a property on our new form before showing it:

```
class MyFirstApp {
  static void Main() {
    Form form = new Form();
    form.Text = "Hello, Windows Forms!";
    Application.Run(form);
  }
}
```

---

[3] To get a command prompt with the proper PATH environment variable set to access the .NET command line tools, click on Start | Programs | Microsoft Visual Studio 2005 | Visual Studio Tools, and then Visual Studio 2005 Command Prompt. If you don't have VS05 installed, you can set up the PATH using the corvars.bat batch file in your FrameworkSDK\Bin directory.

[4] csc.exe is the command line compiler for C#, and it is located in your c:\Windows\Microsoft.NET \Framework\v2.0.50727 folder.

Like most classes in the .NET Framework, Form has several properties to access, methods to call, and events to handle. In this case, we've set the Text property, which sets a form's caption bar text. We could do the same thing to set other properties on the form, showing it when we were finished, but that's not the way we generally do things in Windows Forms. Instead, each custom form is a class that derives from Form and initializes its own properties:

```
class MyFirstForm : Form {
  public MyFirstForm() {
    this.Text = "Hello, Windows Forms!";
  }
}

class MyFirstApp {
  static void Main() {
    Form form = new MyFirstForm();
    Application.Run(form);
  }
}
```

Notice that the MyFirstForm class derives from Form and then initializes its own properties in the constructor. This gives us a simpler usage model, as shown in the new Main method, which creates an instance of the MyFirstForm class. You also gain the potential for reuse should MyFirstForm be needed in other parts of your application.

Still, our form is pretty boring. It doesn't even include a way to interact with it except for the system-provided adornments. We can add some interactivity by adding a button:

```
class MyFirstForm : Form {
  public MyFirstForm() {
    this.Text = "Hello, Windows Forms!";
    Button button = new Button();
    button.Text = "Click Me!";
    this.Controls.Add(button);
  }
}
```

Adding a button to the form is a matter of creating a new Button object, setting the properties that we like, and adding the Button object to the list of controls that the form manages. This code produces a button on the form that does that nifty 3-D depress thing that buttons do when you press them, but nothing else interesting happens. That's because we're still not handling the button's Click event, which is fired when the user presses the button:

```
using System; // For EventArgs
...
class MyFirstForm : Form {
  public MyFirstForm() {
    this.Text = "Hello, Windows Forms!";
    Button button = new Button();
    button.Text = "Click Me!";
    button.Click += new EventHandler(button_Click);
    this.Controls.Add(button);
  }

  void button_Click(object sender, EventArgs e) {
    MessageBox.Show("That's a strong, confident click you've got...");
  }
}
```

Handling the button's Click event involves two things. The first is creating a handler function with the appropriate signature; we've used the standard naming convention for events (*VariableName_EventName)* to name this method button_Click. The type signature of the vast majority of .NET events is a method that returns nothing and takes two parameters: an object that represents the sender of the event (our button, in this case) and an instance of either the EventArgs class or a class that derives from the EventArgs class.

The second thing that's needed to subscribe to an event in C# is shown by the use of the "+=" operator in the MyFirstForm constructor. This notation means that we'd like to add a function to the list of all the other functions that care about a particular event on a particular object, and that requires an instance of an EventHandler delegate object. A *delegate* is a class that translates invocations on an event into calls on the methods that have subscribed to the event.[5]

For this particular event, we have the following delegate and event defined for us in the .NET Framework:

```
namespace System {
  delegate void EventHandler(object sender, EventArgs e);
}

namespace System.Windows.Forms {
  class Button {
    public event EventHandler Click;
  }
}
```

---

[5] Delegates and events are covered in depth in Appendix C: Delegates and Events.

Notice that the Click event on the Button class stores a reference to an EventHandler delegate. Consequently, to add our own method to the list of subscribers to the button's Click event, we create an instance of the EventHandler delegate. To achieve the same effect with less typing, C# offers a syntactic shortcut that allows you to simply provide the name of the subscribing method:

```
public MyFirstForm() {
  ...
  button.Click += button_Click;
  ...
}
```

Shortcut or not, it can quickly become tedious to add property settings and event handlers by hand for any nontrivial UI. Luckily, it's also unnecessary, thanks to the Windows Forms Application Wizard and the Windows Forms Designer provided by VS05.

Windows Forms in Visual Studio .NET

Most Windows Forms projects start in the New Project dialog, available via File | New | Project (Ctrl+Shift+N) and shown in Figure 1.1.

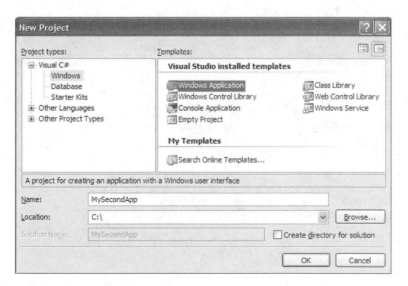

Figure 1.1   Windows Forms Projects

To develop an application, you want the Windows Application project template. To develop a library of custom controls or forms for reuse, you want the Windows Control Library project template. When you run the Windows Application Wizard, choosing whatever you like for the project name, location, and solution name, click OK and you'll get a blank form in the Windows Forms Designer, as shown in Figure 1.2.

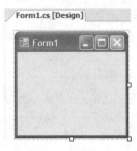

Figure 1.2 **A Windows Forms Application Wizard-Generated Blank Form in the Windows Forms Designer**

Before we start the control drag-and-drop extravaganza that the Windows Forms Designer enables, let's look at a slightly abbreviated version of the code generated by the Windows Forms Application Wizard (available by right-clicking on the design surface and choosing View Code or by pressing F7):[6]

```
// Program.cs
using System.Windows.Forms;

namespace MySecondApp {
  static class Program {
    /// <summary>
    /// The main entry point for the application.
    /// </summary>
    [STAThread]
    static void Main() {
      Application.EnableVisualStyles();
      Application.SetCompatibleTextRenderingDefault(false);
      Application.Run(new Form1());
    }
  }
}

// Form1.cs
using System.Windows.Forms;
namespace MySecondApp {
```

___
[6] The Windows Forms Designer offers two form views: Code and Designer. F7 toggles between them (although this keyboard shortcut is merely the VS05 default and, like any keystroke, depends on your specific settings).

```
  partial class Form1 : Form {
    public Form1() {
      InitializeComponent();
    }
  }
}


// Form1.Designer.cs
namespace MySecondApp {
  partial class Form1 {

    #region Windows Form Designer generated code

    /// <summary>
    /// Required method for Designer support - do not modify
    /// the contents of this method with the code editor.
    /// </summary>
    void InitializeComponent() {
      this.components = new System.ComponentModel.Container();
      this.AutoScaleMode = AutoScaleMode.Font;
      this.Text = "Form1";
    }

    #endregion
  }
}
```

Most of this code should be familiar, including the *using* statements at the top, the form class that derives from the Form base class, the static Main function that provides the entry point to the application, and the Application.Run method. However, four things differ from what we did ourselves.

First, the Windows Forms Designer has dynamic theme support because of the call to Application.EnableVisualStyles, which keeps a UI's appearance consistent with the current Windows theme.

Second, the Windows Forms Designer has also set the default form's AutoScaleMode property to a value of AutoScaleMode.Font, which ensures that the form will automatically retain the correct visual proportions (as discussed in Chapter 4: Layout).

Third, the static Main method is implemented from a static class, Program, which exists in a file, program.cs, that's separate from any of the UI elements in the application. Main is augmented with the STAThread attribute, which enables appropriate communication between Windows Forms and Component Object Model (COM) technology. This is required for several types of Windows Forms functionality, including using the Clipboard, the file dialogs, and drag and drop (shown in Appendix E: Drag and Drop). Because any serious Windows Forms application likely uses some form of COM, the Windows Forms Designer tacks this on to protect you from nasty exceptions that would otherwise arise.

Finally, a call to InitializeComponent is added to the form's constructor to set the form's properties instead of doing it in the constructor itself. InitializeComponent gives the Windows Forms Designer a place to put the code to initialize the form and its controls and components as we visually design the form. For example, dragging a button from the Toolbox onto the form's design surface changes the InitializeComponent implementation to the following, in its entirety:

```
void InitializeComponent() {
    this.button1 = new System.Windows.Forms.Button();
    this.SuspendLayout();
    //
    // button1
    //
    this.button1.Location = new System.Drawing.Point(205, 75);
    this.button1.Name = "button1";
    this.button1.Size = new System.Drawing.Size(75, 23);
    this.button1.TabIndex = 0;
    this.button1.Text = "button1";
    this.button1.UseVisualStyleBackColor = true;
    //
    // Form1
    //
    this.AutoScaleDimensions = new System.Drawing.SizeF(6F, 13F);
    this.AutoScaleMode = System.Windows.Forms.AutoScaleMode.Font;
    this.ClientSize = new System.Drawing.Size(292, 266);
    this.Controls.Add(this.button1);
    this.Name = "Form1";
    this.Text = "Form1";
    this.ResumeLayout(false);
}
```

Notice again that this code is similar to what we built ourselves, although this time created for us by the Windows Forms Designer. Unfortunately, for this process to work reliably, the Windows Forms Designer must have complete control over the InitializeComponent method. In fact, you can notice from the previous sample that the Wizard-generated InitializeComponent code is wrapped in a region that is collapsed to hide the code by default, and is marked with a telling comment:

```
#region Windows Form Designer generated code
/// <summary>
/// Required method for Designer support - do not modify
/// the contents of this method with the code editor.
/// </summary>
...
#endregion
```

To emphasize the need for control, the Windows Forms Designer splits the Form1 class across two files—Form1.cs and Form1.Designer.cs—using partial class support in C#.

The code in InitializeComponent may look like your favorite programming language, but it's actually the serialized form of the object model that the Windows Forms Designer uses to manage the design surface. Although you can make minor changes to this code, such as changing the Text property on the new button, major changes are likely to be ignored—or, worse, thrown away. Feel free to experiment to find out how far you can go by modifying this serialization format by hand, but don't be surprised if your work is lost. I recommend putting custom form initialization into the form's constructor, after the call to Initialize-Component, giving you confidence that your code will be safe from the Windows Forms Designer.

However, we put up with the transgression of the Windows Forms Designer because of the benefits it provides. For example, instead of writing lines of code to set properties on the form or the controls contained therein, all you have to do is to right-click on the object of interest and choose Properties (or press F4) to bring up the Properties window for the selected object, as shown in Figure 1.3.[7]

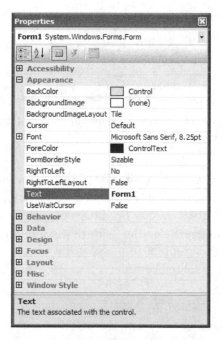

Figure 1.3   Browsing and Editing Properties in the Properties Window

---

[7] Instead of F4, you can press Alt+Enter.

Any properties with nondefault values, as indicated by values in boldface in the browser, are written to the InitializeComponent method for you. Similarly, to choose an event to handle for the form, or a control or component hosted on the form, you can press the Events lightning bolt button at the top of the Properties window to open the corresponding list of events (shown in Figure 1.4).

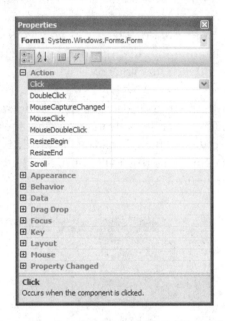

Figure 1.4 Creating Events with the Properties Window

You have a few ways to handle an event from the Properties window. One way is to find the event you'd like to handle on the object selected (say, Click), type the name of the function you'd like to call when this event is fired (say, button_Click), and press Enter. VS05 takes you to the body of an event handler with that name and the correct signature, all ready for you to implement:

```
void button_Click(object sender, System.EventArgs e) {
  }
```

After you've added a handler to a form, that handler will show up in a drop-down list for other events having the same signature. This technique is handy if you'd like the same event for multiple objects to be handled by the same method, such as multiple buttons with the same handler. You can use the sender argument to determine which object fired the event:

```
void button_Click(object sender, System.EventArgs e) {
    Button button = sender as Button;
    MessageBox.Show(button.Text + "was clicked");
}
```

If you'd like each event that you handle for each object to be unique or if you just don't care what the name of the handler is, as is often the case, you can simply double-click on the name of the event in the Properties window; an event handler name is generated for you, based on the name of the control and the name of the event. For example, if you double-clicked on the Load event for the Form1 form, the event handler name would be Form1_Load.

Furthermore, if you want to handle the *default event* of an object, you can create a handler for it automatically by simply double-clicking on the object itself. This generates an event handler name just as if you'd double-clicked on that event name in the Properties window event list. An object's default event is intuitively meant to be the most handled event for a particular type. For example, I'm sure you won't be surprised to learn that the default event for a button is Click and that the default event for a form is Load. Unfortunately, neither the Windows Forms Designer nor the Properties window gives any indication what the default event is for a particular type, but experimentation should reveal few surprises.

Arranging Controls

The beauty of the Windows Forms Designer is that it lets you lay out your controls lovingly within your form, making sure everything lines up nicely with the aid of *snap lines*, as shown in Figure 1.5.

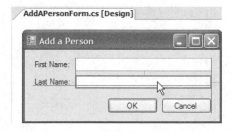

Figure 1.5   Nicely Laid-Out Form at Ideal Size

Snap lines cause controls to "snap" to certain positions as they are dragged around the design surface. These alignments are determined by the target control's proximity to other controls and the edges of the form. Controls can also be snapped to both the vertical (left edge) and horizontal (text baseline) edges of text in other controls. Snapping proximity is visually represented as lines on the design surface.

So building the form is a pleasant experience, although what happens by default when the user resizes it at run-time is less so, as shown in Figure 1.6.

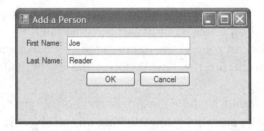

Figure 1.6　Nicely Laid-Out Form Resized

The user isn't resizing the form to get more gray space but to make the controls bigger so that they will hold more visible data. For that to happen, the controls need to resize to take up the newly available space. You can do this manually by handling the form's Resize event and writing the code. Or you can do it with anchoring.

Anchoring is one of the ways Windows Forms gives you automatic layout control of your forms and their controls. By default, all controls are anchored to the upper left, so that as the form is resized and moved, all controls are kept at their position relative to the upper-left corner of the form. In this case, though, we'd clearly like to have the text box controls widen or narrow as the form is resized. We implement this by setting each text box's Anchor property from the Properties window, which displays an editor like the one in Figure 1.7.

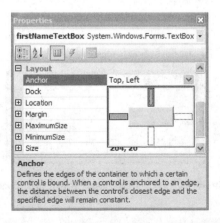

Figure 1.7　Setting the Anchor Property

To change the text boxes so that they anchor to the right edge, as well as the default top and left edges, is a matter of clicking on the anchor rectangle at the right and changing the Anchor property to "Top, Left, Right." This causes the text boxes to resize as the form resizes, as shown in Figure 1.8.

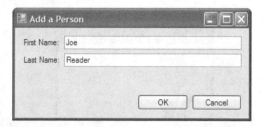

Figure 1.8   Anchoring Text Boxes Top, Left, Right and Buttons Bottom, Right

The default anchoring is "Top, Left," but those edges need not be a part of the anchoring settings at all. For example, notice that Figure 1.8 anchors the OK and Cancel buttons to the bottom right, as is customary in Windows dialogs.

If instead of building a dialog-style form, you'd like to build a window-style form, anchoring is not your best bet. For example, suppose you're building an Explorer-style application: a menu strip and tool strip at the top, a status strip at the bottom, and a tree view and a list view taking up the rest of the space, with a splitter between them. In that kind of application, anchoring won't do. Instead, you want docking.

Docking allows you to "stick" any control on the edge of its container, the way a status strip is stuck to the bottom of a form. By default, most controls have the Dock property set to None. (The default for the StatusStrip control is Bottom.) You can change the Dock property in the Properties window by picking a single edge to dock to, or to take up whatever space is left, as shown in Figure 1.9.

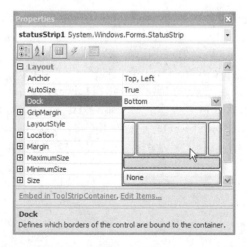

Figure 1.9   Setting the Dock Property

As an example of several types of docking, the form in Figure 1.10 shows the Dock properties for a status strip, a tree view, and a list view, the latter two being separated and managed by a SplitContainer control. You can arrange all this without writing a line of code.

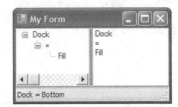

Figure 1.10　Docking and Splitting

Snap lines, anchoring, docking, and splitting are not the only ways to arrange controls on a form. Windows Forms also lets you group controls and handle custom layout for special situations, such as HTML-like tabular and flow layouts. Layout is covered in Chapter 4: Layout. Also, Windows Forms supports arranging windows within a parent, which we call MDI, in addition to several other UI models. These techniques are all covered in detail in Chapter 14.

Controls

After arranging a group of controls just right, you may find that you need that group elsewhere in your application or even in other applications. In that case, you might consider copying and pasting the controls between forms, making sure that all the settings are maintained.

For a more robust form of reuse, however, you can encapsulate the controls into a *user control*, which is a container for other controls. Although you can add one to a Windows Application project, you get one by default when you create a new Windows Control Library project. To add this project to a solution, right-click the solution in Solution Explorer and choose Add | New Project | Windows Control Library. Also make sure that you're creating the new project in the same location as your existing solution, because VS05 defaults to placing new projects one folder too far up the hierarchy in most cases. Figure 1.11 shows how to add a new project called MyFirstControlLibrary to an existing solution called MySecondApp.

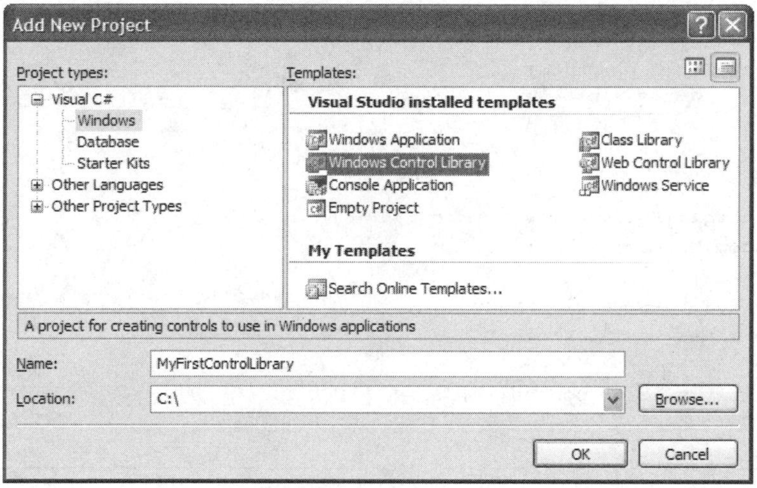

Figure 1.11   Adding a New Project to an Existing Solution

After you've created a Control Library project, you're presented with a user control in a designer that looks very much like the Windows Forms Designer, as shown in Figure 1.12.

Figure 1.12   UserControl Designer

The only real difference is that this designer shows no border or caption, because those features are provided by the form that will host your new control. The code generated by the wizard looks very much like the code generated for a new form except that the base class is UserControl (located in the System.Windows.Forms namespace) instead of Form:

```
// UserControl1.cs
using System.Windows.Forms;

namespace MyFirstControlLibrary {
```

```
partial class UserControl1 : UserControl {
  public UserControl1() {
    InitializeComponent();
  }
}
}
}

// UserControl1.Designer.cs
using System.Windows.Forms;

namespace MyFirstControlLibrary {
  partial class UserControl1 {
    ...
    void InitializeComponent() {...}
  }
}
```

In the UserControl Designer, you can drop and arrange any desired controls on the user control, setting their properties and handling events just as on a form. Figure 1.13 shows a sample user control as seen in the UserControl Designer.

Figure 1.13   A User Control Shown in the UserControl Designer

When you're happy with your user control, build the project and select it from the Toolbox, where you'll find that VS05 has automatically added it to a new tab created especially for your project—in this case, "MyFirstControlLibrary Components." Drag and drop your control onto the forms of your choice, setting properties and handling events via the Properties window just as with any of the built-in components or controls. Figure 1.14 shows the user control from Figure 1.13 hosted on a form.

Figure 1.14   Hosting a User Control

User controls aren't the only kind of custom controls. If you're interested in drawing the contents of your controls yourself, scrolling your controls, or getting more details about user controls, see Chapter 10: Controls. If you need to package reusable code that doesn't have a UI of any kind, see Chapter 9: Components. Either way, you can integrate your custom implementations into the design-time environment of VS05 to take advantage of the Properties window, snap lines, and smart tags, as covered in Chapter 11: Design-Time Integration: The Properties Window, and Chapter 12: Design-Time Integration: Designers and Smart Tags.

Application Settings

After you've assembled your application from the required forms, controls, and components, you build it and deploy it. To run, however, applications need certain information, and that often differs between installations, users, and application sessions. Consequently, you can't compile this information directly into the application assemblies. Instead, the information must reside in a location independent from those assemblies, from which it is read and to which it is written as needed during execution. To solve this problem, .NET provides a complete infrastructure whose fundamental element is the *setting*.

.NET considers there to be two types of settings: those for users and those for applications. *User settings*, such as information you might find in a Tools | Options dialog for an application like VS05, change from one application session to the next. *Application settings*, such as database connection strings, change from one installation to the next. You can add one or more of each type of setting to your application by using the Settings Editor. To open this editor, right-click your project and select Properties | Settings, as shown in Figure 1.15.

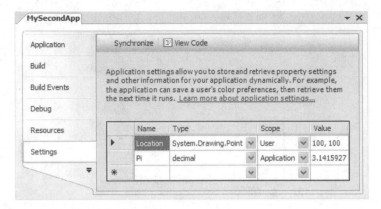

Figure 1.15   Configuring Settings

Each setting has a name, a type, a scope, and a value. The *name* is the way you refer to the setting; *type* specifies the type of value it stores; *scope* determines whether a setting is a user setting or an application setting; and *value* is the setting's initial value. All the settings you create are stored in your project's app.config file, in which they are grouped by scope:

```xml
<?xml version="1.0" encoding="utf-8" ?>
<configuration>
  <configSections>
    ...
  </configSections>

  <userSettings>
    <MySecondApp.Properties.Settings>
      <setting name="WindowLocation" serializeAs="String">
        <value>100, 100</value>
      </setting>
    </MySecondApp.Properties.Settings>
  </userSettings>

  <applicationSettings>
    <MySecondApp.Properties.Settings>
      <setting name="Pi" serializeAs="String">
        <value>3.1415927</value>
      </setting>
    </MySecondApp.Properties.Settings>
  </applicationSettings>

</configuration>
```

When you build your application, the content and settings stored in app.config are copied into your application's configuration file, which is named *ApplicationName*.exe.config.

When your app executes, it needs a way to retrieve these values and, if necessary, save new values. To provide a simple way to do this, VS05 generates a special class, Settings, in your project:

```
namespace MySecondApp.Properties {
    internal sealed class Settings : ApplicationSettingsBase {
      public static Settings Default {
        get {...}
      }
      public Point Location {
        get {...}
        set {...}
      }
      public decimal Pi {
        get {...}
      }
    }
}
```

This class, generated in the *ApplicationName*.Properties namespace, exposes each setting as a property that holds a value of the type specified when the setting was added. Although you could create an instance of this class manually, you can use the static Default method to take on that burden for you. The Settings class derives from ApplicationSettingsBase, a .NET class located in the System.Configuration namespace that implements all the support to read and write settings. This support is encapsulated by the generated properties, so all you need to worry about is the Settings class itself. Additionally, because the properties are strongly typed, you'll receive compile-time errors if you use them incorrectly.

You may have noticed that the user setting is read-write, whereas the application setting is read-only. User settings are read-write to allow users to change values between application sessions. In contrast, application settings are likely to store configuration information; so to prevent developers from writing code that could change them—potentially breaking the application—application settings are generated as read-only properties. The following code shows how you might use both user and application settings at run-time:

```
// Read an application setting
decimal pi = Properties.Settings.Default.Pi;

// Write to an application setting
// NOTE: This won't compile
Properties.Settings.Default.Pi = 3.142;

// Write a user setting
Properties.Settings.Default.WindowLocation = this.Location;
```

When you use the Settings class like this, the settings values are initially retrieved from the application's configuration file and subsequently are operated on in memory. But because user settings need to be persisted across application sessions, all user-scoped property values held by the Settings object should be persisted back to the configuration file if changed. To do this, you call the Save method on the Settings class:

```
void saveSettingsButton_Click(object sender, EventArgs e) {
  // Save all user settings
  Properties.Settings.Default.Save();
}
```

Changed user settings are not stored back to an application's configuration file, as you might expect; the only settings stored in an application's configuration file are application settings and default user settings. Altered user settings are persisted to a file named user.config, which is placed in one of several Windows logo-compliant locations within the file system, depending on where the application is installed and whether the user is roaming. The path to user.config for a locally installed application executed by a nonroaming user conforms to the following:

```
%SystemDrive%\Documents and Settings\UserName\
  Local Settings\Application Data\ProductName\
  ApplicationName.exe_Url_UrlHash\AssemblyVersionNumber
```

Sometimes, users change settings to values they are not happy with and then can't remember what the previous defaults were. Fortunately, the settings infrastructure offers two simple backup options to rollback to the previous settings values. First, you can provide a mechanism for users to revert to the last saved settings by calling the Settings object's Reload method:

```
void reloadSettingsButton_Click(object sender, EventArgs e) {
  // Revert to last saved user settings
  Properties.Settings.Default.Reload();
}
```

Second, if user settings are damaged beyond recovery, you can allow users to revert to the application's default installed user settings—the default values stored in the application's configuration file. Retrieving them is a matter of calling the Settings object's Reset method:

```
void resetSettingsButton_Click(object sender, EventArgs e) {
  // Revert to default installed user settings
  Properties.Settings.Default.Reset();
}
```

User settings are managed so that if the user.config file is deleted, the default values for those settings are loaded into the next application session. This is the same as calling the Reset method.

The settings subsystem comes with more exotic capabilities, including versioning support, settings profiles, and even the ability to create custom settings providers, a feature that lets you save user settings to, for example, a web service. Additionally, you can bind form and control properties directly to settings from the Properties window, a practice that can save a lot of coding effort. To explore these in detail, look at Chapter 15: Settings.

Resources

Application and user settings data is used to control an application's look and feel, as well as its behavior, while remaining separate from the code itself. Alternatively, this kind of application and control data can be stored as part of an assembly's resources. A *resource* is a named piece of data bound into the executable (EXE) or dynamic link library (DLL) at build time. For example, you could set the background image of a form in your application by loading a bitmap from a file:

```
// ResourcesForm.cs
partial class ResourcesForm : Form {
  public ResourcesForm() {
    InitializeComponent();
    this.BackgroundImage =
      new Bitmap(@"C:\WINDOWS\Web\Wallpaper\Azul.jpg");
  }
}
```

Unfortunately, the problem with this code is that not all installations of Windows have Azul.jpg, and even those that have it may not have it in the same place. Even if you shipped this picture with your application, a space-conscious user might decide to remove it, causing your application to fault. The only safe way to make sure that the picture, or any file, stays with code is to embed it as a resource.

Resources can be conveniently embedded in two ways. First, you can use the Resource Editor, which can be opened by right-clicking on your project in Solution Explorer and choosing Properties | Resources. The Resource Editor provides a simplified UI, shown in Figure 1.16, that allows you to manage resources and, just as important, see what your resources will look like at design time.

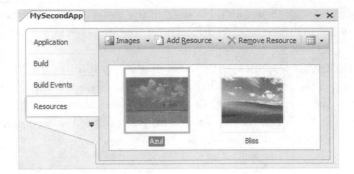

Figure 1.16   The Resource Editor

With the Resource Editor, you can add new and existing resources in a variety of ways, including using the drop-down list shown in Figure 1.17, pasting them from the Clipboard, or dragging and dropping onto the Resource Editor itself.

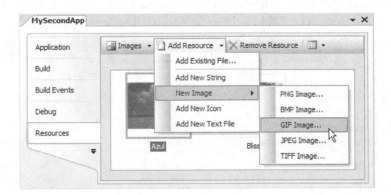

Figure 1.17   Adding a Resource with the Resource Editor

All resources added to and managed by the Resource Editor are categorized by resource type. You can use the drop-down list shown in Figure 1.18 to navigate between categories.

In addition to the categories you would expect to find—strings, images, icons, text files, and sound files—there is another category, Other, for extra resource data such as component-defined serialization of design-time data. Depending on the category, you can

Figure 1.18   Viewing Resource Categories

even view your resources in one of several ways. For example, you can display image resources using the List, Details, or Thumbnails view.

By default, string resources added with the Resource Editor are embedded in Resources.resx, a resource file located in the Properties folder of a Windows Forms project. Other resources are copied into a local project folder named "Resources" and linked (rather than embedded) with a file path reference stored in Resources.resx. As with settings, VS05 exposes your resources as strongly typed properties of the Resources class. Here's the abridged version:

```
internal class Resources {
  ...
  internal static Bitmap Azul { get; }
  ...
}
```

Apart from the advantage of compile-time type checking, the code you write to use resources is simple:

```
// Load strongly typed image resource
this.BackgroundImage = Properties.Resources.Azul;
```

If you are currently working on a form, control, or component, you can avoid having to write this code: Set the value of many properties by using the Properties window directly. For example, to set the background image for a form, you merely press the ellipses (" . . . ")

button in the Properties window next to the BackgroundImage property, opening the Select Resource dialog shown in Figure 1.19.

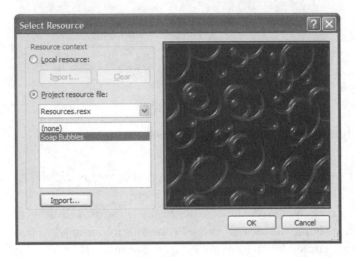

Figure 1.19 Selecting a Resource for a Form Property

This dialog allows you to import or select a resource from the form itself (if you choose Local Resource) or from your project's Resources.resx file (or any additional .resx files you may have added). This action causes the image to be shown in the Designer and generates the code that loads the resource at run time:

```
// Form1.cs
partial class Form1 : Form {
  public Form1() {
    InitializeComponent();
  }
}

// Form1.Designer.cs
partial class Form1 {
  ...
  void InitializeComponent() {
    ...
    this.BackgroundImage = Properties.Resources.Azul;
    ...
  }
}
```

As you can see, the generated code is pretty much the same code you'd write yourself.

For more details about resources and their relationship to localization and internation-alization, see Chapter 13: Resources.

Dialogs

You've seen how to create and show forms, but you can instead show them as dialogs. Although it's not always the case, *dialogs* are typically modal and exist to take information from a user before a task can be completed—in other words, a dialog is a form that has a "dialog" with the user. For example, we created the Options dialog in Figure 1.20 by right-clicking on a project in Solution Explorer and choosing Add Windows Form. Implementing the form was a matter of exposing the favorite color setting as a property, dropping the con-trols onto the form's design surface, and setting the ControlBox property to false so that it looks like a dialog.

Figure 1.20   A Dialog

You can use this form as a modal dialog by calling the ShowDialog method:

```
// OptionsDialog.cs
partial class OptionsDialog : Form {
  public OptionsDialog() {
    InitializeComponent();
  }

  void optionsToolStripMenuItem_Click(object sender, EventArgs e) {
    OptionsDialog dlg = new OptionsDialog();
    dlg.FavoriteColor = this.BackColor;
    if( dlg.ShowDialog() == DialogResult.OK ) {
      this.BackColor = dlg.FavoriteColor;
    }
  }
}
```

Notice that the custom OptionsDialog class is instantiated, but before it's shown, the ini-tial color value is passed in via the FavoriteColor property. When the modal ShowDialog method completes, it returns the value of the DialogResult enumeration—in this case, either OK or Cancel. Although it's possible to implement the Click events for the OK and

Cancel buttons inside the OptionsDialog class, there's a much easier way to make OK and Cancel act as they should: You set each button's DialogResult property appropriately, and set the OptionsDialog form's AcceptButton and CancelButton properties to the OK button and the Cancel button, respectively. In addition to closing the dialog and returning the result to the caller of ShowDialog, setting these properties enables the Enter and Esc keys and highlights the OK button as the default button on the form.

You may still feel the need to handle the OK Click event to validate data captured by the dialog. Although you can do that, Windows Forms provides built-in support for validation. In conjunction with an ErrorProvider component, you can handle the control's Validating event and thereby validate the contents of each control when the user moves focus from the control. For example, if we want the user to specify a color with some green in it, we can drop an ErrorProvider component onto the OptionsDialog form and handle the Validating event for the Change button whenever it loses focus:

```
// OptionsDialog.cs
partial class OptionsDialog : Form {
  ...
  void changeColorButton_Validating(object sender, CancelEventArgs e) {
    byte greenness = this.changeColorButton.BackColor.G;
    string err = "";
    if( greenness < Color.LightGreen.G ) {
      err = "I'm sorry, we were going for leafy, leafy...";
      e.Cancel = true;
    }
    this.errorProvider.SetError(changeColorButton, err);
  }
}
```

In the Validating event handler, notice that we set the CancelEventArgs.Cancel property to true; this cancels the loss of focus from the control that caused the validating event. Also notice the ErrorProvider.SetError invocation; SetError accepts as arguments the control that is being validated and a string, which is the message displayed by the ErrorProvider. When this string is null, the error provider's error indicator for that control is hidden. When this string contains something, the error provider shows an icon to the right of the control and provides a tooltip with the error string, as shown in Figure 1.21.

Figure 1.21   ErrorProvider Providing an Error (See Plate 1)

The Validating event handler is called whenever focus is moved from a control whose CausesValidation property is set to true (the default) to another control whose CausesValidation property is also set to true.

One side effect of setting CancelEventArgs.Cancel to true is that focus is retained on an invalid control until valid data is entered, thereby preventing users from navigating away from the control. The Form class's AutoValidate property dictates this behavior to remain consistent with previous versions of Windows Forms. AutoValidate's default value is EnablePreventFocusChange. If you prefer to let your users navigate away from invalid controls—generally considered better from a user's point of view—you can change AutoValidate to EnableAllowFocusChange in the Properties window, as shown in Figure 1.22.

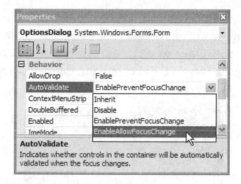

Figure 1.22　Setting the AutoValidate Property to Allow Focus to Change from an Invalid Control

The host form's AutoValidate value applies to all controls hosted by the form that perform validation. AutoValidate and validation are explored further in Chapter 3: Dialogs.

If you do allow free navigation across invalid controls, it means that users can conceivably tab to, or click, a form's AcceptButton without having any valid data on the form. Consequently, you need to write additional code to validate the entire form from the AcceptButton. Fortunately, the Form class exposes the Validate method for this purpose:

```
// OptionsDialog.cs
partial class OptionsDialog : Form {
  ...
  void okButton_Click(object sender, EventArgs e) {
    // Validate form
    bool isValid = this.Validate();
    // Don't close form if data is invalid
    if( !isValid ) this.DialogResult = DialogResult.None;
  }
}
```

The Validate method fires the Validating event for each of the controls hosted on a form, harvesting the results along the way. If any of the Validating event handlers set CancelEventArgs.Cancel to true, Validate returns false.

ErrorProvider and the Validating event give you most of what you need for basic validation, but more complicated validation scenarios require some custom coding. Chapter 3 explores these. It also discusses the standard Windows Forms dialogs and explains how to support communication between your modal and modeless dialogs and other parts of your application.

Drawing

As nifty as all the built-in controls are, and as nicely as you can arrange them, sometimes you need to take things into your own hands and render the state of your form or control yourself. For example, if you want to compose a fancy About dialog, as shown in Figure 1.23, you must handle the form's Paint event and do the drawing yourself.

Figure 1.23   Custom Drawing (See Plate 2)

The following is the Paint event-handling code to fill the inside of the About dialog:

```
// AboutDialog.cs
using System.Drawing;
using System.Drawing.Drawing2D;

partial class AboutDialog : Form {
  ...
  void AboutDialog_Paint(object sender, PaintEventArgs e) {
```

```
    Graphics g = e.Graphics;
    g.SmoothingMode = SmoothingMode.AntiAlias;

    Rectangle rect = this.ClientRectangle;
    int cx = rect.Width;
    int cy = rect.Height;
    float scale = (float)cy / (float)cx;

    LinearGradientBrush brush =
      new LinearGradientBrush(this.ClientRectangle,
                              Color.Empty,
                              Color.Empty,
                              45);
    try {
      ColorBlend blend = new ColorBlend();
      blend.Colors =
        new Color[] { Color.Red, Color.Green, Color.Blue };
      blend.Positions = new float[] { 0, .5f, 1 };
      brush.InterpolationColors = blend;
      Pen pen = new Pen(brush);
      try {
        for( int x = 0; x < cx; x += 7 ) {
          g.DrawLine(pen, 0, x * scale, cx - x, 0);
          g.DrawLine(pen, 0, (cx - x) * scale, cx - x, cx * scale);
          g.DrawLine(pen, cx - x, 0 * scale, cx, (cx - x) * scale);
          g.DrawLine(pen, cx - x, cx * scale, cx, x * scale);
        }
      }
      finally {
        pen.Dispose();
      }

      StringFormat format = new StringFormat();
      try {
        format.Alignment = StringAlignment.Center;
        format.LineAlignment = StringAlignment.Center;
        string s = "Ain't graphics cool?";
        g.DrawString(s, this.Font, brush, rect, format);
      }
      finally {
        format.Dispose();
      }
    }
    finally {
      brush.Dispose();
    }
  }
}
```

Notice the use of the Graphics object from the PaintEventArgs passed to the event handler. This provides an abstraction around the specific device we're drawing on, which we do with constructs like pens, brushes, shapes, and text. All this and more are explored in Chapter 5: Drawing Basics, Chapter 6: Drawing Text, and Chapter 7: Advanced Drawing.

You may be wondering what the try-finally blocks are for. Because the pen and brush objects hold underlying resources managed by Windows, we're responsible for releasing the resources when we're finished, even in the face of an exception. Like many classes in .NET, the Pen and Brush classes implement the IDisposable interface, which serves as a signal for an object's client to call the IDisposable Dispose method when it's finished with an object. This lets the object know that it's time to clean up any unmanaged resources it's holding, such as a file, a database connection, or a graphics resource.

To simplify things in C#, you can replace the try-finally block with a *using* block (shown here for the Brush object):

```
// AboutDialog.cs
using System.Drawing;
using System.Drawing.Drawing2D;

partial class AboutDialog : Form {
  ...
  void AboutDialog_Paint(object sender, PaintEventArgs e) {
    using( LinearGradientBrush brush =
             new LinearGradientBrush(this.ClientRectangle,
                                     Color.Empty,
                                     Color.Empty,
                                     45) ) {
      ...
      // Wrap Pen and StringFormat usage in "using" blocks, too
      ...
    } // brush.Dispose called automatically
  }
}
```

The C# using block instructs the compiler to wrap the code it contains in a try-finally block and call the IDisposable Dispose method at the end of the block for objects created as part of the using clause. This is a convenient shortcut for C# programmers, a good practice to get into, and something you'll see used extensively in the rest of this book.

Printing

Printing is just a matter of getting at another Graphics object that models the printer. We can do that by using the PrintDocument component and handling the events that it fires when the user requests a document to be printed. For example, we can drag the PrintDocument component from the Toolbox onto our AboutDialog form and use it to implement a Print button:

```
void printButton_Click(object sender, EventArgs e) {
  PrintDialog dlg = new PrintDialog();
  dlg.Document = this.printDocument;
  if( dlg.ShowDialog() == DialogResult.OK ) {
    this.printDocument.Print();
  }
}
```

Notice that before we ask the PrintDocument component to print, we use the standard PrintDialog component to ask the user which printer to use. If the user presses the OK button, we ask the document to print. Of course, it can't print on its own. Instead, it fires the PrintPage event, asking us to draw each page:

```
using System.Drawing.Printing;
...
void printDocument_PrintPage(object sender, PrintPageEventArgs e) {
  Graphics g = e.Graphics;
  using( Font font = new Font("Lucida Console", 72) ) {
    g.DrawString("Hello,\nPrinter", font, Brushes.Black, 0, 0);
  }
}
```

If you'd like to print more than one page, set the HasMorePages property of the Print-PageEventArgs class until all pages have been printed. To be notified at the beginning and end of each print request as a whole, you handle the BeginPrint and EndPrint events. To change settings—such as margins, paper size, landscape versus portrait mode, and so on— you handle the QueryPageSettings event.

After you have the PrintDocument events handled, Windows Forms makes adding print preview as easy as using the PrintPreview dialog:

```
void printPreviewButton_Click(object sender, EventArgs e) {
  this.printPreviewDialog.Document = this.printDocument;
  this.printPreviewDialog.ShowDialog();
}
```

For more details on printing, read Chapter 8: Printing.

Data Binding

Dealing with data is one aspect of your application development that may not require you to write custom code. Data-centric applications are fully supported in Windows Forms, and you can manage data sources completely in VS05's Data Sources window, shown in Figure 1.24.

You open the Data Sources window by clicking Data | Show Data Sources (Shift+Alt+D).

Figure 1.24   VS05 Data Sources Window

From the Data Sources window, you can add a new data source to your project either by clicking the Add New Data Source link label (if your project has no data sources) or from the tool strip (to add other data sources). Either action opens the Data Source Configuration Wizard, shown in Figure 1.25.

Figure 1.25   Data Source Configuration Wizard

The Data Source Configuration Wizard allows us to create and configure a data source for tables in a database, objects located in the current assembly, and objects located in another assembly or web service. Figure 1.26 shows the result of creating a data source for the Northwind database's Employees table.

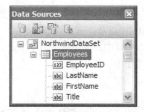

Figure 1.26   Employees Data Source in VS05

After you have a data source, you can perform a variety of additional configurations, as covered in Chapter 16: Data Binding Basics. The most interesting feature is that you can create a fully operational data-bound form simply by dragging data-bound controls straight onto the form from the Data Sources window. Figure 1.27 shows the result of dragging the Employees data source onto a form.

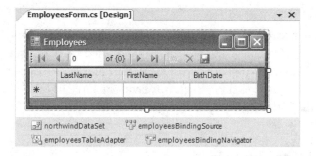

Figure 1.27   Result of Dragging a Data Source onto a Form

The data source is represented by two data components: a *data set*, a DataSet-derived class generated by the Designer to hold Employees data for the Employees table; and a *table adapter* to shuttle data between the data set's Employees table and the Employees table in the Northwind database. The UI is composed of two controls: a *DataGridView* to display the data, and a *BindingNavigator* to provide VCR-style navigation of the data.

Between the data components and the UI controls lies the *BindingSource* component; BindingSource consumes item or collection types and exposes them as data, which can be associated with controls in a special relationship known as *data binding*. Data binding a control to a data source provides for bidirectional communication between the control and the data source so that when the data is modified in one place, it's propagated to the other. Built on top of this basic concept are many additional levels of data binding support that item or collection types can implement, although it is often difficult and time consuming. However, the BindingSource component's major role is to "upgrade" such types to a satisfactory minimum level of data binding support, which includes currency management, inserts, updates, deletes, and change notification.

Figure 1.28 shows the resulting application executing without a single change to the code generated by the Windows Forms Designer.

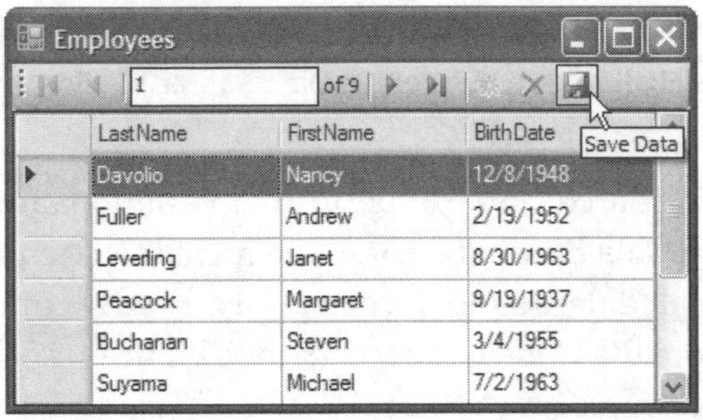

Figure 1.28   Full Data Binding Without Code

We've scratched only the surface of what can be done with data binding. For more, read Chapter 16: Data Binding Basics, and Chapter 17: Applied Data Binding. Also, while some types of applications deal with lists of data located in places like databases, other applications deal with document-style data. Such applications have special requirements that are covered in Appendix F: Document Management.

Multithreaded User Interfaces

Because the Windows Forms Designer provides so much functionality via drag and drop and the Properties window, it might be a while before you get to the meat of your programming chores. When you do, though, you're bound to run into a task that takes long enough to annoy your users if you make them wait while it completes—for example, printing, searching, or calculating the last digit of pi.

It's especially annoying if your application freezes while an operation takes place on the UI thread, showing a blank square where the main form used to be and giving your users time to consider your competitors' applications. To build applications that remain responsive in the face of long-running operations, you need to create and manage worker threads from your main application (UI) thread, as well as ensure safe communication between the UI threads and worker threads. If the thought of doing this fills you with trepidation, then have no fear: Windows Forms encapsulates these complexities within a single component, BackgroundWorker, which you can drop onto a form and configure from the Windows Forms Designer.

For example, consider the application in Figure 1.29, which provides the potentially long-running ability to calculate pi to any number of decimal places.

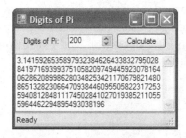

Figure 1.29   Digits of Pi Calculator

To have the pi calculation execute on a worker thread, simply double-click the BackgroundWorker component. The Windows Forms Designer automatically creates an event handler for BackgroundWorker's default DoWork event:

```
// AsyncCalcPiForm.cs
partial class AsyncCalcPiForm : Form {
  ...
  void backgroundWorker_DoWork(object sender, DoWorkEventArgs e) {
    // Pi calculation code
    ...
  }
  ...
}
```

The job of initiating the long-running operation and having the DoWork code execute is left up to you, although it is simply a case of invoking BackgroundWorker.DoWorkAsync:

```
// AsyncCalcPiForm.cs
partial class AsyncCalcPiForm : Form {
  ...
  void calcButton_Click(object sender, EventArgs e) {
    ...
    // Initiate asynchronous worker thread
    this.backgroundWorker.RunWorkerAsync(digits);
  }
  void backgroundWorker_DoWork(object sender, DoWorkEventArgs e) {...}
  ...
}
```

When RunWorkAsync is invoked, BackgroundWorker creates a worker thread from the thread pool, transitions to it, and fires the DoWork event. All this is done behind the scenes and, as long as you follow the golden rule, is thread safe. If you need to update controls on the UI thread from a worker thread—for example, to report the progress of a long-running operation—BackgroundWorker provides additional mechanisms for doing so safely, as well as for canceling a long-running operation mid-execution. These details and more are covered in Chapter 18: Multithreaded User Interfaces.

Deployment

When you have your application just the way you like it, all arranged and responsive and fancy-pants, you'll want to share it. You have several options. You can create an archive of your files and send them as an e-mail to your friends and family, from which they can extract the files into the folder of their choice and run your application. Or if you don't like providing user support because your friends and family inevitably have no idea what they're doing, you can use the VS05 Setup Project template to create a project that produces a Windows Installer (.msi) file containing your application's files. Recipients can use this .msi file to install the application into the desired folder.

The problem with both of these techniques is that as soon as you share your application, that's when you find the crushing bug that, when the moon is full and the sun is in the house of Orion, causes bad, bad things to happen. When problems come up, you need to remember who received your application so that you can let them know to install the new version before the existing version formats C: or resets your boss's Minesweeper high scores. Of course, all this explains why your IT department mandates that all internal applications be web applications.

The web application deployment model is so simple, there is no deployment. Instead, whenever users surf to the web application in the morning, they get the version that the IT department uploaded to the server the night before. This deployment model is now provided for Windows Forms applications, using a technology known as ClickOnce.

At this point, you should stop reading and try the following:

1. Use the New Project dialog to create a new Windows Application called ClickOnceFun.
2. In Solution Explorer, right-click the ClickOnceFun project and choose Publish.
3. In the Publish Wizard, click the Finish button.
4. On the web page that's opened, click the Install ClickOnceFun button.
5. On the Application Install—Security Warning dialog, click the Install button.
6. Bask in the glory of using ClickOnce deployment to publish and install a real Windows application over the web, without any setup required.

You've just used the *ClickOnce* deployment feature of .NET to deploy your Windows Forms application like a web application, except that it's a real Windows application complete with full user control over the frame, the tool strip, the menu strip, the status strip, shortcut keys, and so on. Any libraries your application requires, such as custom or third-party controls, will be downloaded from the same virtual directory that the application came from. When a ClickOnce-deployed application is downloaded, the .NET Framework's *code access security* dictates that the permissions of your code are limited according to the zone from which the application is deployed, such as the Internet, an intranet, or a local machine.

When applications require more permission than their zone allows, users have the option either to prevent the application from installing or to authorize permission elevation to allow the application to execute with increased permissions. This is in contrast to classic Windows security, where code is awarded permissions based on who launched the application, an approach that doesn't work very well when everyone seems to run as Administrator.

If that isn't enough security for you, ClickOnce-deployed applications are downloaded using a model built on trust certificates to identify application publishers; this model allows users to decide whether they should install an application based on whether they trust the application's publisher. If they trust a dodgy publisher and get burned, they have recourse; because the identity of the publisher is stored in the trust certificates themselves, and because trust certificates are handed out only by authorities certified to do so, such as VeriSign, users can be pretty confident in tracking down the perpetrator of any evil crimes that take place.[8]

Overall, ClickOnce deployment offers a slew of support for a wide variety of deployment scenarios that can be configured from VS05. Further, if your deployment needs aren't supported by VS05, you can use code to leverage the System.Deployment namespace to enable them. For the details, turn to Chapter 19: ClickOnce Deployment.

Where Are We?

As this chapter has shown, Windows Forms provides a great deal of functionality. Not only does it give you the basic elements needed to build applications, forms, controls, resources, and dialogs, but it also provides advanced features such as anchoring, docking, user controls, print preview, data binding, and web deployment. Guiding you along the way are a slew of wizards and the Windows Forms Designer, the main vehicle for visually developing the look and feel of your application. Where Windows Forms stops, the rest of the .NET Framework steps in to provide drawing, object serialization, threading, security, and tons of other bits of functionality in thousands of classes and components. One book can't cover all of those, but I'll show you what you need to know to write real Windows Forms applications and controls in the rest of this one.

---

[8] You can reach VeriSign at http://www.verisign.com.

2

Forms

IN A TECHNOLOGY NAMED WINDOWS FORMS, you can expect the form to play a critical role. This chapter explores the basics, including displaying forms, form lifetime, form size and location, nonclient form adornments, menu strips, tool strips, and status strips, as well as advanced topics such as form transparency, nonrectangular forms, and visual inheritance. And if that's not enough, Chapter 3: Dialogs is all about using forms as dialogs.

Some of the material in this chapter discusses child controls, but only where those controls are commonly found on forms, particularly main forms. For a discussion devoted to Windows Forms controls, see Chapter 10: Controls. Chapter 4: Layout covers arranging controls using the myriad of design-time and run-time features offered by .NET.

Showing Forms

Any form—that is, any class that derives from the Form base class—can be shown in one of two ways. Here, a form is shown modelessly:

```
void button_Click(object sender, EventArgs e) {
    AnotherForm form = new AnotherForm();
    form.Show(); // Show form modelessly
}
```

Here, a form is shown modally:

```
void button_Click(object sender, EventArgs e) {
    AnotherForm form = new AnotherForm();
    form.ShowDialog(); // Show form modally
}
```

Form.Show shows the new form modelessly and returns immediately without creating any relationship between the currently active form and the new form. This means that the existing form can be closed, leaving the new form behind.[1] Form.ShowDialog, on the other hand, shows the form modally and does not return control until the created form has been closed, either by using the explicit Close method or by setting the DialogResult property (more on this in Chapter 3).

Owner and Owned Forms

As ShowDialog shows the new form, an implicit relationship is established between the currently active form, known as the *owner* form, and the new form, known as the *owned* form. This relationship ensures that the owned form is the active form and is always shown on top of the owner form, as illustrated in Figure 2.1.

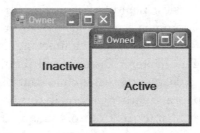

Figure 2.1 Implicit Owner-Owned Relationship Established by ShowDialog Method

One feature of this relationship is that the owned form affects the behavior of its owner form:

- The owner form cannot be minimized, maximized, or even moved.
- The owned form blocks mouse and keyboard input to the owner form.
- The owner form is minimized when the owned form is.
- Only the owned form can be closed.
- If both owner and owned forms are minimized and if the user presses Alt+Tab to switch to the owned form, the owned form is activated.

[1] If the closing form is the main form, by default the other forms close and the application exits.

Unlike the ShowDialog method, however, a call to the Show method does not establish an implicit owner-owned relationship. This means that either form can be the currently active form, as shown in Figure 2.2.

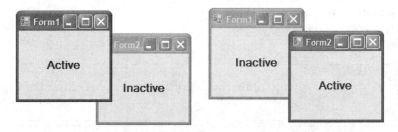

Figure 2.2   No Owner-Owned Relationship Established by Show Method

Without an implicit owner-owned relationship, owner and owned forms alike can be minimized, maximized, or moved. If the user closes any form other than the main form, the most recently active form is reactivated.

Although ShowDialog establishes an implicit owner-owned relationship, there is no built-in way for the owned form to call back to or query the form that opened it. In the modeless case, you can set the new form's Owner property to establish the owner-owned relationship:

```
void button_Click(object sender, EventArgs e) {
    OwnedForm form = new OwnedForm();
    form.Owner = this; // Establish owner-owned relationship
    form.Show();
}
```

As a shortcut, you could pass the owner form as an argument to an overload of the Show method, which also takes an IWin32Window parameter:[2]

```
void button_Click(object sender, EventArgs e) {
    OwnedForm form = new OwnedForm();
    form.Show(this); // Establish owner-owned relationship
}
```

[2] IWin32Window is implemented by Windows Forms UI objects that expose a Win32 HWND property via the IWin32Window.Handle property.

The modal case is similar in that you can either set the Owner property explicitly or pass the owner form as an argument to the ShowDialog override:

```
void button_Click(object sender, EventArgs e) {
    OwnedForm form = new OwnedForm();
    // Establish owner-owned relationship
    // form.Owner = this;
    form.ShowDialog(this);
}
```

An owner form can also enumerate the list of forms it owns using the OwnedForms collection:

```
void button_Click(object sender, EventArgs e) {
    OwnedForm form = new OwnedForm();
    form.Owner = this;
    form.Show();

    foreach( Form ownedForm in this.OwnedForms ) {
        MessageBox.Show(ownedForm.Text);
    }
}
```

The behavior of forms in an explicit modal owner-owned form relationship is the same as its implicit modal counterpart, but the modeless owner-owned relationship provides additional behavior in the non-owner-owned modeless case. First, the modeless owned form always appears on top of the owner form, even though either can be active. This is useful when you need to keep a form, such as a floating tool window, on top of other forms within an application.[3] Second, if the user presses Alt+Tab to switch from the owner, the owned forms follow suit. To ensure that the user knows which form is the main form, minimizing the owner hides the task bar buttons for all owned forms, leaving only the owner's task bar button visible.

You may have noticed that in addition to an optional owner, a form can have an optional parent, as exposed via the Parent property (which is almost always set to null). This property is reserved for Multiple Document Interface (MDI) forms, discussed later in this chapter, and controls. For controls, the parent-child relationship dictates *clipping*—that is, a child's edge is clipped to the edge of the parent, as shown in Figure 2.3.

---

[3] Keeping a form on top of all open forms for all applications depends on z-order, discussed later in this chapter.

Figure 2.3   A Child ListBox Control Clipped to the Client Area of Its Parent Form

Form Lifetime

Although the user can't see a form until either Show or ShowDialog is called, a form comes into existence as soon as a form object is instantiated. From there, its lifetime is measured by a series of events that you can handle to control, manage, or just be notified as appropriate. Figure 2.4 illustrates the sequence of these events, from form construction to form closure.

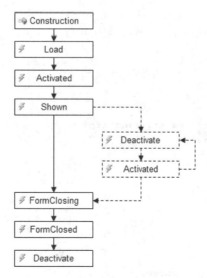

Figure 2.4   Form Lifetime Event Sequence

We now explore a form's lifetime in detail.

Form Opening

A new form object begins waking up when its *constructor* is executed, which in turn calls InitializeComponent to create and initialize all the child controls. InitializeComponent is Designer-generated, and consequently it's a bad idea to put custom code into it because the Designer is likely to throw it away. However, if you'd like to add other controls or change anything set by the InitializeComponent method, you can do so from the constructor after the call to InitializeComponent:

```
public Form1() {
   InitializeComponent();

   // Adding a control
   Button anotherButton = new Button();
   this.Controls.Add(anotherButton);

   // Changing a property to something not known at design-time
   this.Text = DateTime.Now.ToString();
}
```

When either Form.Show or Form.ShowDialog is called, that's the new form's cue to show itself and all its child controls. To be notified just before this happens, you handle the Load event:

```
// Form1.cs
partial class Form1 : Form {
  ...
  void Form1_Load(object sender, EventArgs e) {
    MessageBox.Show("Loading Form1!");
  }
}

// Form1.Designer.cs
partial class Form1 {
  ...
  void InitializeComponent() {
    ...
    this.Load += this.Form1_Load;
    ...
  }
}
```

The Load event is useful for doing any final initialization right before a form is shown. Also, the Load event is a good place to restore any main form settings that need to be remembered from one application session to the next, such as size and location.[4]

When a form is loaded for the first time, it becomes the *active* form, which is the foreground form that receives keyboard input. It's at this point that a form fires the Activated event:

```
// Form1.cs
partial class Form1 : Form {
  ...
  void Form1_Activated(object sender, EventArgs e) {
    MessageBox.Show("Form1 activated!");
  }
}

// Form1.Designer.cs
partial class Form1 {
  ...
  void InitializeComponent() {
    ...
    this.Activated += this.Form1_Activated;
    ...
  }
}
```

After activation, a form broadcasts that opening has completed by firing the Shown event:

```
// Form1.cs
partial class Form1 : Form {
  ...
  void Form1_Shown(object sender, EventArgs e) {
    MessageBox.Show("Form1 shown!");
  }
}

// Form1.Designer.cs
partial class Form1 {
  ...
  void InitializeComponent() {
    ...
    this.Shown += this.Form1_Shown;
    ...
  }
}
```

[4] How to save and restore main form settings is discussed in Chapter 15: Settings.

The story doesn't end here; after a form has finally completed opening, users may switch between your application and others many times.

Form Deactivation and Reactivation

When a user switches away from your application, such as by using Alt+Tab, the current form deactivates and fires the Deactivate event. One reason to handle Deactivate is to pause any activity that can't continue without user involvement, such as game play:

```
// Form1.cs
partial class Form1 : Form {
  ...
  void Form1_Deactivate(object sender, EventArgs e) {
    this.game.Pause();
  }
}

// Form1.Designer.cs
partial class Form1 {
  ...
  void InitializeComponent() {
    ...
    this.Deactivate += this.Form1_Deactivate;
    ...
  }
}
```

When users switch back to the application, the Activated event is fired again, allowing you to resume any activity you may have paused when the form deactivated:

```
// Form1.cs
partial class Form1 : Form {
  ...
  void Form1_Activated(object sender, EventArgs e) {
    this.game.Resume();
  }
}
```

If you write code to handle the Activated and Deactivate events, it needs to be sensitive to the fact that they can be fired multiple times, unlike the other events in a form's lifetime.

Whether a form is active or not is independent of its visibility, which you can change by toggling its Visibility property or by calling either the Hide or the Show method. Hide and Show are helper methods that set the Visible property as appropriate:

```
void hideButton_Click(object sender, EventArgs e) {
    this.Hide(); // Set Visible property indirectly
    this.Visible = false; // Set Visible property directly
}
```

As you might expect, there is an event that you can handle as your form flickers in and out of visual reality. It's called VisibleChanged.

Form Closing

When forms outlive their usefulness, users close them in one of several ways. Figure 2.5 illustrates the ways provided by Windows automatically, including System Menu | Close, Alt+F4, or the close box.

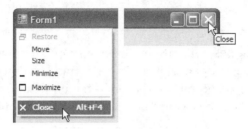

Figure 2.5   System-Provided Mechanisms for Closing a Form

If a form is a main form, it will likely have a menu strip. In this case, you can follow Windows UI consistency by providing either an Exit menu item or, in the case of an MDI child form, a Close menu item. Both of these are normally situated in the File menu, as shown in Figure 2.6.

Figure 2.6   Application-Provided Mechanisms for Closing a Form

In either case, closing the form is handled from the appropriate menu item's Click event handler by a call to the Form's aptly named Close method:

```
void exitToolStripMenuItem_Click(object sender, EventArgs e) {
  this.Close(); // Close this form
}
```

Whichever approach you use, it is possible that an application could prematurely end processing and potentially leave data in an inconsistent state. You can give users the option to change their minds by handling the FormClosing event and setting FormClosingEvent-Args.Cancel to true or false as appropriate:

```
void Form1_FormClosing(object sender, FormClosingEventArgs e) {
  DialogResult result = MessageBox.Show(
    "Abort your game?", "Game In Progress", MessageBoxButtons.YesNo);
  e.Cancel = (result == DialogResult.No);
}
```

FormClosing is also the best place to serialize the properties of a form that you need to remember when the form is reopened, including size and location (as discussed in Chapter 15). On the other hand, the FormClosed event is merely a notification that the form has already gone away even though the form is still visible when FormClosed is fired:[5]

```
void Form1_FormClosed(object sender, FormClosedEventArgs e) {
  MessageBox.Show("Your game was aborted");
}
```

If you need contextual information about who initiated the form closure, you can query the CloseReason property of both FormClosingEventArgs and FormClosed EventArgs:

```
void Form1_FormClosed(object sender, FormClosedEventArgs e) {
  MessageBox.Show(
    "Your game was aborted: " + e.CloseReason.ToString());
}
```

[5] FormClosing and FormClosed supercede Closing and Closed from previous versions of .NET, which are retained to support backward compatibility for applications built before Windows Forms 2.0.

CloseReason can be one of several values:

```
enum CloseReason {
    None, // No reason given, or could not be determined
    WindowsShutDown, // Windows is closing (ShutDown or Logoff)
    MdiFormClosing, // MDI parent form is closing
    UserClosing, // User closed (close box or Alt+F4)
    TaskManagerClosing, // Task Manager | End Task
    FormOwnerClosing, // Owner form is closing
    ApplicationExitCall // Application.Exit invoked
}
```

After FormClosed has been fired, and if form closure wasn't canceled, the form fires the Deactivated event one last time before it winks out of existence.

Form Notification

Some applications, such as games, are unlikely to continue processing while deactivated because they are user-input intensive. Other applications, however, can continue executing in the background and don't need to halt processing. When background applications have something of note to tell the user, such as when they have loaded or an activity has completed, they can use several notification techniques ranging from noninvasive to urgent, depending on how soon user intervention is required.

Flashing Notification

The simplest and least invasive notification technique is to call the form's Activate method:[6]

```
void timer_Tick(object sender, EventArgs e) {
    // Long-running task has completed
    ...
    this.Activate();
}
```

In modern versions of Windows, Activate causes an inactive form's border and task bar button to flash three times in an attempt to grab a user's attention.[7] This is a useful technique if urgent user intervention isn't required. When the application requires more urgent user intervention, such as responding to an MSN Messenger chat request,

[6] Both Form.Visible and Form.IsHandleCreated must be true for Activate to work.
[7] Older versions of Windows allowed an application to set itself active on top of the currently active window, something that could be pretty annoying.

notifications need to be more persistent, perhaps flashing continuously until the user reactivates a form. In these cases, you lean on P/Invoke to call FlashWindowEx from the User32 Windows API.[8]

System Tray Notification

Flashing is a great way to capture a user's attention, particularly if intervention is required. However, some activities can run in the background without requiring user intervention. One such application is Microsoft Outlook, which can be configured to periodically check for new messages, notifying users by placing an icon in the system tray, as shown in Figure 2.7.

Figure 2.7   Microsoft Outlook New Mail Notification

This icon disappears when users read their new mail. You can support the same scenario in Windows Forms by using the NotifyIcon component, shown in Figure 2.8.

Figure 2.8   NotifyIcon Component

NotifyIcon offers several properties for this purpose, including Icon (to specify the system tray icon) and Text (to set the tool tip that appears when the mouse hovers over the icon). From a notification point of view, you should hide the icon until something happens; to do this, you initially set its Visible property to false at design-time. When you need to notify users, you set NotifyIcon.Visible to true:

---

[8] See http://www.pinvoke.net.

```
// MainForm.cs
partial class MainForm : Form {
  ...
  void mailWatcher_NewMail(object sender, EventArgs e) {
    // Show the system tray icon to provide latent access to
    // notification message
    this.newMailNotifyIcon.Visible = true;
  }
}
```

The result is shown in Figure 2.9.

**Figure 2.9   NotifyIcon and Tooltip
in the System Tray**

Further, if an application is currently inactive, you can allow users to reactivate it by double-clicking the system tray icon. To do this, you handle NotifyIcon's DoubleClick event and call Activate on the main form:

```
// MainForm.cs
partial class MainForm : Form {
  ...
  void newMailNotifyIcon_MouseDoubleClick(
    object sender, MouseEventArgs e) {
    this.newMailNotifyIcon.Visible = false;
    this.Activate();
    NewMail();
  }
}
```

If you want to stuff more functionality into a system tray icon, such as opening or closing new mail, you can do so by assigning a context menu to the system tray icon itself. One advantage of this technique is that it allows users to go directly to the desired task.

To add a context menu, drag a context menu strip control onto the form, add the appropriate tool strip menu items, and associate it with the system tray icon. You do the latter by setting the NotifyIcon's ContextMenuStrip property to it, as shown in Figure 2.10.

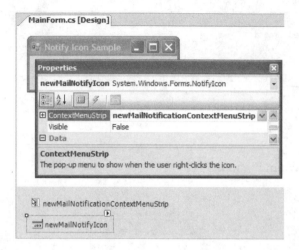

Figure 2.10   NotifyIcon and Context Menu at Design-Time

Figure 2.11 shows what this looks like at run-time

Figure 2.11   NotifyIcon and Context
Menu Strip at Run-Time

System Tray-Only Applications

Although the use of NotifyIcon as a notification device is transient, applications like MSN Messenger and various Windows services are accessible from the system tray for their entire lifetime. Unlike standard Windows Forms applications—which are minimized to and restored from the task bar—applications like MSN Messenger minimize to and restore from the system tray.

Adding this support to an application is similar to setting up a transient notification icon. First, you drag a NotifyIcon control onto your form, this time configuring the Icon property with the application icon. Next, you add a context menu strip to your form to expose the various commands you'd like users to be able to execute from the system tray icon, such as Open to reopen the application, Close to stop application execution, and any shortcut commands you need.[9] Finally, you implement the code that minimizes an application to the system tray. This depends on detecting when a form's WindowState changes to Minimized, after which the form should be hidden and the system tray icon shown:

```
// MainForm.cs
partial class MainForm : Form {
  ...
  void MainForm_Resize(object sender, EventArgs e) {
    // Minimize to system tray
    if( FormWindowState.Minimized == WindowState ) {
      Hide();
      this.appNotifyIcon.Visible = true;
    }
  }
  ...
}
```

Figure 2.12 shows the application's NotifyIcon and Open context menu.

Figure 2.12   NotifyIcon and Open Context Menu

As Figure 2.12 shows, you select the Open command to restore the application. To make this the default command, you can handle NotifyIcon's DoubleClick event. Both are shown here:

```
// MainForm.cs
partial class MainForm : Form {
  ...
  void appNotifyIcon_DoubleClick(object sender, EventArgs e) {
    Open();
  }
```

[9] If your application is purely system tray driven, you should set NotifyIcon.Visible to true, use a context menu strip if required, and consider changing the icon when notification is required.

```
void openToolStripMenuItem_Click(object sender, EventArgs e) {
  Open();
}

void Open() {
  // Restore from system tray
  this.appNotifyIcon.Visible = false;
  this.Show();
  WindowState = FormWindowState.Normal;
}
...
}
```

As you can see, restoring from the system tray involves both hiding the system tray icon and showing the form with a Normal WindowState.[10]

On the other hand, if the application is the kind that receives a notification that doesn't necessitate form reactivation (such as a new mail message), you still need to notify the user visually. Because the main application icon is always visible, you can make it blink using a timer; or you can show another system tray icon, use a pop-up window like Outlook 2003,[11] or use NotifyIcon's balloon tip support, which is designed for this purpose. Balloon tips on system tray icons, such as the one in Figure 2.13, usually pop up for a brief period to let users know something has happened, without interfering with their current activity.

Figure 2.13   NotifyIcon Balloon Tip

The simplest way to create a balloon tip is to set NotifyIcon.Text with the balloon tip message before invoking NotifyIcon.ShowBalloonTip to display the balloon tip:

```
// MainForm.cs
partial class MainForm : Form {
  ...
  void NewMailArrived() {
    // If notify icon is visible, notify user of new mail
```

[10] For an interesting alternative implementation of a system tray icon using custom application contexts, see http://www.windowsforms.net/articles/notifyiconapplications.aspx (http://tinysells.com/4). Custom application contexts are covered in Chapter 14: Applications.

[11] Pop-up windows are affectionately referred to as "toast."

```
      if( !this.appNotifyIcon.Visible ) return;
      this.appNotifyIcon.BalloonTipText = "New mail has arrived!";
      this.appNotifyIcon.ShowBalloonTip(3);
   }
}
```

ShowBalloonTip accepts an integer value that specifies the number of seconds the balloon tip will be visible. NotifyIcon provides several other balloon tip members for more interesting uses:

```
namespace System.Windows.Forms {
   sealed class NotifyIcon : Component {
      ...
      // Properties
      public ToolTipIcon BalloonTipIcon { get; set; }
      public string BalloonTipText { get; set; }
      public string BalloonTipTitle { get; set; }

      // Methods
      public void ShowBalloonTip(int timeout);
      public void ShowBalloonTip(
         int timeout,
         string tipTitle,
         string tipText,
         ToolTipIcon tipIcon);

      // Events
      public event EventHandler BalloonTipClicked;
      public event EventHandler BalloonTipClosed;
      public event EventHandler BalloonTipShown;
   }
}
```

BalloonTipIcon, BalloonTipText, and BalloonTipTitle allow you to configure the various elements of a balloon tip you'd like displayed when ShowBalloonTip is called. ShowBalloonTip has an overload that accepts arguments that allow you to specify these properties if their values change from call to call. Additionally, NotifyIcon provides three events you can handle during the life cycle of a balloon tip.

Form Size and Location

When a form isn't lurking in the background behind a notification icon or task bar button, it is visible in the foreground and takes up space in some location on the screen. A form's initial location is governed by the StartPosition property, which can be one of several FormStartPosition enumeration values:

```
enum FormStartPosition {
   CenterParent = 4, // Center modeless owned forms and modal forms
                     // over owner. Center modeless unowned forms over
                     // currently active form
   CenterScreen = 1, // Centered over the visible desktop
   Manual = 0, // You use code to specify the initial start location
   WindowsDefaultBounds = 3, // Windows is asked for a default location
                             // and size
   WindowsDefaultLocation = 2 // Windows picks a location staggered from
                              // the top-left corner of the screen
                              // (default)
}
```

The size and location of the form are exposed via the Size and Location properties, of type Size and Point, respectively (both from the System.Drawing namespace). As a shortcut, the properties of the size of a form are exposed directly via the Height and Width form properties, and those of the location are exposed via the Left, Right, Top, and Bottom properties. Figure 2.14 shows the basic size and location properties of a form.

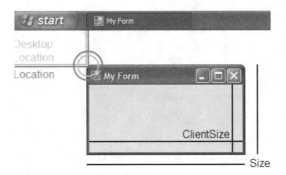

Figure 2.14　The DesktopLocation, Location, ClientSize, and Size Properties (See Plate 3)

When the upper-left corner of a form changes, that's a *move,* which can be handled in either Move or LocationChanged event handlers. When the width or height of a form changes, that's a *resize,* which can be handled in the Resize or the SizeChanged event handler, the latter being fired after the former.[12] You can also handle ResizeBegin and ResizeEnd for more fine-grained control over resizing. Sometimes, one gesture of the mouse can cause all move and size events to happen. For example, resizing a form by dragging the upper-left corner changes the location and the size of the form.

The location of the form is in absolute screen coordinates. If you're interested in the location of the form relative to the desktop, you can instead lean on the DesktopLocation property:

```
void Form1_Load(object sender, EventArgs e) {
  // Could end up under the shell's task bar
  this.Location = new Point(1, 1);

  // Will always be in the desktop
  this.DesktopLocation = new Point(1, 1);

  // A simpler form of the preceding line
  this.SetDesktopLocation(1, 1);
}
```

You might want to do this to ensure that your form's caption never appears underneath the shell's task bar, even if it's on the top edge, as shown in Figure 2.14.

Locations are expressed via the Point structure, the interesting parts of which are shown here:

```
namespace System.Drawing {
  struct Point {
    // Fields
    static readonly Point Empty;

    // Constructors
    Point(int x, int y);

    // Properties
    bool IsEmpty { get; }
    int X { get; set; }
    int Y { get; set; }

    // Methods
    static Point Ceiling(PointF value);
```

[12] Why are there *Xxx*Changed events for Move and Resize? The *Xxx*Changed events are so named to be consistent with data binding. The Move and Resize events are more familiar to Visual Basic programmers and are kept for their benefit. The two events are functionally equivalent.

```
        void Offset(int dx, int dy);
        static Point Round(PointF value);
        override string ToString();
        static Point Truncate(PointF value);
    }
}
```

The PointF structure is very similar to the Point structure, but PointF is used in drawing applications when more precise floating-point measurements are required. Sometimes, you need to convert from a Point to a PointF object to call certain methods or set certain properties. You can do so without any extra effort:

```
// Can convert directly from Point to PointF
Point pt1 = new Point(10, 20);
PointF pt2 = pt1; // Yields PointF(10.0f, 20.0f)
```

However, because floating-point numbers contain extra precision that will be lost in the conversion, you need to be explicit about how to convert from a PointF to a Point object using the static Truncate, Round, and Ceiling methods of the Point class:

```
// Need to be explicit when converting from a PointF to a Point
PointF pt1 = new PointF(1.2f, 1.8f);
Point pt2 = Point.Truncate(pt1); // Yields Point(1, 1);
Point pt3 = Point.Round(pt1); // Yields Point(1, 2);
Point pt4 = Point.Ceiling(pt1); // Yields Point(2, 2);
```

The size of a window is reflected in the Size property (Size also has a SizeF counterpart and provides the same capabilities for conversion):

```
namespace System.Drawing {
    struct Size {
        // Fields
        static readonly Size Empty;

        // Constructors
        Size(int width, int height);

        // Properties
        int Height { get; set; }
        bool IsEmpty { get; }
        int Width { get; set; }

        // Methods
        static Size Add(Size sz1, Size sz2);
```

```
        static Size Ceiling(SizeF value);
        static Size Round(SizeF value);
        override string ToString();
        static Size Truncate(SizeF value);
        static Size Subtract(Size sz1, Size sz2);
    }
}
```

Although the Size property represents the size of the entire window, a form isn't responsible for rendering all of its contents. The form can have edges, a caption, and scroll bars, all of which are drawn by Windows. The area the form is responsible for is marked by ClientSize, as shown in Figure 2.14. It's useful to save the ClientSize property between application sessions because it's independent of the current adornment settings the user has established. Similarly, resizing the form to make sure there's enough space to render your form's state is often related to the client area of the form and not to the size of the form as a whole:

```
void Form1_Load(object sender, EventArgs e) {
    this.ClientSize = new Size(100, 100); // Calls SetClientSizeCore
    this.SetClientSizeCore(100, 100);
}
```

A Rectangle combines a Point and a Size and also has a RectangleF counterpart. Structure RectangleThe Bounds property gives a rectangle of the form relative to the screen, whereas the DesktopBounds property is a rectangle relative to the desktop for top-level windows (and not for child windows). The ClientRectangle property is a rectangle relative to the form itself, describing the client area of the form. Of the three, ClientRectangle tends to be the most used, if only to describe which area to use when drawing:

```
void Form1_Paint(object sender, PaintEventArgs e) {
    Graphics g = e.Graphics )
    g.FillEllipse(Brushes.Yellow, this.ClientRectangle);
    g.DrawEllipse(Pens.DarkBlue, this.ClientRectangle);
}
```

Also, it's sometimes necessary to convert a point that's relative to the screen to one that's relative to the client or vice versa. For example, the HelpRequest event—which is generated when the user clicks on the Help button and then clicks on a control—is passed the mouse position in screen coordinates.[13] However, to determine which control was clicked on, you

---

[13] Adding the Help button to a form is discussed later in this chapter.

must have the mouse position in client coordinates. You can convert between the two coordinate systems by using PointToScreen and PointToClient:

```
void Form1_HelpRequested(object sender, HelpEventArgs e) {
    // Convert screen coordinates to client coordinates
    Point pt = this.PointToClient(e.MousePos);

    // Look for the control that the user clicked on
    foreach( Control control in this.Controls ) {
      if( control.Bounds.Contains(pt) ) {
        Control controlNeedingHelp = control;
        ...
        break;
      }
    }
}
```

To translate an entire rectangle between screen and client coordinates, you can also use RectangleToScreen and RectangleToClient.

Restricting Form Size

Our careful control layouts or rendering requirements often dictate a certain minimum amount of space. Less often, our forms can't be made to take advantage of more than a certain amount of space (although anchoring and docking, described later, should help with that). Either way, it's possible to set a form's minimum and maximum size via the MinimumSize and MaximumSize properties, respectively. The following example sets a fixed height of 200, a minimum width of 300, and a maximum width so large as to be unlimited:

```
void Form1_Load(object sender, EventArgs e) {
    // min width is 300, min height is 200
    this.MinimumSize = new Size(300, 200);

    // max width is unlimited, max height is 200
    this.MaximumSize = new Size(int.MaxValue, 200);
}
```

Notice that the code uses the maximum value of an integer to specify that there is no effective maximum width on the form. You may be tempted to use zero for this value instead, thinking that it is a way of saying "no maximum." However, if either the Width or the Height property of the Size used to set the minimum or maximum is nonzero, then both values of that Size are used for the specified property. That sets the maximum size of our form to zero instead of "no maximum."

One other setting that governs a form's size and location is WindowState, which can be one of the values from the FormWindowState enumeration:

```
namespace System.Windows.Forms {
  enum FormWindowState {
    Maximized = 2,
    Minimized = 1,
    Normal = 0 // default
  }
}
```

By default, the WindowState property is set to Normal, that is, visible but neither maximized nor minimized. Your program can get or set this property at will to manage the state of your form.

Form Z-Order

In addition to being located in terms of x and y, forms live in a third dimension known as the *z-order,* the order that dictates whether one form is drawn above or below another form. Furthermore, z-order is split into two tiers. *Normal* windows are drawn lowest z-order to highest, front to back. On top of all the normal windows are the *topmost* windows, which are also drawn relative to each other, lowest z-order to highest. But no matter the z-order, topmost forms are always drawn on top of any normal window. Figure 2.15 illustrates this two-tiered forms z-order.

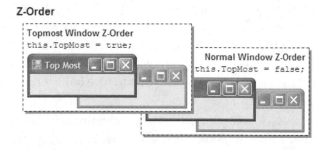

Figure 2.15 Topmost Window Z-Order in Relation to Normal Window Z-Order

For an example of a topmost window, pressing Ctrl+Shift+Esc under many versions of Windows will bring up Task Manager. By default, it's a topmost window and always draws on top of normal windows, whether or not it is the active window. You can change this behavior by unchecking the Options | Always On Top setting.[14] If Task Manager were implemented using Windows Forms, it would implement this feature by toggling the Top-Most property on its main form.

Form Adornments

In addition to size and location, forms have a number of properties that manage various other aspects of their appearance and corresponding behavior. The following settings govern the *nonclient* adornments of a form: those parts of a form outside the client area that are drawn by Windows:

- *FormBorderStyle* sets whether the form has a border, whether it can be resized, and whether it has a normal-sized or small caption. Good forms and dialogs have the default value of Sizable. Annoying dialogs change this property to one of the nonsizable options. Generally, programmers choose nonsizable options because of control-layout issues, but Windows Forms handles that nicely, as discussed in Chapter 4.

  In addition, there are two tool window styles—one fixed and one sizable—for use in building floating tool strip-style windows. You'll find an implementation of this in the sample for Chapter 4.

- *ControlBox* is a Boolean determining whether Windows shows the icon on the upper left corner of the form as well as the close button on the upper right. If ControlBox is set to false, neither left-clicking on the upper-left corner of the form nor right-clicking on the caption shows the System menu. Similarly, when Control-Box is false, the MaximizeBox and MinimizeBox properties are ignored, and those buttons are not shown. This property defaults to true but is often set to false for modal dialogs.

- The *MaximizeBox* and *MinimizeBox* properties determine whether the maximize and minimize buttons are shown on the form's caption. These properties default to true but are often set to false for modal dialogs.

---

[14] Chris always does!

- The *HelpButton* property shows the question mark button next to the close button in the upper right corner, but only if ControlBox is set to true and MaximizeBox and MinimizeBox are both set to false. This property defaults to false but is often set to true for modal dialogs. When the user clicks on the help button and then somewhere else on the form, the HelpRequested event is fired and the form provides the user with help. Whether the HelpButton property is true or false, the HelpRequested event is always fired when the user presses F1.
- The *Icon* property determines the image used as the icon for the form.
- The *ShowIcon* property hides or shows the form's icon.
- The *SizeGripStyle* property allows values from the SizeGripStyle enumeration: Auto, Hide, or Show. A *size grip* is the adornment on the lower-right corner of a window that indicates that it can be resized. The default is Auto and indicates showing the size grip in the lower-right corner "if needed," depending on the form's FormBorderStyle property. The Auto setting judges the size grip needed if the form is sizable and is shown modally. Also, if the form has a status strip control, the form's Size-GripStyle is ignored in favor of the SizingGrip Boolean property on the StatusStrip control (covered later in this chapter), if used.
- *ShowInTaskbar* is a Boolean governing whether the form's Text property appears in a button on the shell's task bar. This property defaults to true but is often set to false for modal forms.

Although most of the properties are independent of each other, not all of these combinations work together. For example, when FormBorderStyle is set to either of the tool window settings, no maximize or minimize box is shown, regardless of the value of the MaximizeBox and MinimizeBox properties. Experimentation will reveal what works and what doesn't.

Form Transparency

In addition to the properties that specify how the nonclient area of a form are rendered by Windows, the Form class provides a set of properties that allow you to change the appearance of the form as a whole, including making it partially transparent or removing pieces of the form altogether.

Opacity is the property that governs transparency for an entire form; it defaults to 1.0, or 100% opaque. A value between 0.0 and 1.0 denotes a degree of opacity using the alpha-blending support in more modern versions of Windows, where any number less than 1.0

results in a partially transparent form.[15] Opacity is mostly a parlor trick, but it's fun for making top-level windows less annoying than they normally are:

```
// MainForm.cs
partial class MainForm : Form {
  ...
  void MainForm_Activated(object sender, EventArgs e) {
    this.timer.Enabled = true;
  }

  void MainForm_Deactivate(object sender, EventArgs e) {
    this.timer.Enabled = false;
    this.Opacity = 0.5;
    this.Text = "Opacity = " + this.Opacity.ToString();
  }

  void timer_Tick(object sender, EventArgs e) {
    if( this.Opacity < 1.0 ) {
      this.Opacity += 0.1;
      this.Text = "Opacity = " + this.Opacity.ToString();
    }
    else this.timer.Enabled = false;
  }
}

// MainForm.Designer.cs
partial class MainForm {
  ...
  void InitializeComponent() {
    ...
    this.Opacity = 0.5;
    this.Text = "Opacity = 0.5";
    this.TopMost = true;
    ...
  }
```

This example shows code from a top-level form whose Opacity property starts at 50%. When the form is activated, it starts a timer that increases the Opacity by 10% on each tick, giving a nice "fade in" effect, as shown in Figure 2.16. When the form is deactivated, it is reset to 50% opaque, making it available for viewing and clicking but hopefully not obscuring too much.

[15] Alpha-blending is the blending of partially transparent elements based on an alpha value denoting the level of transparency.

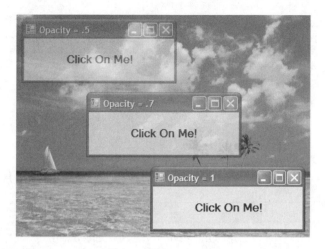

Figure 2.16 Opacity in Action (See Plate 4)

Nonrectangular Forms

Opacity affects the transparency of the entire form. You can also change the shape of the form by making parts of it completely transparent.[16] One way is to use the TransparencyKey property, which lets you designate a color to use in marking transparent pixels. When a pixel on the form is supposed to be drawn with the transparent key color, that pixel instead is removed from the form, in two senses: The pixel is not drawn, and clicking on that spot actually results in a click on what's showing through from underneath.

For example, setting TransparencyKey to the same as BackColor causes a form to lose its background (as well as anything else drawn with that color), as shown in Figure 2.17.

Figure 2.17 Form Shown in Front of Notepad
with TransparencyKey Set to BackColor

[16] For an interesting example of nonrectangular forms, see Mike Harsh's April 2004 MSDN TV presentation at http://msdn.microsoft.com/msdntv/episode.aspx?xml=episodes/en/20040401WinFormsMH/manifest.xml (http://tinysells.com/5).

The novelty of the form shown in Figure 2.17 seems limited until you combine it with FormBorderStyle.None, which removes the nonclient area altogether, as shown in Figure 2.18.

Figure 2.18   TransparencyKey Combined with
FormBorderStyle.None (See Plate 5)

The combination of a transparent color to erase the form's background and the removal of the form border yields a nonrectangular window, which is all the rage with the kids these days. The transparency key color is used to create a *region* that describes the form's visible area to Windows.

As easy as setting TransparencyKey is, you need to be careful. For example, you need to choose a color that you know won't appear in the parts of your form that need to show, or else they'll be made transparent, too. Also, when using TransparencyKey, you must calculate the region each time the form is drawn. Most importantly, TransparencyKey requires certain capabilities of the user's video driver. If they're missing, it fails completely.

So instead of using TransparencyKey, you may want to set the form's Region property directly. This approach is slightly less convenient but much more robust. Regions are covered in detail in Chapter 7: Advanced Drawing, but here's an example of using an ellipse as the form's region:

```
// MainForm.cs
using System.Drawing.Drawing2D;

partial class MainForm : Form {
  ...
  void SetEllipseRegion() {
    // Assume: this.FormBorderStyle = FormBorderStyle.None
    Rectangle rect = this.ClientRectangle;
    using( GraphicsPath path = new GraphicsPath() ) {
      path.AddEllipse(rect);
      this.Region = new Region(path);
```

```
      }
  }

  void MainForm_Load(object sender, EventArgs e) {
    SetEllipseRegion();
  }

  void MainForm_SizeChanged(object sender, EventArgs e) {
    SetEllipseRegion();
  }
  ...
}
```

Notice that our code sets the region both when the form is loaded and whenever the form is resized. However, as careful as we are to handle resizing, with the caption and the edges on the form missing, there's no way for the user to actually move or resize the form. When that's the case, you're on the hook to implement moving and resizing yourself. Here's an example of using the mouse events to move the form around when the user clicks in the form's client area:

```
// MainForm.cs
partial class MainForm : Form {
  ...
  Point downPoint = Point.Empty;

  void MainForm_MouseDown(object sender, MouseEventArgs e) {
    if( e.Button != MouseButtons.Left ) return;
    downPoint = new Point(e.X, e.Y);
  }

  void MainForm_MouseMove(object sender, MouseEventArgs e) {
    if( downPoint == Point.Empty ) return;
    Point location =
    new Point(
      this.Left + e.X - downPoint.X,
      this.Top + e.Y - downPoint.Y);
    this.Location = location;
  }

  void MainForm_MouseUp(object sender, MouseEventArgs e) {
    if( e.Button != MouseButtons.Left ) return;
    downPoint = Point.Empty;
  }
  ...
}
```

When the user clicks on the form's client area, the MouseDown event is fired, which we're handling to cache the point on the screen where the user clicked. When the user moves the mouse, the MouseMove event is fired, which we handle to move the form based on the difference between the current mouse location and the point where the user first clicked. Finally, when the user releases the mouse button, we handle the consequently fired MouseUp event to stop the move. Resizing requires a similar implementation. The details of mouse events, as well as keyboard events, are covered in Chapter 10.

Form and Context Menus

As interesting as forms themselves are—with their lifetime, adornments, transparency settings, and input options—they're all the more interesting when they contain controls. Apart from system-provided adornments like the control box and minimize and maximize buttons, the most likely adornment to appear on a main form is the menu strip. You can add a menu strip to your form by dragging a MenuStrip component onto it from the Toolbox.[17] The MenuStrip Designer allows you to build a menu strip interactively using MenuStrip's design surface, illustrated in Figure 2.19.

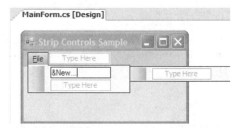

Figure 2.19   The VS05 MenuStrip Control Designer

[17] For an in-depth discussion of MenuStrip's key features, see Chapter 10. MenuStrip (and the other *Xxx*Strip controls discussed later) also support advanced layout capabilities, which are covered in Chapter 4.

To save yourself some effort, you can use MenuStrip's handy "Insert Standard Items" smart tag option, shown in Figure 2.20.[18]

Figure 2.20 MenuStrip Smart Tag Option for Inserting Standard Items

This feature automatically generates a complete set of typical menus and menu items, including File, Edit, Tools, and Help, as shown in Figure 2.21.

Figure 2.21 MenuStrip with Standard Menus and Menu Items Inserted

[18] Many new controls support configuration with smart tags as well as with the Properties window.

Your form can host one or more menu strips, all of which can be visible at run time. You can hide or show a MenuStrip by setting its Visible property:

```
// MainForm.cs
partial class MainForm : Form {
  public MainForm() {
    InitializeComponent();
    this.mainMenuStrip.Visible = true;
    this.alternateMenuStrip.Visible = false;
  }
  ...
}
```

new Sometimes, forms require knowledge of a particular menu strip to perform special, integrated behavior, such as MDI menu merging as discussed later in this chapter. You provide this knowledge to a form by setting its MainMenuStrip property with the appropriate menu strip, which also specifies which menu receives shortcut keys (Alt+...). The Windows Forms Designer automatically sets MainMenuStrip in InitializeComponent to the first menu strip dropped onto a form:

```
// MainForm.Designer.cs
partial class MainForm {
  ...
  void InitializeComponent() {
    ...
    this.MainMenuStrip = this.mainMenuStrip;
    ...
  }
}

public MainForm() {
  InitializeComponent();

  this.MainMenuStrip = this.mainMenuStrip;
}
```

Additionally, you can set MainMenuStrip to any menu strip control either by writing code like this or by using the Properties window.

The MenuStrip control can contain zero or more top-level menus via its Items property, which is of type ToolStripItemCollection. By default, the Designer automatically adds a ToolStripMenuItem. However, you can use the Windows Forms Designer to add several types of tool strip items, including ToolStripMenuItem, ToolStripComboBox, and

ToolStripTextBox for the top-level menu, and the same with the additional ToolStripSeparator for drop-down menus.[19]

Each top-level menu that is a ToolStripMenuItem can also contain zero or more MenuStripItemTypes, which are stored in the DropDownItems property. If a menu item contains zero or more menu items of its own, they show up in a cascading menu, as shown in Figure 2.22.

Figure 2.22   Cascading Menu Items

Figure 2.23 shows the objects used to provide the menu strip in Figure 2.22.

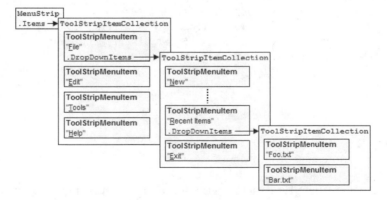

Figure 2.23   Internal Structure of MenuStrip, ToolStripItemCollection, and ToolStripMenuItems

---

[19] Technically, you can add any tool strip items to any strip control. However, the Windows Forms Designer offers only the ability to choose from a subset of these for each strip control, as determined by their appropriateness to a particular tool strip and as indicated using the ToolStripItemDesignerAvailability attribute.

The MenuStrip designer transforms your menu structure into an equivalent set of initialization code, appropriately stored in InitializeComponent (something that really makes you appreciate the Designer):

```
// MainForm.Designer.cs
using System.Windows.Forms;

partial class MainForm : Form {
  ...
  MenuStrip mainMenuStrip;
  ToolStripMenuItem fileToolStripMenuItem;
  ...
  void InitializeComponent() {
    ...
    this.mainMenuStrip = new MenuStrip();
    this.fileToolStripMenuItem = new ToolStripMenuItem();
    ...
    // mainMenuStrip
    this.mainMenuStrip.Items.AddRange(
      new ToolStripItem[] {
        this.fileToolStripMenuItem, ... } );
    this.mainMenuStrip.Location = new System.Drawing.Point(0, 0);
    this.mainMenuStrip.Name = "mainMenuStrip";
    this.mainMenuStrip.Size = new System.Drawing.Size(244, 24);
    this.mainMenuStrip.TabIndex = 0;
    ...
    // fileToolStripMenuItem
    this.fileToolStripMenuItem.DropDownItems.AddRange(
      new ToolStripItem[] { this.newToolStripMenuItem, ... } );
    this.fileToolStripMenuItem.Name = "fileToolStripMenuItem";
    this.fileToolStripMenuItem.Text = "&File";
    ...
    // MainForm
    ...
    this.Controls.Add(this.mainMenuStrip);
  }
  ...
}
```

The ToolStripMenuItem type includes the following interesting properties and events:

```
namespace System.Windows.Forms {
  class ToolStripMenuItem : ToolStripDropDownItem {

    // Properties
    bool Checked { get; set; }
    bool CheckOnClick { get; set; }
    CheckState CheckState { get; set; }
```

```
        override bool Enabled { get; set; }
        virtual Image Image { get; set; }
        ContentAlignment ImageAlign { get; set; }
        MergeAction MergeAction { get; set; }
        int MergeIndex { get; set; }
        ToolStripItemOverflow Overflow { get; set; }
        Keys ShortcutKeys { get; set; }
        bool ShowShortcutKeys { get; set; }
        string ShortcutKeyDisplayString { get; set; }
        bool Visible { get; set; }
        virtual string Text { get; set; }

        // Events
        event EventHandler CheckedChanged;
        event EventHandler CheckStateChanged;
        event EventHandler Click;
        event EventHandler DropDownClosed;
        event ToolStripItemClickedEventHandler DropDownItemClicked;
        event EventHandler DropDownOpened;
    }
}
```

Here are the major properties to focus on:

- *Checked* and *CheckOnClick* mark an item as chosen and determine whether an item can be checked.
- *Enabled* and *Visible* determine whether the item can be chosen or whether it will be shown.
- *Image* assigns images to your strip item.
- *MergeAction* and *MergeIndex* are MDI-related (discussed later in this chapter).
- *ShortcutKeys* allows you to assign a keyboard shortcut to a menu item, such as Ctrl+S for Save.
- *Text* is what's shown to the user. (A Text property that includes an "&" (ampersand) underlines the subsequentcharacter; for example, "&Save" shows as "Save," thereby giving users a visual cue for keyboard menu navigation via the Alt key.)
- *TextAlign* and *TextImageRelation* specify text alignment without or with an image.

Of course, the Click event handler is the big celebrity in the menu item list of events, because it gets fired when the user clicks on a menu item:

```
void exitToolStripMenuItem_Click(object sender, EventArgs e) {
    this.Close();
}
```

```
void helpToolStripMenuItem_Click(object sender, EventArgs e) {
    MessageBox.Show("Ain't menus cool?", "About...");
}
```

MenuStrips normally provide access to all available menu commands at once, no matter what's happening on a form. Sometimes, however, you may need to show a subset of the available menu commands that is specific to what is happening on the form, depending on the context of the current activity. For this, you use context menus.[20]

Context Menus

Whereas forms can have zero or more menus, forms and controls can have at most one context menu each, the value of which is stored in the ContextMenuStrip property:

```
public MainForm() {
    InitializeComponent();

    this.ContextMenuStrip = this.editContextMenuStrip;
}
```

Like a MenuStrip control, a ContextMenuStrip can contain zero or more tool strip items, also exposed by a ToolStripItemCollection Items property. Unlike the MenuStrip, however, ContextMenuStrip items have no concept of items "across the top"; context menus are always vertical at every level. Therefore, every ToolStripItem in the Items property is a ToolStripMenuItem, as reflected in the ContextMenuStrip Designer illustrated in Figure 2.24.

Figure 2.24   ContextMenuStrip Designer

[20] .NET 1.x veterans may be wondering where MainMenu and ContextMenu went; MenuStrip, ContextMenuStrip, ToolStrip, and StatusStrip supercede MainMenu, ContextMenu, Toolbar, and Statusbar, respectively, and the latter remain for backward compatibility with Windows Forms 1.x applications.

As you can see, the top-level menu item, ContextMenuStrip, is only a temporary place-holder supplied by the Context Menu Designer to enable visual editing of the context menu. Figure 2.25 shows how these are arranged internally to construct the context menu in Figure 2.24.

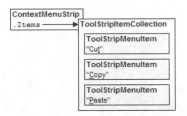

Figure 2.25   Internal Structure of ContextMenuStrip, ToolStripItemCollection, and ToolStripMenuItems

The one remaining behavioral difference between MenuStrip objects and ContextMenuStrip objects is that both forms and controls have a ContextMenuStrip property to let you specify the ContextMenuStrip that appears when the right mouse button is clicked, whereas only forms have a MainMenuStrip property. After a context menu is assigned, users can display it by right-clicking over the form or control it was assigned to, such as the text box in Figure 2.26.

Figure 2.26   ContextMenuStrip in Action

Although many controls have their own context menus—for example, the context menu of a TextBox has things such as Copy and Paste—you can replace a control's built-in context menu by setting the control's ContextMenuStrip property. As a rule, most of the operations available from any control's context menu are also available as methods on the control.

Because of this, while you can't augment a control's context menu, you can replace it with your own and still provide the operations that the control's menu would provide, implementing those options by sending the command to the control itself:

```
void copyToolStripMenuItem_Click(object sender, EventArgs e) {
   this.textBox.Copy();
}
```

Tool Strips

As an application offers a greater number of commands, the associated menu items can become more deeply hidden within a burgeoning menu strip hierarchy. This means that users likely spend more time searching for a specific command. If you encounter this situation, you can save users time by providing access to the most commonly used commands from a tool strip, which displays them as single-click buttons.

new You can add a tool strip to a form by dragging a ToolStrip control onto it from the Toolbox. As with the MenuStrip control, you can manually add items on the design surface, or you can insert a standard set of tool strip buttons automatically by selecting "Insert Standard items" from the ToolStrip's smart tag, resulting in the form shown in Figure 2.27.

Figure 2.27   ToolStrip with Standard Tool Strip Buttons Inserted

ToolStrip is a container for zero or more tool strip items, which are stored in the Items property of type ToolStripItemCollection. The Windows Forms Designer provides a rich selection of tool strip items for the ToolStrip, including ToolStripButton, ToolStripLabel, ToolStripSplitButton, ToolStripDropDownButton, ToolStripSeparator, ToolStripComboBox, ToolStripTextBox, and ToolStripProgressBar.

The most common item is ToolStripButton, which exposes the following interesting design time properties and events:

```
namespace System.Windows.Forms {
   class ToolStripButton : ToolStripItem {

      // Properties
      ToolStripItemAlignment Alignment { get; set; }
      bool AutoSize { get; set; }
      bool AutoToolTip { get; set; }
      bool Checked { get; set; }
      bool CheckOnClick { get; set; }
      CheckState CheckState { get; set; }
      ToolStripItemDisplayStyle DisplayStyle { get; set; }
      virtual bool Enabled { get; set; }
      virtual Image Image { get; set; }
      ContentAlignment ImageAlign { get; set; }
      MergeAction MergeAction { get; set; }
      int MergeIndex { get; set; }
      ToolStripItemPlacement Placement { get; }
      virtual bool Pressed { get; }
      virtual bool Selected { get; }
      virtual string Text { get; set; }
      virtual ContentAlignment TextAlign { get; set; }
      virtual ToolStripTextDirection TextDirection { get; set; }
      TextImageRelation TextImageRelation { get; set; }
      string ToolTipText { get; set; }
      bool Visible { get; set; }

      // Events
      event EventHandler CheckedChanged;
      event EventHandler CheckStateChanged;
      event EventHandler Click;
      event EventHandler DoubleClick;
      event MouseEventHandler MouseDown;
      event EventHandler MouseEnter;
      event EventHandler MouseHover;
      event EventHandler MouseLeave;
      event MouseEventHandler MouseMove;
      event MouseEventHandler MouseUp;
   }
}
```

Here are the properties you'll encounter most often:

- *Image* and *ImageAlign* display an image and align it within the displayable area.
- *Text* lets you show text. (As discussed earlier, you can use an "&" (ampersand) to help users with keyboard menu navigation.)

- *TextAlign* governs how the text is aligned.
- *TextImageRelation* specifies where text should appear in relation to an image.
- *DisplayStyle* lets you choose whether to display text or an image or both.
- *Checked* enables toggle-style button support.
- *Enabled* and *Visible* determine whether the item can be chosen or whether it will be shown, respectively.
- *MergeAction* and *MergeIndex* are MDI-related (discussed later in this chapter).

As with ToolStripMenuItem, the Click event handler is likely the most often used because it is fired whenever a tool strip button is clicked:

```
void newToolStripButton_Click(object sender, EventArgs e) {
    MessageBox.Show("Out with the old, in with the new!", "File | New");
}
```

Status Strips

Whereas tool strips provide visual shortcuts to application commands, *status strips* provide visual shortcuts to details about application status and context. For example, VS05 itself uses the status strip effectively by providing information such as row and column positions when you're editing, and both textual and graphical cues when an application build is in progress, as shown in Figure 2.28.

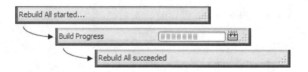

Figure 2.28　VS05 Build Progress Reported Via Status Strip

　Windows Forms provides a StatusStrip control that you can use to similar effect, simply by dragging it onto your form and configuring as needed. StatusStrip is a container for zero or more status strip items, including ToolStripStatusLabel, ToolStripProgressBar, ToolStripDropDownButton, and ToolStripSplitButton.

I've re-created VS05's status strip compilation experience using a text-only ToolStrip-StatusLabel to display the progress text, a ToolStripProgressBar to display compilation progress, and an image-only ToolStripStatusLabel with an appropriate animated GIF. These are shown in the Windows Forms Designer in Figure 2.29.

Figure 2.29   StatusStrip with a Text Panel, a
Progress Strip, and a Panel with an Animated GIF

Note that ToolStripStatusLabel consumes the space not filled by the ToolStripProgressBar and the second ToolStripStatusLabel combined. To do this, you set its Spring property to true. Springing is a nice way to keep tool strip items on the status strip spaced for maximum effect, called *springing*.[21] Also note that you should hide ToolStripProgressBar and the second ToolStripLabel until required by setting their Visible properties to true. This hides both items in the Windows Forms Designer unless their host, StatusStrip, is selected, as is the case in Figure 2.29. All these StatusStrip items are used during a simulated build process:

```
delegate void BuildProgress(object sender, int progressPercent);
  ...

// MainForm.Designer.cs
partial class MainForm : Form {

  event BuildProgress BuildProgress;
  event EventHandler BuildComplete;

  void rebuildButton_Click(object sender, EventArgs e) {
    // Kick rebuild off
    this.readyToolStripStatusLabel.Text = "Rebuild All started...";
    this.animationToolStripStatusLabel.Visible = true;
    this.statusToolStripProgressBar.Visible = true;
    this.buildSimulatorTimer.Enabled = true;
```

---

[21] Only the StatusBar tool strip has native support for springing of its tool strip items. See Chapter 4 to learn how to add this support programmatically to other strip controls.

```
      this.BuildProgress += BuildProgressHandler;
      this.BuildComplete += BuildCompleteHandler;
    }

  void buildSimulatorTimer_Tick(object sender, EventArgs e) {
    // Report progress
    this.readyToolStripStatusLabel.Text = "Build Progress";
    BuildProgress(this, this.statusToolStripProgressBar.Value + 10);
    if( this.statusToolStripProgressBar.Value == 100 ) {
      this.buildSimulatorTimer.Enabled = false;
      this.statusToolStripProgressBar.Value = 0;
      BuildComplete(this, null);
    }
  }

  void BuildProgressHandler(object sender, int progress) {
    // Show progress
    this.statusToolStripProgressBar.Value = progress;
  }

  void BuildCompleteHandler(object sender, EventArgs e) {
    // Show completion
    this.readyToolStripStatusLabel.Text = "Rebuild All succeeded";
    this.statusToolStripProgressBar.Visible = false;
    this.animationToolStripStatusLabel.Visible = false;
  }
}
```

As with MenuStrip and ToolStrip items, you can manipulate StatusStrip items directly. Here are the key properties and events implemented by the ToolStripStatusLabel type:

```
namespace System.Windows.Forms {
  class ToolStripStatusLabel : ToolStripLabel {

    // Properties
    ToolStripStatusLabelBorderSides BorderSides { get; set; }
    Border3DStyle BorderStyle { get; set; }
    ToolStripItemDisplayStyle DisplayStyle { get; set; }
    virtual bool Enabled { get; set; }
    virtual Font Font { get; set; }
    virtual Image Image { get; set; }
    ContentAlignment ImageAlign { get; set; }
    MergeAction MergeAction { get; set; }
    int MergeIndex { get; set; }
    bool Spring { get; set; }
    virtual string Text { get; set; }
    virtual ContentAlignment TextAlign { get; set; }
```

```
        virtual ToolStripTextDirection TextDirection { get; set; }
        TextImageRelation TextImageRelation { get; set; }
        string ToolTipText { get; set; }
        bool Visible { get; set; }

        // Events
        event EventHandler Click;
    }
}
```

The most interesting properties are as follows:

- *Image* and *ImageAlign* display an image and align it within the displayable area.
- *Text* is used to show text. (As discussed earlier, you can use an "&" (ampersand) to help users with keyboard menu navigation.)
- *DisplayStyle* lets you choose whether to display text or an image or both.
- *TextImageRelation* specifies where text should appear in relation to an image.
- *IsLink* and *LinkBehavior* display the specified text as a hyperlink and govern how it acts with regard to the mouse.
- *Checked* enables toggle-style button support.
- *Enabled* and *Visible* determine whether the item can be chosen or whether it will be shown, respectively.
- *Spring* specifies whether the ToolStripStatusLabel fills as much of the StatusStrip as possible, instead of at the same width as ToolStripStatusLabel's contents.
- *MergeAction* and *MergeIndex* are MDI-related (discussed next).

One other important feature of the tool strip suite of controls is their ability to merge tool strip items when operating in an MDI application.

Multiple Document Interface Applications

Menu merging is one of several important features commonly supported by MDI applications. VS05 and the .NET Framework provide a variety of tools for you to use in implementing these features.

MDI Form Configuration

The MDI style of application was invented as a way to contain a set of related windows in a single frame, as shown in Figure 2.30.

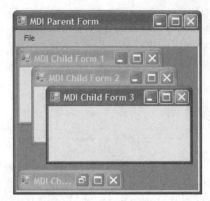

Figure 2.30   Sample MDI Form

An MDI form has two pieces: a parent and a child. You designate the MDI *parent* form by setting the IsMdiContainer property to true, and you designate the MDI *child* form by setting the MdiParent property before showing the form:

```
// MDIParentForm.Designer.cs
partial class MDIParentForm {
  ...
  void InitializeComponent() {
    ...
    this.IsMdiContainer = true;
    ...
  }
}


// MDIParentForm.cs
partial class MDIParentForm : Form {

  static int formCount = 0;

  public MDIParentForm() {
    InitializeComponent();
  }

  void newToolStripMenuItem_Click(object sender, EventArgs e) {
    // Create and show MDI child form with nice title
    MDIChildForm mdiChildForm = new MDIChildForm();
    mdiChildForm.MdiParent = this;
    mdiChildForm.Text = "MDI Child Form " + (++formCount).ToString();
    mdiChildForm.Show();
  }
}
```

The Form class has several MDI-related members. For example, just as the parent has a property indicating that it's an MDI parent, the child form can tell whether it's being shown as an MDI child by inspecting the IsMdiChild property. And just as a form is a collection of controls, an MDI parent form has a collection of MDI children called MdiChildren. When a child is activated, either by direct user input or by the Activate method, the MDI parent receives the MdiChildActivate event. To see or change which of the MDI children is currently active, each MDI parent form provides an ActiveMdiChild property.

Note that MDI children can appear only where the MDI parent directly exposes its form surface. For example, if you cover the entire MDI parent form with a ToolStripContainer or SplitContainer, MDI children will be hidden. Instead of using ToolStripContainer, you can use individual ToolStripPanels to host tool strip controls (see Chapter 4). For splitting, you can use the Windows Forms 1.*x* Splitter strip instead.

Special MDI Menus

An MDI parent is expected to have two sets of special menu items: one to arrange the children inside the parent frame, and a second one to list the active MDI children and select from them. Figure 2.31 shows a typical menu.

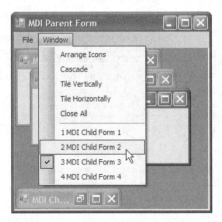

Figure 2.31 The Window Menu with MDI Child Management Commands

To implement the items that arrange the children inside the parent, the Form class provides the LayoutMdi method, which takes one of the four MdiLayout enumeration values:

```
// MDIParentForm.cs
partial class MDIParentForm : Form {
  ...
  void arrangeIconsToolStripMenuItem_Click(
    object sender, EventArgs e) {
    this.LayoutMdi(MdiLayout.ArrangeIcons);
  }

  void cascadeToolStripMenuItem_Click(object sender, EventArgs e) {
    this.LayoutMdi(MdiLayout.Cascade);
  }

  void tileChildrenVerticallyToolStripMenuItem_Click(
    object sender, EventArgs e) {
    this.LayoutMdi(MdiLayout.TileVertical);
  }

  void tileChildrenHorizontallyToolStripMenuItem_Click(
    object sender, EventArgs e) {
    this.LayoutMdi(MdiLayout.TileHorizontal);
  }
}
```

One other Window menu that you may need is Close All, but it isn't supported by the LayoutMdi method. Instead, you enumerate the MDI child forms, closing them one by one:

```
// MDIParentForm.cs
partial class MDIParentForm : Form {
  ...
  void closeAllToolStripMenuItem_Click(object sender, EventArgs e) {
    foreach( Form mdiChildForm in MdiChildren ) {
      mdiChildForm.Close();
    }
  }
}
```

Implementing the active MDI child menu list is almost a code-free affair. You first specify the top-level Window menu strip item as the MenuStrip's MDIWindowListItem, as shown in Figure 2.32.

Figure 2.32 Declaratively Configuring the MDI Child Windows List

This action ensures that a separator is automatically shown between the last window list menu item you manually added at design-time and any dynamically added menu items for MDI children.

However, when all MDI children are closed, the separator does not disappear. To cope, you write code like this:

```
// MDIParentForm.cs
partial class MDIParentForm : Form {
  ...
  public MDIParentForm() {
    InitializeComponent();

    this.menuStrip.MdiWindowListItem.DropDownOpening +=
      MdiWindowListItem_DropDownOpening;
  }

  void MdiWindowListItem_DropDownOpening(object sender, EventArgs e) {
    // Hide separator if it is the last menu strip item in
    // the window list menu
    ToolStripItemCollection items =
      this.menuStrip.MdiWindowListItem.DropDownItems;
```

```
    if( items[items.Count - 1] is ToolStripSeparator ) {
      items.RemoveAt(items.Count - 1);
    }
  }
  ...
}
```

If you prefer to avoid spending the time it takes in VS05 to get an MDI application to this point, you can lean on VS05's MDI Parent project item template to create a reasonably comprehensive MDI parent form with all the MDI trimmings for you.[22]

Using the MDI Parent Project Item Template

The MDI Parent template is available by right-clicking your project and choosing Add | New Item, which opens the Add New Item dialog shown in Figure 2.33.

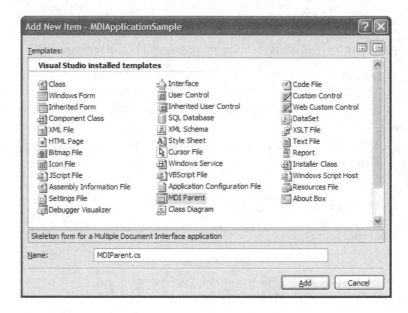

Figure 2.33　Using the VS05 MDI Template

Provide the desired form name and click Add, and a new form is added to your project, like the one shown in Figure 2.34.

---

[22] One way to present MDI children is with a tabbed layout, much like the one VS05 uses. For more information on how to set that up, take a look at http://www.windowsforms.net/Samples/download.aspx?PageId=1&ItemId=174&tabindex=4 (http://tinysells.com/6).

Figure 2.34   A VS05 MDI Template-Generated Form

A complete set of basic UI elements is added to the form, including a menu strip, a tool strip, and a status strip. The form's IsMdiContainer property is set to true, and the Windows menu (which should really be called Window, as per most other applications) is set as the menu strip's MdiWindowListItem. Additionally, all the items on the Windows menu are implemented.

Don't forget that even though the project item template helps a lot, it's really just a skeleton that you need to flesh out to get working the way you want. For example, the code to open a new form operates over the base Form class rather than any specific MDI child form you've created:

```csharp
// MDIParent.cs
partial class MDIParent : Form {

  int childFormNumber = 0;

  public MDIParent() {
    InitializeComponent();
  }

  void ShowNewForm(object sender, EventArgs e) {
    // Create a new instance of the child form.
    Form childForm = new Form();
    // Make it a child of this MDI form before showing it.
    childForm.MdiParent = this;
    childForm.Text = "Window " + childFormNumber++;
    childForm.Show();
  }
  ...
}
```

But as a starting point, you may find the code produced by the MDI Parent template a great big first step, so you should take time to familiarize yourself with it. You can also familiarize yourself with the MDI application model in Chapter 14: Applications.

Menu Merging

Whether the MDI parent form is generated by a project template or built manually by you, it typically has one main menu, which is specified by setting the MainMenuStrip property that we saw earlier. Additionally, the Windows Forms Designer automatically does this on our behalf when the first menu strip is dropped onto a form:

```
// MDIParentForm.Designer.cs
using System.Windows.Forms;
...
partial class MDIParentForm {
  ...
  MenuStrip menuStrip;
  ...
  void InitializeComponent() {
    ...
    this.menuStrip = new MenuStrip();
    ...
    // MDIParentForm
    ...
    this.MainMenuStrip = this.menuStrip;
    ...
  }
}
```

This relationship is fundamental to *merging*, which deals with the special situations that arise when an MDI child form is maximized within an MDI parent form. For example, if an MDI child form that's devoid of controls is maximized within an MDI parent form whose MainMenuStrip property is set, the two forms become one, at least from a caption and menu strip point of view, as shown in Figure 2.35.

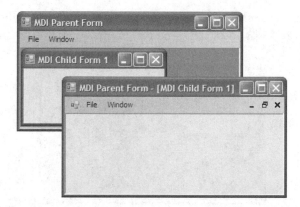

Figure 2.35   MDI Child Form Maximized in MDI Parent Form

The MDI child form's title bar text has been merged into the MDI parent form's title bar, enclosed within square brackets. Additionally, the MDI child form's system menu and maximize, minimize, and close buttons have all been merged into the MDI parent form's main menu strip. Even though the MDI parent form has no special knowledge about main menu strips, the title bar text merges without trouble. However, the MDI child form's title bar doesn't merge, as Figure 2.36 demonstrates.

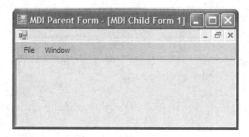

Figure 2.36   Not So Attractive Merging

To ensure an MDI child form's title bar merges, you should set the MDI parent form's MainMenuStrip property.

An MDI parent form's main menu strip typically exposes application-wide commands, but MDI child forms often have menu strips to suit their own purposes. Why not simply put everything into the parent's main menu to start with? The reason is that lots of menu items don't make sense without a child—for example, File | Close—so showing them isn't helpful. Similarly, the set of operations may vary between MDI children, so the merged menu should consist only of the items from the parent that always make sense—such as File | Exit—and the items from the currently active child.

For example, Figure 2.37 shows an MDI parent form's File menu when there are no MDI child forms, and Figure 2.38 shows the same File menu when there is one MDI child form.

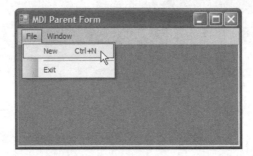

Figure 2.37   MDI Parent Form's File Menu and No MDI Child Forms

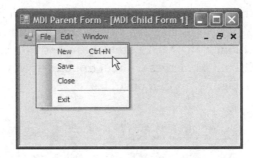

Figure 2.38   MDI Parent Form's File Menu and One Maximized MDI Child Form

In the Windows Forms Designer, both the parent and the child forms have a main menu, as shown in Figure 2.39.

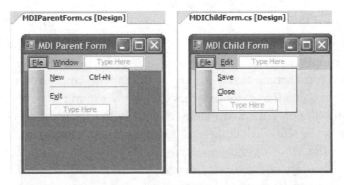

Figure 2.39   The MDI Parent Form and MDI Child Form Menus in the Windows Forms Designer

Notice that the MDI child form's menu items don't contain all of the items shown in Figure 2.38 when the MDI child form is active at run-time. Instead, the MDI child form has only the new items that are to be added to the MDI parent form's menu. For the merging to work, two things must happen. First, we hide the MDI child form's menu strip; otherwise, it would remain visible when merging occurs. This is simply a case of setting the menu strip's Visible property to false. Second, we configure two sets of properties on the menu items to be merged: at the top level (for example, File) and at the lower levels (for example, File | New).

Merging is governed on a per-item basis via the MergeAction and MergeIndex properties that appear on each menu strip item. The MergeAction is one of the following Merge-Action enumeration values:

```
namespace System.Windows.Forms {
    enum MergeAction {
        Append = 0,  // Merge menu item at the end of the menu items
                     // at the same level in the merge target (default)
        Insert = 1,  // Merge menu item into the menu items at same level
                     // in the merge target, at the position specified
                     // by MergeIndex
        MatchOnly = 4,  // If menu item is matched, merge it
                        // (appending child menu items by default)
        Remove = 3,  // If menu item is matched, remove matched menu
                     // item from the merge target
        Replace = 2  // If menu item is matched, replace matched menu
                     // item with it, consuming (not removing) child
                     // menu items of the matched menu item
    }
}
```

Menu merging occurs in two phases: first at the top level and, if matches are found, then at the submenu level.

In the first phase, the MergeAction on each of the MDI child form's top-level menus dictates how they are merged into the MDI parent form's top-level menus. Because the default MergeAction is *Append*, the MDI child form's top-level menus are tacked onto the end of the MDI parent's top-level menus. When the MergeAction is set to *Insert* on a top-level menu item, it isn't actually merged until you also specify a MergeIndex. This is the position in the MDI parent form's top-level menu that it will be inserted into.

A MergeAction of *MatchOnly* means that if a top-level menu item on the MDI child form matches a top-level menu item on the MDI parent form by name, then the child menu items are merged from the MDI child form's menu into the MDI parent form's menu. In the same situation, but with a MergeAction of *Remove*, the MDI parent form's matched top-level menu item disappears, and the MDI child form's top-level menu item stays where it is (which should be hidden along with the menu strip).

Finally, when top-level menu items match by name and the MergeAction is *Replace*, the MDI parent form's top-level menu item is removed and replaced with the MDI child form's top-level menu item.

The only option that merges the menu items from both the MDI parent and the MDI child menus is Match, and, when that occurs, the second phase of menu merging occurs.

In the second phase, submenu items from the MDI child form's matching top-level menu item are merged into the matched top-level menu item on the MDI parent form. Merging of submenu items is also governed by MergeAction, which basically follows the same behavior we just described with regard to Append, MatchOnly, Remove, and Replace. However, when you specify a MergeAction of Insert, you must configure the MergeIndex on each submenu item in the matching and matched menus to ensure that they appear in the correct order.

To see how menu merging works, let's look at Tables 2.1 and 2.2, which illustrate the combined MergeAction and MergeIndex settings for the menus on both MDI parent and MDI child forms.

Table 2.1 MDI Parent Form Menu Merge Settings

MDI Parent Form Menu Item	MergeAction	MergeIndex
File	Append	−1
File | New Child	Append	−1
File | Separator	Append	−1
File | Exit	Append	−1
Window	Append	−1

Table 2.2 MDI Child Form Menu Merge Settings

MDI Child Form Menu Item	MergeAction	MergeIndex
File	MatchOnly	−1
File | Save	Insert	1
File | Close	Insert	2
Edit	Insert	1

In this case, establishing basic menu merging involves only setting the MDI child menu strip's Visible property, and the MergeAction and MergeIndex properties of its menu strip items. The combination of MergeAction and MergeIndex supports a wide variety of merging possibilities that you can experiment with to get the desired effect.[23]

Visual Inheritance

After all the settings and behavior details you've learned to pack into forms, you may decide to keep some of your hard work in a form-derived base class for easy reuse, and you can certainly do that. If you follow the convention that forms initialize their own properties and the properties of their child controls in a function called InitializeComponent, then the Designer provides direct support for your *visual inheritance:* the reuse of a form base class via inheritance.

The goal of visual inheritance is to allow a base class to capture common UI elements, which are then shared and augmented by derived classes. For example, imagine a Base-Form class that derives from Form and provides an icon, a menu strip, a status strip, an open file dialog, and a save file dialog, as shown in the Designer in Figure 2.40.

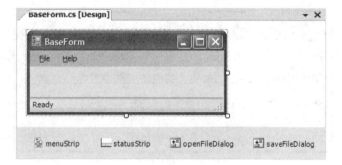

Figure 2.40   Base Class Used in Visual Inheritance

BaseForm can now serve as a base class for all forms that contain at least this functionality, such as the EditorForm shown in Figure 2.41.[24]

---

[23] New to tool strips in Windows Forms 2.0, merging is also supported on tool strips, which you configure using the same techniques you use for menu strips and menu strip items.

[24] Make sure your project is compiled before you use the Designer on inherited forms.

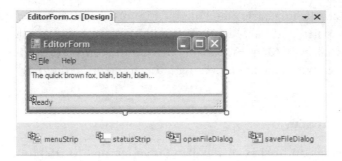

Figure 2.41   EditorForm Derived from BaseForm

I created the EditorForm class by deriving from BaseForm, overriding the Text property, adding the TextBox control to the form, and overriding the various properties of the open and save file dialogs from the base class. Rather than do this work by hand, I used VS05. I right-clicked on the project in Solution Explorer, chose Add | Add New Item, and chose Inherited Form from the Add New Item dialog. Then, I set the form's name and chose Base-Form from the list of forms in the project displayed in the Inheritance Picker dialog, as shown in Figure 2.42.

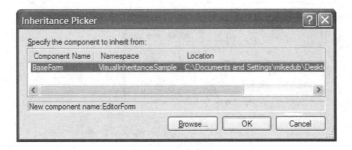

Figure 2.42   The Inheritance Picker Dialog

The initial EditorForm looked just like BaseForm except for the little arrows over the menu and status strips and the open and save file dialogs (as shown in the bottom pane of Figure 2.41). This arrow indicates a control inherited from the base. After inheriting the new form class from the existing form class, I used the Toolbox to add the new controls, and I used the Properties window to change the form's Text property.

However, to configure the file dialogs, I first had to change their access modifiers. By default, the Designer adds all fields as private, and this means that they're accessible only from that class—in our example, the BaseForm class. If you want to use the Designer to set a property on one of the controls in the base class from the deriving class, by default you can't until you change the access modifier in the field declaration in the base class:

```
private OpenFileDialog openFileDialog;
private SaveFileDialog saveFileDialog;
```

To allow access by deriving classes, you change the private keyword to protected:

```
protected OpenFileDialog openFileDialog;
protected SaveFileDialog saveFileDialog;
```

If you're really into Cooperesque visual design, you can change this keyword by using the Designer to select a control on BaseForm and changing the Modifiers property.[25]

The purpose of this exercise in reuse is that when you need a new feature from the set of forms that derive from BaseForm or when you find a bug, you can make the changes to the base form, automatically benefiting the derived forms. For example, BaseForm could be updated to include generic serialization and deserialization that would automatically propagate to derived forms like EditorForm the next time BaseForm is compiled.

As nifty as visual inheritance is, it's not without limitations. For example, although you can completely replace the context menu of a base form in a derived form, you can't change the configurations of inherited tool strip controls, layout-panel controls, and DataGridView because they are all locked. Also, multilevel visual inheritance can lead to brittleness, perhaps forcing you to write more code in your derivations than you had hoped to save by using visual inheritance.

One good rule of thumb is to add only inheritable functionality that's required by all direct and indirect derivations. Additionally, if you provide an area for derivations to insert their own controls—as BaseForm allowed EditorForm to do with a text box—the functionality you add should support any possible combination of added controls.

With judicious use, visual inheritance is definitely worth your consideration as a template mechanism to avoid duplicating controls and code.

[25] Alan Cooper invented the drag-and-drop visual design mechanism for Visual Basic.

Where Are We?

We've explored how to show forms; control their lifetime, size, and location; dictate their nonclient adornments; manage main menus, context menus, tool strips, and status strips; make whole forms partially transparent and parts of forms completely transparent; and package forms for reuse via visual inheritance. You might think that you know all there is to know about forms. If you do, you're mistaken. Chapter 3: Dialogs is all about using forms as dialogs, Chapter 4: Layout covers form and control layout, and Chapter 14: Applications covers how forms are employed to build various styles of Windows Forms applications, including single-instance SDI, MDI, and multi-SDI.

3
Dialogs

A DIALOG IS DEFINED BY ITS USE. If a form is the application's main window, it's a window and not a dialog. However, if a form pops up in response to a user request for service, such as a request to open a file, and stops all other user interactions with the application, it's a dialog (specifically, a modal dialog).

However, things get a little murky when we consider modeless dialogs, such as Outlook's Send/Receive Progress dialog. Modeless dialogs don't stop the user from interacting with the rest of the application, but they do provide a means of interaction outside the main window.

The Windows Forms terminology makes things even murkier. Standard dialogs are exposed by the *Xxx*Dialog family of components, such as OpenFileDialog. Most of these components support only modal activation using ShowDialog, but a couple of them support modeless activation using Show. In contrast, custom dialogs are classes that derive from the Form base class and can be shown modally or modelessly based on whether they're activated using ShowDialog or Show.

No matter how a dialog is defined, this chapter covers things you'd normally think of as dialog-related, including standard dialogs, custom forms to be used as dialogs, modal and modeless activation and lifetime, transferring data in and out, validating user-entered data, and providing help. To aid you in making the transition to the unification of dialog-like functionality with forms, I use the term "dialog" only when I'm referring to the standard dialog components.

Standard Dialogs

Windows Forms ships with several standard dialogs (sometimes known as "common dialogs") provided as components located in the System.Windows.Forms namespace. Here's how to manually create and show an instance of a dialog component like ColorDialog:

```
// ColorDialogForm.cs
partial class ColorDialogForm : Form {
  ...
  void colorDialogButton_Click(object sender, EventArgs e) {
    ColorDialog dlg = new ColorDialog();
    dlg.Color = Color.Red;
    DialogResult result = dlg.ShowDialog();
    if( result == DialogResult.OK ) {
      MessageBox.Show("You picked " + dlg.Color.ToString());
    }
  }
}
```

However, the common dialog components are also located on the Toolbox in VS05, and this means that you can drag them onto a form and configure them from the Properties window. This allows you to show them without writing the initialization code manually:

```
// ColorDialogForm.Designer.cs
partial class ColorDialogForm {
  ...
  void InitializeComponent() {
    ...
    this.colorDialog.Color = System.Drawing.Color.Red;
    ...
  }
}

// ColorDialogForm.cs
partial class ColorDialogForm : Form {
  public ColorDialogForm() {
    InitializeComponent();
  }

  void colorDialogButton_Click(object sender, EventArgs e) {
    DialogResult result = colorDialog.ShowDialog();
    if( result == DialogResult.OK ) {
      MessageBox.Show(
        "You picked " + this.colorDialog.Color.ToString());
    }
  }
}
```

I tend to prefer the latter approach because I like to set properties like Color visually with the Properties window, which you'll notice is also stored in InitializeComponent, thereby saving you the coding. But either approach works just fine. The following standard dialogs come with Windows Forms:[1]

- *ColorDialog* allows the user to pick a color exposed by the Color property of type System.Drawing.Color (see Chapter 9).
- *FolderBrowserDialog* allows the user to pick a folder exposed by the SelectedPath property of type string (see Chapter 9).
- *FontDialog* allows the user to choose a font and its properties, such as bold, italics, and so on. The user-configured font object of type System.Drawing.Font is available from the Font property of the component (see Chapter 9).
- *OpenFileDialog* and *SaveFileDialog* allow the user to pick a file to open or save, as appropriate for the dialog. The chosen file name is available from the FileName property of type string (see Chapter 9).
- *PageSetupDialog, PrintDialog,* and *PrintPreviewDialog* are related to printing and are discussed in Chapter 8: Printing.

Excluding PrintPreviewDialog, the standard dialogs are wrappers around existing common dialogs in Windows. Because these dialogs don't support modeless operation, neither do the Windows Forms components. However, PrintPreviewDialog provides a new dialog and supports both modal and modeless operation using ShowDialog and Show, respectively.

Form Styles

Chapter 2: Forms introduced the important dialog-related properties: ControlBox, FormBorderStyle, HelpButton, MaximizeBox, MinimizeBox, ShowIcon, and ShowInTaskbar. By default, a new form shows the control box, is sizable, doesn't show the help button, can be minimized and maximized, and is shown in the shell's task bar. For a main window, these are fine settings, and they yield a form that looks like the one in Figure 3.1.

---

[1] Neither a FindDialog nor a FindReplaceDialog exists natively in Windows Forms. However, you can download a sample implementation as part of the Genghis class library available from http://www.genghisgroup.com (http://tinysells.com/8).

Figure 3.1   Typical Main Window Form Settings

A typical modal dialog, on the other hand, is more likely to hide both the minimize and the maximize boxes, show the help button, hide the icon, and not show up in the task bar (the parent is already there), as shown in Figure 3.2.

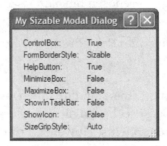

Figure 3.2   Typical Sizable Modal Form Settings

Interestingly, even though SizeGripStyle is set to its default of Auto, the size grip is automatically shown for modal forms (Figure 3.2), but it is not shown for main windows (Figure 3.1). Also, while the ControlBox property remains true when the border style is changed to FixedDialog, the icon is not shown when ShowIcon is set to true, as you can see in Figure 3.3.

Figure 3.3   Typical Fixed Modal Form Settings

Clearly, Windows Forms has its own ideas about what to show along the edge of your form, sometimes disregarding your preferences. Except for FormBorderStyle, typical modeless form settings are just like the sizable modal form settings (from Figure 3.2) except that calling Show instead of ShowDialog causes the size grip to go away.

These examples should serve most of your needs, although it's possible to vary form properties to get a few more variations. For example, you can use the border styles Fixed-ToolWindow and SizableToolWindow to show the caption in miniature (handy for floating tool strip or tool box windows).

Deciding on Modal Versus Modeless at Run-Time

If you'd like your form to change its settings based on whether it's being shown modally, check its Modal property:

```
void ModalOrModelessDialog_Load(object sender, EventArgs e) {
  if( this.Modal ) {
    // Show as a fixed-sized modal dialog
    this.FormBorderStyle = FormBorderStyle.FixedDialog;
  }
  else {
    // Show as a sizable modeless dialog
    this.FormBorderStyle = FormBorderStyle.Sizable;
  }
}
```

Depending on whether the form is shown using ShowDialog or Show, the Modal property is true or false, respectively. However, because the way a form is shown isn't known until after it has been created, you can't use the Modal property when it is inspected from a form's constructor, because it is always false at that time. However, you can use the Modal property value during and after the Load event.

Data Exchange

No matter what kind of form you have, you need to get data into it and out of it. Although it is possible for a form to update an application's data directly when the user presses OK or Apply, it is generally considered bad practice for anything except the main form of your application. The problem is that changes in one part of the application might adversely affect your code, so forms should be as stand-alone as possible.[2] This means that forms should have a set of properties they manage, letting the form's client populate the initial

---

[2] As should classes and components of all kinds, but that's a discussion for another book.

property values and pulling out the final values as appropriate, just as you saw earlier in the typical use of ColorDialog.

Because most properties managed by a form are actually properties of the controls hosted by a form, you may be tempted to make the control field declarations public to allow a form client to do this:[3]

```
LoanApplicationDialog dlg = new LoanApplicationDialog();
dlg.applicantNameTextBox.Text = "Joe Borrower"; // DON'T!
DialogResult result = dlg.ShowDialog();
if( result == DialogResult.OK ) { /* user pressed OK */ }
```

The problem with this approach is the same one you encounter when making any field public: If LoanApplicationDialog wants to change the way the applicant's name is displayed, such as from a TextBox control to a Label control, all users of the LoanApplicationDialog class must now be updated. To avoid this problem, the general practice is to expose public custom form properties that get and set the form's child control properties:

```
string ApplicantName {
  get { return this.applicantNameTextBox.Text; }
  set { this.applicantNameTextBox.Text = value; }
}
```

The form client can access these properties in the same way it can access a field. However, unlike a field, getting or setting a property allows your form to change how the code executes without requiring a code change in the form client. Furthermore, using properties results in a simpler usage model for the form client, because you no longer need to concern yourself with the implementation details best left to the form:

```
LoanApplicationDialog dlg = new LoanApplicationDialog();
dlg.ApplicantName = "Joe Borrower";
DialogResult result = dlg.ShowDialog();
if( result == DialogResult.OK ) { /* user pressed OK */ }
```

Handling OK and Cancel

Before data can be retrieved from the property of a modal form, ShowDialog must first return, and this means that the form must first be closed. To do this, you call the Form.Close function inside each button's Click event handler:

[3] Because the dialog's constructor calls InitializeComponent, which creates the dialog's child controls, any client of the dialog is free to get and set properties as soon as the dialog object is created.

```
void okButton_Click(object sender, EventArgs e) {
  this.Close();
}

void cancelButton_Click(object sender, EventArgs e) {
  this.Close();
}
```

After a form is closed, ShowDialog returns a value that specifies the condition under which the form was closed, allowing the form client code to respond accordingly. This value, exposed from a form as the DialogResult property, is one of the following Dialog-Result enumeration values:

```
namespace System.Windows.Forms {
  enum DialogResult {
    None = 0, // default
    OK = 1,
    Cancel = 2, // result when calling Form.Close()
    Abort = 3,
    Retry = 4,
    Ignore = 5,
    Yes = 6,
    No = 7,
  }
}
```

A new form instance's DialogResult value defaults to None. A closed form—whether closed by the Close method, a click on the form's close button, or Alt+F4—automatically has its DialogResult value set to Cancel. The Abort, Ignore, No, and Retry values are used mostly by MessageBox.Show, but you should feel free to use them for your own custom forms.[4] Of course, the desired value returned from ShowDialog when the OK button is pressed is OK, which our client code checks for:

```
dlg.ShowDialog();
DialogResult result = dlg.DialogResult;
if( result == DialogResult.OK ) { /* user pressed OK */ }
```

As a coding shortcut, you can check the return value from ShowDialog, which happens to be the modal dialog's DialogResult property value:

```
DialogResult result = dlg.ShowDialog();
if( result == DialogResult.OK ) { /* user pressed OK */ }
```

---

[4] In contrast with Form.Show, MessageBox.Show is modal, not modeless, exposing an inconsistency between the two methods with the same name.

To return a value other than Cancel from ShowDialog, you set the form's DialogResult property before closing the form:

```
void okButton_Click(object sender, EventArgs e) {
  this.DialogResult = DialogResult.OK;
  this.Close();
}
```

A call to the Close method is unnecessary when you set a form's DialogResult property, because a modal form interprets that to mean it should close automatically:

```
void okButton_Click(object sender, EventArgs e) {
  this.DialogResult = DialogResult.OK; // Close automatically
}
```

The equivalent for a Cancel button is to set DialogResult to Cancel:

```
void cancelButton_Click(object sender, EventArgs e) {
  this.DialogResult = DialogResult.Cancel; // Close automatically
}
```

With this code in place, clicking either OK or Cancel dismisses a form such as the one shown in Figure 3.4.

Figure 3.4   A Sample Form Used as a Dialog

Unfortunately, we don't have quite all the behavior we need from our OK and Cancel buttons. In Figure 3.4, notice that the OK button is not drawn as the default button. The *default button* is the one invoked when the Enter key is pressed, and it's typically drawn with a thicker border than nondefault buttons. In addition, the Cancel button should be invoked when the Esc key is pressed. Enabling this behavior is a matter of designating which buttons on the form should be invoked when Enter and Esc are pressed. You set these by configuring the form's AcceptButton and CancelButton, respectively, as shown in Figure 3.5.

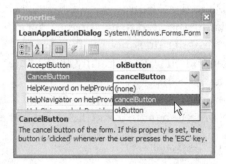

**Figure 3.5   Using the Properties Window to
Set a Form's AcceptButton and CancelButton**

This is handy because the Properties window allows you to choose from a drop-down list of all the buttons currently on the form, and because your choice is automatically persisted to InitializeComponent:

```csharp
// LoanApplicationDialog.Designer.cs
partial class LoanApplicationDialog {
  ...
  void InitializeComponent() {
    ...
    this.AcceptButton = this.okButton;
    this.CancelButton = this.cancelButton;
    ...
  }
}

// LoanApplicationDialog.cs
partial class LoanApplicationDialog : Form {
  public LoanApplicationDialog() {
    InitializeComponent();
  }

  void okButton_Click(object sender, EventArgs e) {
    this.DialogResult = DialogResult.OK;
  }

  void cancelButton_Click(object sender, EventArgs e) {
    this.DialogResult = DialogResult.Cancel;
  }
}
```

When you use the Properties window to set the form's CancelButton property, you don't actually need to set the DialogResult property in the Cancel button's Click event handler. This works because when you set the form's CancelButton property, the Windows Forms Designer sets the DialogResult property of the Cancel button itself to DialogResult.Cancel, thereby obviating the need to handle the Cancel button's Click event. However, the Windows Forms Designer does not set the form's AcceptButton DialogResult property in the same manner, so you must manually change the OK button's default value of DialogResult.None to DialogResult.OK.[5]

With the DialogResult properties set for both the OK and the Cancel buttons, you can dismiss the form without having to handle their Click events at all:

```
// LoanApplicationDialog.Designer.cs
partial class LoanApplicationDialog {
  ...
  void InitializeComponent() {
    ...
    this.okButton.DialogResult = DialogResult.OK;
    ...
    this.cancelButton.DialogResult = DialogResult.Cancel;
    ...
    this.AcceptButton = this.okButton;
    this.CancelButton = this.cancelButton;
    ...
  }
}

// LoanApplicationDialog.cs
partial class LoanApplicationDialog : Form {
  ...
  // okButton_Click handler not needed
  // cancelButton_Click handler not needed
  ...
}
```

Even though it's possible to implement the client event handlers for the OK and Cancel buttons, you can often get away with simply setting the form's AcceptButton and CancelButton properties and setting the DialogResult property of the OK button. This

---

[5] There's an open debate in the Windows Forms community as to which is a bug: that the Windows Forms Designer sets the DialogResult of the CancelButton, or that the Designer doesn't set the DialogResult of the AcceptButton. As for me, I think it's a bug that the Windows Forms Designer doesn't do the same thing for both buttons.

technique gives you all the data exchange behavior you need in a modal form (except for data validation, which is covered later in this chapter).

Modeless Form Data

Modeless forms require a different strategy from that of modal forms to communicate user-updated data to the form's client. For one thing, setting the DialogResult property of a modeless form doesn't automatically dismiss it, as it does for a modal form. For another thing, because Show returns immediately, the client usage model is different. Finally, modeless forms acting as dialogs usually have Apply and Close buttons, so data entered into the form can be used before the modeless form even goes away.

What's needed is a way to notify the client of a modeless form when the Accept button is pressed. Luckily, standard .NET events can be used for this purpose:[6]

```
// PropertiesDialog.cs
partial class PropertiesDialog : Form {
  ...
  // Event to fire when Accept is pressed
  public event EventHandler Accept;

  void acceptButton_Click(object sender, EventArgs e) {
    // Fire event when Accept is pressed
    if( Accept != null ) Accept(this, EventArgs.Empty);
  }

  void closeButton_Click(object sender, EventArgs e) {
    this.Close();
  }
}
```

In this example, PropertiesDialog exposes a public event called Accept using the standard EventHandler delegate signature. When the Accept button is pressed, the modeless form fires the Accept event to notify any interested parties that the Accept button has been pressed. The form client can subscribe to the event when the form is created:

```
// Client creates, connects to, and shows modeless form
void showProperties_Click(object sender, EventArgs e) {
  PropertiesDialog dlg = new PropertiesDialog();
  dlg.Accept += Properties_Accept;
  dlg.Show();
}
```

[6] For more information about .NET delegates and events, see Appendix C: Delegates and Events.

```
// Client handles event from form to access accepted values
void Properties_Accept(object sender, EventArgs e) {
  PropertiesDialog dlg = (PropertiesDialog)sender;
  MessageBox.Show(dlg.SomeProperty);
}
```

The client subscribes to the Accept event after the form is created, but before it's shown. When the Accept button is pressed, the notification shows up in the client's event handler. By convention, the form passes itself when it fires the event so that the receiver of the event can use a simple cast operation to get back the reference to the form. The only thing left to do is to make the modeless form's Close button call the Close method, and you've got yourself a modeless form.

Data Validation

Even though you may have a nice modal or modeless form, it doesn't mean you can trust your users. I don't mean you can't trust them to pay (a separate issue that I won't go into here); I mean you can't trust the data they enter. They may not give you all the data you need, or they may not give you data in the correct format. List boxes, radio buttons, and all the other controls that give users choices ensure that they provide data in the correct format. However, free-form data entry controls such as text boxes sometimes require you to validate them, because users can provide any sort of data. For that, you handle a control's Validating event:

```
void applicantNameTextBox_Validating(object sender, CancelEventArgs e) {
  // Check that applicant name exists
  if( ((Control)sender).Text.Trim().Length == 0 ) {
    MessageBox.Show("Please enter a name", "Error");
    e.Cancel = true;
  }
}
```

The Validating event is fired when the focus is moved from one control on the form whose CausesValidation property is set to true to another control whose CausesValidation property is set to true—in this case, from the Applicant Name text box control to the OK button. The Validating event lets the handler cancel the moving of the focus by setting the CancelEventArgs.Cancel property to true. In this example, if the user doesn't enter a name into the text box, the Validating event handler notifies the user of the transgression, cancels the event, and retains focus on the invalid text box.

If the Validating event is not canceled, the form is notified via the Validated event:

```
void applicantNameTextBox_Validated(object sender, EventArgs e) {
  MessageBox.Show(
    "Nice name, " + this.applicantNameTextBox.Text, "Thanks!");
}
```

Each control has CausesValidation set to true by default. To allow the user to click the Cancel button to close the form without entering valid data, you must set the CausesValidation property to false for your Cancel or Close button. Doing so from the Properties window generates the following code:

```
// LoanApplicationDialog.Designer.cs
partial class LoanApplicationDialog {
  ...
  void InitializeComponent() {
    ...
    this.cancelButton.CausesValidation = false;
    ...
  }
}
```

Regular Expressions and Validation

One handy tool for data validation that's not specific to Windows Forms but is provided by .NET is the regular expression interpreter encapsulated as the Regex class in the System.Text.RegularExpressions namespace. A *regular expression* is a general-purpose way to describe the format of string data so that, among other things, you can check a string to make sure that it fits a required format.

Although the regular expression language is beyond the scope of this book, let's take a look at a small example.[7] A string to check that the format of a phone number fits the Australian format, (02) 9999-1234, including area code, parentheses, spaces, and hyphens, would look like this:

```
^\(\d{2}\) \d{4}-\d{4}$
```

---

[7] For an overview of regular expressions in .NET, read "Regular Expressions in .NET," by Michael Weinhardt and Chris Sells, *Windows Developer*, November 2002, http://www.wd-mag.com/documents/s=7547/win0212d/ (http://tinysells.com/10).

This regular expression breaks down as follows:

- The leading "^" means to start checking the string from the beginning. Without this, any leading characters that don't match the regular expression are ignored, something that could lead to improperly formatted phone numbers.
- The "\(" means to match against a literal "(" character. The "\" prefix escapes the "(," which otherwise would be treated specially by the Regex class.
- The "\d{2}" means to match two digits.
- The "\) " means to match a ")" character followed by a space character.
- The "\d{4}-\d{4}" means to match four more digits, followed by a "-" character, followed by four more digits.
- The trailing "$" means to match the string all the way to the end so that no other characters can come after the phone number.

This regular expression can be used in a Validating event handler to check for an Australian phone number:

```
Regex rgxOzPhone = new Regex(@"^\(\d{2}\) \d{4}-\d{4}$");
...
void applicantPhoneNoTextBox_Validating(
  object sender, CancelEventArgs e) {

  // Check that a valid Australian application phone exists
  if( !rgxOzPhone.IsMatch(((Control)sender).Text) ) {
    MessageBox.Show(
      "Please enter an Australian phone number: (xx) xxxx-xxxx",
      "Error");
    e.Cancel = true;
  }
}
```

If the string entered into the phone number text box does not match the regular expression in its entirety, the IsMatch method of the Regex class returns false, letting the handler indicate to the user that the data is not in the correct format. Taken together, regular expressions and validation provide a powerful tool to check a wide range of input strings provided by the user.[8]

[8] An implementation of ASP.NET-like validation controls for Windows Forms is available from Genghis at http://www.genghisgroup.com (http://tinysells.com/8).

Masked Text Entry and Validation

One downside of using regular expressions is that the required data format is not visually apparent to the user because the control itself is empty. This is where a MaskedTextBox comes into its own. MaskedTextBox allows you to specify a visual *mask* that helps users understand the type and range of the required data. A mask is composed of a sequence of mask characters, each of which specifies an expected data type and range and shows how it should be displayed in the text box as a placeholder character. Masks are stored in the MaskedTextBox control's Mask property and, for the Australian phone number example, would look like this:

```
(00) 0000-0000
```

The MaskedTextBox uses "0" to specify a required number, and "(" ")" and "-" are treated as string literal placeholders and turn out to be useful visual guides. Wherever a mask character accepts data, a prompt character (specified by the PromptChar property and defaulting to "_") is displayed when MaskedTextBox is active, as shown in Figure 3.6.

Figure 3.6   An Active MaskedTextBox
Control with Prompt Characters

By default, the prompts disappear when MaskedTextBox loses focus, although you can set the HidePromptOnLeave property to true to retain them in this situation.

MaskedTextBox has many useful features and a rich set of mask characters to choose from.

Using MaskedTextBox controls gives you two advantages. First, it gives users visual cues to assist with data entry. Second, many data formats are simple, and using mask characters is likely to be simpler and more self-explanatory than using regular expressions. On the other hand, the richness of regular expressions supports more complex data-formatting requirements, particularly when data can be entered in multiple formats. In these cases, regular expressions may be more maintainable than the equivalent code, and it's worth the investment to learn how to use them.

Data Format Notification

If users enter invalid data, they need to be notified in some fashion. As much as I lean on the message box in my test development, I prefer not to use it for actual applications; if a form has several controls that are invalid, it quickly becomes difficult for the user to remember which controls are invalid in what way, because message boxes don't stick around. This problem is exacerbated by increasing levels of data-formatting complexity.

One alternative is to use a status strip, but status strips tend to be ignored because they're at the bottom of the screen, far away from what the user is looking at.[9] A better way is to use the ErrorProvider component, which provides a visual indicator from which a tool tip can be displayed, as shown in Figure 3.7.

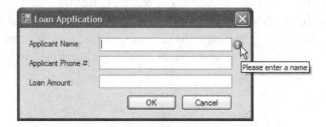

Figure 3.7   Sample Use of the ErrorProvider Component

When users attempt to change focus from the empty text box, we use an instance of the ErrorProvider component to set an error associated with that text box, causing the icon to be displayed to the right of the text box and making the tool tip available. To implement this behavior, you drag an ErrorProvider component onto the form and handle the Validating event for the desired control:

```
void applicantNameTextBox_Validating(object sender, CancelEventArgs e) {

  // Check that applicant name exists
  string error = null;
  if( ((Control)sender).Text.Trim().Length == 0 ) {
    error = "Please enter a name";
    e.Cancel = true;
  }
  this.errorProvider.SetError((Control)sender, error);
}
```

[9] According to legend, Microsoft did a usability study awarding people $50 if they would look under their chairs, putting the notification for this award in the status strip. The $50 went unclaimed during the testing.

Notice the call to ErrorProvider.SetError. The first argument is the control that the error is associated with, which we get from the Validating event's sender argument. The second argument is the error string, which turns into the tool tip. If the control's data is valid, you hide the error indicator by setting the error string to null.

Combined Validation

Validation is not always on a per-control basis. In some cases, several controls capture a set of data that needs to be validated in its entirety, rather than each individual control. For example, consider the update to the Loan Application dialog shown in Figure 3.8. Now it accepts a repayment percentage split across two payments, where the combined percentage must, of course, add up to 100.

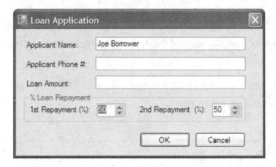

Figure 3.8   Combined Controls Requiring Single Validation

In this example, it doesn't make sense to validate each numeric up/down control, because it's the combined value that needs to be validated. It's much nicer to group those controls within a container control, such as a group box, and validate collectively:

```
void applicantLoanAmountRepaymentGroupBox_Validating(
  object sender, CancelEventArgs e) {

  // Check that 1st and 2nd percentages sum up to 100
  string error = null;
  if( (this.firstNumericUpDown.Value +
      this.secondNumericUpDown.Value != 100) ) {
    error = "First and second repayments must add up to 100%";
    e.Cancel = true;
  }
  this.errorProvider.SetError((Control)sender, error);
}
```

Here, we handle the group box's Validating event to validate the combined values of the contained controls. If the data is invalid, we pass the group box to the ErrorProvider.SetError invocation to display the error provider icon for the group box as a whole, rather than any individual controls, as shown in Figure 3.9.

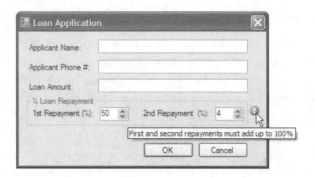

Figure 3.9   Combined Controls Being Validated as One

As with validating a single control at a time, we hide the error by setting the error string passed to ErrorProvider.SetError to null.

Thorough Validation

As useful as the Validating event is, especially when combined with ErrorProvider, there is one validation issue you must deal with separately: If a control has invalid data but never receives focus, it is never validated, because the Validating event is triggered only when focus is moved from one control to another. For example, the form in Figure 3.9 has three text boxes and two numeric up/down controls. Even if you were to handle the Validating event for all five controls, the user could still enter valid data into the first one (assuming it gets focus first) and press OK, causing the form to close and return DialogResult.OK. The problem is that the other two text boxes never get focus, never receive the Validating event, and, therefore, never get a chance to cancel the acceptance of the form.

One solution is to make sure that all controls start with valid data, although there are lots of cases when you can't provide reasonable and valid initial data. What's a good default for a phone number? Or an e-mail address? For these cases, you need to manually write the code to validate the form via the OK button's Click event handler:

```
void okButton_Click(object sender, EventArgs e) {
  if( !this.Validate() ) {
    this.DialogResult = DialogResult.None;
  }
}
```

The Validate method causes the form to enumerate the controls on the form. For each control found, the Validating event is fired, thereby executing your validation logic. Validate is also implemented by container controls such as SplitContainer, ToolStripContainer, and UserControl. If you need to validate subsets of controls on a form, such as those in container controls like group boxes, you can call ValidateChildren, which accepts a ValidationConstraints enumeration value that specifies the control subset of interest:

```
namespace System.Windows.Forms {
  enum ValidationConstraints {
    None = 0, // No child controls
    Selectable = 1, // All selectable controls
    Enabled = 2, // All enabled controls on the form
    Visible = 4, // All visible controls
    TabStop = 8, // All tabbable controls
    ImmediateChildren = 16, // Controls whose parent is this form
  }
}
```

For example, validating the selectable controls on a form would look like this:

```
void okButton_Click(object sender, EventArgs e) {
  if( !this.ValidateChildren(ValidationConstraints.Selectable) ) {
    this.DialogResult = DialogResult.None;
  }
}
```

As a shortcut for validating selectable child controls, you can invoke ValidateChildren without passing a ValidationConstraints value:

```
void okButton_Click(object sender, EventArgs e) {
  if( !this.ValidateChildren() ) {
    this.DialogResult = DialogResult.None;
  }
}
```

You can even use more than one ValidationConstraints value if necessary. For example, the following code validates only immediate child controls of the validating container that can be tabbed to:

```
void okButton_Click(object sender, EventArgs e) {
  if( !this.ValidateChildren(ValidationConstraints.ImmediateChildren |
    ValidationConstraints.TabStop) ) {
    this.DialogResult = DialogResult.None;
  }
}
```

Although Validate validates all controls on a form by default, it may never be called because of an interesting validation quirk: If the control that has focus is invalid, focus is prevented from leaving that control and moving to any other control with CausesValidation set to true, including other data entry controls and the OK button. This also means that the Esc key can't be pressed to close the form (even though you can press the form's close button or select Close from its system menu). Retaining focus on a control is inconsistent with general Windows user experience practice, which is to typically allow unfettered navigation across a form's landscape. Consequently, retaining focus in this way can potentially confuse your users. Presumably, this behavior is the default in order to be consistent with previous versions of Windows Forms.

new

You can avoid this situation by preventing both Validating and Validated events from firing until either the Validate or the ValidateChildren method is called. Use the form's AutoValidate property:

```
// LoanApplicationDialog.Designer.cs
using System.Windows.Forms;
...
partial class LoanApplicationDialog {
  ...
  void InitializeComponent() {
    ...
    // Allow focus to shift away from invalid controls
    this.AutoValidate = AutoValidate.EnableAllowFocusChange;
    ...
  }
}
```

You can set AutoValidate to one of four AutoValidate enumeration values:

```
namespace System.Windows.Forms {
  enum AutoValidate {
    Inherit = -1 // Use parent control's AutoValidate value
    Disable = 0, // Don't validate any control
    EnablePreventFocusChange = 1, // Keep focus if invalid (default)
    EnableAllowFocusChange = 2, // Don't keep focus if invalid
  }
}
```

Because controls have their CausesValidation property set to true by default, their Validating and Validated events fire automatically. To prevent this behavior for all controls on a form or a user control, you set AutoValidate to AutoValidate.Disable. This is easier than setting each and every control's CausesValidation property to false, and it easily allows you to turn validation back on by setting AutoValidate to EnableAllowFocusChange, EnablePreventFocusChange, or Inherit. Inherit is for controls that implement AutoValidate and wish to use the same AutoValidate behavior of their containers.

With AutoValidate set to EnableAllowFocusChange and with Validate being called when the OK button is pressed, you can validate an entire form in one fell swoop, resulting in the dialog shown in Figure 3.10.

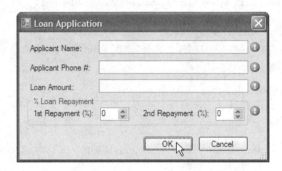

Figure 3.10   Single-Click Formwide Validation Using Validate and AutoValidate.EnableAllowFocusChange

In summary, you should consider several principles when including form validation: First, always include validation. Even a little can go a long way to helping users understand what is required for individual fields and entire forms. Second, to avoid an unpleasant user experience, don't retain focus in any control. Third, implement dialog-wide validation via the OK button's Click event handler; client code on the form that created the dialog processes your data, and the more accurate it is, the less likely it is that an exception will occur or bad data will be allowed through. Finally, because validation is usually specific to controls and container controls, you should deploy your validation logic to their Validating event handlers, especially because formwide validation ensures that this logic is called.[10] These considerations are summarized in the following code:

---

[10] User controls, discussed in Chapter 10, can simplify the deployment of multiple controls and validations into a single, reusable control, thereby saving you a lot of trouble.

```
// LoanApplicationDialog.cs
partial class LoanApplicationDialog : Form {
  public LoanApplicationDialog() {
    InitializeComponent();

    // Configure AcceptButton and CancelButton
    this.AcceptButton = this.okButton;
    this.CancelButton = this.cancelButton;
    this.okButton.DialogResult = DialogResult.OK;
    this.cancelButton.DialogResult = DialogResult.Cancel;

    // Allow focus to shift away from invalid controls
    this.AutoValidate = AutoValidate.EnableAllowFocusChange;
  }
  ...
  void applicantNameTextBox_Validating(
    object sender, CancelEventArgs e) {
    // Check that applicant name exists
    string error = null;
    if( ((Control)sender).Text.Trim().Length == 0 ) {
      error = "Please enter a name";
      e.Cancel = true;
    }
    this.errorProvider.SetError((Control)sender, error);
  }
  // Other Validating event handlers
  ...
  void okButton_Click(object sender, EventArgs e) {
    if( !this.Validate() ) {
      this.DialogResult = DialogResult.None;
    }
  }
}
```

The built-in Windows Forms validation infrastructure provides a fine framework for applying these principles.

Implementing Help

As noticeable as the ErrorProvider user interface is (at least compared with the status strip), it's nice to provide user help that doesn't take the form of a reprimand. It also is useful to give users help without making them try something that fails. Windows Forms supports these goals in several ways.

Tool Tips

One simple way is to provide each control with relevant instructions via a tool tip that appears when users hover the mouse pointer over the control, as shown in Figure 3.11.

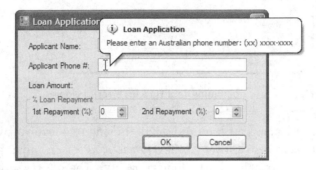

Figure 3.11   Using Tool Tips

The Tool tip component allows you to add tool tips to any control in a form; when dropped onto a form, Tool tip adds a new property to each control that shows up as "ToolTip on toolTip" in the Properties window. Any new property added by one object to another object on a form is called an *extender property,* because the former object extends the latter with additional functionality via a property.[11]

Setting the Tool tip extender property for a control gives it a tool tip as provided by the Tool tip component. You can also configure the Tool tip component to appear either as a rectangular tool tip or as a balloon with an icon and a title, as shown in Figure 3.11.

Using ErrorProvider for General Information

The problem with tool tips displayed after hovering is that the user may not know that they're available. (When was the last time you hovered your mouse pointer over a text box looking for help?) Luckily, ErrorProvider is really good at providing a visual indicator, so it can be used with a different icon, as shown in Figure 3.12.[12]

---

[11] Extender properties are covered in detail in Chapter 11: Design-Time Integration: The Properties Window.

[12] I got the sample icon from Common7\VS2005ImageLibrary\icons\WinXP\INFO.ICO in my VS05 installation directory. Feel free to use whatever icon makes you happy.

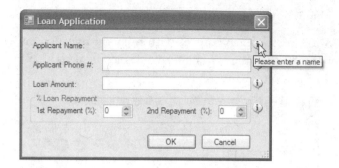

Figure 3.12   Combining Tool Tip with ErrorProvider

If you like this approach, you can implement it using two error providers: one with a friendly information icon, also known as the *information provider,* and another with a mean error icon (as set using ErrorProvider's Icon property). The information provider is displayed without blinking when a form first loads and when there's no error. Otherwise, the error provider is used:

```
void LoanApplicationDialog_Load(object sender, EventArgs e) {
  // Use tool tips to populate the "information provider"
  this.infoProvider.BlinkStyle = ErrorBlinkStyle.NeverBlink;
  foreach( Control control in this.Controls ) {
    string toolTip = this.toolTip.GetToolTip(control);
    if( toolTip.Length == 0 ) continue;
    this.infoProvider.SetError(control, toolTip);
  }
}

void applicantNameTextBox_Validating(object sender, CancelEventArgs e)
{
  // Check that applicant name exists
  string toolTip = this.toolTip.GetToolTip((Control)sender);
  if( ((Control)sender).Text.Trim().Length == 0 ) {
    // Show the error when there is no text in the text box
    this.errorProvider.SetError((Control)sender, toolTip);
    this.infoProvider.SetError((Control)sender, null);
    e.Cancel = true;
  }
  else {
    // Show the info when there is text in the text box
    this.errorProvider.SetError((Control)sender, null);
    this.infoProvider.SetError((Control)sender, toolTip);
  }
}
```

Just as the ToolTip component adds the ToolTip extender property to each control on the form, ErrorProvider adds an Error property to each control. Setting a control's Error property in the Properties window is the equivalent of calling ErrorProvider.SetError, passing the control and an error string as the arguments. However, the Error property is not a good place to store a message, because clearing the message is the only way to hide an ErrorProvider's icon for a particular control. Instead, given that the Tool tip property never needs clearing, the example uses it whenever a message should be displayed: when the mouse is hovered over a control, when the information provider is showing, or when the error provider is showing. This has the added benefit of keeping hard-coded strings out of code and in a place that can easily be made localizable, as discussed in Chapter 13: Resources.

If you use this technique, each Validating event handler is likely to use the same code to determine whether to enable or disable the ErrorProvider controls appropriately. Thus, it makes sense to provide a generic solution to save extra coding:

```
void applicantNameTextBox_Validating(
  object sender, CancelEventArgs e) {
  UpdateErrorStatus(
    ((Control)sender).Text.Trim().Length != 0, (Control)sender, e);
}

void applicantPhoneNoTextBox_Validating(
  object sender, CancelEventArgs e) {
  UpdateErrorStatus(
    rgxOzPhone.IsMatch(((Control)sender).Text), (Control)sender, e);
}

void applicantLoanAmountTextBox_Validating(
  object sender, CancelEventArgs e) {
  UpdateErrorStatus(
    rgxLoanAmount.IsMatch(((Control)sender).Text), (Control)sender, e);
}

void UpdateErrorStatus(
  bool isValid, Control control, CancelEventArgs e) {
  string toolTip = this.toolTip.GetToolTip(control);
  if( isValid ) {
    // Show the info when there is text in the text box
    this.errorProvider.SetError(control, null);
    this.infoProvider.SetError(control, toolTip);
  }
  else {
    // Show the error when there is no text in the text box
    this.errorProvider.SetError(control, toolTip);
    this.infoProvider.SetError(control, null);
    e.Cancel = true;
  }
}
```

Handling the Help Button and F1

Although the little icons on the forms are useful, the standard way to provide this kind of information is to use the help button (the question mark) located in the upper-right corner of the form, as shown in Figure 3.13.

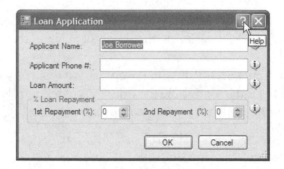

Figure 3.13   Adding a Help Button to a Form

You enable the help button by setting the HelpButton property of the form to true. When the button is pressed, the cursor changes as a visual cue for the user to click on the desired control, as shown in Figure 3.14.

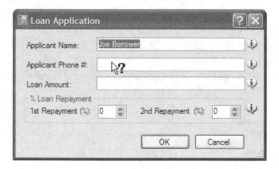

Figure 3.14   The Help Cursor

When the user clicks on a control, the HelpRequested event is fired to the form. You handle this event to find the clicked control and display appropriate help:

```
void LoanApplicationDialog_HelpRequested(
  object sender, HelpEventArgs e) {
  // Convert screen coordinates to client coordinates
  Point pt = this.PointToClient(e.MousePos);
```

```
  // Look for control user clicked on
  Control control = FindChildAtPoint(this, pt);
  if( control == null ) return;

  // Show help
  string help = this.toolTip.GetToolTip(control);
  if( string.IsNullOrEmpty(help) ) return;
  MessageBox.Show(help, "Help");
  e.Handled = true;
}

// More useful version of GetChildAtPoint
Control FindChildAtPoint(Control parent, Point pt) {
  // Find a child
  Control child = parent.GetChildAtPoint(pt);

  // If no child, this is the control at the mouse cursor
  if( child == null ) return parent;

  // If a child, offset our current position to be relative to the child
  Point childPoint =
    new Point(pt.X - child.Location.X, pt.Y - child.Location.Y);

  // Find child of child control at offset position
  return FindChildAtPoint(child, childPoint);
}
```

The HelpRequested handler uses both of the HelpEventArgs properties:

```
namespace System.Windows.Forms {
  class HelpEventArgs : EventArgs {
    public bool Handled { get; set; }
    public Point MousePos { get; }
  }
}
```

MousePos represents the screen coordinates where the user clicked, and Handled lets us stop the HelpRequested event from going any further if we handle it. In the example, we convert MousePos, provided in screen coordinates, to client coordinates and call FindChild-AtPoint to find the control the user clicked on. The Form class's GetChildAtPoint method searches only the immediate children of a form, but our custom FindChildAtPoint method searches through all containers to find the clicked control, taking containers such as group boxes into account. For example, if a user clicks the first repayment percentage numeric up/down control, GetChildAtPoint returns the container group box, whereas FindChildAtPoint returns the numeric up/down control. If FindChildAtPoint finds the clicked control, we put the control's tool tip into a message box and stop the event from propagating elsewhere.

The help button is useful to most users, but keyboard-oriented Windows users are more familiar with the F1 key, which is meant to communicate to the application that help is requested on whatever is currently active, which is normally the control with focus. Pressing F1 also fires the HelpRequested event. However, you'll notice that the HelpEventArgs class provides no indication of how the event was fired. Therefore, if we want to do something such as open an HTML file when F1 is pressed, we must check whether it was a mouse button that triggered the event:

```
void LoanApplicationDialog_HelpRequested(
  object sender, HelpEventArgs e) {

  // If no mouse button was clicked, F1 got us here
  if( Control.MouseButtons == MouseButtons.None ) {
    // open a help file...
  }
  // Help button got us here
  else {
    // show the message box...
  }
}
```

Because we know that a mouse click triggers the HelpRequested event when it comes from the help button, we need to know whether any mouse buttons were pressed when the HelpRequested event was fired. Consequently, we check the Control.MouseButtons property, which provides the state of the mouse buttons during the current event. If no buttons were pressed to fire this event, the user got to the handler using the F1 key; otherwise, the user pressed the help button.

Using HTML Help

When you implement F1, it is not hard to launch a uniform resource locator (URL) to show an HTML page. However, when using the help button, users are accustomed to seeing help messages in shadowed tool tips, known as *pop-up help*, as shown in Figure 3.15.

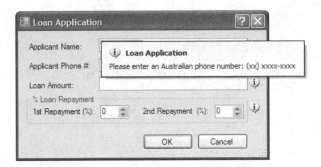

Figure 3.15   Using HelpProvider to Implement the Help Button

You implement pop-up help with a call to the Tool tip component's Show method:

```
void LoanApplicationDialog_HelpRequested(
  object sender, HelpEventArgs e) {

  if( Control.MouseButtons == MouseButtons.None ) {
    // Open a help file...
  }
  // Help button got us here
  else {
    // Convert screen coordinates to client coordinates
    Point pt = this.PointToClient(e.MousePos);

    // Look for control user clicked on
    Control control = FindChildAtPoint(this, pt);
    if( control == null ) return;

    // Show help
    string help = this.toolTip.GetToolTip(control);
    if( string.IsNullOrEmpty(help) ) return;
    this.toolTip.Show(help, this, pt, 3000);
    e.Handled = true;
  }
}
```

If you want to implement opening an HTML file using the F1 key, Tool tip doesn't help you. However, you'll find joy with the Help class, because it wraps the HTML Help functions provided by Windows and exposes them as one of the following methods for you to enjoy:

```
namespace System.Windows.Forms {
  class Help {
    public static void ShowHelp(Control parent, string url);
```

```
    public static void ShowHelp(Control parent,
      string url, HelpNavigator command, object parameter);
    public static void ShowHelp(Control parent,
      string url, string keyword);
    public static void ShowHelp(Control parent,
      string url, HelpNavigator navigator);
    public static void ShowHelpIndex(Control parent, string url);
    public static void ShowPopup(Control parent,
      string caption, Point location);
  }
}
```

The following example uses the simplest variation of ShowHelp to display the HTML help file:

```
void LoanApplicationDialog_HelpRequested(
  object sender, HelpEventArgs e) {

  if( Control.MouseButtons == MouseButtons.None ) {
    // Open a help file...
    string file = Path.GetFullPath("loanApplicationDialog.htm");
    Help.ShowHelp(this, file);
  }
  ...
}
```

This code uses the Path.GetFullPath method (from the System.IO namespace) to turn a relative path name into a full path name. The URL argument to the ShowHelp method can be a full file path or a full URL, but ShowHelp doesn't seem to like relative path names. If you use this technique, F1 takes users to a page of HTML describing the form as a whole. However, users pressing F1 would probably prefer help that is specific to the currently active control; in other words, if they press F1 while in the Loan Amount field, they should see help for the Loan Amount field. For that to happen against a file in the local file system, you must move from HTML to Microsoft's compiled and indexed HTML Help format.

Compiled HTML Help

When it was clear that HTML files were more flexible than the WinHelp help file format, Microsoft decided to switch from WinHelp to something HTML-based. However, WinHelp had a number of advantages over raw HTML, including tools for indexing and searching and support for having multiple pages in a single file. Merging the flexibility of HTML with the convenience of WinHelp yielded HTML Help, which consists of a set of functions, a set of tools, and a file format that compiles all pages into a single file with a .chm extension. The details of how to build real HTML Help files are beyond the scope of this book, so I recommend downloading the HTML Help Workshop from the Microsoft Developer Network site to experiment with it yourself.[13]

To create a minimal HTML Help file with the HTML Help Workshop, follow these steps:

1. Run the HTML Help Workshop.
2. Create a new project. This is the list of files used to create a .chm file.
3. Create a new HTML file. Add some text to the <body> tag and save the file. This file will become a topic page.
4. Make sure the Project tab is selected, and click the Add/Remove Topic Files button. Add the HTML file you created and saved in step 3. This action adds the topic file to the project.
5. Click the Contents tab and choose Create a New Contents File. This enables the table of contents.
6. Make sure the Contents tab is selected, and click the Insert a Page button. Add the HTML file from the previous steps, and make sure that the Entry Title field has a value before pressing OK. This adds an entry to the table of contents.
7. Click the Index tab and choose Create a New Index File. This enables the index. Feel free to add a keyword or two to populate the index.
8. Click the Project tab again, and then click the Change Project Options button. Choose the Compiler tab. Enable the Compile Full-Text Searching Information option. This enables search.
9. Compile and view.

When you have an HTML Help file, you can integrate it into your form using the Help class by passing the name of the .chm file to the ShowHelp function. Furthermore, you can enable scrolling to a particular subtopic inside a topic by using the HTML <a> tag to name a subtopic:

```html
<!-- loanapplicationdialog.htm -->
<html>
  <head>
    <title>loan application dialog</title>
  </head>
  <body>
    <h1><a name="name">Applicant Name</a></h1>
    Please enter a name
    <h1><a name="phoneno">Applicant Phone #</a></h1>
```

---

[13] http://msdn.microsoft.com/library/default.asp?url=/library/en-us/htmlhelp/html/ hwMicrosoftHTMLHelpDownloads.asp (http://tinysells.com/11).

```
     Please enter an Australian phone number: (xx) xxxx-xxxx
     <h1><a name="loanamount">Applicant Loan Amount</a></h1>
     Please enter a valid loan amount: x.xx
     <h1><a name="firstrepaymentpercent">% Repayment</a></h1>
     Please enter a % of the loan amount to repay first
     <h1><a name="secondrepaymentpercent">% Repayment</a></h1>
     Please enter a % of the loan amount to repay second
  </body>
</html>
```

Now you can map the name of the subtopic to the control when F1 is pressed:

```
void LoanApplicationDialog_HelpRequested(
  object sender,
  HelpEventArgs e) {
  // If no mouse button was clicked, F1 got us here
  if( Control.MouseButtons == MouseButtons.None ) {

    string subtopic = null;

    if(
      this.ActiveControl == this.applicantNameTextBox ) {
      subtopic = "name";
    }
    else if( this.ActiveControl == this.applicantPhoneNoTextBox ) {
      subtopic = "phoneNo";
    }
    else if( this.ActiveControl == this.applicantLoanAmountTextBox ) {
      subtopic = "loanAmount";
    }
    else if( this.ActiveControl == this.firstNumericUpDown ) {
      subtopic = "firstrepaymentpercent";
    }
    else if( this.ActiveControl == this.secondNumericUpDown ) {
      subtopic = "secondrepaymentpercent";
    }
    Help.ShowHelp(
      this, "dialogs.chm", "loanApplicationDialog.htm#" + subtopic);

    e.Handled = true;
  }
  ...
}
```

Now when F1 is pressed and focus is on a specific control, the topic is brought up in the help viewer window, and the specific subtopic is scrolled into view, as shown in Figure 3.16.

**Figure 3.16   Showing the Applicant Phone Number ("phoneNo")
Subtopic**

F1-Style Help with the Help Button

Some applications, such as VS05, provide the same behavior for clicking a dialog's help button as by pressing F1 (namely, displaying context-sensitive help). If your application's help
system uses this model, you must detect when the help button is clicked, prevent the special icon from being displayed, and open the help for the active control in the same way
pressing F1 does. To do this, you handle the form's HelpButtonClicked event:

```
void LoanApplicationDialog_HelpButtonClicked(
  object sender, CancelEventArgs e) {

  // Show help for currently active control
  string subtopic = null;
  if( this.ActiveControl == this.applicantNameTextBox ) {
    subtopic = "name";
  }
  else if( this.ActiveControl == this.applicantPhoneNoTextBox ) {
    subtopic = "phoneNo";
  }
  else if( this.ActiveControl == this.applicantLoanAmountTextBox ) {
    subtopic = "loanAmount";
  }
  else if( this.ActiveControl == this.firstNumericUpDown ) {
    subtopic = "firstrepaymentpercent";
  }
  else if( this.ActiveControl == this.secondNumericUpDown ) {
    subtopic = "secondrepaymentpercent";
  }

  Help.ShowHelp(this, "dialogs.chm", "loanApplicationDialog.htm#" + subtopic);

  // Don't allow users to click a control to find its help,
  // because we just did that for the active control
  e.Cancel = true;
}
```

Here, we use the same code we did to handle the F1 button. Note that we want to prevent the HelpRequested event from being fired to avoid further help processing, including allowing the user to select a control to find its help and changing the cursor after opening the help file. We do this by setting the CancelEventArgs argument's Cancel property to true.

Notice that we're back to mapping between controls and strings (subtopics, in this case); such mapping is better facilitated by a component that provides extender properties, allowing you to set the help information for each control using the Properties window and keeping that information out of the code. The component that provides extender properties to manage this information is HelpProvider.

Using the HelpProvider Component

HelpProvider implements both topic navigation support for the F1 key and pop-up help for the help button. HelpProvider is a wrapper around the Help class for a specific file, so it works well only for HTML Help. After dropping a HelpProvider component onto your form, you set its HelpNamespace property to the name of the file it is to manage, such as dialogs.chm. HelpProvider extends the host form and its controls with the following properties:

```
string HelpKeyword; // Defaults to ""
HelpNavigator HelpNavigator; // Defaults to AssociateIndex
string HelpString; // Defaults to ""
bool ShowHelp; // Defaults to true
```

When F1 is pressed, an empty HelpKeyword displays the HelpString from pop-up help. Otherwise, F1 is detected by HelpProvider, which subsequently passes the HelpKeyword to ShowHelp and uses it in a manner determined by the HelpNavigator property, which can be one of the following:

```
enum HelpNavigator {
   AssociateIndex = -2147483643,
   Find = -2147483644,
   Index = -2147483645, // What ShowHelpIndex does
   KeywordIndex = -2147483642,
   TableOfContents = -2147483646,
   Topic = -2147483647, // The default when ShowHelp is set to true
   TopicId = -2147483641
}
```

For example, if HelpNavigator is Topic, then HelpKeyword is the name of the topic to show—say, loanApplicationDialog.htm. ShowHelp is a Boolean that determines whether HelpProvider should handle the HelpRequested event for the control. Setting ShowHelp to false allows you to handle the HelpRequested event manually, as we've done so far.

However, after dropping a HelpProvider component onto our sample form, we don't have to handle the HelpRequested event at all. Instead, given that the HelpNamespace property is set to dialogs.chm, we can set the HelpProvider properties on each control on the form (as shown in Table 3.1) , causing F1 and the help button to be handled automatically.

Showing Help Contents, Index, and Search

Dialogs don't often have menus—let alone Help menus with Contents, Index, and Search menu items—but while we're on the topic of integrating help with forms, I thought it would be a good idea to mention how to implement these help menu items. You can do this easily by using the Help class:

```
void helpContentsMenuItem_Click(object sender, EventArgs e) {
  Help.ShowHelp(this, "dialogs.chm", HelpNavigator.TableOfContents);
}

void helpIndexMenuItem_Click(object sender, EventArgs e) {
  Help.ShowHelpIndex(this, "dialogs.chm");
}

void helpSearchMenuItem_Click(object sender, EventArgs e) {
  Help.ShowHelp(this, "dialogs.chm", HelpNavigator.Find, "");
}
```

Where Are We?

This chapter deals with topics that are often dialog-related: getting data in and out, validating data, and letting users know about the required data format (including providing access to online help). But none of these topics is specific to "dialogs" (which is a slippery term anyway). However, in this chapter and Chapter 2: Forms, we've covered almost everything a programmer needs to know about modal and modeless forms. If you haven't seen

Table 3.1 Sample HelpProvider Settings

Control	HelpKeyword	HelpNavigator	HelpString	ShowHelp
applicantNameTextBox	loanApplicationDialog.htm#name	Topic	"Please enter a name"	True
applicantPhoneNoTextBox	loanApplicationDialog.htm#phoneNo	Topic	"Please enter an Australian phone number: (xx) xxxx-xxxx"	True
applicantLoanAmount	loanApplicationDialog.htm#loanAmount	Topic	"Please enter a valid loan amount: x.xx"	True
firstNumericUpDown	loanApplicationDialog.htm#firstRepaymentPercent	Topic	"Please enter a % of the loan amount to repay first"	True
secondNumericUpDown	loanApplicationDialog.htm#secondRepaymentPercent	Topic	"Please enter a % of the loan amount to repay second"	True

topics that interest you, such as form localization and drag and drop, read on, especially Chapter 13: Resources (for form localization) and Appendix E: Drag and Drop (for drag and drop). If, however, you're more interested in arranging controls, you'll want to read the next chapter, Chapter 4: Layout, to see how much time you can save by using the vast array of layout support capabilities in Windows Forms.

■4■
Layout

I N CHAPTER 2: FORMS AND CHAPTER 3: DIALOGS, we explored the lion's share of form- and dialog-related issues, which are all ably supported by the Form class. But forms have another important, obvious role: They are canvases on which you compose controls. In all but the most trivial cases, it would require a serious investment of time to compose controls and make sure everything's laid out just right—it would, that is, if it weren't for the layout support present in Windows Forms and VS05. Additionally, this support helps a form and its controls gracefully retain their layouts in the face of user resizing, localization, and, in some cases, control rearrangement at run time.

This chapter explores the range of layout support offered by VS05, the Windows Forms Designer, and forms and controls, collectively known as the *layout system*. The goal is to dramatically simplify the layout process and make your life much easier.

Fixed Layout

The fundamental elements of the layout system assist control positioning, sizing, and ordering to establish a basic composition. One of the key requirements, therefore, is to ensure that the basic composition is retained, something that depends on the Windows Forms Designer "remembering" your composition.

Position and Size

When controls are dropped onto a form, moved into position, and resized as necessary, the Windows Forms Designer needs a mechanism that allows it to accurately compose and recompose a form and its controls at design-time and run-time. For example, consider the four controls hosted on a form in Figure 4.1.

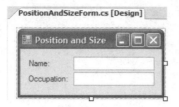

Figure 4.1   Controls Contained by a Form

The Windows Forms Designer generates the code to instantiate, position, and size each of these controls. This code is added to the form's Designer-managed InitializeComponent method:

```
// PositionAndSizeForm.designer.cs
using System.Drawing;
using System.Windows.Forms;
...
partial class PositionAndSizeForm {
  ...
  void InitializeComponent() {
    this.nameLabel = new Label();
    this.nameTextBox = new TextBox();
    this.occupationLabel = new Label();
    this.occupationTextBox = new TextBox();
    ...
    // nameLabel
    this.nameLabel.Location = new Point(12, 15);
    this.nameLabel.Size = new Size(34, 13);
    ...
    // nameTextBox
    this.nameTextBox.Location = new Point(79, 12);
    this.nameTextBox.Size = new Size(110, 20);
    ...
    // occupationLabel
    this.occupationLabel.Location = new Point(12, 42);
    this.occupationLabel.Size = new.Size(61, 13);
    ...
    // occupationTextBox
    this.occupationTextBox.Location = new Point(79, 39);
    this.occupationTextBox.Size = new Size(110, 20);
    ...
  }
  Label nameLabel;
  TextBox nameTextBox;
  Label occupationLabel;
  TextBox occupationTextBox;
}
```

Position, with respect to the upper-left corner of each control's parent, is stored in the Location property, which is of type System.Drawing.Point. Size is captured by the Size property, which is of type System.Drawing.Size.

Dragging controls around and resizing them to establish a composition can be quite an endeavor, particularly as you try to ensure that they are nicely spaced and aligned with respect to each other and the form. Fortunately, the Windows Forms Designer offers specialized layout support to assist this process.

Layout Mode

One aspect of form composition is to make sure that controls are nicely aligned with respect to each other. Another is to ensure that appropriate and consistent amounts of white space are maintained between controls and the edges of a form. For this, the Windows Forms Designer provides two layout modes: SnapToGrid and SnapLines.

You configure the layout mode by setting the LayoutMode property via Tools | Options | Windows Forms Designer | General. Either mode causes controls to snap to certain locations determined by the mode; a control *snaps* when the Designer detects that it is within a certain proximity to a predefined location and automatically aligns it to that location.

SnapToGrid supports snapping to a predefined grid whose dimensions you can set in the same location you configure the layout mode. However, real-world composition is more complicated and flexible than SnapToGrid accommodates. This is why we have the SnapLines layout mode, Windows Forms Designer's default. When controls are dragged onto or around a form or resized, snap lines are manifested as one or more "sticky" lines that guide controls to alignment with other controls in close proximity, including to horizontal and vertical edges, to common text baselines, and to text margins. These snap lines are all illustrated in Figure 4.2.

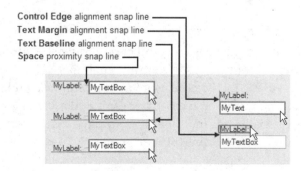

Figure 4.2   SnapLines Layout Mode with Control Edge, Text Margin, Text Baseline, and Space Snap Lines

The Windows Forms Designer easily determines control edge, text margin, and text baseline snap lines without your help. However, you determine space proximity, which is a combination of two pieces of information for each control and the form: padding and margin.

Padding

Padding is the internal distance in pixels from the edge of a form or control's client area that child controls (and also things like text, images, and so on) can't intrude on. You configure this using the Padding property, which is of type Padding:

```
namespace System.Windows.Forms {
    struct Padding {

        // No padding
        public static readonly Padding Empty;

        // Constructors
        Padding(int all);
        Padding(int left, int top, int right, int bottom);

        // Properties (Properties window and code)
        int All { get; set; } // Get/Set all padding edges
        int Bottom { get; set; } // Get/Set bottom padding edge only
        int Left { get; set; } // Get/Set left padding edge only
        int Right { get; set; } // Get/Set right padding edge only
        int Top { get; set; } // Get/Set top padding edge only

        // Properties (Code only)
        int Horizontal { get; } // Sum of Left and Right padding
        int Vertical { get; } // Sum of Top and Bottom padding
        Size Size { get; } // Horizontal + Vertical
    }
}
```

Padding is implemented on the base Control class and most controls that derive from it, including most common controls, user controls, container controls, and forms. Some controls—including TextBox, ListBox, ListView, and MonthCalendar—don't support padding, because padding is either fixed or doesn't make sense for them. For those controls that do support padding, the default is to have zero padding, although you can change this by setting the Padding property with the desired values, as shown in Figure 4.3.

Figure 4.3   Setting a Control's Padding

You can set each dimension individually, or you can use the Padding.All shortcut if all the desired padding dimensions are the same. Either way, the Windows Forms Designer generates the appropriate code:

```
// PositionAndSizeForm.designer.cs
using System.Windows.Forms;
...
partial class PositionAndSizeForm {
  ...
  void InitializeComponent() {
    ...
    this.paddedLabel.Padding = new Padding(3);
    ...
  }
}
```

Note that the Padding structure's Horizontal, Vertical, and Size properties are read-only and consequently not available from the Properties window. However, you may find them useful when rendering a custom control, as discussed in Chapter 11: Design-Time Integration: The Properties Window.

Margins

A *margin* defines the spacing between adjacent controls. You configure margins by using a control's Margin property, which is also of type Padding and is configured in the same manner. All controls implement the Margin property except for Form, because margins are useful only within a form's client area.

Calculating Space SnapLines

When the Windows Forms Designer calculates the size and location of the space proximity snap lines (as shown in Figure 4.2), it adds the padding and margin values for each relevant dimension of the control being dragged or resized and the controls around it. Figure 4.4 illustrates how various combinations of padding and margins are used by the Windows Forms Designer in its calculations.

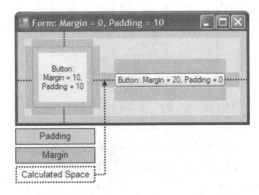

Figure 4.4   Using the Margin and Padding Properties to Calculate the Space Snap Line (See Plate 6)

Location, Size, Padding, and Margin constitute the basic set of information that allows the Windows Forms Designer to accurately reconstruct and lay out your form at design-time, and allows Windows Forms to do the same at run-time.

However, even though this information keeps controls positioned nicely with respect to each other and to their host form, it has no effect when controls appear on top of other controls. In these situations, we need to remember which controls appear above which. For this, the Windows Forms Designer supports control positions within a vertical dimension known as the z-order.

Control Z-Order

Although a control's location specifies its upper-left position in a container relative to the container's upper-left corner, all controls in the same container are logically ordered in a vertical stack, with controls higher in the stack being rendered on top of controls lower in the stack. The position of a control within this stack is defined by its z-order and is implicitly determined by the order in which controls are added to their container. For example, consider the following code:

```
// ZOrderForm.designer.cs
partial class ZOrderForm {
  void InitializeComponent() {
    ...
    this.Controls.Add(this.zorder0button3);
    this.Controls.Add(this.zorder1button2);
```

```
      this.Controls.Add(this.zorder2button1);
      ...
    }
}
```

The resulting z-order of these controls is shown in Figure 4.5.

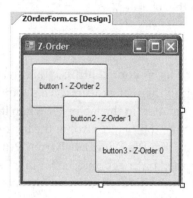

Figure 4.5　Z-Order in Action

As you can see, controls are rendered in last-to-first order, although their z-order is calculated in first-to-last order. The first control to be added to the Controls collection, and the last control to be drawn on the form, has the highest z-order in the vertical stack, which equates to a z-order number of zero. Controls lower down in the stack may have a higher z-order number but are considered lower in the z-order itself.

If you need to change the z-order at design time, you can right-click on a control and choose Bring To Front (which brings the control to z-order zero) or Send To Back (which sets the z-order to the last item in the collection). At run-time, you can use the Control.BringToFront and Control.SendToBack methods. For more control, you can use the SetChildIndex property of the Controls collection. But the easiest approach is to use Document Outline in VS05 (View | Other Windows | Document Outline), as shown in Figure 4.6.

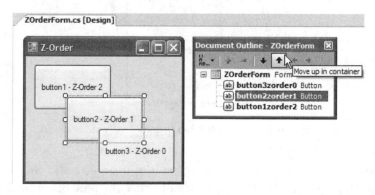

Figure 4.6　Managing Z-Order with Document Outline

Document Outline visualizes the containment hierarchy of all controls on a form, including z-order within each container. Additionally, it lets you change a control's container and z-order directly. For example, Figure 4.6 shows a control's z-order about to be moved up in the container to cover the other controls in the same container. You'll also find Document Outline useful for shuffling tool strip items left and right within tool strip controls, which are discussed later in this chapter.

Control Tab Order

Just as you can control the visual order of your controls, you can also control the sequence in which a user can navigate through them at run-time. This sequence is known as the *tab order*. A control is registered to be included in the tab order when its Boolean TabStop property is set to true, the default. The position of a control in the tab order is determined by its TabIndex property, an integer value that the Windows Forms Designer automatically generates for controls as they are dropped onto a form. The *tab index* starts at zero for the first control dropped and increases for each subsequently dropped control.

To change the tab order, you can either programmatically set the TabIndex properties for all controls, or declaratively using the Properties window. However, you may find the programmatic technique laborious because you have to write code, while using the Properties window can be monotonous as you iteratively navigate between it and controls on a form, one control at a time, setting the TabIndex and remembering the tab order as you go. These problems are exacerbated when UI changes require an update to the tab order.

Instead, you can visually set the tab order from the Windows Forms Designer by clicking View | Tab Order, as illustrated in Figure 4.7.

Figure 4.7   Editing the Tab Order Visually

Each control's tab order is displayed in a blue box, irrespective of the value of its TabStop property. To change the tab order, you simply click the blue boxes with the crosshair cursor in the desired tab order. The Windows Forms Designer updates the indices after each click. You can stop visual tab order editing by again clicking View | Tab Order (or pressing Esc).

A control's tab index is relative to other controls within the container, and this means that you set its TabIndex property with a single integer value. However, when you visually edit the tab order, the tab order for each control prefixes the tab index of each container control up the containment hierarchy, as shown in Figure 4.6. For example, both TabIndex property values for the Name and Street address text boxes would be 1, even though they are displayed as "1" and "4.1," respectively, in the Windows Forms Designer. This is much easier to work with than writing code or using the Properties window.

One nice side effect of setting the tab order is that the first control in the tab order automatically receives the focus when a form is loaded. If your form is related to data entry, this simple UI optimization allows your users to start entering data immediately without having to navigate to the first data entry field.

Dynamic Layout

After controls are positioned, sized, and z-ordered the way you like, you might think that's all you need to do. That is, until a user resizes your form. For example, suppose users want to enter a long string into a text box. They may attempt to widen your form, as shown in Figure 4.8.

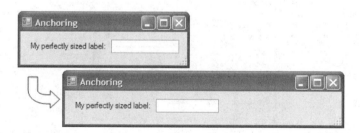

Figure 4.8   All Controls Anchored Top, Left

Users aren't likely to be happy with this less-than-professional resizing; ideally, the text box should expand as the form does.

Anchoring

Preserving the distance between the edge of a control and the adjacent edge of a control's container is a technique known as *anchoring*. By default, all controls are anchored to the top, left edges of their containers. We're accustomed to Windows moving child controls to keep this anchoring intact as the container's left or top edge changes. However, Windows does only so much; it doesn't resize controls to anchor them to other edges. Fortunately, Windows Forms does so without any coding required on your part.

For example, you can change the edges to which a control is anchored by changing the Anchor property to any bitwise combination of the values in the AnchorStyles enumeration:

```
namespace System.Windows.Forms {
  enum AnchorStyles {
    None = 0,
    Top = 1, // default
    Bottom = 2,
    Left = 4, // default
    Right = 8,
  }
}
```

Getting our text box to resize as the form is resized, we change the Anchor property to include the right edge as well as the left and the top edges. Using the Properties window, you even get the fancy drop-down editor shown in Figure 4.9.

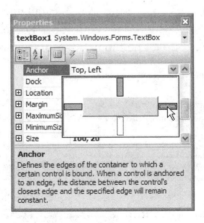

Figure 4.9 Setting the Anchor Property in the Properties Window

When we set the text box from Figure 4.8 to be anchored to the top, left, and right, the Windows Forms Designer generates the following (elided) code:

```
// AnchoringForm.designer.cs
partial class AnchoringForm {
  ...
  void InitializeComponent() {
    ...
    this.anchoredTextBox.Anchor =
      AnchorStyles.Top |
```

```
        AnchorStyles.Left |
        AnchorStyles.Right;
    ...
    }
}
```

This code makes sure that the text box resizes so that its right edge always resides the same distance from the right edge of the host form's client area, as illustrated in Figure 4.10.

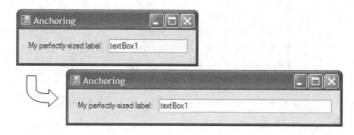

Figure 4.10   Automatic Control Resizing with the Anchor Property

Even though the default for Windows Forms controls is to anchor to the top and left edges of a form, anchoring does not have to include either of those edges. For example, it's common to anchor a modal dialog's OK and Cancel buttons to only the bottom and right edges; in this way, these buttons stay at the bottom-right corner as the dialog is resized but aren't resized themselves. A control is resized if the user has selected two opposing edges. If neither of the opposing edges is selected, neither left nor right, then the control is not resized in that dimension but instead maintains the same proportion of space between the opposing edges. The middle square in Figures 4.11 and 4.12 shows this behavior as well as several other anchoring combinations.

Figure 4.11   Anchoring Settings Before Widening

Figure 4.12   Anchoring Settings After Widening

So far, we've concentrated on what happens when a form increases in size. However, you may need to pay special attention when a form's size decreases. For example, consider what happens when the form in Figure 4.11 is made smaller, resulting in the form shown in Figure 4.13.

Figure 4.13   Anchor Settings After Narrowing

The way the controls are anchored causes controls to overlap as the edges they are anchored to come close together. You can resolve this by setting your form to a suitable minimum size using its MinimumSize property.

Docking

As powerful as anchoring is, it doesn't do everything by itself. For example, if you wanted to build a text editor, you'd probably like to have a menu, a tool strip, and a status strip hugging the edges with a text box that takes up the rest of the client area not occupied by the other controls. Anchoring would be tricky in this case, because some controls need more or less space depending on the run-time environment they find themselves in.

Because anchoring depends on keeping a control a fixed number of pixels away from a form's edge, we'd have to do some programming at run-time to figure out, for example, how high the status strip was and then set that as the distance to anchor the text box away from the edge. Instead, it is far easier to tell the form that the text box should simply take whatever space remains in the client area. For that, we have docking.

Docking is a way to identify the edge that we want a control to "stick" itself to. For example, Figure 4.14 shows a form with three controls, all docked. The menu strip is docked to the top edge, the status strip is docked to the bottom edge, and the text box is docked to fill the rest.

Figure 4.14   A Docking Example

You configure docking behavior in the Properties window (shown in Figure 4.15) by setting a control's Dock property, which is one of the DockStyle enumeration values:

```
namespace System.Windows.Forms {
  enum DockStyle {
    None = 0, // default
    Top = 1,
    Bottom = 2,
    Left = 3,
    Right = 4,
    Fill = 5,
  }
}
```

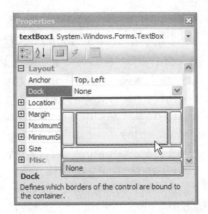

Figure 4.15   Setting the Dock Property in the Properties Window

Docking can also be affected by z-order and needs special consideration.

Docking and Z-Order

As a form resizes, the docking settings keep the controls along their designated edges (or the rest of the space, as determined by the Fill DockStyle). It's even possible to have multiple controls docked to the same edge, as shown in Figure 4.16.

Figure 4.16   Two Status Strips Docked to the Bottom Edge

Although I don't recommend docking two status strips to the same edge, it's certainly possible. Docking is done in reverse z-order priority. In other words, for statusStrip1 to be closest to the bottom edge, it must be further down in the z-order than statusStrip2. The following Add calls give statusStrip1 edge priority over statusStrip2:

```
// DockingForm.designer.cs
partial class DockingForm {
  ...
  void InitializeComponent() {
    ...
    this.Controls.Add(this.textBox1); // z-order 0
    this.Controls.Add(this.menuStrip1); // z-order 1
    this.Controls.Add(this.statusStrip2); // z-order 2
    this.Controls.Add(this.statusStrip1); // z-order 3
    ...
  }
}
```

Given the drag-and-drop Windows Forms Designer model, which inserts each new control with a z-order of 0, it makes sense that docking priority is the reverse of z-order. However, as you add new controls on the form and need to adjust the z-order, you may find a conflict between controls along a certain edge and those set to fill. In that case, the fill control needs to have the lowest edge priority on the form, or else it will dock all the way to an edge that is set to be used by another control. Figure 4.17 shows an example.

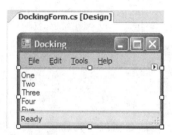

Figure 4.17   TextBox Whose DockStyle.Fill Has Higher Docking Priority Than a StatusStrip

Notice that the text in the bottom part of the text box is cut off by the status strip along the bottom edge. This indicates that the status strip has a lower docking priority than the text box. However, docking priority isn't set directly in the Designer. Instead, you set the z-order. In our example, right-clicking on the text box in the Designer and choosing Bring To Front pushes the text box to the top of the z-order but to the bottom of the docking priority, letting the status strip own the bottom edge and removing it from the client area that the text box is allowed to fill, as Figure 4.18 illustrates.

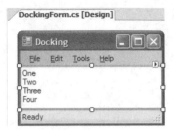

**Figure 4.18　TextBox Whose DockStyle.Fill Has
Lower Docking Priority Than a StatusStrip**

Whenever you see a visual anomaly like this on your form, you can usually resolve the problem by bringing to the front the control whose Dock property is set to DockStyle.Fill. Alternatively, you can use Document Outline from the View | Other Windows menu.

 DockStyle.Fill has special significance in Windows Forms because there are several controls that should naturally fill their containers as soon as they are dropped onto a form. It's common for these controls, including Panel, to implement smart tags, with an option to toggle a control's Dock property between DockStyle.Fill and the previous DockStyle value, as shown in Figure 4.19.

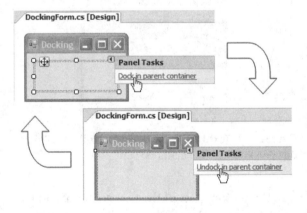

Figure 4.19　Setting the Dock Property via a Smart Tag

The set of controls that actually provides the "Dock in parent container" smart tag is somewhat smaller than you might expect. For example, DataGridView and Panel offer this, but GroupBox, ListBox, and TabControl don't.[1]

Some controls, such as MenuStrip, ToolStrip, and StatusStrip, take it one step further by automatically docking to the most logical edge when dropped onto a form; MenuStrip

---

[1] Those .NET Framework controls that do support this feature are augmented with the Docking attribute, which is covered in Chapter 12: Design Time Integration: Designers and Smart Tags.

and ToolStrip dock to the top, and StatusStrip docks to the bottom. The default dock settings can be changed as necessary, although they suffice for most scenarios.

Docking with Tool Strip Controls

After most controls are docked to a particular edge at design time, they remain there after compilation until the UI needs an update or an application becomes obsolete. In this respect, tool strip controls are special because they allow users to dynamically redock them at run-time. For example, Figure 4.20 shows a ToolStrip control being dragged from a form's top edge to the same form's bottom edge by the user at run-time.

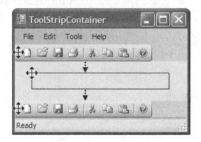

Figure 4.20   Dragging a ToolStrip Control at Run-Time

Rather than force you to handle the complexities of dynamically juggling the Dock property values of all controls to cope with run-time tool strip dragging, System. Windows.Forms comes with the ToolStripContainer control. Its purpose is to simplify design-time tool strip composition and enable run-time tool strip dragging independently of the docked arrangement of other controls on a form.

ToolStripContainer

When you drag a ToolStripContainer onto your form, the first thing you should do is set its Dock property to DockStyle.Fill, as shown in Figure 4.21.

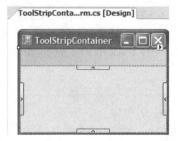

Figure 4.21   Form Filled with a ToolStripContainer
(with the top ToolStripPanel visible)

By its nature, ToolStripContainer should be dock-filled to cover the entire surface area of a form, because it provides special docking semantics to the form itself, independent of controls hosted on the form. However, ToolStripContainer provides a special area for those controls known as the *content panel.* The content panel is abstracted as the ToolStripContent-Panel, which derives from Panel. ToolStripContainer exposes the content panel through its ContentPanel property.

ToolStripContainer provides four special areas to host the tool strip controls, one for each edge of the ToolStripContainer. Each of these is a ToolStripPanel hosted by ToolStrip-Container and exposed via four properties: TopToolStripPanel, BottomToolStripPanel, Left-ToolStripPanel, and RightToolStripPanel.[2] By default, all tool strip panels are visible, although you can hide or show each by setting one of the four following properties as appropriate: TopToolStripPanelVisible, BottomToolStripPanelVisible, LeftToolStripPanel-Visible, and RightToolStripPanelVisible. Alternatively, you can use the ToolStripContainer's Properties window or smart tag, as shown in Figure 4.22.

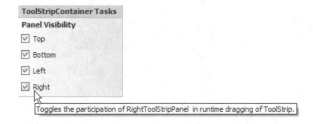

Figure 4.22   Configuring Which Edges That Tool Strip Controls Can Be Dragged to at Run-Time

Users can drag tool strip controls across any tool strip panels that remain visible after your configurations.

Each tool strip panel needs to be expanded before you can drop tool strip controls onto it by clicking its expand or collapse button, shown in Figure 4.21. By default, the top tool strip panel is expanded so that you can drag a tool strip control right onto it without manually expanding it.

Figure 4.23 shows a form that uses a ToolStripContainer hosting a MenuStrip and Tool-Strip control in its top tool strip panel, and a StatusStrip in its bottom tool strip panel. It supports tool strip dragging across only the top and bottom tool strip panels.

---

[2] You can also use ToolStripPanels individually by adding them to the Toolbox. Click Choose Items | .NET Framework Components | ToolStripPanel. From there, you can drag them onto your form and treat them like any other control. This is especially useful if you don't need full ToolStripContainer support.

Figure 4.23   A ToolStripContainer with Three Tool Strip Controls and Dragging Supported Between Top and Bottom Panels

As you can see, tool strip panels can host multiple tool strips, stacking them either horizontally or vertically to match the tool strip panel in which they're hosted. Also, one or more tool strip controls can be hosted in the same row; they do not have to be positioned flush against another tool strip control in the same row, or flush against the adjacent form edge. The Windows Forms Designer allows you to drag and position tool strips within these constraints, storing the final design-time position of each using the Location property.

Run-Time Tool Strip Support

At run-time, a tool strip can be dragged from one tool strip panel to another, as long as it has a drag grip, as determined by a tool strip's GripStyle property. GripStyle can be one of two ToolStripGripStyle enumeration values: Visible or Hidden. By default, ToolStrip.GripStyle is set to ToolStripGripStyle.Visible, whereas MenuStrip.GripStyle and StatusStrip.GripStyle are set to ToolStripGripStyle.Hidden.

Additionally, you can allow users to drag tool strip items around their host tool strip. You enable this by setting a tool strip's AllowItemReorder property to true. At run-time, users drag a tool strip item by pressing the Alt key and dragging the item using the left mouse button.

Of course, when users can move tool strips and tool strip items around, they'll want them to appear in the same position they left them in the previous application session when they start a new session. Consequently, you need to store pertinent tool strip details such as size, location, visibility, and order of tool strip items at the end of a session, refreshing them at the beginning of the next. This support is dependent on the settings system and is discussed in Chapter 15: Settings.

ToolStrip Overflow

There is one side effect you should consider when allowing users to drag tool strips around a form: Tool strips might end up being aligned to edges that are too small to display them in their entirety. Some tool strip items may overflow the edge of a form and their functionality become hidden. The solution is to give users a visual cue that more tool strip items are available and then provide access to them.

Such support is native to all tool strip controls via a special drop-down menu, called a *chevron*, shown on a ToolStrip in Figure 4.24.

Figure 4.24   ToolStrip Control with Overflowing Tool Strip Items

Whether a tool strip supports overflow is determined by its Boolean CanOverflow property, which is set to true by default.

But that's only half the story; hosted tool strip items are also responsible for instructing their containing tool strip how they should be treated if visual overflow is enabled. To do this, each tool strip item exposes an Overflow property, which stores one of the following values of the ToolStripItemOverflow enumeration:

```
namespace System.Windows.Forms {
    enum ToolStripItemOverflow {
        Never = 0 // Never overflow
        Always = 1, // Always overflow, even if enough space to show
        AsNeeded = 2, // Overflow space runs out (default)
    }
}
```

For ToolStrip, CanOverflow defaults to true, and the Overflow property for most tool strip items defaults to ToolStripItemOverflow.AsNeeded. As a result, most of your tool strip resizing needs are handled out of the box, at both design-time and run-time.

MenuStrip exposes CanOverflow, although it's false by default and can't be set from the various Designer windows such as the Properties window. However, you can programmatically set it to true, and you need to update the Overflow property for any hosted tool strip menu items because their default Overflow value is Never.

StatusStrip has the same design as MenuStrip with regard to its CanOverflow property, so if you need it to overflow, you must do so programmatically. You also need to change its layout style to StackWithOverflow (discussed later), because the default is Table, which doesn't support overflowing. Fortunately, the various tool strip items you can host on a

StatusStrip have their Overflow properties set to AsNeeded, so you don't need to recon-figure them.

Tool strip item alignment also plays a role in overflow behavior by determining which tool strip items overflow before others. Tool strip alignment is governed by the Alignment property, which is implemented by tool strip items to allow you to specify that they glue themselves to the left or right edge of a tool strip control, as shown in Figure 4.25.

Figure 4.25   Tool Strip Items with Left and Right Alignment

For a tool strip whose items are all left-aligned, the right-most item is the first to over-flow, followed by its siblings in right-to-left order as their host tool strip's width decreases. When a combination of left- and right-aligned tool strip items coexists on a tool strip, the set of right-aligned items overflows starting with the leftmost tool strip item, and then each tool strip item overflows in left-to-right order. When all right-aligned items have over-flowed, the set of left-aligned items overflows in right-to-left order.

ToolStrip Layout Styles

Sometimes, it is preferable to show all tool strip items irrespective of the size of a host form. One common example is the menu strip, which typically increases in height to make room for tool strip items that would otherwise become hidden as the width decreases. Figure 4.26 illustrates the default behavior of MenuStrip.

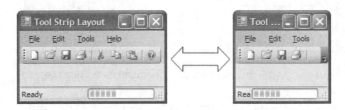

Figure 4.26   Collapsing MenuStrip Control

As the form's width decreases, the MenuStrip hides its items while providing an over-flow chevron to access them. A tool strip's behavior is determined by its LayoutStyle prop-erty, whose value comes from ToolStripLayoutStyle:

```
namespace System.Windows.Forms {
   enum ToolStripLayoutStyle {
      StackWithOverflow = 0, // MenuStrip and ToolStrip default
      HorizontalStackWithOverflow = 1, // Items placed horizontally,
                                       // with overflow
      VerticalStackWithOverflow = 2, // Items laid out vertically,
                                     // with overflow
      Flow = 3, // Items wrap horizontally, in either RTL or LTR order
      Table = 4 // Items arranged in rows and columns
                // (StatusStrip default)
   }
}
```

By default, MenuStrip and ToolStrip controls have a ToolStripLayoutStyle of StackWith-Overflow, whose effect is to automatically switch between HorizontalStackWithOverflow and VerticalStackWithOverflow as either MenuStrip or ToolStrip is dragged to a horizontal or vertical edge, respectively. If you want your MenuStrip's or ToolStrip's items to always be laid out either horizontally or vertically, irrespective of the orientation of the edge to which they are aligned, you can explicitly choose HorizontalStackWithOverflow or VerticalStackWithOverflow as required. All three of these options automatically set a MenuStrip or ToolStrip to overflow its items as necessary.

While a MenuStrip might be set to horizontally stack with overflow by default, but it doesn't actually provide overflow behavior (by showing the overflow chevron). Instead, items become hidden as a form's width decreases, which is fine because the default behavior for a MenuStrip is to expand its height to provide extra space for the overflow items. You configure this by setting the MenuStrip's LayoutStyle to Flow, which yields the effect illustrated in Figure 4.27.

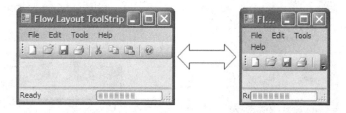

Figure 4.27   MenuStrip Wrapping ToolStrip Items Horizontally

With this layout style, items flow from left to right by default, and, as they wrap, they do so starting from the top-left corner of the tool strip. You can swap the flow order to right-to-left by setting the tool strip's RightToLeft property to true.[3] Note that ToolStrip doesn't

---

[3] If you want some of your tool strip items to be displayed right-to-left and others displayed left-to-right, you can use the Alignment property on each top-level tool strip item to instruct it to align itself to either the left or the right edge of the host tool strip.

support flowing if hosted by a ToolStripContainer, whereas MenuStrip does. Additionally, if you're using the Windows Form Designer, you can configure flow layout only to support horizontal flowing. If you need vertical flowing, you must write code. For example, the following code supports vertical flowing for a MenuStrip control that's docked to the left edge of the form.

```csharp
// MainForm.cs
partial class MainForm : Form {
  public MainForm() {
    InitializeComponent();

    // MenuStrip docked left with vertical flow
    MenuStrip ms = this.menuStrip1;
    ms.LayoutStyle = ToolStripLayoutStyle.Flow;
    FlowLayoutSettings flowLayout =
      ms.LayoutSettings as FlowLayoutSettings;
    flowLayout.FlowDirection = FlowDirection.TopDown;
    ms.Dock = DockStyle.Left;
  }
}
```

As you can see, we set the LayoutStyle to ToolStripLayoutStyle.Flow. But that's not enough; items on a vertical tool strip don't automatically flow vertically when the LayoutStyle is ToolStripLayoutStyle.Flow. To ensure that they do, you update the tool strip's LayoutSettings property, which references the LayoutSettings object, whose job is to manage layout for the tool strip. When a tool strip is set to the StackWithOverflow, HorizontalStackWithOverflow, or VerticalStackWithOverflow layout style, the LayoutSettings property is null, because this support is implemented natively by the tool strip. When you set the layout style of a tool strip to Flow, however, LayoutSettings is provided with an instance of the FlowLayoutSettings object, which supports tool strip content flowing. The key feature is the direction in which the items can flow, which is specified by the FlowDirection property. For vertical flowing, we set the FlowDirection to TopDown, resulting in the form shown in Figure 4.28.

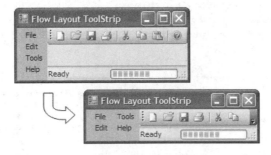

Figure 4.28   MenuStrip Wrapping ToolStrip Items Vertically

FlowLayoutSettings.FlowDirection can be one of several values of the FlowDirection enumeration, which is discussed in detail later in this chapter.

The final LayoutStyle is Table, which allows you to construct a tool strip in a tabular fashion using rows, columns, and cells. This is the default LayoutStyle for StatusStrip, and for good reason: to support springing of tool strip items, which we discussed in Chapter 2. You may also need springing in a MenuStrip or ToolStrip, although neither supports it natively. Instead, you write the code to handle it if, for example, you'd like an Internet Explorer-like Address tool strip, shown in Figure 4.29.

Figure 4.29   ToolStrip with Internet Explorer-like Address ToolStrip

The important thing is to ensure that the drop-down list expands and shrinks as the form resizes, which is shown in Figure 4.29. You could probably handle the ToolStrip's Resize event and update the length of the drop-down list to suit, but there is an easier way: You set the ToolStrip's LayoutStyle property to Table and write some additional code:[4]

```
// Configure table structure
partial class MainForm : Form {
  public MainForm() {
    InitializeComponent();

    ToolStrip ts = this.toolStrip1;

    // Configure table structure
    ts.LayoutStyle = ToolStripLayoutStyle.Table;
    TableLayoutSettings tableLayout =
      ts.LayoutSettings as TableLayoutSettings;
    tableLayout.ColumnCount = 3;
    tableLayout.RowCount = 1;
    tableLayout.ColumnStyles.Add(new ColumnStyle());
    // Spring contents of this column, which will be the drop-down list
```

[4] You'll find a discussion of tabular layout using the TableLayoutPanel control later in this chapter.

```
    tableLayout.ColumnStyles.Add(
      new ColumnStyle(SizeType.Percent, 100F));
    tableLayout.ColumnStyles.Add(new ColumnStyle());
    tableLayout.RowStyles.Add(new RowStyle(SizeType.Absolute, 25F));

    // Fill the entire cell
    foreach( ToolStripItem toolStripItem in ts.Items ) {
      toolStripItem.Dock = DockStyle.Fill;
    }
  }
}
```

When a ToolStrip control's LayoutStyle is set to Table, a custom table-oriented Layout-Settings object is created and set as the LayoutSettings object. This allows us to configure the table's rows and columns using the ColumnCount and RowCount properties. In our example, the table contains three columns and one row, just enough to fit each tool strip item.

To enable springing, we make sure that the column that contains the drop-down list takes up 100% of the space on the ToolStrip not used by the other tool strip items. You configure this using ColumnStyle objects that you add to the TableLayoutSettings.Column-Styles collection. You must create one style for each column, in column order; for example, if you created a column style for the third column but it was the only style you added, it would be applied to the first column. That's why the code creates three. The second column style applies to the second column and uses the ColumnStyle class's constructor overload to pass in a SizeType of Percent, and specifies it to size to 100% automatically.

However, configuring columns and rows to resize appropriately is not enough. We also need the cell contents to resize, so we enumerate the table's tool strip item contents and dock, filling them within their cells. This code generates the UI shown in Figure 4.29. When you set tool strip items hosted on a StatusStrip to spring, the behavior is basically implemented in the same fashion as in our springing ToolStrip example.

When you choose either LayoutStyle.Flow or LayoutStyle.Table, you should be aware of three limitations in the current tool strip implementation. First, flow layout and springing contents in ToolStrips don't work when tool strips are hosted in ToolStripContentPanels. Second, a tool strip's grip disappears irrespective of the value you've specified for the GripStyle property. Third, you can't support tool strip item overflowing and alignment, irrespective of your tool strip's CanOverflow property setting and the Overflow property setting for each tool strip item.

Automatic Resizing

When containers are resized around content, you need to take steps to make sure that the content is still visible. Conversely, when content is resized, you need to take steps to make sure that containers still display the content, something that isn't happening in Figure 4.30.

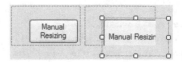

Figure 4.30　Resized Control Becoming Hidden

When controls become hidden as a result of a move or resize, you need to resize the container control to show the hidden parts of the resized or moved control. When many controls are involved, this is a tedious process.

Instead, you can use the AutoSize and AutoSizeMode properties to do it for you. Auto-Size is a Boolean property that, when set to true, specifies that a control will resize automatically to fit its contents. AutoSizeMode governs how the control resizes, as specified by the GrowOnly and GrowAndShrink values of the AutoSizeMode (System.Windows.Forms) enumeration.

GrowOnly tells a container to automatically resize if the new size of the contained control will be the same size or bigger than its size, as shown in Figure 4.31.

Figure 4.31　Automatic Resizing with AutoSize = True and AutoSizeMode = GrowOnly

GrowAndShrink tells a container to increase and decrease in size in response to a contained control's resizing and moving, as illustrated in Figure 4.32.

Figure 4.32　Automatic Resizing with AutoSize = True and AutoSizeMode = GrowAndShrink

Automatic resizing is triggered when the edges of a resizing or repositioning control come close enough in proximity to the host container's right and bottom edges that their margins overlap. A variety of controls supports AutoSize alone, or AutoSize and AutoSize-Mode together. Form supports both AutoSize and AutoSizeMode, but only at run-time. You need to experiment with each control to determine its level of automatic resizing support.

Automatic Scaling

Automatic resizing allows forms to resize to accommodate relocated or resized controls. But forms also come equipped to resize in the face of the needs of different users with respect to system font size and dpi (dots per inch).

For example, if you lay out a form with the system font size set to Normal (96 dpi) in the Display control panel, what happens when your users are using Large (120 dpi) or one of the custom settings?[5] Figure 4.33 illustrates the default for a Windows Forms application.

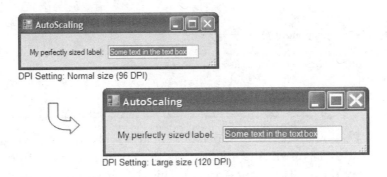

Figure 4.33   Form Scaling Up from Smaller to Larger dpi

As you can see, the changed dpi setting not only increases the size of all fonts displayed on the form and its title bar, but also increases the form's overall size as well as increases control sizes and changes locations to maintain the same proportional sizing and spacing. The best part is that this happened without your configuring anything, and without the application being recompiled.

Two key elements are required if you want to maintain the same proportions, or scale, across multiple dpi settings: The first is to tell the form to automatically scale, and the second is to acquire a scale factor that can be applied to the widths and heights to scale a form and its controls proportionally. By default, a form automatically scales because its AutoScale property is set to true. The type of scale factor is specified by the AutoScaleMode property and defaults to Font, meaning that the scale factor is based on the ratio between the average widths and heights of the default system font when the form was created and when the form executes.

[5] Click Control Panel | Display | Settings | Advanced | General | DPI Setting.

For example, if a form was created under Windows XP Normal fonts (96 dpi), the default font is 8.25-point MS Sans Serif and has an average width and height of 6 points × 13 points. (A point is a traditional unit of measure for type characters. For more, see Chapter 6: Drawing Text.) This information is stored by the Windows Forms Designer in InitializeComponent against the form's AutoScaleDimensions property:

```
// AutoScalingForm.designer.cs
partial class AutoScalingForm {
  ...


  void InitializeComponent() {
    ...
    this.AutoScaleDimensions = new SizeF(6F, 13F);
    ...
  }
}
```

Then, if the form is re-opened or executed under Large fonts (120 dpi), where the default font is 7.8-point MS Sans Serif, the average width and height of the font increases to 8 × 16 (that is why they call it "Large" fonts). This data is stored in a form's read-only CurrentAutoScaleDimensions property. When the form is loaded into the Windows Forms Designer or executed, it notices the difference between AutoScaleDimensions and CurrentAutoScaleDimensions by calling its own PerformAutoScale method to adjust the height and width of itself and its controls, along with the positions of the controls. This keeps the "feel" of the form roughly the same, no matter what the system font settings are.

In our sample, the form's client area width increased from 293 to 391 (~33%) as the width of the font went from 6 to 8 (~33%). Similarly, the height increased from 50 to 62 (~24%) as the height of the font went from 13 to 16 (~23%). As you can see, the form's client area scaled horizontally and vertically to almost exactly the same degree, yielding a form that looks good at both 96 dpi and 120 dpi, especially given the amount of work you had to do to achieve the effect (~0%).

AutoScale Modes

Our example so far has used a scaling factor based on font size, although three other autoscaling modes can be set via the AutoScaleMode property. These are determined by the AutoScaleMode enumeration:

```
namespace System.Windows.Forms {
  enum AutoScaleMode {
    None = 0 // Don't scale
    Font = 1, // Scale in relation to font size at current dpi (default)
    Dpi = 2, // Scale in relation to dpi
    Inherit = 3, // Inherit container's AutoScaleMode
  }
}
```

So, if you want your form to resize in direct proportion to the dpi setting itself, you change the AutoScaleMode value to AutoScaleMode.Dpi. This changes the values captured by AutoScaleDimensions to match the dpi at the time the form was created:

```
this.AutoScaleDimensions = new SizeF(96F, 96F);
```

If the sample were changed like this, the form's client area width would increase from 293 to 366 (~24%) as the dpi x dimension increased from 96 to 120 (25%). Similarly, the height would increase from 50 to 62 (24%) as the dpi y dimension increased from 96 to 120 (25%).

Both AutoScaleMode.Font and AutoScaleMode.Dpi are driven by a change in dpi setting, but the comparative ratios between the two may differ. Specifically, the average width and height of a font may not change from one dpi setting to another in the same proportion as a change in the dpi settings themselves. This is because fonts vary in the widths and heights of their characters. Consequently, you can get away with AutoScaleMode.Dpi when your applications run over various dpi settings on computers having the same language version. However, if an application needs to scale in the face of different fonts and therefore different font widths and heights, your life is made easy because the recommended setting is also the default—that is, AutoSizeMode.Font.

Figure 4.34 illustrates the difference between AutoSizeMode.Font and AutoSizeMode. Dpi.

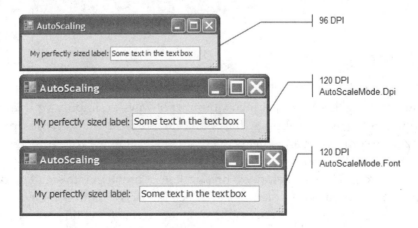

Figure 4.34 AutoScaleMode.Dpi and AutoScaleMode.Font Autoscaling from 96 dpi to 120 dpi

AutoScaleMode is implemented internally on the ContainerControl class, and you can programmatically set it on container controls. However, when using the Properties window, you can set AutoScaleMode only for those container controls that have their own designers, including Form and UserControl. Because user controls are typically hosted on forms, you can set a user control's AutoScaleMode to Inherit to make sure it picks up the host form's AutoScaleMode to scale consistently. If the host form has a different AutoScale-Mode value from that of the contained user control, scaling is unlikely to be pretty.

AutoScaleMode.None turns off scaling altogether, the equivalent of setting AutoScale to false, and it doesn't look pretty at all if an application runs in a dpi that differs from the dpi it was created in. Figure 4.35 should scare you.

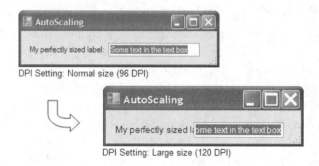

Figure 4.35   Form Scaling Up from Smaller to Larger dpi (Using AutoScaleMode.None)

When considering the various AutoScaleMode options, you'll find that AutoScale-Mode.Font is the least likely to cause scaling issues, and that is why you should prefer it as the default.

Layout Controls

So far, we've covered the basic building blocks of the Windows Forms layout system. In general, you can bring them together in any number of ways to simplify your layout experience. As powerful as they are, though, they don't cater to all layout scenarios, particularly those that require complex arrangements of controls, which may prove difficult to configure adequately using the features you've seen so far.

In these situations, it can be helpful to break a layout problem into smaller, more manageable pieces. For this purpose, you can use a special subset of controls known as *container controls*. Just like forms, container controls can act as parents for child controls, including other container controls. Container controls share the same layout characteristics of forms in that child controls can be anchored or docked. Because of this, the anchoring and docking settings of a container control aren't relative to the edges of the form, but rather to the edges of the container.

Additionally, each of the container controls comes with its own special layout characteristics. You've seen one container control, the Panel, that you use to add automatic scrolling support to a tool strip content panel. Now, we cover several other container controls that let you incorporate splitting, grouping, flow layout, and tabular layout.

Splitting

Often, you'd like to let users resize some controls independently of the size of the form. For example, Windows Explorer splits the space between the toolstrip and the status strip, with a tree view on the left and a list view on the right. To resize these controls, Explorer provides a *splitter*, which is a bar that separates two controls. Users can drag the bar to change the proportion of the space shared between the controls.

Figure 4.36 shows a simple example of how this can be achieved in Windows Forms, using a SplitContainer control; a TreeView control is docked to fill the SplitContainer's left panel, and a ListView control is docked to fill the SplitContainer's right panel.

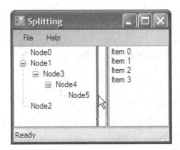

Figure 4.36   An Example of Splitting (with Cursor Indicating a Potential Drag)

By default, SplitContainer is configured to vertical splitting, as specified by its Orientation property. Thus, you can implement horizontal splitting by simply changing the value of the Orientation property from Vertical to Horizontal. Horizontal splitting is illustrated in Figure 4.37. We've added another SplitContainer to the form from Figure 4.36, added a GroupBox control docked to fill the new SplitContainer's top panel, and moved the existing SplitContainer into the new SplitContainer's bottom panel, setting it to dock-fill.

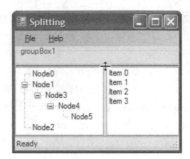

Figure 4.37   Horizontal Splitting

By default, if the container or form that hosts a split container resizes, the sizes of both SplitContainer panels remain in proportion, as illustrated in Figure 4.38.

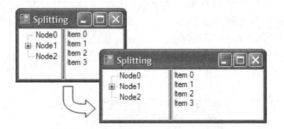

Figure 4.38   Proportional Resizing of SplitContainer

However, you can specify that one of the panels remain a fixed size by setting the Fixed-Panel property to either of the two panels. If you specify the right panel, the splitter moves with it, leaving the left panel to resize in its wake, and vice versa for the left panel. Either way, the user can still drag the splitter as appropriate. If you want to prevent splitter bar dragging altogether, set SplitContainer.IsSplitterFixed to true.

Note that even though SplitContainer is highly useful and saves a lot of design-time effort, you may need to use the pre-Windows Forms 2.0 Splitter control for MDI applications, as discussed in Chapter 14: Applications.

Grouping

Another way to divide UI real estate is to group controls. For example, imagine a form showing a list of people on the left and a list of details about the current selection on the right, as shown in Figure 4.39.

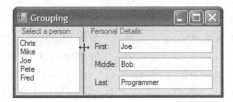

Figure 4.39   Grouping, Docking, Anchoring, and Splitting

You can't tell by looking at this single picture, but as the group boxes in Figure 4.39 change size, the controls inside the group boxes also change size; both group boxes are set to dock-fill their respective SplitContainer panels, and, because they are container controls, their contained controls can use anchoring to ensure nice resizing. And because the group box is a container control, it essentially encapsulates a portion of the UI that you can drag around a form, rather than piece by piece. To do this and to acquire a reusable portion of the UI that you can add to any form, you can create a user control, as discussed in Chapter 10.

The GroupBox control is one of several container controls that Windows Forms provides specifically for grouping other controls, including Panels and TabPages. The Panel control is just like a group box except that it has no label and no frame. A panel is handy if you want something that looks and acts like a *subform*, or a form within a form. TabControl hosts one or more TabPage controls, each of which is a container control with a tab at the top, as shown in Figure 4.40.

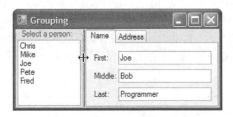

Figure 4.40   A TabControl with Two TabPage Controls

Container controls such as group boxes and tab pages provide a basic level of layout support that allows you to neatly decompose a complex layout problem into smaller, more manageable pieces. In general, though, they are blank canvases from a layout point of view, in that you must still provide the layout of their contained controls by using techniques like docking, anchoring, and automatic resizing. Two controls—FlowLayoutPanel and Table-LayoutPanel—go one step further by overlaying the Panel control with additional support for highly customized layout scenarios.

Flow Layout

If your form is comprised of controls that you want to participate in consistently ordered collapsing and expanding as their container resizes, then you need to use FlowLayoutPanel, which provides flow-style resizing in much the same way as web pages do. Figure 4.41 shows FlowLayoutPanel used to lay out four labels in left-to-right order and to retain that order as best it can during a resize.

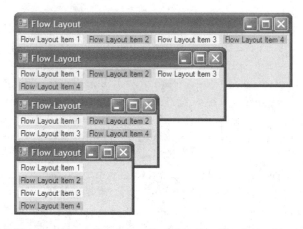

Figure 4.41   A FlowLayoutPanel Laying Out Controls
in Left-to-Right Order (See Plate 7)

Although this example uses labels, any control can be placed within a FlowLayoutPanel, including other FlowLayoutPanels for more granular flow control.

The key property of FlowLayoutPanel is FlowDirection, which specifies the order in which the contained controls are arranged. FlowDirection can be one of four FlowDirection enumeration values:

```
namespace System.Windows.Forms {
  enum FlowDirection {
    LeftToRight = 0, // default
    TopDown = 1
    RightToLeft = 2,
    BottomUp = 3,
  }
}
```

Figure 4.42 illustrates each of these values being applied.

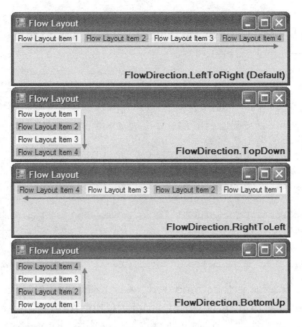

Figure 4.42 All Four FlowDirection Enumeration Values in Action

For each FlowDirection, the first element in the flow is rendered in the position closest to the logical corner of the FlowLayoutPanel implied by FlowDirection, in conjunction with the current locale's reading order (right-to-left or left-to-right). Table 4.1 shows the starting corners for each of the possible combinations.

Table 4.1   Flow Starting Corner, Determined by FlowDirection and Locale Reading Order

	Flow Starting Corner	
FlowDirection	**Reading Left-to-Right**	**Reading Right-to-Left**
Left-Right	Top, Left	Top, Right
Top-Down	Top, Left	Top, Right
Right-Left	Top, Right	Top, Left
Bottom-Up	Bottom, Left	Bottom, Right

The way in which controls are rendered to the FlowLayoutPanel away from the starting corner is determined by the order in which they were added to the FlowLayoutPanel's Controls collection—namely, first-to-last:

```
void InitializeComponent() {
   ...
   // Rendered first
   this.flowLayoutPanel.Controls.Add(this.label1);
   // Rendered second
   this.flowLayoutPanel.Controls.Add(this.label2);
   // Rendered third
   this.flowLayoutPanel.Controls.Add(this.label3);
   // Rendered fourth
   this.flowLayoutPanel.Controls.Add(this.label4);
   this.flowLayoutPanel.FlowDirection = FlowDirection.LeftRight;
   ...
}
```

Each subsequent control is then rendered away from the first control in the direction also dictated by FlowDirection and reading order; the horizontal flow directions—left-right and right-left—render in rows, and the vertical flow directions—top-down and bottom-up—render in columns. If there are more controls than can fit into the remaining column or row—as dictated by FlowLayoutPanel's width or height, respectively—then subsequent controls are rendered in a new row or column, in the same order as the first, as you saw in Figure 4.42.

The proximity of one control to another control or to the edge of FlowLayoutPanel is determined by a combination of FlowLayoutPanel's padding settings and the margin settings of all contained controls. You would expect this, because FlowLayoutPanel is a container control. Figure 4.43 illustrates FlowLayoutPanel with top, right, bottom, and left padding of 10, each contained control with a top, right, bottom, and left margin of 20, and one control set as a flow break.

Figure 4.43　FlowLayoutPanel with Margins, Padding, and Flow Breaking

To extend any control placed in a FlowLayoutPanel, you use the FlowBreak property, which, when true, instructs FlowLayoutPanel to treat the control as a break between controls in the current flow. In Figure 4.43, you can see that the third and fourth items do not continue flowing from the flow break; instead, the flow begins anew in a location dictated by FlowDirection.

You can also use docking and anchoring to lay out flowing controls. Although it sounds a bit weird, essentially you dock and anchor flowing controls relative to the largest control in the same line of flow whose direction is determined by FlowDirection, as Figure 4.44 illustrates.

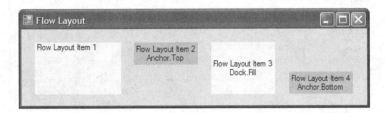

Figure 4.44   Anchoring and Docking in a FlowLayoutPanel

Although FlowLayoutPanel solves an interesting type of layout problem, its layout heuristics are somewhat akin to ordered chaos. If you're a control freak, you may need more order than chaos; if so, you need TableLayoutPanel.[6]

TableLayoutPanel

As you would expect, TableLayoutPanel provides a tabular layout experience built on columns, rows, and cells. Figure 4.45 shows a form with a single dock-filled TableLayout-Panel, with three columns, three rows, and, implicitly, nine cells.

**Figure 4.45   TableLayoutControl with Three Columns,
Three Rows, and Nine Cells**

[6] However, if you can use FlowLayoutPanel, you may receive better layout performance than if you use TableLayoutPanel. As usual, you should test your specific scenarios.

Because the primary layout units in a table are the rows and columns, TableLayoutPanel goes out of its way to make it as easy as possible to configure these. Smart tag tasks allow you to add and remove columns one at a time, or you can open the Column and Row Styles dialog to do them at once, as shown in Figure 4.46.

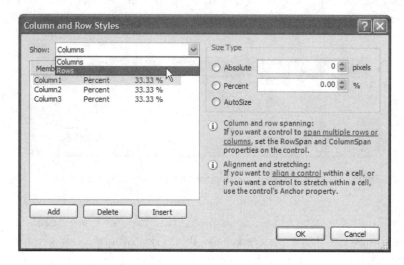

Figure 4.46   The Column and Row Styles Dialog

As you can see, the Column and Row Styles dialog allows you to add and remove columns to and from the end of the table or insert them between existing columns, a feature that's not available directly from the smart tag panel.

Each column and row has a *size* type, which allows you to specify size in terms of an absolute pixel value, a percentage, or a size that's relative to the spacing of other columns or rows. For columns, the size applies to width, whereas it applies to height for rows. Table-LayoutPanel allocates space based on these settings in the following order: absolute (fixed size), AutoSize, and remaining space by percent; if any space is left over, it expands the last row or column to fill it. In the example in Figure 4.45, all columns and all rows are set to 33%, the overall width and height, respectively, of the TableLayoutPanel. This setting ensures that the columns and rows resize to match as TableLayoutPanel resizes. If you need columns and rows to remain fixed in size, you specify their sizes with an absolute value.

TableLayoutPanel also allows you to span multiple rows and columns, a common requirement of table layouts. You can't set this using the Column and Row Styles dialog, but you can set the ColumnSpan and RowSpan properties, which are added to each control that resides in a cell. To span two columns, for example, you would select the control in the cell where you wanted to start the span and then set the ColumnSpan property to 2, the number of columns you want spanned. The same goes for the RowSpan property. Both are illustrated in Figure 4.47.

Figure 4.47   TableLayoutControl Column and Row Spanning

When you've created your tabular structure, you fill its cells with the desired controls; as with the other panels, you can use any type of control. The key limitation is that each cell can contain, at most, one control; although, you can host multiple controls in a single cell by adding them to a container control that you then place into the cell. If you need to, you can use anchoring and docking to manage the way your controls are resized in conjunction with TableLayoutPanel's resizing configuration. Figure 4.48 shows the table from Figure 4.47 with each of the contained controls dock-filling its cell, allowing them to resize proportionally just as the table's cells do.

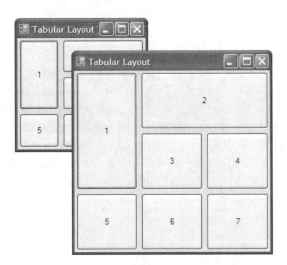

Figure 4.48   Resizing Dock-Filled Controls Within a TableLayoutPanel

Note that each cell contains some padding; the amount of padding is determined by each control's Margin property, which you can use to fine-tune your overall layout.

Layout Optimization

For any form with a nontrivial number of controls, the layout and corresponding initialization code generated by the Windows Forms Designer into InitializeComponent can become quite involved, and can have a detrimental effect on performance because the form refreshes itself visually as each control is added to its Controls property.

In response to this situation, the Windows Forms Designer employs a special optimization that relies on two methods: SuspendLayout and ResumeLayout. Calls to these methods are placed in InitializeComponent for any form that has at least one control:

```
// ContainmentForm.cs
partial class ContainmentForm {
  ...
  void InitializeComponent() {
    // Hosted control and component instantiation
    ...
    this.SuspendLayout();
    // Hosted control, component, and form initialization
    ...
    // Controls added to form
    ...
    this.ResumeLayout(true);
    ...
  }
}
```

By bracketing several tasks—the child control creation and initialization as well as the addition of the controls to the control collection—in SuspendLayout and ResumeLayout, we prevent the form from trying to draw itself until everything is set up. However, SuspendLayout and ResumeLayout operate only one level deep, so if your form hosts controls within container controls like Panel, you also need to call SuspendLayout and ResumeLayout on the panel. You can do this if you need to make a nontrivial set of changes to the form's properties or controls yourself, a situation you'll encounter when the layout system can't do quite what you need.

Custom Layout

Yes, even with all the layout support that exists in VS05, the Windows Forms Designer, and the .NET Framework, you may still encounter situations that are complex enough to make it difficult or impossible to use it. It's at times like these that you need to roll up your sleeves, dive down into code, and take advantage of the Layout event, which is fired whenever a control or form needs to reposition its child controls—that is, when controls are added and removed, or the form is resized.

The following Layout event handler re-creates the tabular layout from Figure 4.45 by programmatically arranging the nine button controls proportionally as the form is resized:

```
Button[] buttons =
  new Button[] {
    this.button1, this.button2, this.button3,
    this.button4, this.button5, this.button6,
    this.button7, this.button8, this.button9 };
...
void LayoutEventForm_Layout(object sender, LayoutEventArgs e) {

  // Arrange the buttons in a grid on the form
  int cx = this.ClientRectangle.Width / 3;
  int cy = this.ClientRectangle.Height / 3;
  for( int row = 0; row != 3; ++row ) {
    for( int col = 0; col != 3; ++col ) {
      Button button = buttons[col * 3 + row];
      button.SetBounds(cx * row, cy * col, cx, cy);
    }
  }

  // Set form client size to be multiple of width/height
  this.SetClientSizeCore(cx * 3, cy * 3);



}
```

Although you can use the Layout event to handle all the layout needs of a form, it's much easier to use anchoring, docking, and grouping and fall back on the Layout event only to handle special cases. One advantage of handling the Layout event, however, is that it is protected by SuspendLayout and ResumeLayout, whereas the Resize event is not.[7]

Where Are We?

As you've seen, Windows Forms and VS05 offer an abundance of layout support for forms and controls. This support starts when controls are added to parent forms or parent controls, whether by designer-generated code in InitializeComponent or programmatically by you. After the controls are contained, a host of designer features makes life easier when it comes to ordering, positioning, grouping, and resizing your controls, either at design time

---

[7] See http://blogs.msdn.com/jfoscoding/archive/2005/03/04/385625.aspx (http://tinysells.com/12) for more information.

or at run-time. If these myriad features aren't enough for you, you can take advantage of several container controls to handle specific resizing requirements, including splitting, grouping, flow layout, and tabular layout. You can also easily handle the Layout event or build your own layout panel control to take up the slack, although you'll seldom need to employ these techniques.

As nicely and easily as you can do layout, you often need to change certain aspects of a UI, particularly for out-of-the box .NET Framework controls. This is where the ability to paint your own UIs comes in handy, a topic we cover next.

■ 5 ■
Drawing Basics

A S HANDY AS FORMS are and as rich as the set of built-in controls is, sometimes neither is sufficient to render the state of your application.[1] In that case, you need to draw the state yourself. You may be drawing to the screen, to a file, or to a printer, but wherever you're drawing to, you're dealing with the same primitives—colors, brushes, pens, and fonts—and the same kinds of things to draw: shapes, images, and strings. This chapter starts by examining the fundamentals of drawing to the screen and the basic building blocks of drawing.

Note that all the drawing techniques discussed in this chapter and in the next two chapters relate equally well to controls as to forms. For information about building custom controls, see Chapter 10: Controls.

Also note that the System.Drawing namespace is implemented on top of GDI+ (Graphics Device Interface+), the successor to GDI. The original GDI has been a mainstay in Windows since there was a Windows, providing an abstraction over screens and printers to make writing GUI-style applications easy.[2] GDI+ is a Win32 DLL (gdiplus.dll) that ships with Windows XP and is available for older versions of Windows. GDI+ is also an unmanaged C++ class library that wraps gdiplus.dll. Because the System.Drawing classes share many of the same names with the GDI+ C++ classes, you may very well stumble onto the unmanaged classes when looking for the .NET classes in the online documentation. The concepts are the same, but the coding details are very different between unmanaged C++ and managed anything else, so keep an eye out.

---

[1] The standard controls that come with Windows Forms are listed in Appendix D: Component and Control Survey.

[2] GDI programming certainly isn't easy when compared with System.Drawing programming, but it is tremendously easier than supporting printers and video display adapters by hand, something DOS programmers had to do to put food on the table.

Drawing to the Screen

No matter what kind of drawing you're doing, the underlying abstraction is the Graphics class from the System.Drawing namespace. The Graphics class provides the abstract surface on which you're drawing, whether the results of your drawing operations are displayed on the screen, stored in a file, or spooled to the printer. The Graphics class is too large to show here, but we return to it throughout the chapter.

One way to obtain a Graphics object is to use CreateGraphics to create a new one that's associated with a form:

```csharp
bool drawEllipse = false;

void drawEllipseButton_Click(object sender, EventArgs e) {
  ...
  // Toggle whether or not to draw the ellipse
  this.drawEllipse = !this.drawEllipse;

  using( Graphics g = this.CreateGraphics() ) {
    if( this.drawEllipse ) {
      // Draw the ellipse
      g.FillEllipse(Brushes.DarkBlue, this.ClientRectangle);
    }
    else {
      // Erase the previously drawn ellipse
      g.FillEllipse(SystemBrushes.Control, this.ClientRectangle);
    }
  }
}
```

After we have a Graphics object, we can use it to draw on the form. Because we're using the button to toggle whether to draw the ellipse, we either draw an ellipse in dark blue or use the system color as the background of the form, as illustrated in Figure 5.1.

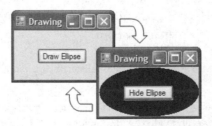

Figure 5.1 Ellipse Form Before Resizing

Unfortunately, when the form is resized, or covered and uncovered, the ellipse is not automatically redrawn.

Handling the Paint Event

To deal with this, Windows asks a form (and all child controls) to redraw newly uncovered content via the Paint event, whose PaintEventArgs argument provides a Graphics object for us:

```
namespace System.Windows.Forms {
  class PaintEventArgs {
    public Rectangle ClipRectangle { get; }
    public Graphics Graphics { get; }
  }
}
```

Taking advantage of this requires moving the ellipse drawing logic to the Paint event handler:

```
bool drawEllipse = false;

void drawEllipseButton_Click(object sender, EventArgs e) {
  this.drawEllipse = !this.drawEllipse;
}

void DrawingForm_Paint(object sender, PaintEventArgs e) {
  if( !this.drawEllipse ) return;
  Graphics g = e.Graphics;
  g.FillEllipse(Brushes.DarkBlue, this.ClientRectangle);
}
```

By the time the Paint event is fired, the background of the form has already been drawn, so any ellipse that was drawn during the last Paint event will be gone; this means that we must draw the ellipse only if the flag is set to true.[3] However, even if we set the flag to draw the ellipse, Windows doesn't know that the state of the flag has changed, so the Paint event isn't triggered and the form doesn't get a chance to draw the ellipse. To avoid the need to draw the ellipse in both the button's Click event and the form's Paint event, we must request a Paint event and let Windows know that the form needs to be redrawn.

---

[3] A form or control can draw its own background by overriding the OnPaintBackground method.

Triggering the Paint Event

To request a Paint event, we use the Invalidate method:

```
void drawEllipseButton_Click(object sender, EventArgs e) {
    drawEllipse = !drawEllipse;
    // Ask Windows for a Paint event for the form and its children
    this.Invalidate(true);
}
```

Now, when the user toggles the drawEllipse flag, we call Invalidate to let Windows know that a part of the form needs to be redrawn. Passing true to the form's Invalidate method ensures that Paint events are fired for the form and its child controls, whereas passing false or nothing at all fires a Paint event only for the form.[4]

Because drawing is one of the more expensive operations, Windows first handles all other events—such as mouse movements, keyboard entry, and so on—before firing the Paint event, just in case multiple areas of the form need to be redrawn at the same time. To avoid this delay, we use the Update method to force Windows Forms to trigger the Paint event immediately. Because both invalidating and updating the entire client area of a form are common, forms also have a Refresh method that combines the two:

```
void drawEllipseButton_Click(object sender, EventArgs e) {
    drawEllipse = !drawEllipse;

    // Either ask Windows Forms for a Paint event
    // for both form and children
    this.Invalidate(true);

    // Or force the Paint event to happen now
    this.Update();

    // Or do both at once
    this.Refresh(); // Invalidate(true) + Update
}
```

However, if you can wait, it's best to let Windows request the Paint event in its own sweet time. It's delayed for a reason: It's the slowest thing that the system does. Forcing all paint operations to happen immediately eliminates an important optimization. However, letting Windows combine paint requests and then handle them in Windows Forms when it's ready results in less drawing and consequently a potentially more responsive application.

---

[4] Optimized use of the Invalidate method is covered in Chapter 7: Advanced Drawing.

If you've been following along with this simple example, you'll be pleased to see that pressing the button toggles nicely whether or not the ellipse is shown on the form, and covering and uncovering the form redraws as expected. However, if you resize the form, you'll be disappointed by the results shown by Figure 5.2.

Figure 5.2   Ellipse Form After Resizing

In Figure 5.2, it seems as if the ellipse has been drawn several times as the form is resized, incompletely each time. What's happening is that, as the form is being expanded, Windows is drawing only the newly exposed area, under the assumption that the existing rectangle doesn't need to be redrawn. Although we're redrawing the entire ellipse during each Paint event, Windows is ignoring everything outside the *clip region*—that part of the form that needs redrawing—and that leads to the strange drawing behavior. Luckily, you can set a *style* to request that Windows redraw the entire form during a resize:

```
// DrawingSampleForm.cs
partial class DrawingSampleForm : Form {
  public DrawingSampleForm() {
    InitializeComponent();

    // Trigger a Paint event when the form is resized
    this.SetStyle(ControlStyles.ResizeRedraw, true);
  }
}
```

Forms (and controls) have several drawing styles (you'll see more in Chapter 7). The ResizeRedraw style causes Windows to redraw the entire client area whenever the form is resized. Of course, this is less efficient, and that's why Windows defaults to the original behavior.

Colors

So far, I've been drawing the ellipse in my form using a built-in dark blue brush. A *brush*, as you'll see, is for filling the interior of a shape, whereas a *pen* is used to draw the edge of a shape. Either way, suppose I'm not quite happy with the dark blue brush. Instead, I'd like a brush composed from one of the more than 16 million colors available to me. Color is modeled in .NET via the Color structure:

```
namespace System.Drawing {
  struct Color {

    // No color
    public static readonly Color Empty;

    // Built-in colors
    public static Color Transparent { get; }
    public static Color AliceBlue { get; }
    ...
    public static Color YellowGreen { get; }

    // Properties
    public byte A { get; }
    public byte R { get; }
    public byte G { get; }
    public byte B { get; }
    public bool IsEmpty { get; }
    public bool IsKnownColor { get; }
    public bool IsNamedColor { get; }
    public bool IsSystemColor { get; }
    public string Name { get; }

    // Methods
    public static Color FromArgb(int argb);
    public static Color FromArgb(int alpha, Color baseColor);
    public static Color FromArgb(int red, int green, int blue);
    public static Color FromArgb(
       int alpha, int red, int green, int blue);
    public static Color FromKnownColor(KnownColor color);
    public static Color FromName(string name);
    public float GetBrightness();
    public float GetHue();
    public float GetSaturation();
    public int ToArgb();
    public KnownColor ToKnownColor();
  }
}
```

A Color object represents four values: the amount of red, green, and blue color and the amount of opacity. The red, green, and blue elements are often referred to together as RGB (red-green-blue), and each ranges from 0 to 255, with 0 being the smallest amount of color and 255 being the greatest. The degree of opacity is specified by an *alpha* value, which is sometimes seen together with RGB as ARGB (Alpha-RGB). The alpha value ranges from 0 to 255, where 0 is completely transparent and 255 is completely opaque.

Instead of using a constructor, you create a Color object by using the static Color. FromArgb method, passing brightness settings of red, green, and blue:

```
Color red = Color.FromArgb(255, 0, 0); // 255 R, 0 G, 0 B
Color green = Color.FromArgb(0, 255, 0); // 0 R, 255 G, 0 B
Color blue = Color.FromArgb(0, 0, 255); // 0 R, 0 G, 255 B
Color white = Color.FromArgb(255, 255, 255);
Color black = Color.FromArgb(0, 0, 0);
```

If you'd like to specify the degree of transparency as well, you pass an alpha value:

```
Color blue25PercentOpaque = Color.FromArgb(255 * 1/4, 0, 0, 255);
```

The three 8-bit color values and the 8-bit alpha value make up the four parts of a single value that defines the 32-bit color that modern video display adapters can handle. If you prefer to pass the four values combined into the single 32-bit value, you can use another of the overloads, although it's fairly awkward and therefore usually avoided:

```
// A=191, R=0, G=0, B=255
Color blue75PercentOpaque = Color.FromArgb(-1090518785);
```

Known Colors

Often, the color you're interested in already has a well-known name, and this means that it is already available from the static fields of Color that define known colors, or from the KnownColor enumeration, or by name:

```
Color blue1 = Color.BlueViolet;
Color blue2 = Color.FromKnownColor(KnownColor.ActiveBorder);
Color blue3 = Color.FromName("ActiveBorder");
```

In addition to 141 colors with names such as AliceBlue and OldLace, the KnownColor enumeration has 33 values describing the current colors assigned to various parts of the Windows UI, such as the color of the border on the active window and the color of the default background of a control. These colors are handy when you're doing custom drawing and you'd like to match the rest of the system. The system color values of the KnownColor enumeration are shown here:

updated

```
namespace System.Drawing {
    enum KnownColor {
        // Nonsystem colors elided...
        ActiveBorder = 1,
        ActiveCaption = 2,
        ActiveCaptionText = 3,
        AppWorkspace = 4,
        ButtonFace = 168, // New
        ButtonHighlight = 169, // New
        ButtonShadow = 170, // New
        Control = 5,
        ControlDark = 6,
        ControlDarkDark = 7,
        ControlLight = 8,
        ControlLightLight = 9,
        ControlText = 10,
        Desktop = 11,
        GradientActiveCaption = 171, // New
        GradientInactiveCaption = 172, // New
        GrayText = 12,
        Highlight = 13,
        HighlightText = 14,
        HotTrack = 15,
        InactiveBorder = 16,
        InactiveCaption = 17,
        InactiveCaptionText = 18,
        Info = 19,
        InfoText = 20,
        Menu = 21,
        MenuBar = 173, // New
        MenuHighlight = 174, // New
        MenuText = 22,
        ScrollBar = 23,
        Window = 24,
        WindowFrame = 25,
        WindowText = 26
    }
}
```

If you'd like to use one of the system colors without creating your own instance of the Color class, they are already created for you and exposed as properties of the SystemColors class:

```
namespace System.Drawing {
  sealed class SystemColors {
    public static Color ActiveBorder { get; }
    public static Color ActiveCaption { get; }
    public static Color ActiveCaptionText { get; }
    public static Color AppWorkspace { get; }
    public static Color ButtonFace { get; }// New
    public static Color ButtonHighlight { get; } // New
    public static Color ButtonShadow { get; } // New
    public static Color Control { get; }
    public static Color ControlDark { get; }
    public static Color ControlDarkDark { get; }
    public static Color ControlLight { get; }
    public static Color ControlLightLight { get; }
    public static Color ControlText { get; }
    public static Color Desktop { get; }
    public static Color GradientActiveCaption { get; } // New
    public static Color GradientInactiveCaption { get; } // New
    public static Color GrayText { get; }
    public static Color Highlight { get; }
    public static Color HighlightText { get; }
    public static Color HotTrack { get; }
    public static Color InactiveBorder { get; }
    public static Color InactiveCaption { get; }
    public static Color InactiveCaptionText { get; }
    public static Color Info { get; }
    public static Color InfoText { get; }
    public static Color Menu { get; }
    public static Color MenuBar { get; } // New
    public static Color MenuHighlight { get; } // New
    public static Color MenuText { get; }
    public static Color ScrollBar { get; }
    public static Color Window { get; }
    public static Color WindowFrame { get; }
    public static Color WindowText { get; }
  }
}
```

As an accessibility feature for vision-impaired users, you should use the SystemColors enumeration when your application needs to support high-contrast UIs.[5]

---

[5] High-contrast support is a requirement for Windows Logo certification (see http://www.microsoft.com/windowsxp/using/accessibility/highcontrast.mspx (http://tinysells.com/14)), and it is active if SystemInformation.HighContrast is true.

The following two lines yield Color objects with the same color values, and you can use whichever one you like:

```
Color color1 = Color.FromKnownColor(KnownColor.GrayText);
Color color2 = SystemColors.GrayText;
```

Color Translation

If you have a color in one of three other formats—HTML, Object Linking and Embedding (OLE), or Win32—or you'd like to translate to one of these formats, you can use Color-Translator, as shown here for HTML:

```
Color htmlBlue = ColorTranslator.FromHtml("#0000ff");
string htmlBlueToo = ColorTranslator.ToHtml(htmlBlue);
```

When you have a Color, you can get its alpha, red, blue, and green values (Color.A, Color.R, Color.B, Color.G) as well as the color's name (Color.Name), whether it's a known color (Color.IsKnownColor) or a system color (Color.IsSystemColor). You can also use these values to fill and frame shapes using brushes and pens, respectively.

Brushes

The System.Drawing.Brush class serves as a base class for several kinds of brushes to suit a variety of needs. Figure 5.3 shows the five derived brush classes provided in the System.Drawing and System.Drawing.Drawing2D namespaces.

Figure 5.3   Sample Brushes

As you can see, each derived brush exhibits its own peculiarities, and they're worth delving into.

Solid Brushes

A SolidBrush is constructed with a color used to fill in the shape being drawn. As a convenience, because solid-color brushes are heavily used, the Brushes class contains 141 Brush properties, one for each of the named colors in the KnownColor enumeration. These properties are handy because their resources are cached and managed by .NET itself, making them a bit easier to use than brushes you have to create yourself:[6]

```
// Managed by .NET
Brush whiteBrush = System.Drawing.Brushes.White;

// Managed by your program
using( Brush brush = new SolidBrush(Color.White) ) { ... }
```

Similarly, all 33 system colors from the SystemColors enumeration are provided in the SystemBrushes class. This is handy if you want to use one of the system colors to create a brush but prefer to let Windows Forms handle the underlying resource.

Texture Brushes

A TextureBrush is constructed with an image, such as a bitmap:

```
// Draw TextureBrush
string file = @"c:\windows\santa fe stucco.bmp";
using( Brush brush = new TextureBrush(new Bitmap(file)) ) { ... }
```

By default, the image is used repeatedly to tile the space inside the shape being drawn. You can change this behavior by choosing a member of the WrapMode enumeration:

```
namespace System.Drawing.Drawing2D {
    enum WrapMode {
        Tile = 0, // default
        TileFlipX = 1, // flip image horizontally along X axis
        TileFlipY = 2, // flip image vertically along Y axis
        TileFlipXY = 3, // flip image along X and Y axes
        Clamp = 4, // draw only once
    }
}
```

[6] In fact, if you attempt to dispose of one of the .NET-provided resources, such as pens, brushes, and so on, you'll eventually get an exception, either when you dispose of it in the first place or later when you try to use it again after it's been disposed of.

Figure 5.4 shows the various modes.

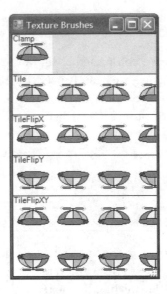

Figure 5.4   Various TextureBrush WrapMode Values

Hatch Brushes

A HatchBrush is used to fill space using one of several built-in two-color patterns, where the two colors are used to draw the foreground and the background of the pattern:

```
// Draw HatchBrush
using( Brush brush =
   new HatchBrush(HatchStyle.Divot, Color.DarkBlue, Color.White) ) {
   ...
}
```

Figure 5.5 shows the 56 hatches in the HatchStyle enumeration using black as the foreground color and white as the background color.

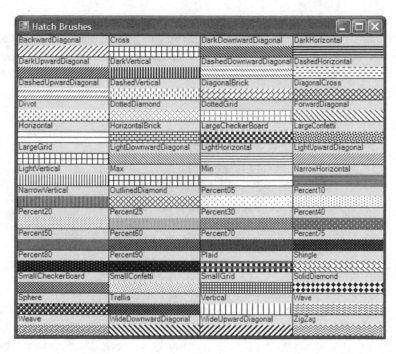

Figure 5.5   Available Hatch Brush Styles Shown with Black Foreground and White Background

Linear Gradient Brushes

A LinearGradientBrush is used to draw a smooth blending between two end points and between two colors. The resulting gradations are drawn at a specified angle:

```
// Draw LinearGradientBrush
Rectangle area = new Rectangle(x, y, width, height);
Color startColor = Color.DarkBlue;
Color endColor = Color.White;
using( Brush brush =
  new LinearGradientBrush(area, startColor, endColor, 45.0f) ) { ... }
```

The angle you specify can either be a float, as shown in the example, or one of four LinearGradientMode values:

```
namespace System.Drawing.Drawing2D {
  enum LinearGradientMode {
    Horizontal = 0, // 0 degrees
    Vertical = 1 // 90 degrees
    ForwardDiagonal = 2, // 45 degrees
    BackwardDiagonal = 3, // 135 degrees
  }
}
```

The angle is used to set up a *blend*, which governs the transition between colors over the area of the brush along the angle of the line. You can set this blend either directly or indirectly. In the direct technique, you use a Blend property, which determines positions and factors of fallout between the two colors. To set the blend indirectly, you use a *focus* point for the end color and a fallout rate toward the start color, as shown in Figure 5.6.

Figure 5.6   Normal, Triangle, Bell Linear Gradient and Normal
Custom Color Brushes (See Plate 8)

Notice that the normal linear gradient brush transitions between the start and end colors, whereas the triangle version transitions from the start color to the end color at some specified focus (in this example, it is set right in the middle). Furthermore, the bell shape transitions toward the end color using a normal bell curve distribution. The following code draws the first three brushes (notice the use of the SetBlendTriangularShape and SetSigmaBellShape methods to adjust the blend):

```
using(
  LinearGradientBrush brush =
    new LinearGradientBrush(
      this.ClientRectangle,
      Color.White,
      Color.Black,
      LinearGradientMode.Horizontal) ) {

  // Normal: focus set at the end
  g.FillRectangle(brush, x, y, width, height);
  g.DrawString("Normal", this.Font, blackBrush, x, y);
  y += height;

  // Triangle: focus set in the middle
  brush.SetBlendTriangularShape(0.5f);
  g.FillRectangle(brush, x, y, width, height);
  g.DrawString("Triangle", this.Font, blackBrush, x, y);
  y += height;

  // Bell: focus set in the middle
  brush.SetSigmaBellShape(0.5f);
  g.FillRectangle(brush, x, y, width, height);
```

```
    g.DrawString("Bell", this.Font, blackBrush, x, y);
    y += height;
    ...
}
```

At the bottom of Figure 5.6, we're still transitioning from white to black, but we're transitioning through red in the middle. This is because we took over the blending with an instance of a ColorBlend object that lets us set custom colors and positions:

```
// Custom colors
ColorBlend blend = new ColorBlend();
blend.Colors = new Color[] { Color.White, Color.Red, Color.Black };
blend.Positions = new float[] { 0.0f, 0.5f, 1.0f };
brush.InterpolationColors = blend;
g.FillRectangle(brush, x, y, width, height);
g.DrawString("Custom Colors", this.Font, blackBrush, x, y);
```

Path Gradient Brushes

In the unlikely event that your linear gradient brush is not defined for the entire shape you're drawing, the brush will be tiled just like a texture brush, as governed by the WrapMode. If you want to get even fancier than linear gradients along a single angle, you can use the PathGradientBrush, as shown in Figure 5.7.

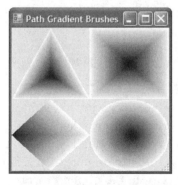

Figure 5.7   Four Sample Uses of the PathGradientBrush Class

PathGradientBrush is defined by a set of points that define the surrounding edges of the path, a center point, and a set of colors for each point. By default, the color for each edge point is white, and for the center point is black. The gradient color transitions along each edge are defined by the points toward the center. Both triangle and square brushes were created this way:

```
Point[] triPoints = new Point[] { new Point(width/2, 0),
                                    new Point(0, height),
                                    new Point(width, height), };
using( PathGradientBrush brush = new PathGradientBrush(triPoints) ) {
  int x = 0;
  int y = 0;
  g.FillRectangle(brush, x, y, width, height);
}

Point[] quadPoints = new Point[] { new Point(0, 0),
                                    new Point(width, 0),
                                    new Point(width, height),
                                    new Point(0, height), };
using( PathGradientBrush brush =
  new PathGradientBrush(quadPoints) ) { ... }
```

Notice that although we defined the surrounding points in a Point array in both cases, we didn't define the center point explicitly. The center point is calculated based on the surrounding points; but it doesn't need to be in the midpoint between all points, as shown by the diamond brush and the following code:

```
Point[] diamondPoints = new Point[] { ... };
using( PathGradientBrush brush =
        new PathGradientBrush(diamondPoints) ) {
  brush.WrapMode = WrapMode.Tile;
  brush.CenterPoint = new Point(0, height / 2);
  int x = 0;
  int y = height;
  g.FillRectangle(brush, x, y, width, height);
}
```

Notice that we use the CenterPoint property to set the gradient end point along the left edge of the diamond. The center of a path gradient brush doesn't even have to be inside the polygon described by the points if you don't want it to be.

Notice also the use of the WrapMode property. By default, this is set to Clamp, which causes the brush to draw only once in the upper-left corner. The points on the brush are relative to the client area, not to where they're being used to fill, so we must set WrapMode if we want the brush to draw anywhere except in the upper-left corner. Another way to handle this is to apply a transform on the Graphics object before drawing, a technique described in Chapter 7.

Although it's possible to describe a circle with a lot of points, it's far easier to use a GraphicsPath object instead. A GraphicsPath is actually a data structure that contains zero or more shapes (the GraphicsPath class is discussed in more detail later in this chapter). It's useful for describing an area for drawing, just as we're doing with the set of points describing our brush. The points are used by the PathGradientBrush to create a GraphicsPath internally (hence the name of this brush), but we can create and use a GraphicsPath directly:

```
using( GraphicsPath circle = new GraphicsPath() ) {
   circle.AddEllipse(0, 0, width, height);
   using( PathGradientBrush brush = new PathGradientBrush(circle) ) {
     brush.WrapMode = WrapMode.Tile;
     brush.SurroundColors = new Color[] { Color.White }; // default
     brush.CenterColor = Color.Black;
     int x = width;
     int y = height;
     g.FillRectangle(brush, x, y, width, height);
   }
}
```

After we create an empty GraphicsPath object, notice the addition of an ellipse to the path before we use it to create a brush. The center of whatever set of shapes is in the path is used as the brush's center point, just as you'd expect, but the center color defaults to white when we use a GraphicsPath; that's why the code manually sets the CenterColor property to black.

Notice also the use of the SurroundColors property, which is an array of colors, one for each point on the gradient path. If there are more points than colors (as is clearly the case when we're providing only a single color for all the points around the edge of a circle), the last color in the array is used for all remaining points. For example, this code draws a red gradient from the first point of the triangle but uses blue for the other two points, as shown in Figure 5.8:

```
using( PathGradientBrush brush = new PathGradientBrush(triPoints) ) {
   brush.SurroundColors = new Color[] { Color.Red, Color.Blue };
   int x = 0;
   int y = 0;
   g.FillRectangle(brush, x, y, width, height);
}
```

Figure 5.8   A PathGradientBrush with One Red Surrounding
Point and Two Blue Ones (See Plate 9)

Like linear gradient brushes, path gradient brushes allow you to adjust the blend as well as the colors used to transition between start and end points.

Pens

Whereas the Brush classes are used to fill shapes, the Pen class is used to frame shapes. The interesting members are shown here:

```
namespace System.Drawing {
   sealed class Pen : IDisposable, ... {
     // Constructors
     public Pen(Brush brush);
     public Pen(Brush brush, float width);
     public Pen(Color color);
     public Pen(Color color, float width);

     // Properties
     public PenAlignment Alignment { get; set; }
     public Brush Brush { get; set; }
     public Color Color { get; set; }
     public float[] CompoundArray { get; set; }
     public CustomLineCap CustomEndCap { get; set; }
     public CustomLineCap CustomStartCap { get; set; }
     public DashCap DashCap { get; set; }
     public float DashOffset { get; set; }
     public float[] DashPattern { get; set; }
     public DashStyle DashStyle { get; set; }
     public LineCap EndCap { get; set; }
     public LineJoin LineJoin { get; set; }
     public float MiterLimit { get; set; }
     public PenType PenType { get; }
     public LineCap StartCap { get; set; }
     public float Width { get; set; }
```

```
      // Transformation members elided...

      // Methods
      public void SetLineCap(...);
   }
}
```

Pens have several interesting properties, including a width, a color or a brush, start and end cap styles, and a dash pattern for the line itself. One note of interest is that the width of a pen is specified in the units of the underlying Graphics object being drawn on (more information about Graphics units is available in Chapter 7). However, no matter what the underlying units, a pen width of 0 always translates into a width of 1 physical unit on the underlying Graphic surface. This lets you specify the smallest visible pen width without worrying about the units of a particular surface.

Notice that the Pen class is sealed. This means that it can't be used as a base class for deriving further penlike functionality. Instead, each pen has a type that governs its behavior, as determined by the PenType enumeration from the System.Drawing.Drawing2D namespace:

```
namespace System.Drawing.Drawing2D {
   enum PenType {
      SolidColor = 0, // Created from a color or a SolidBrush
      HatchFill = 1, // Created from a HatchBrush
      TextureFill = 2, // Created from a TextureBrush
      PathGradient = 3, // Created from a PathGradientBrush
      LinearGradient = 4, // Created from a LinearGradientBrush
   }
}
```

If you're interested in common, solid-color pens, the 141 named pens are provided as static Pen properties on the Pens class, and 33 system pens are provided as static Pen properties on the SystemPens class, providing the same usage as the corresponding Brushes and SystemBrushes classes. As with SystemBrushes, the FromSystemColor method of the SystemPens class returns a pen in one of the system colors that's managed by .NET.

Line Caps

In addition to their brushlike behavior, pens have behavior at their ends, at their joints, and along their length that brushes don't have. For example, each end can be capped in a different style, as determined by the LineCap enumeration shown in Figure 5.9.

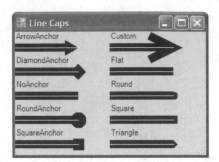

Figure 5.9   Examples from the LineCap Enumeration

All these lines were generated with a black pen of width 12 passed to the Graphics. DrawLine method. We drew the white line of width 1 in the middle by using a separate call to Graphics.DrawLine to show the two end points that define the line. Each black pen is defined with the EndCap property set to a value from the LineCap enumeration:

```
using( Pen pen = new Pen(Color.Black, 12) ) {
  pen.EndCap = LineCap.Flat; // default
  g.DrawLine(
    pen, x, y + height * 2/3, x + width * 2/3, y + height * 2/3);
  g.DrawLine(
    whitePen, x, y + height * 2/3, x + width * 2/3, y + height * 2/3);
  ...
}
```

The default line cap style is flat, which is what all the StartCap properties are set to. You'll notice some familiar line cap styles, including flat, round, square, and triangle, which have no anchor, as well as arrow, diamond, round, and square, which have anchors. An *anchor* indicates that part of the line cap extends beyond the width of the pen. The difference between square and flat, on the other hand, dictates whether the line cap extends beyond the end of the line (as square does, but flat does not).

You can manage these kinds of drawing behaviors independently by using the LineCap.Custom enumeration value and setting the CustomStartCap or CustomEndCap field to a class that derives from the CustomLineCap class (from the System.Drawing. Drawing2D namespace). The custom line cap in Figure 5.9 shows a pen created using an instance of the AdjustableArrowCap class, the only custom end cap class that .NET provides:

```
using( Pen pen = new Pen(Color.Black, 12) ) {
  pen.EndCap = LineCap.Custom;
  // width and height of 3 and unfilled arrowhead
  pen.CustomEndCap = new AdjustableArrowCap(3f, 3f, false);
  ...
}
```

Dashes

In addition to the ends having special styles, a line can have a dash style, as defined by the DashStyle enumeration, shown in Figure 5.10.

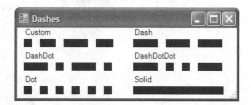

Figure 5.10   Examples Using the DashStyle Enumeration

Each of the lines was created by setting the DashStyle property of the pen. The DashStyle.Custom value is used to set custom dash and space lengths, where each length is a multiplier of the width. For example, the following code draws the increasing-length dashes shown in Figure 5.10 with a constant space length:

```
using( Pen pen = new Pen(Color.Black, 12) ) {
    pen.DashStyle = DashStyle.Custom;
    // Set increasing dashes with constant spaces
    pen.DashPattern = new float[] { 1f, 1f, 2f, 1f, 3f, 1f, 4f, 1f };
    g.DrawLine(
      pen, x + 10, y + height * 2/3, x + width - 20, y + height * 2/3);
    ...
}
```

If you'd like to exercise more control over your custom dash settings, you can set the DashCap property on the pen to any of the values in the DashCap enumeration, which is a subset of the values in the LineCap enumeration with only Flat (the default), Round, and Triangle.

To exercise more control over the line itself, in addition to dash settings you can define *compound* pens using the CompoundArray property. This allows you to provide lines and spaces parallel to the lines being drawn instead of perpendicularly, as dash settings do. For example, Figure 5.11 was drawn with a pen set up this way:

```
using( Pen pen = new Pen(Color.Black, 20) ) {
    // Set percentages of width where line starts, then space starts,
    // then line starts again, etc., in alternating pattern
    pen.CompoundArray =
      new float[] { 0.0f, 0.25f, 0.45f, 0.55f, 0.75f, 1.0f, };
    g.DrawRectangle(pen, new Rectangle(...));
}
```

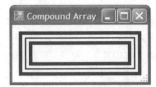

Figure 5.11   A Single Rectangle Drawn with a Pen Using a Compound Array

Pen Alignment

Most of the examples, including Figure 5.11, show pens of width greater than 1. When you draw a line of width greater than 1, the question is, where do the extra pixels go—above the line being drawn, below it, or somewhere else? The default pen alignment is *centered*, which means that half the width goes inside the shape being drawn, and the other half goes outside. The alignment can also be *inset*, which means that the entire width of the pen is inside the shape being drawn, as shown in Figure 5.12.

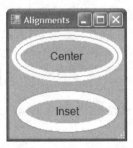

Figure 5.12   Pen Alignment Options (See Plate 10)

In Figure 5.12, both ellipses are drawn using a rectangle of the same dimensions (as shown by the red line), but the different alignments determine where the width of the line is drawn. There are actually five values in the PenAlignment enumeration, but only Center and Inset are currently supported, and Inset is used only for closed shapes (an open figure has no "inside"). The other three—Left, Outset, and Right—render as if you had used Center.

Joins

One final consideration when you draw figures that have angles is what to do with the line at the angle. In Figure 5.13, the four values in the LineJoin enumeration have been set in the Pen class's LineJoin property before the rectangles were drawn (again, a white line of width 1 is used to show the shape being drawn).

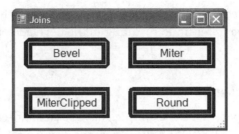

Figure 5.13   Sample LineJoin Values

In Figure 5.13, each corner provides a different join. The one exception is MiterClipped, which changes between Bevel and Miter dynamically based on the limit set by the Miter-Limit property. The length of a miter is the distance between the inner corner and the outer corner of a join, where the distance is a function of line thickness and the angle of the corner. When the ratio of the line thickness to the miter length exceeds the miter limit, the join is beveled; otherwise, it's mitered.

For example, consider the following combination of pen size and miter limit:

```
// MiterClipped Join
using( Pen blackPen = new Pen(Color.Black, 10) ) {
   blackPen.LineJoin = LineJoin.MiterClipped;
   blackPen.MiterLimit = 5.0F; // Default is 10.0f
   // Draw four sets of angled lines of increasing angle size
   ...
}
```

Figure 5.14 illustrates the results.

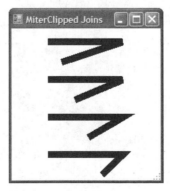

Figure 5.14   Effects of MiterLimit Property on Joins

As the corner angle decreases, the miter length increases to the point where its ratio to the line thickness tops the miter limit, resulting in the beveled corner that's applied to the top two sets of angled lines.

Creating Pens from Brushes

So far in this section on pens, all the examples have used solid-color pens. However, you can also create a pen from a brush and thereby employ any effect you can create using the multitude of brushes provided by System.Drawing, including textures, hatches, and gradients. For example, Figure 5.15 shows an image you first encountered in Chapter 1: Hello, Windows Forms.

Figure 5.15   Creating a Pen from a LinearGradientBrush (See Plate 2)

The pen used to draw the lines in Figure 5.15 was created from a LinearGradientBrush:

```
using( LinearGradientBrush brush =
  new LinearGradientBrush(
    this.ClientRectangle,
    Color.Empty,
    Color.Empty,
    45) ) {
  ColorBlend blend = new ColorBlend();
  blend.Colors = new Color[] { Color.Red, Color.Green, Color.Blue };
  blend.Positions = new float[] { 0, .5f, 1 };
  brush.InterpolationColors = blend;
  using( Pen pen = new Pen(brush) ) { ... }
  ...
}
```

Shapes

Now that you know how to frame and fill shapes with pens and brushes, you might be interested in the shapes themselves. Figure 5.16 shows what's available.

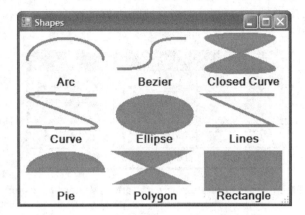

Figure 5.16   The Basic Shapes (See Plate 11)

The edges of all the shapes in Figure 5.16 were rendered by one of several DrawXxx functions implemented by the Graphics object, including DrawArc and DrawEllipse. The shapes that can be filled were rendered using an appropriate FillXxx function, such as FillEllipse and FillPie. Not all shapes can be filled, because not all of them are closed shapes; for example, there is no FillCurve. However, all the open shapes (except the Bezier) have closed-shape equivalents; for example, a filled arc is called a pie.

You could draw the Lines shape using multiple calls to DrawLine, but it turns out to be simpler to use DrawLines; this helper method can draw multiple lines at once, as the plural name suggests. DrawRectangle and DrawBezier have equivalent helpers: DrawRectangles and DrawBeziers, respectively. In addition to being convenient, these helpers handle the appropriate mitering at intersections that you'd otherwise have to do by hand. Finally, just as you can fill a single rectangle, you can fill multiple rectangles at once using the extra FillRectangles method. Lines and Beziers can't be filled and consequently don't have equivalent helper methods.

Curves

Most of the shapes are specified as you'd expect. You specify the rectangle and the ellipse using an x, y, width, and height, or a Rectangle object. You specify the arc and the pie as with a rectangle, but you also include a start and a length of *sweep,* both specified in degrees (the shown arc and pie start at 180 degrees and sweep for 180 degrees). You specify the lines, polygon, and curves using an array of points, although the curves are a little different.

The curve (also known as a *cardinal spline*) acts just like a set of lines, except as a point is approached, there's a curve instead of a sharp point. In addition to a set of points, you specify the curve using a *tension*, which is a value that determines how "curvy" the curve is around the points. A tension of 0 indicates no curve, and a tension of 0.5 is the default. You can set the tension as high as allowed by the floating-point type. Figure 5.17 shows some common variations.

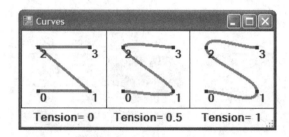

Figure 5.17   Curves Drawn with Various Values of Tension

Figure 5.17 shows the same set of points (as indicated by the black dots and index number) drawn using the DrawCurve function with three different values of tension. As the tension increases, so does the amount of curve at each point.

Unlike normal curves, Bezier curves are specified with exactly four points: one start point, followed by two *control* points, followed by an end point. If you use the DrawBeziers function to draw multiple curves, the end point of the preceding curve becomes the start point of the next. Figure 5.18 shows three Bezier curves drawn using the same set of points, but in different orders.

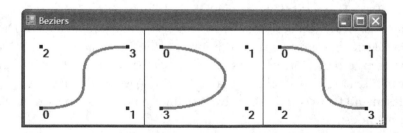

Figure 5.18   Three Bezier Curves Drawn Using the Same Set of Points in Different Orders

In each case, the Bezier is drawn between the start point and the end point, but the two control points are used to determine the shape of the curve by exerting more "control" over the curve as they get farther away.

Smoothing Modes

When drawing shapes, you may want the smooth rendering you've seen in the really cool applications. The shapes in Figures 5.16, 5.17, and 5.18 were all drawn without any kind of "smoothing," as evidenced by the jagged edges. The jagged edges are caused by the swift transition between the color of the shape being drawn and the color of the background. A technique known as *antialiasing* uses additional colored pixels to provide a smoother transition between the shape color and the background color, in much the same way that a gradient brush provides a smooth transition from one color to another. To turn on antialiasing for shapes subsequently drawn on the Graphics object, you set the SmoothingMode property:

```
g.SmoothingMode = SmoothingMode.AntiAlias;
```

The default value of the SmoothingMode property is SmoothingMode.None. In addition to the AntiAlias value, SmoothingMode has four other values: Default, HighSpeed, HighQuality, and Invalid. The first three are merely aliases for None, None, and AntiAlias, depending on your system settings, and Invalid cannot be set by you. Figure 5.19 shows the difference between using and not using antialiasing.

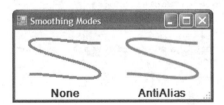

Figure 5.19   The Effect of Changing the SmoothingMode from None to AntiAlias

Notice that setting the SmoothingMode has no effect on the text drawn on the Graphics object. You set the rendering effects of text using the TextRenderingHint property, which I discuss in Chapter 6: Drawing Text.

Saving and Restoring Graphics Settings

Setting the SmoothingMode in the preceding section is the first time we've changed a property on the Graphics object that affects subsequent operations. When you change a

Graphics object property like this, you need to be especially careful. For example, consider the following:

```
void DrawingWithHelpForm_Paint(object sender, PaintEventArgs e) {
  // Draw some smooth things
  DrawSomethingSmooth(e.Graphics);

  // Draw other things unsmoothed, or so I think...
}

void DrawSomethingSmooth(Graphics g) {
  // Make things draw smoothly
  g.SmoothingMode = SmoothingMode.AntiAlias;

  // Draw things...
}
```

The Paint event handler calls the DrawSomethingSmooth helper method and passes it the Graphics object, which is subsequently set to paint smoothly. However, when Draw-SomethingSmooth returns, the Paint event handler is expecting to continue painting roughly, although that isn't the case. To avoid unexpected situations like this, it's a good idea to save the initial values of any properties you change on the Graphics object and restore them before the method returns:

```
void DrawSomethingSmooth(Graphics g) {
  // Save old smoothing mode
  SmoothingMode oldMode = g.SmoothingMode;

  // Make things draw smoothly
  g.SmoothingMode = SmoothingMode.AntiAlias;

  // Draw things...

  // Restore smoothing mode
  g.SmoothingMode = oldMode;
}
```

As you'll see in further topics, a variety of Graphics object properties affect subsequent operations. This technique quickly becomes painful if you need to save and restore several of these properties. Luckily, you can save yourself the trouble by taking a snapshot of a Graphics object state in a GraphicsState object from the System.Drawing.Drawing2D namespace:

```
void DrawSomethingSmooth(Graphics g) {
  // Save old graphics state
  GraphicsState oldState = g.Save();

  // Make things draw smoothly
  g.SmoothingMode = SmoothingMode.AntiAlias;

  // Draw things...

  // Restore old graphics state
  g.Restore(oldState);
}
```

The Save method on the Graphics class returns the current state of the properties in the Graphics object. The call to Restore takes a GraphicsState object and sets the Graphics object to the state cached in that object. The code shows a pair of calls to Save and Restore, but it's not necessary to keep them in balance, something that's handy for switching a lot between two or more states.

Paths

In addition to using the basic shapes, you can compose and draw shapes together using a path. A *path,* modeled via the GraphicsPath class, is very much like a Graphics object, in that it's a logical container of zero or more shapes (called *figures* or *subpaths*). The main difference is that the figures can be started and ended arbitrarily.[7]

This means that you can compose one or more complicated figures from a set of basic shapes. You collect figures into a path so that you can frame or fill them as a unit using a single brush or pen, which is applied when the path is drawn. For example, Figure 5.20 shows a rounded rectangle (a shape that the Graphics object can't draw for you directly).

Figure 5.20 A Rounded Rectangle Composed of Arc Figures in a GraphicsPath Object

---

[7] Another important difference is that a Graphics object is backed by a surface such as a screen or a printer.

Imagine a method called GetRoundedRectPath that takes a rectangle and the radius of an arc describing the curve. Calling the function returns a path, which can be filled and framed using the Graphics methods FillPath and DrawPath:

```
Graphics g = e.Graphics;
int width = this.ClientRectangle.Width;
int height = this.ClientRectangle.Height;
Rectangle rect = new Rectangle(10, 10, width - 20, height - 20);
 using( GraphicsPath path = GetRoundedRectPath(rect, width / 10) ) {
   g.FillPath(Brushes.Yellow, path);
   g.DrawPath(Pens.Black, path);
 }
```

Even though the rounded rectangle path is composed of eight shapes (four arcs and four lines), the entire path is filled with one brush and framed with one pen. Here is the implementation of the method that composes the rounded rectangle:

```
GraphicsPath GetRoundedRectPath(Rectangle rect, int radius) {
   int diameter = 2 * radius;
   Rectangle arcRect =
     new Rectangle(rect.Location, new Size(diameter, diameter));

   GraphicsPath path = new GraphicsPath();

   // top left
   path.AddArc(arcRect, 180, 90);

   // top right
   arcRect.X = rect.Right - diameter;
   path.AddArc(arcRect, 270, 90);

   // bottom right
   arcRect.Y = rect.Bottom - diameter;
   path.AddArc(arcRect, 0, 90);

   // bottom left
   arcRect.X = rect.Left;
   path.AddArc(arcRect, 90, 90);

   path.CloseFigure();

   return path;
}
```

This function adds four arcs to the path—one at each of the corners of the rectangle. Each shape added to the path is filled or framed as appropriate when the path is drawn or filled. In fact, notice that no pen or brush is used to add each shape. The pen or brush is provided when the path is drawn, and not when the shapes are added.

Also, notice that none of the lines are added explicitly. The first three lines are added implicitly by the path itself. As each new unclosed shape is added, the starting point of the new shape is joined to the ending point of the last unclosed shape, creating a connected figure. After the last arc is added, we call the CloseFigure method to join the ending point of that arc to the starting point of the first arc. If CloseFigure had not been called, we'd still have a closed figure when the path was filled and framed, but the line connecting the top-left arc with the bottom-left arc would be missing. On the other hand, adding a closed shape, such as a rectangle or an ellipse, will close itself, so there's no need to call CloseFigure.

If, after calling CloseFigure, we were to add another shape, then another figure would be started for us implicitly. If you'd like to start a new figure without closing the current figure, you can do so by calling StartFigure. Figure 5.21 shows what would happen if Start-Figure were called after the second arc at the top right is added to the path. Notice that there would be two figures in the path, the first one unclosed because the second figure was started without closing the first.

Figure 5.21   Starting a New Figure in a Path
Without Closing the Current Figure

Paths can add any of the shapes that the Graphics class can draw or fill. In fact, paths are handy because they can be used to create closed figures that aren't normally closed. For example, the following function returns a closed Bezier, another shape that the Graphics class doesn't provide directly:

```
GraphicsPath GetClosedBezierPath(Rectangle rect, Point[] points) {
    GraphicsPath path = new GraphicsPath();
    path.AddBeziers(points);
    path.CloseFigure();
    return path;
}
```

Fill Modes

When you compose a path of multiple figures that overlap, the overlap is subtractive by default. For example, the following code produces the donut in Figure 5.22:

```
GraphicsPath GetDonutPath(Rectangle rect, int holeRadius) {
    GraphicsPath path = new GraphicsPath();
    path.AddEllipse(rect);
    Point centerPoint = new Point(...);
    Rectangle holeRect = new Rectangle(...);
    path.StartFigure(); // not needed: an ellipse will close itself
    path.AddEllipse(holeRect);
    return path;
}
```

Figure 5.22   Figures That Overlap Completely Act Subtractively

However, notice that when the donut is resized, as in Figure 5.23, only the overlapping parts subtract from each other.

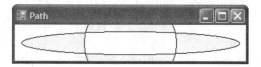

Figure 5.23   Overlapping Figures and the Alternate FillMode (See Plate 12)

This behavior is governed by the FillMode property on the GraphicsPath, of type FillMode. The FillMode enumeration has two values: Alternate and Winding. Alternate, the default, changes how shapes are filled by noticing when lines cross. Switching to Winding mode, in this case, would fill both circles, because Winding mode changes how shapes are filled based on a complicated scheme of line segment direction that wouldn't be invoked in our case. You can also set the FillMode on a polygon and a closed curve, but the default Alternate FillMode is the overwhelming favorite and is seldom changed.

Images

As useful as curves and lines are, most modern applications also include the need to load and display professionally produced, prepackaged images. Also, some applications themselves produce images that can be saved to a file for later display. Both kinds of applications are supported by the two kinds of images in .NET: bitmaps and metafiles.

A *bitmap* is a set of pixels at certain color values stored in a variety of standard *raster* formats such as Graphics Interchange Format (GIF) (.gif files), Joint Picture Experts Group (JPEG) (.jpg files), and Portable Network Graphics (PNG) (.png files), as well as Windows-specific formats such as Windows bitmap (.bmp files) and Windows icon (.ico files). A *metafile* is a set of shapes that make up a *vector* format, such as a GraphicsPath, but can also be loaded from Windows metafile (.wmf) and enhanced Windows metafile (.emf) formats. In general, raster formats provide more detail, whereas metafiles offer better resizing support.

Loading and Drawing Images

Bitmaps and metafiles can be loaded from files in the file system as well as files embedded as resources.[8] However, you must use the appropriate class. The Bitmap class (from the System.Drawing namespace) handles only raster formats and doesn't support alpha channels for 32 bits per pixel (BPP) ARGB images, and the Metafile class (from the System.Drawing.Imaging namespace) handles only vector formats.[9] Both the Bitmap class and the Metafile class derive from a common base class, the Image class. Image objects are what you deal with most of the time, whether you're drawing them into a Graphics object or setting a Form object's BackgroundImage property.

The easiest way to load the image is to pass a file name to the appropriate class's constructor. After an image has been loaded, it can be drawn using the Graphics.DrawImage method:

```
using( Metafile wmf = new Metafile(@"2DARROW3.WMF") ) {
    // Draw the full image, unscaled and
    // clipped only to the Graphics object
    g.DrawImage(wmf, new PointF(0, 0));
}

using( Bitmap bmp = new Bitmap(@"c:\windows\soap bubbles.bmp") ) {
    g.DrawImage(bmp, new PointF(100, 100));
}

using( Bitmap ico = new Bitmap(@"POINT10.ICO") ) {
    g.DrawImage(ico, new PointF(200, 200));
}
```

---

[8] For details of loading images from resources, see Chapter 13: Resources.

[9] Bitmap does support alpha channels for .png files, but not for .bmp files. Alpha channels aren't officially part of the bitmap specification, even though some applications (like Adobe Photoshop) do support alpha channels on bitmaps.

Drawing an image using a point causes the image to be rendered at its native size and clipped only by the Graphics object. You can be explicit about this desire by calling Draw-ImageUnscaled, but it acts no differently from passing only a point to DrawImage. If you'd like to draw your image both unscaled and clipped, you can call the Graphics.Draw-ImageUnscaledAndClipped method, passing an image and the target rectangle.

Scaling, Clipping, Panning, and Skewing

Drawing an image unscaled, although useful, is somewhat boring. Often, you'd like to perform operations on the image as it's drawn to achieve effects. For example, to *scale* an image as it's drawn to fit into a rectangle, you pass a rectangle instead of a point to DrawImage:

```
// Scale the image to the rectangle
Rectangle rect = new Rectangle(...);
g.DrawImage(bmp, rect);
```

Going the other way, if you'd like to *clip* an image but leave it unscaled, you can use the DrawImage method, which takes both a source and a destination rectangle of the same size (Figure 5.24 shows the difference):

```
// Clip the image to the destination rectangle
Rectangle srcRect = new Rectangle(...);
Rectangle destRect = srcRect;
g.DrawImage(bmp, destRect, srcRect, g.PageUnit);
```

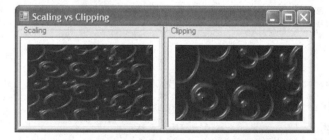

Figure 5.24   Scaling an Image Versus Clipping an Image

The code that does the clipping specifies a source rectangle to take from the image, and a destination rectangle on the Graphics object. Because both rectangles were the same size, there was no scaling, but this technique allows any chunk of the image to be drawn (and scaled) to any rectangle on the Graphics object. This technique also allows for *panning*, which offsets the upper-left corner of the image being drawn from the client rectangle of the surface the image is being drawn to (as shown in Figure 5.25):

```
Bitmap bmp = new Bitmap(@"c:\windows\soap bubbles.bmp");
Size offset = new Size(0, 0); // Adjusted by buttons

void panningPanel_Paint(object sender, PaintEventArgs e) {
  Graphics g = e.Graphics;
  Rectangle destRect = this.panningPanel.ClientRectangle;
  Rectangle srcRect =
    new Rectangle(this.offset.Width, this.offset.Height,
                  destRect.Width, destRect.Height);
  g.DrawImage(this.bmp, destRect, srcRect, g.PageUnit);
}
```

Figure 5.25　A Form That Pans an Image in Four Directions

Not only can you scale an image (or part of an image) to a rectangle, but also you can scale an image (or part of an image) to an arbitrary parallelogram. Several of the Draw-Images overloads take an array of three PointF objects that describe three points on a parallelogram, which in turn acts as the destination (the fourth point is extrapolated to make sure that it's a real parallelogram). Scaling to a nonrectangular parallelogram is called *skewing* because of the skewed look of the results. For example, here's a way to skew an entire image (as shown in Figure 5.26):

```
Bitmap bmp = new Bitmap(@"c:\windows\soap bubbles.bmp");
Size offset = new Size(0, 0); // Adjusted by buttons

void skewingPanel_Paint(object sender, PaintEventArgs e) {
  Graphics g = e.Graphics;
  Rectangle rect = this.skewingPanel.ClientRectangle;
  Point[] points = new Point[3];
  points[0] =
    new Point(rect.Left + this.offset.Width,
              rect.Top + this.offset.Height);
```

```
    points[1] = new Point(rect.Right, rect.Top + this.offset.Height);
    points[2] = new Point(rect.Left, rect.Bottom - this.offset.Height);
    g.DrawImage(this.bmp, points);
}
```

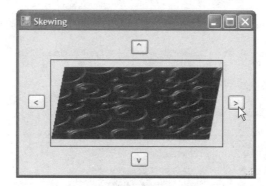

Figure 5.26   An Example of Skewing an Image (See Plate 13)

Rotating and Flipping

Two other kinds of transformation that you can apply to an image are rotating and flipping. *Rotating* an image allows it to be turned in increments of 90 degrees—that is, 90, 180, or 270. *Flipping* an image allows an image to be flipped along either the X or the Y axis. You can perform these two transformations together using the values from the RotateFlipType enumeration, as shown in Figure 5.27.

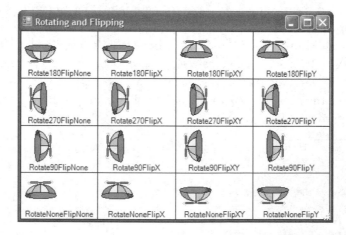

Figure 5.27   The Rotating and Flipping Types from the RotateFlipType Enumeration

Notice in Figure 5.27 that both RotateNoneFlipNone and Rotate180FlipXY are the original image. All the others are either rotated or flipped, or both. To rotate only, you pick a type that includes FlipNone. To flip only, you pick a type that includes RotateNone. The values from the RotateFlipType enumeration affect an image itself using the RotateFlip method:

```
// Rotate 90 degrees
bitmap1.RotateFlip(RotateFlipType.Rotate90FlipNone);

// Flip along the X axis
bitmap2.RotateFlip(RotateFlipType.RotateNoneFlipX);
```

The effects of rotation and flipping are cumulative. For example, rotating an image 90 degrees twice rotates it a total of 180 degrees.

Recoloring

Rotating and flipping aren't merely effects applied when drawing; rather, these operations affect the contents of the image. You can also transform the contents using an ImageAttributes object that contains information about what kind of transformations to make. For example, one of the things you can do with an ImageAttributes class is to map colors:

```
void mappedColorsPanel_Paint(object sender, PaintEventArgs e) {
   Graphics g = e.Graphics;
   using( Bitmap bmp = new Bitmap(this.GetType(), "INTL_NO.BMP") ) {
      // Set the image attribute's color mappings
      ColorMap[] colorMap = new ColorMap[1];
      colorMap[0] = new ColorMap();
      colorMap[0].OldColor = Color.Lime;
      colorMap[0].NewColor = Color.White;
      ImageAttributes attr = new ImageAttributes();
      attr.SetRemapTable(colorMap);

      // Draw using the color map
      Rectangle rect = new Rectangle(0, 0, bmp.Width, bmp.Height);
      rect.Offset(...);
      g.DrawImage(
         bmp, rect, 0, 0, rect.Width, rect.Height, g.PageUnit, attr);
   }
}
```

This code first creates an array with a single ColorMap object, which contains the old color to transform from and the new color to transform to. The color map array is passed to a new ImageAttribute class via the SetRemapTable. The ImageAttribute object is then passed to the DrawImage function, which does the color mapping as the image is drawn. Figure 5.28 shows an example.

Figure 5.28   An Example of Mapping Color.Lime to Color.White

Notice that in addition to mapping the colors, the sample code uses the Width and Height properties of the Bitmap class. The Bitmap class, as well as the Image base class and the Metafile class, provides a great deal of information about the image.

Another useful piece of information is the color information at each pixel. For example, instead of hard-coding lime as the color, we could use the pixel information of the bitmap itself to pick the color to replace:

```
ColorMap[] colorMap = new ColorMap[1];
colorMap[0] = new ColorMap();
colorMap[0].OldColor = bmp.GetPixel(0, bmp.Height - 1);
colorMap[0].NewColor = Color.White;
```

In this case, we're mapping whatever color is at the bottom left as the pixel to replace. In addition to replacing colors, the ImageAttributes object can contain information about remapping palettes, setting gamma correction values, mapping color to grayscale, and other color-related options as well as the wrap mode (as with brushes).

Transparency

Unfortunately, simply mapping to white or any other color isn't useful if the image needs to be drawn on top of something else that you'd like to show through. For this case, a special color called Transparent allows the mapped color to disappear instead of being replaced with another color:

```
ColorMap[] colorMap = new ColorMap[1];
colorMap[0] = new ColorMap();
colorMap[0].OldColor = bmp.GetPixel(0, bmp.Height - 1);
colorMap[0].NewColor = Color.Transparent;
```

Figure 5.29 shows the effects of using Color.Transparent.

Figure 5.29   Using Color.Transparent in a Color Map

Again, I used the bottom-left pixel as the color to replace, the convention used in other parts of .NET. In fact, if you're going to always draw a bitmap with a transparent color and if the color to be made transparent is in the bitmap itself in the bottom-left pixel, you can save yourself the trouble of building a color map and instead use the MakeTransparent method:

```
// Make the bottom-left pixel the transparent color
bmp.MakeTransparent();
g.DrawImage(bmp, rect);
```

If the pixel you'd like to use as the transparency color isn't in the bottom left of the bitmap, you can also use the MakeTransparent overload, which takes a color as an argument. Calling MakeTransparent actually replaces the pixels of the transparency color with the Color.Transparent value. Some raster formats, such as the GIF and Windows icon formats, allow you to specify a transparency color value as one of their legal values. However, even if the raster format itself doesn't support a transparency color, all Bitmap objects, regardless of the raster format, support the MakeTransparent method.

Animation

Just as some raster formats support transparency as a native color, some also support animation. One in particular is the GIF format. Images expose support for animation by supporting more than one image in a single file. GIFs support animation by storing two or more images in an array that represents a time dimension, but other formats (such as TIFF files) can support different resolutions or multiple images as pages. You can count how many pages are in each "dimension" by calling the GetFrameCount method with FrameDimension objects exposed by properties from the FrameDimension class:

```
// Will throw exceptions if image format doesn't support
// multiple images along requested dimension
Bitmap gif = new Bitmap(typeof(AnimationForm), "animatedgif.gif");
int timeFrames = gif.GetFrameCount(FrameDimension.Time);
```

```
int pageFrames = gif.GetFrameCount(FrameDimension.Page);
int resolutionFrames =
  gif.GetFrameCount(FrameDimension.Resolution);
```

Selecting which frame to be displayed when the image is drawn is a matter of selecting the "active" frame along a dimension:

```
int frame = 4; // Needs to be between 0 and frame count -1
gif.SelectActiveFrame(FrameDimension.Time, frame);
g.DrawImage(gif, this.ClientRectangle);
```

In addition to the multiple frames, the GIF format encodes timing information for each frame. However, that's where things get tricky. Because different image formats support different information, the Image class exposes "extra" information via its GetPropertyItem method. This method takes a numeric ID and returns a generic PropertyItem object. The IDs themselves are defined only in a GDI+ header file and the PropertyItem object's Value property. The Value property exposes the actual data as an array of bytes that must be interpreted, making usage from .NET difficult. For example, here's how to get the timings for a GIF file:

```
// Get bytes describing each frame's time delay
int PropertyTagFrameDelay = 0x5100; // From GdiPlusImaging.h
PropertyItem prop = gif.GetPropertyItem(PropertyTagFrameDelay);
byte[] bytes = prop.Value;

// Convert bytes into an array of time delays
int frames = gif.GetFrameCount(FrameDimension.Time);
int[] delays = new int[frames];
for( int frame = 0; frame != frames; ++frame ) {
  // Convert each 4-byte chunk into an integer
  delays[frame] = BitConverter.ToInt32(bytes, frame * 4);
}
```

After you have the time delays, you can start a timer and use the SelectActiveFrame method to do the animation. If you do it that way, make sure to convert the delays to milliseconds ($\frac{1}{1000}$ second), which is what .NET timers like, from centiseconds ($\frac{1}{100}$ second), which is what GIF time delays are specified in. Or just use the ImageAnimator helper class, which can do all this for you:

```
// Load animated GIF
Bitmap gif = new Bitmap(@"c:\animatedgif.gif");

void AnimationForm_Load(object sender, EventArgs e) {
  ...
```

```
    // Check whether image supports animation
    if( ImageAnimator.CanAnimate(gif) ) {
      // Subscribe to an event indicating the next frame should be shown
      ImageAnimator.Animate(gif, gif_FrameChanged);
    }
    ...
  }

  void gif_FrameChanged(object sender, EventArgs e) {
    if( this.InvokeRequired ) {
      // Transition from worker thread to UI thread
      this.BeginInvoke(
        new EventHandler(gif_FrameChanged),
        new object[] { sender, e });
    }
    else {
        currentFrame++;
        this.toolStripStatusLabel1.Text =
          string.Format("Frame {0} of {1}", currentFrame, frameCount);
        if( currentFrame == frameCount ) currentFrame = 0;

      // Trigger Paint event to draw next frame
      this.Invalidate();
    }
  }

  void AnimationForm_Paint(object sender, PaintEventArgs e) {
    // Update image's current frame
    ImageAnimator.UpdateFrames(gif);

    // Draw image's active frame
    Graphics g = e.Graphics;
    Rectangle rect = this.ClientRectangle;
    rect.Height -= this.statusStrip1.Height;
    g.DrawImage(gif, rect);
  }
```

The ImageAnimator knows how to pull the timing information out of an image and call you back when it's time to show a new frame, which is what calling ImageAnimator.Animate does. When the event is fired, invalidating the rectangle being used to draw the animated GIF triggers the Paint event. The Paint event sets the next active frame by calling ImageAnimator.UpdateFrames before drawing the active frame. Figure 5.30 shows an image being animated.

Figure 5.30   Sample Animation, Showing First, Middle, and Last Frames

The only thing that's a bit tricky is that the animated event is called back on a worker thread, not on the main UI thread, because it's not legal for the former to make any method calls on objects executing from the latter, such as forms. To avoid breaking the law, we used the BeginInvoke method to transition back from the worker thread to the UI thread to make the call. This technique is discussed in gory detail in Chapter 18: Multithreaded User Interfaces.

Many of the animation capabilities discussed so far are automatically provided by the PictureBox control, which basically wraps the appropriate ImageAnimator method calls, such as Animate. All you need to do is set the PictureBox's Image property with an image that supports animation, and it takes care of the rest:

```
void AnimatedPictureBoxForm_Load(object sender, EventArgs e) {
   Bitmap gif = new Bitmap(@"c:\animatedgif.gif");
   this.animatedPictureBox.Image = gif; // Automatically begins animating
}
```

PictureBox is perfect if all you need is to simply animate your image. Unfortunately, PictureBox doesn't provide hooks into the animation process (as the FrameChanged event does). This means that you need to code directly against ImageAnimator for such support. However, some controls, including Button, Label, and ToolStripItem, do support animation natively. Simply set the control's Image property to the animated GIF directly:

```
this.animatedLabel.Image = Image.FromFile(@"c:\animatedgif.gif");
```

Drawing to Images

Certain kinds of applications need to create images on-the-fly, often requiring that they be saved to a file. The key is to create an image with the appropriate starting parameters, which for a Bitmap means the height, width, and pixel depth. The image is then used as the "backing store" of a Graphics object. If you're interested in getting the pixel depth from the screen itself, you can use a Graphics object when creating a Bitmap:

```
// Get current graphics object for display
Graphics displayGraphics = this.CreateGraphics();

// Create bitmap to draw into, based on existing Graphics object
Image image = new Bitmap(rect.Width, rect.Height, displayGraphics);
```

After you have an image, you can use the Graphics.FromImage method to wrap a Graphics object around it:

```
// Wrap Graphics object around image to draw into
Graphics imageGraphics = Graphics.FromImage(image);
```

After you have a Graphics object, you can draw on it as you would normally. One thing to watch out for, however, is that a Bitmap starts with all pixels set to the Transparent color. That may be exactly what you want, but if it's not, then a quick FillRectangle across the entire area of the Bitmap will set things right.

After you've done the drawing on the Graphics object that represents the image, you can draw that image to the screen or a printer, or you can save it to a file using the Save method of the Image class:

```
// Save created image to a file
image.Save(@"c:\image.png");
```

Unless otherwise specified, the file is saved in PNG format, regardless of the extension on the file name.[10] If you prefer to save it in another format, you can pass an instance of the ImageFormat class as an argument to the Save method. You create an instance of the ImageFormat class using the GUID (globally unique ID) of the format, but the ImageFormat class comes with several properties prebuilt for supported formats:

```
namespace System.Drawing.Imaging {
  sealed class ImageFormat {
    // Constructors
    public ImageFormat(Guid guid);

    // Properties
    public static ImageFormat Bmp { get; }
    public static ImageFormat Emf { get; }
    public static ImageFormat Exif { get; }
    public static ImageFormat Gif { get; }
```

---

[10] You might consider storing images in Portable Network Graphics (PNG) format because it is royalty-free, unlike the Graphics Interchange Format (GIF).

```
    public Guid Guid { get; }
    public static ImageFormat Icon { get; }
    public static ImageFormat Jpeg { get; }
    public static ImageFormat MemoryBmp { get; }
    public static ImageFormat Png { get; }
    public static ImageFormat Tiff { get; }
    public static ImageFormat Wmf { get; }
  }
}
```

As an example of creating images on-the-fly and saving them to a file, the following code builds the bitmap shown in Figure 5.31:

```
void saveButton_Click(object sender, EventArgs e) {
  Rectangle rect = new Rectangle(0, 0, 100, 100);

  // Get current graphics object for display
  using( Graphics displayGraphics = this.CreateGraphics() )

  // Create bitmap to draw into based on existing Graphics object
  using( Image image =
    new Bitmap(rect.Width, rect.Height, displayGraphics) )

  // Wrap Graphics object around image to draw into
  using( Graphics imageGraphics = Graphics.FromImage(image) ) {

    imageGraphics.FillRectangle(Brushes.Black, rect);
    imageGraphics.DrawString("Drawing to an image", ... );

    // Save created image to a file
    image.Save(@"c:\image.png");
  }
}
```

Figure 5.31   Example of Drawing to an Image

Screen Copying

 Some applications need to copy a portion of the screen to either save to file or to copy to an image-editing application for further processing. The Graphics object now implements the CopyFromScreen methods to help you do just that. The basic process is to define an area of the screen to copy from, create a copy target, copy from the screen to the target, and do something with it. The following example copies the entire screen to a Bitmap that is then scaled and displayed in a picture box control:

```
void captureButton_Click(object sender, EventArgs e) {
  // Dump screen to bitmap
  Rectangle screenRect = Screen.PrimaryScreen.WorkingArea;
  Bitmap dumpBitmap = new Bitmap(screenRect.Width, screenRect.Height);
  using( Graphics targetGraphics = Graphics.FromImage(dumpBitmap) ) {
    targetGraphics.CopyFromScreen(
      0, 0, 0, 0, new Size(dumpBitmap.Width, dumpBitmap.Height));
  }

  // Display screen dump
  this.screenPictureBox.BackgroundImage = dumpBitmap;
  this.screenPictureBox.BackgroundImageLayout = ImageLayout.Stretch;
}
```

Although this technique allows you to capture any area of the screen, you can use a more granular approach that relies on the DrawToBitmap method, implemented by Control. The DrawToBitmap method encapsulates the work of copying any portion of a control's UI to a bitmap, including resource management. And because DrawToBitmap is implemented by Control, and because controls, container controls, user controls, and forms all derive from Control, you can enjoy the benefit of inheritance:

```
void captureButton_Click(object sender, EventArgs e) {
  // Dump form UI to a bitmap
  Rectangle rect =
    new Rectangle(0, 0, form.Size.Width, form.Size.Height);
  Bitmap dumpBitmap = new Bitmap(form.Size.Width, form.Size.Height);
  form.DrawToBitmap(dumpBitmap, rect);

  // Display screen dump
  this.screenPictureBox.BackgroundImage = dumpBitmap;
  this.screenPictureBox.BackgroundImageLayout = ImageLayout.Stretch;
}
```

This example invokes DrawToBitmap on a form, capturing the entire form area and displaying it to a picture box control.

Icons

Before I wrap up the images section, I want to mention two kinds of images for which .NET provides special care: icons and cursors. You can load a Windows icon (.ico) file directly into an Icon object. The Icon class is largely a direct wrapper class around the Win32 HICON type and is provided mainly for interoperability. Unlike the Bitmap or Metafile class, the Icon class doesn't derive from the base Image class:

updated

```
namespace System.Drawing {
    sealed class Icon : IDisposable, ... {
        // Constructors
        public Icon(Stream stream);
        public Icon(string fileName);
        public Icon(Icon original, Size size);
        public Icon(Stream stream, Size size); // New
        public Icon(string fileName, Size size); // New
        public Icon(Type type, string resource);
        public Icon(Icon original, int width, int height);
        public Icon(Stream stream, int width, int height);
        public Icon(string fileName, int width, int height); // New

        // Properties
        public IntPtr Handle { get; }
        public int Height { get; }
        public Size Size { get; }
        public int Width { get; }

        // Methods
        public static Icon ExtractAssociatedIcon(string filePath); // New
        public static Icon FromHandle(IntPtr handle);
        public void Save(Stream outputStream);
        public Bitmap ToBitmap();
    }
}
```

When setting the Icon property of a Form, for example, you use the Icon class, not the Bitmap class. Icons support construction from files and resources as well as from raw streams (if you want to create an icon from data in memory) and expose their Height and Width. For interoperability with Win32, Icons also support the Handle property and the FromHandle method. FromHandle is particularly useful if you need to convert a Bitmap to an Icon:

```
void ConvertBitmapToIcon() {
    // Get source bitmap
    Bitmap bitmap = new Bitmap(@"c:\windows\soap bubbles.bmp");

    // Get source bitmap's icon handle
    IntPtr hIcon = bitmap.GetHicon();

    // Convert bitmap to icon
    Icon icon = Icon.FromHandle(hIcon);

    this.Icon = icon;
}
```

On the other hand, creating a Bitmap from an Icon is as simple as calling Icon's ToBitmap method, which copies the data to a new Bitmap object. After you've loaded an icon, you can draw it to a Graphics object using the DrawIcon or DrawIconUnstretched method:

```
Icon ico = new Icon("POINT10.ICO");
g.DrawIcon(ico, this.ClientRectangle); // Stretch
g.DrawIconUnstretched(ico, this.ClientRectangle); // Don't stretch
```

As well as stand-alone .ico files, icons can be compiled into assemblies as resources. To acquire the first icon resource from an assembly (index 0), you can pull it out using Icon's ExtractAssociatedIcon method:[11]

```
Icon icon = Icon.ExtractAssociatedIcon(@"c:\windows\notepad.exe");
```

Several icons used by the system come prepackaged for you as properties of the SystemIcons class for your own use, as shown in Figure 5.32.

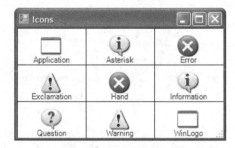

Figure 5.32   Icon Properties from the SystemIcons Class as Shown Under Windows XP

Cursors

The other Win32 graphics type that Windows Forms provides is the Cursor type. As with icons, Cursor doesn't derive from the Image base class:

```
namespace System.Windows.Forms {
  sealed class Cursor : IDisposable, ... {
    // Constructors
    public Cursor(IntPtr handle);
    public Cursor(Stream stream);
    public Cursor(string fileName);
    public Cursor(Type type, string resource);

    // Properties
    public static Rectangle Clip { get; set; }
    public static Cursor Current { get; set; }
```

[11] Icon contains a static overload of ExtractAssociatedIcon that accepts an additional index argument, although, for no apparent reason, it is marked as private.

```
    public IntPtr Handle { get; }
    public Point HotSpot { get; } // New
    public static Point Position { get; set; }
    public Size Size { get; }
    public object Tag { get; set; } // New

    // Methods
    public IntPtr CopyHandle();
    public void Draw(Graphics g, Rectangle targetRect);
    public void DrawStretched(Graphics g, Rectangle targetRect);
    public static void Hide();
    public static void Show();
  }
}
```

A Cursor is a graphic that represents the position of the mouse on the screen. It can take on several values based on the needs of the window currently under the cursor. For example, by default, the cursor is an arrow to indicate that it should be used to point. However, when the cursor passes over a text-editing window, it often turns into an I-beam to provide for better positioning between characters. Cursors also have a *hot spot*, which is the pixel in the icon image that actually cause an action. For example, the hot spot of the default arrow cursor is in the tip of the arrow, and that is why you can't click or double-click using the arrow's tail.

A cursor can be loaded from one of the system-provided cursors in the Cursors class, as shown in Figure 5.33.[12]

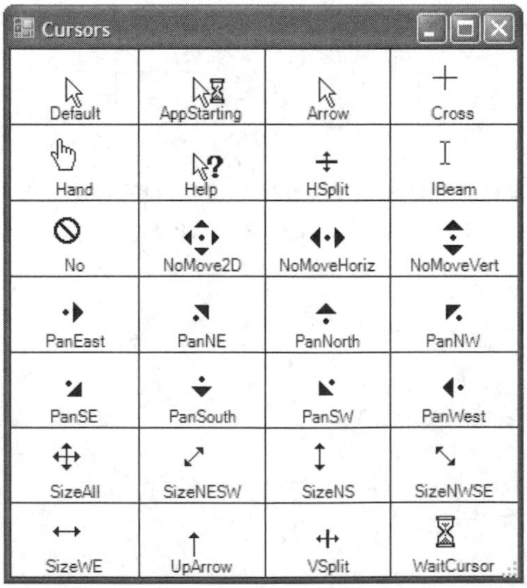

Figure 5.33 System Cursors from the Cursors Class

[12] Note that .ani files are not supported.

You can draw a cursor manually using the Draw or DrawStretched method of the Cursor class, but most of the time you draw a cursor by setting it as the current cursor using the static Current property of the Cursor class. Setting the current cursor remains in effect only during the current event handler and only when the cursor is over windows of that application. Changing the cursor doesn't stop another window in another application from changing it to something it finds appropriate. For example, the following code changes the application's cursor to the WaitCursor during a long operation:

```
void CursorsForm_Click(object sender, EventArgs e) {
   try {
      // Change the cursor to indicate that we're waiting
      Cursor.Current = Cursors.WaitCursor;

      // Do something that takes a long time...
   }
   finally {
      // Restore current cursor
      Cursor.Current = this.Cursor;
   }

} // Cursor restored after this event handler anyway...
```

Notice the use of the form's Cursor property to restore the current cursor after the long operation completes. Every form and every control has a Cursor property. This cursor becomes the default when the mouse passes over the window. For example, the following code sets a form's default cursor to the Cross:

```
// CursorsForm.Designer.cs
partial class CursorsForm {
   ...
   void InitializeComponent() {
      ...
      this.Cursor = System.Windows.Forms.Cursors.Cross;
      ...
   }
}
```

Notice the use of InitializeComponent to set the Form's cursor, indicating that this is yet another property that can be set in the Properties window, which shows a drop-down list of all the system-provided cursors to choose from.

Using Animated and Colored Cursors

Beyond the black-and-white cursors available from the Cursors class, the cursor world is full of color and animation. Typically, colored and animated cursors are created in third-party applications and are generated as .cur and .ani files, respectively. Unfortunately, you can't create a Cursor object using either of these file types directly. Instead, you must call the LoadCursorFromFile User32 API function to load them and return a handle with which you can instantiate a Cursor. The following code shows how (for animated cursors):

```csharp
// AnimatedCursorForm.cs
using System.Runtime.InteropServices;
...
partial class AnimatedAndColoredCursorsForm : Form {

    [DllImport("user32.dll")]
    static extern IntPtr LoadCursorFromFile(string lpFileName);

    static Cursor ColoredCursor;
    static Cursor AnimatedCursor;

    static AnimatedAndColoredCursorsForm() {
        // Load animated cursor
        IntPtr cursor =
            LoadCursorFromFile(@"c:\windows\cursors\hourglas.ani");
        AnimatedCursor = new Cursor(cursor);

        // Load colored cursor
        IntPtr cursor =
            LoadCursorFromFile(@"c:\windows\cursors\3dgarro.cur");
        ColoredCursor = new Cursor(cursor);
    }

    public AnimatedAndColoredCursorsForm() {
        InitializeComponent();
    }

    void Form_MouseEnter(object sender, EventArgs e) {
        this.Cursor = this.ColoredCursor;
    }

    void Form_MouseLeave(object sender, EventArgs e) {
        this.Cursor = Cursors.Default;
    }

    void ALongRunningOperation() {
        this.Cursor = this.AnimatedCursor;
        ...
        this.Cursor = Cursors.Default;
    }
}
```

Animated and colored cursors are a nice option when your application needs a visual flavor not afforded by the standard cursors.

Where Are We?

In this chapter, we've discussed the basics of drawing, including colors, brushes, pens, shapes, paths, and images. Of course, that's not all you need to know about drawing in your Windows Forms applications and controls. Chapter 6: Drawing Text is dedicated to fonts and drawing strings.

▪6▪

Drawing Text

P ROBABLY THE MOST USEFUL THING to draw in any application is text. Sometimes, you draw text yourself and, sometimes, text is drawn for you by the controls you're using. No matter who does the drawing, you can often specify the font, and that's what the first part of this chapter is about. The second part deals with drawing text yourself into a Graphics object, into a GraphicsPath object, or via the TextRenderer.

Fonts

A *font* is an instance of the System.Drawing.Font class, which for each font includes a family, a style, and a size. And, as you might expect, a *font family* is an instance of the FontFamily class, which encapsulates a group of typefaces that differ only in style. A *typeface* is a named collection of drawing strokes that make up the outlines of the characters, such as those you're reading right now. It's the typeface name that you're used to seeing in the "Font" menu of most programs. The *font style* constitutes the variations within a typeface, such as bold, italics, underline, and size. So, a typeface would be Arial, a font family would include Arial Regular and Arial Bold, and a font would be 12-point Arial Bold.

Fonts can be measured in several sizes other than points, including pixels, ems, and design units. A *pixel* is a point of light on a screen or a point of ink on a printer. Pixels are often packed into inches for measurement. For example, the resolution of video display adapters and printers is typically specified in *dots per inch* (dpi), where a dot is the same as a pixel. Pixels are device-dependent, so a pixel on a 72-dpi display bears no size relationship to a pixel on a 300-dpi printer.

A point, on the other hand, is $\frac{1}{72}$ inch no matter what device it's drawn on, and the Graphics object scales appropriately as text is drawn. If you want to ensure that a font is rendered to the target device in the correct size, you need to convert between points and pixels. This requires knowing the dpi of the device you're drawing on, which is conveniently available via the Graphics.DpiY property:[1]

```
using( Graphics g = this.CreateGraphics() ) {
    // A 12-point font is 16 pixels high on a 96-dpi monitor
    float dpi = g.DpiY;
    float points = 12f;
    float pixels = (points * dpi)/72f; //=16f
    ...
}
```

The *em* unit of measure is so named because metal typesetters used uppercase *M* as the guide against which all other letters were measured. *M* was used because it took up the most vertical and horizontal space. Consequently, the number of points specified for a font represents "one em" for that font.

Finally, *design units* are a font designer's way to specify a font family's dimensions regardless of the resolution of the rendering device or the size of the rendered font. For example, Arial has a height of 2,048 design units. The design units are used to scale a font family to a point size when individual strokes of the font are rendered (more on this later).

The Font class is shown here:

```
namespace System.Drawing {
    sealed class Font : IDisposable, ... {

    // Constructors
    public Font(...); // Several overloads

      // Properties
      public bool Bold { get; }
      public FontFamily FontFamily { get; }
      public byte GdiCharSet { get; }
      public bool GdiVerticalFont { get; }
      public int Height { get; }
      public bool IsSystemFont { get; } // New
      public bool Italic { get; }
      public string Name { get; }
      public float Size { get; }
      public float SizeInPoints { get; }
      public bool Strikeout { get; }
      public FontStyle Style { get; }
      public string SystemFontName { get; } // New
      public bool Underline { get; }
      public GraphicsUnit Unit { get; }
```

updated

[1] There's also a Graphics.DpiX property, but that's used for measuring width and is not useful as related to font height.

```
        // Methods
        public static Font FromHdc(IntPtr hdc);
        public static Font FromHfont(IntPtr hfont);
        public static Font FromLogFont(...);
        public float GetHeight(...);
        public IntPtr ToHfont();
        public void ToLogFont(...);
    }
}
```

Creating Fonts

You can create a Font object by specifying, at a minimum, the typeface and the size in points:

```
using( Font font = new Font("Arial", 12) ) {...}
```

If you specify a font that's not available, you get an instance of the MS Sans Serif font in the size you specify. To specify the font in a unit other than points, you use an overload of the Font constructor that takes a value from the GraphicsUnit enumeration:

```
namespace System.Drawing {
    enum GraphicsUnit {
        World = 0, // discussed in Chapter 7: Advanced Drawing
        Display = 1, // 1/75 inch (1/100 inch for printers)
        Pixel = 2, // 1 device-dependent pixel
        Point = 3, // 1/72 inch
        Inch = 4, // 1 inch
        Document = 5, // 1/300 inch
        Millimeter = 6, // 1 millimeter
    }
}
```

Except for GraphicsUnit.Pixel and GraphicsUnit.World, all the units are variations of a point, because they're all specified in device-independent units. Using these units, all the following specify 12-point Arial:[2]

```
// Can't use GraphicsUnit.Display for creating font
// because Display varies based on where shapes are drawn
Font font1 = new Font("Arial", 12, GraphicsUnit.Point);
Font font2 = new Font("Arial", 16, GraphicsUnit.Pixel);
Font font3 = new Font("Arial", 0.1666667f, GraphicsUnit.Inch);
Font font4 = new Font("Arial", 50, GraphicsUnit.Document);
Font font5 = new Font("Arial", 4.233334f, GraphicsUnit.Millimeter);
```

---

[2] A dpi of 96 is assumed, which yields 16 pixels for a 12-point font.

To specify a style other than regular, you pass a combination of the values from the FontStyle enumeration:

```
namespace System.Drawing {
   enum FontStyle {
      Regular = 0, // default
      Bold = 1,
      Italic = 2,
      Underline = 4,
      Strikeout = 8,
   }
}
```

For example, the following creates Arial Bold Italic:

```
Font font = new Font("Arial", 12, FontStyle.Bold | FontStyle.Italic);
```

If the font family you're specifying with the typeface argument to the Font constructor doesn't support the styles you specify, a run-time exception is thrown.

If you have a font but you don't like the style, you can create a Font based on another Font. This is handy when you'd like to base a new font on an existing font but need to make a minor adjustment:

```
Font font = new Font(this.Font, FontStyle.Bold | FontStyle.Italic);
```

Note that you can't set font properties like Bold and Italic directly on a Font object because they are read-only.

Font Families

When creating a font, you use the typeface name to retrieve a font family from the list of fonts currently installed on the system. The typeface name is passed to the constructor of the FontFamily class. The FontFamily class is shown here:

```
namespace System.Drawing {
   sealed class FontFamily : IDisposable, ... {
      // Constructors
      public FontFamily(GenericFontFamilies genericFamily);
      public FontFamily(string name);
      public FontFamily(string name, FontCollection fontCollection);

      // Properties
      public static FontFamily[] Families { get; }
      public static FontFamily GenericMonospace { get; }
      public static FontFamily GenericSansSerif { get; }
```

```
    public static FontFamily GenericSerif { get; }
    public string Name { get; }

    // Methods
    public int GetCellAscent(FontStyle style);
    public int GetCellDescent(FontStyle style);
    public int GetEmHeight(FontStyle style);
    public static FontFamily[] GetFamilies(Graphics graphics);
    public int GetLineSpacing(FontStyle style);
    public string GetName(int language);
    public bool IsStyleAvailable(FontStyle style);
  }
}
```

Creating a Font from a FontFamily looks like this:

```
FontFamily family = new FontFamily("Arial");
Font font = new Font(family, 12, FontStyle.Bold | FontStyle.Italic);
```

Creating a Font from a FontFamily object is useful if you'd like to pick a font family based on general characteristics instead of a specific typeface name. You can construct a FontFamily using one of several values provided by the GenericFontFamilies enumeration:

```
namespace System.Drawing.Text {
   enum GenericFontFamilies {
      Serif = 0, // Times New Roman
      SansSerif = 1, // Microsoft Sans Serif
      Monospace = 2, // Courier New
   }
}
```

Constructing a FontFamily using a value from GenericFontFamilies is useful if you'd like to avoid the risk that a more specific font won't be available on the system. In fact, the FontFamily class even provides properties that you can use directly for each of these FontFamilies:

```
// The hard way
Font font1 = new Font(new FontFamily(GenericFontFamilies.Serif), 12);

// The easy way
Font font2 = new Font(FontFamily.GenericMonospace, 12);
```

To let users pick their favorite font instead of hard-coding a font family (even a generic one), you present a UI that lets them pick from the font families they have installed. The

FontFamily class provides the Families property for determining the currently installed font families:

```
foreach( FontFamily family in FontFamily.Families ) {
   // Can filter based on available styles
   if( !family.IsStyleAvailable(FontStyle.Bold) ) continue;

   familiesListBox.Items.Add(family.Name);
}
```

You can also construct a Font object from an HDC, an HFONT, or a LOGFONT, all features that support interoperability with Win32.

System Fonts

One special subset of all the font families installed on your computer is the *system fonts*, those fonts that are the same for all specific Windows UI items such as the active form's title bar. You can configure system fonts from the Advanced Appearance dialog (Control Panel | Display | Appearance | Advanced), as shown in Figure 6.1.

Figure 6.1   Setting Systemwide Fonts

System fonts are automatically used by Windows Forms, but sometimes you may require system font information for your own purposes, such as building a custom control (see Chapter 10: Controls). In these cases, you should use the SystemFonts class, which exposes a subset of eight of the system fonts you can set via Display Properties as static properties:

```
namespace System.Drawing {
  sealed class SystemFonts {
    // Properties
    public static Font CaptionFont { get; }
    public static Font DefaultFont { get; }
    public static Font DialogFont { get; }
    public static Font IconTitleFont { get; }
    public static Font MenuFont { get; }
    public static Font MessageBoxFont { get; }
    public static Font SmallCaptionFont { get; }
    public static Font StatusFont { get; }

    // Methods
    public static Font GetFontByName(string systemFontName);
  }
}
```

Figure 6.2 shows each of the SystemFont properties along with the default Windows XP fonts to which they map.

Figure 6.2   Windows XP Default SystemFonts

Unlike other System*Xxx* classes, SystemFonts aren't cached by .NET, so you must dispose of any you use:

```
using( Font systemFont = SystemFonts.CaptionFont ) {
  // Draw some text
  ...
}
```

Font Characteristics

Whichever way you get a Font object, after you have it, you can interrogate it for all kinds of properties, such as its family, its name (which is the same as the family name), and a couple of GDI properties for Win32 interoperability. Most importantly, you probably want to know about a font's style, using either the Style property of type FontStyle or using individual properties:

```
// The hard way
bool bold1 = (this.Font.Style & FontStyle.Bold) == FontStyle.Bold;


// The easy way
bool bold2 = this.Font.Bold;
```

Another important characteristic of a Font is its dimensions. The width of a character in a specific font varies from character to character, unless you've used a *monospace* font such as Courier New, in which all characters are padded as necessary so that they're the same width. The Graphics object provides the MeasureString method for measuring the maximum size of a string of characters of a specific font:

```
using( Graphics g = this.CreateGraphics() ) {
    SizeF size = g.MeasureString("Howdy", this.Font);
    float length = size.Width;
}
```

When it's called this way, MeasureString assumes that the string is clipped to a single line; this means that the width varies with the width of the string, but the height is a constant.[3] Because the Graphics object can wrap multiline strings to a rectangle, you can also measure the rectangle needed for a multiline string. You do this by calling the Measure-String method and specifying a maximum layout rectangle for the string to live in:

```
SizeF layoutArea = this.ClientRectangle.Size;
// New line character '\n' forces text to next line
string s = "a string that will\ntake at least two lines";
SizeF size = g.MeasureString(s, this.Font, layoutArea);
```

The Width property returned in the SizeF object is the width of the longest wrapped line, and the Height is the number of lines needed to show the string multiplied by the height of the font (up to the maximum height specified in the layout area). The height used as the multiplier isn't the height of the font as specified. For example, 12 points would be 16 pixels at 96 dpi, but that's not the value that's used. Instead, the height is approximately 115% of that, or about 18.4 pixels for a 12-point font at 96 dpi. This expanded value is

---

[3] Although individual character heights vary, the vertical space reserved for them does not.

exposed from the Font.GetHeight method and is meant to maximize readability when lines of text are drawn one after another. For example, if you wanted to handle wrapping yourself, you could lay out text one line at a time, incrementing the y value by the result of Font.GetHeight:

```
foreach( string line in
    multiline.Split(Environment.NewLine.ToCharArray()) ) {

    float width = manualPanel.ClientRectangle.Width;
    float height = manualPanel.ClientRectangle.Height - y;
    RectangleF layoutRect = new RectangleF(0, y, width, height);

    // Turn off autowrapping (we're doing it manually)
    using( StringFormat format =
      new StringFormat(StringFormatFlags.NoWrap) ) {
      g.DrawString(line, this.Font, Brushes.Black, layoutRect, format);
      ...
      // Get ready for the next line
      y += this.Font.GetHeight(g);
    }
}
```

In this code, we split the string into multiple lines using the embedded new line characters, just as DrawString does when it does the wrapping for us. We also set up a StringFormat (more about that later) that turns off wrapping; otherwise, DrawString wraps at word boundaries for us. After we draw the string at our chosen rectangle, we increment y by the result of Font.GetHeight so that the next line of text is far enough below the text we just drew to make it pleasing to read. Figure 6.3 shows what DrawString would do with a multiline string automatically, and what our manual code does.

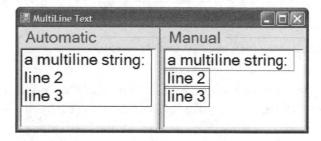

Figure 6.3   Automatic Word Wrap Performed by DrawString
Compared with Manual Word Wrap Using Font.GetHeight

In addition to the strings, Figure 6.3 shows the rectangles obtained by measuring each string: one rectangle when DrawString wraps the text for us, and one rectangle per line when we do it ourselves. Notice also that the rectangle produced by MeasureString is a bit bigger than it needs to be to draw the text. This is especially evident in the overlapping rectangles shown on the manual side. MeasureString is guaranteed to produce a size that's big enough to hold the string but sometimes produces a size that's larger than it needs to be to meet that guarantee.

Font Height

While we're on the subject of font height, it turns out that there are a lot of ways to measure the height of a font. The Font class provides not only the GetHeight method but also the Size property, which stores the base size provided in the units passed to the Font object's constructor (the GraphicsUnit value specified at construction time is available via the Font's Unit property).[4] As I mentioned, the height of a font is determined from the base size. The height of the font is further broken down into three parts called *cell ascent, cell descent*, and *leading* (so named because typesetters used to use strings of lead to separate lines of text and prevent letters from touching each other). Two of these three measures are available in design units from the FontFamily class (available via the Font's FontFamily property) and are shown in Figure 6.4. Together, these three values make up the *line spacing*, which is also provided as a property on FontFamily and is used to calculate the font's height and leading (leading isn't available directly).

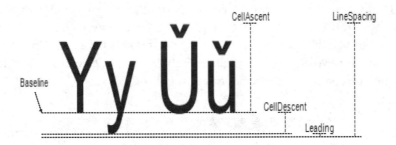

Figure 6.4   The Parts of a Font Family's Height

The line spacing is expressed in design units but is used at run time to determine the result of calling Font.GetHeight. The magic of the conversion between design units and pixels is managed by one more measure available from the FontFamily class: the em height. The *em height* is a logical value but is equivalent to the font's size in points, so scaling between design units and pixels is performed using the proportion between the font's size

---

[4] The Font also provides a Height property, but it should be avoided in favor of the GetHeight method. The GetHeight method scales to a specified Graphics object, whereas the Height property scales only to the current video adapter's dpi, making it largely worthless for anything except the nontransformed video adapter.

and the font family's em height. For example, the scaling factor between Arial's em height (2,048) and its 12-point pixel height (16 at 96 dpi) is 128. Dividing Arial's line spacing (2,355) by 128 yields 18.39844, which is the same as the result of calling GetHeight on 12-point Arial at 96 dpi. Table 6.1 shows the various measures of font and font family height.

Table 6.1 Font and FontFamily Sizes (Sample Font Is Arial 12 Point at 96 dpi)

Measure	Units	Example	Description
FontFamily.GetEmHeight	Design Units	2,048	Base size, equivalent to Size
FontFamily.GetCellAscent	Design Units	1,854	Height above base line
FontFamily.GetCellDescent	Design Units	434	Height below base line
FontFamily.GetLineSpacing	Design Units	2,355	CellAscent + CellDescent + Leading, normally about 115% of EmHeight
Leading	Design Units	67	Extra space below bottom of CellDescent for readability, not exposed by any property
Font.Size	GraphicsUnit passed to Font ctor (defaults to Point)	16 pixels	Base size, equivalent to EmHeight
Font.SizeInPoints	Points	12 points	Base size in points, equivalent to Size and EmHeight
Font.GetHeight	Pixels	18.39844	Equivalent to LineSpacing scaled to either Graphics object or dpi
Font.Height	Pixels	19	Equivalent to LineSpacing scaled to system dpi and rounded to next highest integer value
Scaling Factor	Design Unit or Pixels	128	Used to convert design units to physical or logical values for rendering

Strings

Of course, deciding on a font is only half the fun. The real action is drawing strings after a font has been picked. For that, you use the DrawString method of the Graphics object:

```
using( Font font = new Font("Arial", 12) ) {
   // This wraps at new line characters
   g.DrawString("line 1\nline 2", font, Brushes.Black, 10, 10);
}
```

The DrawString method takes, at a minimum, a string, a font, a brush to fill in the font characters, and a point. DrawString starts the drawing at the point and keeps going until it hits the edges of the region in the Graphics object. This includes translating new line characters as appropriate but does not include wrapping at word boundaries. To get the wrapping, you specify a layout rectangle:

```
using( Font font = new Font("Arial", 12) ) {
   // This automatically wraps long lines and
   // it wraps at new line characters
   g.DrawString("A long string ...", font, Brushes.Black,
      this.ClientRectangle);
}
```

Formatting

If you'd like to turn off wrapping or set other formatting options, you use an instance of the StringFormat class:

```
namespace System.Drawing {
   sealed class StringFormat : IDisposable, ... {

      // Constructors
      public StringFormat(...); // various overloads

   // Properties
      public StringAlignment Alignment { get; set; }
      public int DigitSubstitutionLanguage { get; }
      public StringDigitSubstitute DigitSubstitutionMethod { get; }
      public StringFormatFlags FormatFlags { get; set; }
      public static StringFormat GenericDefault { get; }
      public static StringFormat GenericTypographic { get; }
      public HotkeyPrefix HotkeyPrefix { get; set; }
      public StringAlignment LineAlignment { get; set; }
      public StringTrimming Trimming { get; set; }
```

```
      // Methods
      public float[] GetTabStops(out float firstTabOffset);
      public void SetDigitSubstitution(
         int language, StringDigitSubstitute substitute);
      public void SetMeasurableCharacterRanges(CharacterRange[] ranges);
      public void SetTabStops(float firstTabOffset, float[] tabStops);
   }
}
```

A StringFormat object lets you set all kinds of interesting text characteristics, such as the tab stops and the alignment (vertically and horizontally) as well as whether to wrap. Because StringFormat implements IDisposable, you create it inside a *using* statement:

```
// Turn off autowrapping
using( StringFormat format =
   new StringFormat(StringFormatFlags.NoWrap) ) {
   g.DrawString("...", font, brush, rect, format);
}
```

The StringFormatFlags enumeration provides a number of additional formatting options:

```
namespace System.Drawing {
   enum StringFormatFlags {
      0, // No flags (default)
      DirectionRightToLeft = 1, // Draw text right-to-left
      DirectionVertical = 2, // Draw text top-to-bottom
      FitBlackBox = 4, // Characters can overhang the layout rectangle5
      DisplayFormatControl = 32, // Show format control character glyphs6
      NoFontFallback = 1024, // Don't fall back for characters missing
                             // from font
      MeasureTrailingSpaces = 2048, // MeasureString includes trailing spaces
      NoWrap = 4096, // Don't interpret \n or \t (implied when no rect)
      LineLimit = 8192, // Show only whole lines
      NoClip = 16384, // Don't clip text partially outside
                      // layout rectangle
   }
}
```

[5] You would think that FitBlackBox implies characters *can't* overhang, but this is not the case, as stated in the installed version of the MSDN Library: "The FitBlackBox field was misnamed and its behavior is similar to the NoFitBlackBox field in the original GDI+ implementation."

[6] In this context, a *glyph* is a symbol that conveys information that can't be conveyed by normal letters, numbers, and punctuation, like the additional characters that are displayed when formatting is shown in a Word document.

You can combine and set one or more StringFormatFlags on a StringFormat object by using either the StringFormat constructor or the FormatFlags property. For example, the following draws text top-to-bottom and disables automatic wrapping:

```
using( StringFormat format = new StringFormat() ) {
  format.FormatFlags = StringFormatFlags.DirectionVertical |
                       StringFormatFlags.NoWrap;
  g.DrawString("...", font, brush, rect, format);
}
```

If the string is too tall to fit into the allotted space, you have three choices. You can clip to the layout rectangle, letting partial lines show, which is the default. You can show only complete lines if they fit inside the layout rectangle—the behavior you get with String-FormatFlags.LineLimit. Finally, you can decide to show complete lines even if they lie outside the layout rectangle, which is what you get with StringFormatFlags.NoClip. Combining LineLimit with NoClip is not useful, because the behavior is the same as LineLimit. The three options are shown in Figure 6.5.

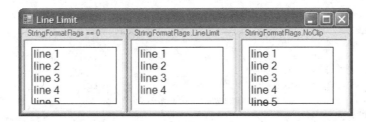

Figure 6.5   The Effect of the LineLimit StringFormatFlags Value

String Trimming

If, on the other hand, the string is too long, you can dictate what happens by setting the Trimming property of the StringFormat object to one of the StringTrimming enumeration values:

```
namespace System.Drawing {
  enum StringTrimming {
    None = 0, // No trimming (acts like Word for single lines)
    Character = 1, // Trim to nearest character (the default)
    Word = 2, // Trim to nearest word
    EllipsisCharacter = 3, // Trim to nearest character
                           // and show ellipsis
    EllipsisWord = 4, // Trim to nearest word and show ellipsis
    EllipsisPath = 5, // Trim file path by putting ellipsis
                      // in the middle
  }
}
```

Figure 6.6 shows the results of applying the StringTrimming values when you draw a string.

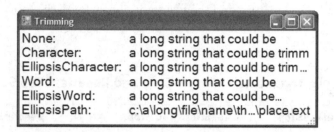

Figure 6.6   Examples of the StringTrimming Enumeration

Tab Stops

Something else of interest in Figure 6.6 is the use of tabs to line up the string, instead of forcing the text to be in a monospaced font and aligning the text with space characters. You set tabs using the SetTabStops method of the StringFormat class:

```
using( StringFormat format = new StringFormat() ) {
    SizeF size =
      g.MeasureString(
        StringTrimming.EllipsisCharacter.ToString(), this.Font);
    format.SetTabStops(0, new float[] { size.Width + 10 });
}
```

This call to SetTabStops sets a single tab stop to be the width of the longest string, plus a pleasing amount of padding. When tab stops are specified and when StringFormat-Flags.NoWrap is absent from the StringFormat object, then the tab character (ASCII 9 or "\t") causes the characters that follow to be drawn starting at the tab stop offset (unless the string has already passed that point). If the StringFormat object has not been given any tab stops, then the tab character is not interpreted. If DrawString is called without any String-Format object at all, it builds one internally that defaults tab width to four times the size of the font; for example, a 12-point font will have tab stops every 48 points.

There are several ways to specify tab stops logically. For example, imagine that you'd like a tab stop at every 48 units, as DrawString does by default when no StringFormat is provided. You might also imagine that you'd like to specify only a certain number of tab stops at specific locations. Finally, you might imagine that you'd like to have an array of tab stops but use an offset determined at run time to calculate the actual tab stops. All these techniques are supported, but you must use a single SetTabStops method, and that makes things somewhat unintuitive.

The array of floating-point values passed to set the tab stops represents the spaces between successive tab stops. The first value in this array is added to the first argument to

SetTabStops to get the first tab stop, and each successive value is added to the preceding value to get the next tab stop. Finally, when more tabs are found than tab stops, the last value of the array is added repeatedly to get successive tab stops. Table 6.2 shows various arguments passed to SetTabStops and the resultant offsets for each stop.

Table 6.2   Sample Arguments to SetTabStop and Resultant Tab Stops

Arguments to SetTabStop	Resultant Tab Stops	Description
0, { 100 }	100, 200, 300, . . .	Tab stops every 100 units
0, { 100, 0 }	100, 100, 100, . . .	One tab stop at 100 units
0, { 50, 75, 100 }	50, 125, 225, 325, 425, . . .	A tab stop at 50, 125, and 225 and then one every 100 units
0, { 50, 75, 100, 0 }	50, 125, 225, 225, 225, . . .	A tab stop at 50, 125, and 225 units
50, { 100 }	150, 250, 350, . . .	One tab stop at 150 units and then one every 100 units
50, { 100, 0 }	150, 150, 150, . . .	One tab stop at 150 units
50, { 50, 75, 100 }	100, 175, 275, 375, 475, . . .	A tab stop at 100, 175, and 275 and then one every 100 units
50, { 50, 75, 100, 0 }	100, 175, 275, 275, 275, . . .	A tab stop at 100, 175, and 275 units

You may have noticed the GetTabStops method on the StringFormat class, but unfortunately it hands back only the same tab stop settings handed to SetTabStops in the first place. It would have been handy to get back the resultant tab stops so that you could make sure you've set them correctly.

Hotkey Prefixes

In addition to new lines and tab characters, DrawString can substitute other characters, including ampersands and digits. Substitution of ampersands is a convenience for specifying Windows hotkeys for menu items and form fields. For example, by default the string

"&File" is output as "&File" (but without the quotation marks). However, you can specify that the ampersand be dropped or that the next character be underlined, as governed by the HotkeyPrefix enumeration:

```
namespace System.Drawing.Text {
  enum HotkeyPrefix {
    None = 0, // Show all & characters (default)
    Show = 1, // Drop & characters and underline next character
    Hide = 2, // Drop all & characters
  }
}
```

For example, the following translates "&File" into "File" (no quotation marks) as the string is drawn:

```
using( StringFormat format = new StringFormat() ) {
  format.HotkeyPrefix = HotkeyPrefix.Show;
  g.DrawString("&File", font, brush, rect, format);
}
```

Digit Substitution

One other substitution that DrawString can perform is for digits. Most languages have adopted the Arabic digits (0, 1, 2, 3, ...) when representing numbers, but some also have traditional representations. Which representation to show is governed by the method and language, as determined by a call to the SetDigitSubstitution method on the StringFormat class:

```
CultureInfo culture = new CultureInfo("th-TH"); // Thailand Thai
using( StringFormat format = new StringFormat() ) {
  format.SetDigitSubstitution(
    culture.LCID, StringDigitSubstitute.Traditional);
  g.DrawString("0 1 2...", font, brush, rect, format);
}
```

The substitution method is governed by StringDigitSubstitute (and can be discovered using the DigitSubstitutionMethod on the StringFormat class), as shown in Figure 6.7.

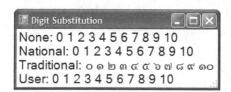

Figure 6.7 StringDigitSubstitute Values as Applied to Thailand Thai

The integer language identifier comes from the LCID (language and culture ID) of an instance of the CultureInfo class. It can be constructed with a two-part name: a two-letter country code followed by a two-letter language code, separated by a hyphen.[7] The methods applied to the national and traditional languages of Thailand are shown in Figure 6.7.

Alignment

In addition to substitution, tabs, wrapping, and clipping, you can use StringFormat to set text alignment (both horizontally and vertically) by setting the Alignment and LineAlignment properties, respectively, using one of the StringAlignment enumeration values:

```
namespace System.Drawing {
  enum StringAlignment {
    Near = 0, // Depends on right-to-left setting
    Center = 1,
    Far = 2, // Depends on right-to-left setting
  }
}
```

Notice that instead of Left and Right alignment, the StringAlignment enumeration values are Near and Far and depend on whether the RightToLeft string format flag is specified. The following code centers text in a rectangle horizontally and vertically:

```
// Center horizontally
format.Alignment = StringAlignment.Center;

// Center vertically
format.LineAlignment = StringAlignment.Center;
```

Two combinations on a StringFormat object are so commonly needed that they're set up for you and are exposed via the GenericDefault and GenericTypographic properties of the StringFormat class. The GenericDefault StringFormat object is what you get when you create a new StringFormat object, so it saves you the trouble if that's all you're after. The GenericTypographic StringFormat object is useful for showing text as text, not as part of drawing a UI element. The properties you get from each are shown in Table 6.3.

---

[7] The country code and language codes are defined by ISO standards.

Table 6.3   The Settings of the Built-In StringFormat Classes

GenericDefault	GenericTypographic
StringFormatFlags = 0	StringFormatFlags = LineLimit, NoClip
Alignment = Near	Alignment = Near
LineAlignment = Near	LineAlignment = Near
DigitSubstitutionMethod = User	DigitSubstitutionMethod = User
HotkeyPrefix = None	HotkeyPrefix = None
No tab stops	No tab stops
Trimming = Character	Trimming = None

Antialiasing

All the strings I've shown in the sample figures in this section have been nice and smooth. That's because I'm using Windows XP with ClearType turned on. If I turn that off, I go back to the old, blocky way of looking at things. However, when I'm drawing strings, I don't have to settle for what the user specifies. Before I draw a string, I can set the TextRenderingHint property of the Graphics object to one of the TextRenderingHint enumeration values, as shown in Figure 6.8.

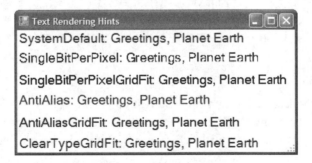

Figure 6.8   Examples of the TextRenderingHint Enumeration

In this case, SystemDefault shows what text looks like without any smoothing effects. The SingleBitPerPixel setting does just what it says, although it's clearly not useful for anything that needs to look great. The AntiAlias and ClearType settings are two different algorithms for smoothing that are meant to make the text look good: one for any monitor, and one specifically for LCD displays. The grid fit versions of the algorithms use extra hints to improve the appearance, as you can see from the examples.

Of course, as the quality improves, the rendering time also increases, and that's why you can set the option as appropriate for your application. Furthermore, when drawing using one of the antialiasing algorithms, you can adjust the TextContrast property of a Graphics object:

```
for( int i = 0; i <= 12; i += 4 ) {
   // Set the current text contrast
   g.TextContrast = i;
   string line = string.Format("TextContrast = {0}", i.ToString());
   g.DrawString(line, this.Font, Brushes.Black, 0, 0, format);
   ...
}
```

The contrast ranges from 0 to 12, where 0 is the most contrast and 12 is the least, with 4 being the default. The contrast makes fonts at smaller point sizes stand out more against the background. Figure 6.9 demonstrates the broad spectrum of text contrasts.

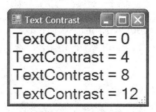

Figure 6.9   Examples of the TextContrast Property

Strings and Paths

One more string-drawing trick that might interest you is the ability to add strings to graphics paths. Because everything that's added to a path has both an outline and an interior that can be drawn separately, you can add strings to a path to achieve outline effects, as shown in Figure 6.10:

```
// Need to pass in DPI = 100 for GraphicsUnit == Display
GraphicsPath GetStringPath(
   string s,
   float dpi,
   RectangleF rect,
   Font font,
   StringFormat format) {
```

```
GraphicsPath path = new GraphicsPath();
// Convert font size into appropriate coordinates
float emSize = dpi * font.SizeInPoints / 72;
path.AddString(
  s, font.FontFamily, (int)font.Style, emSize, rect, format);
return path;
}

void OutlineFontsForm_Paint(object sender, PaintEventArgs e) {
  Graphics g = e.Graphics;
  string s = "Outline";
  RectangleF rect = this.ClientRectangle;
  Font font = this.Font;
  float dpi = g.DpiY;
  using( GraphicsPath path =
    GetStringPath(
      s, dpi, rect, font, StringFormat.GenericTypographic) ) {
    g.DrawPath(Pens.Black, path);
  }
}
```

Figure 6.10   Using a GraphicsPath Object to Simulate an Outline-Only Font

Even though I have ClearType on and the TextRenderingHint set to SystemDefault, the outline path was not drawn smoothly. As soon as the string was used to create a path, it stopped being text and became a shape, which is drawn smoothly or not based on the SmoothingMode property. Also, notice that I showed an example of a really big font (72-point). The string-as-path trick doesn't work very well at lower resolutions because of the translation of font family characters into a series of lines and curves.

Even more interesting uses of paths are available when you apply transformations, which you'll read about in Chapter 7: Advanced Drawing.

The TextRenderer

The TextRenderer class, located in the System.Windows.Forms namespace, is an alternative to the Graphics class for text rendering. Although Graphics and TextRenderer provide similar levels of text-rendering capabilities, the key difference between the two technologies is the underlying rendering API each one encapsulates; the Graphics class uses GDI+, and TextRenderer wraps GDI directly. Thus, when you need to render text using GDI, you can use TextRenderer to save the effort of writing interop code.

TextRenderer provides two methods—DrawText and MeasureText—each of which has plenty of overloads that almost parallel their Graphics DrawString and MeasureString counterparts:

```
namespace System.Windows.Forms {
  sealed class TextRenderer {
    // Methods
    public static void DrawText(IDeviceContext dc, ...);
    public static Size MeasureText(IDeviceContext dc, ...}
    public static Size MeasureText(string text, ...);
  }
}
```

Both DrawText and MeasureText, the equivalents of Graphics.DrawString and Graphics.MeasureString, respectively, wrap GDI invocations outside the graphics scope that is native to your applications via GDI+, whose main element is the surface you're drawing to via the Graphics object.[8] But GDI doesn't know anything about that drawing surface, so you need to pass it a device context handle that's wrapped by an IDeviceContext reference to the surface you want to draw text on. This is why several overloads of both DrawText and MeasureText accept an IDeviceContext. Fortunately, the Graphics class implements IDeviceContext, so you can simply pass it to either method.

There is another set of MeasureText overloads that don't require an IDeviceContext. However, you should prefer those that do because it allows MeasureText to more accurately determine the size needed to display a chunk of text.

Here's how to determine how much space a chunk of text actually needs:

```
void TextRendererForm_Paint(object sender, PaintEventArgs e) {
  Graphics g = e.Graphics;
  Size proposedSize = this.ClientRectangle.Size;

  // Calculate rendered text size
  Size size = TextRenderer.MeasureText(
              g, "Text To Measure", this.Font, proposedSize);
}
```

As you can see, calling the MeasureText method is quite similar to calling Graphics.MeasureString. In addition to support for passing an IDeviceContext object reference, the other important difference between MeasureText and MeasureString is that the former

---

[8] Although they are conceptually equivalent, it is highly recommended that you don't mix calls between Graphics and TextRenderer Draw*Xxx* and Measure*Xxx* methods.

returns a Size object, and the latter returns SizeF; the entire TextRenderer implementation works with integers only.

To render a string with DrawText is almost the same as using Graphics.DrawString, apart from passing an IDeviceContext reference:

```
void TextRendererForm_Paint(object sender, PaintEventArgs e) {
    Graphics g = e.Graphics; // IDeviceContext
    Size proposedSize = this.ClientRectangle.Size;

    // Calculate rendered text size
    Size size =
      TextRenderer.MeasureText(
        g, "Text To Measure", this.Font, proposedSize);

    // Render text to calculated size
    Rectangle rect = new Rectangle(0, 0, size.Width, size.Height);
    TextRenderer.DrawText(
        g, "Text To Measure", this.Font, rect, Color.Black);
}
```

Figure 6.11 illustrates the result.

Figure 6.11   Measuring and Drawing Text with TextRenderer

Of course, this is pretty plain, particularly from the point of view of formatting. Therein lies another consistency with Graphics: the ability to pass special formatting details to both MeasureText and DrawText.

Formatting with TextRenderer

As with Graphics.DrawString, overloads of both the TextRenderer.MeasureText method and the TextRenderer.DrawText method allow you to pass in a special formatting-oriented argument of type TextFormattingFlags:

```
namespace System.Windows.Forms {
    [Flags]
    enum TextFormatFlags {
        // Default (Top, Left, and GlyphOverhangPadding)
        Default = 0,
        // Align text to top
        Top = 0,
```

```
// Align text to left
Left = 0,
// Use glyph overhang in text line height
GlyphOverhangPadding = 0,
// Align text to horizontal center of the rectangle
HorizontalCenter = 1,
// Align text to right
Right = 2,
// Align text to vertical center of rectangle
VerticalCenter = 4,
// Align text to bottom
Bottom = 8,
// Word wrapping
WordBreak = 16,
// Render all text to a single line
SingleLine = 32,
// "\t" characters in text are turned into tabs
ExpandTabs = 64,
// Don't clip text partially outside layout rect
NoClipping = 256,
// Use external leading in text line height
ExternalLeading = 512,
// Don't show underscores at all
NoPrefix = 2048,
// Calculate text metrics using system font
Internal = 4096,
// Render text as if rendered to a TextBox
TextBoxControl = 8192,
// Trim file path by putting ellipsis in the middle
PathEllipsis = 16384,
// Trim to nearest character and show ellipsis
EndEllipsis = 32768,
// Copy the displayed string to source string
ModifyString = 65536,
// Render text in right-to-left order
RightToLeft = 131072,
// Trim to nearest word and show ellipsis
WordEllipsis = 262144,
// Don't line break wide chars
NoFullWidthCharacterBreak = 524288,
// Hide "&" chars intended as underscores
HidePrefix = 1048576,
// Only draw underscores in place of "&"
PrefixOnly = 2097152,
// Use Graphics object clipping
PreserveGraphicsClipping = 16777216,
// Use Graphics object transformations
PreserveGraphicsTranslateTransform = 33554432,
// Don't pad text
```

```
    NoPadding = 268435456,
    // Pad text left and right edges
    LeftAndRightPadding = 536870912,
}
```

Using TextFormatFlags, it's easy to center-align a chunk of text that collapses lines of text on a word-by-word basis, replacing hidden text with ellipsis characters:

```
void TextRendererForm_Paint(object sender, PaintEventArgs e) {
    Graphics g = e.Graphics;
    Rectangle rect = this.ClientRectangle;
    TextFormatFlags flags = TextFormatFlags.HorizontalCenter|
                            TextFormatFlags.VerticalCenter|
                            TextFormatFlags.WordEllipsis;
    TextRenderer.DrawText(
      g, "Text To Measure", this.Font, rect, Color.Black, flags);
}
```

The output of this code is shown in Figure 6.12.

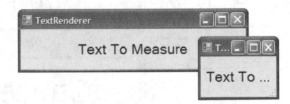

Figure 6.12   Measuring and Drawing Centered Text with TextRenderer

In general, you will find a lot of crossover between the two text-rendering technologies, particularly from the formatting perspective. Furthermore, knowledge you gain using one technology will serve you well with the other. However, there are also differences between the two technologies that you need to be aware of.

A Tale of Two Technologies

In general, text is rendered with a specific font to a specific location, and both Graphics and TextRenderer do that quite nicely. So, you might be wondering why there are two text-rendering technologies in the .NET Framework.

The Graphics class's text-rendering capabilities are powerful, but they suffer from several key problems, including weak internationalization support for complex scripts (such as Arabic), a lack of visual consistency between Windows Forms applications and the Windows shell, and performance. Unfortunately, although Microsoft tried, it could not refactor Graphics to solve these problems, because of inherent limitations in the technology.

These problems are solved by GDI, however, so Microsoft created TextRenderer to provide a managed wrapper around GDI that, for Windows Forms applications, simplifies access to those features missing from Graphics. The resulting implementation is powerful, and the union of functionality between the two technology sets is reasonably large.

As with most competing technologies, however, the union is not 100%. Instead, each technology is the best tool for a particular job. What follows is a discussion of the key issues you should consider to help you decide.

Shell Consistency

The Windows shell uses GDI to render certain UI elements with a consistent font. For example, given a shell default button font of "Tahoma 8pt," Graphics and TextRenderer produce slightly different results, as illustrated in Figure 6.13.

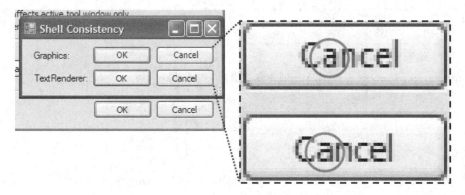

Figure 6.13 Comparing Shell Consistency (with VS05 | Tools | Options Dialog Buttons) (See Plate 14)

If you look closely, you can see that the TextRenderer output is consistent with the font used in the VS05 dialog, unlike Graphics, even though the same font is used:

```
// ShellConsistencyForm.cs
partial class ShellConsistencyForm : Form {

  // Draw OK button using Graphics
  void gOKButton_Paint(object sender, PaintEventArgs e) {
    // Draw button background
    ...
    // Render text
    using( StringFormat format = new StringFormat() )
    using( Font font = new Font("Tahoma", 8) ) {
      format.Alignment = StringAlignment.Center;
      format.LineAlignment = StringAlignment.Center;
```

```
      e.Graphics.DrawString(
        "OK",
        font,
        Brushes.Black,
        this.gOKButton.ClientRectangle,
        format);
    }
  }

  // Draw OK button using TextRenderer
  void tOKButton_Paint(object sender, PaintEventArgs e) {
    // Draw button background
    ...
    using( Font font = new Font("Tahoma", 8) ) {
      TextFormatFlags format = TextFormatFlags.VerticalCenter |
                               TextFormatFlags.HorizontalCenter;
      TextRenderer.DrawText(
        e.Graphics,
        "OK",
        font,
        this.tOKButton.ClientRectangle,
        this.ForeColor,
        format);
    }
  }
  ...
}
```

Being consistent with the shell is a great feature for applications in general and for reusable controls in particular. If you need to ensure that your visuals are consistent with the shell, you should prefer TextRenderer.

Internationalization

Shell integration is also important for internationalization-ready applications, which must deal with rendering in a variety of languages, including complex scripts, that are determined by the shell.

A *script* is the set of characters for a particular language, and a complex script is a script with special processing requirements, including the following:[9]

- **Character reordering.** Characters are ordered right-to-left or left-to-right.
- **Contextual shaping.** Characters render differently depending on their position within a word or the surrounding characters.

[9] An outline of complex scripts can be found at http://www.microsoft.com/globaldev/DrIntl/faqs/Complex.mspx#E6 (http://tinysells.com/17).

- **Combined characters**. One character is composed from several other characters.
- **Diacritics**. Character accents that alter the pronunciation of individual characters.

Support for handling these issues is native to GDI and is used by Windows to render text for multiple languages.[10] If you've played with the Windows XP Language Bar and installed various language packs, you're familiar with this. Because TextRenderer wraps GDI, it naturally inherits the ability to render complex scripts with the same accuracy as Windows. Although you can render text for complex scripts using Graphics, you are unlikely to achieve the same level of quality as TextRenderer because of GDI+ limitations. Figure 6.14 demonstrates the difference in quality when you render Sinhala script using an appropriate font.

Figure 6.14   Comparing Complex Script Output (Script=*Sinhala*, Font=*DinaminaUniWeb 30pt*)

In Figure 6.14, you can see that Sinhala uses combined characters, and Graphics can't combine characters while TextRenderer can.[11] From this example, it is clear that you should favor TextRenderer if your Windows Forms applications or custom controls require custom text rendering and need to support internationalization.

Device-Independent Drawing

Internationalization attempts to provide language independence. Another type of independence that is a key feature of GDI+ and the Graphics object is device independence. This means that you render to a logical surface provided by the Graphics object, which wraps and paints to a physical surface, such as a screen or a printer. Consequently, the Graphics object you are handed has intimate knowledge of the physical surface, including the units to draw in, such as pixels (screen) or dpi (printer). Such intimacy allows you to

[10] Specifically, the Windows Unicode Script Processor, or Uniscribe (usp10.dll) in Windows XP.

[11] http://si.wikipedia.org/wiki/Wikipedia:Sinhala_font (http://tinysells.com/18). Thanks to Miguel Lacouture-Amaya from Microsoft for help in creating the complex script sample.

draw to the Graphics object, which then performs scaling as required to match the units of the physical surface to which your stylings are eventually rendered. Thus WYSIWYG (what you see is what you get) is enabled. Figure 6.15 shows that what you see in a text box is what you get when printed, without the need to write any code other than drawing a string to a Graphics object using Graphics.DrawString.

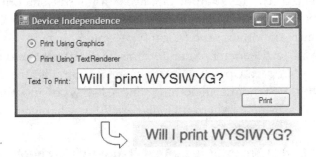

Figure 6.15 Graphics.DrawString Rendering Text to a Printer (Output Scanned) at Same Font as Text Box

From a device point of view, TextRenderer has no concept of independence. It was designed and built to render to one device, the screen, and this means that it knows only one set of units (pixels) and one scale. This subverts WYSIWYG, as shown in Figure 6.16.

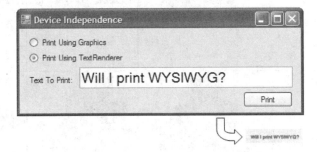

Figure 6.16 TextRenderer.DrawText Rendering Text to a Printer (Output Scanned) at Same Font as Text Box

If you want to use a TextRenderer to output to a different device, such as a printer, you need to convert the scale of your output to suit the target device. Although it's possible to do this, it's problematic for two reasons. First, you need to write one set of code to scale your TextRenderer output for each device you intend to target. Second, any manual scaling may lead to a loss of precision that will affect your ability to support WYSIWYG output.

Therefore, for WYSIWYG output to multiple devices, Graphics provides a more accurate and simplified model.

Font Edge Smoothing Support

Certain devices have special text-rendering considerations beyond scaling. For example, LCD screens produce blocky text output that needs font edge smoothing technology to make it more visually appealing. Windows XP supports three smoothing modes: no smoothing, "Standard" smoothing, and "ClearType" smoothing.[12]

Both Graphics and TextRenderer render text to suit the current smoothing mode without intervention on your part. Up to a point, they are comparable. Table 6.4 illustrates the effect of no smoothing, Standard smoothing, and ClearType smoothing for both text-rendering technologies, using a "Microsoft Sans Serif 70 pt" character.

Table 6.4 Font Edge Smoothing by Text-Rendering Technology

Text-Rendering Technology	Font Edge Smoothing Type		
	None	Standard	ClearType
Graphics			
TextRenderer			

As you can see, the two technologies are equivalent for no smoothing and Standard smoothing. However, things go awry when ClearType is the smoothing mode.

---

[12] These can be set from Control Panel | Display | Appearance | Effects.

For no apparent reason, text rendered by Graphics using Microsoft Sans Serif (66 points and up) loses the antialiasing effect of ClearType. You can use text-rendering hints to influence the antialiasing applied to Graphics-rendered text, but you fall out of the sphere of influence exerted by the shellwide font edge smoothing mode. If you need your custom-rendered text to conform to the current shell smoothing mode, TextRenderer is the more consistent option.

Performance

The performance of your output can be as important as how it eventually looks on your target device, particularly to screens, which often need to support high paint and refresh speeds. Because TextRenderer wraps GDI directly, it provides a higher-performance experience than using GDI+. For example, testing on the machine on which this chapter was typed demonstrated that text-rendering speeds for TextRenderer were approximately three times as fast as equivalent rendering by the Graphics object. Make sure you test appropriately if performance is an issue for your applications.

Integration with GDI+ Graphical Rendering

Often, rendering performance is a factor of rendering both textual and graphical output together. One benefit of rendering text using a Graphics object is the ability it gives you to integrate text output with the graphical capabilities of GDI+. A simple example that you've already seen is the ability to turn on antialiasing to ensure smoothly printed fonts; in this case, what was applied to the Graphics object was implicitly applied to the rendered text, along with all the other nontextual graphical output. Similarly, we cited a more complex example in which we used a GraphicsPath object to simulate an outline-only font. Unfortunately, this benefit isn't available using TextRenderer because it bypasses GDI+ and, by association, the capability of both Graphics and GraphicsPath objects to integrate with it.

Text-Formatting Comparison

Although both Graphics and TextRenderer offer a truckload of formatting options, if you use the StringFormat class and TextFormatFlags enumeration, respectively, a one-to-one parity does not exist, as outlined in Table 6.5.

Table 6.5 StringFormat Class Versus TextFormatFlags Enumeration

Member	StringFormat Class Type and Value	TextFormatFlags Enumeration Value
Alignment	StringAlignment.Near	Left (TextFormatFlag.Default)
	StringAlignment.Center	HorizontalCenter
	StringAlignment.Far	Right
DigitSubstitutionMethod	StringDigitSubstitute.User	*No Equivalent*
	StringDigitSubstitute.None	*No Equivalent*
	StringDigitSubstitute.National	*No Equivalent*
	StringDigitSubstitute.Traditional	*No Equivalent*
FormatFlags	StringFormatFlags.DirectionRightToLeft	RightToLeft
	StringFormatFlags.DirectionVertical	*No Equivalent*
	StringFormatFlags.DisplayFormatControl	*No Equivalent*
	StringFormatFlags.FitBlackBox	NoPadding
	StringFormatFlags.LineLimit	WordBreak | TextBoxControl
	StringFormatFlags.MeasureTrailingSpaces	*No Equivalent*
	StringFormatFlags.NoClip	NoClipping
	StringFormatFlags.NoFontFallback	*No Equivalent*
	StringFormatFlags.NoWrap	SingleLine
	Default Behavior	WordBreak
HotkeyPrefix	HotKeyPrefix.None	NoPrefix
	HotKeyPrefix.Show	*Default Behavior*
	HotKeyPrefix.Hide	HidePrefix
LineAlignment	StringAlignment.Near	Top (TextFormatFlag.Default)
	StringAlignment.Center	VerticalCenter
	StringAlignment.Far	Bottom
Trimming	StringTrimming.None	*Default Behavior*
	StringTrimming.Character	*No Equivalent*
	StringTrimming.Word	*No Equivalent*
	StringTrimming.EllipsisCharacter	EndEllipsis
	StringTrimming.EllipsisWord	WordEllipsis
	StringTrimming.EllipsisPath	PathEllipsis
	No Equivalent	GlyphOverhangPadding (TextFormatFlag.Default)
	No Equivalent	ExternalLeading
	No Equivalent	Internal
	No Equivalent	ModifyString
	No Equivalent	NoFullWidthCharacterBreak
	No Equivalent	PrefixOnly
	No Equivalent	PreserveGraphicsClipping
	No Equivalent	PreserveGraphicsTranslateTransform
	No Equivalent	LeftAndRightPadding
SetTabStops()		ExpandTabs
GetTabStops()		*No Equivalent*
SetDigitSubstitution()		*No Equivalent*
SetMeasurableCharacterRanges()		*No Equivalent*

Note: This table is inspired by work done by Miguel Lacouture-Amaya, from Microsoft.

One other feature notably missing from TextRenderer is text-rendering hints, because these are set via the Graphics object and thus have no effect on TextRenderer output.

Integration

Because of TextRenderer's ability to paint text that's consistent with the Windows shell and because it supports internationalization, TextRenderer is now responsible for handling text-rendering duties for several Windows Forms controls, including Button, Label, TextBox, RadioButton, and CheckBox.

However, this could be a problem if your application, overall, uses the Graphics text-rendering approach; there could be perceivable visual inconsistencies between the Windows Forms controls and your custom text-painting output. This is a likely scenario for all applications written for Windows Forms 1.x that you upgrade to Windows Forms 2.0.

Fortunately, those controls that do paint their text elements with TextRenderer come with a compatibility switch that you can use to determine which text-rendering technology to use. The switch is exposed from each of these controls as the Boolean UseCompatibleTextRendering property. By default, UseCompatibleTextRendering is set to false, indicating that TextRenderer should be used. You set it to true to ensure that these controls instead render text using Graphics, most easily from the Properties window, as shown in Figure 6.17.

Figure 6.17   Configuring a Control to Use Graphics Instead of TextRenderer

A nice benefit of setting UseCompatibleTextRendering from the Properties window is that you see the results immediately in the Windows Forms Designer. But if you have a lot of controls to change compatibility on, this approach could become tedious. Instead, you can invoke the Application.SetCompatibleTextRenderingDefault method to force all controls to use one model irrespective of the values of their own UseCompatibleTextRendering properties. By default, VS05 includes the call to SetCompatibleTextRenderingDefault in the wizard-generated Program.cs file:

```
// Program.cs
static class Program {
  /// <summary>
  /// The main entry point for the application.
  /// </summary>
  [STAThread]
  static void Main() {
    Application.EnableVisualStyles();
    // Make controls use TextRenderer
    Application.SetCompatibleTextRenderingDefault(false);
    Application.Run(new MainForm());
  }
}
```

As with UseCompatibleTextRendering, passing false to SetCompatibleTextRendering-Default means that TextRenderer is used, and passing true ensures that Graphics is used.

If you're developing for Windows Forms 2.0 right off the bat, it's unlikely you'll need to fiddle with these settings unless you decide to use Graphics to render text in your applications or custom controls.

Where Are We?

We've finished the basics of drawing that we started in Chapter 5: Drawing Basics. In Chapter 7: Advanced Drawing, we talk about advanced drawing topics, such as coordinate systems, regions, and transformations.

7

Advanced Drawing

C HAPTER 5: DRAWING BASICS AND CHAPTER 6: DRAWING TEXT cover the basics of drawing, including colors, pens, brushes, shapes, paths, images, fonts, and string drawing. This chapter looks at advanced topics such as page units, world transforms, regions, and optimization techniques. And as if that weren't enough, Chapter 8: Printing wraps up the tour of the System.Drawing namespace with a look at printing.

Page Units

In Chapters 5 and 6, we've concentrated on drawing to the screen. By default, if you're drawing in the Paint event handler, you're drawing in units of pixels. Even if you create a Graphics object from a form using Form.CreateGraphics, you draw in units of pixels. This is handy because the units of the various user interface elements (such as the client rectangle) and the position and sizes of the controls are all in pixels.

Pixels translate into real-world coordinates based on system settings for Normal or Small (versus Large or Custom) fonts, the resolution at which the display adapter runs, and the size of the monitor. Taking all that into account, only some of which is available programmatically, it would be remarkably difficult to display physically correct sizes on a monitor—for example, the ruler you see at the top of a word processing program. Luckily, because you can usually adjust all this using various systemwide and application-specific settings, people generally size things so that they are comfortable, and the real-world sizes are not so important. That is, they're not important until you need to output to a specific physical size (such as to a printer).

For example, it's not important that the ruler at the top of the document I'm typing this sentence into is currently showing an inch as 1%₆ inches.[1] What is important is the proportion of the dimensions of each line to the units shown as "inches" as compared to the width of each line as I type. The principle of WYSIWYG (what you see is what you get) dictates that I should be able to print something very similar to what I'm seeing on the screen. When my word processing program shows a line wrapping at a certain word when I get close to the 6.5-inch area inside my margins (standard 8.5-inch wide paper with a 1-inch margin on each side), I want that same wrap to happen at the same word when I print the document. To make that happen, we need to write programs that can wrap text at units other than pixels, like the one shown in Figure 7.1.

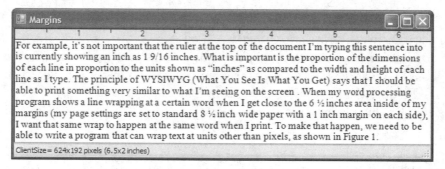

Figure 7.1   Manually Drawing in Inches

Figure 7.1 shows a ruler marked off in half-inch increments and text wrapped to a right margin of 6.5 inches. The numbers in the status strip represent the dimensions of the form's client area in both pixels and the real-world inch values they equate to. We accomplish this by using the following function to manually convert coordinates and sizes to inches:[2]

```
float InchesToPixels(float inches) {
  using( Graphics g = this.CreateGraphics() ) {
    return inches * g.DpiX;
  }
}
```

This function is used to calculate the width of the ruler, the half-inch tick marks, and the width of the text box. For example, the code that draws the outline of the ruler looks like this:

[1] I measured it with a ruler from the physical world.

[2] See Chapter 6 for further discussion of Graphics.DpiX and Graphics.DpiY.

```
using( Font rulerFont = new Font("MS Sans Serif", 8.25f) ) {
  int pixelsPerInch = 72;

  // Inches
  float rulerFontHeight = rulerFont.SizeInPoints / pixelsPerInch;

  // Specify units in inches
  RectangleF rulerRect =
    new RectangleF(0, 0, 6.5f, rulerFontHeight * 1.5f);

  // Draw in pixels
  g.DrawRectangle(
    Pens.Black,
    InchesToPixels(rulerRect.X),
    InchesToPixels(rulerRect.Y),
    InchesToPixels(rulerRect.Width),
    InchesToPixels(rulerRect.Height));
  ...
}
```

The conversion from inches to pixels is necessary because the units of the Graphics object passed to the Paint event are pixels, which represent the *device units* for the display adapter. All units eventually need to be translated to device units for rendering, but this doesn't mean that you need to specify drawing in device units. Instead, the Graphics object draws with *page units*, which default to pixels in the Paint event but don't need to stay that way. The PageUnit and PageScale properties of the Graphics object allow you to specify different units in which to draw:

```
// Set page units and scale
g.PageUnit = GraphicsUnit.Inch;
g.PageScale = 1; // 1 unit is 1 inch

using( Font rulerFont = new Font("MS Sans Serif", 8.25f) )
using( Pen blackPen = new Pen(Color.Black, 0) ) {
  float rulerFontHeight = rulerFont.GetHeight(g); // Inches

  // Specify units in inches
  RectangleF rulerRect =
    new RectangleF(0, 0, 6.5f, rulerFontHeight * 1.5f);

  // Draw in inches
  g.DrawRectangle(
    blackPen,
    rulerRect.X,
    rulerRect.Y,
    rulerRect.Width,
    rulerRect.Height);
  ...
}
```

Before the code does any drawing, the first thing it does is to set the page unit for the graphics object to GraphicsUnit.Inch and the page scale to 1, which turns every 1 unit (whether it's specified for a position or a size) into 1 inch.[3] Notice that we're using floating-point numbers to enable fractional inches; the floating-point numbers are converted to device units by the Graphics object. The PageUnit property can be any value from the GraphicsUnit enumeration, so units can be in points or millimeters as well as pixels or inches. The PageScale can be a floating-point number, so if we wanted to specify a scale of 0.1 when specifying a PageUnit of Inch, then 1 unit would equal 0.1 inch, and 10 units would equal 1 inch.

Note the use of a new black pen, in spite of the presence of the Pens.Black pen that was used in the earlier example. All the default pens default to 1 unit in width. When the unit was pixels, that was fine, but when the unit is inches, a 1-unit pen became 1-inch wide. Pens are specified in units that are interpreted when the pen is used. To avoid having a very wide pen, the code specifies 0 for the width of the pen, and that causes the pen to be 1 device unit wide no matter what the page unit is currently set to.

Also note that the Font object is not affected by the page units. Instead, recall from Chapter 6 that we specify Fonts using a GraphicsUnit argument passed to the constructor, and they default to GraphicsUnit.Point. Finally, notice that the code uses the GetHeight method of the Font class, passing the Graphics object. Unlike the Height property, the GetHeight method is scaled appropriately to the current units of the Graphics object.

Converting Pixels to Page Units

If a method doesn't take a Graphics object as an argument, then it isn't affected by the page units. For example, the ClientRectangle of the form or control being drawn is always specified in pixels, making some consideration necessary when you use units other than pixels. To convert back and forth between device and page units, the Graphics object provides the TransformPoints method:

```
using( Graphics g = this.CreateGraphics() ) {
  // Set page unit to inches
  g.PageUnit = GraphicsUnit.Inch;
  g.PageScale = 1;

  PointF[] bottomRight =
    new PointF[] {
      new PointF(this.ClientSize.Width, this.ClientSize.Height) };
```

[3] The GraphicsUnit enumeration is covered in Chapter 5.

```
    // Convert client size from pixels to inches
    g.TransformPoints(
      CoordinateSpace.Page, // Destination
      CoordinateSpace.Device, // Source
      bottomRight);
    ...
}
```

This code converts to page units (set to inches in this example) from device units (also known as pixels) using the TransformPoints method, which can convert between any type of coordinates from the CoordinateSpace enumeration. CoordinateSpace has the following values:

```
namespace System.Drawing.Drawing2D {
  enum CoordinateSpace {
    Device = 2,
    Page = 1,
    World = 0,
  }
}
```

The value we haven't yet discussed is CoordinateSpace.World, which is a whole other world of coordinates (if you'll excuse the pun).

Transforms

Page units are useful for conveniently specifying things and letting the Graphics object sort it out, but there are all kinds of effects that can't be achieved with such a simple transform. A *transform* is a mathematical function by which units are specified and then transformed into other units. So far, we've talked about transforming from page units to device units, but a more general-purpose transform facility is provided via the Transform property of the Graphics object, which is an instance of the Matrix class:

```
namespace System.Drawing.Drawing2D {
  sealed class Matrix : IDisposable, ... {
    // Contructors
    public Matrix( ... );

    // Properties
    public float[] Elements { get; }
    public bool IsIdentity { get; }
    public bool IsInvertible { get; }
    public float OffsetX { get; }
    public float OffsetY { get; }
```

```
      // Methods
      public void Invert();
      public void Multiply( ... );
      public void Reset();
      public void Rotate( ... );
      public void RotateAt( ... );
      public void Scale( ... );
      public void Shear( ... );
      public void TransformPoints( ... );
      public void TransformVectors( ... );
      public void Translate( ... );
      public void VectorTransformPoints(Point[] pts);
    }
  }
```

The Matrix class provides an implementation of a 3x3 mathematical *matrix*, which is a rectangular array of numbers. The specifics of what make up a matrix in math are beyond the scope of this book, but the Matrix class provides all kinds of interesting methods that let you use a matrix without doing any of the math.[4]

The graphics transformation matrix is used to transform *world coordinates*, which is what units involved with graphics operations are really specified in. Graphical units are passed as world coordinates, transformed by the transformation matrix into page units, and finally transformed again from page units to display units. As you've seen, the default page units for the screen are pixels, and that's why no page unit conversion happens without our changing the page unit or the scale or both. Similarly, the default transformation matrix is the *identity matrix*, which means that it doesn't actually do any conversions.

Scaling

Using an instance of a Matrix object instead of page units, we could perform the simple scaling we did in the preceding example:

```
// Set units to inches using a transform
Matrix matrix = new Matrix();
matrix.Scale(g.DpiX, g.DpiY);
g.Transform = matrix;

using( Font rulerFont = new Font("MS Sans Serif", 8.25f / g.DpiY) )
using( Pen blackPen = new Pen(Color.Black, 0) ) {
  float rulerFontHeight = rulerFont.GetHeight(g); // Inches
```

[4] As with all technology, understanding the underlying principles is always helpful. Martin Heller recommends *Introduction to Computer Graphics*, by James D. Foley, Andries Van Dam, and Steven K. Feiner (Addison-Wesley, 1993), for the details of matrix math as related to graphics programming.

```
// Specify units in inches
RectangleF rulerRect =
  new RectangleF(0, 0, 6.5f, rulerFontHeight * 1.5f);
// Draw in inches
g.DrawRectangle(
  blackPen,
  rulerRect.X,
  rulerRect.Y,
  rulerRect.Width,
  rulerRect.Height);
...
}
```

This code creates a new instance of the Matrix class, which defaults to the identity matrix.[5] Instead of directly manipulating the underlying 3x3 matrix numbers, the code uses the Scale method to put the numbers in the right place to scale from inches to pixels using the dpi settings for the current Graphics object. This transformation is exactly the same result that we got by setting the page unit to inches and the page scale to 1, except for one detail: the font. Although the page unit and scale do not affect the size of fonts, the current transform affects everything, including fonts. This is why the point size being passed to the Font's constructor in the sample code is first scaled back by the current dpi setting, causing it to come out right after the transformation has occurred. I'd show you the result of using the transform instead of page units, but because it looks just like Figure 7.1, it'd be pretty boring.

Scaling Fonts

Because the world transform works with fonts as well as everything else, scaling fonts is an interesting use of the world transform all by itself. Usually, fonts are specified by height only, but using transforms allows us to adjust a font's height and width independently of each other, as shown in Figure 7.2.

Figure 7.2   Scaling Font Height Independently of Font Width

[5] Also demonstrated is a technique that allows you to tie multiple *using* statements to the life of a single block, a practice that makes for neater code.

Notice that scaling can even be used in the negative direction, as shown on the far right of Figure 7.2, although you must specify the rectangle appropriately:

```
Matrix matrix = new Matrix();
matrix.Scale(-1, -1);
g.Transform = matrix;
g.DrawString(
  "Scale(-1, -1)",
  this.Font,
  Brushes.Black,
  new RectangleF(-x - width, -y - height, width, height),
  ...);
```

Because scaling by –1 in both dimensions causes all coordinates to be multiplied by –1, we use negative coordinates to get a rectangle at the appropriate place in the window. Notice that the width and height are still positive, however, because a rectangle needs positive dimensions to have positive area.

Rotation

Scaling by a negative amount can look very much like rotation, but only in a limited way. Luckily, matrices support rotation directly, as in this code sample, which draws a line rotated along a number of degrees (see Figure 7.3):

```
for( int i = 0; i <= 90; i += 10 ) {
  Matrix matrix = new Matrix();
  matrix.Rotate(i);
  g.Transform = matrix;
  g.DrawLine(Pens.Black, 0, 0, 250, 0);
  g.DrawString(i.ToString(), ... );
}
```

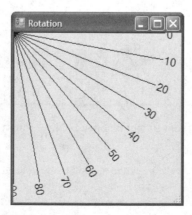

Figure 7.3   Line from (0, 0) to (250, 0) Rotated by Degrees 0–90

Notice that rotation takes place starting to the right horizontally and proceeding clockwise. Both shapes and text are rotated, as would anything else drawn into the rotated Graphics object.

Rotate works well if you're rotating around graphical elements with origins at (0, 0), but if you're drawing multiple lines originating at a different origin, the results may prove unintuitive (although mathematically sound), as shown in Figure 7.4.

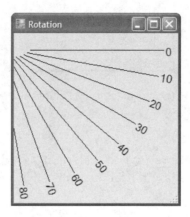

Figure 7.4 Line from (25, 25) to (275, 25) Rotated by Degrees 0–90

To rotate more intuitively around a point other than (0, 0), use the RotateAt method (as shown in Figure 7.5):

```
for( int i = 0; i <= 90; i += 10 ) {
   Matrix matrix = new Matrix();
   matrix.RotateAt(i, new PointF(25, 25));
   g.Transform = matrix;
   g.DrawLine(Pens.Black, 25, 25, 275, 25);
   g.DrawString(
     i.ToString(), this.Font, Brushes.Black, textRect, format);
}
```

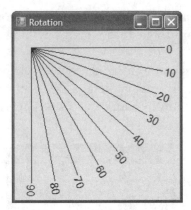

Figure 7.5   Line from (25, 25) to (275, 25) Rotated by Degrees 0–90 at (25, 25)

Translation

Instead of moving our shapes relative to the origin, as we did when drawing the lines, it's often handy to move the origin itself by translating the matrix (as demonstrated in Figure 7.6).

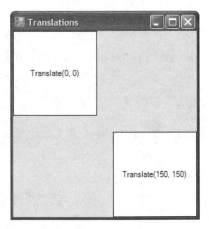

Figure 7.6   Rectangle (0, 0, 125, 125) Drawn at Two Origins

Translation is very handy when you have a figure to draw that can take on several positions around the display area. You can always draw starting from the origin and let the translation decide where the figure actually ends up:

```
void DrawLabeledRect(Graphics g, string label) {
    // Always draw at (0, 0) and let the client
    // set the position using a transform
    RectangleF rect = new RectangleF(0, 0, 125, 125);
```

```
    StringFormat format = new StringFormat();
    format.Alignment = StringAlignment.Center;
    format.LineAlignment = StringAlignment.Center;
    g.FillRectangle(Brushes.White, rect);
    g.DrawRectangle(Pens.Black, rect.X, rect.Y, rect.Width, rect.Height);
    g.DrawString(label, this.Font, Brushes.Black, rect, format);
  }

  void TranslationForm_Paint(object sender, PaintEventArgs e) {
    Graphics g = e.Graphics;

    // Origin at (0, 0)
    DrawLabeledRect(g, "Translate(0, 0)");

    // Move origin to (150, 150)
    Matrix matrix = new Matrix();
    matrix.Translate(150, 150);
    g.Transform = matrix;
    DrawLabeledRect(g, "Translate(150, 150)");
  }
```

In fact, you can use this technique for any of the matrix transformation effects covered so far, in addition to the one yet to be covered: shearing.

Shearing

Shearing is like drawing on a rectangle and then pulling along an edge while holding the opposite edge down. Shearing can happen in both directions independently. A shear of zero represents no shear, and the "pull" is increased as the shear increases. The shear is the proportion of the opposite dimension from one corner to another.

For example, the rectangle (0, 0, 200, 50) sheared 0.5 along the x dimension has its top-left edge at (0, 0) but its bottom-left edge at (25, 50). Because the shear dimension is x, the top edge follows the coordinates of the rectangle, but the bottom edge is offset by the height of the rectangle multiplied by the shear value:

```
bottomLeftX = height * xShear = 50 * 0.5 = 25
```

Here's the code that results in the middle sheared rectangle and text in Figure 7.7:

```
RectangleF rect = new RectangleF(0, 0, 200, 50);
Matrix matrix = new Matrix();
matrix.Shear(.5f, 0f); // Shear in x dimension only
matrix.Translate(200, 0);
g.Transform = matrix;
g.DrawString("Shear(.5, 0)", this.Font, Brushes.Black, rect, format);
g.DrawRectangle(Pens.Black, rect.X, rect.Y, rect.Width, rect.Height);
```

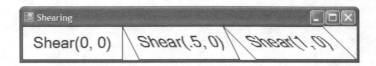

Figure 7.7   Drawing a Constant-Size Rectangle at Various Shearing Values

Combining Transforms

In addition to a demonstration of shearing, the preceding code snippet offers another interesting thing to notice: the use of two operations—a translation and a shear—on the matrix. Multiple operations on a matrix are cumulative. This is useful because the translation allows you to draw the sheared rectangle in the middle at a translated (0, 0) without stepping on the rectangle at the right (and the rectangle at the right is further translated out of the way of the rectangle in the middle).

It's a common desire to combine effects in a matrix, but be careful, because order matters. In this case, because translation works on coordinates and shear works on sizes, the two operations can come in any order. However, because scaling works on coordinates as well as sizes, the order in which scaling and translation are performed matters very much. For example, this code results in Figure 7.8:

```
Matrix matrix = new Matrix();
matrix.Scale(2, 3); // Scale x/width and y/width by 2 and 3
matrix.Translate(10, 20); // Move origin to (20, 60)
```

Figure 7.8   Scale Before Translate

However, swapping the Translate and Scale method calls produces a different result, shown in Figure 7.9:

```
Matrix matrix = new Matrix();
matrix.Translate(10, 20); // Move origin to (10, 20)
matrix.Scale(2, 3); // Scale x/width and y/width by 2 and 3
```

Figure 7.9   Translate Before Scale

If you'd like to reuse a Matrix object but don't want to undo all the operations you've done so far, you can use the Reset method to set it back to the identity matrix. Similarly, you can check whether it's already the identity matrix:

```
Matrix matrix = new Matrix(); // Starts as identity
matrix.Rotate( ... ); // Touched by inhuman hands
if( !matrix.IsIdentity ) matrix.Reset(); // Back to identity
```

Transformation Helpers

If you've been following along with this section on transformations, you may have been tempted to reach into the Graphics object's Transform property and call Matrix methods directly:

```
Matrix matrix = new Matrix();
matrix.Shear(.5f, .5f);
g.Transform = matrix; // works

g.Transform.Shear(.5f, .5f); // compiles, but doesn't work
```

Although the Transform property returns its Matrix object, it's returning a copy, so performing operations on the copy has no effect on the transformation matrix of the Graphics object. However, instead of creating Matrix objects and setting the Transform property all the time, you can use several helper methods of the Graphics class that affect the transformation matrix directly:

```
namespace System.Drawing {
    sealed class Graphics : IDisposable, ... {
        ...
        // Transformation methods of the Graphics class
        public void ResetTransform();
        public void RotateTransform( ... );
        public void ScaleTransform( ... );
        public void TranslateTransform( ... );
    }
}
```

These methods are handy for simplifying transformation code because each call is cumulative (although there's no ShearTransform method):

```
// No new Matrix object required
g.TranslateTransform(200, 0);
g.DrawString("(0, 0)", this.Font, Brushes.Black, 0, 0);
```

Path Transformations

As you've seen in previous chapters, GraphicsPath objects are very similar to Graphics objects, and the similarity extends to transformations. A GraphicsPath object can be transformed just as a Graphics object can, and that's handy when you'd like some parts of a drawing, as specified in paths, to be transformed but not others.

Because a path is a collection of figures to be drawn as a group, a transformation isn't a property to be set and changed; instead, it is an operation that is applied. To transform a GraphicsPath, you use the Transform method:

```
GraphicsPath CreateLabeledRectPath(string label) {
    GraphicsPath path = new GraphicsPath();
    // Add rectangle and string
    ...
    return path;
}

void PathTranslationForm_Paint(object sender, PaintEventArgs e) {
Graphics g = e.Graphics;
using( GraphicsPath path = CreateLabeledRectPath("My Path") ) {

    // Draw at (0, 0)
    g.DrawPath(Pens.Black, path);

    // Translate all points in path by (150, 150)
    Matrix matrix = new Matrix();
    matrix.Translate(150, 150);
    path.Transform(matrix);
    g.DrawPath(Pens.Black, path);
}
```

In addition, GraphicsPath provides transformations that do flattening, widening, and warping via the Flatten, Widen, and Warp methods, respectively (as shown in Figure 7.10).

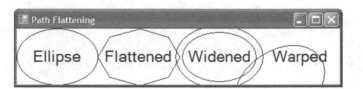

Figure 7.10   Path Flattening, Widening, and Warping

Each of these methods takes a Matrix object in case you'd like to, for example, translate and widen at the same time. Passing the identity matrix allows each of the specific operations to happen without an additional transformation. The Flatten method takes a flatness value; the larger the value, the fewer the number of points used along a curve and, therefore, the flatter the curve. Figure 7.10 shows an ellipse flattened by 10:

```
// Pass the identity matrix as the first argument to
// stop any transformation except for the flattening
path.Flatten(new Matrix(), 10);
g.DrawPath(Pens.Black, path);
```

The Widen method takes a Pen whose width is used to widen the lines and curves along the path. Figure 7.10 shows an ellipse widened by a pen of width 10:

```
using( Pen widenPen = new Pen(Color.Empty /* ignored */, 10) ) {
    path.Widen(widenPen);
    g.DrawPath(Pens.Black, path);
}
```

One of the overloads of the Widen method takes a flatness value, in case you'd like to widen and flatten simultaneously, in addition to the matrix that it also takes for translation.

The Warp method acts like the skewing of an image discussed in Chapter 5. Warp takes, at a minimum, a set of points that defines a parallelogram that describes the target, and a rectangle that describes a chunk of the source. It uses these arguments to skew the source chunk to the destination parallelogram. Figure 7.10 shows the top half of an ellipse skewed left:

```
// Draw warped
PointF[] destPoints = new PointF[3];
destPoints[0] = new PointF(width / 2, 0);
destPoints[1] = new PointF(width, height);
destPoints[2] = new PointF(0, height / 2);
RectangleF srcRect = new RectangleF(0, 0, width, height / 2);
path.Warp(destPoints, srcRect);
g.DrawPath(Pens.Black, path);
```

Regions

Whereas paths define a set of figures, with both a frame and an area, a *region* defines only an area. A region can be used for filling or, most importantly, clipping. A region is modeled in .NET with the Region class:

```
namespace System.Drawing {
    sealed class Region : IDisposable, ... {
        // Constructors
        public Region( ... );

        // Methods
        public void Complement( ... );
        public void Exclude( ... );
        public static Region FromHrgn(IntPtr hrgn);
        public RectangleF GetBounds(Graphics g);
        public IntPtr GetHrgn(Graphics g);
        public RegionData GetRegionData();
        public RectangleF[] GetRegionScans(Matrix matrix);
        public void Intersect( ... );
        public bool IsEmpty(Graphics g);
        public bool IsInfinite(Graphics g);
        public bool IsVisible( ... );
        public void MakeEmpty();
        public void MakeInfinite();
        public void ReleaseHRgn(IntPtr regionHandle); // New
        public void Transform( ... );
        public void Translate( ... );
        public void Union( ... );
        public void Xor( ... );
    }
}
```

Constructing and Filling a Region

Because the underlying Win32 implementation also has a construct that represents a region (managed using the Win32 HRGN data type), the Region class can be translated back and forth for interoperability reasons. In addition to constructing a region from an HRGN, you can construct regions from Rectangle objects or, more generally, from GraphicsPath objects:

```
using( GraphicsPath path = new GraphicsPath() ) {
    path.AddEllipse(rect);
    path.Flatten(new Matrix(), 13f);
    path.AddString("Flattened Ellipse", ...);
```

```
   using( Region region = new Region(path) ) {
      g.FillRegion(Brushes.Red, region);
   }
}
```

You might be curious about what might drive you to fill a region, especially given that paths can be drawn or filled but regions can only be filled. The answer is that you probably won't use regions to draw. You'll probably use regions to decide what not to draw.

Clipping to a Region

Every Graphics object has a region to which all drawing is *clipped*; any drawing outside the clip region is ignored. By default, the clip region is an *infinite* region, and this means that it has no bounds and nothing inside the region being drawn will be thrown out. Windows itself clips outside the region that isn't part of the invalid region that triggered the Paint event, but that's a separate region from the region exposed by the Graphics object. You can set the clip region on the Graphics object by setting the Clip property (as shown in Figure 7.11):

```
using( GraphicsPath path = new GraphicsPath() ) {
   path.AddEllipse(this.ClientRectangle);
   using( Region region = new Region(path) ) {
      // Frame clipping region
      g.DrawPath(Pens.Red, path);

      // Don't draw outside the ellipse region
      g.Clip = region;

      // Draw a rectangle
      Rectangle rect = this.ClientRectangle;
      rect.Offset(10, 10);
      rect.Width -= 20;
      rect.Height -= 20;
      g.FillRectangle(Brushes.Black, rect);
      g.DrawString("Rectangle clipped to Ellipse", ...);
   }
}
```

Figure 7.11   Rectangle Clipped to an Ellipse Region

If you'd rather call a method than set a property when setting the clip region, you can use the SetClip method. It has overloads that take rectangles and paths and create the underlying clip region itself from those. If you'd like to go back to no clipping, you can use the ResetClip method. There are also several clip-related methods on the Region class that deal with intersecting and combining clip regions. All these operate on the underlying methods of the Region class itself, which supports various combination techniques.

Region Combination Operations

Regions support several combination operations for creating more complicated regions from several combined simpler regions. These operations are complement, exclude, intersect, union, and xor, as shown in Figure 7.12.

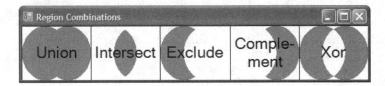

Figure 7.12   Region Combination Operations

Each region combination method takes a path, a region, or a rectangle and combines it with the existing region. By default, a Region with no constructor argument is infinite, but you can make it empty by calling MakeEmpty. Creating a Region with a constructor argument is like creating it as empty and then using the Union method to add a new shape to the region. The following are equivalent:

```
// Intersect the easy way
using( Region region = new Region(path1) ) {
  region.Intersect(path2);
  g.FillRegion(Brushes.Red, region);
}

// Intersect the hard way
using( Region region = new Region() ) {
  // Defaults to region.IsInfinite(g) == true
  if( !region.IsEmpty(g) ) region.MakeEmpty();
  region.Union(path1); // Add a path
  region.Intersect(path2); // Intersect with another path
  g.FillRegion(Brushes.Red, region);
}
```

Taken together, these combining operations provide a complete set of ways to combine regions for filling and clipping.

Optimized Drawing

If you're drawing using page units, transformations, and regions, it's likely that you're seriously into drawing. If that's the case, you'll be interested in ways to optimize your drawings for responsiveness and smooth operation. First and foremost, you should avoid drawing anything that doesn't need drawing. You can do that in one of two ways: redraw only what needs to be redrawn, or don't draw unnecessarily in the first place.

First, invalidate only the portion of your drawing surface that needs to be refreshed. In other words, when drawing the internal state of your form or control, don't invalidate the entire thing if only a small part of the state has changed:

```
float[] lotsOfNumbers;

Region GetRegionWhereNumberIsShown(int number) { ... }

public float OneNumber {
  set {
    lotsOfNumbers[1] = value;

    // Don't do this:
    this.Invalidate();

    // Do this:
    this.Invalidate(GetRegionWhereNumberIsShown(1));
  }
}
```

The Invalidate function takes an optional rectangle or region as the first argument, so you must invalidate only the portion that needs redrawing, not the entire client area. Now, when the Paint event is triggered, all drawing outside the invalid rectangle is ignored:

```
void NumbersForm_Paint(object sender, PaintEventArgs e) {
  for( int i = 0; i != lotsOfNumbers.Length; ++i ) {
    DrawNumber(g, i); // Will draw only in invalid rectangle
  }
}
```

Also, there's an optional second argument that says whether to invalidate children. If the state of your children doesn't need updating, don't invalidate.

What's even better than having drawing operations ignored for efficiency? Not drawing at all. Sometimes, the client area is too small to show all of the state.[6] When that happens, there's no need to draw something that lies entirely outside the visible clip region. To determine whether that's the case, you can use the IsVisible method of the Graphics object, which checks to see whether a point or any part of a rectangle is visible in the current clipped region:

```
Rectangle GetNumberRectangle(int i) { ... }

void DrawNumber(Graphics g, int i) {
    // Avoid something that takes a long time to draw
    if( !g.IsVisible(GetNumberRectangle(i)) ) return;

    // Draw something that takes a long time...
}
```

Be careful when calculating the region to invalidate or checking to see whether a hunk of data is in the invalid region; it may take more cycles to do the checking than it does to simply do the drawing. As always, when performance is what you're after, your best bet is to profile various real-world scenarios.

Double Buffering

Another way to make your graphics-intensive programs come out sweet and nice is to eliminate flicker. *Flicker* is a result of the three-phase painting process Windows employs to render a form, where each phase renders directly to the screen. When flickering occurs, you are seeing the rendering results of each phase in quick succession. The first phase erases the invalid region by painting it with a Windows-level background brush. The second phase sends the PaintBackground event for your form or control to paint the background, something that your base class generally handles for you using the BackColor and BackgroundImage properties. But you can handle it yourself:

```
// There is no PaintBackground event, only this virtual method
protected override void OnPaintBackground(PaintEventArgs e) {
    // Make sure to paint the entire client area or call the
    // base class, or else you'll have stuff from below showing through
    // base.OnPaintBackground(e);
    e.Graphics.FillRectangle(Brushes.Black, this.ClientRectangle);
}
```

The third and final phase of painting is the Paint event handler itself.

---

[6] This often involves scrolling, which is covered in Chapter 10: Controls.

Double buffering is a technique by which you can combine the three phases into a single paint operation and thereby eliminate flicker. To make this work, you apply the three painting phases to a second, internally managed graphics buffer, and, when they're all finished, they're rendered to the screen in one fell swoop. You can enable double buffering in a form or a control by setting the AllPaintingInWmPaint and OptimizedDoubleBuffer styles from the System.Windows.Forms.ControlStyles enumeration to true:[7]

```
// Form1.cs
partial class Form1 {
   public Form1() {
      InitializeComponent();

      // Enable double buffering
      this.SetStyle(ControlStyles.OptimizedDoubleBuffer, true);
      this.SetStyle(ControlStyles.AllPaintingInWmPaint, true);
   }
   ...
}
```

To save time, you can implement double buffering by opening your form in the Windows Forms Designer and setting its DoubleBuffered property to true from the Properties window.[8] DoubleBuffered is false by default and is implemented by the base Control class and marked with the protected modifier, so only classes that derive from Control can set it—unless, like Form and UserControl, they shadow it. Consequently, you should set DoubleBuffered to true on all custom controls and user controls to ensure that double buffering is enabled:

```
public partial class CustomControl : Control {
   public CustomControl() {
      InitializeComponent();

      // Enable double buffering: equivalent to setting
      // AllPaintingInWmPaint and OptimizedDoubleBuffer
      // control styles
      base.DoubleBuffered = true;
   }
}
```

---

[7] The OptimizedDoubleBuffer style replaces the DoubleBuffer style from previous versions of .NET. You should avoid the DoubleBuffer style except for backwards compatibility.

[8] You can do the same for user controls from the UserControl Designer.

Manual Double Buffering

Requesting double buffering using either ControlStyles or the DoubleBuffered property is an all-or-nothing approach; each paint operation creates a new buffer, renders to it, renders from the buffer to the screen, and releases the buffer. The more intensive your rendering requirements are, the more likely it is that you'll demand more fine-grained control and flexibility from double buffering. When animating, for example, you probably prefer to retain your double buffer across paints—rather than create and dispose of each paint operation—and thus avoid costly memory allocation.

For this, you can do as ControlStyles.OptimizedDoubleBuffer does and use buffered graphics support from System.Drawing. In most cases, you create a buffered graphics context from which you allocate one or more buffered graphics drawing surfaces, each of which represents a graphics surface to which you'll render.

The buffered graphics context is actually the off-screen buffer that you render to. It is exposed via System.Drawing.BufferedGraphicsContext:

```
namespace System.Drawing {
    sealed class BufferedGraphicsContext : IDisposable {

        // Constructor
        BufferedGraphicsContext();

        // Properties
        Size MaximumBuffer { get; set; }

        // Methods
        BufferedGraphics Allocate(
          Graphics targetGraphics, Rectangle targetRectangle);
        BufferedGraphics Allocate(IntPtr targetDC, targetRectangle);
        void Invalidate();
    }
}
```

Your first step is to instantiate BufferedGraphicsContext and specify the size of the off-screen buffer using the MaximumBuffer property:

```
// MainForm.cs
partial class MainForm : Form {

    // Keep buffered graphics context open across method calls
    // and event handling
    BufferedGraphicsContext bufferContext;
    ...
    public MainForm() {

        InitializeComponent();
```

```
      // Allocate the buffer context for a maximum desired size
      bufferContext = new BufferedGraphicsContext();
      bufferContext.MaximumBuffer = this.ClientRectangle.Size;

      // Animate the gif, if possible
      if( ImageAnimator.CanAnimate(gif) ) {
        ImageAnimator.Animate(gif, gif_FrameChanged);
      }
    }
    void gif_FrameChanged(object sender, EventArgs e) { ... }
  }
```

After you've created the off-screen graphics buffer, you create a Graphics object that allows you to render to it. You also specify the target graphics surface that your buffered graphics will ultimately render to. Both needs are satisfied by calling BufferedGraphics-Context's Allocate method:

```
// MainForm.cs
class MainForm : Form {

  // Keep buffered graphics context open across method calls
  // and event handling
  BufferedGraphicsContext bufferContext;
  ...
  public MainForm() { ... }

  void gif_FrameChanged(object sender, EventArgs e) {

    // Create a graphics buffer drawing surface and associate it
    // with the target graphics surface, which is the host form's
    // drawing surface in this example
    Graphics g = this.CreateGraphics();
    using( BufferedGraphics frame =
      bufferContext.Allocate(g, this.ClientRectangle) ) {
      ...
    }
  }
  ...
}
```

As you can see, Allocate returns a BufferedGraphics object instance:

```
namespace System.Drawing {
  sealed class BufferedGraphics : IDisposable {

    // Constructor
    static BufferedGraphics();
```

```
      // Properties
      public Graphics Graphics { get; }

      // Methods
      public void Render();
      public void Render(Graphics target);
      public void Render(IntPtr targetDC);
    }
  }
```

Using the BufferedGraphics instance is a two-step process. First, you paint to the off-screen buffer, using the Graphics object that you acquire from the Graphics property. Then, you call the Render method to blast the bits from your off-screen buffer to the target drawing surface. Both steps are shown here:

```
void gif_FrameChanged(object sender, EventArgs e) {

  // Create a graphics buffer drawing surface and associate it
  // with the target graphics surface, which is the host form's
  // drawing surface in this example
  Graphics g = this.CreateGraphics();
  using( BufferedGraphics frame =
    bufferContext.Allocate(g, this.ClientRectangle) ) {

    // Get next gif frame
    ImageAnimator.UpdateFrames(gif);

    // Render to buffered graphics
    frame.Graphics.DrawImage(gif, this.ClientRectangle);

    // Render buffered graphics to target drawing surface
    frame.Render();
  }
}
```

By creating a BufferedGraphics object instance, you avoid the effort involved in re-creating a new off-screen graphics buffer for every paint cycle. Notice that the BufferedGraphics object is actually created within a *using* block to ensure that system drawing resources are disposed of as soon as possible. You should also remember to dispose of your BufferedGraphicsContext instance:

```
void AnimationBufferingForm_FormClosing(
    object sender, FormClosingEventArgs e) {
    // Release outstanding system drawing resources
    bufferContext.Dispose();
}
```

Double Buffering Performance Considerations

Although double buffering (without the initial erasing of the background) can make all the difference in the user experience, double buffering requires enough memory to capture the entire visible region at the current color quality. At 32 bits per pixel, a 200 × 200 region requires 156 K in additional memory per drawing operation for that region. In memory-constrained systems, this extra memory usage could degrade instead of improve the user experience.

Other Drawing Options

There are a few other drawing-related ControlStyles you may be interested in:

```
namespace System.Drawing {
  enum ControlStyles {
  ...
  // Drawing-related control styles
    UserPaint = 2, // Control that paints itself specially
    Opaque = 4, // OnPaintBackground skipped, Paint draws
                // the entire client area
    ResizeRedraw = 16, // Invalidate entire client area on resize
    SupportsTransparentBackColor = 2048, // Simulated transparent
                                         // controls
    AllPaintingInWmPaint = 8192, // Collapse drawing phases into
                                 // Paint event
    OptimizedDoubleBuffer = 131072, // Hide drawing until Paint
                                    // event returns
  }
}
```

For example, it's common for controls that need double buffering to want to automatically redraw when they're resized. For this, you use the ResizeRedraw style:

```
// Form1.cs
partial class Form1 {
  public Form1() {
    InitializeComponent();

    // Double buffering
    this.DoubleBuffered = true;

    // Redraw when resized
    this.SetStyle(ControlStyles.ResizeRedraw, true);
  }
  ...
}
```

The ControlStyles settings apply at the point where Windows Forms starts wrapping the functionality of Windows itself, which is the Control base class (Forms ultimately derive from Control). Several of the ControlStyles settings have nothing to do with drawing but rather govern how the Control class interacts with the underlying operating system. For more information, see the reference documentation for the ControlStyles enumeration.

Where Are We?

If Chapter 5: Drawing Basics, Chapter 6: Drawing Text, and this chapter haven't convinced you of .NET's rich support for drawing, then Chapter 8: Printing, on drawing to the printer, should do the trick.

8.

Printing

DRAWING TO THE SCREEN is usually easy because screen settings are generally constant during the run of the application. Drawing to a printer, on the other hand, is more complicated because users may change the printer or the printer settings many times, even for a single document. Similarly, paper costs money and can't be sent through the printer twice (unless you don't care what's on the back), so before users print their documents, they want to see what they will look like. The actual drawing is largely the same for a printer as it is for the screen, but the printer settings are the interesting part, and they are covered in this chapter.

Print Documents

The basic unit of printing in Windows Forms is the print document. A *print document* describes the characteristics of what's to be printed, such as the document title, and provides events at various parts of the printing process, such as when it's time to print a page. .NET models the print document using the PrintDocument component (available from the VS05 Toolbox via the Windows Forms tab):

```
namespace System.Drawing.Printing {
  class PrintDocument : Component {
    // Constructor
    public PrintDocument();

    // Properties
    public PageSettings DefaultPageSettings { get; set; }
    public string DocumentName { get; set; }
    public bool OriginAtMargins { get; set; }
    public PrintController PrintController { get; set; }
    public PrinterSettings PrinterSettings { get; set; }
```

```
    // Methods
    public void Print();

    // Events
    public event PrintEventHandler BeginPrint;
    public event PrintEventHandler EndPrint;
    public event PrintPageEventHandler PrintPage;
    public event QueryPageSettingsEventHandler QueryPageSettings;
  }
}
```

To use a PrintDocument component, you create an instance, subscribe to at least the PrintPage event, call the Print method, and handle the PrintPage event:

```
// MainForm.Designer.cs
partial class MainForm {
  ...
  PrintDocument printDocument;
  ...
  void InitializeComponent() {
    ...
    this.printDocument = new PrintDocument();
    ...
    this.printDocument.PrintPage += this.printDocument_PrintPage;
    ...
  }
}

// MainForm.cs
using System.Drawing.Printing;
...
partial class MainForm : Form {
  string fileName = "myFile.txt";

  void printButton_Click(object sender, EventArgs e) {
    this.printDocument.DocumentName = this.fileName;
    this.printDocument.Print();
  }

  void printDocument_PrintPage(object sender, PrintPageEventArgs e) {
    // Draw to the e.Graphics object that wraps the print target
    Graphics g = e.Graphics;
    using( Font font = new Font("Lucida Console", 72) ) {
      g.DrawString("Hello,\nPrinter", font, Brushes.Black, 0, 0);
    }
  }
}
```

The PrintPage event is triggered by a call to the PrintDocument object's Print method. The PrintPage event is responsible for actually rendering the state of the document to the printer surface using the Graphics object. The actual drawing is just like drawing on any other Graphics object, as discussed in Chapter 5: Drawing Basics, Chapter 6: Drawing Text, and Chapter 7: Advanced Drawing.

Notice that this sample sets the DocumentName property of the document. This string shows up in the queue for the printer so that the user can manage the document being printed.

Print Controllers

The name of the print document also shows up in the dialog displayed by the print document during printing. The Printing dialog lets the user cancel the print job as it's being spooled to the printer, as shown in Figure 8.1.

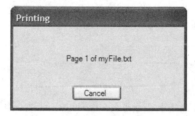

Figure 8.1   The Printing Dialog Shown by PrintControllerWithStatusDialog

The Printing dialog is provided by a print controller. The print controller, modeled as the PrintController abstract base class (from the System.Drawing.Printing namespace) and exposed via the PrintController property of the PrintDocument object, manages the underlying printing process and fires the events as printing progresses. Because printing is fundamentally the rendering of graphics to a printer, a Graphics object that wraps the printer device is required so that drawing commands make it to the printer.

This is the job of the StandardPrintController (from the System.Drawing.Printing namespace), although the default print controller is actually an instance of the PrintControllerWithStatusDialog class (from the System.Windows.Forms namespace), which is the one that shows the Printing dialog in Figure 8.1. PrintControllerWithStatusDialog doesn't do anything except show the dialog; it relies on StandardPrintController to communicate with the printer. In fact, creating an instance of PrintControllerWithStatusDialog requires an instance of the StandardPrintController class as a constructor argument. So, by default, the print controller provided by the print document acts as if you'd written this code:

```
void printButton_Click(object sender, EventArgs e) {
   PrintController standard = new StandardPrintController();
   PrintController status =
      new PrintControllerWithStatusDialog(standard, "Print Status");
   printDocument.PrintController = status;
   printDocument.DocumentName = fileName;
   printDocument.Print();
}
```

If you prefer to print without showing a dialog—for example, when you're printing in the background—you can use StandardPrintController directly:

```
void printButton_Click(object sender, EventArgs e) {
   // Suppress the Printing dialog
   PrintController standard = new StandardPrintController();
   printDocument.PrintController = standard;
   printDocument.DocumentName = fileName;
   printDocument.Print();
}
```

Print Preview

Another print controller that .NET provides is PreviewPrintController (from the System. Drawing.Printing namespace), which is used for previewing a document before it's printed. Figure 8.2 shows a preview print controller being used to prepare a document for preview.

Figure 8.2   PreviewPrintController in Use by PrintPreviewControl

PreviewPrintController is primarily used by PrintPreviewControl (from the System. Windows.Forms namespace), which shows document previews one page at a time by default. PrintPreviewControl is available on the Toolbox and uses the drawing commands performed in PrintDocument's PrintPage event handler to display the client area for a standard print preview-style dialog, as shown in Figure 8.3.

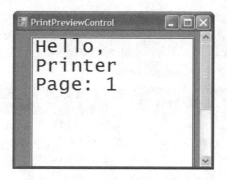

Figure 8.3   The PrintPreviewControl Hosted in a Custom Form

The client area in Figure 8.3 consists of a PrintPreviewControl set to fill the client area (using DockStyle.Fill). Notice that it draws what looks like a piece of paper in miniature, showing the drawing performed by the PrintPage event handler. The PrintPreviewControl class has all kinds of interesting properties and methods for implementing a print preview-style dialog:

```
namespace System.Windows.Forms {
    class PrintPreviewControl : Control {

        // Constructors
        static PrintPreviewControl();
        public PrintPreviewControl();

        // Properties
        public bool AutoZoom { get; set; }
        public int Columns { get; set; }
        public PrintDocument Document { get; set; }
        public override RightToLeft RightToLeft { get; set; } // New
        public int Rows { get; set; }
        public int StartPage { get; set; }
        public override string Text { get; set; }
        public bool UseAntiAlias { get; set; }
        public double Zoom { get; set; }

        // Methods
        public void InvalidatePreview();
        public override void ResetBackColor();
        public override void ResetForeColor();

        // Events
        public event EventHandler StartPageChanged;
        public event EventHandler TextChanged;
    }
}
```

The only requirement is that the Document property be set to an instance of a Print-Document so that the preview control can get the contents of each page to be displayed. Displaying multiple pages at once is a matter of setting the Rows and Columns properties. Figure 8.4 shows a PrintPreviewControl with Rows set to 1 and Columns set to 2.

Figure 8.4   Previewing Multiple Pages at Once in PrintPreviewControl

Displaying the next page (or the next set of pages) is a matter of setting the StartPage property to dictate the page shown in the upper left portion of the control. In addition, PrintPreview Control interprets Page Up and Page Down to move between pages.

The Zoom property is a multiplier: A Zoom of 1.0 is 100%, a Zoom of 0.5 is 50%, and a Zoom of 2.0 is 200%. The AutoZoom property is handy when PrintPreviewControl can resize. When AutoZoom is true (the default), PrintPreviewControl sets the Zoom property to scale the page (or pages) to a size as large as possible inside the control.

Finally, the UseAntiAlias property applies antialiasing to the preview image (this defaults to false to let the printer's higher resolution print smoothly without the need to antialias).

Although it's useful to implement a custom print preview-style dialog with zooming, page count, and multipage support, often a "standard" print preview dialog is all that's required. In those cases, the PrintPreviewDialog component is your friend. Figure 8.5 shows the PrintPreviewDialog component in action.

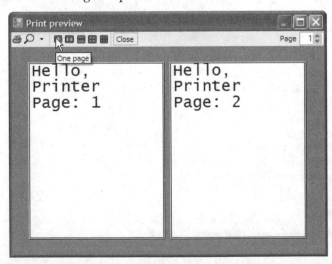

Figure 8.5   The PrintPreviewDialog Component

The PrintPreviewDialog component uses PrintPreviewControl and your PrintDocument instance to provide a full-featured, preview-style dialog:

```
PrintPreviewDialog printPreviewDialog;

void InitializeComponent() {
  ...
  this.printPreviewDialog = new PrintPreviewDialog();
  ...
}

void printPreviewDialogButton_Click(object sender, EventArgs e) {
  this.printPreviewDialog.Document = this.printDocument;
  this.printPreviewDialog.ShowDialog();
}
```

PrintPreviewDialog Control Box Icon

Additionally, PrintPreviewDialog allows you to hide or show a control box icon (shown by default) using the Boolean ShowIcon property. Further, although PrintPreviewDialog exposes an Icon property, it is hidden from the Windows Forms Designer and Properties window.[1] However, you can still set Icon programmatically:

```
void printPreviewDialogButton_Click(object sender, EventArgs e) {
  this.printPreviewDialog.Document = this.printDocument;
  // Change icon
  this.printPreviewDialog.Icon = Properties.Resources.printpreview;
  this.printPreviewDialog.ShowDialog();
}
```

This yields the icon shown in Figure 8.6.

Figure 8.6   PrintPreviewDialog with Updated Control Box Icon

PrintDialog and PageSetupDialog, discussed later, provide no way to specify an icon or influence whether they show an icon.

---

[1] The Icon property is "hidden" via attribution with both the Browsable and EditorBrowsable attributes, which are covered in Chapter 11: Design-Time Integration: The Properties Window.

Basic Print Events

All print controller implementations rely on the print document's print events to gather the drawing commands into the Graphics object, either to spool to the printer or to show on the screen:

```
void printDocument_PrintPage(object sender, PrintPageEventArgs e) {
  // Draw to the e.Graphics object that wraps the print target
  Graphics g = e.Graphics;
  using( Font font = new Font("Lucida Console", 72) ) {
    g.DrawString("Hello,\nPrinter", font, Brushes.Black, 0, 0);
  }
}
```

Notice that this sample PrintPage event handler creates a font only for printing. For a single page, this code is fine, because it creates the font and then reclaims the font resources when the printing is complete. However, if we're printing more than one page, it's wasteful to create the font anew on each page. On the other hand, creating a font for printing and then caching it in a field seems wasteful if the font is never used again after the print job. What we need is to be notified when a print job is started and ended so that we can have tight control over print-related resources. For this, we use the print document's BeginPrint and EndPrint events:

```
Font printerfont = null;

void printDocument_BeginPrint(object sender, PrintEventArgs e) {
  // Create font for printing
  printerfont = new Font("Lucida Console", 72);
}

void printDocument_EndPrint(object sender, PrintEventArgs e) {
  // Reclaim font
  printerfont.Dispose();
  printerfont = null;
}
```

Notice that the BeginPrint and EndPrint event handlers are passed an instance of the PrintEventArgs class:

```
namespace System.Drawing.Printing {
  class PrintEventArgs : CancelEventArgs {
    // Properties
    public bool Cancel { get; set; }
    public PrintAction PrintAction { get; } // New
  }
}
```

updated

PrintEventArgs derives from CancelEventArgs to allow you to cancel a print operation if certain conditions aren't met—for example, a lack of data to print:

```
void printDocument_BeginPrint(object sender, PrintEventArgs e) {
  ...
  // Don't print if data not available to print
  if( myDataObject == null ) e.Cancel = true;
}
```

PrintEventArgs.PrintAction provides information about the type of printing that is taking place, and is one of the values of the PrintAction enumeration:

```
namespace System.Drawing.Printing {
  enum PrintAction {
    PrintToFile = 0,
    PrintToPreview = 1,
    PrintToPrinter = 2
  }
}
```

This value is ultimately determined by the print controller that's being used; if PreviewPrintController is processing a print document, PrintAction has a value of Print-ToPreview. Thus, PrintAction allows you to determine the type of print before printing takes place, information that PrintPage can use if it needs to tailor the output it generates on a per-target basis. The following code checks for a print preview, which receives special attention later in this chapter:

```
bool preview;
...
void printDocument_BeginPrint(object sender, PrintEventArgs e) {
  ...
  // Print preview?
  preview = (e.PrintAction == PrintAction.PrintToPreview);
}
```

Like BeginPrint, EndPrint is passed a PrintEventArgs object. Unlike BeginPrint and EndPrint, the PrintPage event comes with an instance of the PrintPageEventArgs class:

```
namespace System.Drawing.Printing {
  class PrintPageEventArgs : EventArgs {
    // Constructors
    public PrintPageEventArgs(
      Graphics graphics,
      Rectangle marginBounds,
      Rectangle pageBounds,
      PageSettings pageSettings);
```

```
    // Properties
    public bool Cancel { get; set; }
    public Graphics Graphics { get; }
    public bool HasMorePages { get; set; }
    public Rectangle MarginBounds { get; }
    public Rectangle PageBounds { get; }
    public PageSettings PageSettings { get; }
  }
}
```

As you've seen, the Cancel property is used to cancel a print job, and the Graphics property is used for drawing. HasMorePages defaults to false. If there are more pages to print, you set HasMorePages to true during the PrintPage handler for all pages except the last page of a multipage document:

```
int totalPages = 13;
int page;
int maxPage;

void printDocument_PrintPage(object sender, PrintPageEventArgs e) {

  // Draw to the e.Graphics object that wraps the print target
  Graphics g = e.Graphics;
  using( Font font = new Font("Lucida Console", 72) ) {
    g.DrawString("Hello,\nPrinter\nPage: " + page.ToString(), ...);
  }

  // Check whether there are more pages to print
  ++page;
  e.HasMorePages = ( page <= maxPage );
}

void printPreviewDialogButton_Click(object sender, EventArgs e) {
  // Calculate print preview range
  page = 1;
  maxPage = totalPages;
  // Print
  this.printPreviewDialog.Document = this.printDocument;
  this.printPreviewDialog.ShowDialog();
}
```

This example has 13 pages, and as many as 6 can be shown in the print preview dialog at once (as shown in Figure 8.7).

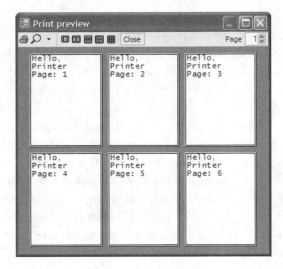

Figure 8.7   Printing Multiple Pages

Margins

The PageBounds rectangle property of the PrintPageEventArgs class represents the entire rectangle of the page, all the way to the edge. The MarginBounds rectangle represents the area inside the margins. Figure 8.8 shows the difference.

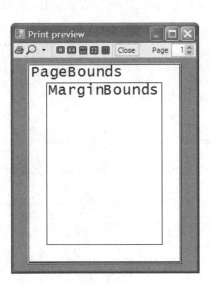

Figure 8.8   PageBounds Versus MarginBounds

Both PageBounds and MarginBounds are always scaled to units of 100 dpi, so a standard 8.5 × 11 inch piece of paper will always have a PageBounds rectangle {0, 0, 850, 1100}. With the default margin of 1 inch all the way around, the MarginBounds is at {100, 100, 750, 1000}. To match the bounds, by default the GraphicsUnit for the Graphics object is 100 dpi, too, and is scaled to whatever is appropriate for the printer resolution. For example, my laser printer is 600 × 600 dpi.

The margin is useful not only because users often want some white space around their printed pages, but also because many printers can't print to the edge of the page, so anything printed all the way to the edge is bound to be cut off to some degree. To avoid this, the Graphics object you get when you're printing starts at the top-left corner of the printable area of the page. That's useful for printing outside the margins, such as for headers or footers.

However, because printers normally can't print to the edge of the page, the PageBounds rectangle will be too large. To get the actual size of the bounding rectangle, you can use the Graphics object's VisibleClipBounds rectangle:

```
// Get a page bounds with an accurate size
RectangleF visibleClipBounds = e.Graphics.VisibleClipBounds;


// Draw a header
g.DrawString("header", printerfont, Brushes.Black, visibleClipBounds);
```

If the Graphics object is using a nondefault PageUnit[2], then VisibleClipBounds will be in different units than PageBounds (which is always in units of 100 dpi). To handle these variables, it's useful to have a helper method to return the "real" page bounds in a consistent unit of measure:

```
// Get real page bounds based on printable area of the page
static Rectangle GetRealPageBounds(PrintPageEventArgs e, bool preview) {
  // Return in units of 1/100 inch
  if( preview ) return e.PageBounds;

  // Translate to units of 1/100 inch
  RectangleF vpb = e.Graphics.VisibleClipBounds;
  PointF[] bottomRight = {
    new PointF(vpb.Size.Width, vpb.Size.Height)
  };
  e.Graphics.TransformPoints(
    CoordinateSpace.Device, CoordinateSpace.Page, bottomRight);
  float dpiX = e.Graphics.DpiX;
  float dpiY = e.Graphics.DpiY;
  return new Rectangle(0, 0, (int)(bottomRight[0].X * 100 / dpiX),
                             (int)(bottomRight[0].Y * 100 / dpiY));
}
```

[2] PageUnit is discussed in Chapter 7.

GetRealPageBounds returns the PageBounds rectangle if in preview mode and always scales the returned Rectangle in the same units. This helper allows you to write your printing code to stay within the real bounds of the page:

```
void printDocument_PrintPage(object sender, PrintPageEventArgs e) {
    // Draw to the e.Graphics object that wraps the print target
    Graphics g = e.Graphics;

    // Get the real page bounds
    Rectangle realPageBounds = GetRealPageBounds(e, preview);

    // Draw a header in the upper left
    g.DrawString("header", printerfont, Brushes.Black, realPageBounds);

    // Draw a footer in the lower right
    StringFormat farFormat = new StringFormat();
    farFormat.Alignment = StringAlignment.Far;
    farFormat.LineAlignment = StringAlignment.Far;
    g.DrawString(
      "footer",
      printerfont,
      Brushes.Black,
      realPageBounds,
      farFormat);
}
```

For the bulk of the printed content, however, you should print inside the MarginBounds rectangle:

```
void printDocument_PrintPage(object sender, PrintPageEventArgs e) {
    // Draw to the e.Graphics object that wraps the print target
    Graphics g = e.Graphics;
    ...
    g.DrawString("Content", printerfont, Brushes.Black, e.MarginBounds);
}
```

Unfortunately, because MarginBounds is offset from PageBounds and because PageBounds is offset to stay inside the printable region of the page, MarginBounds is often lined up at offsets that don't match the user-specified margins along the edge of the page.

For example, on my Hewlett-Packard LaserJet 2100, the left edge of the PageBounds rectangle is actually ¼ inch in from the left edge, and the top edge is ⅙ inch down from the top. This affects the MarginBounds, lining up the 1-inch margin I expect at 1¼ inches from the left edge of the page. This poses a problem because neither the PageBounds nor the VisibleClipBounds actually tells you how much the offset of the PageBounds is from the actual edge of the paper. The PageSettings class does tell you—via its PrintableArea property, which returns a RectangleF (the PageBounds plus the printer offsets).

However, it turns out to be just a little bit easier to determine a printer's physical X and Y offsets from the top left by using PageSettings.HardMarginX and PageSettings.HardMarginY. You can then use these values to adjust the margins appropriately. However, the X and Y offsets are in printer coordinates, which may not be the same units as the MarginBounds, so you must convert those units as well. The following helper methods do all that work:

```
// Adjust MarginBounds rectangle when printing based
// on the physical characteristics of the printer
static Rectangle GetRealMarginBounds(
    PrintPageEventArgs e, bool preview) {

    if( preview ) return e.MarginBounds;

    // Get printer's offsets
    float cx = e.PageSettings.HardMarginX;
    float cy = e.PageSettings.HardMarginY;

    // Create the real margin bounds by scaling the offset
    // by the printer resolution and then rescaling it
    // back to 1/100 inch
    Rectangle marginBounds = e.MarginBounds;
    float dpiX = e.Graphics.DpiX;
    float dpiY = e.Graphics.DpiY;
    marginBounds.Offset((int)(-cx * 100 / dpiX), (int)(-cy * 100 / dpiY));
    return marginBounds;
}
```

The GetRealMarginBounds method takes preview mode into account and, when you use a real printer, adjusts MarginBounds using the physical offsets, always returning a rectangle in the same units. With this in place, you can safely print inside the margins based on the edges of the paper, as you'd expect:

```
void printDocument_PrintPage(object sender, PrintPageEventArgs e) {
    // Draw to the e.Graphics object that wraps the print target
    Graphics g = e.Graphics;
    ...
    RectangleF realMarginBounds = GetRealMarginBounds(e, preview);
    g.DrawString(
        "Content", printerfont, Brushes.Black, realMarginBounds);
}
```

As an alternative to using these helper functions, the .NET 2.0 Framework provides a property on PrintDocument called OriginAtMargins. This property defaults to false, but setting it to true sets the offset of the PageBounds rectangle to be at the margin offset from the physical edge of the page, letting you print at the appropriate margins using the Page-Bounds rectangle. However, this property doesn't have any effect in preview mode, doesn't adjust the PageBounds size, and keeps the MarginBounds as offset from the now further offset PageBounds. For these reasons, I don't find it particularly useful when compared with the GetRealPageBounds and GetRealMarginBounds helper methods.

Page Settings

You may have noticed that both the MarginBounds and the PageSettings properties of the PrintPageEventArgs class are read-only. Changing PageSettings (including the margins) on-the-fly requires handling the print document's QueryPageSettings event, which is fired before each page is printed:

```
void printDocument_QueryPageSettings(
    object sender, QueryPageSettingsEventArgs e) {
    // Set margins to 0.5" all the way around
    // (measured in hundredths of an inch)
    e.PageSettings.Margins = new Margins(50, 50, 50, 50);
}
```

QueryPageSettingsEventArgs exposes only the Cancel and PageSettings properties. The latter is an instance of the PageSettings class:

```
namespace System.Drawing.Printing {
    class PageSettings : ICloneable {

        // Constructors
        public PageSettings();
        public PageSettings(PrinterSettings printerSettings);

        // Properties
        public Rectangle Bounds { get; }
        public bool Color { get; set; }
        public float HardMarginX { get; } // New
        public float HardMarginY { get; } // New
        public bool Landscape { get; set; }
        public Margins Margins { get; set; }
        public PaperSize PaperSize { get; set; }
        public PaperSource PaperSource { get; set; }
```

updated

```
    public RectangleF PrintableArea { get; } // New
    public PrinterResolution PrinterResolution { get; set; }
    public PrinterSettings PrinterSettings { get; set; }

    // Methods
    public object Clone();
    public void CopyToHdevmode(IntPtr hdevmode);
    public void SetHdevmode(IntPtr hdevmode);
    public override string ToString();
  }
}
```

In addition to setting the margins, you can set the PageSettings object to indicate whether color is allowed, the size and source of the paper, the printer resolution, and other printer-specific settings. You could adjust these properties programmatically during the printing process, but it's friendlier to let the user do it before the printing begins. For that, you use the PageSetupDialog component, from System.Windows.Forms, as shown in Figure 8.9.

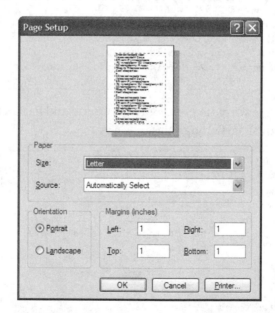

Figure 8.9   PageSetupDialog Component with Default Page Settings

Before you can show the Page Setup dialog, you must set the Document property:

```
PageSetupDialog pageSetupDialog;

void InitializeComponent() {
  ...
  this.pageSetupDialog = new PageSetupDialog();
  ...
}

void pageSetupButton_Click(object sender, EventArgs e) {
  // Let the user select page settings
  this.pageSetupDialog.Document = this.printDocument;
  this.pageSetupDialog.ShowDialog();
}
```

When the user presses OK, the PageSettings properties are adjusted for that instance of the PrintDocument and are used at the next printing. PageSetupDialog itself provides some useful options:

```
namespace System.Windows.Forms {
  sealed class PageSetupDialog : CommonDialog {

    // Properties
    public bool AllowMargins { get; set; }
    public bool AllowOrientation { get; set; }
    public bool AllowPaper { get; set; }
    public bool AllowPrinter { get; set; }
    public PrintDocument Document { get; set; }
    public bool EnableMetric { get; set; } // New
    public Margins MinMargins { get; set; }
    public PageSettings PageSettings { get; set; }
    public PrinterSettings PrinterSettings { get; set; }
    public bool ShowHelp { get; set; }
    public bool ShowNetwork { get; set; }

    // Methods
    public PageSetupDialog();
    public override void Reset();

    // Events
    public event EventHandler HelpRequest;
  }
}
```

The Allow*Xxx* properties dictate whether the dialog allows the user to change things such as the margins or the orientation (all these properties default to true). The MinMargins property sets minimum margins that the user can't set smaller. EnableMetric, when true, specifies that the PageSetupDialog will display printer measurements in metric if that's what the current locale demands; by default, EnableMetric is false.

The ShowHelp property indicates whether the help button should be shown. By default it isn't shown, because there's no built-in help to show (other than the pop-up help). If you set ShowHelp to true, make sure to subscribe to the HelpRequest event so that when the user presses the help button, you can provide help. Finally, the ShowNetwork property determines whether the user can navigate the network to find a printer after pressing the Printer button (assuming AllowPrinter is set to true).

Printer Settings

So far, all the printing in this chapter has been done to the default printer, as defined by Windows. The user can change the printer for a document via the printer button on the PageSetupDialog. It's more common, however, to allow the user to choose the printer after choosing the Print item from the File menu. For this you use the PrintDialog component, from the System.Windows.Forms namespace, as shown in Figure 8.10.

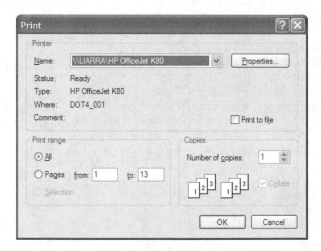

Figure 8.10   The PrintDialog Component

Here's how you use the PrintDialog component:

```csharp
// MainForm.Designer.cs
partial class MainForm {
  ...
  PrintDialog printDialog;
  ...
  void InitializeComponent() {
    ...
    this.printDialog = new PrintDialog();
    ...
  }
}

// MainForm.cs
partial class MainForm : Form {
  ...
  void printButton_Click(object sender, EventArgs e) {
    // Let the user choose the printer
    this.printDialog.Document = this.printDocument;
    if( this.printDialog.ShowDialog() == DialogResult.OK ) {
      this.printDocument.DocumentName = fileName;
      this.printDocument.Print();
    }
  }
}
```

Like PageSetupDialog, the PrintDialog component allows you to set a number of options before it is shown:

```csharp
namespace System.Windows.Forms {
  sealed class PrintDialog : CommonDialog {
    // Methods
    public PrintDialog();
    public override void Reset();

    // Properties
    public bool AllowCurrentPage { get; set; } // New
    public bool AllowPrintToFile { get; set; }
    public bool AllowSelection { get; set; }
    public bool AllowSomePages { get; set; }
    public PrintDocument Document { get; set; }
    public PrinterSettings PrinterSettings { get; set; }
    public bool PrintToFile { get; set; }
    public bool ShowHelp { get; set; }
    public bool ShowNetwork { get; set; }
    public bool UseEXDialog { get; set; } // New
```

updated

```
    // Events
    public event EventHandler HelpRequest;
  }
}
```

You must set the Document property before showing a PrintDialog object. The UseEX-Dialog property can be set to true if you prefer to display the extended, better-looking Print dialog shown in Figure 8.11.[3]

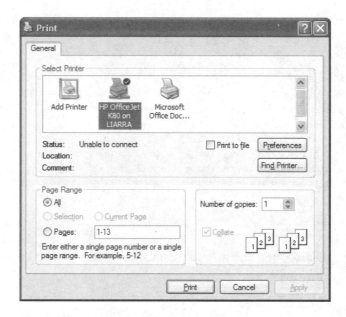

Figure 8.11   The Extended PrintDialog Component

The other PrintDialog properties are similar in function to the PageSetupDialog properties. A couple of properties are special, however, because they determine what to print. Let's take a look.

Print Range

The AllowSelection property of PrintDialog lets the user print only the current selection, and AllowSomePages allows the user to decide on a subset of pages to be

[3] Users must be running versions no older than Windows 2000 or Windows XP.

printed.[4] Both settings require you to print specially, based on the PrintRange property of the PrinterSettings class (discussed in a moment), which is of type PrintRange:

```
namespace System.Drawing.Printing {
  enum PrintRange {
    // Fields
    AllPages = 0, // Print all pages (default)
    Selection = 1, // Print only the current selection
    SomePages = 2, // Print pages from FromPage to ToPage
    CurrentPage = 4194304 // Print the current page (New)
  }
}
```

Before you can set a print range that's different from AllPages, you must set AllSelection or AllowSomePages (or both) to true (they both default to false). AllowSomePages also requires that the PrinterSettings' FromPage and ToPage be set greater than the default of zero:

```
int totalPages = 13;
int page;

void printButton_Click(object sender, EventArgs e) {
  // Let the user choose the printer
  this.printDocument.PrinterSettings.FromPage = 1;
  this.printDocument.PrinterSettings.ToPage = totalPages;
  this.printDocument.PrinterSettings.MinimumPage = 1;
  this.printDocument.PrinterSettings.MaximumPage = totalPages;
  this.printDialog.AllowSomePages = true;
  this.printDialog.Document = this.printDocument;
  if( this.printDialog.ShowDialog() == DialogResult.OK ) {
    this.printDocument.DocumentName = fileName;
    this.printDocument.Print();
  }
}
```

When you set AllowSomePages to true, it's a good idea to also set MinimumPage and MaximumPage; while not required, this prevents users from accidentally asking for a page out of the allowed range. If AllowSelection or AllowSomePages is set to true, the

---

[4] What, if anything, the "current selection" means is application-specific. However, Betsy Hardinger, the copy editor for this book, made an impassioned plea that when the print dialog is invoked while there is a current selection, the print dialog default to printing only the selection and not all 75 pages of the document (which Betsy often finds herself printing when she doesn't want to). Thank you.

PrintPage event must check the PrintRange and FromPage and ToPage properties to see what to print:

```
int totalPages = 13;
int page;
int maxPage;

void printButton_Click(object sender, EventArgs e) {
  ...
  if( this.printDialog.ShowDialog() == DialogResult.OK ) {
    if( this.printDialog.PrinterSettings.PrintRange ==
          PrintRange.SomePages ) {
      // Set first page to print to FromPage
      page = this.printDocument.PrinterSettings.FromPage;

      // Set last page to print to ToPage
      maxPage = this.printDocument.PrinterSettings.ToPage;
    }
    else {
      // Print all pages
      page = 1;
      maxPage = totalPages;
    }

    // Print from first page to last page
    this.printDocument.DocumentName = fileName;
    this.printDocument.Print();
  }
}

void printDocument_PrintPage(object sender, PrintPageEventArgs e) {
  // Draw to the e.Graphics object that wraps the print target
  Graphics g = e.Graphics;

  // Print current page
  ...

  // Check whether there are more pages to print
  ++page;
  e.HasMorePages = ( page <= maxPage );
}
```

In addition to the PrintRange, FromPage, and ToPage properties, the PrinterSettings class has many more settings for use in determining exactly how the user would like to print:

```
namespace System.Drawing.Printing {
   class PrinterSettings : ICloneable {
     // Properties
     public bool CanDuplex { get; }
     public bool Collate { get; set; }
     public short Copies { get; set; }
     public PageSettings DefaultPageSettings { get; }
     internal string DriverName { get; }
     public Duplex Duplex { get; set; }
     public int FromPage { get; set; }
     public static StringCollection InstalledPrinters { get; }
     public bool IsDefaultPrinter { get; }
     public bool IsPlotter { get; }
     public bool IsValid { get; }
     public int LandscapeAngle { get; }
     public int MaximumCopies { get; }
     public int MaximumPage { get; set; }
     public int MinimumPage { get; set; }
     public PaperSizeCollection PaperSizes { get; }
     public PaperSourceCollection PaperSources { get; }
     public string PrinterName { get; set; }
     public PrinterResolutionCollection PrinterResolutions { get; }
     public string PrintFileName { get; set; } // New
     public PrintRange PrintRange { get; set; }
     public bool PrintToFile { get; set; }
     public bool SupportsColor { get; }
     public int ToPage { get; set; }

     // Methods
     public PrinterSettings();
     public object Clone();
     public Graphics CreateMeasurementGraphics(...); // New
     public IntPtr GetHdevmode(...);
     public IntPtr GetHdevnames();
     public bool IsDirectPrintingSupported(...); // New
     public void SetHdevmode(IntPtr hdevmode);
     public void SetHdevnames(IntPtr hdevnames);
   }
}
```

Of particular interest is the CreateMeasurementGraphics method, which returns a Graphics object based on the printer and its settings. You can use this Graphics object for making measurement calculations and for enumerating the font families (using the FontFamily.GetFamilies method), all without having to actually start a print operation.

PrinterSettings represents the last major piece of the printing infrastructure, which includes print controllers, print documents, and page settings. Figure 8.12 illustrates the basic relationship between them.

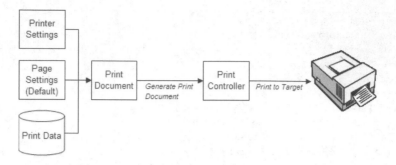

Figure 8.12   Relationship Between the Major Elements of the Printing Infrastructure

Targeting the Printer

Recall that because the drawing happens on a Graphics object, all the drawing techniques from Chapter 5, Chapter 6, and Chapter 7 work just as well with printers as they do with screens. However, unlike the screen, where page units default to Pixel, the page units for the printer default to Display. Furthermore, whereas Display means Pixel on the screen, Display maps the printer resolution to a logical 100 dpi for the printer.

Because printers often have different resolutions both vertically and horizontally and are almost never 100 dpi anyway, this may seem unintuitive. However, the default system font setting is 96 dpi on the screen, so mapping the printer to a logical 100 dpi means that the default mappings for both screen and printer yield a quick and dirty near-WYSIWYG without your having to change a thing. If you want something even closer, you're free to use page units such as inches or millimeters, as discussed in Chapter 7.

If you do change the units, remember to convert PageBounds and MarginBounds to the new units as well. You can use the Graphics method TransformPoints:

```
static RectangleF TranslateBounds(Graphics g, Rectangle bounds) {
  // Translate from units of 1/100 inch to page units
  float dpiX = g.DpiX;
  float dpiY = g.DpiY;
  PointF[] pts = new PointF[2];
  pts[0] = new PointF(bounds.X * dpiX / 100, bounds.Y * dpiY / 100);
  pts[1] = new PointF(
    bounds.Width * dpiX / 100, bounds.Height * dpiX / 100);
  g.TransformPoints(CoordinateSpace.Page, CoordinateSpace.Device, pts);
  return new RectangleF(pts[0].X, pts[0].Y, pts[1].X, pts[1].Y);
}
```

The TranslateBounds helper method uses the current Graphics object to translate a PageBounds or MarginBounds rectangle from units of 100 dpi to whatever the page unit is set to. This helper is meant to be used from the PrintPage handler:

```
void printDocument_PrintPage(object sender, PrintPageEventArgs e) {
  // Draw to the e.Graphics object that wraps the print target
  Graphics g = e.Graphics;
  g.PageUnit = GraphicsUnit.Inch;
  ...
  using( Pen thinPen = new Pen(Color.Black, 0) ) {
    RectangleF pageBounds = GetRealPageBounds(e, preview);
    pageBounds = TranslateBounds(g, Rectangle.Truncate(pageBounds));
    g.DrawRectangle(
      thinPen,
      pageBounds.X,
      pageBounds.Y,
      pageBounds.Width,
      pageBounds.Height);
    ...
  }
  ...
}
```

Notice that PageUnit is set on the Graphics object to the appropriate GraphicsUnit enumeration value right away so that any drawing that takes place in the PrintPage handler is in the specified unit. Notice also the creation of a new Pen object with a thickness of zero. By default, all the pens exposed from the Pens class have a width of 1, which is 1 unit thick, or, in this example, 1 inch thick. A Pen of width zero, on the other hand, is always 1 device unit thick, something that is more useful for framing a rectangle.

Finally, notice that the PrintPage handler sets the PageUnit during each page being printed. Each time the PrintPage handler is called, it gets a fresh Graphics object, so don't forget to set its options every time.

Useful Printing Techniques

Our tour of the printing landscape has so far negotiated the spectrum of fundamental concepts, types, and techniques you typically need when you start building a printing solution. Now, we build on these to create useful techniques for solving several printing problems you may encounter, including word wrapping and pagination, configuration of page settings on a per-page basis, and dynamic page counting.

Word Wrapping and Pagination

As you've seen, printing is a graphical process built on a PrintDocument and its PrintPage event. We've dealt only with highly specific, simple scenarios where we knew that the output would fit within a page. But the norm is more complex, even if you are dealing with a simple text file. Printing algorithms must ensure that all file data is displayed—that is, no data disappears beyond any of the margins.

You've seen how to determine the printable area of a page, but you haven't seen how to handle situations when file data doesn't fit within the area, most commonly when a line of text you want printed with a specific font is wider than the printable area at hand. The common solution to this is *word wrapping,* in which any pieces of text that don't fit are printed onto, or wrapped to, the following line. As you saw in Chapter 6, Graphics.Measure-String and Graphics.DrawString provide native word wrapping.

DrawString automatically wraps text if it doesn't fit into an area defined by a SizeF object that you've specified. But that's the easy part. The hard part is to determine where the next line of text needs to be printed; its start location depends on how high the previous line of text ended up being, and whether it fitted on a single line or needed to be wrapped over multiple lines.

One technique for handling this is to maintain the size and location of the printable area, adjusting it after every line of text printed so that its adjusted size represents the location and size of the remaining area of print in which we will attempt to render the next line of text. Figure 8.13 illustrates this idea.

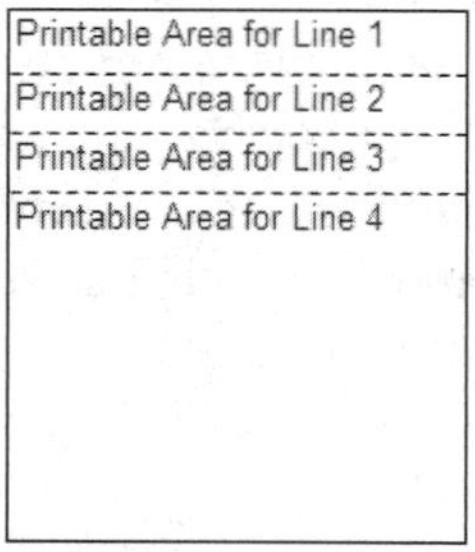

Figure 8.13   Maintaining Printable Area Information

As each line is printed, the printable area needs to increase its Top property by the height of the previous printed line of text, and reduce its height by the same value. The height of the text is nicely calculated by MeasureString:

```
// MainForm.cs
partial class MainForm : Form {
  ...
   int rowCount;
```

```
Font textFont;
bool preview;
List<String> fileRows = new List<string>(); // Text file

public MainForm() {
  InitializeComponent();
  // "Load" text file
  ...
  // Preview text file
  this.printPreviewControl.InvalidatePreview();
}

void printDocument_BeginPrint(object sender, PrintEventArgs e) {

  // Don't print if nothing to print
  if( fileRows == null ) e.Cancel = true;

  // Preprinting configuration
  this.textFont = new Font("Arial", 25);
  this.preview = (e.PrintAction == PrintAction.PrintToPreview);
}

void printDocument_PrintPage(
  object sender, Printing.PrintPageEventArgs e) {

  Graphics g = e.Graphics;
  ...
  // Print page text
  Rectangle printableArea = GetRealMarginBounds(
    e, this.printDocument.PrinterSettings, preview);

  while( this.rowCount < fileRows.Count ) {

    string line = fileRows[rowCount];

    // Get size for word wrap
    SizeF printSize =
      g.MeasureString(line, this.textFont, printableArea.Width);

    // Print line
    g.DrawString(line, this.textFont, Brushes.Black, printableArea);

    // Calculate and reduce remaining printable area
    printableArea.Y += (int)printSize.Height;
    printableArea.Height -= (int)printSize.Height;

    ++this.rowCount;
  }
```

```
      // Keep printing while more rows
      e.HasMorePages = (this.rowCount < fileRows.Count);
  }

  void printDocument_EndPrint(object sender, PrintEventArgs e) {
    // Postprinting cleanup
    this.textFont.Dispose();
  }
  ...
}
```

Now, we ensure that each line of text is printed on a new line in the document, but we don't handle what happens when there are more lines than will fit on a page. The ability during printing (or rendering to screen like a word processor) to determine when a new page needs to start and, if required, creating a new page and continuing printing, is known as *pagination*.

A new page basically starts when the remaining printable area is less than the height of the next line to output. Our word-wrapping code actually contains the two pieces of information that we need if we are to determine this for ourselves: the height of the remaining line and the height of the remaining printable area. If the former is greater than the latter, we simply exit the *while* loop. If there's more file data left, we set HasMorePages to whether or not we have reached the end of the stream, ensuring that we print a new page. The updates are shown here:

```
public partial class MainForm : Form {
  ...
  int pageCount;
  ...
  Font headerFont;
  ...
  void printDocument_BeginPrint(object sender, PrintEventArgs e) {
    // Preprinting configuration
    this.headerFont = new Font("Arial", 50);
    ...
  }
  ...
  void printDocument_PrintPage(object sender, PrintPageEventArgs e) {

    Graphics g = e.Graphics;

    // Print page header
    string headerText = "Page " + this.pageCount;
    Rectangle marginBounds = GetRealMarginBounds(e, preview);
    RectangleF headerArea =
      new RectangleF(
        marginBounds.Left, 0, marginBounds.Width, marginBounds.Top);
```

```csharp
  using( StringFormat format = new StringFormat() ) {
    format.LineAlignment = StringAlignment.Center;
    g.DrawString(
      headerText, headerFont, Brushes.Black, headerArea, format);
  }
  ...
  while( this.rowCount < fileRows.Count ) {

    string line = fileRows[rowCount];

    // Get size for word wrap
    SizeF printSize =
      g.MeasureString(line, this.textFont, printableArea.Width);

    if( printableArea.Height > printSize.Height ) {

      // Print line
      g.DrawString(line, this.textFont, Brushes.Black, printableArea);

      // Calculate and reduce remaining printable area
      printableArea.Y += (int)printSize.Height;
      printableArea.Height -= (int)printSize.Height;

      ++this.rowCount;
    }
    else break;
  }

  // Increment page count
  ++this.pageCount;

  // Keep printing while more rows
  e.HasMorePages = (this.rowCount < fileRows.Count);

}

void printDocument_EndPrint(object sender, PrintEventArgs e) {
  // Postprinting cleanup
  this.headerFont.Dispose();
  ...
}
}
```

One trick you may have noticed in this code is the buffering of the last read-in line, which happens in the event that the last line read doesn't fit in the remaining area. Because we can't reset the buffer to the position it was in before reading a line that doesn't fit, we need to store it somewhere else and use it during the next read.

Figure 8.14 shows the results of our machinations, with the source text file rendered to a print preview using the PrintPreviewControl.

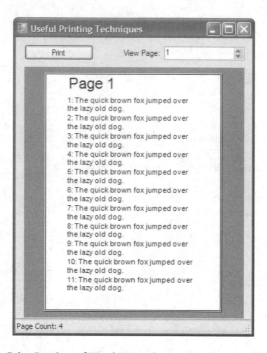

Figure 8.14   Print Preview of Word-Wrapping and Paginating Print Algorithm

The pagination algorithm is simple, unlike the algorithms in applications like Microsoft Word, which support much more comprehensive editing, previewing, and printing scenarios. That discussion is beyond the scope of this book.

After your print algorithm accommodates pagination, you can easily support the application of page settings to individual pages rather than the entire document.

Per-Page Page Setting Configuration

It is always possible that a document printed to multiple pages might need different settings from one page to the next. For example, for report-style documents, users may prefer to show text using portrait orientation and show graphs and images using landscape orientation. To support this, you need to solve three problems. First, you need to identify individual pages before your print them, a situation we have already enabled through pagination. Second, you need to allow users to assign specific PageSettings to each page. Third, you need to use PageSettings objects while printing.

Using the PrintPreviewControl from the previous example, we easily determine the page that users are on. Then, we use the Page Setup dialog to allow users to specify a specific set of page settings, returned from PageSetup via its PageSettings property. Finally, we internally use a hashtable to store PageSettings, using the page number as the hashtable key value:

```
Hashtable pageSettings = new Hashtable();
...
void editPageSettingsButton_Click(object sender, EventArgs e) {

  // Set Page Setup dialog with page settings for current page
  PageSettings pageCountSettings = (PageSettings)
    pageSettings[(int)this.previewPageNumericUpDown.Value];
  if( pageCountSettings != null ) {
    this.pageSetupDialog.PageSettings = pageCountSettings;
  }
  else this.pageSetupDialog.PageSettings = new PageSettings();

  // Edit page settings
  if( this.pageSetupDialog.ShowDialog() == DialogResult.OK ) {
    // Store new page settings and apply
    pageSettings[(int)this.previewPageNumericUpDown.Value] =
      (PageSettings)this.pageSetupDialog.PageSettings.Clone();
  }
}
```

If the PageSettings change, your UI should reflect those changes, whether the user is previewing or editing a document. If you use PrintPreviewControl, you make a call to its InvalidatePreview method:

```
void editPageSettingsButton_Click(object sender, EventArgs e) {
  ...
  // Edit page settings
  if( this.pageSetupDialog.ShowDialog() == DialogResult.OK ) {
    ...
    this.printPreviewControl.InvalidatePreview();
  }
}
```

InvalidatePreview causes PrintPreviewControl to repaint itself. During this process, and when printing, we need to pass the appropriate updated PageSettings object to the Print-Controller for the currently printing page. As you saw earlier, this is what PrintDocument's QueryPageSettings event is for, and here's how you use it:

```
void printDocument_QueryPageSettings(
    object sender, QueryPageSettingsEventArgs e) {
  // Get page settings for the page that's currently printing
```

```
    PageSettings pageCountSettings =
      (PageSettings)pageSettings[pageCount];
    if( pageCountSettings != null ) {
      e.PageSettings = pageCountSettings;
    }
    else e.PageSettings = new PageSettings();
  }
```

Figure 8.15 shows a previewed page whose orientation was switched from portrait to landscape.

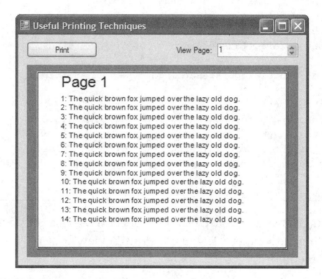

Figure 8.15   Custom PageSettings Applied

You may have noticed that the QueryPageSettings event handler returns a default Page-Settings object if a custom one doesn't exist for the currently printing page. If you don't do this, PrintController uses the last passed PageSettings object, which may not contain the appropriate state.

Dynamic Page Counting

Many of the operations we've discussed, especially applying custom page settings to specific pages, rely on determining the page number and the total number of pages in a document when it is previewed or printed. The most common example of this is to preset the PrintDialog with the correct page range, as shown in Figure 8.16.

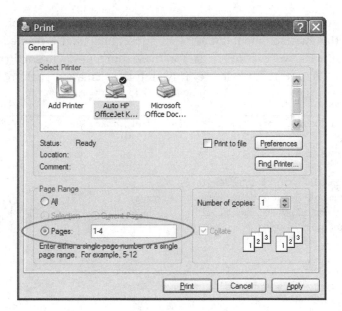

Figure 8.16   Setting the Page Range

You'd think you could just count pages with a numeric variable that's incremented every time you handle a PrintDocument's PagePrint event, but there's an issue you should consider: The page count is accurate only for the most recently printed document. However, the page range value you display in PrintDialog needs to accurately reflect the document you're about to print. Between the time you last printed a document and the next time it's printed, the number of pages may have changed as a result of editing.

As it turns out, the most reliable technique for determining the page count at any one time is to actually print the document, counting each page generated from a PrintDocument's PagePrint event handler. The problem is that you don't want to have to run a print preview or a print just to count the number of pages. Either of these tasks is performed by a PrintController, of which you've already seen SimpleDocumentPrintController, PreviewPrintController, and PrintControllerWithStatusDialog. Because they all derive from PrintController, we can do the same thing to create a custom PageCountPrintController class, allowing us to abstract away page-counting code into a single, reusable class that relies on actual generated print output to determine the page count.[5]

---

[5] Even though PageCountPrintController provides the most accurate page count without generating printed output, it does require your print algorithm to execute. This can raise performance issues you should consider for your own applications.

To count the number of pages, we initialize a page count variable when printing commences, and then we increment it when each subsequent page is printed. PrintController provides two methods we can override for these purposes: OnStartPrint and OnStart Page, respectively. With this knowledge, it is simple to create a custom PageCountPrint Controller:

```
class PageCountPrintController : PreviewPrintController {

  int pageCount = 0;

  public override void OnStartPrint(
    PrintDocument document, PrintEventArgs e) {
    base.OnStartPrint(document, e);
    this.pageCount = 0;
  }

  public override System.Drawing.Graphics OnStartPage(
    PrintDocument document, PrintPageEventArgs e) {
    // Increment page count
    ++this.pageCount;
    return base.OnStartPage(document, e);
  }

  public int PageCount {
    get { return this.pageCount; }
  }

  // Helper method to simplify client code
  public static int GetPageCount(PrintDocument document) {
    // Must have a print document to generate page count
    if( document == null )
      throw new ArgumentNullException("PrintDocument must be set.");

    // Substitute this PrintController to cause a Print to initiate the
    // count, which means that OnStartPrint and OnStartPage are called
    // as the PrintDocument prints
    PrintController existingController = document.PrintController;
    PageCountPrintController controller =
      new PageCountPrintController();
    document.PrintController = controller;
    document.Print();
    document.PrintController = existingController;
    return controller.PageCount;
  }
}
```

The PageCount property simply makes the result available to client code. On the client, you substitute the PageCountPrintController for the PrintDocument's current Print Controller before calling PrintDocument's Print method. The code should be familiar:

```
void getPageCountButton_Click(object sender, EventArgs e) {
  int pageCount =
    PageCountPrintController.GetPageCount(this.printDocument);
  MessageBox.Show(pageCount.ToString());
}
```

PrintController is a great base class from which you can derive your own custom print controllers to tackle all manner of printing chores. Even better, you can take it a step further and convert them into full-blown design-time components and thereby enjoy the productivity benefits of declarative configuration. In fact, you'll find the implementation in the sample code for this chapter, and you'll also find an in-depth discussion of the fundamentals of design-time component development in Chapter 9: Components.

Where Are We?

The nucleus around which the entire .NET printing architecture revolves is the print document. It's the one that initiates the printing process, fires the print events (through the use of a print controller), holds the page and printer settings, and gathers the drawing commands for rendering to the printer or to the print preview control. You implement the actual drawing using the Graphics object, and this drawing is governed by the settings held by the print document. For more complex scenarios, you can use the printing building blocks contained within the nucleus.

9
Components

PACKAGING CODE into classes is an effective way to promote code reuse and save coding effort. VS05 and the Windows Forms Designer take this one step further by providing an infrastructure that trades a programmatic experience for a declarative one, enabling you to drag a class from the Toolbox onto a form and configure it using a host of Windows Forms Designer features, including the Properties window to set properties and manage event handlers. It takes a special type of class known as a component to use such support.

This chapter defines what components are, the capabilities they possess, and the ways in which you can use them, customize them, or create your own.

Components Defined

A *component* is a class that implements the IComponent interface, located in the System.ComponentModel namespace. Any class that implements IComponent can be integrated with a component-hosting environment, such as VS05. In this way, components like ErrorProvider show up on the Toolbox and can be dragged onto a form, as shown in Figure 9.1.

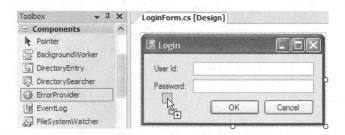

Figure 9.1   Dragging an ErrorProvider Component onto a Form

Essentially, components are reusable, configurable classes. Consequently, they do not provide native support for user interaction via a form, such as by exposing a UI that's hosted by a form or handling keyboard and mouse input. Intrinsic support for UI interaction is provided by controls, which are covered in Chapter 10: Controls. This distinction is further reinforced by the location where components are hosted on a form, specifically in an area known as the *nonvisual design surface*, or *component tray*, shown in Figure 9.2.

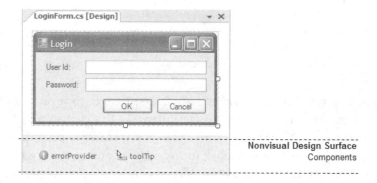

Figure 9.2   Components Hosted on Nonvisual Design Surface (a.k.a. the Component Tray)

Two kinds of components do expose UIs in special situations. First, there are components like ErrorProvider and Tool tip that show their UIs infrequently enough that it doesn't make sense for them to be hosted on a form next to other controls that are usually visible all the time. Second, the behavior of components like OpenFileDialog and SaveFileDialog requires the creation of an entirely new window. However, the UIs presented by these components do not come under the purview of the host form.

Some controls, such as tool strips, also manifest themselves on the nonvisual design surface as pseudo-components. When the Visible property on a tool strip is set to false, it actually becomes hidden on the form at design time, thereby precluding developers from selecting and configuring it. However, this ability is given back via the nonvisual design surface.

Either way, all components reside on the nonvisual design surface.

Using Components

After a component is dropped onto a form, you can use it just like any regular class. For example, imagine that you'd like users to be able to set an alarm in your application and be notified when it goes off. You can easily implement this functionality with a Timer component, from the System.Windows.Forms namespace.[1] When a Timer is dropped onto a form, the Windows Forms Designer generates the following code to InitializeComponent:

```csharp
// AlarmForm.Designer.cs
partial class AlarmForm {
  ...
  /// <summary>
  /// Required designer variable.
  /// </summary>
  System.ComponentModel.IContainer components = null;
  Timer timer;
  ...
  void InitializeComponent() {
    ...
    this.components = new System.ComponentModel.Container();
    this.timer = new Timer(this.components);
    ...
  }
}

// AlarmForm.cs
partial class AlarmForm : Form {
  public AlarmForm() {
    InitializeComponent();
  }
}
```

When a new component is created, it's placed in a container-managed list with the other components on the form. This allows forms to keep track of hosted components and to provide automatic resource management.

Because the Windows Forms Designer takes care of these issues behind the scenes, you need only write the code to use the component, as with a normal class. For a timer component, this might involve setting its Enabled and Interval properties and handling its Tick event:

```csharp
// AlarmForm.cs
partial class AlarmForm : Form {
  public AlarmForm() {
    InitializeComponent();
```

[1] Several timers are available from the .NET Framework. When and how to use them are discussed at http://msdn.microsoft.com/msdnmag/issues/04/02/TimersinNET/default.aspx (http://tinysells.com/15).

```
        // Configure the Timer component
        this.timer.Enabled = true;
        this.timer.Interval = 1000;
        this.timer.Tick += this.timer_Tick;
    }
    void timer_Tick(object sender, EventArgs e) {...}
}
```

The real beauty of using components is their integration with the Windows Forms Designer, which allows you to configure them declaratively. Making sure the desired component is selected, in this case the Timer, you set properties and register event handlers using the Properties window, as shown in Figure 9.3.

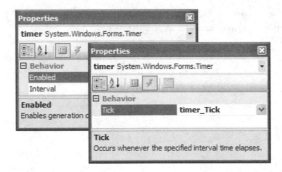

Figure 9.3   Declaratively Configuring a Component with the Properties Window

As properties are set and events are registered, the Windows Forms Designer generates the necessary code to reflect your configuration requirements, and, as you have probably come to expect by now, the result looks remarkably similar to what you would write yourself:

```
// AlarmForm.Designer.cs
partial class AlarmForm {
    ...
    void InitializeComponent() {
        ...
        // timer
        this.timer.Enabled = true;
        this.timer.Interval = 1000;
        this.timer.Tick += this.timer_Tick;
        ...
    }
}
```

```
// AlarmForm.cs
partial class AlarmForm : Form {
  public AlarmForm() {
    InitializeComponent();
  }

  void timer_Tick(object sender, EventArgs e) {...}
}
```

In our alarm example, the Windows Forms Designer has generated most of the Timer-related code for us, so we implement the rest of the alarm functionality for our form:

```
// AlarmForm.cs
partial class AlarmForm : Form {
  ...
  DateTime alarm = DateTime.MaxValue; // No alarm

  void setAlarmButton_Click(object sender, EventArgs e) {
    this.alarm = this.dateTimePicker.Value;
  }

  void timer_Tick(object sender, EventArgs e) {
    // Check to see whether we're within 1 second of the alarm
    double seconds = (DateTime.Now - this.alarm).TotalSeconds;
    if( (seconds >= 0) && (seconds <= 1) ) {
      this.alarm = DateTime.MaxValue; // Show alarm only once
      MessageBox.Show("Wake Up!");
    }
  }
}
```

Here, we use DateTimePicker to allow users to specify an alarm time. When the timer goes off every second, we check to see whether we're within one second of the alarm time. If we are, we turn off the alarm and notify the user, as shown in Figure 9.4.

Figure 9.4   The Alarm Code Responding to the Timer Component's Tick Event

To help you write less code in a wide variety of scenarios, Windows Forms implements a multitude of intrinsic components. Appendix D: Component and Control Survey outlines the standard Windows Forms components and refers you to locations in the book where they are covered in more detail.

Creating Custom Components

Although the .NET Framework offers a wide variety of standard components, it can't possibly cover every scenario where a component makes sense. When you need a component that's beyond the scope of the intrinsic .NET Framework components, or when you have reusable code that would benefit from the Windows Forms Designer support enabled by a component, you can easily create your own custom components. For example, the single-fire alarm we constructed earlier might be useful in more than just your application and would be better repackaged as a custom component.

Deriving Directly from System.ComponentModel.Component

The easiest way to create a new component is to right-click on a project, choose Add | Add Component, enter the name of your component class (our example is AlarmComponent), and press OK. You're greeted with a blank, nonvisual design surface, as shown in Figure 9.5.

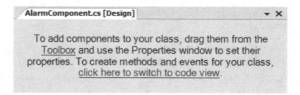

Figure 9.5   A New Component's Wholly Nonvisual Design Surface

Much like the nonvisual design surface of a form, this design surface is meant to host the components you need in order to implement your new component. For example, we can drop a Timer component from the Toolbox onto the AlarmComponent's design surface. In this way, we can create and configure a timer just as if we were hosting the timer on a form. Figure 9.6 shows the alarm component with a timer component configured for our needs.

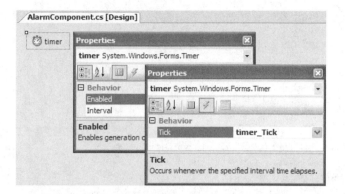

Figure 9.6   A Timer Component Hosted on a Custom Component's Nonvisual Design Surface

Switching to Code view for the component displays the following skeleton,[2] which is generated by the component project item template and filled in by the Windows Forms Designer for the timer:

```
// AlarmComponent.Designer.cs
partial class AlarmComponent {
  ...
  Timer timer;
  ...
  #region Component Designer generated code
  /// <summary>
  /// Required method for Designer support - do not modify
  /// the contents of this method with the code editor.
  /// </summary>
  void InitializeComponent() {
    this.components = new Container();
    this.timer = new Timer(this.components);
    ...
    // timer
    this.timer.Enabled = true;
    this.timer.Interval = 1000;
    this.timer.Tick += this.timer_Tick;
  }
  #endregion
}

// AlarmComponent.cs
using System;
using System.ComponentModel;
```

---

[2] You can switch to Code view from Windows Forms Designer view by choosing View | Code, and switch back by choosing View | Designer. You can toggle between the two by pressing F7.

```
using System.Collections.Generic;
using System.Diagnostics;
using System.Text;

partial class AlarmComponent : Component {
  public AlarmComponent() {
    InitializeComponent();
  }

  public AlarmComponent(IContainer container) {
    container.Add(this);
    InitializeComponent();
  }

  void timer_Tick(object sender, EventArgs e) {...}
}
```

Notice that a default custom component derives from the Component class from the System.ComponentModel namespace. Component is the base implementation of IComponent, which enables integration with VS05 features such as the Properties window and automatic resource management.

Component Resource Management

The Windows Forms Designer also generates code that enables components to automatically add them to their container's list of components. When the container shuts down, it uses this list to notify all the components that they can release any managed and native resources that they're holding. To let the Windows Forms Designer know that it would like to be notified when its container goes away, a component can implement a public constructor that takes a single argument of type IContainer:

```
// AlarmComponent.cs
partial class AlarmComponent : Component {
  ...
  public AlarmComponent(IContainer container) {
    // Add object to container's list so that
    // we get notified when the container goes away
    container.Add(this);
    InitializeComponent();
  }
  ...
}
```

Notice that the component uses the container passed to its constructor to add itself to its host and become a contained component. In the presence of this constructor, the Windows Forms Designer generates code that uses this constructor, passing it a container for the component to add itself to. Because the AlarmComponent implements this special constructor, the following code is generated when an AlarmComponent is added to a form:

```
// AlarmComponentSampleForm.Designer.cs
partial class AlarmComponentSampleForm {
  ...
  AlarmComponent alarmComponent;
  IContainer components = null;
  ...
  void InitializeComponent() {
    this.components = new Container();
    this.alarmComponent = new AlarmComponent(this.components);
    ...
  }
}


// AlarmComponentSampleForm.cs
partial class AlarmComponentSampleForm : Form {
  public AlarmComponentSampleForm() {
    InitializeComponent();
  }
}
```

Several VS05-generated classes can contain components: forms, user controls, controls, and components themselves. When classes of these types are disposed of, they automatically notify their contained components as part of the Dispose method implementation:

```
// AlarmComponentSampleForm.Designer.cs
partial class AlarmComponentSampleForm {
  ...
  // Overridden from the base class Component.Dispose method
  protected override void Dispose(bool disposing) {
    if( disposing && (components != null) ) {
      components.Dispose();
    }
    base.Dispose(disposing);
  }
  ...
}
```

A component that has added itself to the container can override the Component base class's Dispose method to catch the notification that it is being disposed of. In this way, components like AlarmComponent's contained Timer component can release its own resources:

```
// AlarmComponent.Designer.cs
partial class AlarmComponent {
  ...
  Timer timer;
  IContainer components = null;
  ...
  protected override void Dispose(bool disposing) {
    if( disposing ) {
      // Release managed resources
      ...

      // Let contained components know to release their resources
      if( components != null ) {
        components.Dispose();
      }
    }

    // Release native resources
    ...
  }
  ...
  void InitializeComponent() {
    this.components = new Container();
    this.timer = new Timer(this.components);
    ...
  }
}
```

Notice the call to components.Dispose. This call walks the list of contained components, calling each component's Dispose(bool) method much like this:

```
namespace System.ComponentModel {
  ...
  class Container : IContainer { // IContainer inherits IDisposable
    void Dispose() {
      // Container is being proactively disposed of from client code
      Dispose(true);
      ...
    }

    // Logical implementation of Container's Dispose(bool) method
    void Dispose(bool disposing) {
      if( disposing ) {
        foreach( Component component in this.components ) {
```

```
            component.Dispose();
          }
        }
      }
      ...
    }
    ...
  }
```

Each component implements IComponent, which extends IDisposable so that it can be used in just this way. The Component base class routes the implementation of IDisposable. Dispose() to call its own Dispose(bool) method, passing true.

When true is passed to Dispose (bool), it means that was called by a client that remembered to properly dispose of the component. In the case of our alarm component, the only managed resources we have to reclaim are those of the timer component we're using to provide our implementation, so we ask our own component list (the "components" field) to dispose of the components it's holding on our behalf. Because the Windows Forms Designer-generated code added the timer to our container, that's all we need to do.

A disposing argument of false means that the client forgot to properly dispose of the object and that the .NET Garbage Collector (GC) is calling our object's finalizer. The *finalizer* is the method that the GC calls when it's about to reclaim the memory associated with the object (called Finalize and defined in Object, the ultimate base class of all .NET classes). Because the GC calls the finalizer at some indeterminate time—potentially long after the component is no longer needed (perhaps hours or days later)—the finalizer is a bad place to reclaim resources, but it's better than not reclaiming them at all.

The Component base class's finalizer implementation calls the Dispose method, passing a disposing argument of false, which indicates that the component shouldn't touch any of the managed objects it may contain. The other managed objects should remain untouched because the GC may have already disposed of them, and their state is undefined. Consequently, the only resources that should be released at this stage are native resources.

Any component that contains other objects that implement IDisposable, or handles to native resources, should implement the Dispose(bool) method to properly release those objects' resources when the component itself is being released by its container.

Implementing IComponent

As you've seen, automatic resource management and Properties window integration are both features we get by deriving from Component's implementation of IComponent and IDisposable. In most cases, Component should serve you well as the starting point for building custom components, though, at times is not possible. For example, suppose you have a class that you'd like to drop onto a form and offer the same level of integration with VS05 offered by existing components like Timer. If the class already derives from a base class other than Component and if that base class doesn't implement IComponent, you must implement it. Likewise with IDisposable, the base of IComponent.

For example, in Chapter 8: Printing, we created the PageCountPrintController class, which derives from PreviewPrintController:

```
// PageCountPrintController.cs
class PageCountPrintController : PreviewPrintController {

  #region PageCountPrintController implementation
  ...
  #endregion
}
```

To provide consistency with other print-oriented components, it would be great to drop this class onto a form in the Windows Forms Designer. However, PreviewPrintController implements neither IComponent nor IDisposable. To do so requires implementing IComponent:

```
namespace System.ComponentModel {
  ...
  interface IComponent : IDisposable {
    // Properties
    ISite Site { get; set; }

    // Events
    event EventHandler Disposed;
  }
  ...
}
```

The Site property is what enables VS05 and Windows Forms Designer integration, a topic that's explored in detail in Chapter 11: Design-Time Integration: The Properties Window, and Chapter 12: Design-Time Integration: Designers and Smart Tags. The Disposed event is fired by a component to let its hosts know it's going away, something that is particularly useful to containers that need to remove it from their list of managed components when that happens. Consequently, the implementation of IComponent is relatively simple:

```
// PageCountPrintController.cs
class PageCountPrintController : PreviewPrintController, IComponent {

  public PageCountPrintController() {}
  public PageCountPrintController(IContainer container) {
    container.Add(this);
```

```
    }

    #region PageCountPrintController implementation
    ...
    #endregion

    #region IComponent

    public event EventHandler Disposed;
    private ISite site;

    [Browsable(false)]
    [DesignerSerializationVisibility(
      DesignerSerializationVisibility.Hidden)]
    public ISite Site {
      get { return this.site; }
      set { this.site = value; }
    }

    #endregion

    #region IDisposable
    ...
    #endregion
  }
```

Because the Site property is configured by VS05, and not developers, it should be hidden from the Properties window via attribution with both the Browsable and Designer-SerializationVisibility attributes, which are discussed in Chapter 11.

To complete our custom IComponent, we also need to implement IDisposable.

Implementing IDisposable

IDisposable declares only one method, Dispose, which client code calls to notify the component that it should release its managed and native resources immediately:

```
// PageCountPrintController.cs
class PageCountPrintController : PreviewPrintController, IComponent {

  #region PageCountPrintController implementation
  ...
  #endregion

  #region IComponent
  ...
  #endregion
  #region IDisposable
```

```
    private bool disposed;

    public void Dispose() {
      if( !this.disposed ) {
        // Release managed and native resources
        ...

        // Release resources only once
        this.disposed = true;

        // Let interested parties know
        if( this.Disposed != null ) this.Disposed(this, EventArgs.Empty);
      }
    }

    #endregion
  }
```

The use of the disposed flag ensures that we release resources only once. When disposal occurs, we also fire the Disposed event, as required by our implementation of IComponent, to ensure that interested parties are kept in the loop.

This implementation of Dispose is a fine one, as long as it is called. If client code forgets to do so, then we must implement the Finalize method as backup, as discussed earlier. Also discussed was the fact that by the time Finalize is called, managed resources are in an indeterminate state and shouldn't be touched. Thus, the component needs to distinguish whether it's being disposed of or finalized when it releases resources:

```
// PageCountPrintController.cs
class PageCountPrintController : PreviewPrintController, IComponent {

  public PageCountPrintController() { }
  public PageCountPrintController(IContainer container) {
    container.Add(this);
  }

  #region PageCountPrintController implementation
  ...
  #endregion

  #region IComponent
  ...
  #endregion

  #region IDisposable

  bool disposed;
```

```
   public void Dispose() {
      Dispose(true);
   }


   // Finalize method in C# is implemented using destructor syntax
   ~PageCountPrintController() {
      // Finalizer is called in case Dispose wasn't, although we
      // can release only native resources at this stage
      Dispose(false);
   }

   // Dispose of managed and native resources
   protected virtual void Dispose(bool disposing) {
      if( !this.disposed ) {

         // If IDisposable.Dispose() was called
         if( disposing ) {
            // Release managed resources
            ...
         }

         // If IDisposable.Dispose() or finalizer was called,
         // release native resources
         ...

         // Only release resources once
         this.disposed = true;

         // Let interested parties know
         if( this.Disposed != null ) this.Disposed(this, EventArgs.Empty);
      }
   }
   #endregion
}
```

Here, we create an overload of the Dispose method that accepts a Boolean argument indicating whether the class is being disposed of from client code (true) or during finalization (false), and it is called from both the Dispose and the Finalize (implemented as a destructor) methods. If the class is being disposed of, true is passed, and both managed and native resources are released. If the class is being finalized, however, false is passed to ensure that only native resources are released. The Dispose method overload is marked as protected virtual, so any derivations of PageCountPrintController can override the Dispose method and extend it as needed (remembering to call the base's Dispose implementation, of course).

An appropriate constructor is also provided to allow VS05 to add this component to its container's component list, ensuring that the disposal logic is automatically called when the container goes away. If PageCountPrintController is hooked up to a host by the Windows Forms Designer, then Dispose is automatically called as part of the resource management chain created on our behalf. However, because our component may be created manually by developers, we still need to support finalization.

Disposal Optimization

Finalizers must ensure that native resources are released, but implementing them can have an undesirable performance hit, as described in the MSDN Library: "Reclaiming the memory used by objects with Finalize methods requires at least two garbage collections."[3]

If Dispose is not called by client code, this performance hit must be taken on the component's chin. However, if Dispose(bool) is proactively called from client code, there is no need to call Finalize, because native resources have been released. In this case, you can take advantage of this knowledge and influence the Garbage Collector's treatment of your component instance by instructing it not to execute Finalize. You call the SuppressFinalize method of the .NET Framework's Garbage Collector wrapper class, GC, from Dispose:

```
// PageCountPrintController.cs
class PageCountPrintController : PreviewPrintController, IComponent {
  #region PageCountPrintController implementation
  ...
  public void Dispose() {
    Dispose(true);

    // Prevent Finalize method from being called
    GC.SuppressFinalize(this);
  }

  // NOT CALLED IF COMPONENT IS ALREADY DISPOSED OF
  // Finalize method in C# is implemented using destructor syntax
  ~PageCountPrintController() {
    // Finalizer is called in case Dispose wasn't, although we
    // can release only native resources at this stage
    Dispose(false);
  }
  ...
}
```

[3] See http://msdn.microsoft.com/library/default.asp?url=/library/en-us/cpguide/html/ cpconfinalizemethodscdestructors.asp (http://tinysells.com/16).

Implementing IComponent with proper IDisposable finalization in mind is a necessary but onerous task if you have to do it manually. It is certainly easier to derive from Component when you can—as AlarmComponent does—to inherit this support automatically.

Adding a Custom Component to the Toolbox

Having had all the code to create, manage, and dispose of a component automatically generated on our behalf, we now have the most basic possible implementation that we could drop into a form. Before this can happen, though, a component should be made available from VS05's Toolbox. Fortunately, VS05 makes this easy for you if your component is in the same project as your Windows Forms application; after you recompile a project that contains one or more components, they are automatically added to the Toolbox under a new tab, which lists all the components in the currently active project, as shown in Figure 9.7.

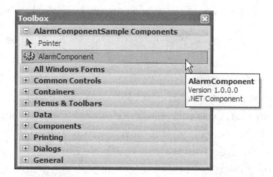

Figure 9.7   Alarm Component Automatically Added to Toolbox after Compilation

If your component is deployed to a different assembly outside the scope of your project, you need to spend a little more effort adding it to the Toolbox. You right-mouse-click the Toolbox and select Choose Items, which opens a dialog where you select either .NET or COM components, as shown in Figure 9.8.

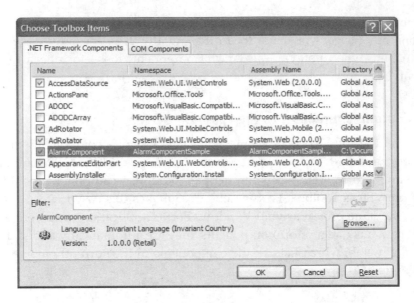

Figure 9.8   Selecting Components and Controls to Add to the Toolbox

If your component doesn't appear in the list by default, simply browse to and select the assembly (.dll or .exe) that contains it. The public components in your assembly are added to the list and selected and checked by default.[4] Uncheck the components you don't want, and click OK to add the remaining checked components to the Toolbox. By default, the components are added to whichever Toolbox tab you have currently selected, which could be either one of the defaults or a custom tab you created by right-mouse-clicking the Toolbox and choosing Add Tab. It can be very handy to have custom tabs for custom controls so that they don't get lost among the standard controls and components.

Once you've got a component onto the Toolbox, you can drag it onto a form and use the Properties window to set properties and hook up events.

Custom Functionality

Properties, events, and, indeed, methods comprise the ways in which a component, like any other .NET class, exposes custom functionality to solve the problem at hand.

---

[4] Chapter 11 discusses how to control whether public components can be added to the Toolbox at all using special design-time attributes.

Custom Properties

The only way AlarmComponent can make itself useful is by letting users actually set an alarm date/time value. You can use either fields or properties in .NET to store values, but the Properties window shows any public property without your doing anything special to make it work. It's an easy way to simplify the design-time experience of your component. AlarmComponent implements the Alarm property:

```
// AlarmComponent.cs
partial class AlarmComponent : Component {
  ...
  DateTime alarm = DateTime.MaxValue; // No alarm
  ...
  public DateTime Alarm {
    get { return this.alarm; }
    set { this.alarm = value; }
  }
}
```

Components need to be recompiled before public properties appear in the Properties window, after which they appear the way Alarm does in Figure 9.9.

Figure 9.9   A Custom Property Shown in the Properties Window

Not only does the Properties window display the custom Alarm property without extra code, but it has also determined that the property is a date/time value and provides additional property-editing support with a date/time picker-style UI.

Custom Events

As with properties, the Properties window shows any public event without a lick of additional code.[5] For example, if you want to fire an event when the alarm sounds, you can expose a public event such as AlarmSounded:

```
// AlarmComponent.cs
partial class AlarmComponent : Component {
  ...
  public event EventHandler AlarmSounded;
  ...
  void timer_Tick(object sender, EventArgs e) {
    // Check to see whether we're within 1 second of the alarm
    double seconds = (DateTime.Now - this.alarm).TotalSeconds;
    if( (seconds >= 0) && (seconds <= 1) ) {
      this.alarm = DateTime.MaxValue; // Show alarm only once
      if( this.AlarmSounded != null ) {
        AlarmSounded(this, EventArgs.Empty);
      }
    }
  }
}
```

AlarmSounded is an event of the EventHandler delegate type. When it's time to sound the alarm, as determined by code inside the timer control's Tick event handler, the code looks for event subscribers. If there are any, it lets them know that the alarm has sounded, passing the sender (AlarmComponent) and an empty EventArgs object.

When your component has a public event like AlarmSounded, it shows up as just another event in the Properties window, as shown in Figure 9.10.

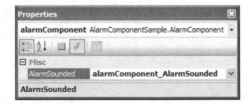

Figure 9.10　A Custom Event Shown in the Properties Window

Just like handling any other event, handling a custom event causes the Windows Forms Designer to generate a code skeleton for you to fill.

---

[5] For an introduction to delegates and events, see Chapter 1: Hello, Windows Forms. For a thorough explanation, refer to Appendix C: Delegates and Events.

When defining your event, you may find that you'd like to pass contextual information about the event to the event handler. If that's the case, you need to create a custom delegate type to operate over a custom arguments class with the information you'd like to pass:

```
// AlarmSoundedEventArgs.cs
public class AlarmSoundedEventArgs : EventArgs {
  DateTime alarm;
  public AlarmSoundedEventArgs(DateTime alarm) {
    this.alarm = alarm;
  }
  public DateTime Alarm {
    get { return this.alarm; }
  }
}

// AlarmSoundedEventHandler.cs
public delegate void AlarmSoundedEventHandler(
  object sender, AlarmSoundedEventArgs e);

// AlarmComponent.cs
partial class AlarmComponent : Component {
  ...
  // AlarmSounded event
  public event AlarmSoundedEventHandler AlarmSounded;

  void timer_Tick(object sender, EventArgs e) {
    // Check to see whether we're within 1 second of the alarm
    double seconds = (DateTime.Now - this.alarm).TotalSeconds;
  if( (seconds >= 0) && (seconds <= 1) ) {
      DateTime alarm = this.alarm;
    this.alarm = DateTime.MaxValue; // Show alarm only once
    if( this.AlarmSounded != null ) {
        AlarmSounded(this, new AlarmSoundedEventArgs(alarm));
      }
    }
  }
}
```

Notice the custom delegate we created, AlarmSoundedEventHandler, which uses the same pattern—no return value, an object sender argument, and an EventArgs-derived type—as the last argument. This is the pattern that .NET follows, and it's a good one for you to emulate with your own custom events. In our case, AlarmSoundedEventHandler accepts a custom AlarmSoundedEventArgs as its event argument. AlarmSoundedEventArgs derives from EventArgs and extends it with a property to store and pass the alarm time.

You can, and should, define new event argument classes by deriving from an appropriate .NET event arguments class. For example, in this case, it was fine to derive from EventArgs, because we extended it only with a new property. However, if you want your custom event arguments to support cancellation, you can instead derive from CancelEventArgs because it extends EventArgs with cancellation functionality.

Custom Methods

Although methods don't appear in the Properties window, they are slightly easier to use because you don't have to worry about creating and managing a component instance to call them against. In general, creating methods like DelayAlarm for components is the same as creating methods for plain types:

```
// AlarmComponent.cs
partial class AlarmComponent : Component {
  ...
  DateTime DelayAlarm(double minutes) {
    // Delay alarm by specified minutes if less than maximum date/time
    if( this.alarm < DateTime.MaxValue.AddMinutes(-minutes) ) {
      this.alarm = this.alarm.AddMinutes(minutes);
    }
    return this.alarm;
  }
}
```

However, in some scenarios, you may need to take special care when creating methods, particularly if they need to distinguish between design time and run time. Events and properties need to make this consideration, which is discussed in depth in Chapter 11: Design-Time Integration: The Properties Window.

Putting the Alarm property, the AlarmSounded event, and the DelayAlarm method together produces a design-time experience that's much less time and code intensive than would be possible using a Timer and code. With the Windows Forms Designer generating code on our behalf to create and configure the AlarmComponent, as well as hook up the AlarmSounded event, the only code we need to write is to allow users to set and delay the alarm and to respond when the alarm is sounded:

```
// AlarmComponentSampleForm.cs
partial class AlarmComponentSampleForm : Form {
  public AlarmComponentSampleForm() {
    InitializeComponent();
  }

  void setAlarmButton_Click(object sender, EventArgs e) {
    // Set the Alarm property
    this.alarmComponent.Alarm = dateTimePicker.Value;
    ...
  }
}
```

```
void alarmComponent_AlarmSounded(
  object sender, AlarmSoundedEventArgs e) {
  // Handle the alarm sounded event
  MessageBox.Show("It's " + e.Alarm.ToString() + ". Wake up!");
}

void delayAlarmButton_Click(object sender, EventArgs e) {
  // Call the DelayAlarm method
  double minutes = (double)this.numericUpDown.Value;
  DateTime newAlarm = this.alarmComponent.DelayAlarm(minutes);
  this.dateTimePicker.Value = newAlarm;
}
}
```

Figure 9.11 shows the form-hosted, custom AlarmComponent in action.

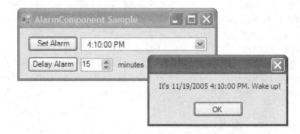

Figure 9.11   An Alarming AlarmComponent in Action

Extending Existing Components

Custom components require you to write a complete implementation from scratch. In some cases, that may result in your writing code that mostly implements a subset of properties, events, and methods already provided by an existing component. In these situations, a better approach is to extend the existing component with your specific functionality and save a lot of effort. As you may have guessed, all you need to do is derive from the desired component.

For example, instead of creating a completely custom alarm component, it may be sufficient to derive directly from a Timer. To derive from an existing component, you first add a new component to your project just as you would to create a custom component. Then, you update the generated code to derive from the desired component:

```
// AlarmComponent.cs
partial class AlarmComponent : Timer {...}
```

After this is in place, you add your custom members as needed. The following is the alarm component implementation, refactored as a subclass of the Timer class:

```
// AlarmComponent.cs
public partial class AlarmComponent : Timer {
  public AlarmComponent() {
    InitializeComponent();
  }

  public AlarmComponent(IContainer container) {
    container.Add(this);
    InitializeComponent();
  }

  // Alarm property
  DateTime alarm = DateTime.MaxValue; // No alarm
  public DateTime Alarm {
    get { return this.alarm; }
    set {
      this.alarm = value;
      // Enable timer for tenth of a second intervals
      this.Interval = 100;
      this.Enabled = true;
    }
  }

  protected override void OnTick(EventArgs e) {
    // Check to see whether we're within 1 second of the alarm
    double seconds = (DateTime.Now - this.alarm).TotalSeconds;
    if( (seconds >= 0) && (seconds <= 1) ) {
      this.alarm = DateTime.MaxValue; // Show alarm only once
      MessageBox.Show("Wake Up!");
      // Disable timer
      this.Enabled = false;
    }
  }
}
```

One key difference is that we override Timer's protected virtual OnTick method rather than handle its Tick event. Most base classes provide protected virtual methods for public, protected, and internal events to save your having to write event registration code and to improve performance.

When you extend an existing component in this fashion, you enjoy all the Windows Forms Designer support that custom components provide, including form containment and automatic resource management. Both features are enabled when a component is dragged onto a form from the Toolbox.

Where Are We?

Custom components are a great way to package reusable Windows Forms code that typically doesn't have a UI or handle user input. Creating a custom component is much like creating a standard class, except that components come with built-in resource management and are the cornerstone of the Windows Forms design-time experience. Components are added to the Toolbox in one of two ways: either automatically by VS05 (if a component is located in the current project) or by an extra, manual step to pull in a component from another assembly. Components can be dragged from the Toolbox onto the nonvisual design surface of a form, and that allows them to receive design-time support provided by VS05 and Windows Forms Designer, including property configuration and event handling via the Properties window. Ultimately, the overall productivity and usability of a component are an order of magnitude greater than those of a simple class.

When reusable Windows Forms code does need a region of its host container to render a UI and handle user input, like text boxes and labels, it needs to become a control, which you can acquaint yourself with in Chapter 10: Controls.

10
Controls

A S YOU SAW IN CHAPTER 9: Components, it is possible to create specialized classes, known as *components*, which can be hosted on a form's nonvisual design surface. Components can be configured using Windows Forms Designer features such as the Properties window and generally make lighter work for developers. What components don't do, however, is provide a UI that's painted directly to a region on a container, such as a form or panel, which they are directly responsible for. Also, components cannot directly process user input. The weapon of choice in these situations is the control.

Controls Defined

A *control* is a reusable class that derives from the System.Windows.Forms.Control base implementation (either directly or indirectly) and whose main purpose in life is to interact with users on behalf of a *container*, which can be either a form or a container control.[1] A control's user interaction takes two forms: acceptance of user input via mice and keyboards, and presentation of processing results and state as UI output.

System.Windows.Forms.Control itself derives from System.ComponentModel.Component, which is great news for you because it provides all the design-time capabilities that components enjoy (as you saw in Chapter 9) and paints a UI right on the container's surface.

In addition to presenting a UI at run time, controls need to present a UI at design time to aid developers in form composition. All controls are composed on a part of the VS05 Windows Forms Designer aptly known as the *visual design surface,* shown in Figure 10.1.

[1] See Chapter 4: Layout for further discussion on container controls.

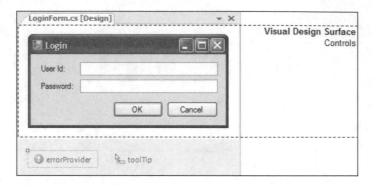

Figure 10.1   Components Versus Controls in the Windows Forms Designer

After they are on the form, you can proceed to configure controls in exactly the same fashion as you configure components; although with controls, you can see the results immediately.

Using Controls

When a control such as a CheckBox is dropped onto a container, the Windows Forms Designer generates the following code to InitializeComponent:

```
// UsingControlsSampleForm.Designer.cs
partial class UsingControlsSampleForm {
  ...
  CheckBox checkBox1;
  ...
  void InitializeComponent() {
    this.checkBox1 = new CheckBox();
    ...
    // checkBox1
    this.checkBox1.AutoSize = true;
    this.checkBox1.Location = new System.Drawing.Point(185, 100);
    this.checkBox1.Name = "checkBox1";
    this.checkBox1.Size = new System.Drawing.Size(80, 17);
    this.checkBox1.TabIndex = 0;
    this.checkBox1.Text = "checkBox1";
    this.checkBox1.UseVisualStyleBackColor = true;
    ...
    // UsingControlsSampleForm
    ...
    this.Controls.Add(this.checkBox1);
    ...
  }
}
```

This code declares and creates an instance of the CheckBox control with an initial, default state. It also brings the control under the purview of its container (in this case, the form) by adding it to the Controls collection. This also implicitly sets the control's Parent property to the container and allows the container to manage it and provide support for features such as layout and z-ordering.

Because the Windows Forms Designer's efforts are transparent, generally you need to concentrate only on writing code to configure and use controls. This process is typically driven by the Properties window, shown in Figure 10.2.

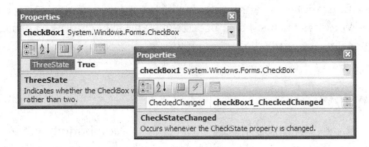

Figure 10.2   Declaratively Configuring a Control in the Properties Window

The Windows Forms Designer applies your configuration automatically, producing code similar to what you'd write yourself:

```
// UsingControlsSampleForm.Designer.cs
partial class UsingControlsSampleForm {
  ...
  void InitializeComponent() {
    ...
    // checkBox1
    this.checkBox1.ThreeState = true;
    this.checkBox1.CheckedChanged += this.checkBox1_CheckedChanged;
    ...
  }
}

// UsingControlsSampleForm.cs
partial class UsingControlsSampleForm : Form {
  ...
  void checkBox1_CheckedChanged(object sender, EventArgs e) {}
}
```

The result leaves you to fill in the remaining code. In this example, you need to fill in only the CheckedChanged event handler:

```
// UsingControlsSampleForm.cs
partial class UsingControlsSampleForm : Form {
  ...
  void checkBox1_CheckedChanged(object sender, EventArgs e) {
    MessageBox.Show("I am being appropriately handled!");
  }
}
```

The same configuration ease applies to any of the myriad controls that come prepackaged in System.Windows.Forms. For a list of the standard Windows Forms controls and where to find more information about them in this book, see Appendix D: Component and Control Survey.

Themed Controls

All common Windows controls—TextBox, CheckBox, RadioButton, and so on—support Windows themes. A *Windows theme* specifies how the basic elements of the desktop UI are rendered. Modern versions of Windows, such as Windows XP, support controls that are rendered to a particular Windows theme, such as "Windows Classic" or "Windows XP." The theme they render to is specified via the Display Properties dialog, shown in Figure 10.3.

Figure 10.3   Changing the Windows Theme

One of the main aspects of a theme is that a user can adjust the way the basic controls are drawn at any time and expect the entire desktop and all applications to automatically update themselves to support the new theme. For example, when buttons aren't themed, they look like those in Figure 10.4.

Figure 10.4   Unthemed Buttons in Windows XP

However, when the Windows XP theme is applied in the Display Properties control panel, buttons (and other standard controls) render themselves to match, as shown in Figure 10.5.

Figure 10.5   Themed Buttons in Windows XP

To let you render the standard Windows controls in Windows themes, Windows Forms uses the EnableVisualStyles method (implemented by the System.Windows.Forms.Application class). When you create a new Windows Forms application, themed rendering is enabled by default in a generated application entry point:[2]

```
// Program.cs
[STAThread]
static void Main() {
  Application.EnableVisualStyles();
  ...
}
```

The call to EnableVisualStyles ensures that your controls render to the current Windows theme when loaded, and, after they're running, they automatically update themselves to reflect further theme changes.

[2] If you use the VS05 Windows Application project template to create your project, the main entry point for the application is created in Program.cs.

Tool Strip Render Modes

By default, the MenuStrip, ToolStrip, and StatusStrip controls all support theme-sensitive rendering, in that they have the same look as the Office 2003 tool strips across the various themes. However, tool strips offer additional rendering modes that allow you to override the current theme using special renderer classes.

The type of renderer class used at any given time by a tool strip is determined by the RenderMode property, which is exposed by all tool strips. RenderMode can be one of the four ToolStripRenderMode enumeration values:

```
namespace System.Windows.Forms {
  enum ToolStripRenderMode {
    [Browsable(false)]
    Custom = 0, // Can't set this RenderMode property in
                // the Properties window
    System = 1 // Windows apps appearance (default for StatusStrip)
    Professional = 2, // Office 2003 appearance
    ManagerRenderMode = 3,  // Renderer determined by ToolStripManager
                   // (default for MenuStrip and ToolStrip)
  }
}
```

Windows Forms comes with two stock tool strip renderers: ToolStripSystemRenderer and ToolStripProfessionalRenderer.[3] The former is used when RenderMode is set to System, and the latter is used when RenderMode is set to Professional. To see the difference, look at Figure 10.6.

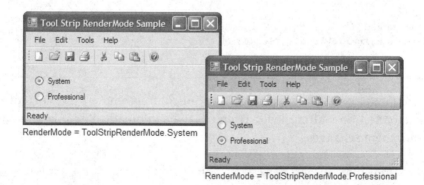

RenderMode = ToolStripRenderMode.System

RenderMode = ToolStripRenderMode.Professional

Figure 10.6　Tool Strip System and Professional Render Modes

---

[3] Windows Forms also comes with two specialized renderers for high-contrast and low-resolution scenarios: ToolStripHighContrastRenderer and ToolStripProfessionalLowResolutionRenderer. However, these are marked as internal and are unavailable for your use.

The System render mode gives the look and feel you'd expect to find on a variety of applications that come with Windows, including Calculator (calc.exe) and WordPad (wordpad.exe). Professional, on the other hand, renders in the same way as Office 2003 applications.

By default, both MenuStrip and ToolStrip actually have their RenderMode properties set to ManagerRenderMode, and this means that they yield the choice of renderer to ToolStripManager. The renderer used by ToolStripManager is set via its Renderer property, which defaults to ToolStripProfessionalRenderer. When ToolStripManager.Renderer is set to a tool strip renderer, ToolStripManager applies it to all tool strips on a form whose RenderMode is set to ManagerRenderMode. This gives you a shortcut for swapping renderers and applying them in one fell swoop, rather than individually for each tool strip.

On the other hand, StatusStrip's RenderMode property is set to System by default. This causes StatusStrip to render as gray, with the rounded shading style that you find in VS05 rather than the flatter style in Office 2003. You can make the StatusStrip render flat, too, when its RenderMode is Professional, but, as you can see in Figure 10.6, it's colored blue with a highlight on the top edge. If you want it flat but colored gray with a highlight, you have a fourth RenderMode option: Custom. However, setting the RenderMode property to Custom actually causes an exception, and that is why the RenderMode.Custom enumeration value is hidden from the Properties window using the Browsable attribute.[4] RenderMode is set to Custom implicitly as a result of using a custom tool strip renderer.

Custom Tool Strip Rendering

If you need custom tool strip rendering, you create a custom tool strip renderer class to paint the StatusStrip (or any tool strip) the way you want. A custom tool strip renderer derives from the abstract ToolStripRenderer base class, which offers a host of protected virtual methods you can override to paint the various elements of a tool strip:

```
namespace System.Windows.Forms {
  abstract class ToolStripRenderer {
    ...
    protected virtual void OnRenderArrow(...);
    protected virtual void OnRenderButtonBackground(...);
    protected virtual void OnRenderDropDownButtonBackground(...);
    protected virtual void OnRenderGrip(...);
    protected virtual void OnRenderImageMargin(...);
    protected virtual void OnRenderItemBackground(...);
    protected virtual void OnRenderItemCheck(...);
```

---

[4] BrowsableAttribute is one of many attributes that influence how types operate in the Windows Forms Designer's design-time environment. These attributes are discussed in Chapter 11: Design-Time Integration: The Properties Window.

```
    protected virtual void OnRenderItemImage(...);
    protected virtual void OnRenderItemText(...);
    protected virtual void OnRenderLabelBackground(...);
    protected virtual void OnRenderMenuItemBackground(...);
    protected virtual void OnRenderOverflowButtonBackground(...);
    protected virtual void OnRenderRaftingContainerBackground(...);
    protected virtual void OnRenderSeparator(...);
    protected virtual void OnRenderSplitButtonBackground(...);
    protected virtual void OnRenderStatusStripSizingGrip(...);
    protected virtual void OnRenderToolStripBackground(...);
    protected virtual void OnRenderToolStripBorder(...);
    protected virtual void OnRenderToolStripContentPanelBackground(...);
    protected virtual void OnRenderToolStripPanelBackground(...);
    protected virtual void OnRenderToolStripStatusLabelBackground(...);
    ...
  }
}
```

Each of these methods is passed an argument that provides a Graphics object that wraps the underlying tool strip's drawing surface. It also provides several additional properties specific to the piece of the UI being rendered. To create a custom tool strip renderer that paints a tool strip's background gray with a highlight, you derive from ToolStripRenderer and override its OnRenderToolStripBackground:

```
class CustomStatusStripRenderer : ToolStripRenderer {
  protected override void OnRenderToolStripBackground(
    ToolStripRenderEventArgs e) {

    Rectangle backgroundRect = e.AffectedBounds;
    Graphics g = e.Graphics;

    // Fill rectangle
    g.FillRectangle(SystemBrushes.Control, backgroundRect);

    // Draw highlight
    using( Pen highlightPen =
      new Pen(SystemColors.ControlLightLight) ) {
      g.DrawLine(highlightPen, 0, 0, backgroundRect.Width, 0);
    }
  }
}
```

The area to which you need to paint the background is defined as a Rectangle that you retrieve from the AffectedBounds property of the ToolStripRenderEventArgs argument. Then it's painting as usual, à la Chapter 5: Drawing Basics and Chapter 7: Advanced Drawing.

To use your custom tool strip renderer, you set your tool strip's Renderer property to point to an instance of it:

```
void customRadioButton_CheckedChanged(object sender, EventArgs e) {
    this.statusStrip1.Renderer = new CustomStatusStripRenderer();
}
```

The result is shown in Figure 10.7.

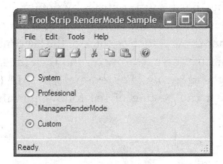

Figure 10.7   StatusBar with Custom Renderer (see the white line along the top of the StatusBar)

When you set the Renderer property of a tool strip to a custom renderer, the tool strip automatically changes its RenderMode to Custom. So, even though you can't set the RenderMode property yourself, you can at least detect whether a tool strip is using a custom renderer.

ToolStripSystemRenderer and ToolStripProfessionalRenderer also derive from Tool-StripRenderer, and that's how they get their unique tool strip rendering services. Consequently, you may need to write less code in your custom tool strip renderers if you derive from either, especially when they provide the basic appearance you require. Either way, there are many more ways to alter the appearance of both a tool strip and its items, although that discussion is beyond the scope of this book.[5]

Custom tool strip rendering lets you take over the painting of tool strip controls. This ability is also available for a variety of common Windows Forms controls using a technique known as owner-draw.

[5] You will find a great introduction sample and discussion of custom tool strip rendering at http://www.windowsforms.com/Samples/Go%20To%20Market/Tool%20Strips/ToolStrip%20GTM.doc#Toc116357041 (http://tinysells.com/19).

Owner-Drawn Controls

The appearance of most of the standard controls is consistent with those exposed by the underlying operating system. Where possible, you should use these controls to ensure that your applications are equally consistent, although some styles of applications, such as Windows Media Player, demand UIs that differ from the norm.

When an existing control provides all the functionality you need but not the desired UI, you can take over the drawing by using a control feature known as owner-draw. An *owner-drawn control* provides events that allow a control's owner (or the control itself) to take over the drawing chores from the control in the underlying operating system.

Controls that allow owner-draw—such as some of the list controls, TabControl, and Tool tip—expose a property that turns owner-draw on and then fires events to let the container know that it should do the drawing. For example, the ListBox control exposes the DrawMode property, which can be one of the following values from the DrawMode enumeration:

```
namespace System.Windows.Forms {
   enum DrawMode {
     Normal = 0, // Control draws its own items (default)
     OwnerDrawFixed = 1, // Fixed-size custom drawing of each item
     OwnerDrawVariable = 2, // Variable-size custom drawing of each item
   }
 }
```

Figure 10.8 shows an owner-drawn ListBox control that changes the style to Italics when it's drawing the selected item.[6]

Figure 10.8   Owner-Drawn ListBox

---

[6] Owner-draw is how Microsoft turns a ListBox control into a CheckedListBox control.

To handle the drawing of a ListBox, you first set the DrawMode property to something other than Normal (the default), and then you handle the ListBox control's DrawItem event:

```csharp
// OwnerDrawFixedSampleForm.Designer.cs
partial class OwnerDrawFixedSampleForm {
  ...
  void InitializeComponent() {
    ...
    // listBox
    this.listBox.DrawMode = DrawMode.OwnerDrawFixed;
    ...
  }
}

// OwnerDrawFixedSampleForm.cs
partial class OwnerDrawFixedSampleForm : Form {
  public OwnerDrawnFixedSampleForm() {
    InitializeComponent();
  }
  void listBox_DrawItem(object sender, DrawItemEventArgs e) {
    // Draw the background
    e.DrawBackground();

    // Get the default font
    Font drawFont = e.Font;
    bool ourFont = false;

    // Draw in italics if selected
    if( (e.State & DrawItemState.Selected) == DrawItemState.Selected ) {
      ourFont = true;
      drawFont = new Font(drawFont, FontStyle.Italic);
    }

    using( Brush brush = new SolidBrush(e.ForeColor) ) {
      // Draw the list box item
      e.Graphics.DrawString(
        listBox.Items[e.Index].ToString(), drawFont, brush, e.Bounds);
        if( ourFont ) drawFont.Dispose();
      }

      // Draw the focus rectangle
      e.DrawFocusRectangle();
    }
  }
}
```

This code uses several members of the DrawItemEventArgs object that's passed to the DrawItem event handler:

```
namespace System.Windows.Forms {
  class DrawItemEventArgs : EventArgs {
    // Properties
    public Color BackColor { get; }
    public Rectangle Bounds { get; }
    public Font Font { get; }
    public Color ForeColor { get; }
    public Graphics Graphics { get; }
    public int Index { get; }
    public DrawItemState State { get; }

    // Methods
    public virtual void DrawBackground();
    public virtual void DrawFocusRectangle();
  }
}
```

The DrawItem event is called whenever the item is drawn or when the item's state changes. The DrawItemEventArgs object provides all the information you need to draw the item in question, including the index of the item, the bounds of the rectangle to draw in, the preferred font, the preferred color of the foreground and background, and the Graphics object to do the drawing on. DrawItemEventArgs also supplies the selection state so that you can draw selected items differently (as our example does). DrawItemEventArgs also gives you a couple of helper methods for drawing the background and the focus rectangle if necessary. You usually use the latter to bracket your own custom drawing.

When you set DrawMode to OwnerDrawFixed, each item's size is set for you. If you'd like to influence the size, too, you set DrawMode to OwnerDrawVariable, and, in addition to doing the drawing in the DrawItem handler, you specify the height in the MeasureItem handler:

```
// OwnerDrawVariableSampleForm.Designer.cs
partial class OwnerDrawVariableSampleForm {
  ...
  void InitializeComponent() {
    ...
    // listBox
    this.listBox.DrawMode = DrawMode.OwnerDrawVariable;
    ...
  }
}
```

```
// OwnerDrawVariableSampleForm.cs
partial class OwnerDrawVariableSampleForm : Form {
  public OwnerDrawnVariableSampleForm() {
    InitializeComponent();
  }
  void listBox_MeasureItem(object sender, MeasureItemEventArgs e) {
    // Make every even item twice as high
    if( e.Index % 2 == 0 ) e.ItemHeight *= 2;
  }
}
```

The MeasureItem event provides an instance of the MeasureItemEventArgs class, which gives you useful properties for getting and setting each item's height:

```
namespace System.Windows.Forms {
  class MeasureItemEventArgs : EventArgs {
    // Properties
    public Graphics Graphics { get; }
    public int Index { get; }
    public int ItemHeight { get; set; }
    public int ItemWidth { get; set; }
  }
}
```

Figure 10.9 shows the effects of doubling the heights of the event items (as well as continuing to show the selection in italics).

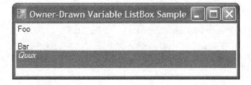

Figure 10.9   An Owner-Drawn List Box Using Variable Height

Unlike the DrawItem event, the MeasureItem event is called only once for every item in the control, so things such as selection state can't be a factor when you decide how big to make the space for the item.

ControlPaint

Often, owner-draw is used to draw a control that looks just like an existing Windows control but has one minor addition, such as drawing disabled text in a list box. In those cases, you'd like to avoid spending any time duplicating the way every version of Windows draws its controls. For that purpose, you can use the ControlPaint helper class. ControlPaint, has static members for drawing common controls, lines, grids, and types of text:

```
namespace System.Windows.Forms {
   sealed class ControlPaint {
      // Properties
      public static Color ContrastControlDark { get; }

      // Methods
      public static IntPtr CreateHBitmap16Bit(...);
      public static IntPtr CreateHBitmapColorMask(...);
      public static IntPtr CreateHBitmapTransparencyMask(...);
      public static Color Dark(...);
      public static Color DarkDark(...);
      public static void DrawBorder(...);
      public static void DrawBorder3D(...);
      public static void DrawButton(...);
      public static void DrawCaptionButton(...);
      public static void DrawCheckBox(...);
      public static void DrawComboButton(...);
      public static void DrawContainerGrabHandle(...);
      public static void DrawFocusRectangle(...);
      public static void DrawGrabHandle(...);
      public static void DrawGrid(...);
      public static void DrawImageDisabled(...);
      public static void DrawLockedFrame(...);
      public static void DrawMenuGlyph(...); // New
      public static void DrawMixedCheckBox(...);
      public static void DrawRadioButton(...);
      public static void DrawReversibleFrame(...);
      public static void DrawReversibleLine(...);
      public static void DrawScrollButton(...);
      public static void DrawSelectionFrame(...);
      public static void DrawSizeGrip(...);
      public static void DrawStringDisabled(...); // New
      public static void DrawVisualStyleBorder(...); // New
      public static void FillReversibleRectangle(...);
      public static Color Light(...);
      public static Color LightLight(...);
   }
}
```

updated

To use ControlPaint to draw disabled text in an owner-drawn ListBox, you need only invoke ControlPaint.DrawStringDisabled from the DrawItem event handler for each disabled item:

```
// OwnerDrawVariableSampleForm.cs
partial class OwnerDrawnVariableSampleForm: Form {
  ...
  void listBox_DrawItem(object sender, DrawItemEventArgs e) {
    ...
    using( Brush brush = new SolidBrush(e.ForeColor) ) {
      // Draw every even item as disabled
      if( e.Index % 2 == 0 ) {
        ControlPaint.DrawStringDisabled(
          e.Graphics,
          listBox.Items[e.Index].ToString(),
          drawFont,
          this.ForeColor,
          e.Bounds,
          null);
      }
      else {
        e.Graphics.DrawString(
          listBox.Items[e.Index].ToString(),
          drawFont,
          brush,
          e.Bounds);
      }
      if( ourFont ) drawFont.Dispose();
    }
    ...
  }
}
```

The effect of using ControlPaint is shown in Figure 10.10.

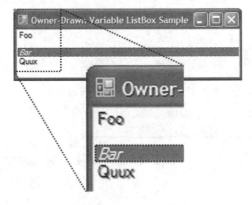

Figure 10.10 An Owner-Drawn Variable ListBox Using ControlPaint

Owner-draw is great for scenarios when an existing control's functionality is exactly what you need but you need to alter the UI it generates. However, you do need to be careful when using ControlPaint as part of your owner-draw regime; ControlPaint does not paint theme-sensitive UI elements. If you need to support theme sensitivity, you use themed control rendering.

Themed Control Rendering

All the Windows Forms common controls are rendered theme-sensitive using a slew of custom renderer classes located in System.Windows.Forms. You get one renderer for each common control, including ButtonRenderer, CheckBoxRenderer, TextBoxRender, and so on. The nice thing about the *Xxx*Renderer classes is that they are publicly available for you to exploit. This allows you to ensure that any control-style rendering you do is consistent not only with Windows Forms but also with the current theme. The following is a sample use of ButtonRenderer:

```
// ThemedControlRenderingSampleForm.cs
public partial class ThemedControlRenderingSampleForm : Form {
  ...
  void themedPanel_Paint(object sender, PaintEventArgs e) {
    // Render themed button with the ButtonRenderer
    ButtonRenderer.DrawButton(
      e.Graphics,
      this.themedPanel.ClientRectangle,
      VisualStyles.PushButtonState.Normal);
  }
}
```

Figure 10.11 illustrates the difference between ControlPaint—rendering an unthemed button—and ButtonRenderer—rendering a themed button—and shows how both react to theme change.

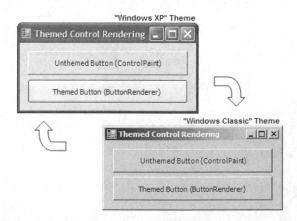

Figure 10.11   Theme-Sensitive Rendering Using the ButtonRenderer

As you can see, ButtonRenderer automatically adapts to the new theme, without any additional code from you.[7]

Where possible, it's best to lean on the renderers for your custom control rendering to ensure that you maintain theme consistency. For raw themed rendering support, however, you'll want to use the same API used by the *Xxx*Renderers: System.Windows.Forms.VisualStyles. This API wraps the shell's UxTheme API and exposes the common controls and accoutrements via static types nested within the VisualStyleElement class. You render these in conjunction with VisualStyleRenderer:

```csharp
// ThemedControlRenderingSampleForm.cs
public partial class ThemedControlRenderingSampleForm : Form {
  ...
  void themedPanel_Paint(object sender, PaintEventArgs e) {
    // Render themed button with the VisualStyleRenderer
    VisualStyleRenderer renderer =
      new VisualStyleRenderer(
        VisualStyleElement.Button.PushButton.Normal);
    renderer.DrawBackground(
      e.Graphics, this.themedPanel.ClientRectangle);
  }
}
```

Although a thorough exploration of the expansive VisualStyles namespace is beyond the scope of this book, you should familiarize yourself with it if you are rendering custom controls. A good place to start is the MSDN Library.[8]

Extending Existing Controls

Further down the spectrum of customization from owner-drawn controls are those controls that have exactly the UI you require but not the functionality you need. You can approach such situations by using a different technique: Identify a suitable existing control, derive from it, and add your desired functionality.

For example, let's assume that you want to create a FileTextBox control that's just like the TextBox control except that it indicates to the user whether the currently entered file exists. Figures 10.12 and 10.13 show the FileTextBox control in use.

---

[7] Also observe that the fonts rendered for the two buttons are slightly different. The new TextRenderer is used to paint text on the themed button that is consistent with both the shell and the current theme. TextRenderer is covered in Chapter 6: Drawing Text.

[8] See http://msdn2.microsoft.com/en-us/library/system.windows.forms.visualstyles.visualstylerenderer.aspx (http://tinysells.com/20).

Figure 10.12   FileTextBox with a
File That *Does Not* Exist

Figure 10.13   FileTextBox with a
File Name That *Does* Exist

By putting this functionality into a reusable control, you can drop it onto any form without making the form itself provide the functionality. By deriving FileTextBox from the TextBox base control class, you get most of the behavior you need without any effort, and thus you can focus on the interesting new functionality:

```
class FileTextBox : TextBox {
  protected override void OnTextChanged(EventArgs e) {
    // Let the base class process changed text first
    base.OnTextChanged(e);

    // If the file does not exist, color the text red
    if( !File.Exists(this.Text) ) {
      this.ForeColor = Color.Red;
    }
    else { // Make it black
      this.ForeColor = Color.Black;
    }
  }
}
```

Notice that implementing FileTextBox is merely a matter of deriving from the TextBox base class (which provides all the editing capabilities that users expect) and overriding the OnTextChanged method (instead, you could handle the TextChanged event). When the text changes, we use the Exists method of the System.IO.File class to check whether the currently entered file exists in the file system; then, we set the foreground color of the control accordingly.

Often, you can use as little code as this to easily create new controls that have application-specific functionality because the bulk of the code is provided by the base control class.

Custom Controls

Owner-drawn and extended controls allow you to leverage the .NET Framework's control base to produce slightly customized variations with little effort. Sometimes, however, the standard controls simply don't provide a UI or an implementation that comes close to what you need. In these situations, your best option is to bite the bullet and create a complete *custom control* from scratch. There are two main kinds of custom controls:

1. Controls that derive directly from the Control base class, allowing you to handle your control's input and output completely
2. Controls that derive from ScrollableControl, which are like controls that derive from Control but also provide built-in support for scrolling

The kind of control you choose depends on the kind of functionality you need.

Deriving Directly from System.Windows.Forms.Control

Consider the AlarmClockComponent from Chapter 9. .NET gives you no controls that offer alarm clock functionality, and none that render a clock face UI to boot. Turning AlarmClockComponent into a custom control to add the UI is the only way to go.

In VS05, you start by right-clicking your project in Solution Explorer and choosing Add | New Item | Custom Control, calling it AlarmClockControl. You get the following skeleton:

```
// AlarmClockControl.Designer.cs
partial class AlarmClockControl {
  ...
  void InitializeComponent() {...}
  ...
}


// AlarmClockControl.cs
using System;
using System.Collections.Generic;
using System.ComponentModel;
using System.Data;
using System.Drawing;
using System.Text;
using System.Windows.Forms;

partial class AlarmClockControl : Control {
  public AlarmClockControl() {
    InitializeComponent();
  }
```

```
protected override void OnPaint(PaintEventArgs e) {
    // TODO: Add custom paint code here

    // Calling the base class OnPaint
    base.OnPaint(pe);
}
}
```

This skeleton derives from the Control base class and provides an override of the virtual OnPaint method responsible for painting its content. It even includes a helpful comment that lets you know where to add your custom code to render your custom control's state.

Notice that the generated constructor includes a call to InitializeComponent; controls, like components, provide a nonvisual design surface for you to drag components onto as required, as shown in Figure 10.14.

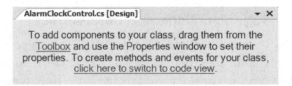

Figure 10.14 A New Control's Nonvisual Design Surface

The Windows Forms Designer generates the necessary InitializeComponent code to support use of the nonvisual design surface. In our case, if we want to add a UI to Chapter 9's AlarmComponent, it's likely we'll use the nonvisual design surface. That's because we'll require a timer again to build the AlarmClockControl, as shown in Figure 10.15.

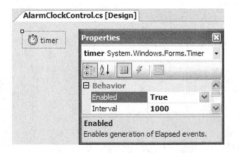

Figure 10.15 A Timer Component Hosted on a Control's Nonvisual Design Surface

After configuring the Timer as needed, we next provide a UI.

Control Rendering

As you look back at the skeleton code generated by the Windows Forms Designer for a custom control, remember that it handles the Paint event by deriving from the Control base class and overriding the OnPaint method. Because we're deriving from the Control class, we have two options when deciding how to handle a event.

The first option is to write an event handler and register it with the event. This is the only option available when you're not deriving from Control. When you are deriving, the second option is to override the virtual method provided by the base class both to perform any relevant processing and to fire the associated event. By convention, these methods are named On*EventName* and take an object of the EventArgs (or EventArgs-derived) class as a parameter. When you override an event method, remember to call the base class's implementation of the method so that all the event subscribers will be notified.

For example, here's how to implement OnPaint for the custom AlarmClockControl:

```csharp
// AlarmClockControl.cs
partial class AlarmClockControl : Control {
    ...
  protected override void OnPaint(PaintEventArgs e) {

    Graphics g = e.Graphics;

    // Get current date/time
    DateTime now = DateTime.Now;

    // Calculate required dimensions
    Size faceSize = this.ClientRectangle.Size;
    int xRadius = faceSize.Width / 2;
    int yRadius = faceSize.Height / 2;
    double degrees;
    int x;
    int y;

    // Make things pretty
    g.SmoothingMode = System.Drawing.Drawing2D.SmoothingMode.AntiAlias;

    // Paint clock face
    using( Pen facePen = new Pen(Color.Black, 2) )
    using( SolidBrush faceBrush = new SolidBrush(Color.White) ) {
      g.DrawEllipse(facePen, facePen.Width, facePen.Width,
                faceSize.Width - facePen.Width * 2,
                faceSize.Height - facePen.Width * 2);
      g.FillEllipse(faceBrush, facePen.Width, facePen.Width,
                faceSize.Width - facePen.Width * 2,
                faceSize.Height - facePen.Width * 2);
    }
```

```
    // Paint hour hand, minute hand, second hand, and digital time
    ...
    // Let the base class fire the Paint event
    base.OnPaint(e);
  }

  void timer_Tick(object sender, EventArgs e) {
    // Refresh clock face
    this.Invalidate();
  }
}
```

In this code, the Graphics object passed with the PaintEventArgs to this override is used to paint the clock face and hands to display the current time. To ensure that clients can handle AlarmClockControl's Paint event to overlay its UI with additional UI elements, we call the base class's OnPaint method to fire the Paint event after AlarmClockControl's paint logic executes.

To add a control to the Toolbox, we compile the project that houses the control. Follow the steps discussed in Chapter 9 to see how. Figure 10.16 shows an AlarmClockControl in action.

Figure 10.16   The AlarmClockControl in Action

Although it's pretty, this UI goes only halfway to solving the alarm setting and sounding problem.

Custom Implementation

The original AlarmComponent was gifted with several custom members to enable its operational capability. Controls are equally capable when it comes to implementing custom properties, events, and methods, and AlarmClockControl re-implements one of each from

AlarmComponent, including the Alarm property, AlarmSoundedEvent, and the Delay-Alarm method:

```csharp
// AlarmSoundedEventArgs.cs
public class AlarmSoundedEventArgs : EventArgs {
  DateTime alarm;
  public AlarmSoundedEventArgs(DateTime alarm) {
    this.alarm = alarm;
  }
  public DateTime Alarm {
    get { return this.alarm; }
  }
}

// AlarmSoundedEventHandler.cs
public delegate void AlarmSoundedEventHandler(
  object sender, AlarmSoundedEventArgs e);

// AlarmClockControl.cs
partial class AlarmClockControl : Control {
  ...
  DateTime alarm = DateTime.MaxValue; // No alarm
  DateTime Alarm {
    get { return this.alarm; }
    set { this.alarm = value; }
  }

  event AlarmSoundedEventHandler AlarmSounded;

  DateTime DelayAlarm(double minutes) {
    if( this.alarm < DateTime.MaxValue ) {
      this.alarm = this.alarm.AddMinutes(minutes);
    }
    return this.alarm;
  }
  ...
  void timer_Tick(object sender, EventArgs e) {
    // Check to see whether we're within 1 second of the alarm
    double seconds = (DateTime.Now - this.alarm).TotalSeconds;
    if( (seconds >= 0) && (seconds <= 1) ) {
      DateTime alarm = this.alarm;
      this.alarm = DateTime.MaxValue; // Show alarm only once
      if( this.AlarmSounded != null ) {
        // Sound alarm async so clock can keep ticking
        this.AlarmSounded.BeginInvoke(
          this,
          new AlarmSoundedEventArgs(alarm),
```

```
        null,
        null);
    }
  }
  ...
}
}
```

As you would expect, a control that's hosted on the Toolbox can be dragged onto a form and configured by using the Properties window. With a clock face beaming at us and additional controls to set and delay the alarm, we can quickly produce the form shown in Figure 10.17.

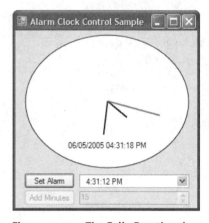

Figure 10.17   The Fully Functional AlarmClockControl in Action

The code to make this work is similar to the client code we built for Chapter 9's AlarmComponent:

```
// AlarmClockControlSampleForm.cs
partial class AlarmClockControlSampleForm : Form {
  public AlarmClockControlSampleForm() {
    InitializeComponent();
  }

  void setAlarmButton_Click(object sender, EventArgs e) {
    this.alarmClockControl.Alarm = this.dateTimePicker.Value;
    this.addMinutesButton.Enabled = true;
    this.numericUpDown.Enabled = true;
  }
```

```
   void alarmClockControl_AlarmSounded(
     object sender, AlarmSoundedEventArgs e) {
     System.Media.SystemSounds.Exclamation.Play();
     MessageBox.Show("It's " + e.Alarm.ToString() + ". Wake up!");
   }

   void addMinutesButton_Click(object sender, EventArgs e) {
     double minutes = (double)this.numericUpDown.Value;
     DateTime newAlarm = this.alarmClockControl.DelayAlarm(minutes);
     this.dateTimePicker.Value = newAlarm;
   }
 }
```

So, for the same code, your users are treated to a more visually appealing experience.

Event*Changed*

Part of any user experience is choice. One choice that AlarmClockControl users might like to have is to hide or show the second hand, particularly when they've had more than their daily allowance of caffeine and any movement distracts them from their game of Minesweeper. You can easily let users toggle the visibility of the second hand:

```
// AlarmClockControl.cs
partial class AlarmClockControl : Control {
  ...
  bool showSecondHand = true;
  public bool ShowSecondHand {
    get { return this.showSecondHand; }
    set {
      this.showSecondHand = value;
      this.Invalidate();
    }
  }

  protected override void OnPaint(PaintEventArgs e) {
    Graphics g = e.Graphics;
    ...
    // Paint second hand, if so configured
    if( this.showSecondHand ) {
      using( Pen secondHandPen = new Pen(Color.Red, 2) ) {
        ...
      }
    }
    ...
    string nowFormatted = ( this.showSecondHand ?
                            now.ToString("dd/MM/yyyy hh:mm:ss tt") :
                            now.ToString("dd/MM/yyyy hh:mm tt"));
    ...
  }
```

```
void timer_Tick(object sender, EventArgs e) {
  ...
  // If we're showing the second hand, we need to refresh every second
  if( this.showSecondHand ) {
    this.Invalidate();
  }
  else {
    // Otherwise, we need to refresh only every minute, on the minute
    if( (DateTime.Now.Second == 59) || (DateTime.Now.Second == 0) ) {
      this.Invalidate();
    }
  }
}
}
```

The ShowSecondHand property controls whether the analog clock's second hand and the digital clock's seconds element are rendered, and it refreshes the UI immediately when changed. Additionally, if the second hand isn't shown, AlarmClockControl refreshes its UI only once a minute.

One advantage of implementing a custom property like ShowSecondHand is the ability it gives you to immediately repaint the control's UI. However, when a property such as Padding from the base Control class is set, there's a little problem: AlarmClockControl's padding does not change, for two reasons.

First, AlarmClockControl's painting logic doesn't take padding into account, something that is easy to update:

```
// AlarmClockControl.cs
partial class AlarmClockControl : Control {
  ...
  protected override void OnPaint(PaintEventArgs e) {
    Graphics g = e.Graphics;
    ...
    // Calculate required dimensions
    Size faceSize = this.ClientRectangle.Size;
    ...
    // Paint clock face
    using( Pen facePen = new Pen(Color.Black, 2) ) {
      g.DrawEllipse(
        facePen,
        facePen.Width + this.Padding.Left,
        facePen.Width + this.Padding.Top,
        faceSize.Width - facePen.Width * 2,
        faceSize.Height - facePen.Width * 2);
      ...
    }
    ...
```

```
      // Calling the base class OnPaint
      base.OnPaint(pe);
  }
  ...
}
```

Second, even though the painting logic handles padding, setting it via the Properties window doesn't have an immediate effect because we're not forcing a repaint when the Padding property is changed. Instead, we need to wait until AlarmClockControl is requested to repaint itself. If we had implemented the Padding property on AlarmClock-Control ourselves, we could apply the principles of drawing and invalidation (from Chapter 5) to keep the control visually up to date by calling Invalidate from its set accessor. However, because the base Control class implements Padding, that option isn't available to us.[9]

Fortunately, the base Control class does implement the Padding property, which, when set, causes Control to fire the PaddingChanged event via the virtual OnPaddingChanged method. We can override OnPaddingChanged to invalidate the UI immediately:

```
// AlarmClockControl.cs
partial class AlarmClockControl : Control {
  ...
  protected override void OnPaddingChanged(EventArgs e) {
    base.OnPaddingChanged(e);
    this.Invalidate();
  }
  ...
}
```

Several events—including BackColorChanged, FontChanged, ForeColorChanged, and CusrorChanged—don't need to be tracked in this fashion because the base class knows to invalidate the client area of the control in those cases for us. Those properties are special.

Ambient Properties

The reason that the base class knows to treat some properties specially is that they are ambient properties. An *ambient property* is one that, if it's not set in the control, is "inherited" from the container. Of all the standard properties provided by the Control base class, only four are ambient: BackColor, ForeColor, Font, and Cursor.

For example, consider the AlarmClockControl host form, with all its glorious controls on proud display in Figure 10.18.

---

[9] Technically, we could shadow (hide) the base class's Padding property with C#'s *new* keyword, although shadowing is a shady technique; the technique shown here achieves the same effect without creating the confusion of hidden base class members.

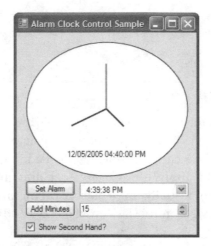

Figure 10.18 AlarmClockControl Host Form with Many Controls

All the settings for the Form, AlarmClockControl, and other controls are the defaults with respect to the Font property; this means that on my Windows XP machine running at normal-sized fonts, the two controls use the MS Sans Serif 8.25-point font. The Alarm-ClockControl control takes its own Font property into account when drawing, and therefore changing its Font property to 9.75-point Impact in the Properties window yields this code:

```
// AlarmClockControlSampleForm.Designer.cs
partial class AlarmClockControlSampleForm {
  ...
  void InitializeComponent() {
    ...
    this.alarmClockControl.Font = new Font("Impact", 9.75F);
    ...
  }
}
```

The result looks like Figure 10.19.

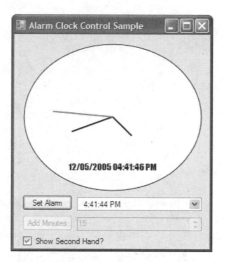

**Figure 10.19   Setting the Font Property
on the AlarmClockControl Host Form**

This works great if you're creating a funhouse application in which different controls have different fonts, but more commonly, all the controls in a container share the same font. Although it's possible to use the Windows Forms Designer to set the fonts for each of the controls individually, it's even easier to leave the controls' fonts alone and set the font on the form:

```
// AlarmClockControlSampleForm.Designer.cs
partial class AlarmClockControlSampleForm {
  ...
  void InitializeComponent() {
    ...
    this.Font = new Font("Impact", 9.75F);
    ...
  }
}
```

Because the Font property is ambient, setting the font on the container also sets the fonts on the contained controls, as shown in Figure 10.20.[10]

---

[10] By default, the form automatically resizes to accommodate the font change. This is a result of scaling, as covered in Chapter 4.

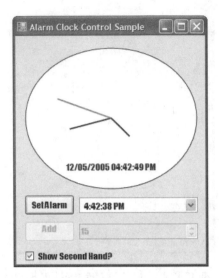

Figure 10.20   Setting the Font Property on the Hosting Form

When you set the Font property on the container and leave the Font property at the default value for the controls, the control "inherits" the Font property from the container. Similarly, a contained control can "override" an ambient property if you set it to something other than the default:

```
// AlarmClockControlSampleForm.Designer.cs
partial class AlarmClockControlSampleForm {
  ...
  void InitializeComponent() {
    ...
    this.alarmClockControl.Font =
      new Font("Times New Roman", 9.75F);
    ...
    this.Font = new Font("Impact", 9.75F);
    ...
  }
}
```

Notice that the form's font is set after the AlarmClockControl's font. It doesn't matter in which order the ambient properties are set. If a control has its own value for an ambient property, that value is used instead of the container's value. The result of the contained AlarmClockControl overriding the ambient Font property is shown in Figure 10.21.

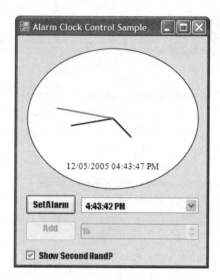

Figure 10.21   A Contained Control
Overriding the Value of the Ambient
Font Property

Also, if you need to reset the ambient properties to a default value, you can do this by right-clicking the desired ambient property in the Properties window and choosing Reset.[11]

Ambient properties allow container controls to specify an appearance shared by all contained controls without any special effort. However, a control can also override a property inherited from its container without incident.

Control Input

In addition to providing output and exposing custom properties, events, and methods, custom controls often handle input, whether it's mouse input, keyboard input, or both.

Mouse Input

For example, let's say we wanted to let users click on AlarmClockControl and, as they drag, adjust the color of the current digital time text. We do this by overriding the

---

[11] A complete discussion of how resetting works is provided in Chapter 11, where you'll learn how to implement your own support for this on custom components and controls.

OnMouseDown, OnMouseMove, and OnMouseUp methods:

```
// Track whether mouse button is down
bool mouseDown = false;

protected override void OnMouseDown(MouseEventArgs e) {
  this.mouseDown = true;
  this.SetForeColor(e);
  base.OnMouseDown(e);
}

protected override void OnMouseMove(MouseEventArgs e) {
  if( this.mouseDown ) this.SetForeColor(e);
  base.OnMouseMove(e);
}

protected override void OnMouseUp(MouseEventArgs e) {
  this.SetForeColor(e);
  this.mouseDown = false;
  base.OnMouseUp(e);
}

void SetForeColor(MouseEventArgs e) {
  int red = (e.X * 255 / (this.ClientRectangle.Width - e.X)) % 256;
  if( red < 0 ) red = -red;
  int green = 0;
  int blue = (e.Y * 255 / (this.ClientRectangle.Height - e.Y)) % 256;
  if( blue < 0 ) blue = -blue;
  this.ForeColor = Color.FromArgb(red, green, blue);
}
```

The MouseDown event is fired when the mouse is clicked inside the client area of the control. The control continues to get MouseMove events until the MouseUp event is fired, even if the mouse moves out of the region of the control's client area. The code sample watches the mouse movements when the button is down and calculates a new ForeColor using the X and Y coordinates of the mouse as provided by the MouseEventArgs argument to the events:

```
namespace System.Windows.Forms {
  class MouseEventArgs : EventArgs {
    public MouseButtons Button { get; } // Which buttons are pressed
    public int Clicks { get; } // How many clicks since the last event
    public int Delta { get; } // How many mouse wheel ticks
    public Point Location { get; } // Screen x,y position (New)
    public int X { get; } // Current X pos. relative to the screen
    public int Y { get; } // Current Y pos. relative to the screen
  }
}
```

updated

MouseEventArgs is meant to give you the information you need in order to handle mouse events. For example, to eliminate the need to track the mouse button state manually, we could use the Button property to check for a click of the left mouse button:

```
// Track whether mouse button is down
// bool mouseDown = false; // use MouseEventArgs.Button instead

protected override void OnMouseDown(MouseEventArgs e) {...}
protected override void OnMouseMove(MouseEventArgs e) {...}
protected override void OnMouseUp(MouseEventArgs e) {...}

void SetForeColor(MouseEventArgs e) {
  if( (e.Button & MouseButtons.Left) == MouseButtons.Left ) {
    int red = (e.X * 255 / (this.ClientRectangle.Width - e.X)) % 256;
    if( red < 0 ) red = -red;
    int green = 0;
    int blue = (e.Y * 255 / (this.ClientRectangle.Height - e.Y)) % 256;
    if( blue < 0 ) blue = -blue;
    this.ForeColor = Color.FromArgb(red, green, blue);
  }
}
```

Additional mouse-related input events are MouseEnter, MouseHover, and Mouse-Leave, which tell you that the mouse is over the control, that it's hovered for "a while" (useful for showing tool tips), and that it has left the control's client area.

If you'd like to know the state of the mouse buttons or the mouse position outside a mouse event, you can access this information from the static MouseButtons and MousePosition properties of the Control class. In addition to MouseDown, MouseMove, and MouseUp, there are seven other mouse-related events. MouseEnter, MouseHover, and MouseLeave allow you to track when a mouse enters, loiters in, and leaves the control's client area. Click and DoubleClick, and MouseClick and MouseDoubleClick, indicate that the user has clicked or double-clicked the mouse in the control's client area.

Keyboard Input

In addition to providing mouse input, forms (and controls) can capture keyboard input via the KeyDown, KeyUp, and KeyPress events. For example, to make the keys i, j, k, and l move our elliptical label around on the container, the AlarmClockControl class could override the OnKeyPress method:

```
protected override void OnKeyPress(KeyPressEventArgs e) {

    Point location = new Point(this.Left, this.Top);

    switch( e.KeyChar ) {
```

```
    case 'i':
      --location.Y;
      break;

    case 'j':
      --location.X;
      break;

    case 'k':
      ++location.Y;
      break;

    case 'l':
      ++location.X;
      break;
  }

  this.Location = location;

  base.OnKeyPress(e);
}
```

The KeyPress event takes a KeyPressEventArgs argument:

```
namespace System.Windows.Forms {
  class KeyPressEventArgs : EventArgs {
    public bool Handled { get; set; } // Whether this key is handled
    public char KeyChar { get; set; } // Key pressed char (set is New)
  }
}
```

updated

The KeyPressEventArgs object has two properties. The Handled property defaults to false but can be set to true to indicate that no other handlers should handle the event. The KeyChar property is the character value of the key after the modifier has been applied.

For example, if the user presses the I key, the KeyChar is i, but if the user presses Shift and the I key, the KeyChar property is I. On the other hand, if the user presses Ctrl+I or Alt+I, we don't get a KeyPress event at all, because those are special sequences that aren't sent via the KeyPress event. To handle these kinds of sequences, along with other special characters such as F-keys or arrows, you override the OnKeyDown method:

```
protected override void OnKeyDown(KeyEventArgs e) {

  Point location = new Point(this.Left, this.Top);

  switch( e.KeyCode ) {
```

```
      case Keys.I:
      case Keys.Up:
        --location.Y;
        break;

      case Keys.J:
      case Keys.Left:
        --location.X;
        break;

      case Keys.K:
      case Keys.Down:
        ++location.Y;
        break;

      case Keys.L:
      case Keys.Right:
        ++location.X;
        break;
    }

    this.Location = location;

    base.OnKeyDown(e);
  }
```

Notice that the KeyDown event takes a KeyEventArgs argument (as does the KeyUp event), which is shown here:

```
namespace System.Windows.Forms {
  class KeyEventArgs : EventArgs {
    public bool Alt { virtual get; } // Whether Alt is pressed
    public bool Control { get; } // Whether Ctrl is pressed
    public bool Handled { get; set; } // Whether this key is handled
    public Keys KeyCode { get; } // The pressed key, w/o the modifiers
    public Keys KeyData { get; } // The key and the modifiers
    public int KeyValue { get; } // KeyData as an integer
    public Keys Modifiers { get; } // Only the modifiers
    public bool Shift { virtual get; } // Whether Shift is pressed
    public bool SuppressKeyPress { get; set; } // No KeyPressed
                                                // No KeyUp
                                                // (New)
  }
}
```

updated

By default, the KeyPressed and KeyUp events are still fired even if KeyEventArgs.Handled is set to true by the KeyDown event handler. To prevent these events from being fired, you additionally set KeyEventArgs.SuppressKeyPress to true.

Although it looks as if the KeyEventArgs object contains a lot of data, it really contains only one thing: a private field exposed via the KeyData property. KeyData is a bit field of the combination of the keys being pressed (from the Keys enumeration) and the modifiers being pressed (also from the Keys enumeration). For example, if the I key is pressed by itself, KeyData is Keys.I, whereas if Ctrl+Shift+F2 is pressed, KeyData is a bitwise combination of Keys.F2, Keys.Shift, and Keys.Control.

The rest of the properties in the KeyEventArgs object are handy views of the KeyData property, as shown in Table 10.1. Also shown is the KeyChar that would be generated in a corresponding KeyPress event.

Table 10.1 KeyEventArgs and KeyPressEventArgs Examples

Keys Pressed	KeyData	KeyCode	Modifiers	Alt	Ctrl	Shift	KeyValue	KeyChar
I	Keys.I	Keys.I	Keys.None	false	false	false	73	i
Shift+I	Keys.Shift + Keys.I	Keys.I	Keys.Shift	false	false	true	73	I
Ctrl+Shift+I	Keys.Ctrl + Keys.Shift + Keys.I	Keys.I	Keys.Ctrl + Keys.Shift	false	true	true	73	n/a
Ctrl	Keys. ControlKey + Keys.Ctrl	Keys. ControlKey	Keys. Control	false	true	false	17	n/a

Even though we're handling the KeyDown event specifically to get special characters, some special characters, such as arrows, aren't sent to the control by default. To enable them, the custom control overrides the IsInputKey method from the base class:

```
protected override bool IsInputKey(Keys keyData) {
  // Make sure we get arrow keys
  switch( keyData ) {
    case Keys.Up:
    case Keys.Left:
    case Keys.Down:
    case Keys.Right:
      return true;
  }

  // The rest can be determined by the base class
  return base.IsInputKey(keyData);
}
```

The return from IsInputKey indicates whether the key data should be sent in events to the control. In this example, IsInputKey returns true for all the arrow keys and lets the base class decide what to do about the other keys.

IsInputKey can only be overridden, which is useful when you're handling events in your own custom control or form. However, if you are simply using a control and you'd like to get your fingers into its keyboard events, you can handle the PreviewKeyDown event:

```
protected override void OnPreviewKeyDown(PreviewKeyDownEventArgs e) {

  // Specify the arrow keys as input chars
  switch( e.KeyData ) {
    case Keys.Up:
    case Keys.Left:
    case Keys.Down:
    case Keys.Right:
      e.IsInputKey = true;
      return;
  }

  // The rest can be determined by the base class
  base.OnPreviewKeyDown(e);
}
```

Here, we inspect the KeyData property exposed from the PreviewKeyDownEventArgs argument; if we decide that the key we are after should be considered an input key, we set PreviewKeyDownEventArgs.IsInputKey to true. When the IsInputKey property is set here, the call to the IsInputKey override doesn't even occur; the keypress is routed straight to the KeyDown event.

If you'd like to know the state of a modifier key outside a key event, you can access the state in the static ModifierKeys property of the Control class. For example, the following checks to see whether the Ctrl key is the only modifier to be pressed during a mouse click event:

```
void alarmClockControl_Click(object sender, EventArgs e) {
  if( Control.ModifierKeys == Keys.Control ) {
    MessageBox.Show("Ctrl+Click detected");
  }
}
```

Scrolling

Deriving from Control provides a broad base of functionality, although scrolling isn't supported. Scrolling is needed when the space that is required by one or more controls is greater than the space provided by a container control. Scrollbars were invented for just this situation. A scrolling control provides scroll bars to allow users to navigate to hidden bits of a control's content.

You could use a custom control to handle the logic involved in creating scroll bars and handling repainting correctly as the user scrolls across the drawing surface, but you're much better off deriving your custom control implementation from ScrollableControl:

```
class AlarmClockControl : ScrollableControl {...}
```

When you implement a scrolling control, ClientRectangle represents the size of the control's visible surface, but there could be more of the control that isn't currently visible because it's been scrolled out of range. To get to the area of the control that represents the size of its scrollable surface, use the DisplayRectangle property instead. DisplayRectangle is a property of the ScrollableControl class that represents the virtual drawing area. Figure 10.22 shows the difference between ClientRectangle and DisplayRectangle.

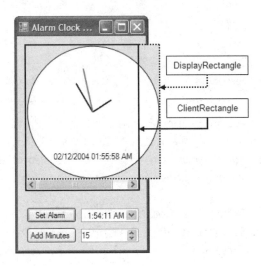

Figure 10.22 DisplayRectangle Versus ClientRectangle

An OnPaint method for handling scrolling should look something like this:

```
protected override void OnPaint(PaintEventArgs e) {
    ...
    // Calculate required dimensions
    Size faceSize = this.DisplayRectangle.Size;
    ...
    // Calling the base class OnPaint
    base.OnPaint(pe);
}
```

The only difference between this OnPaint method and the custom control is that we paint to DisplayRectangle instead of ClientRectangle.

Setting the Scroll Dimension

Unlike ClientRectangle, which is determined by the container of the control, DisplayRectangle is determined by the control itself. The scrollable control gets to decide the minimum when you set the AutoScrollMinSize property from the ScrollableControl base class or from the Properties window, as shown in Figure 10.23.

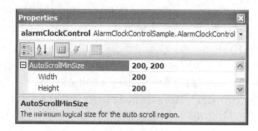

Figure 10.23   Setting the AutoScrollMinSize Property

The AutoScrollMinSize property is used to tell the control when to show the scroll bars. If DisplayRectangle is larger in either dimension than ClientRectangle, scroll bars appear.

The ScrollableControl base class has a few other interesting properties. The AutoScroll property (set to true by the Windows Forms Designer by default) enables DisplayRectangle to be a different size than ClientRectangle. Otherwise, the two are always the same size.

The AutoScrollPosition property lets you programmatically change the position within the scrollable area of the control. The AutoScrollMargin property is used to set a margin around scrollable controls that are also container controls. The DockPadding property is similar but is used for child controls that dock. Container controls can be controls such as GroupBox or Panel, or they can be custom controls, such as user controls (covered later in this chapter).

If a child control of a scrollable control is partially or completely hidden beyond the edges of the scroll bars, you can force the scrollable control to scroll to show the child control in its entirety. To do this, you invoke ScrollControlIntoView on the scrollable control. This technique is useful when a scrollable control contains so many controls that you need to provide a UI mechanism for quickly navigating among them.

Calling ScrollControlIntoView or allowing similar behavior is not a good idea when users switch away from and back to your form. Such behavior may be surprising to users because the form they switch back to looks different from the one they switched away from. To prevent scrolling in these situations, you set the AutoScrollOffset property of your controls. AutoScrollOffset, of type Point, specifies a location (in relation to the top-left corner of the host scrollable control), and your control scrolls no closer than that point.

If you'd like to know when your scrollable control scrolls, you can handle the Scroll event. Except for the scrolling capability, scrollable controls are just like controls that derive from the Control base class.

Windows Message Handling

The paint event, the mouse and keyboard events, and most of the other events handled by a custom control come from the underlying Windows operating system. At the Win32 level, the events start out life as Windows messages. A *Windows message* is most often generated by Windows because of some kind of hardware event, such as the user pressing a key, moving the mouse, or bringing a window from the background to the foreground. The window that needs to react to the message gets the message queued in its *message queue*. That's where Windows Forms steps in.

The Control base class is roughly equivalent to the concept of a window in the operating system. It's the job of Windows Forms to take each message off the Windows message queue and route it to the Control class responsible for handling it. The base Control class turns the message into an event, which Control then fires by calling the appropriate method in the base class. For example, the WM_PAINT Windows message eventually turns into a call on the OnPaint method, which, in turn, fires the Paint event to all interested listeners.

However, not all Windows messages are turned into events by Windows Forms. For those cases, you can drop down to a lower level and handle the messages as they come into the Control class. You do this by overriding the WndProc method:

```
public class MyControl : Control {
  ...
  protected override void WndProc(ref Message m) {
    // Process and/or update message
    ...

    // Let the base class process the message if you don't want to
    base.WndProc(ref m);
  }
}
```

As a somewhat esoteric example of handling Windows messages directly, the following is a rewrite of the code from Chapter 2: Forms to move the nonrectangular form around the screen:

```
public partial class MainForm : Form {
  ...
  public MainForm() {
    InitializeComponent();
  }

  const int WM_NCHITTEST = 0x84; // winuser.h
  const int HTCLIENT = 1;
```

```
    const int HTCAPTION = 2;

    protected override void WndProc(ref Message m) {
      switch( m.Msg ) {
        case WM_NCHITTEST:
          // Let the base class have first crack
          base.WndProc(ref m);
          // If the user clicked on the client area,
          // ask the OS to treat it as a click on the caption
          if( m.Result.ToInt32() == HTCLIENT ) {
            m.Result = (IntPtr)HTCAPTION;
          }
          break;
        default:
          base.WndProc(ref m);
          break;
      }
    }
  }
}
```

This code handles the WM_NCHITTEST message, which is one of the few that Windows Forms doesn't expose as an event. In this case, the code calls to the Windows-provided handler (also known as its *window procedure*) with this message to see whether the user is moving the mouse over the client area of the form. If that's the case, the code pretends that the entire client area is the caption so that when the user clicks and drags on it, Windows takes care of moving the form for us.

There aren't very many reasons to override the WndProc method and handle the Windows message directly, but it's nice to know that the option is there in case you need it.

User Controls

Although one benefit of custom controls is that they allow you to create a reusable UI, the most popular form of UI reuse for a control is simple containment, as you're accustomed to using when you build custom forms using existing controls. A *user control* derives from System.Windows.Forms.UserControl and is a way to contain a set of other controls for reuse as a set, producing a kind of "subform." For example, imagine that we want a control that composes our FileTextBox control from earlier with a "…" button to browse the file system.

To create a custom user control, you right-click on your project in Solution Explorer, choose Add | User Control, enter an appropriate name, and press OK.[12] When you do, you get the design surface for your user control, where you can arrange controls, as shown in Figure 10.24.

---

[12] If you'd like to start a new project to hold user controls, you can use the Windows Controls Library project template in the New Project dialog.

Figure 10.24 A New UserControl

Building a user control that brings the FileTextBox together with a browse button is a matter of dropping each onto the form and arranging to taste. Also, to enable browsing, you'll want to use an instance of the OpenFileDialog component, capturing all that functionality into a single user control for reuse, as shown in Figure 10.25.

Figure 10.25 The FileBrowseTextBox User Control in the Windows Forms Designer

All the control arranging that you're accustomed to—such as anchoring and docking—works the same way in a user control as in a custom form. You also use the same techniques for setting properties or handling events. After arranging the existing controls and components on the user control design surface, you simply write a tiny chunk of code to handle the click on the browse button to make it all work:

```
// FileBrowseTextBox.cs
partial class FileBrowseTextBox : UserControl {
  ...
  void openFileButton_Click(object sender, EventArgs e) {
    if( this.openFileDialog.ShowDialog() == DialogResult.OK ) {
      fileTextBox.Text = this.openFileDialog.FileName;
    }
  }
}
```

This code, along with a couple of controls, converts into a single user control form that can be run without any further effort, resulting in Figure 10.26.

Figure 10.26   The FileBrowseTextBox User Control in Action

User controls allow you to build reusable controls using the same tools you use when building forms, but with the added advantage that you can drop a user control onto anything that can contain controls, including container controls, forms, and even other user controls.

Testing User Controls

One issue with testing controls is that you need to create a control library and a control library test client. Furthermore, you also have to fiddle around with referencing between the two projects, which can lead to potential run-time errors; this can be a little awkward.

VS05 helps out by allowing you to test your custom user controls in a generic user control test container, shown in Figure 10.27.

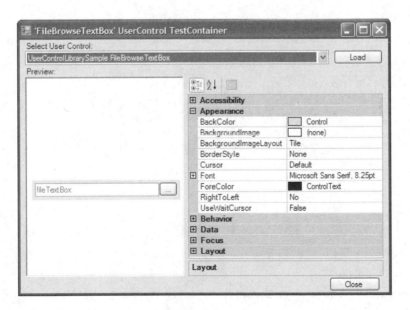

Figure 10.27   VS05's UserControl TestContainer

You select the user control you want to test from the Select User Control drop-down. You can test the various properties exposed by your user control, and you can see how the resulting configuration affects its function. You can also load user controls from other assemblies by clicking the Load button.

To enable this, you create a control library and make sure it is configured to be the start-up project, as shown in Figure 10.28.

Figure 10.28   Configuring a Control Library to Use the UserControl TestContainer

Hosting COM Controls

As wonderful and varied as Windows Forms controls are, especially considering the burgeoning third-party Windows Forms control market, Component Object Model (COM) controls have been around a lot longer, and you may still need to use some of them in your Windows Forms applications.[13] Windows Forms has built-in support for hosting COM controls, and VS05 makes it easy to take advantage of that support.

The first step is to get your COM control of choice to show up on the Toolbox so that you can drag it onto your forms. To do that, right-click on the Toolbox and click Choose Items. This action brings up the Choose Toolbox Items dialog, as shown in Figure 10.29.

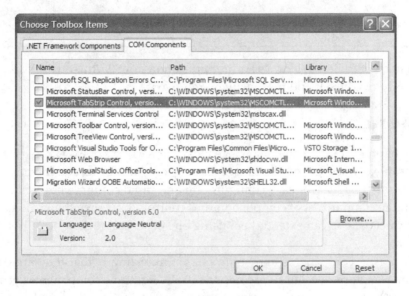

Figure 10.29   Choose Toolbox Items Dialog

All the items under the COM Components tab are COM controls registered on your machine. Checking any of them and pressing OK adds the control to the Toolbox, as shown in Figure 10.30.

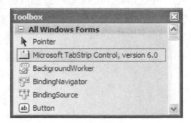

Figure 10.30   COM Component Added to the Toolbox

[13] COM controls are also known as OLE controls and ActiveX controls.

After a COM control has been added to the Toolbox, you can drop an instance onto a form, set the properties, and handle the events. Any COM control added to your Windows Forms project causes a pair of interop assemblies to be generated by VS05 and added to the project.[14] It's the code in these assemblies that you're referencing and that forwards your calls to the underlying COM control.[15]

Also, COM controls need COM initialized in a UI-friendly manner, so make sure that the STAThread attribute adorns your Main method:

```
// Program.cs
[STAThread]
static void Main() {
  ...
  Application.Run(new MainForm());
}
```

When you create a new Windows Forms application in VS05, this attribute is applied by default, so to hurt yourself you must actively remove it.

Where Are We?

In both Chapter 9 and this chapter, we've looked at a variety of ways you can create specialized reusable classes that can be hosted directly on your forms and integrated into the Windows Forms Designer for easy configuration and rapid coding. The .NET Framework provides a huge standard set of components and controls, but when they're inadequate for your specific needs, you can extend them using one of several techniques. Or you can create your own.

Another reason components and controls are interesting is that they are collectively known by another name: design-time components. Design-time components get some Windows Forms Designer integration, such as having public properties and events exposed from the Properties window, for free. However, using design-time components allows you to integrate with a whole lot more of the Windows Forms Designer, as covered in the next two chapters.

---

[14] The aximp.exe command line tool generates COM control interop assemblies in the same way that VS05 does.

[15] For more information about COM interop, see *Essential .NET, Volume I: The Common Language Runtime* (Addison-Wesley, 2003), by Don Box, with Chris Sells.

11
Design-Time Integration: The Properties Window

Windows Forms applications are designed and built primarily for a user-driven mode of execution commonly known as the *run time*. A subset of Windows Forms classes, including components, controls, and user controls, is designed and built to support an additional developer-driven mode of execution known as the design time. The *design time* comprises VS05, the Windows Forms Designer, and the .NET Framework, and it supports the creation and management of design-time components as developers drag them onto forms and user controls, configure them, arrange them, and delete them.

Because components support two modes of execution, component developers should ensure that their implementations provide an adequate experience for both users and developers. Although the rest of this book focuses on what developers must do to target the run time, both this chapter and the next one show how developers can take full advantage of design-time integration support, which includes Properties window augmentation, code serialization, extender provider properties, rich property-editing support with UI type editors, custom designers, and smart tags.

Design-Time Components

Before components, controls, and user controls can start using design-time features, they must integrate with the design time itself. As discussed in Chapter 9: Components, the point of integration between a class and the design time is modeled by the *IComponent* interface:

```
namespace System.ComponentModel {
   interface IComponent : IDisposable {
    ISite Site { get; set; }
```

```
    event EventHandler Disposed;
  }
}
```

IComponent is the fundamental building block of the entire design-time infrastructure, on which all the design-time features we discuss in this book depend. Consequently, your custom components, controls, and user controls must implement IComponent.

In Chapter 9: Components, we looked at a custom IComponent implementation, although we found we could save the effort in most cases by deriving from .NET's base IComponent implementation, System.ComponentModel.Component. In both Chapter 9 and Chapter 10: Controls, you saw that all .NET Framework and custom components and controls implicitly implement IComponent as long as they derive from Component, Control, or UserControl, as shown in Figure 11.1.

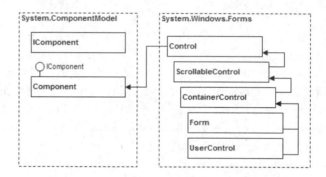

Figure 11.1   Types That Directly or Indirectly Implement IComponent

Figure 11.1 also shows that neither UserControl nor Form directly inherits from Control. Instead, they both derive from ContainerControl, itself deriving from ScrollableControl, both of which overlay Control with control containment and scrolling support commonly required by user control containers, including user controls and forms. Both ScrollableControl and ContainerControl are base classes for implementations that require specific types of support, but you'll find that your classes typically derive from Component, Control, or UserControl.

No matter how a class comes to implement IComponent, it is known as a *design-time component* if it does.[1]

Hosts, Containers, and Sites

In VS05, when a component is dragged onto a Windows Forms design surface, it is instantiated by the Windows Forms Designer, which also grabs a reference to its IComponent interface. At the highest level, the Windows Forms Designer manages a form's UI and code

---

[1] For the sake of readability, design-time components are simply referred to as "components" for the remainder of this chapter.

views; the Windows Forms Designer's internal IDesignerHost (from the System.Component Model.Design namespace) implementation, the *designer host,* has the specific responsibility of managing design-time objects and providing design-time services.

The designer host stores IComponent references to all design-time objects hosted on a form, including the form itself; as Figure 11.1 shows, forms are also components because they indirectly implement IComponent. The resulting collection of design-time objects is available from the IDesignerHost interface through the Container property, which is of type System.ComponentModel.IContainer (from the System.ComponentModel namespace):

```
namespace System.ComponentModel {
  interface IContainer : IDisposable {
    ComponentCollection Components { get; }
    void Add(IComponent component);
    void Add(IComponent component, string name);
    void Remove(IComponent component);
  }
}
```

Implementing IContainer provides the mechanism by which the designer host can access and manage components. Similarly, contained components can access the designer host and each other through their container at design time. Figure 11.2 illustrates this two-way relationship.

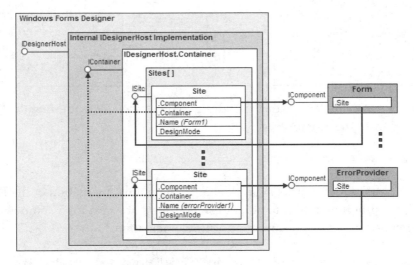

Figure 11.2   Design-Time Architecture (See Plate 15)

Figure 11.2 shows that the relationship between a component and its designer host is established via the ISite interface (from the System.ComponentModel namespace):

```
namespace System.ComponentModel {
  interface ISite : IServiceProvider {
    IComponent Component { get; }
    IContainer Container { get; }
    bool DesignMode { get; }
    string Name { get; set; }
  }
}
```

Internally, a container stores a list of sites. When each component is added to the container, the designer host creates a new site and connects the component to it by setting the latter's IComponent.Site property implementation to the new site's ISite reference.[2] By establishing this relationship, IComponent implementations acquire direct access to their site. Additionally, the Component class provides direct access to the container, and this avoids the complexity of navigating to it via the ISite reference:

```
namespace System.ComponentModel {
  class Component : MarshalByRefObject, IComponent, IDisposable {
    ...
    public IContainer Container { get; } // Direct container access
    public virtual ISite Site { get; set; }
    protected bool DesignMode { get; }
    protected EventHandlerList Events { get; }
    public event EventHandler Disposed;
    ...
  }
}
```

A component can also access the VS05 designer host itself by requesting the IDesigner-Host interface from the container:

```
IDesignerHost designerHost = this.Container as IDesignerHost;
```

In VS05, the Windows Forms Designer has its own implementation of the IDesigner-Host interface, although to fit into other designer hosts, it's best for a component to rely only on the interface and not on any specific implementation.

---

[2] Whenever you read about a *sited* component in any design-time literature, you are reading about a component whose Site property is set.

To demonstrate the various services provided by the VS05 designer host to components, let's build on the AlarmClockControl created in Chapter 10: Controls:

```
// AlarmClockControl.cs
partial class AlarmClockControl : ScrollableControl {
   // Properties
   public DateTime Alarm { get; set; }
   // Methods
   public DateTime DelayAlarm(double minutes);
   // Events
   public event AlarmSoundedEventHandler AlarmSounded;
}
```

Figure 11.3 shows the control in action.

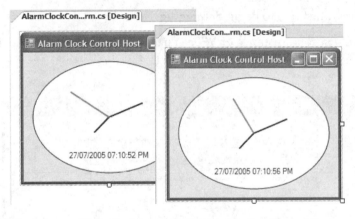

Figure 11.3   AlarmClockControl in Action, Albeit at Design Time

While there's a strange satisfaction in knowing that AlarmClockControl works at design time as well as run time, such behavior should occur only at run time. To track down why and where this is occurring, we need to perform a little debugging.

Debugging Design-Time Functionality

Because components implement functionality for both run time and design time, you need to test and debug them in both modes. To test run-time functionality, you simply set a breakpoint in your component's code and run a test application, relying on the VS05 debugger to break at the right moment.

Debugging design-time functionality is different because components are hosted within another application's design-time environment, and thus debugging is unavailable by default. To debug in the design time, you create a special environment that requires a design-time host to debug against. Because the hands-down hosting favorite is VS05 itself, this means that you use one instance of VS05 to debug another instance of VS05 with a running instance of the component loaded. This may sound confusing, but it's easy to set up:

1. Open the VS05 solution that contains both the component and the hosting application.

2. Set a second instance of VS05 as your debug application by going to Project | Properties | Debug and setting the following properties on your component project:

   - Set Start Action to Start External Program.

   - Set the external program to *VS05IDEPath*\devenv.exe.

   - Set Command Line Arguments to *SolutionPath**SolutionName*.sln.

3. Choose Set As StartUp Project on the project that contains your component.

4. Set a breakpoint in the component code.

5. Use Debug | Start (F5) to begin debugging.

At this point, a second instance of VS05 starts up with your solution, allowing you to break and debug at will, as illustrated in Figure 11.4.

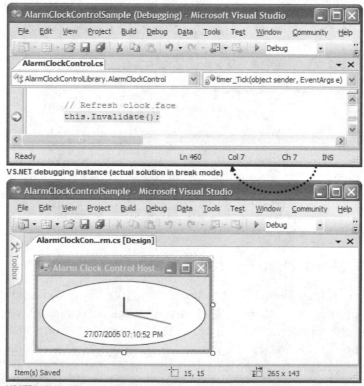

VS.NET debugging instance (actual solution in break mode)

VS.NET instance with running control (simulated solution in design-time mode)

Figure 11.4   Design-Time Debugging

Using this debugging technique, it becomes obvious that the timer's Tick event is firing at design time, leading to constant control repainting. Somehow, AlarmClockControl needs to determine when it's executing at design time and, if it is, prevent such behavior.

The DesignMode Property

To change the behavior of a component depending on whether it's executing at design time or run time, you need to know that you're running in a designer. This information is provided by Component's DesignMode property, which returns true at design time or returns false at run time and during the execution of a component's constructor at design time.

Using DesignMode makes it relatively simple to prevent AlarmClockControl from constantly repainting at design time:

```
void timer_Tick(object sender, EventArgs e) {
  ...
  // Don't do anything if executing at design time
  if( this.DesignMode ) return;
  ...
  // Refresh clock face
  this.Invalidate();
}
```

Note that Component.DesignMode reports that a component is operating in the design time only if the component has been sited. Because the design time sets the ISite reference after it instantiates a component, you can't inspect Component.DesignMode from a component's constructor.

Attributes

Design-time functionality is available to controls in one of two ways: programmatically or declaratively. Checking the DesignMode property is an example of the programmatic approach. One side effect of using a programmatic approach is that your implementation takes on some of the design-time responsibility, resulting in a blend of design-time and run-time code within the component implementation.

On the other hand, the declarative approach relies on attributes to request design-time functionality provided by the designer host.

Changing the Toolbox Icon

For example, consider the default Toolbox icon for AlarmClockControl, shown in Figure 11.5 residing in the AlarmClockControlLibrary's Toolbox tab. Recall from Chapter 9 that this tab is automatically created for you after a project build and is filled with all the public components in your solution.

Figure 11.5   Default Toolbox Icon

Typically, a custom component prefers a more appropriate icon. To substitute your own icon, you start by adding a 16 × 16, 16-color icon or bitmap to your project. Next, you set its Build Action to Embedded Resource (embedded resources are discussed in Chapter 13: Resources).[3] Finally, you add the ToolboxBitmap attribute to associate the icon with your component:

```
// AlarmClockControl.cs
[ToolboxBitmap(
   typeof(AlarmClockControl), "AlarmClockControl.ico")]
partial class AlarmClockControl : ScrollableControl {...}
```

Whenever you add or change the ToolboxBitmap attribute, the icon for your component is automatically updated in both the Toolbox and the nonvisual design surface after a project rebuild, resulting in something like Figure 11.6.

Figure 11.6   New and Improved Toolbox Icon

You can achieve the same result without using the ToolboxBitmap attribute: Simply place a 16 × 16, 16-color bitmap in the same project folder as the component, give it the same name as the component, select the file in Solution Explorer, and set its Build Action to Embedded Resource from the Properties window. This is a special shortcut for the

---

[3] The Toolbox supports transparent colors, too. The transparent color for icons and bitmaps is determined by the color of their bottom-left pixel.

ToolboxBitmap attribute only; don't expect to find similar shortcuts for other design-time attributes.

It is possible that not all of the public component implementations in your assembly specifically target the design time. In these cases, you probably don't want them to be available from the Toolbox at all. To hide them, you adorn them with the DesignTimeVisible attribute, passing false to its constructor:[4]

```
// IDontWantToAppearInTheToolboxComponent.cs
[ToolboxBitmap(false)]
partial class DontAppearInTheToolboxComponent : Component {...}
```

Passing true to the constructor is the same as not using the DesignTimeVisible attribute at all.

Properties Window Integration

Just as we use an attribute to influence which icon the design time displays in the Toolbox, we can use attributes to influence how properties and events appear. This is worth considering because the defaults can be quite uninformative, as shown in Figure 11.7.

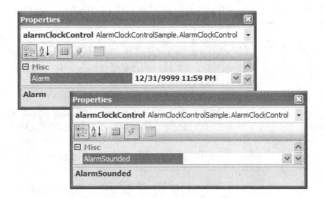

Figure 11.7   Default Appearance of Public Properties
and Events in the Properties Window

For a more informative experience, you can use special design-time attributes to enhance the look and feel of your component in the Properties window, describing and categorizing your properties and events. The System.ComponentModel namespace provides a comprehensive set of attributes, as shown in Table 11.1, that you can use to influence your custom component's behavior within the Properties window as well as its interactions with other design-time features like the Toolbox and the Windows Forms Designer.

---

[4] You can also use the ToolboxItem and ToolboxItemFilter attributes, although a discussion of these is beyond the scope of this book.

Table 11.1 Design-Time Properties Window-Influencing Attributes

Attribute	Description
AmbientValue	Specifies the value for this property that causes it to acquire its value from another source, usually its container (see the section "Ambient Properties" in Chapter 10: Controls).
Bindable	Most properties can be data-bound. The Bindable attribute allows you to control whether this is true for your custom properties and, if so, whether a property supports one-way or two-way binding. Additionally, properties adorned with the Bindable attribute appear in the Properties window under Properties Window | Data | (DataBindings) Property; here, you can highlight them as recommended for data binding, which is usually reserved for key properties. See Chapter 17: Applied Data Binding for further information.
Browsable	Determines whether the property is visible in the Properties window. Covered in this chapter.
Category	Tells the Properties window which group to include this property in. Covered in this chapter.
DefaultEvent	When a component is double-clicked, this attribute determines which event the Windows Forms Designer automatically registers with and creates an event handler for. Covered in this chapter.
DefaultProperty	When a component is selected, the property that is selected by default is specified by this attribute. Covered in this chapter.
DefaultValue	Stipulates the default property value. Covered in this chapter.
Description	Provides text for the Properties window to display in its description bar. Covered in this chapter.
DesignerCategory	Can be used to force Code view to be displayed for forms, components, controls, and user controls, which would normally open to Designer view.* Note that you must use the full name (e.g., System.ComponentModel.DesignerCategoryAttribute) for this to work.
DesignerSerializationVisibility	Influences how property values are serialized to InitializeComponent, if at all. Covered in this chapter.

Table 11.1 Continued

Attribute	Description
DesignOnly	Specifies that the design-time value of this property is serialized to the form's resource file. This attribute is typically used on properties that do not exist at run time.
DesignTimeVisible	You apply this to a component to specify whether it can be visible in a visual designer, such as the Windows Forms Designer. Covered in this chapter.
DisplayName	By default, the name used by the Properties window is the actual property's name. Using the DisplayName attribute allows you to specify a more human-readable property name to be displayed by the Properties window. This is particularly useful for extender provider properties, which are covered in this chapter.
Editor	Assigns a custom UI-type editor to a property to provide rich editing support. Covered in this chapter.
EditorBrowsable	Shows or hides a property or method in IntelliSense. Useful for discouraging developers from writing code against either type of member, or from viewing them with IntelliSense. You need to pass to the EditorBrowsable attribute one of the EditorBrowsableState enumeration values: Never (to always hide it), Always (to always show it), and Advanced (to allow developers to configure their IDEs to hide or show members, if supported). The EditorBrowsable attribute should be used in conjunction with the Browsable attribute.
MergableProperty	Allows this property to be combined with properties from other objects when two or more are selected for editing.
NotifyParentProperty	When this attribute is applied to a child property (such as Size) that is a child property of the Font property, a change to the child property sends a notification to the parent property to update itself. Parent-child properties are covered later. Note that, for this to work, you must use the full name (e.g., System.ComponentModel.NotifyParentPropertyAttribute). Covered in this chapter.
ParenthesizePropertyName	Specifies whether this property should be surrounded by parentheses in the Properties window.
PasswordPropertyText	Replaces the string representation of a property value with password replacement characters, which are either dots or asterisks.

(Continued)

Table 11.1 Continued

Attribute	Description
ProvideProperty	Configures a component to provide an extended property to other components hosted on either the visual or the nonvisual design surface. Covered in this chapter.
ReadOnly	Specifies that this property cannot be edited in the Properties window.
RefreshProperties	When a property is refreshed, you can use this attribute to instruct the Properties window to refresh itself in one of several ways specified by the RefreshProperties enumeration value: All (to refresh all properties), Repaint (to refresh only the visible properties), and None (to refresh no properties). Covered in this chapter.
SettingsBindable	All properties can be bound to application and user settings, but by applying the SettingsBindable attribute to a component's property, you force it to appear as a "recommended" property for settings purposes. A property with this attribute appears under Properties Window	Data	(Application Settings), which alleviates the need to open the Property Binding UI type editor. See Chapter 15: Settings for more information on application and user settings.
TypeConverter	Assigns a type converter to a component property to facilitate conversion between that property type and the string that's displayed in the Properties window. Covered in this chapter.

new

* Ian Griffiths has a great explanation at http://www.interact-sw.co.uk/iangblog/2004/06/10/codeviewinvs (http://tinysells.com/31).

By default, public read-only and read-write properties—such as the Alarm property highlighted in Figure 11.7—are displayed in the Properties window under the Misc category. If a property is intended for run time only, as Alarm is, you can prevent it from appearing in the Properties window by adorning the property with the Browsable attribute:

```
[Category("Behavior")]
public DateTime Alarm {
  get {...}
  set {...}
}
```

You can use the Description attribute to provide a description for the Properties window to display, thereby improving the situation:

```
[Category("Behavior")]
[Description("Alarm for late risers")]
public DateTime Alarm {
  get {...}
  set {...}
}
```

If you really want to, you can even change the property label text in the Properties window; the value of the property label text is the name of the underlying component's property implementation. You can do this by using the DisplayName attribute, which also allows you to use spaces and punctuation characters:

```
[Category("Behavior")]
[Description("Alarm for late risers.")]
[DisplayName("Alarm!!!")]
public DateTime Alarm {
  get {...}
  set {...}
}
```

After you add these attributes and rebuild, the Alarm property is categorized appropriately and described nicely in the Properties window, as shown in Figure 11.8.

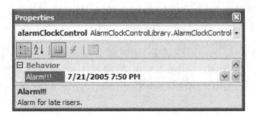

Figure 11.8   Alarm Property Augmented with Category, Description, and DisplayName Attributes

Note that you can use the Category attribute to create new categories, but you should do so only if the existing categories don't suitably describe a property's purpose. Otherwise, you'll confuse developers who look for your properties in the most intuitive category.

In Figure 11.8, some property values are shown in boldface and others are not. Boldface values are those that differ from the property's default value. For example, if we had a property, ShowDigitalTime that allowed us to hide or show the digital time value on the clock face, and if the default value was true, we could use the DefaultValue attribute to specify that it be bolded when false:

```
bool showDigitalTime = true;
...
[Category("Appearance")]
[Description("Whether digital time is shown")]
[DefaultValue(true)]
public bool ShowDigitalTime {
   get {...}
   set {...}
}
```

Using the DefaultValue attribute also allows you to reset a property to its default value using the Properties window, which is available from the property's context menu, as shown in Figure 11.9.

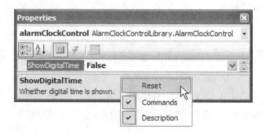

Figure 11.9   Resetting a Property to Its Default Value

This option is disabled if the current property is already the default value. Default values represent the most common value for a property. Some properties, such as Alarm or Text, simply don't have a default that's possible to define, whereas others, such as Enabled and ControlBox, do.

Just like properties, a class can have defaults. You can specify a default event by adorning a class with the DefaultEvent attribute:

```
// AlarmClockControl.cs
[DefaultEvent("AlarmSounded")]
partial class AlarmClockControl : ScrollableControl {...}
```

Double-clicking the component causes the Windows Forms Designer to automatically hook up the default event; it does this by serializing code to register with the specified event in InitializeComponent and providing a handler for it:

```csharp
// AlarmClockControlHostForm.cs
partial class AlarmClockControlHostForm : Form {
  ...
  void alarmClockControl_AlarmSounded(
    object sender,
    AlarmClockControlLibrary.AlarmSoundedEventArgs e) {...}
  ...
}

// AlarmClockControlHostForm.Designer.cs
partial class AlarmClockControlHostForm {
  ...
  void InitializeComponent() {
    ...
    this.alarmClockControl.AlarmSounded +=
      this.alarmClockControl_AlarmSounded;
    ...
  }
}
```

You can also adorn your component with the DefaultProperty attribute:

```csharp
// AlarmClockControl.cs
[DefaultProperty("ShowDigitalTime")]
partial class AlarmClockControl : ScrollableControl {...}
```

This attribute causes the Windows Forms Designer to highlight the default property when the component's property is first edited. Default properties aren't terribly useful, but properly setting the correct default event can save a developer's time when using your component.

Code Serialization

Whereas the DefaultEvent and DefaultProperty attributes affect only the behavior of the Properties window, the DefaultValue attribute serves a dual purpose: It also plays a role in helping the Windows Forms Designer determine which code is serialized to Initialize-Component. Properties that don't have a default value are automatically included in InitializeComponent, but those that do are included only if their configured values differ from their default values. To avoid unnecessarily changing a property, you should set your initial property values to match the value set by the DefaultValue attribute.

The DesignerSerializationVisibility attribute is another attribute that affects the code serialization process, as determined by the DesignerSerializationVisibility enumeration value passed to its constructor:

```
namespace System.ComponentModel {
   enum DesignerSerializationVisibility {
      Hidden = 0, // Don't initialize property
      Visible = 1, // Initialize property if nondefault value (default)
      Content = 2 // Initialize sets of properties on a subobject
   }
}
```

The default, Visible, causes a property's value to be set in InitializeComponent if the value of the property is not the same as the value of the default. But if you prefer that no code be generated to initialize a property—you might prefer this for a property like IsAlarmSet, which is useful only at run time—use Hidden:

```
[DesignerSerializationVisibility(
   DesignerSerializationVisibility.Hidden)]
public bool IsAlarmSet {
   get {...}
   set {...}
}
```

You can use Hidden in conjunction with the Browsable attribute set to false for run-time-only properties. Although the Browsable attribute determines whether a property is visible in the Properties window, its value may still be serialized unless you prevent that by using Hidden.

By default, properties that maintain a collection of custom types cannot be serialized to code. Such a property is implemented by the clock control in the form of a "messages to self" feature, which captures a set of messages and displays them at the appropriate date and time. To enable serialization of a collection, you can apply DesignerSerialization Visibility.Content to instruct the Windows Forms Designer to walk into the property and serialize its internal structure:

```
[Category("Behavior")]
[Description("Stuff to remember for later.")]
[DesignerSerializationVisibility(
   DesignerSerializationVisibility.Content)]
public Collection<MessageToSelf> MessagesToSelf {
   get {...}
   set {...}
}
```

The generated InitializeComponent code for a single message looks like this:

```
// AlarmClockControl.Designer.cs
partial class AlarmClockControl {
  ...
  void InitializeComponent() {
    ...
    this.alarmClockControl.MessagesToSelf.Add(
      new AlarmClockControlLibrary.MessageToSelf(
        new System.DateTime(2005, 12, 8, 21, 59, 23, 577),
        "My First Message"));
    ...
  }
}
```

This code also needs a translator class to help the Windows Forms Designer serialize the proper code to construct a MessageToSelf type. This is covered in detail in the section "Type Converters" later in this chapter.

Batch Initialization

As you may have noticed, the code that's eventually serialized to InitializeComponent is laid out as an alphabetically ordered sequence of property sets, grouped by object. Order may become problematic if your component exposes range-dependent properties, such as Min/Max or Start/Stop pairs. For example, the clock control also has two dependent properties: PrimaryAlarm and BackupAlarm. (The Alarm property was split into two for extra-sleepy people who work too hard writing books.)

Internally, the clock control instance initializes the two properties 15 minutes apart, starting from the current date and time:

```
DateTime primaryAlarm = DateTime.Now;
DateTime backupAlarm = DateTime.Now.AddMinutes(15);
```

Both properties should check to ensure that the values are valid:

```
public DateTime PrimaryAlarm {
  get { return this.primaryAlarm; }
  set {
    if( value >= this.backupAlarm ) {
      throw new ArgumentOutOfRangeException(
        "Primary alarm must be before Backup alarm");
    }
    ...
  }
}
```

```
public DateTime BackupAlarm {
  get { return this.backupAlarm; }
  set {
    if( value < this.primaryAlarm ) {
      throw new ArgumentOutOfRangeException(
        "Backup alarm must be after Primary alarm");
    }
    ...
  }
}
```

With this dependence checking in place, at design time the Properties window shows an exception in an error dialog if an invalid property is entered, as shown in Figure 11.10.

Figure 11.10   Invalid Value Entered into the Properties Window

This error dialog is great at design time, because it shows the developer the relationship between the two properties. However, there's a problem when the properties are serialized into InitializeComponent alphabetically:

```
// AlarmClockControl.Designer.cs
partial class AlarmClockControl {
  ...
  void InitializeComponent() {
    ...
    this.alarmClockControl.BackupAlarm =
      new System.DateTime(2005, 12, 8, 23, 21, 37, 607);
    this.alarmClockControl.PrimaryAlarm =
      new System.DateTime(2005, 12, 8, 23, 8, 0, 0);
    ...
  }
}
```

Notice that even if the developer sets the two alarms properly, as soon as BackupAlarm is set and is checked against the value of PrimaryAlarm, a run-time exception results if BackupAlarm comes before the default PrimaryAlarm value.

To avoid this, you'll want to ensure that the component is notified when its properties are being set from InitializeComponent in "batch mode" so that they can be validated all at the same time at the end. Implementing the ISupportInitialize interface provides this capability, with two notification methods to be called before and after initialization:

```
namespace System.ComponentModel {
    interface ISupportInitialize {
        void BeginInit();
        void EndInit();
    }
}
```

When a component implements this interface, calls to BeginInit and EndInit are serialized to InitializeComponent:

```
// AlarmClockControl.Designer.cs
partial class AlarmClockControl {
    ...
    void InitializeComponent() {
        ...
        ((System.ComponentModel.ISupportInitialize)
          (this.alarmClockControl)).BeginInit();
        ...
        this.alarmClockControl.BackupAlarm =
            new System.DateTime(2005, 12, 8, 23, 21, 37, 607);
        this.alarmClockControl.PrimaryAlarm =
            new System.DateTime(2005, 12, 8, 23, 8, 0, 0);
        ...
        ((System.ComponentModel.ISupportInitialize)
          (this.alarmClockControl)).EndInit();
        ...
    }
}
```

The call to BeginInit signals the entry into initialization batch mode, a signal that is useful for turning off value checking:

```
// AlarmClockControl.cs
partial class AlarmClockControl : ISupportInitialize, ... {
    ...
    bool initializing = false;
```

```
  void BeginInit() { this.initializing = true; }
public DateTime PrimaryAlarm {
  get {...}
  set {
    if( !this.initializing ) { /* check value */ }
    ...
  }
}

public DateTime BackupAlarm {
  get {...}
  set {
    if( !this.initializing ) { /* check value */ }
    ...
  }
}
}
```

Placing the appropriate logic into EndInit performs batch validation:

```
// AlarmClockControl.cs
partial class AlarmClockControl : ISupportInitialize, ... {
  ...
  void EndInit() {
    // Check alarm values
    if( this.primaryAlarm >= this.backupAlarm ) {
        throw new ArgumentOutOfRangeException(
          "Primary alarm must be before Backup alarm");
    }
    this.initializing = false;
  }
  ...
}
```

EndInit also turns out to be a better place to avoid the timer's Tick event, which currently fires once every second during design time. Although the code inside the Tick event handler doesn't run at design time (because it's protected by a check of the DesignMode property), it would be better to not even start the timer at all until run time. However, because DesignMode can't be checked in the constructor, a good place to check it is in the EndInit call, which is called after all properties have been initialized at run time or at design time:

```
// AlarmClockControl.cs
partial class AlarmClockControl : ISupportInitialize, ... {
  ...
  void EndInit() {
    if( !this.DesignMode ) {
      ...
```

```
        // Initialize timer
        this.timer.Interval = 1000;
        this.timer.Tick += new System.EventHandler(this.timer_Tick);
        this.timer.Enabled = true;
      }
      ...
    }
    ...
  }
```

InitializeComponent nicely guarantees that ISupportInitialize.EndInit is invoked after your component's child components have initialized.

ISupportInitializeNotification

ISupportInitialize, however, doesn't guarantee that it will be invoked before or after other components have completed their own initialization. This could be an issue when your component initialization is dependent on another component being initialized. For example, some controls, such as DataGridView, have a DataSource property, which is usually a reference to another component hosted by the form, such as a BindingSource.[5] In these situations, you can implement ISupportInitializeNotification on your component to provide initialization information to dependent components:

```
namespace System.ComponentModel {
  interface ISupportInitializeNotification : ISupportInitialize {
    // Properties
    bool IsInitialized { get; }
    // Events
    event EventHandler Initialized;
  }
}
```

ISupportInitializeNotification exposes the IsInitialized property, which dependent components can check to see whether your component has initialized. If IsInitialized returns true, the dependent components initialize as usual. If false is returned, they register with the Initialized event to be notified when the component they're depending on initializes. If AlarmClockControl anticipates that other components will be dependent on it for initialization, it implements ISupportInitializeNotification:

```
// AlarmClockControl.cs
partial class AlarmClockControl : ISupportInitializeNotification, ... {
  ...
  #region ISupportInitializeNotification Members
```

---

[5] DataGridView and BindingSource are explored in depth in Chapter 16: Data Binding Basics and Chapter 17: Applied Data Binding.

```
public event EventHandler Initialized;

public bool IsInitialized {
  get { return !this.initializing; }
}

#endregion

#region ISupportInitialize

public void BeginInit() { this.initializing = true; }
public void EndInit() {
  ...
  this.initializing = false;

  // Notify dependent components
  if( this.Initialized != null ) {
    this.Initialized(this, EventArgs.Empty);
  }
}

#endregion
...
}
```

The code on a dependent component that uses this implementation would look something like this:

```
public class MyDependentComponent : Component, ISupportInitialize {
  #region ISupportInitialize Members

  public void BeginInit() {...}
  public void EndInit() {
    ISupportInitializeNotification notifier =
      this.alarmClockControl as ISupportInitializeNotification;
    // Is the component we're depending on initialized?
    if( (notifier != null) && !notifier.IsInitialized ) {
      // If not, ask it to let us know when it does, so we
      // can complete our own initialization as per normal
      notifier.Initialized += this.notifier_Initialized;
    }
    else {
      // Initialize as per normal
      ...
    }
  }

  #endregion

  void notifier_Initialized(object sender, EventArgs e) {
```

```
if( sender == this.alarmClockControl ) {
  // Initialize as per normal
  ...
  // Unregister event
  ISupportInitializeNotification notifier =
    sender as ISupportInitializeNotification;
  if( notifier != null ) {
    notifier.Initialized -= this.notifier_Initialized;
  }
}
}
}
```

As you've seen, the Windows Forms Designer and the Properties window provide all kinds of declarative and programmatic design-time help to augment a component's design-time experience, including establishing how a property is categorized and described, how its state is serialized to the InitializeComponent method, and how the initialization process can be coordinated in special scenarios.

Extender Property Providers

The discussion to this point has focused on the properties implemented by a component for itself. One example of such a property, TimeZoneModifier, allows AlarmClockControl to be time zone sensitive, allowing it to display the time in each time zone where an organization has offices. This allows each office to be visually represented with a picture box and an AlarmClockControl, as illustrated in Figure 11.11, with appropriate configuration of the TimeZoneModifier property on each AlarmClockControl.

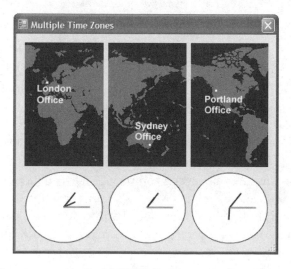

Figure 11.11   Form with Multiple Time Zones (See Plate 16)

This works quite nicely but could lead to real estate problems, particularly if you have one AlarmClockControl for each of the 24 time zones globally and consequently 24 implementations of the same logic on the form. If you are concerned about resources, this also means 24 system timers. Figure 11.12 shows what it might look like.

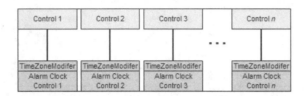

Figure 11.12   One Provider Control for Each Client Control

Another approach is to have a single AlarmClockControl and update its TimeZoneModifier property with the relevant time zone from the Click event of each picture box. This is a cumbersome approach because it requires developers to write the code associating a time zone offset with each control, a situation controls are meant to help you avoid. Figure 11.13 illustrates this approach.

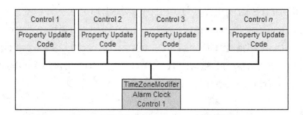

Figure 11.13   One Provider Control for All Client Controls, Accessed with Code

A nicer way to handle this situation is to provide access to a single implementation of the AlarmClockControl without forcing developers to write additional property update code. And .NET offers extender property support to do just this, allowing components to extend property implementations to other components.

Logically, an *extender property* is a property exposed by an *extender provider*, such as the AlarmClockControl, to other components in the same container, such as picture boxes. Extender properties are useful whenever a component needs data from a set of other components in the same host. For example, Windows Forms itself provides several extender provider components, including ErrorProvider, HelpProvider, and ToolTip. With respect to ToolTip, it makes a lot more sense to set the ToolTip property on each component than it does to set tool tip information for all components using an editor provided by ToolTip itself.

In our case, by implementing TimeZoneModifier as an extender property, we allow each picture box control on the form to get its own value, as shown in Figure 11.14.

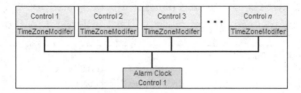

Figure 11.14   One Provider Control for All Client Controls, Accessed with a Property Set

Such a solution allows us to create a form with a single AlarmClockControl that services multiple other controls, as illustrated in Figure 11.15.

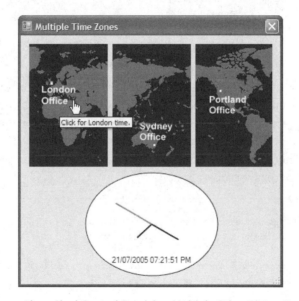

Figure 11.15   AlarmClockControl Servicing Multiple Other PictureBox Controls

Exposing an extender property from your component requires that you first use the ProvideProperty attribute to declare the property to be extended:

```
// AlarmClockControl.cs
[ProvideProperty("TimeZoneModifier", typeof(PictureBox))]
partial class AlarmClockControl : ScrollableControl, ... {...}
```

The first parameter to the attribute is the name of the property to be extended. The second parameter is the *receiver* type, which specifies the type of object to extend, such as PictureBox. Only components of the type specified by the receiver can be extended. If you want to implement a more sophisticated algorithm, such as supporting picture boxes and panels, you must implement the IExtenderProvider CanExtend method:

```
// AlarmClockControl.cs
[ProvideProperty("TimeZoneModifier", typeof(PictureBox))]
partial class AlarmClockControl : IExtenderProvider, ... {
  ...
  public bool CanExtend(object extendee) {
    // Don't extend self
    if( extendee == this ) return false;

    // Extend suitable controls
    return ((extendee is PictureBox) ||
            (extendee is Panel));
  }
  ...
}
```

As illustrated in Figure 11.15, an extender provider can support one or more *extendee* components. Consequently, the extender provider must be able to store and distinguish one extendee's property value from that of another. It does this in the Get*PropertyName* and Set-*PropertyName* methods, where *PropertyName* is the name you provided in the Provide-Property attribute. Then, GetTimeZoneModifier simply returns the property value when requested by the Properties window:

```
// AlarmClockControl.cs
[ProvideProperty("TimeZoneModifier", typeof(PictureBox))]
partial class AlarmClockControl : IExtenderProvider, ... {
  ...
  // Mapping of components to numeric time zone offsets
  Hashtable timeZoneModifiers = new Hashtable();
  ...
  public int GetTimeZoneModifier(Control extendee) {
    // Return component's time zone offset
    return Convert.ToInt32(this.timeZoneModifiers[extendee]);
  }
  ...
}
```

SetTimeZoneModifier has a little more work to do. First, it stores an extender provider property value on behalf of every extendee that chooses to set it. Second, it removes the value when an extendee chooses to unset it. Both actions operate over the same hashtable as used by GetTimeZoneModifier:

```
// AlarmClockControl.cs
[ProvideProperty("TimeZoneModifier", typeof(PictureBox))]
partial class AlarmClockControl : IExtenderProvider, ... {
  ...
  int timeZoneModifier = 0;
  ...
  public void SetTimeZoneModifier(Control extendee, object value) {
    // If property isn't provided
    if( value == null ) {
      // Remove it
      this.timeZoneModifiers.Remove(extendee);
    }
    else {
      // Add the time zone modifier as an integer
      this.timeZoneModifiers[extendee] = Convert.ToInt32(value);
    }
  }
  ...
}
```

When an extender property value has been set for one or more extendees, the clock control needs to make sure the property values are applied for each extendee. To do this, the extender provider is notified that the extendee is currently active in some shape or form, and this is why SetTimeZoneModifier registers an extendee's Click event to be handled by the AlarmClockControl:

```
// AlarmClockControl.cs
[ProvideProperty("TimeZoneModifier", typeof(PictureBox))]
partial class AlarmClockControl : IExtenderProvider, ... {
  ...
  public void SetTimeZoneModifier(Control extendee, object value) {
    // If property isn't provided
    if( value == null ) {
      // Remove it
      timeZoneModifiers.Remove(extendee);
      if( !this.DesignMode ) this.extendee.Click -= extendee_Click;
    }
    else {
      // Add the time zone modifier as an integer
      timeZoneModifiers[extendee] = Convert.ToInt32(value);
      if( !this.DesignMode ) this.extendee.Click += extendee_Click;
    }
  }
  ...
  void extendee_Click(object sender, System.EventArgs e) {
    // Update the time zone
    this.timeZoneModifier = this.GetTimeZoneModifier((Control)sender);
  }
```

```
  ...
  protected override void OnPaint(PaintEventArgs e) {
    ...
    // Get specified date/time if control is in design time,
    // or current date/time if control is in run time
    DateTime now;
    if( this.DesignMode ) {
      // Get pretty date/time for design time
      now = new DateTime(2005, 12, 31, 15, 00, 20, 0);
    }
    else {
      // Get current date/time and apply the time zone modifier
      now = DateTime.Now.AddHours(timeZoneModifier);
    }
    ...
  }
}
```

As with other properties, you can affect the appearance of an extender property in the Properties window by adorning the Get*PropertyName* method with attributes:

```
// AlarmClockControl.cs
[ProvideProperty("TimeZoneModifier", typeof(PictureBox))]
partial class AlarmClockControl : IExtenderProvider, ... {
  ...
  [Category("Behavior")]
  [Description("Sets the time zone difference from the current time.")]
  [DefaultValue(0)]
  public int GetTimeZoneModifier(Control extendee) {...}
  public void SetTimeZoneModifier(Control extendee, object value) {...}
  ...
}
```

These attributes are applied to the extendee's Properties window view after compilation. Extended properties appear as an entry in the extendee component's Properties Window view with the following default naming format:

ExtendedPropertyName on *ExtenderProviderName*

This format, however, may not be as readable as you'd like, and it is inconsistent with the vast majority of property names you'll find in the Properties window. Luckily, you can use the DisplayName attribute to override the default name with something prettier:

```
// AlarmClockControl.cs
[ProvideProperty("TimeZoneModifier", typeof(PictureBox))]
partial class AlarmClockControl : IExtenderProvider, ... {
  ...
```

```
    [Category("Behavior")]
    [Description("Sets the time zone difference from the current time.")]
    [DefaultValue(0)]
    [DisplayName("TimeZoneModifier")]
    public int GetTimeZoneModifier(Control extendee) {...}
    public void SetTimeZoneModifier(
      Control extendee, object value) {...}
    ...
  }
```

Note that for extender properties, you must adorn the Get*PropertyName* method with the DisplayName attribute. Figure 11.16 shows the TimeZoneModifier extender property behaving like any other property on a PictureBox control.

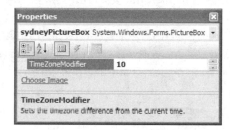

Figure 11.16   Extended Property in Action

Now that we've made the TimeZoneModifier property pretty, users will be so attracted to it that they'll be drawn to the Properties window to change it. If the changed value is not the default value, it is serialized to InitializeComponent, although this time as a SetTimeZoneModifier method call on the extender provider component, which is actually grouped with the extendee component:

```
// MultipleTimeZonesForm.Designer.cs
partial class MultipleTimeZonesForm {
  ...
  void InitializeComponent() {
    ...
    // sydneyPictureBox
    this.sydneyPictureBox.Name = "sydneyPictureBox";
    this.sydneyPictureBox.Size = new System.Drawing.Size(117, 184);
    this.alarmClockControl.SetTimeZoneModifier(
      this.sydneyPictureBox, 10);
    ...
  }
}
```

Extender properties allow one component—the extender—to add properties to another component, the extendee. However, even though logically the extendee gets one or more additional properties, storage and property access are managed by the extender.

Type Converters

When you select a component on a design surface, the entries in the Properties window are rendered from an internal instance of that component. When you edit properties in the Properties window, the component instance is updated with the new property values. This synchronicity isn't as straightforward as it seems, however, because the Properties window displays properties only as text, even though properties can be of any type. As values shuttle between the Properties window and the component instance, they must be converted back and forth between the string type and the type of the property.

Enter the *type converter*, the translator droid of .NET, whose main goal in life is to convert between types. For string-to-type conversion, a type converter is used for each property displayed in the Properties window, as shown in Figure 11.17.

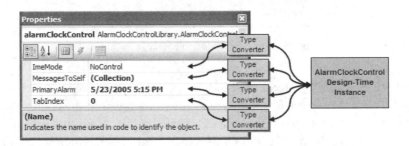

Figure 11.17   The Properties Window and Design-Time Conversion

.NET offers the TypeConverter class (from the System.ComponentModel namespace) as the base implementation type converter. And .NET also gives you several derivations—including StringConverter, Int32Converter, and DateTimeConverter—that support conversion between one common .NET type and one or more other common .NET types. If you know the type that needs conversion at compile time, you can create an appropriate converter directly:

```
// Type is known at compile time
TypeConverter converter = new Int32Converter();
```

Or, if you don't know the type that needs conversion until run time, let the Type-Descriptor class (from the System.ComponentModel namespace) make the choice for you:

```
// Don't know the type before run time
object myData = 0;
TypeConverter converter = TypeDescriptor.GetConverter(myData.GetType());
```

The TypeDescriptor class provides information about a particular type or object, including methods, properties, events, and attributes. TypeDescriptor.GetConverter evaluates a type to determine a suitable TypeConverter based on the following:

1. Checking whether a type is adorned with an attribute that specifies a particular type converter

2. Comparing the type against the set of built-in type converters

3. Returning the TypeConverter base if no other type converters are found

Because the Properties window is designed to display the properties of any component, it can't know specific property types in advance. Consequently, it relies on TypeDescriptor.GetConverter to dynamically select the most appropriate type converter for each property.

After a type converter is chosen, the Properties window and the component instance perform the required conversions, using the same principle expressed in the following code:

```
public void PretendDesignerConversion() {
    // Create the appropriate type converter
    object myData = 0;
    TypeConverter converter =
      TypeDescriptor.GetConverter(myData.GetType());
    // Can converter convert int to string?
    if( converter.CanConvertTo(typeof(string)) ) {
      // Convert it
      object intToString = converter.ConvertTo(42, typeof(string));
    }
    // Can converter convert string to int?
    if( converter.CanConvertFrom(typeof(string)) ) {
      // Convert it
      object stringToInt = converter.ConvertFrom("42");
    }
}
```

When the Properties window renders itself, it uses the type converter to convert each component instance property to a string representation using the following steps:

1. CanConvertTo: Can you convert from the design-time property type to a string?

2. ConvertTo: If so, please convert the property value to a string.

The string representation of the source value is then displayed at the property's entry in the Properties window. If the property is edited and the value is changed, the

Properties window uses the next steps to convert the string back to the source property value:

1. **CanConvertFrom:** Can you convert back to the design-time property type?
2. **ConvertFrom:** If so, please convert the string to the property value.

Some intrinsic type converters can do more than just convert between simple types. To demonstrate, let's upgrade AlarmClockControl's ShowDigitalTime property to a new Face property of type ClockFace that allows developers to decide how the clock is displayed, including options for Analog, Digital, or Both:

```csharp
// ClockFaceEnumeration.cs
enum ClockFace {
  Analog = 0,
  Digital = 1,
  Both = 2
}


// AlarmClockControl.cs
partial class AlarmClockControl : ... {
  ...
  ClockFace face = ClockFace.Both;
  ...
  [Category("Appearance")]
  [Description("Determines the clock face type to display.")]
  [DefaultValue(ClockFace.Both)]
  public ClockFace Face {
    get {...}
    set {...}
  }
  ...
}
```

TypeDescriptor.GetConverter returns an EnumConverter, which has the smarts to examine the source enumeration and convert it to a drop-down list of descriptive string values, as shown in Figure 11.18.

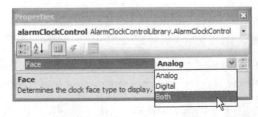

Figure 11.18 Enumeration Type Displayed in the Properties Window via EnumConverter

Custom Type Converters

Although the built-in type converters are useful, they aren't enough when components expose properties based on custom types, such as AlarmClockControl's HourHand, MinuteHand, and SecondHand properties:

```csharp
// Hand.cs
class Hand {
  Color color = Color.Black;
  int width = 1;
  public Hand(Color color, int width) {
    this.color = color;
    this.width = width;
  }
  public Color Color {
    get {...}
    set {...}
  }
  public int Width {
    get {...}
    set {...}
  }
}


// AlarmClockControl.cs
partial class AlarmClockControl : ... {
  ...
  Hand hourHand = new Hand(Color.Black, 1);
  Hand minuteHand = new Hand(Color.Black, 1);
  Hand secondHand = new Hand(Color.Red, 1);
  ...
  [Category("Appearance")]
  [Description("Sets the color and size of the Hour Hand.")]
  public Hand HourHand {
    get {...}
    set {...}
  }
  [Category("Appearance")]
  [Description("Sets the color and size of the Minute Hand.")]
  public Hand MinuteHand {
    get {...}
    set {...}
  }
  [Category("Appearance")]
  [Description("Sets the color and size of the Second Hand.")]
  public Hand SecondHand {
```

```
    get {...}
    set {...}
  }
  ...
}
```

The idea is to give developers the option to pretty up the clock's hands with color and width values. If we had no custom type converter, the result would be rather unfortunate, as shown in Figure 11.19.[6]

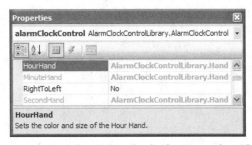

Figure 11.19   Complex Properties in the Properties Window

Just as the Properties window can't know which types it will display, .NET can't know which custom types you'll develop. Consequently, there aren't any type converters capable of handling your custom types. However, the type converter infrastructure is extensible enough that you can leverage it to provide your own. To build a custom type converter, you start by deriving from the TypeConverter base class:

```
// HandConverter.cs
class HandConverter : TypeConverter {...}
```

To support conversion, HandConverter must override CanConvertTo, CanConvert-From, ConvertTo, and ConvertFrom:

```
// HandConverter.cs
class HandConverter : TypeConverter {

  public override bool CanConvertTo(
    ITypeDescriptorContext context,
    Type destinationType) {...}

  public override bool CanConvertFrom(
    ITypeDescriptorContext context,
    Type sourceType) {...}
```

[6] Be careful when you use custom types for properties. If the value of the property is null, you won't be able to edit it in the Properties window at all.

```
  public override object ConvertFrom(
    ITypeDescriptorContext context,
    CultureInfo info,
    object value) {...}

  public override object ConvertTo(
    ITypeDescriptorContext context,
    CultureInfo culture,
    object value,
    Type destinationType) {...}
}
```

CanConvertFrom lets clients know which types it can convert from. In this case, Hand-Converter reports that it can convert from a string type to a Hand type:

```
// HandConverter.cs
class HandConverter : TypeConverter {
  public override bool CanConvertFrom(
    ITypeDescriptorContext context,
    Type sourceType) {

    // We can convert from a string to a Hand type
    if( sourceType == typeof(string) ) { return true; }
    return base.CanConvertFrom(context, sourceType);
  }
}
```

Whether the string type is in the correct format is left up to ConvertFrom, which actually performs the conversion. HandConverter expects a multivalued string, which it splits into its atomic values before it uses them to instantiate a Hand object:

```
// HandConverter.cs
class HandConverter : TypeConverter {
  ...
  public override object ConvertFrom(
    ITypeDescriptorContext context,
    CultureInfo info,
    object value) {

    // If converting from a string
    if( value is string ) {
      // Build a Hand type
      try {
        // Get Hand properties
        string propertyList = (string)value;
        string[] properties = propertyList.Split(';');
        return new Hand(Color.FromName(properties[0].Trim()),
                        Convert.ToInt32(properties[1]));
      }
```

```
      catch { }
      throw new ArgumentException("The arguments were not valid.");
    }
    return base.ConvertFrom(context, info, value);
  }
}
```

To convert a Hand type back to a string, we first need to let clients know we can, and we do that by overriding CanConvertTo:

```
// HandConverter.cs
class HandConverter : TypeConverter {
  ...
  public override bool CanConvertTo(
    ITypeDescriptorContext context,
    Type destinationType) {

    // We can convert from a Hand type to a string
    return (destinationType == typeof(string));
  }
}
```

Then, we override ConvertTo to perform the actual conversion:

```
// HandConverter.cs
class HandConverter : TypeConverter {
  ...
  public override object ConvertTo(
    ITypeDescriptorContext context,
    CultureInfo culture,
    object value,
    Type destinationType) {

    // If source value is a Hand type
    if( value is Hand ) {
      // Convert to string
      if( (destinationType == typeof(string)) ) {
        Hand hand = (Hand)value;
        string color;
        if( hand.Color.IsNamedColor ) {
          color = hand.Color.Name;
        }
        else {
          color = string.Format("{0}, {1}, {2}", hand.Color.R,
                                                  hand.Color.G,
                                                  hand.Color.B);
```

```
      }
      return string.Format("{0}; {1}", color, hand.Width.ToString());
    }
  }
  // Base ConvertTo if string isn't required
  return base.ConvertTo(context, culture, value, destinationType);
  }
}
```

When the Properties window looks for a custom type converter, it looks at each property for a TypeConverter attribute:

```
// AlarmClockControl.cs
partial class AlarmClockControl : ... {
  ...
  [TypeConverter(typeof(HandConverter))]
  public Hand HourHand {...}
  [TypeConverter(typeof(HandConverter))]
  public Hand MinuteHand {...}
  [TypeConverter(typeof(HandConverter))]
  public Hand SecondHand {...}
  ...
}
```

However, this code can be quite cumbersome. Sometimes it's simpler to decorate the type itself with the TypeConverter attribute:

```
// Hand.cs
[TypeConverter(typeof(HandConverter))]
class Hand {...}

// AlarmClockControl.cs
partial class AlarmClockControl : ... {
  ...
  public Hand HourHand {...}
  public Hand MinuteHand {...}
  public Hand SecondHand {...}
  ...
}
```

Figure 11.20 shows the effect of the custom HandConverter type converter.

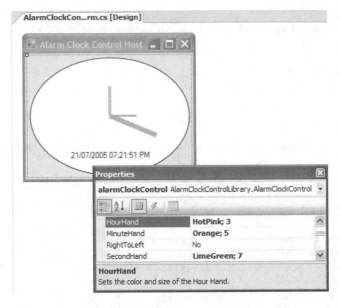

Figure 11.20   HandConverter in Action (See Plate 17)

Expandable Object Converter

Although using the UI shown in Figure 11.20 is better than not being able to edit the property at all, there are still ways it can be improved. For example, put yourself in a developer's shoes; although it might be obvious what the first part of the property is, it's disappointing not to be able to pick the color from one of those pretty drop-down color pickers. And what is the second part of the property meant to be? Length? Width? Degrees? Thingamajigs?

As an example of what you'd like to see, the Font type supports browsing and editing of its subproperties, as shown in Figure 11.21.

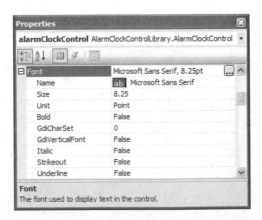

Figure 11.21   Expanded Property Value

This ability to expand a property of a custom type makes it a lot easier to understand what the property represents and what sort of values you need to provide. To allow sub-property editing, you change the base type from TypeConverter to ExpandableObjectConverter (from the System.ComponentModel namespace):

```
// HandConverter.cs
class HandConverter : ExpandableObjectConverter {...}
```

This trivial change supports both multivalue and nested property editing, as illustrated in Figure 11.22.

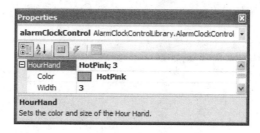

Figure 11.22   HandConverter Derived from ExpandableObjectConverter

Although you don't have to write any code to make this property expandable, you need to fix an irksome problem: a delay in property updating. In expanded mode, a change to the parent property value (e.g., SecondHand) is automatically reflected in its child property values (e.g., Color and Width). This occurs because the parent property value refers to the design-time property instance, whereas its child property values refer directly to the design-time instance's properties, as shown in Figure 11.23.

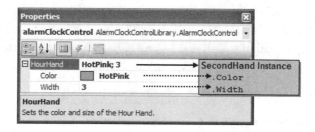

Figure 11.23   Relationship Between Parent and Child Properties and Design-Time Property Instance

When the parent property is edited, the Properties window calls HandConverter.ConvertFrom to convert the Properties window's string entry to a new SecondHand instance, and that results in a refresh of the Properties window. However, changing the child property values only changes the current instance's property values, rather than creating a new instance. Consequently, there isn't an immediate refresh of the parent property.

However, you can force the parent property value to be refreshed through the use of the NotifyParentProperty attribute. When a property type is a class with one or more other properties, such as SecondHand, you adorn each of the child properties of that class with the NotifyParentProperty attribute, passing true to its constructor:

```csharp
// Hand.cs
[TypeConverter(typeof(HandConverter))]
class Hand {
  ...
  [System.ComponentModel.NotifyParentProperty(true)]
  [Description("Sets the color of the clock Hand.")]
  public Color Color {
    get {...}
    set {...}
  }

  [System.ComponentModel.NotifyParentProperty(true)]
  [Description("Sets the width of the clock Hand.")]
  public int Width {
    get {...}
    set {...}
  }
}
```

TypeConverters also offer a mechanism by which you can force the creation of a new instance whenever instance property values change, and this is a great alternative in complex scenarios that require code to refresh a property. To implement refreshing of the parent property value, you override TypeDescriptor's GetCreateInstanceSupported and CreateInstance methods. The GetCreateInstanceSupported method returns a Boolean indicating whether this support is available and, if it is, calls CreateInstance to implement it:

```csharp
// HandConverter.cs
class HandConverter : ExpandableObjectConverter {
  ...
  public override bool GetCreateInstanceSupported(
    ITypeDescriptorContext context) {

    // Always force a new instance
    return true;
  }
```

```
public override object CreateInstance(
  ITypeDescriptorContext context,
  IDictionary propertyValues) {

  // Use the dictionary to create a new instance
  return new Hand((Color)propertyValues["Color"],
                  (int)propertyValues["Width"]);
  }
}
```

If GetCreateInstanceSupported returns true, then CreateInstance is used to create a new instance whenever any of the subproperties of an expandable object are changed. The propertyValues argument to CreateInstance provides a set of name/value pairs for the current values of the object's subproperties, and you can use them to construct a new instance.

Both the NotifyParentProperty attribute and TypeDescriptor techniques apply only to a single property; this keeps the parent property value synchronized with changes made to the child property values. Sometimes, however, you may need to refresh several properties when one property changes. In this case, the simplest approach is to use the RefreshProperties attribute to force the Properties window to update itself, retrieving new property values in the process. To control how the Properties window does that, if at all, you pass in one of three RefreshProperties enumeration values:

```
namespace System.ComponentModel {
  enum RefreshProperties {
    None = 0, // Don't refresh at all
    All = 1,  // Refresh property values for all properties in the
              // Properties window
    Repaint = 2 // Refresh property values for only those properties
                // that are visible in the Properties window
  }
}
```

To refresh all property values, you use the RefreshProperties attribute and RefreshProperties.All:

```
[RefreshProperties(RefreshProperties.All)]
public string SomeProperty {
  get {...}
  set {...}
}
```

Custom Type Code Serialization with TypeConverters

Although the Hand type now plays nicely with the Properties window, it doesn't yet play nicely with code serialization. In fact, at this point, its values are not being serialized to

InitializeComponent at all. To enable serialization of properties of complex types, you must expose a public ShouldSerialize*PropertyName* method that returns a Boolean:

```
// AlarmClockControl.cs
partial class AlarmClockControl : ... {
  ...
  public Hand HourHand {...}
  bool ShouldSerializeHourHand() {
    // Serialize only nondefault values
    return ((this.hourHand.Color != Color.Black) ||
            (this.hourHand.Width != 1));
  }
  ...
}
```

Internally, the Windows Forms Designer looks for a method named ShouldSerialize*PropertyName* to ask whether the property should be serialized. From the Windows Forms Designer's point of view, it doesn't matter whether your ShouldSerialize*PropertyName* is public or private, but choosing private removes it from client visibility.

To programmatically implement the Properties window reset functionality, you use the Reset*PropertyName* method:

```
// AlarmClockControl.cs
partial class AlarmClockControl : ... {
  ...
  public Hand HourHand {...}
  bool ShouldSerializeHourHand() {
    // Serialize only nondefault values
    return ((this.hourHand.Color != Color.Black) ||
            (this.hourHand.Width != 1));
  }
  void ResetHourHand() {
    HourHand = new Hand(Color.Black, 1);
    // Refresh clock face
    this.Invalidate();
  }
  ...
}
```

Implementing ShouldSerialize lets the design-time environment know whether the property should be serialized, but you also need to write custom code to assist in the generation of appropriate InitializeComponent code. Specifically, the Windows Forms Designer needs an *instance descriptor*, which provides the information needed to create an instance of a particular type. The code serializer gets an InstanceDescriptor object for a Hand by asking the Hand type converter:

```csharp
// HandConverter.cs
class HandConverter : ExpandableObjectConverter {
  ...
  public override bool CanConvertTo(
    ITypeDescriptorContext context,
    Type destinationType) {

    // We can be converted to a string or an InstanceDescriptor
    if( destinationType == typeof(string) ) return true;
    if( destinationType == typeof(InstanceDescriptor) ) return true;
    return base.CanConvertTo(context, destinationType);
  }
  ...
  public override object ConvertTo(
    ITypeDescriptorContext context,
    CultureInfo culture,
    object value,
    Type destinationType) {

    // If source value is a Hand type
    if( value is Hand ) {
      // Convert to string
      if( destinationType == typeof(string) ) {...}
      // Convert to InstanceDescriptor
      if( (destinationType == typeof(InstanceDescriptor)) ) {
        Hand hand = (Hand)value;
        object[] properties = new object[2];
        Type[] types = new Type[2];

        // Color
        types[0] = typeof(Color);
        properties[0] = hand.Color;

        // Width
        types[1] = typeof(int);
        properties[1] = hand.Width;

        // Build constructor
        ConstructorInfo ci = typeof(Hand).GetConstructor(types);
        return new InstanceDescriptor(ci, properties);
      }
    }
    // Base ConvertTo if InstanceDescriptor not required
    return base.ConvertTo(context, culture, value, destinationType);
  }
  ...
}
```

To be useful, an instance descriptor requires two pieces of information. First, it needs to know what the constructor looks like. Second, it needs to know which property values should be used if the object is instantiated. The former is described by the ConstructorInfo type, and the latter is simply an array of values, which should be in constructor parameter order. After the component is rebuilt, and assuming that ShouldSerialize*PropertyName* permits, all Hand type properties are serialized using the information provided by the HandConverter-provided InstanceDescriptor:

```
// AlarmClockControlHostForm.Designer.cs
partial class AlarmClockControlHostForm {
  ...
  void InitializeComponent() {
    ...
    this.alarmClockControl.SecondHand =
      new AlarmClockControlLibrary.Hand(
        System.Drawing.Color.LimeGreen, 7);
    ...
  }
  ...
}
```

Type converters provide all kinds of help for the Properties window and the Windows Forms Designer to display, convert, and serialize properties of custom types for components that use such properties.

UI Type Editors

ExpandableObjectConverters help break down a complex multivalue property into a nested list of its atomic values. Although this technique simplifies editing of a complicated property, it may not be suitable for other properties that exhibit the following behavior:

- Hard to construct, interpret, or validate, such as a regular expression
- One of a list of values so large it would be difficult to remember all of them
- A visual property—such as ForeColor or BackColor—that is better represented as something other than a string

Actually, ForeColor satisfies all three points. First, it would be hard to find the color you wanted by typing comma-separated integers like 33, 86, 24 or guessing a named color, like PapayaWhip. Second, there are a lot of colors to choose from. Finally, colors are just plain visual.

In addition to supporting in-place editing in the Properties window, properties such as ForeColor help the developer by providing an alternative UI-based property-editing mechanism. You access this tool, shown in Figure 11.24, from a drop-down arrow in the Properties window.

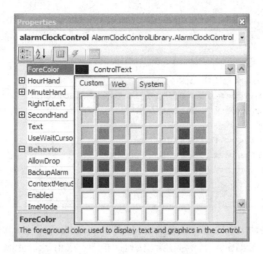

Figure 11.24   Color Property Drop-Down UI Editor (See Plate 18)

The result is a prettier, more intuitive way to select a property value. This style of visual editing is supported by the *UI type editor,* a design-time feature that you can use to similar effect. There are two kinds to choose from: modal or drop-down. Drop-down editors support single-click property selection from a drop-down UI attached to the Properties window. This UI might be a nice way to enhance the AlarmClockControl's Face property, allowing developers to visualize the clock face style as they make their selection, as illustrated in Figure 11.25.

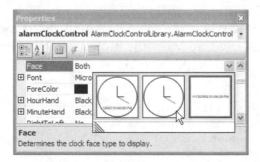

Figure 11.25   Custom View Drop-Down UI Editor

You begin implementing a custom UI editor by deriving from the UITypeEditor class (from the System.Drawing.Design namespace):

```
// FaceEditor.cs
class FaceEditor : UITypeEditor {...}
```

Next, you override the GetEditStyle and EditValue methods from the UITypeEditor base class:

```
// FaceEditor.cs
class FaceEditor : UITypeEditor {
  public override UITypeEditorEditStyle GetEditStyle(
    ITypeDescriptorContext context) {...}

  public override object EditValue(
    ITypeDescriptorContext context,
    IServiceProvider provider,
    object value) {...}
}
```

As with type converters, the appropriate UI type editor—provided by the GetEditor method of the TypeDescription class—is stored with each property. When the Properties window updates itself to reflect a control selection in the Windows Forms Designer, it queries GetEditStyle to determine whether it should show a drop-down button, an open dialog button, or nothing in the property value box when the property is selected. This behavior is determined by a value from the UITypeEditorEditStyle enumeration:

```
namespace System.Drawing.Design {
  enum UITypeEditorEditStyle {
    None = 1 // Don't display a UI (default)
    Modal = 2, // Display a modal dialog UI
    DropDown = 3, // Display a drop-down UI
  }
}
```

Not overriding GetEditStyle is the same as returning UITypeEditorEditStyle.None, which is the default edit style. To show the drop-down UI editor, AlarmClockControl returns UITypeEditorEditStyle.DropDown:

```
// FaceEditor.cs
class FaceEditor : UITypeEditor {
  public override UITypeEditorEditStyle GetEditStyle(
    ITypeDescriptorContext context) {
    // Specify a drop-down UITypeEditor
    return UITypeEditorEditStyle.DropDown;
  }
  ...
}
```

ITypeDescriptorContext is passed to GetEditStyle to provide contextual information regarding the execution of this method, including the following:

- The container and, subsequently, the designer host and its components
- The component design-time instance being shown in the Properties window
- A PropertyDescriptor type describing the property, including the TypeConverter and UITypeEditor assigned to the component

Whereas GetEditStyle is used to initialize the way the property behaves, EditValue actually implements the defined behavior. Whether the UI editor is drop-down or modal, you follow the same basic steps to edit the value:

1. Access IWindowsFormsEditorService, the Properties window's UI display service.
2. Create an instance of the editor UI implementation, which is a control that the Properties window will display.
3. Pass the current property value to the UI editor control.
4. Ask the Properties window to display the UI editor control.
5. Let the user choose the value and close the UI editor control.
6. Return the new property value from the editor.

Drop-Down UI Type Editors

Here's how AlarmClockControl implements these steps to show a drop-down editor for the Face property:

```
// FaceEditor.cs
class FaceEditor : UITypeEditor {
  ...
  public override object EditValue(
    ITypeDescriptorContext context,
    IServiceProvider provider,
    object value) {

    if( (context != null) && (provider != null) ) {
      // Access the Properties window's UI display service
      IWindowsFormsEditorService editorService =
        (IWindowsFormsEditorService)
          provider.GetService(typeof(IWindowsFormsEditorService));

      if( editorService != null ) {
        // Create an instance of the UI editor control,
        // passing a reference to the editor service
```

```
        FaceEditorControl dropDownEditor =
          new FaceEditorControl(editorService);

        // Pass the UI editor control the current property value
        dropDownEditor.Face = (ClockFace)value;

        // Display the UI editor control
        editorService.DropDownControl(dropDownEditor);

        // Return the new property value from the UI editor control
        return dropDownEditor.Face;
      }
    }
    return base.EditValue(context, provider, value);
  }
}
```

When it comes to displaying the UI editor control, you must play nicely in the design-time environment, particularly regarding UI positioning in relation to the Properties window. Specifically, drop-down UI editors must appear flush against the bottom of the property entry.

To facilitate this, the Properties window exposes a service—an implementation of the IWindowsFormsEditorService interface—to manage the loading and unloading of UI editor controls as well as their positioning inside the development environment. The FaceEditor type references this service and calls its DropDownControl method to display the FaceEditorControl, relative to the Properties window edit box. When displayed, FaceEditorControl captures the user selection and returns control to EditValue with the new value. This requires a call to IWindowsFormsEditorService.CloseDropDown from FaceEditor-Control, something you do by passing to FaceEditorControl a reference to the IWindows-FormsEditorService interface via its constructor:

```
// FaceEditorControl.cs
partial class FaceEditorControl : UserControl {
  ...
  ClockFace face = ClockFace.Both;
  IWindowsFormsEditorService editorService = null;
  ...
  public FaceEditorControl(IWindowsFormsEditorService editorService) {
    InitializeComponent();
    this.editorService = editorService;
  }

  public ClockFace Face {
    get { return this.face; }
    set { this.face = value; }
  }
```

```
    void bothPictureBox_Click(object sender, EventArgs e) {
      this.face = ClockFace.Both;
      // Close the UI editor upon value selection
      this.editorService.CloseDropDown();
    }

    void analogPictureBox_Click(object sender, EventArgs e) {
      this.face = ClockFace.Analog;
      // Close the UI editor upon value selection
      this.editorService.CloseDropDown();
    }

    void digitalPictureBox_Click(object sender, EventArgs e) {
      this.face = ClockFace.Digital;
      // Close the UI editor upon value selection
      this.editorService.CloseDropDown();
    }
    ...
}
```

The final step is to associate FaceEditor with the Face property by adorning the property with the Editor attribute:

```
[Category("Appearance")]
[Description("Determines the clock face type to display.")]
[DefaultValue(ClockFace.Both)]
[Editor(typeof(FaceEditor), typeof(UITypeEditor))]
public ClockFace Face {...}
```

Now FaceEditor is in place for the Face property. When a developer edits that property in the Properties window, it shows a drop-down arrow and the FaceEditorControl as the UI the developer uses to choose a value of the ClockFace enumeration.

If the UI editor control you are using is resizable friendly, you can override UIType-Editor's IsDropDownResizable property to return true, rather than the default of false:

```
// FaceEditor.cs
partial class FaceEditor : UITypeEditor {
    ...
    // If the UI editor control is resizable, override this
    // property to include a sizing grip on the Properties
    // window drop-down
    public override bool IsDropDownResizable {
      get { return true; }
    }
    ...
}
```

This tiny update ensures that the UITypeEditor adds a size grip to your UI editing control, as illustrated in Figure 11.26.

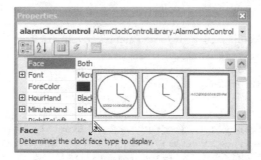

Figure 11.26   Custom View Drop-Down UI Editor with Size Grip

Drop-down editors are a great way to enhance the usability of single-click value selection.

Modal UI Type Editors

Sometimes, single-click selection isn't the most appropriate; sometimes, unrestricted editing is more desirable. In such situations, you use a modal UITypeEditor implemented as a modal form. For example, AlarmClockControl's digital time format is sufficiently complex to edit in a separate dialog outside the Properties window:

```
// AlarmClockControl.cs
partial class AlarmClockControl : ... {
  ...
  string digitalTimeFormat = "dd/MM/yyyy hh:mm:ss tt";
  ...
  [Category("Appearance")]
  [Description("The digital time format, ... ")]
  [DefaultValue("dd/MM/yyyy hh:mm:ss tt")]
  public string DigitalTimeFormat {
    get {...}
    set {...}
  }
  ...
}
```

Date and Time format strings are composed of a complex array of format specifiers that are not easy to remember and certainly aren't intuitive in a Properties window, as shown in Figure 11.27.

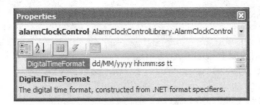

Figure 11.27   The DigitalTimeFormat Property

Modal UITypeEditors are an ideal way to provide a more intuitive way to construct hard-to-format property values. By providing a custom form, you give developers whatever editing experience is the most suitable for that property type. Figure 11.28 illustrates how the Digital Time Format Editor dialog makes it easier to edit AlarmClockControl's DigitalTimeFormat property.

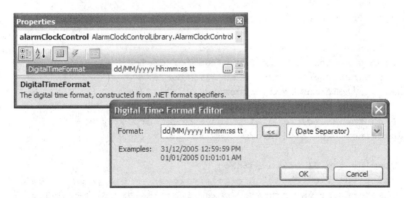

Figure 11.28   Custom DigitalTimeFormat Modal UI Editor

A modal UITypeEditor actually requires slightly different code from that of its drop-down counterpart. You follow the same logical steps as with a drop-down editor, with three minor implementation differences:

- You return UITypeEditorEditStyle.Modal from UITypeEditor.GetEditStyle.
- You call IWindowsFormsEditorService.ShowDialog from EditValue to open the UI editor dialog.
- You don't pass the dialog an editor service reference—to call its CloseDropDown method—because Windows Forms can close themselves, unlike user controls.

AlarmClockControl's modal UI type editor is shown here:

```
// DigitalTimeFormatEditor.cs
class DigitalTimeFormatEditor : UITypeEditor {
  public override UITypeEditorEditStyle GetEditStyle(
    ITypeDescriptorContext context) {
    // Specify a modal UITypeEditor
    return UITypeEditorEditStyle.Modal;
  }
  public override object EditValue(
    ITypeDescriptorContext context,
    IServiceProvider provider,
    object value) {

    if( (context != null) && (provider != null) ) {
      // Access the Properties window's UI display service
      IWindowsFormsEditorService editorService =
        (IWindowsFormsEditorService)
          provider.GetService(typeof(IWindowsFormsEditorService));

      if( editorService != null ) {
        // Create an instance of the UI editor dialog
        DigitalTimeFormatEditorForm modalEditor =
          new DigitalTimeFormatEditorForm();

        // Pass the UI editor dialog the current property value
        modalEditor.DigitalTimeFormat = (string)value;

        // Display the UI editor dialog
        if( editorService.ShowDialog(modalEditor) == DialogResult.OK ) {
          // Return the new property value from the UI editor dialog
          return modalEditor.DigitalTimeFormat;
        }
      }
    }
    return base.EditValue(context, provider, value);
  }
}
```

At this point, normal dialog activities (as covered in Chapter 3: Dialogs) apply for the UI editor's modal form:

```
// DigitalTimeFormatEditorForm.cs
partial class DigitalTimeFormatEditorForm : Form {
  ...
  string digitalTimeFormat = "dd/MM/yyyy hh:mm:ss tt";
  ...
  public string DigitalTimeFormat {
    get { return this.digitalTimeFormat; }
```

```
      set { this.digitalTimeFormat = value; }
    }
    ...
    void okButton_Click(object sender, EventArgs e) {
      this.digitalTimeFormat = this.formatTextBox.Text;
    }
    ...
  }
```

Again, to associate the new UI type editor with the property, you apply the Editor attribute:

```
[Category("Appearance")]
[Description("The digital time format, ...")]
[DefaultValue("dd/MM/yyyy hh:mm:ss tt")]
[Editor(typeof(DigitalTimeFormatEditor), typeof(UITypeEditor))]
public string DigitalTimeFormat {...}
```

After the Editor attribute is applied, developers access the modal UITypeEditor via an ellipsis-style button displayed in the Properties window, as shown in Figure 11.29.

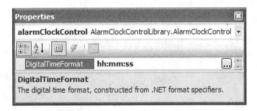

Figure 11.29   Accessing a Modal UITypeEditor

UI type editors allow you to give developers a customized editing environment on a per-property basis, whether it's a drop-down UI to support selection from a list of possible values or a modal dialog to provide an entire editing environment outside the Properties window.

Where Are We?

Although a component gains a default level of integration with the VS05 design-time environment with no work on your part, .NET gives you a rich supporting infrastructure that can be used to enhance a component's design-time experience in the Properties window.

In Chapter 12: Design-Time Integration: Designers and Smart Tags, we look at several design-time features that provide further integration with the Windows Forms Designer, including custom designers, smart tags, and context menus.

12

Design-Time Integration: Designers and Smart Tags

T HE PROPERTIES WINDOW is part of a broad set of design-time services that includes component designers and smart tags and which allow you to enhance the behavior of your components in many ways. Designers allow you to completely separate design-time behavior from a component, thereby simplifying the implementation of design-time-only functionality.

Designers are also the design-time entry point for smart tags, a feature that enhances Properties window integration by making key configurations available for a design-time component right on the design surface, visual or nonvisual. This chapter concludes our journey through the immense landscape of the design time by showing how to use custom designers and smart tags to add polish to your components.

Designers

In Chapter 11: Design-Time Integration: The Properties Window, you saw how properties are exposed to the developer at design-time, plus the set of design-time services that allow your components to integrate with it. The goal of these features is to replace programmatic configuration experience with a comparatively easier declarative configuration experience.

Configuration targets properties are required to manage state at run time and, in the case of controls, to help render UIs. However, there are times when a component requires functionality that is useful only at design-time. In these situations, it is much cleaner to separate design-time only code from that executes at run time. To help in this endeavor, we have designers.

A *Designer* is a class that implements the IDesigner interface:

```
namespace System.ComponentModel.Design {
  interface IDesigner : IDisposable {
    void DoDefaultAction();
    void Initialize(IComponent component);
    IComponent Component { get; }
    DesignerVerbCollection Verbs { get; }
  }
}
```

A component uses the Designer attribute to associate themselves with a designer which, at design-time, is created and used by the Windows Forms Designer.

The reason you haven't yet needed to think about designers is that all the types from which your custom components will most likely derive—Component, Control, UserControl, and Form—have exactly two designers associated with them:

```
using System.ComponentModel; // Designer attribute
using System.ComponentModel.Design; // ComponentDesigner
using System.Windows.Forms.Design; // ControlDesigner
                                    // ComponentDocumentDesigner
                                    // UserControlDocumentDesigner
                                    // FormDocumentDesigner

[Designer(typeof(ComponentDesigner))]
[Designer(typeof(ComponentDocumentDesigner))]
interface IComponent : IDisposable {...}

class Component : IComponent, ... {...}

[Designer(typeof(ControlDesigner))]
class Control : Component, ... {...}

[Designer(typeof(ControlDesigner))]
[Designer(typeof(UserControlDocumentDesigner))]
class UserControl : ContainerControl {...}

[Designer(typeof(FormDocumentDesigner))]
class Form : ContainerControl, ... {...}
```

Only two of these classes have the two required designers defined; that's because if you don't define exactly two designers, the ones you don't associate with a component are associated by the base class, all the way up to IComponent. Each component needs two designers because there are two contexts in which you use designers. The first is the Designer tab in VS05, which is shown by default when you double-click a Form, UserControl, or Component in Solution Explorer. The Designer tab hosts the *component document designer* that provides the full document-viewing experience (hence its name).[1]

The second designer context is provided by a *component designer*, which is the designer you get when you interact with the component as contained by a document designer. For example, if you have a Timer in the component tray of a Form, the Timer's designer is a component designer (specifically the default ComponentDesigner provided by the IComponent interface). A normal component designer implements only the IDesigner interface.

If you'd like to replace either the component document designer or the plain component designer, you implement the appropriate interface and associate it with your component using the Designer attribute. Although the implementation of a full-blown component document designer is beyond the scope of this book, it's easy to add a plain old custom designer to your custom components to deploy design-time-only functionality.

ComponentDesigner

Consider the ability of a control to gain access to its parent at run time, using either the Find-Form method or the Parent property. Either of these is suitable if the child control wants to gain access to functionality provided by its parent (such as the parent's caption text):

```
Control host = this.Parent; // Find parent
MessageBox.Show("My parent says: " + host.Text);
```

Further, it's not hard to imagine the need for a noncontrol component to gain access to the functionality exposed by the parent. Unfortunately, components don't offer any support for discovering their host container. An IComponent implementation can be hosted by any ISite implementation, but the site is not the same as the component's hosting form or user control.

For example, suppose the AlarmComponent from Chapter 9: Components needs the name of its container to use as a caption for any message boxes it may need to display. In this case, we need AlarmComponent to store a reference to its host container and to use the host container's Text property for all message boxes:

```
// AlarmComponent.cs
...
partial class AlarmComponent : Component {
  ...
  ContainerControl host;
```

---

[1] The component document designer is also known as the root designer because it implements the IRootDesigner interface (from the System.ComponentModel.Design namespace) to separate it from a plain component designer.

```
      // Hide from Properties window and persist any value
      // to container's InitializeComponent
      [Browsable(false)]
      [DefaultValue(null)]
      public ContainerControl Host {
        get { return this.host; }
        set { this.host = value; }
      }

      void timer_Tick(object sender, System.EventArgs e) {
        ...
        // If no handlers, display a message box
        MessageBox.Show("Wake up!", this.host.Text);
        ...
      }
    }
    ...
  }
```

AlarmComponent can't determine its host container on its own, so its default value is null. However, this means that we must supply the value for use at run time. To do this, we influence the Windows Forms Designer's serialization behavior to persist the host reference to the host's InitializeComponent method at design time:

```
// MainForm.Designer.cs
partial class MainForm {
  ...
  void InitializeComponent() {
    ...
    this.alarmComponent =
      new AlarmComponent (this.components);
    ...
    // alarmComponent
    this.alarmComponent.Host = this;
  }
}
```

Unfortunately, we can't use the specific serialization techniques you saw in Chapter 11 because they rely on interaction with the Properties window; we don't want developers to have to risk proper functioning of the component by making them responsible for setting it, particularly when the information is available already.

A custom designer helps solve this problem, but rather than implement IDesigner directly, we're better off deriving from ComponentDesigner. ComponentDesigner not only happens to implement IDesigner, but also lets us grab a component's host container and ensure that its value is serialized to InitializeComponent:

```
// HostComponentDesigner.cs
using System.ComponentModel.Design; // From System.Design.dll
...
class HostComponentDesigner : ComponentDesigner { }
```

We then use the Designer attribute to assign our new designer to a component:

```
// AlarmComponent.cs
[Designer(typeof(HostComponentDesigner))]
partial class AlarmComponent : Component {...}
```

The next step is to identify which property on the component will store the host container reference that HostContainerComponentDesigner will look for. A custom attribute is perfect for this job, which has been assigned to the component:

```
// HostPropertyAttribute.cs
class HostPropertyAttribute : Attribute {
  string propertyName;
  public HostPropertyAttribute(string propertyName) {
    this.propertyName = propertyName;
  }

  public string PropertyName {
    get { return this.propertyName; }
  }
}

// HostComponentDesigner.cs
[Designer(typeof(HostComponentDesigner))]
[HostProperty("Host")]
partial class HostContainerComponent : Component {...}
```

Finally, we need for the custom designer to acquire a reference to the component and to set the property specified by the HostProperty attribute to its container component. For components and container components, ComponentDesigner helps by providing the Component and ParentComponent properties:

```
// HostComponentDesigner.cs
using System.ComponentModel.Design; // From System.Design.dll
...
class HostComponentDesigner : ComponentDesigner {

  public override void InitializeNewComponent(
    System.Collections.IDictionary defaultValues) {

    base.InitializeNewComponent(defaultValues);
```

```
      IComponent customComponent = this.Component;
      IComponent parentComponent = this.ParentComponent;

      // Don't bother if parent is not a container
      if( !(parentComponent is ContainerControl) ) return;

      // Get the name of the property on the component
      // that will store the host reference, defaulting
      // to "Host" if not found
      string propertyName = "Host";
      AttributeCollection attributes =
        TypeDescriptor.GetAttributes(customComponent);
      foreach( Attribute attribute in attributes ) {
        if( attribute is HostPropertyAttribute ) {
          HostPropertyAttribute hpAttribute =
            (HostPropertyAttribute)attribute;
          if( !string.IsNullOrEmpty(hpAttribute.PropertyName) ) {
            propertyName = hpAttribute.PropertyName;
          }
          break;
        }
      }

      // Set property with host container
      PropertyInfo property =
        customComponent.GetType().GetProperty(propertyName);
      if( property != null ) {
        property.SetValue(
          customComponent, (ContainerControl)parentComponent, null);
      }
    }
  }
```

This code is deployed to an override of ComponentDesigner's InitializeNewCompo-nent method, which is called by the designer host when a component is first dropped onto a form, and turns out to be a nice time to do our processing. We then grab the parent com-ponent, check whether it's a container control, and, if it is, set the specified property on the component (in our case, AlarmComponent). This ensures that the desired code is serial-ized to InitializeComponent. By default, our implementation of InitializeNewComponent automatically looks for a property named "Host" on the component if the HostProperty attribute isn't provided.

The next time AlarmComponent is dropped onto a container control's designer surface, the desired property initialization is automatically serialized via InitializeComponent. Because the code in both HostComponentDesigner and the HostProperty attribute is generic, the only code that we need to write is a property to store a reference to the host and, of course, the code to use the reference after it's been acquired. Further, if the property you add to your component is called "Host," you don't need to use the HostProperty attribute at all:

```csharp
// AlarmComponent.cs
...
[Designer(typeof(HostComponentDesigner))]
partial class AlarmComponent : Component {
  ...
  // Set by HostComponentDesigner
  // ("Host" is the default property name used by our custom designer)
  ContainerControl host;
  [Browsable(false)]
  [DefaultValue(null)]
  public ContainerControl Host {
    get { return this.host; }
    set { this.host = value; }
  }

  void timer_Tick(object sender, System.EventArgs e) {
    ...
    // Use the host set by the designer
    MessageBox.Show("Wake up!", this.host.Text);
    ...
    }
  }
  ...
}
```

In addition to leveraging a nice design-time feature, the key reason to use a custom designer is to create a clean separation of design-time and run-time code. This practice follows the tradition honored by type converters and UI type editors, as you saw in Chapter 11.[2]

ControlDesigner

Beyond capturing design-time information for run-time processing, designers are well suited to performing design-time-only processing on behalf of a custom control, such as rendering additional design-time UI elements to optimize its appearance in the Windows Forms Designer.

For example, the SplitContainer control displays a dashed border when its BorderStyle is set to BorderStyle.None. This design makes it easier for developers to find it on the form's design surface in the absence of a visible border and to spot the areas within which they can place other controls, as illustrated in Figure 12.1.

---

[2] As an alternative, you can use the same technique used by System.Timers.Timer: It implements the SynchronizingObject property, which contains the code to find Timer's parent component using design-time services. Your favorite decompiler will help here.

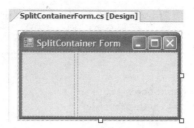

Figure 12.1   SplitContainer Dashed Border When BorderStyle Is None

Because BorderStyle.None means "Don't render a border at run time," the dashed border is drawn only at design time for the developer's benefit. Of course, if BorderStyle is set to BorderStyle.FixedSingle or BorderStyle.Fixed3D, the dashed border is not necessary, as illustrated in Figure 12.2.

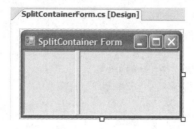

Figure 12.2   SplitContainer with BorderStyle.Fixed3D

Although it's not obvious, the dashed border is not actually rendered from the control implementation. Instead, this work is conducted on its behalf by a custom control designer.

The AlarmClockControl from Chapter 11 could benefit from this capability; when it has an Analog clock face, it's difficult to determine where the edges and corners of the control are when it's not selected on the design surface. To help out, we can render a SplitContainer-style dashed border at design time, which would look something like Figure 12.3.

Figure 12.3   Border Displayed from AlarmClockControlDesigner

ControlDesigner doesn't implement the required dashed border functionality, so we create a custom designer and associate it with AlarmClockControl. Because AlarmClockControl derives from ScrollableControl, the most suitable way to start is to derive from ScrollableControlDesigner itself:

```
class AlarmClockControlDesigner : ScrollableControlDesigner {...}
```

To paint the dashed border, AlarmClockControlDesigner overrides the OnPaintAdornments method:

```
class AlarmClockControlDesigner : ScrollableControlDesigner {
  ...
  protected override void OnPaintAdornments(PaintEventArgs e) {...}
  ...
}
```

You could manually register with the Control.Paint event to add your design-time UI, but overriding OnPaintAdornments is a better option because it is called only after the control's design-time or run-time UI is painted, letting you put the icing on the cake:

```
class AlarmClockControlDesigner : ScrollableControlDesigner {
  ...
  protected override void OnPaintAdornments(PaintEventArgs e) {

    base.OnPaintAdornments(e);

    // Draw border
    Graphics g = e.Graphics;
    using( Pen pen = new Pen(Color.Gray, 1) ) {
      pen.DashStyle = DashStyle.Dash;
      g.DrawRectangle(
        pen,
        0,
        0,
        this.AlarmClockControl.Width - 1,
        this.AlarmClockControl.Height - 1);
    }
  }

  // Helper property to acquire an AlarmClockControl reference
  AlarmClockControl AlarmClockControl {
    get { return (AlarmClockControl)this.Component; }
  }
}
```

Then, we associate AlarmClockControlDesigner with AlarmClockControl, aided by the Designer attribute:

```
[Designer(typeof(AlarmClockControlDesigner))]
partial class AlarmClockControl : ScrollableControl, ... {...}
```

The result is that AlarmClockControl's design-time-only dashed border is now displayed, just like the one shown in Figure 12.3.

Design-Time-Only Properties

One way to improve on the dashed border is to give developers the option of not showing it (maybe it offends their WYSIWIG sensibilities). Because this is not a feature that should be accessible at run time, what's needed is a design-time-only property, ShowBorder. And designers are exactly the right location to implement them.

You start by adding the basic property implementation to the custom AlarmClockControlDesigner with the appropriate attributes:

```
class AlarmClockControlDesigner : ScrollableControlDesigner {
  ...
  bool showBorder = true;
  ...
  protected override void OnPaintAdornments(PaintEventArgs e) {
    ...
    // Don't show border if hidden or does not have an Analog face
    if( (!this.showBorder) ||
        (this.alarmClockControl.Face == ClockFace.Digital) ) return;
    ...
  }

  // Provide implementation of ShowBorder to provide
  // storage for created ShowBorder property
  [Category("Design")]
  [DesignOnly(true)]
  [DefaultValue(true)]
  [Description("Show/Hide a border at design time.")]
  public bool ShowBorder {
    get { return this.showBorder; }
    set {
      // Change property value
      PropertyDescriptor property = TypeDescriptor.GetProperties(
        typeof(AlarmClockControl))["ShowBorder"];
```

```
      this.RaiseComponentChanging(property);
      this.showBorder = value;
      this.RaiseComponentChanged(
        property, !this.showBorder, this.showBorder);

      // Update clock UI
      this.AlarmClockControl.Invalidate();
    }
  }
}
```

The ShowBorder set accessor stores the new value and invalidates the control to request a repaint. Additionally, it hooks into the design time's *component change service*, which broadcasts the property change in a manner that ensures the use of certain designer features, including an immediate Properties window refresh and undo.

This isn't enough on its own, however, because the Properties window doesn't examine a custom designer for properties when the associated component is selected. The Properties window acquires a list of a component's properties using the TypeDescriptor class's static GetProperties method (which in turn uses reflection to acquire the list of properties from the type). To inject a design-time-only property into the list of properties returned by GetProperties, a custom designer can override the PreFilterProperties method and add the property manually:

```
class AlarmClockControlDesigner : ScrollableControlDesigner {
  ...
  protected override void PreFilterProperties(IDictionary properties) {

    base.PreFilterProperties(properties);

    // Create design-time-only property entry and add it to the
    // Properties window's Design category
    properties["ShowBorder"] =
      TypeDescriptor.CreateProperty(typeof(AlarmClockControlDesigner),
                                    "ShowBorder",
                                    typeof(bool),
                                    null);

  }
  ...
}
```

The IDictionary argument of the PreFilterProperties method allows you to populate new properties by creating PropertyDescriptor objects using TypeDescriptor's CreateProperty method, passing arguments that appropriately describe the new property. Although we pass null as the last argument, you can pass an array of Attributes instead of adorning the custom designer property with those attributes:

```
// Create design-time-only property entry and add it to the
// Properties window's Design category
properties["ShowBorder"] =
  TypeDescriptor.CreateProperty(
    typeof(AlarmClockControlDesigner),
    "ShowBorder",
    typeof(bool),
    new Attribute[] {
      new CategoryAttribute("Design"),
      new DesignOnlyAttribute(true),
      new DefaultValueAttribute(true),
      new DescriptionAttribute("Show/Hide a border at design time.")
    }
  );
```

Either way, because the property is adorned with a DesignOnly attribute whose constructor is passed a value of true, ShowBorder's value is serialized to the form's resource file rather than to InitializeComponent when its value differs from the default (is false), as shown in Figure 12.4.

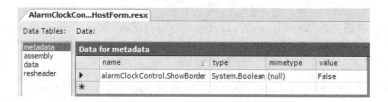

Figure 12.4 ShowBorder Property Value Serialized to the Host Form's Resource File

This also has the effect of clearly delineating the difference between design-time-only properties and those that can be set at design time and run time.

If you need to alter or remove existing properties, you override PostFilterProperties and act on the list of properties after TypeDescriptor has filled it using reflection. Pre and Post filter pairs can also be overridden for events if necessary. Figure 12.5 shows the result of adding the ShowBorder design-time property.

PLATE 1 (FIGURE 1.21): ErrorProvider Providing an Error

PLATE 2 (FIGURES 1.23 AND 5.15): Custom Drawing

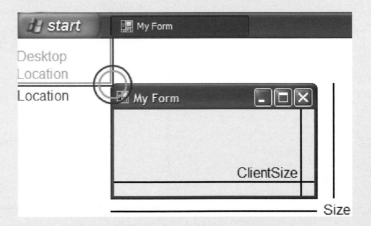

PLATE 3 (FIGURE 2.14): The DesktopLocation, Location,
ClientSize, and Size Properties

PLATE 4 (FIGURE 2.16): Opacity in Action

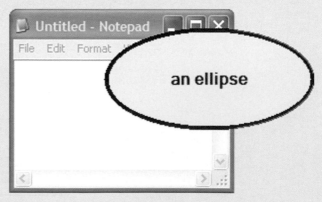

PLATE 5 (FIGURE 2.18): TransparencyKey Combined with FormBorderStyle.None

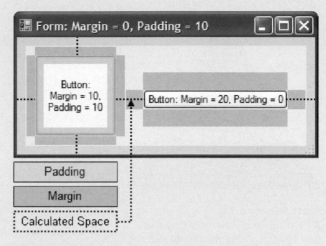

PLATE 6 (FIGURE 4.4): How the Margin and Padding
Properties Are Used to Calculate the Space Snap Line

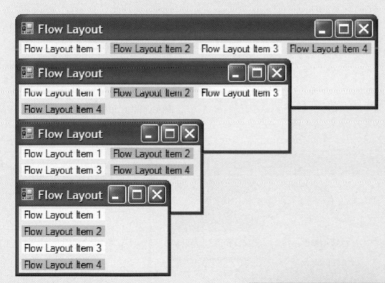

PLATE 7 (FIGURE 4.44):
A FlowLayoutPanel Laying Out
Controls in Left-To-Right Order

PLATE 8 (FIGURE 5.6): Normal, Triangle, Bell
Linear Gradient and Normal Custom Color Brushes

PLATE 9 (FIGURE 5.8):
A PathGradientBrush with One Red
Surrounding Point and Two Blue Ones

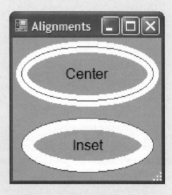

PLATE 10 (FIGURE 5.12):
Pen Alignment Options

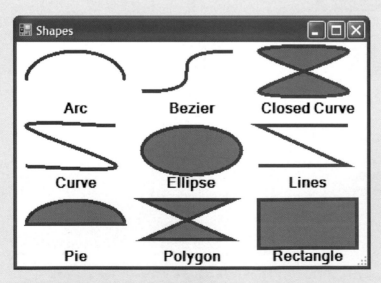

PLATE 11 (FIGURE 5.16): The Basic Shapes

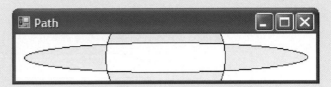

PLATE 12 (FIGURE 5.23): Overlapping Figures and the Alternate FillMode

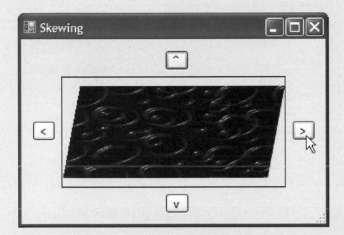

PLATE 13 (FIGURE 5.26): An Example of Skewing an Image

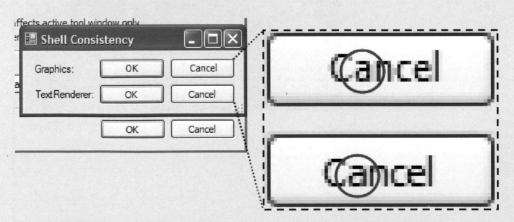

PLATE 14 (FIGURE 6.13): Comparing Shell Consistency (with VS05 | Tools | Options Dialog Buttons)

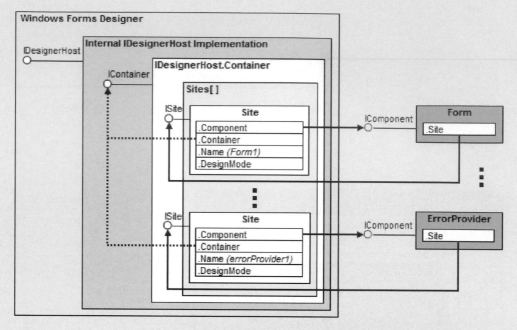

PLATE 15 (FIGURE 11.2): Design-Time Architecture

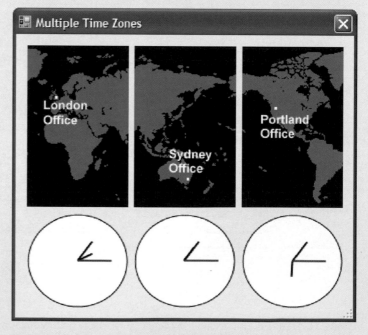

PLATE 16 (FIGURE 11.11): Form with Multiple Time Zones

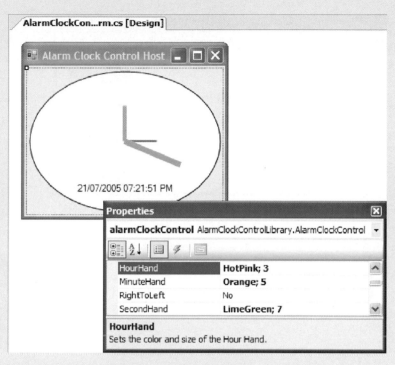

PLATE 17 (FIGURE 11.20): HandConverter in Action

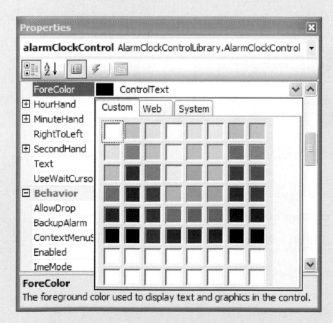

PLATE 18 (FIGURE 11.24): Color Property Drop-Down UI Editor

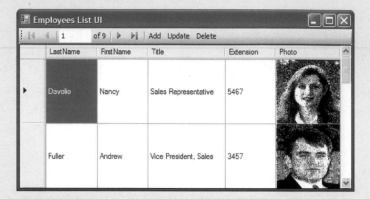

PLATE 19 (FIGURE 17.41): Employees (Sporting 80's Hair Styles) List Form

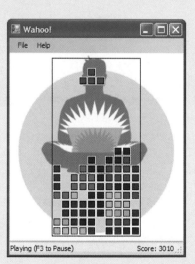

PLATE 20 (FIGURE 19.1):
The Game of Wahoo!

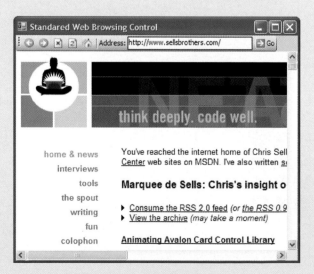

PLATE 21 (FIGURE D.25): The WebBrowser Control
in Action

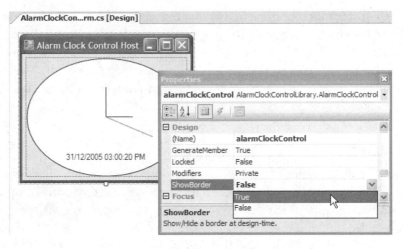

Figure 12.5   ShowBorder Option in the Properties Window

The key concept is that when you have design-time-only functionality, you should first consider custom designers to avoid burdening your components with code that is not useful at run time. You can achieve much with custom designers, although the scope of such possibilities is beyond this chapter. However, one specific feature warrants further attention, particularly if you want your controls to be more usable. That feature is known as smart tags.

Smart Tags

Smart tags are designed to present the most commonly used or contextually relevant configurations for a component right next to the component on the design surface (visual or nonvisual). Figure 12.6 shows the smart tag for the DataGridView control.

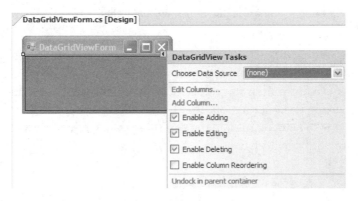

Figure 12.6   DataGridView's Smart Tag

Presenting configuration options in this manner makes the design-time experience for developers much more focused and efficient because they avoid sifting through the entire set of properties available from the Properties window to find the few they are most likely to use. Many Windows Forms components provide smart tag support by leveraging a subset of types in the System.ComponentModel.Design namespace (in System.Design.dll). These types are known collectively as *designer actions*.

Designer Actions

The Windows Forms Designer notices whether a component implements designer actions and, if so, renders a clickable *smart tag glyph* at the top-right edge of the component when it's selected on the design surface. The glyph is clicked to display the *smart tag panel*, a special UI managed by the Windows Forms Designer; to provide access to one or more *smart tag items* for a component. Figure 12.7 highlights these elements on the DataGridView's smart tag.

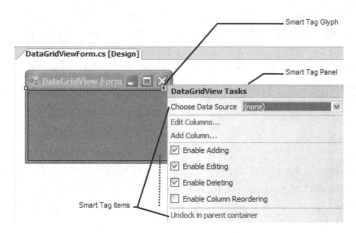

Figure 12.7   Smart Tag Glyph, Panel, and Items

In designer action infrastructure parlance, smart tag items are referred to as *designer action items*, which are shuttled around the design time in groups known as *designer action lists*. If a component requires smart tag support, it must pass at least one designer action list containing at least one designer action item to the Windows Forms Designer. The same designer action list is then forwarded to the smart tag panel, which converts each designer action item into an equivalent visual task.

Designer Action Lists

Because you must package designer action items in designer action lists, the best place to start adding smart tag support to your component is to build a designer action list. The designer action infrastructure implements a special class to represent designer action lists, appropriately called DesignerActionList:

```
namespace System.ComponentModel.Design {
  class DesignerActionList {
    public DesignerActionList(IComponent component);
    public virtual bool AutoShow { get; set; }
    public IComponent Component { get; }
    public object GetService(Type serviceType);
    public virtual DesignerActionItemCollection GetSortedActionItems();
  }
}
```

The DesignerActionList class is designed to associate one or more designer action items with a single component. You make the association via its constructor, which expects a component's IComponent reference and is available from the read-only Component property after construction.

Designer action lists aren't lists in the sense that they implement IList or ICollection. Instead, designer action lists implement the GetSortedActionItems method to return a list of designer action items stored in a DesignerActionItemCollection. The smart tag panel converts this list into one or more smart tag items. If GetSortedActionItems returns an empty DesignerActionItemCollection, the smart tag glyph isn't displayed for the associated component.

To implement a list of designer action items for your component, you create a custom DesignerActionList, which you start by deriving from it:

```
class AlarmClockControlDesignerActionList : DesignerActionList {...}
```

Smart Tag Properties

Because a component is primarily about setting properties, it follows that the most common type of smart tag item to be displayed on the smart tag panel is a smart tag *property item*. In similar fashion to the Properties window, each property item is composed of a label that describes the property, and a control that allows developers to edit the property.

Creating a Smart Tag Property Item

Using the AlarmClockControl as an example, let's consider the Face property. Recall from Chapter 11 that the Face property is used to determine whether the AlarmClockControl's face is rendered as analog or digital (or both). Because Face is one of the properties most likely to be configured at design time on the AlarmClockControl, it is an ideal smart tag candidate.

To provide a way for GetSortedActionItems to create a DesignerActionItem object for this property, we implement a Face property on the custom DesignerActionList:

```
class AlarmClockControlDesignerActionList : DesignerActionList {
  ...
  // Face proxy property
  public ClockFace Face {
    get { return this.AlarmClockControl.Face; }
    set { ... }
  }
  ...
  // Helper property to acquire an AlarmClockControl reference
  AlarmClockControl AlarmClockControl {
    get { return (AlarmClockControl)this.Component; }
  }
}
```

The reason we implement the property on DesignerActionList—rather than use the component's own implementation—is that the smart tag panel is geared to operate on DesignerActionList objects rather than directly with the components themselves. In reality, DesignerActionItems are pointers to members on the DesignerActionList that the smart tag panel needs to expose. Thus, DesignerActionLists must implement a public property that exposes the component's property, by proxy, that the smart tag panel can read from and write to. The role of the proxy property is illustrated in Figure 12.8.

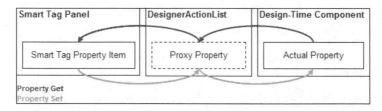

Figure 12.8   Intermediary Designer Action List with Proxy Property

In light of this requirement, there is another consideration. The proxy property cannot set the actual property on the component directly; when you set properties using this technique, design-time services—such as immediately refreshing the Properties window to reflect a change to the property, and supports undoing property sets—are circumvented.

You can avoid such naughtiness by using TypeDescriptor to set the component's property safely:

```
class AlarmClockControlDesignerActionList : DesignerActionList {
  ...
  // Face proxy property
  public ClockFace Face {
    get { return this.AlarmClockControl.Face; }
    set { this.SetProperty("Face", value); }
  }

  // Helper method to safely set a component's property
  void SetProperty(string propertyName, object value) {
    // Get property
    PropertyDescriptor property =
      TypeDescriptor.GetProperties(this.AlarmClockControl)
        [propertyName];
    // Set property value
    property.SetValue(this.AlarmClockControl, value);
  }
  ...
}
```

This has the same effect as using the Windows Forms Designer's component change service to update a property, as you saw earlier, although the code to use TypeDescriptor is more concise.

The proxy Face property, in conjunction with the custom DesignerActionList's base GetSortedActionItems method implementation, comprises the minimum implementation required by a designer action list. GetSortedActionItems is called from the smart tag panel before the panel opens and when it is refreshed, in both cases converting the proxy Face property into a designer action item that's eventually displayed as an equivalent smart tag task. The initial value of the smart tag property item is retrieved from the component's Face property via the proxy Face property we implemented on AlarmClockControlDesigner ActionList. When the Face property is edited via the smart tag panel, the component's Face property is set using the same proxy property.

Of course, since we haven't yet passed our designer action list to the smart panel, nothing is displayed.

Using Custom Designers to Expose Designer Action Lists

Designer actions are classified as design-time-only functionality; this means they are provided to, and used by, a component solely from within the design-time environment. A custom designer makes perfect sense as the means for exposing a custom designer action list. Luckily, the custom designer we baked earlier in this chapter has just popped out of the oven:

```
class AlarmClockControlDesigner : ScrollableControlDesigner {...}

[Designer(typeof(AlarmClockControlDesigner))]
class AlarmClockControl : ScrollableControl, ... {...}
```

As you can see, AlarmClockControlDesigner derives from ScrollableControlDesigner, which indirectly derives from ComponentDesigner. ComponentDesigner implements a read-only property, ActionLists, that returns an instance of DesignerActionListCollection. By default, the base ComponentDesigner class's ActionList property returns an empty DesignerActionListCollection, which is viewed by the Windows Forms Designer as "Smart Tags Not Required" for the component in question. However, you can change that to "Smart Tags Required" by overriding ActionLists to return an instance of the Designer-ActionListCollection class that contains at least one DesignerActionList object:[3]

```
class AlarmClockControlDesigner : ScrollableControlDesigner {
  ...
  DesignerActionListCollection dalc; // Cache action list collection
  ...
  public override DesignerActionListCollection ActionLists {
    get {
      // Create action list collection
      if( this.dalc == null ) {
        this.dalc = new DesignerActionListCollection();
        // Add custom action list
        this.dalc.Add(
          new AlarmClockControlDesignerActionList(this.Component));
      }

    }
  }
  ...
}
```

As a performance measure, this code creates a designer action list collection field that needs to be initialized only once, even though ActionLists are inspected multiple times.

That's all the implementation you need to edit a property from the smart tag panel. After rebuilding the updated AlarmClockControl solution and dragging the new Alarm-ClockControl onto the form, you should be able to edit the Face property from the smart tag panel of AlarmClockControl, as shown in Figure 12.9.

---

[3] You may be wondering about the need to return multiple DesignerActionList objects; this is useful from a management point of view when you need to break a large number of smart tag items into distinct lists, which is discussed later in this chapter.

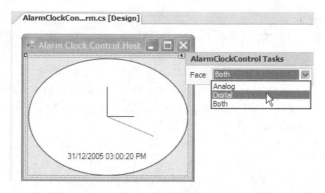

Figure 12.9   The Modern Face of Smart Tag Property Items

Under the covers, the smart tag panel inspects ActionLists for a DesignerActionList-Collection object and calls the GetSortedActionItems method on each designer action list in the collection, using the results to populate the smart tag.

One feature of the smart tag panel that you have no control over is its title field. However, in lieu of developer-configurable support, the Windows Forms Designer uses a reasonable default that conforms to the following naming convention:

```
ComponentTypeName Tasks
```

The Windows Forms Designer also takes care of determining which controls are used to provide display and editing of designer action property items.

Displaying Smart Tag Property Items

In Figure 12.9, you can see that the smart tag panel renders enumeration types like the Face type, as drop-down lists. The heuristics employed by the smart tag panel to translate property types to editable controls include the following:

- If a property is an enumeration, a drop-down list with all the values of the enumeration is shown.
- If a property has an associated UI type editor—as specified automatically by the property type or as specified manually by applying the Editor attribute to the proxy property—the editor is shown.
- If a property is a Boolean, a check box is shown.
- Properties other than enumerations and Booleans are displayed as text boxes.
- If a property is of a type that isn't supported by any of these mechanisms, it is displayed as read-only text sourced from the type's ToString method.

Although you have no influence over the control that's chosen by the Windows Forms Designer, you can use many of the design-time attributes you saw in Chapter 11 to enhance the appearance and usage of smart tag property items.

For example, recall that the AlarmClockControl implements FaceEditor, a custom UITypeEditor for the Face property, to enable a more aesthetic experience. We can associate FaceEditor with the proxy Face property by adorning it with the Editor attribute, just as we did with the actual Face property:

```
using System.Drawing.Design;
...
class AlarmClockControlDesignerActionList : DesignerActionList {
  ...
  // Face proxy property
  [Editor(typeof(FaceEditor), typeof(UITypeEditor))]
  public ClockFace Face {
    get { return this.AlarmClockControl.Face; }
    set { this.SetProperty("Face", value); }
  }
  ...
}
```

We do a quick rebuild, and now editing the Face property on the smart tag panel is somewhat prettier, as shown in Figure 12.10.

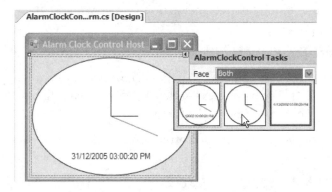

Figure 12.10   The Face Property Item's FaceEditor in Action

FaceEditor is a drop-down style of UI type editor, but you can use the same technique with modal UI type editors, such as the DigitalTimeFormatEditor that AlarmClockControl associates with the DigitalTimeFormat property:

```
class AlarmClockControlDesignerActionList : DesignerActionList {
  ...
  // DigitalTimeFormat proxy property
```

```
[Editor(typeof(DigitalTimeFormatEditor), typeof(UITypeEditor))]
public string DigitalTimeFormat {
  get { return this.AlarmClockControl.DigitalTimeFormat; }
  set { this.SetProperty("DigitalTimeFormat", value); }
}
...
}
```

A modal UI type editor behaves the same from the smart tag panel as it would from the Properties window, including being opened from an ellipses button, as shown in Figure 12.11.

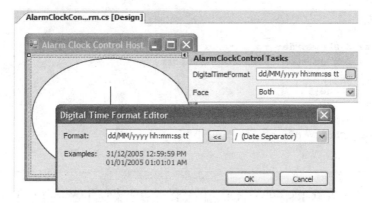

Figure 12.11   The DigitalTimeFormat Property Item's DigitalTimeFormatEditor in Action

If a proxy property is one of the .NET Framework's intrinsic types that have UI type editors associated with them, such as DateTime, the smart tag panel automatically provides access to UI type editors, as shown in Figure 12.12 for the BackupAlarm and PrimaryAlarm properties.

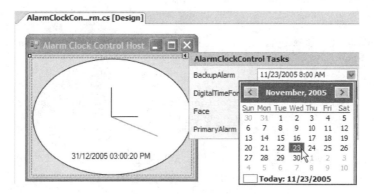

Figure 12.12   Intrinsic .NET Framework Types with UI Type Editors

The basic process of adding designer action property items to the smart tag panel and providing additional support like UI type editors is straightforward. A variety of more exotic scenarios is supported, however, and we take a look at some of those next.

Design-Time-Only Smart Tag Property Items

There is no rule that says designer action property items must expose properties implemented by a component. They can also be used to expose design-time-only properties implemented by a custom designer. One such property is ShowBorder, which, as you saw earlier, is implemented by AlarmClockControlDesigner:

```
class AlarmClockControlDesigner : ScrollableControlDesigner {
  ...
  // Implement ShowBorder to provide
  // storage for created ShowBorder property
  [Category("Design")]
  [DesignOnly(true)]
  [DefaultValue(true)]
  [Description("Show/Hide a border at design time.")]
  public bool ShowBorder { get; set; }
  ...
}
```

The principles of implementing a proxy property for ShowBorder are the same as you've seen, although the property that's wrapped by the proxy property originates on AlarmClockControlDesigner rather than the component:

```
class AlarmClockControlDesignerActionList : DesignerActionList {
  ...
  // ShowBorder proxy property
  public bool ShowBorder {
    get { return this.Designer.ShowBorder; }
    set { this.Designer.ShowBorder = value; }
  }
  ...
  // Helper method to acquire an AlarmClockControlDesigner reference
  AlarmClockControlDesigner Designer {
    get {
      IDesignerHost designerHost =
        this.GetService(typeof(IDesignerHost)) as IDesignerHost;
      if( designerHost == null ) return null;
      return
        (AlarmClockControlDesigner)
          designerHost.GetDesigner(this.AlarmClockControl);
    }
  }
  ...
}
```

The proxy ShowBorder property uses a helper property to acquire a reference to the AlarmClockControl's designer, because it isn't natively available from DesignerActionList. It then gets and sets the actual ShowBorder property directly, rather than use the Set-Property helper introduced earlier. In this case, SetProperty isn't necessary because we rely on the actual AlarmClockControlDesigner's ShowBorder property implementation to issue change notifications against the component change service:

```
class AlarmClockControlDesigner : ScrollableControlDesigner {
  ...
  public bool ShowBorder {
    get { return this.showBorder; }
    set {
      // Change property value
      PropertyDescriptor property = TypeDescriptor.GetProperties(
        typeof(AlarmClockControl))["ShowBorder"];
      this.RaiseComponentChanging(property);
      this.showBorder = value;
      this.RaiseComponentChanged(
        property, !this.showBorder, this.showBorder);

      // Update clock UI
      this.AlarmClockControl.Invalidate();
    }
  } ...
}
```

It's important to leave this change notification code implemented by AlarmClockControlDesigner to ensure that when design-time code other than our designer action list updates the property value, correct change behavior is applied. The only thing left to do is rebuild the solution, and, as if by magic, ShowBorder appears on the smart tag panel, shown conjured up in Figure 12.13.

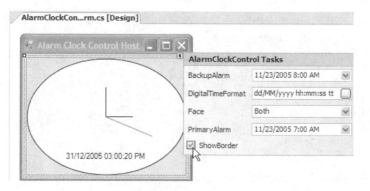

Figure 12.13 Hey, Presto! ShowBorder Design-Time-Only Smart Tag Property Items

Because ShowBorder is a Boolean, it appears as a check box in the smart tag panel. If you play with the sample, you'll notice that, besides the border appearing and disappearing as the ShowBorder smart tag property is toggled, the Properties window's ShowBorder field is updated immediately to reflect the change. This is the expected result of the actual Show-Border property's component change service integration.

Multivalue Smart Tag Property Items

One other type of smart tag property item you might need to handle is one whose type is multivalued. Examples include the HourHand, MinuteHand, and SecondHand properties implemented by AlarmClockControl, as shown in Figure 12.14.

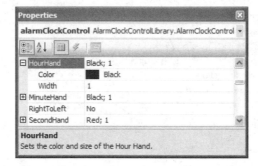

Figure 12.14   Multivalued Property Editing with the Properties Window

As you may recall from Chapter 11, expandable properties are a great way to simplify multivalue property editing, thanks to ExpandableObjectConverter. Unfortunately, unlike the Properties window, the smart tag panel doesn't allow expandable property editing because such a feature doesn't fit into the less-is-more style of the smart tag panel's UI. However, the smart tag panel still relies on HandConverter, the custom Hand class's type converter, to facilitate conversion between a Hand object and a multivalued string representation of a Hand object, as shown in Figure 12.15.

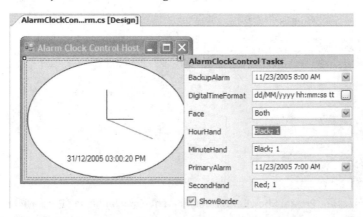

Figure 12.15   Not-So-Pretty Multivalued Property Editing

Developers can change the multivalued property and, if they get the format right, HandConverter converts it and sets the associated component's property correctly. But without expandable property editing, we still have the same problem we had in Chapter 11. The string format is not user friendly.

One way to increase usability is to create a new modal UITypeEditor (HandEditor) to display a dialog (HandEditorForm) for editing both the Color and the Width properties with a bit more style, such as the one shown in Figure 12.16.

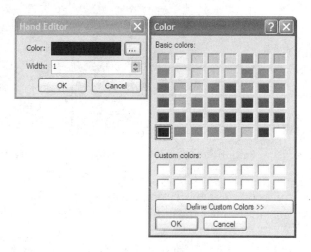

Figure 12.16 The Hand UI Type Editor

You can create HandEditor and HandEditorForm using techniques from Chapter 11, which also discusses how to hook HandEditor up to the Hand class using the Editor attribute:

```
// HandEditorForm.cs
partial class HandEditorForm : Form {...}

// HandEditor.cs
class HandEditor : UITypeEditor {...}

// Hand.cs
[Editor(typeof(HandEditor), typeof(UITypeEditor))]
[TypeConverter(typeof(HandConverter))]
class Hand {...}
```

After we rebuild the AlarmClockControl project, HandEditor is available from all three Hand smart tag items via ellipses buttons, as shown in Figure 12.17.

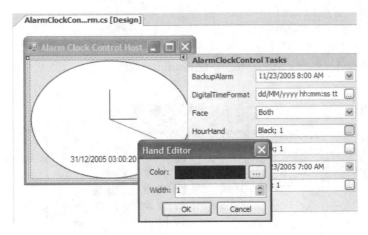

Figure 12.17   Editing Hand Smart Tag Property Items with Style

At least this technique provides a more usable way to edit multivalue properties, something that becomes more important as the number of values increases, as with a property of type Font.

If developers wanted to reconfigure one of the Hand properties away from its default value, it's likely that they'd reconfigure all Hand properties. Although, thanks to Hand-Editor, they can do so, they must open and close the editor three times. It would be easier to combine the configuration of all three Hand properties into a single step. The smart tag solution is to change our strategy from using smart tag property items and to using smart tag method items.

Smart Tag Method Items

When a configuration is more complex than setting only a single property, you can use smart tag method items to reduce the complexity through the use of additional UIs, much as the PictureBox control does to allow developers to choose an image, as shown in Figure 12.18.

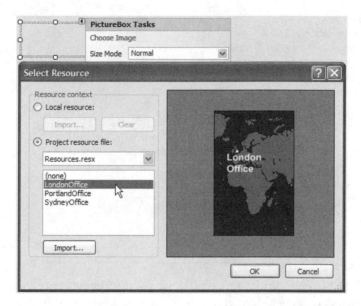

Figure 12.18   Editing Smart Tag Items by Using a Modal UITypeEditor

Smart tag method items are presented as link labels (like the Choose Image link label in Figure 12.18). When they are clicked, they perform an action—in this case, to display the Select Resource dialog. And, quite nicely, hooking up designer action method items turns out to be quite similar to using designer action property items.

Creating a Smart Tag Method Item

To add a smart tag method item to the smart tag panel that supports editing all clock hands at once, you add a method to your custom designer action list:

```
class AlarmClockControlDesignerActionList : DesignerActionList {
  void EditClockHands() {
    // Create form
    HandsEditorForm form = new HandsEditorForm();

    // Set current hand values
    form.HourHand = this.AlarmClockControl.HourHand;
    form.MinuteHand = this.AlarmClockControl.MinuteHand;
    form.SecondHand = this.AlarmClockControl.SecondHand;
```

```
    // Update new hand values of OK button was pressed
    if( form.ShowDialog() == DialogResult.OK ) {
      IDesignerHost designerHost =
        this.GetService(typeof(IDesignerHost)) as IDesignerHost;
      if( designerHost != null ) {
        DesignerTransaction t = designerHost.CreateTransaction();
        try {
          this.SetProperty("HourHand", form.HourHand);
          this.SetProperty("MinuteHand", form.MinuteHand);
          this.SetProperty("SecondHand", form.SecondHand);
          t.Commit();
        }
        catch { t.Cancel(); }
      }
    }
  }
  ...
```

EditClockHands creates an instance of HandsEditorForm before passing it the three current Hand property values. If a DialogResult of OK is returned, the current Hand values are replaced with the new Hand values. Note that this method interacts with the components in the same way the proxy properties do, ensuring nice Windows Forms Designer behavior.

Additionally, because setting three properties is really a single logical unit of activity, we need to support one-click undoing of all the changes made. That's why we wrap the property sets in a designer transaction using a DesignerTransaction object. If the transaction is successful, we commit the set of changes and turn them into a single undoable action. If the transaction fails, we attempt to cancel any changes made while the transaction was active.[4]

Figure 12.19 shows how the EditClockHands smart tag method item appears on the smart tag panel, replacing the three individual Hand properties with a single link label.

[4] For more information on designer transactions, see http://msdn2.microsoft.com/en-us/library/ system.componentmodel.design.designertransaction.aspx (http://tinysells.com/21).

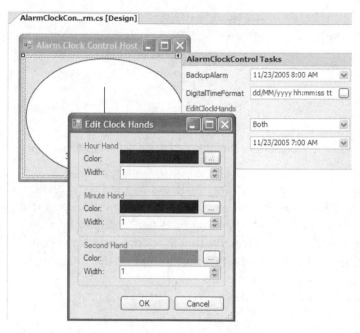

Figure 12.19   Edit Clock Hands Designer Action Method Item

Unlike smart tag property items, the method implementation of a designer action method item can be private, protected, internal, or public. Also, the method must not accept any arguments because the smart tag panel doesn't provide a mechanism to capture and pass them to the designer action method implementation. Conversely, the designer action method implementation must not return a value because the smart tag panel can't receive or process it.

Poor Man's Smart Tag Panel Appearance

We've created smart tag property and method items and, to this point, have relied on the base GetSortedActionItems method of our custom designer action list to assemble a list of designer action items that ultimately winds up with the smart tag panel. The layout of those items on the smart tag panel is determined by the order in which GetSortedActionItems adds them to the DesignerActionItemCollection collection. This turns out to be alphabetical, as shown in Figure 12.20.

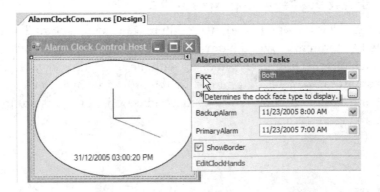

Figure 12.20   GetSortedActionItems-Dictated Smart Tag Panel Appearance

The smart tag panel is certainly functional, but it ain't pretty; for starters, the smart tag items are neither categorized nor described, two features we expect from our component in the Properties window. However, using the same Category and Description attributes we've come to know and love, we can create a Properties window-equivalent experience on the smart tag panel. We apply both attributes to each of the smart tag methods and smart tag properties on the custom designer action list:

```
class AlarmClockControlDesignerActionList : DesignerActionList {
  ...
  [Category("Appearance")]
  [Description("Determines the clock face type to display.")]
  public ClockFace Face {...}
  ...
  [Category("Appearance")]
  [Description("Edit analog clock hand properties.")]
  public void EditClockHands() {...}
  ...
}
```

The updated and better-looking smart tag panel is shown in Figure 12.21.

Figure 12.21   Better-Looking Smart Tag Panel Appearance

Because the smart tag panel is about using the minimum amount of real estate, smart tag item descriptions are displayed as tool tips rather than constantly visible text on the smart tag panel itself. The tool tips are activated (not necessarily obviously) when the mouse is hovered over the smart tag items. Also, the smart tag sorts the smart tag items by category and then by smart tag item name.

Another way you can alter the appearance is to use the DisplayName attribute to make the smart tag item labels a little more human, including spaces and whatnot:

```
class AlarmClockControlDesignerActionList : DesignerActionList {
  ...
  [Category("Appearance")]
  [Description("The digital time format, ...")]
  [DisplayName("Digital Time Format")]
  [Editor(typeof(DigitalTimeFormatEditor), typeof(UITypeEditor))]
  public string DigitalTimeFormat {...}

  // EditClockHands method
  [Category("Commands")]
  [Description("Configure the AlarmClockControl's hour, ...")]
  [DisplayName("Edit Clock Hands...")]
  public void EditClockHands() {...}
  ...
}
```

Figure 12.22 shows the result.

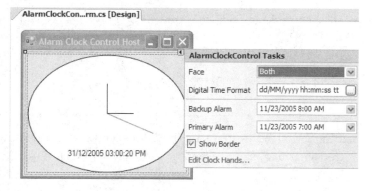

Figure 12.22   Even Better-Looking Smart Tag Panel

Using the DisplayName attribute also means that we can use ellipses to indicate that smart tag methods open dialogs, keeping the smart tag panel consistent with other UI elements like menu items.

You may be able to get away with the look and feel you can cobble together with attributes and the base GetSortedActionItems method implementation, although there are some things you can't do. For example, the categories are not labeled automatically, so it's a little more difficult to see which smart tag items belong in which category. Also, there are no attributes to provide descriptive text labels. Finally, you can't control the order in which smart tag items appear, something you may want to do in some situations.

You can address all these issues by overriding GetSortedActionItems.

Custom Smart Tag Panel Appearance

To customize the appearance of your smart tag panel, you construct your own Designer-ActionItemCollection. You do this in GetSortedActionItems, the same place used by the base DesignerActionList class. This means overriding it in your custom designer action list implementation:

```
class AlarmClockControlDesignerActionList : DesignerActionList {
  ...
  public override DesignerActionItemCollection GetSortedActionItems() {

    // Create list to store designer action items
    DesignerActionItemCollection actionItems =
      new DesignerActionItemCollection();

    // Fill list of designer action items
    ...

    // Return list of designer action items (for smart tag panel)
    return actionItems;
  }

  // Method and proxy property implementations
  ...
}
```

Just as the base GetSortedActionItems method does, you create a DesignerActionItem object for each desired smart tag property and method. However, DesignerActionItem is an abstract class:

```
abstract class DesignerActionItem {...}
```

DesignerActionItem implements functionality that's common to all designer action items, but it doesn't implement enough functionality to support the specifics of all designer action items. Instead, there are several DesignerActionItem derivations that specialize DesignerActionItem for specific purposes. As you might guess, two of those are for smart tag property items and smart tag method items:

```
sealed class DesignerActionPropertyItem : DesignerActionItem {...}
class DesignerActionMethodItem : DesignerActionItem {...}
```

DesignerActionPropertyItem provides a constructor that accepts two string arguments: member name and display name. *Member name* is the name of the public proxy property implementation on the custom designer action list class. *Display name* is how you want the smart tag property item's label to be formatted, just as if you'd used the DisplayName attribute. To create a designer action property item, you instantiate DesignerActionPropertyItem, passing the appropriate arguments to its constructor and adding it to Designer-ActionItemCollection, shown here for the Face property:

```
class AlarmClockControlDesignerActionList : DesignerActionList {
  ...
  public override DesignerActionItemCollection GetSortedActionItems() {
    // Create list to store designer action items
    DesignerActionItemCollection actionItems =
      new DesignerActionItemCollection();

    // Fill list of designer action items
    // Add Face designer action property item
    actionItems.Add(new DesignerActionPropertyItem("Face", "Face"));
    ...

    // Return list of designer action items (for smart tag panel)
    return actionItems;
  }
  ...
}
```

DesignerActionMethodItem implements a constructor that also accepts both member name and display name strings, as well as a reference to the designer action list that implements the member.[5] Using a DesignerActionMethodItem is quite similar to using a DesignerActionPropertyItem:

```
class AlarmClockControlDesignerActionList : DesignerActionList {
  ...
  public override DesignerActionItemCollection GetSortedActionItems() {
    // Create list to store designer action items
    DesignerActionItemCollection actionItems =
      new DesignerActionItemCollection();

    // Fill list of designer action items
    ...
```

[5] It's unclear why DesignerActionMethodItem needs a reference to its host DesignerActionList, while Designer-ActionPropertyItem doesn't. Both refer to members on the DesignerActionList.

```
    // EditClockHands designer action method item
    actionItems.Add(
      new DesignerActionMethodItem(
        this,
        "EditClockHands",
        "Edit Clock Hands..."));
    ...
    // Return list of designer action items (for smart tag panel)
    return actionItems;
  }
  ...
}
```

To assemble a complete list in this fashion, you place the items in the order you want them to appear on the smart tag panel. So, right off the bat, you can order them by category, yielding Figure 12.23.

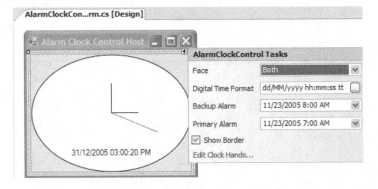

Figure 12.23   Manually Created Smart Tag Appearance

You may be wondering what happened to the categories we assigned earlier. And, although you can't see it, you should also wonder why tool tips no longer appear. The reason is that both category and description information must be included with a DesignerActionItem. When the base GetSortedActionItems method builds this list, it uses reflection to acquire category and description details from the attributes we used, passing the values to DesignerActionItems as it creates them. When you construct your own DesignerActionItem objects, this responsibility is placed squarely on your shoulders.

Categories and Descriptions

Both DesignerActionPropertyItem and DesignerActionMethodItem implement constructor overloads that accept two extra string arguments to collect category and description data. Here's how to provide both kinds of designer action items:

```
class AlarmClockControlDesignerActionList : DesignerActionList {
  ...
  public override DesignerActionItemCollection GetSortedActionItems() {
    ...
    // Add Face designer action property item
    actionItems.Add(
      new DesignerActionPropertyItem(
        "Face",
        "Face",
        "Appearance", // Category string argument
        "Determines the clock ...")); // Description string argument
    ...
    // EditClockHands designer action method item
    actionItems.Add(
      new DesignerActionMethodItem(
        this,
        "EditClockHands",
        "Edit Clock Hands...",
        "Commands",// Category string argument
        "Configure the ...")); // Description string argument
  }
  ...
}
```

The result of updating all our designer action items is shown in Figure 12.24.

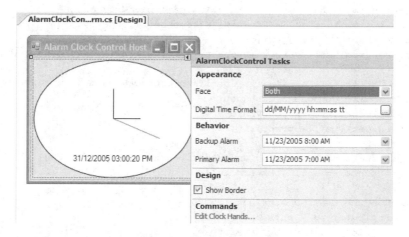

Figure 12.24   Categorized and Described Face Smart Tag Item

Figure 12.24 looks like what we could achieve without overriding GetSortedAction-Items, and indeed, if this is all the appearance you need, you wouldn't need to. However, if you do override GetSortedActionItems, there is a host of smart tag features you can take advantage of, including sucking category and description information right off your components.

Usually, components like AlarmClockControl apply both the Category and the Description attributes to their properties to influence their appearance in the Properties window. Consequently, when you provide both category and description string values, you must ensure that they are consistent with those supplied to the Category and Description attributes, respectively. Generics and reflection enable one way to do so:

```
class AlarmClockControlDesignerActionList : DesignerActionList {
  ...
  public override DesignerActionItemCollection GetSortedActionItems() {
    ...
    // Add Face designer action property item
    actionItems.Add(
      new DesignerActionPropertyItem(
        "Face",
        "Face",
        this.GetAttributeString<CategoryAttribute>(
          this.AlarmClockControl, "Face", "Category"),
        this.GetAttributeString<DescriptionAttribute>(
          this.AlarmClockControl, "Face", "Description")));
    ...
  }
  ...

  // Helper method that returns the value of a property exposed
  // by an attribute that is adorning a component property
  string GetAttributeString<T>(
    object source, string sourceProperty, string attributeProperty) {

    // Get attribute adorning the specified property of a
    // particular component instance
    PropertyInfo sourcePropertyInfo =
      source.GetType().GetProperty(sourceProperty);
    T attribute =
      (T)sourcePropertyInfo.GetCustomAttributes(typeof(T), false)[0];
    if( attribute == null ) return null;

    // Return the desired attribute's property value
    Type attributeType = attribute.GetType();
    PropertyInfo attributePropertyInfo =
      attributeType.GetProperty(attributeProperty);
    return (string)attributePropertyInfo.GetValue(attribute, null);
  }
  ...
}
```

The Description attribute actually has a property on it called Description, which represents the value we passed to the constructor. To retrieve the description from the attribute, we use the GetAttributeString helper function and pass it four pieces of information: the object (AlarmClock), the name of the property on the alarm clock (Face), the type of attribute (the Description attribute, which is passed in as T), and the name of the property on the attribute that contains the value (Description). GetAttributeString then uses this information in conjunction with reflection to discover the desired attribute information.

Null strings passed to the DesignerActionPropertyItem class's constructor are treated as if they weren't provided; the corresponding smart tag task is placed in the default category and doesn't have a tool tip. In general, properties that you expose from your components that can be configured from the design time should be adorned with both Category and Description attributes, especially because they influence the Properties window in the same manner to provide the same benefits.

Why does GetAttributeString expect an object parameter to describe the source object rather than internally relying on an AlarmClockControl reference? It does so to handle situations where properties are implemented by different types. For example, the Show-Border property is exposed from AlarmClockControlDesigner rather than AlarmClock-Control. To get ShowBorder's Category and Description attribute values, you pass GetAttributeString a reference to AlarmClockControlDesigner:

```
class AlarmClockControlDesignerActionList : DesignerActionList {
  ...
  public override DesignerActionItemCollection GetSortedActionItems() {
    ...
    // ShowBorder designer action property item
    actionItems.Add(
      new DesignerActionPropertyItem(
        "ShowBorder",
        "Show Border",
        this.GetAttributeString<CategoryAttribute>(
          this.Designer, "ShowBorder", "Category"),
        this.GetAttributeString<DescriptionAttribute>(
          this.Designer, "ShowBorder", "Description")));
    ...
  }
  ...
}
```

In general, this technique works well for designer action properties because, as you know, component and designer properties are likely to be adorned with both Category and Description attributes. Designer action methods, on the other hand, are highly likely to be implemented in their entirety on the custom designer action list, rather than act as proxies to underlying implementations. Consequently, you must provide category and description strings when instantiating DesignerActionMethodItem:

```
class AlarmClockControlDesignerActionList : DesignerActionList {
  ...
  public override DesignerActionItemCollection GetSortedActionItems() {
    ...
    // EditClockHands designer action method item
    actionItems.Add(
      new DesignerActionMethodItem(
        this,
        "EditClockHands",
        "Edit Clock Hands",
        "Appearance",
        "Configure the AlarmClockControl's ...",
        true));
    ...
  }
  ...
}
```

Fortunately, these are unlikely to be repeated anywhere else. In those few cases where they might be repeated, you should easily be able to refactor both the GetCategory and the GetDescription methods to operate over method implementations.

The major benefit of acquiring the category and description of each smart tag property item from the component is that it ensures consistency between the smart tag panel and the Properties window, something that can only be considered a benefit for users of your components.

Note that if you want them sorted alphabetically, you must rearrange the order in which you add the designer action property and method items to the DesignerActionItem-Collection object to suit. This can be a bit tricky because designer action method items don't appear among other properties in the Properties window. So you can either subcategorize each category by designer action item type or simply plonk all designer action method items into a single "Commands" category, as the Properties window does.

Headers

Even though you can nicely categorize your designer action items, the category names aren't actually displayed on the smart tag panel (unlike the Properties window), leaving the smart tag item groupings appearing somewhat arbitrary. Fortunately, you can also assign each smart tag item a text header using DesignerActionHeaderItem, another type of designer action item. DesignerActionHeaderItem's constructor accepts a single string value, which must be the same name as the category into which it goes:

```
class AlarmClockControlDesignerActionList : DesignerActionList {
  ...
  public override DesignerActionItemCollection GetSortedActionItems() {
    ...
    actionItems.Add(new DesignerActionHeaderItem("Appearance"));
    // Appearance category designer action items added here ...

    actionItems.Add(new DesignerActionHeaderItem("Behavior"));
    // Behavior category designer action items added here ...

    actionItems.Add(new DesignerActionHeaderItem("Design"));
    // Design category designer action items added here ...
    ...
  }
  ...
}
```

By using the same name as the category, you ensure that the designer action header item is located above all other designer action property and method items in that category. The application of designer action header items yields Figure 12.25.

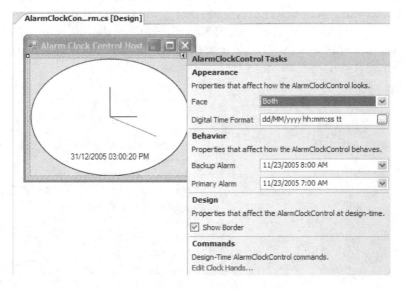

Figure 12.25 Smart Tag Header Items in Action

DesignerActionHeaderItems behave like DesignerActionPropertyItems and Designer-ActionMethodItems with regard to how they appear within a category; if you want the label to appear at the top of your category, you must add it to DesignerActionItem-Collection before all other designer action items in that category.

Text Labels

One final trick is to provide text to describe a category or a smart tag property or method item. To do so, use DesignerActionTextItem, whose constructor accepts a string description argument and a string category name:

```
class AlarmClockControlDesignerActionList : DesignerActionList {
  ...
  public override DesignerActionItemCollection GetSortedActionItems() {
    ...
    actionItems.Add(new DesignerActionHeaderItem("Appearance"));

    actionItems.Add(
      new DesignerActionTextItem(
        "Properties that affect how the AlarmClockControl looks.",
        "Appearance"));
    // Appearance category designer action items added here ...
    ...
  }
  ...
}
```

The two parameter constructors ensure that labels are sorted first by the category they are assigned to, and then in the order in which they are added to the designer action item collection.

The result of applying categories, descriptions, headers, and labels is the nicely titivated smart tag panel shown in Figure 12.26.

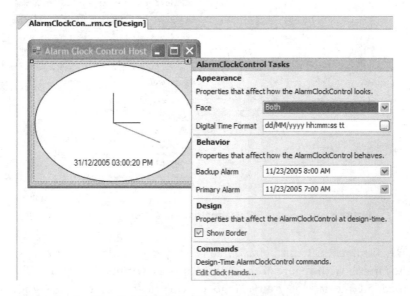

Figure 12.26   Completely Titivated Smart Tag Panel

The smart tag panel in Figure 12.26 is a Rolls-Royce from a look-and-feel point of view, but you can easily mix and match subsets of categories, descriptions, headers, and labels to support a wide variety of scenarios.

Note that the order in which smart tag items appear is determined by category and then the order in which each designer action property, method, header, or text item is added to the DesignerActionItemCollection object, whether or not those items are added contiguously.

Adding a Smart Tag Method Item to the Context Menu

The sphere of influence exerted by designer action method items extends beyond the smart tag panel; they can be configured to be displayed in a component's context menu and in the Properties window. To do this, you use one of the DesignerActionMethodItem class's constructor overloads that accept an additional Boolean argument. When this argument is true, the designer action infrastructure adds a menu item to the underlying component's context menu and adds a link label in the Properties window's Description pane. This takes a little tweak to our existing solution:

```
class AlarmClockControlDesignerActionList : DesignerActionList {
  ...
  public override DesignerActionItemCollection GetSortedActionItems() {
    ...
    // EditClockHands designer action method item
    actionItems.Add(
      new DesignerActionMethodItem(
        this, "EditClockHands", "Edit Clock Hands...", true));
    ...
  }
  ...
}
```

Figure 12.27 shows the new additions to the component's context menu and Properties window.[6]

---

[6] Designer action method items are displayed in the Properties window's Commands panel. Right-clicking Properties window opens a context menu with a Commands menu item that you can check or uncheck to hide or show the Commands panel. The same is true for the Description panel.

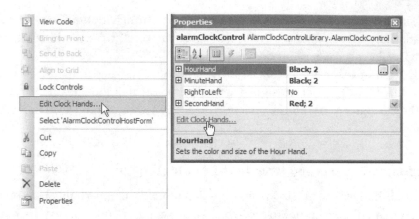

Figure 12.27   Displaying a Designer Action Method Item in Both the Context Menu and the Properties Window

Note that custom designers implement a Verbs property that you can use to add and update context menus and the Properties window. If you built a custom designer before .NET 2.0 that uses designer verbs to add items to a control's design-time context menu, the Windows Forms Designer automatically turns the verbs into smart tag methods without any effort on your part. Unfortunately, you can't categorize designer verbs or lay them out as nicely as native designer action items.

Toggling the Label Text of a Smart Tag Item

One of the common designer action method items you'll find on rectangular controls in Windows Forms lets you dock and undock those controls to and from their parent container via a designer action method item available on the smart tag panel. The trick with the Dock/Undock property is to toggle the display name to reflect the current component's Dock state whenever the designer action method item's link label is clicked, something that ultimately looks like Figure 12.28.

Figure 12.28   Toggling the Smart Tag Panel Dock Property

To begin, we create a new designer action method item with an accompanying method implementation that toggles the Dock property between a DockStyle of Fill and a DockStyle of None:

```
class AlarmClockControlDesignerActionList : DesignerActionList {
  ...
  public override DesignerActionItemCollection GetSortedActionItems() {
    ...
    // Dock/Undock designer action method item
    actionItems.Add(
      new DesignerActionMethodItem(
        this,
        "ToggleDockStyle",
        "Dock/Undock in parent container"));
    ...
  }
  ...
  // Toggle AlarmClockControl's Dock property
  void ToggleDockStyle() {
    if( this.AlarmClockControl.Dock != DockStyle.Fill ) {
      this.SetProperty("Dock", DockStyle.Fill);
    }
    else {
```

```
            this.SetProperty("Dock", DockStyle.None);
        }
    }
    ...
}
```

To toggle the display name of the designer action method item, we need two things: a helper method that calculates and returns the appropriate text, and a way to have it called when the dock style changes. With regard to the latter, the smart tag panel is refreshed whenever a property is changed, resulting in a subsequent call to GetSortedActionItems. So we can invoke the helper method from the DesignerActionMethodItem's constructor. The updated constructor and new helper method are shown here:

```
class AlarmClockControlDesignerActionList : DesignerActionList {
    ...
    public override DesignerActionItemCollection GetSortedActionItems() {
        ...
        // Dock/Undock designer action method item with display name
        // generated from GetDockStyleText helper method
        actionItems.Add(
            new DesignerActionMethodItem(
                this,
                "ToggleDockStyle",
                this.GetDockStyleText()));
        ...
    }
    ...
    // Helper method that returns an appropriate display name for the
    // Dock/Undock property, based on the AlarmClockControl's current Dock
    // property value
    string GetDockStyleText() {
        if( this.AlarmClockControl.Dock == DockStyle.Fill ) {
            return "Undock in parent container";
        }
        else {
            return "Dock in parent container";
        }
    }
    ...
}
```

After a rebuild, the updated smart tag panel with the new designer action method item operates, as shown in Figure 12.28.

Although this toggling technique should serve you well in general, there is a shortcut for docking and undocking that uses the Docking attribute (from the System.Windows.Forms namespace). You augment your custom control with the Docking attribute to automatically grant it docking and undocking smart tag support:

```
[Docking(DockingBehavior.Ask)]
partial class AlarmClockControl : ... {...}
```

You specify the type of docking by passing one of the following DockingBehavior enumeration values:

```
namespace System.Windows.Forms {
  enum DockingBehavior {
    Never = 0, // Never auto dock/undock
    Ask = 1, // Allow dock/undock via smart tag
    AutoDock = 2, // Allow dock/undock via smart tag and automatically
                  // dock-fill when control is dropped onto a form
  }
}
```

Figure 12.29 illustrates the result.

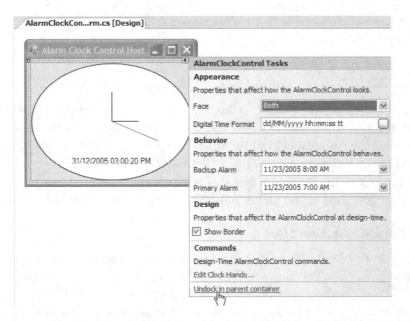

Figure 12.29   Toggling the Smart Tag Panel Dock Property Using the Docking Attribute

Designer Action Lists

To this point, we've spent our time working on a monolithic custom DesignerActionList class that returns all designer action items for a single component. However, designer action lists offer a little more flexibility and capability, which we explore next.

AutoShow

When a component that is likely to be dock-filled is dropped onto a form, you may want to let developers automatically toggle the dock state using the smart tag panel. If you need to, you can use the DesignerActionList class's AutoShow property to automatically pop open the smart tag for a component as soon as it is dropped onto a form. By default, the base implementation of AutoShow returns false, thereby keeping AutoShow turned off. Consequently, we override it to return true:

```
class AlarmClockControlDesignerActionList : DesignerActionList {
  ...
  public AlarmClockControlDesignerActionList(
    ClockControl AlarmClockControl) : base(clockControl) {
    // Automatically display smart tag panel when
    // component is dropped onto a form
    this.AutoShow = true;
  }
  ...
}
```

You can specify whether a design action list automatically shows itself when dropped onto a form, but it is effective only when VS05 is configured appropriately. Specifically, you must ensure that the Automatically Open Smart Tags setting, available from Tools | Options | Windows Forms Designer | General, is set to true (the default). This has the effect of yielding autoshow control to the in-play designer action list. However, if this property is set to false, autoshow is turned off, no matter how the designer action list is configured.

Multiple Designer Action Lists

Currently, the entire AlarmClockControl smart tag panel is constructed from a single custom designer action list. The larger and more complex a designer action list becomes, the less wieldy it becomes to support. In this situation, you can break a single, monolithic designer action list into several smaller and more manageable designer action lists. For example, we can arbitrarily break AlarmClockControlDesignerActionList into four individual custom designer action lists based on category:

```
class AppearanceActionList : DesignerActionList {...}
class BehaviorActionList : DesignerActionList {...}
class DesignActionList : DesignerActionList {...}
class CommandsActionList : DesignerActionList {...}
```

To ensure that all four are passed to the designer action service, we update the custom designer's ActionLists property to return a DesignerActionListCollection containing all four:

```
class AlarmClockControlDesigner : ControlDesigner {
  ...
  DesignerActionListCollection dalc;
  ...
  public override DesignerActionListCollection ActionLists {
    get {
      // Create action list collection
      if( this.dalc == null ) {
        this.dalc = new DesignerActionListCollection();

        // Add custom action lists
        this.dalc.Add(new AppearanceDesignerActionList(this.Component));
        this.dalc.Add(new BehaviorDesignerActionList(this.Component));
        this.dalc.Add(new DesignDesignerActionList(this.Component));
        this.dalc.Add(new CommandsDesignerActionList(this.Component));
      }
      // Return to the designer action service
      return this.dalc;
    }
  }
  ...
}
```

Now the categories are rendered to the smart tag panel in the order in which they are loaded into DesignerActionListCollection, and this smart tag panel actually looks the same as the smart tag panel shown earlier in Figure 12.26.

Note that if a component uses multiple designer action lists at once, all of them are automatically shown if at least one overrides its AutoShow property to return true (and if VS05 is configured appropriately).

Dynamic Designer Actions

Another advantage of splitting one monolithic designer action list into several discrete designer action lists is that it lets you pick and choose which ones to display on a smart tag panel at any one time.[7]

---

[7] The advantage of having a collection of ActionLists instead of a flat collection of Actions is the ability of one component to add its own action lists to another component. One example of this is how the Data Sources window adds data-related smart tag items to the controls it creates when a data source is dragged from it and dropped onto a form (see Chapter 17: Applied Data Binding). The technique requires use of DesignerActionService, and you can find an example of it at http://www.windowsforms.net/Default.aspx?tabindex=4&tabid=49#Windows Forms%20V2%20Demo%20App (http://tinysells.com/22).

Dynamic Designer Action Lists

You might consider adding, removing, or changing which designer action lists are displayed when the value of a smart tag property item on one designer action list affects whether smart tag property or method items are displayed from other designer action lists.

For example, when the AlarmClockControl's Face designer action property on the Appearance designer action list is set to ClockFace.Digital, it doesn't make much sense to edit the clock's hands via the Edit Clock Hands designer action method on the Commands designer action list. Consequently, you'd want to hide or show the Commands designer action list to hide or show the Edit Clock Hands designer action method as necessary. The logic to manage the showing and hiding of the Commands designer action list depends on the value of the Face property, which, when changed, can be used from the custom designer's ActionLists property appropriately:

```
class AlarmClockControlDesigner : ScrollableControlDesigner {
  ...
  DesignerActionListCollection dalc;
  CommandsDesignerActionList cDal;
  ...
  public override DesignerActionListCollection ActionLists {
    get {
      // Create action list collection
      if( this.dalc == null ) {
        this.dalc = new DesignerActionListCollection();

        // Add custom action lists
        this.dalc.Add(new AppearanceDesignerActionList(this.Component));
        this.dalc.Add(new BehaviorDesignerActionList(this.Component));
        this.dalc.Add(new DesignDesignerActionList(this.Component));
      }

      // Hide/Show Commands designer action list as necessary
      if( this.cDal == null )
        this.cDal = new CommandsDesignerActionList(this.Component);
      if( this.dalc.Contains(this.cDal) ) this.dalc.Remove(this.cDal);
      if( this.AlarmClockControl.Face != ClockFace.Digital ) {
        this.dalc.Add(this.cDal);
      }

      // Return to the designer action service
      return this.dalc;
    }
  }
  ...
}
```

We're almost there. The one thing that is missing is to broadcast to the designer action infrastructure that the Face value has changed and that a new set of designer action lists needs to be retrieved and displayed in the smart tag panel. To do this, we acquire a reference to DesignerActionService, which is the design-time service that manages smart tags on behalf of the Windows Forms Designer. DesignerActionService implements a Refresh method that, when invoked, provides exactly the behavior we need. Refresh should be called from the Face proxy property:

```
class AppearanceDesignerActionList : DesignerActionList {
  ...
  // Face proxy property
  [Editor(typeof(FaceEditor), typeof(UITypeEditor))]
  public ClockFace Face {
    get { return this.AlarmClockControl.Face; }
    set {
      this.SetProperty("Face", value);

      // Refresh smart tag panel
      DesignerActionUIService das =
        this.GetService(typeof(DesignerActionUIService)) as
          DesignerActionUIService;
      if( das != null ) das.Refresh(this.Component);
    }
  }
  ...
}
```

Figure 12.30 shows the result.

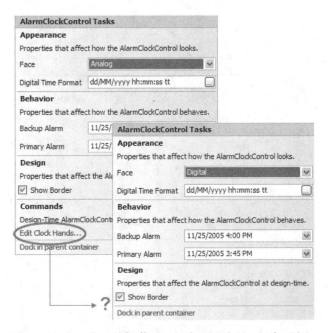

Figure 12.30　Dynamically Swapping Designer Action Lists

Notice in Figure 12.26 that the DigitalTimeFormat smart tag property item is available when the Face property is set to ClockFace.Digital. The DigitalTimeFormat smart tag property item is not really needed when this is the case, and we can dynamically include or exclude it as needed.

Dynamic Designer Action Items

When you need to be selective about which designer action items are displayed at which time, it makes sense to control that selection from GetSortedActionItems, where you can decide which designer action items are added (and which are not added) to the Designer-ActionItemCollection object as the designer action list is built.

For example, we can check whether the AlarmClockControl's Face property is set to Analog (neither of the digital options), and, if it is, we avoid adding the DigitalTimeFormat designer action property item:

```
class AppearanceDesignerActionList : DesignerActionList {
  ...
  public override DesignerActionItemCollection GetSortedActionItems() {
    ...
    // Add DigitalTimeFormat designer action property item
    // if Face is not Analog
    if( this.AlarmClockControl.Face != ClockFace.Analog ) {
      actionItems.Add(
        new DesignerActionPropertyItem("DigitalTimeFormat", ...));
    }
    ...
  }
  ...
}
```

You also need to refresh the designer action service when the Face property value changes; because we already have that in place. However, we've done all that's needed (see Figure 12.31).

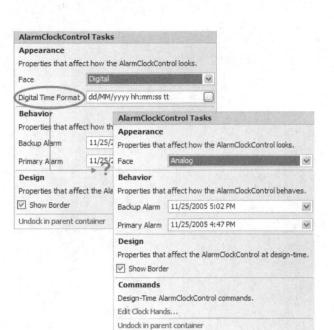

Figure 12.31   Dynamically Hiding Designer Action Items

There might be many scenarios that require you to dynamically add and remove designer action lists or designer action items, and the techniques we've discussed here should provide a solid foundation when you need to. And remember that this technique is not possible unless you override GetSortedActionItems.

Where Are We?

In Chapter 11, we looked at a variety of design-time integration features, most of which target the behavior of a component in the Properties window. In this chapter, we've expanded our integration through the use of custom designers and smart tags. Custom designers are the primary mechanism by which you implement design-time-only functionality for your components. One special type of design-time-only functionality is smart tags, which is enabled by leveraging the .NET Framework's designer action infrastructure.

The key reason to consider using custom designers and smart tags, in addition to nicer integration with the Properties window, is to enhance the usability of your components. To this end, the design-time infrastructure is far richer than what we've uncovered in Chapter 11 and this chapter, although you've seen a vast majority of the fundamental features that you should become familiar with if you intend to build and deploy components that offer enhanced capabilities at design-time.

13
Resources

A RESOURCE IS A NAMED PIECE OF DATA that is bound to an assembly at build time.[1] Resources are an extremely useful way to bundle arbitrary data such as text, graphics, and sounds into your applications and components for use at run time in tasks as diverse as setting the background image on a form and setting the label of a button. And because applications and components can find themselves being used in countries other than those in which they were written, resources also serve as the building block for internationalization to support no-compile deployment of localized resources.

Resource Basics

Imagine setting the background image of a form by loading a bitmap from a file:

```
// MainForm.cs
namespace ResourcesSample {
  partial class MainForm : Form {
    public MainForm() {
      ...
      // Load azul.jpg
      this.BackgroundImage =
        new Bitmap(@"c:\windows\web\wallpaper\azul.jpg");
    }
  }
}
```

The problem with this code is that not all installations of Windows have Azul.jpg, and even those that do have it may not have it in the same place. Even if you shipped this picture with your application, a space-conscious user may decide to remove it, causing your

---

[1] Recall from Chapter 1: Hello, Windows Forms that a .NET assembly is either an executable (.exe) or a library (.dll).

application to fault. The only safe way to make sure that the picture, or any file, stays with your code is to embed it and load it as a resource.

Manifest Resources

Resources are added to an assembly at compile time. To embed a resource into an assembly using VS05, you must add the file to your VS05 project.[2] To add a file to a project, right-click on your project in Solution Explorer, choose Add Existing Item, and choose the file you want to add. If it's not already there, it will be copied into your project's directory. To embed the file as a resource, right-click on the file and choose Properties; then, change Build Action from Content (the default) to Embedded Resource, as shown in Figure 13.1.

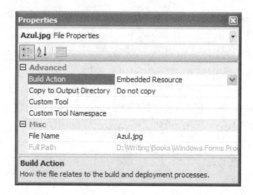

Figure 13.1   Setting a File's Build Action to Embedded Resource

When a file is marked as an Embedded Resource, it becomes embedded in the assembly's set of manifest resources. The *manifest* of an assembly is composed of a set of metadata that describes part of the assembly. Part of that metadata is the name and data associated with each embedded resource.

Naming Manifest Resources

To check that a file has been embedded properly into your project's output assembly, you use the .NET Framework SDK tool ildasm.exe. This tool shows all embedded resources in the Manifest view of your assembly, as shown in Figure 13.2.

---

[2] The .NET Framework SDK command line compilers, such as csc.exe and vbc.exe, provide options for bundling files into assemblies as resources (for csc.exe and vbc.exe, the switch is /resource). In addition, the /embedresource switch for al.exe creates a new assembly from an existing assembly and a set of files to embed as resources.

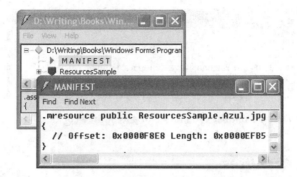

Figure 13.2   The ildasm Utility Showing an Embedded Manifest Resource

As shown in ildasm with the .mresource entry, embedding a file as a resource causes VS05 to name the resource using the project's default namespace, an optional subfolder name, and the resource's file name itself in the following format:

```
defaultNamespace.folderName.fileName
```

The default namespace portion of the resource name is the default namespace of the project itself, as set via Solution Explorer | *projectName* (right-click) | Properties | Application Tab | Default Namespace (see Figure 13.3).

Figure 13.3   A VS05 Project's Default Namespace

If the file happens to be in a subfolder of your project, the folder name of the resource includes a version of that folder name, replacing the backslashes with dots. For example, Figure 13.4 shows the Azul.jpg file in the foo\bar project subfolder, and Figure 13.5 shows the resulting name of the resource in ildasm.

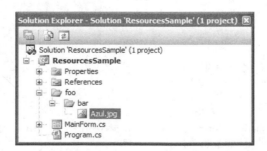

Figure 13.4   The Azul.jpg Resource in the foo\bar Project Subfolder

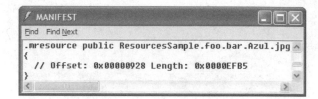

Figure 13.5   How VS05 Composes the Name of a Resource Located in a Project Subfolder

Loading Manifest Resources

To discover the resources embedded in an assembly, you enumerate the list of manifest resources, as ildasm does, by using the GetManifestResourceNames method of the System.Reflection.Assembly class:[3]

```
// MainForm.cs
using System.Reflection;
...
namespace ResourcesSample {
  partial class MainForm : Form {
    public MainForm() {
      ...
      // Get this type's assembly
      Assembly asm = this.GetType().Assembly;

      // Enumerate the assembly's manifest resources
      foreach( string resourceName in asm.GetManifestResourceNames() ) {
        MessageBox.Show(resourceName);
      }
    }
  }
}
```

When you know the name of a manifest resource—either by enumerating the resources or by hard-coding the one you want—you load it as a raw stream of bytes via the Assembly class's GetManifestResourceStream method:

```
// MainForm.cs
using System.IO;
...
namespace ResourcesSample {
  partial class MainForm : Form {
```

---

[3] You can retrieve a type's assembly via the associated Type object's Assembly property. Similarly, the Assembly class itself provides several methods for retrieving assemblies of interest: GetAssembly, GetCallingAssembly, GetEntryAssembly, and GetExecutingAssembly.

```
     public MainForm() {
       ...
       // Get this type's assembly
       Assembly asm = this.GetType().Assembly;

       // Get the stream that holds the resource
       // from the "ResourcesSample.Azul.jpg" resource
       // NOTE1: Make sure not to close this stream,
       //         or the Bitmap object will lose access to it
       // NOTE2: Also be very careful to match the case
       //         on the resource name itself
       Stream stream =
         asm.GetManifestResourceStream("ResourcesSample.Azul.jpg");
       // Load the bitmap from the stream
       this.BackgroundImage = new Bitmap(stream);
     }
   }
 }
```

Note that the resource name passed to GetManifestResourceStream is the full, case-sensitive name of the resource, including the namespace and file name. If the resource is located in a project subfolder, remember to include the "dottified" version of the folder name as well:

```
Stream stream =
  asm.GetManifestResourceStream("ResourcesSample.foo.bar.Azul.jpg");
```

Manifest Resource Namespaces

If you pass a System.Type object to the GetManifestResourceStream method, it uses the type's namespace as the namespace prefix portion of the embedded resource. This is especially useful because, by default, a newly generated class in VS05 is contained in the project's default namespace, allowing for an easy match between a type's namespace and the project's default namespace:

```
// MainForm.cs
namespace ResourcesSample {
  partial class MainForm : Form {
    public MainForm() {
      ...
      // Load the stream for resource "ResourcesSample.Azul.jpg"
      Stream stream =
        asm.GetManifestResourceStream(this.GetType(), "Azul.jpg");
      ...
    }
  }
}
```

This namespace-specification shortcut also works for some types that can directly load files that are embedded as resources. For example, the Bitmap class can load an image from a resource, eliminating the need to get the manifest stream manually:

```
// MainForm.cs
namespace ResourcesSample {
  partial class MainForm : Form {
    public MainForm() {
      ...
      // Get this type's assembly
      Assembly asm = this.GetType().Assembly;

      // Load image from "ResourcesApp.Azul.jpg"
      this.BackgroundImage = new Bitmap(this.GetType(), "Azul.jpg");
    }
  }
}
```

Figure 13.6 shows where all the parts of a manifest resource come from and how they're specified.

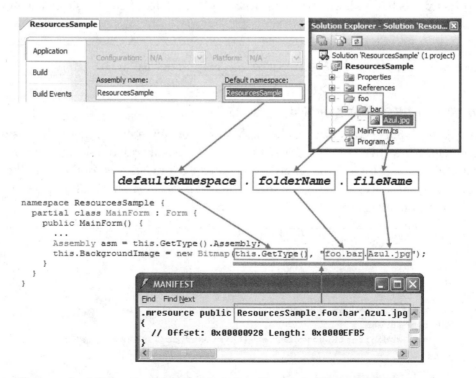

Figure 13.6   A Summary of Manifest Resource Naming and Name Resolution

Although manifest resources are useful, their degree of integration with both VS05 and the type system is limited. However, manifest resources serve as the needed foundation for strongly typed resources, which address both of these issues.

Strongly Typed Resources

Despite the file's extension, manifest resources are embedded with no type information. For example, if the name of the Azul.jpg file were Azul.quux, that would make no difference to the Bitmap class, which is looking at the data itself for the type—JPEG, PNG, GIF, and so on. It's up to you to properly map the type of each resource to the type of the object that's needed to load it. Fortunately, VS05 can do most of the heavy lifting to assist you in this endeavor.

Application Resources (.resx) Files

Because resources do not come with their own type, you need a place where you can tag your resources with appropriate type information. This is the primary job of *application resources files*, or .resx files, so called because they employ a .NET-specific XML schema called ResX to persist resource type information.

By default, a standard VS05 wizard-generated Windows Application project comes with a .resx file, Resources.resx, located in the Properties project folder. If you need to add .resx files to your project, perhaps as a mechanism for segregating subsets of resource data, you choose Add New Item from the Project menu and pick the Resources File template, as illustrated in Figure 13.7.

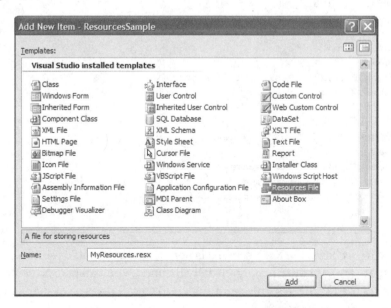

Figure 13.7   Adding a New Resources (.resx) File to a Project

As of this writing, even an empty .resx file is 42 lines of noncomment Extensible Markup Language (XML), most of which is the schema information. The schema allows for any number of entries in the .resx file, each of which has a name, value, comment, type, and Multipurpose Internet Mail Extensions (MIME) type. The following shows the XML for a .resx file with a single string resource, MyString:

```xml
<?xml version="1.0" encoding="utf-8"?>
<root>
  <xsd:schema
    id="root"
    xmlns=""
    xmlns:xsd="http://www.w3.org/2001/XMLSchema"
    xmlns:msdata="urn:schemas-microsoft-com:xml-msdata">
    ...
  </xsd:schema>
  <resheader name="resmimetype">
    <value>text/microsoft-resx</value>
  </resheader>
  <resheader name="version">
    <value>2.0</value>
  </resheader>
  <resheader name="reader">
    <value>
      System.Resources.ResXResourceReader,
      System.Windows.Forms,
      Version=2.0.0.0,
      Culture=neutral,
      PublicKeyToken=b77a5c561934e089</value>
  </resheader>
  <resheader name="writer">
    <value>
      System.Resources.ResXResourceWriter,
      System.Windows.Forms,
      Version=2.0.0.0,
      Culture=neutral,
      PublicKeyToken=b77a5c561934e089</value>
  </resheader>
  <data name="MyString" xml:space="preserve">
    <value>MyStringValue</value>
    <comment>MyStringComment</comment>
  </data>
</root>
```

 In spite of its text basis, the ResX schema is not meant to be read or edited by humans (as few XML formats are). If you are more visually inclined, you can take advantage of VS05's Resources Editor UI to edit .resx files and turn the overall process of managing resources into a relatively painless experience.

Managing Resources

The Resources Editor, shown in Figure 13.8 with the MyResources.resx file open, is the UI
that appears in VS05 when you open a .resx file for editing.

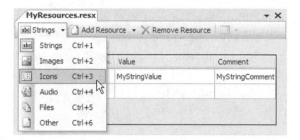

Figure 13.8   The Resources Editor

As you can see in Figure 13.8, the Resources Editor supports categorization of the
resources it manages into strings, images, icons, audio (.wavs), and files (either text or
binary, including text files, Word documents, or .wmv files). Another category, Other, exists
to store extra resource data such as component-defined serialization of design-time data.

Adding Resources

The first way you'll likely use the Resources Editor is to add the desired resources to the
.resx file. The Resources Editor offers several ways to add resources from a variety of locations. First, you can use the Resources Editor's Add Resource menu, shown in Figure 13.9.

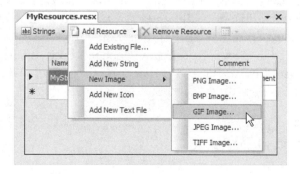

Figure 13.9   Adding Resources to a .resx File Using the Add Resource Menu Button

Depending on whether the resource exists as a file, you can either import existing resources (excluding string resources) by clicking Add Existing File, or create new resources by clicking any of the other Add New *Xxx* menu items.[4] Either way, the Resources Editor determines the type and again categorizes it appropriately.

You can also drag resources onto the Resources Editor from the current project and other applications such as File Explorer. Interestingly, you can even drag selected document text from an application like Word onto the string resources category.

All resource data files added to a .resx file using the Resources Editor are automatically added to a Resources folder in your project. If the folder doesn't already exist, the Resources Editor creates it. As shown in Figure 13.10, this provides a basic, useful segregation of resource data files from the rest of the files in your project.

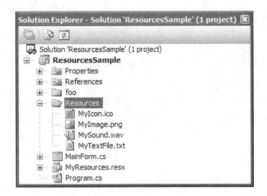

Figure 13.10   Resources Editor-Managed Project Resources Folder

If a resource already within a project is added to a .resx file, it is neither moved nor copied to the Resources folder, but it still works the same. The reason is that each resource data file managed by a .resx through the Resources Editor references a file in the file system, whether each is included in the VS05 project in which it is used. It's important to consider this indirection because, as we discussed earlier, .resx files merely layer type information over actual manifest resources.

---

[4] For some reason, the menu item for adding a new image does not contain the word *Add*, unlike its counterparts, but it still allows you to add a new image.

Deleting Resources

Another example of resource indirection derives from resource deletion. A resource can only be cut or removed from a .resx using the Resources Editor, but not actually deleted. This is because you are cutting or removing only resource metadata rather than the resource file (excluding strings, which can only be embedded). Also, the file remains after being cut or removed from the .resx file. If you want to remove all traces of a file resource, you must remove it from the .resx file and then delete it from the project.

Similarly, if you delete the file from your project, its .resx metadata remains. Upon recompilation, a compile-time exception is raised indicating that the actual file referenced from the .resx file is missing and needs to be rectified, as shown in Figure 13.11.

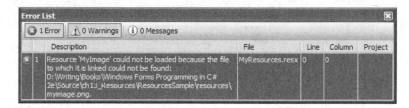

Figure 13.11   Compilation Error Caused by a Named Resource without a Resource File

Consequently, you must make sure that you properly remove all traces of a file resource. The Resources Editor helps out by raising useful exceptions as necessary to help ensure that your project is in a consistent state.

Editing Resources

In some situations, you add resources to your project that are ready for production and require no further editing. In other situations, you may create resources via the Resources Editor, or you may add resources that are not yet complete. Either way, these kinds of resources still need to be edited.

You can edit strings using the Resources Editor. If you are editing your project in VS05, you'll find that VS05 has extra smarts for editing icons, images, and text files. When you double-click resources of these types, VS05 opens an appropriate editor. For icons, it is VS05's own icon editor, for images, it is the Windows Paint application, and for text files, it is a VS05 text editor. By default, double-clicking a sound file opens Windows Media Player to play the .wav file.

However, you aren't limited to VS05's default editors to create and manage resource files; in all cases, you can edit these files with the tools of your choice. In fact, resource support in VS05 is geared toward supporting resource editing in this fashion throughout the development cycle, whether by you, by other developers, or by nontechnical people, such as graphic designers. Support for this hinges on how resources are associated with a project.

Resource Persistence

After an icon, image, or audio resource is added, you can specify the way it is associated with the project either by linking or embedding. You make this choice by setting a resource's Persistence property via the Properties window, as shown in Figure 13.12.

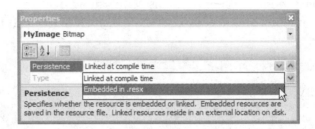

Figure 13.12   Specifying Project Persistence of a File Resource

You'll find that the Persistence property is set to *Linked at compile time* by default for all resources other than strings (which can only be embedded). This means that the resource's data is stored in a separate file and referenced from the .resx file using a relative file path (the file path you add via the Resources Editor). Keeping this separation makes the resource available for editing by anyone, and is incorporated into the executable only when the project is built. The following excerpt from the .resx file shows how a linked resource is persisted:

```xml
<?xml version="1.0" encoding="utf-8"?>
<root>
  ...
  <data
    name="MyImage"
    type="System.Resources.ResXFileRef, System.Windows.Forms">
    <value>
      Resources\MyImage.png;
      System.Drawing.Bitmap,
      System.Drawing,
      Version=2.0.0.0,
      Culture=neutral,
      PublicKeyToken=b03f5f7f11d50a3a
    </value>
  </data>
  ...
</root>
```

If you prefer, you can specify the persistence of your file resource as Embedded, which causes the resource to be sucked into your project and stored in the .resx file for the duration of development:

```xml
<?xml version="1.0" encoding="utf-8"?>
<root>
  . . .
  <assembly
    alias="System.Drawing"
    name="System.Drawing,
          Version=2.0.0.0,
          Culture=neutral,
          PublicKeyToken=b03f5f7f11d50a3a" />
  <data
    name="MyImage"
    type="System.Drawing.Bitmap, System.Drawing"
    mimetype="application/x-microsoft.net.object.bytearray.base64">
    <value>
      iVBORw0KGgoAAAANSUhEUgAAADAAAA ...
    </value>
  </data>
  . . .
</root>
```

Consequently, you can be assured that the resource exists and thereby avoid compilation errors, unless you delete it yourself. When you switch to Embedded persistence, you can delete the resource file from your project and the application still compiles safely. If you switch back to Linked persistence, a file is re-created for your resource, if it doesn't already exist, and is added to the Resources folder. Note that embedding a resource makes it impossible to edit. Instead, to affect an embedded resource, you have to remove the resource and add an updated file as a new resource.

An interesting side effect of adding or creating resources via the Resources Editor is that all resources, including icons, images, and audio files, are given a Build Action of None. But as you saw when we discussed manifest resources, the Build Action must be set to Embedded Resource for the resource to be compiled into the assembly. Yet, if we compile and execute an app whose resources were created with the Resources Editor, they are there in the assembly. This is possible because the .resx file itself has a Build Action that, by default, is set to Embedded Resource. As the visual Resources Editor suggests, a .resx file is a container for one or more resources to be compiled into an application when built. It also reinforces the fact that whether your resources are linked or embedded, the persistence property is only for the design time; either way, both types of resources are ultimately compiled into an assembly.

Using Typed Resources

As interesting and rich as the resource management experience may be, the proof of the pudding is in the eating. There is a variety of things that you can do with a .resx file both directly and indirectly.

Using the .resx File Directly

When a .resx file has been configured, you might like to access it directly—for example, to load and enumerate—something you can do with a little help from the ResXResourceReader class (from the System.Resources namespace):

```
using System.Collections;
using System.Resources;
...
using( ResXResourceReader reader =
  new ResXResourceReader(@"C:\MyResources.resx") ) {
  foreach( DictionaryEntry entry in reader ) {
    string s = string.Format("{0} ({1})= '{2}'",
      entry.Key, entry.Value.GetType(), entry.Value);
    MessageBox.Show(s);
  }
}
```

The ResXResourceReader class parses the XML file and exposes a set of named, typed values, but it provides no random access to them. Pulling out a specific entry requires first finding it:

```
using( ResXResourceReader reader =
  new ResXResourceReader(@"C:\MyResources.resx") ) {
  foreach( DictionaryEntry entry in reader ) {
    if( entry.Key.ToString() == "MyString" ) {
      // Display string resource value and stop searching further
      MessageBox.Show("MyString = " + (string)entry.Value);
      break;
    }
  }
}
```

The benefit of the .resx file is that type information is embedded along with the data itself, requiring a simple cast to get to a typed version of the data. For linked resources, the resource returned by ResXResourceReader is pulled from the relative file path stored as the resource's value.

Using Compiled .resx Resources

Building the project causes the .resx data to be embedded as *nested resources*, which are resources grouped into a named container. When a .resx file is embedded as a resource in a VS05 project, it becomes the container for the nested resources it holds.

As part of that process, the .resx file is compiled from the text format to the .resources binary format. Assuming a project's default namespace of ResourcesSample and a .resx file, MyResources.resx, the container of nested resources is named ResourcesSample.My-Resources.resources, as shown in ildasm in Figure 13.13.

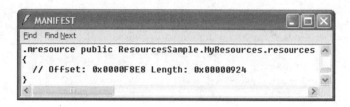

Figure 13.13   An Embedded .resources File

The .resources extension comes from the resgen.exe tool, which VS05 uses on the .resx file before embedding it as a resource. You can compile a .resx file into a .resources file yourself by using the following command line (which produces MyResources.resources in this case):

```
C:\> resgen.exe MyResources.resx
```

After you've compiled a .resx file into a .resources file in the file system, you can load it from the relative path and enumerate it using ResourceReader (from the System.Resources namespace). Except for the name of the class and the input format, usage of the ResourceReader class is identical to that of ResXResourceReader, including the lack of random access for named entries:

```
using( ResourceReader reader =
  new ResourceReader("MyResources.resources") ) {
  foreach( DictionaryEntry entry in reader ) {
    string s = string.Format("{0} ({1})= '{2}'",
      entry.Key, entry.Value.GetType(), entry.Value);
    MessageBox.Show(s);
  }
}
```

You can read a .resources file from the file system, but because VS05 compiles a .resx file and embeds the resulting .resources file for you, it's easier to access a .resources file directly from its manifest resource stream:

```
Assembly asm = Assembly.GetExecutingAssembly();

// Load embedded .resources file
using(
  Stream stream = asm.GetManifestResourceStream(
    this.GetType(),
    "MyResources.resources") ) {

  // Find resource in .resources stream
  using( ResourceReader reader = new ResourceReader(stream) ) {
    foreach( DictionaryEntry entry in reader ) {
      if( entry.Key.ToString() == "MyString" ) {
        // Display string resource value
        MessageBox.Show("MyString = " + (string)entry.Value);
        break;
      }
    }
  }
}
```

This two-step process—first loading either the .resx or the .resources file and then enumerating all values looking for the one you want—is an inconvenience, so .NET provides the ResourceManager class, which supports random access to resources.

The Resource Manager

The ResourceManager class (from the System.Resources namespace) is initialized with an embedded .resources file:

```
// Get this type's assembly
Assembly asm = this.GetType().Assembly;

// Load the .resources file into the ResourceManager
// Assumes a file named MyResources.resx within the current
// project ("ResourcesSample")
ResourceManager resman =
  new ResourceManager("ResourcesSample.MyResources", asm);
```

Notice the use of the project's default namespace appended to the MyResources.resources file. You name your .resources files in exactly the same way you name any other kind of resource, except that the .resources extension is assumed and cannot be included in the name.

Accessing Resources from a Resource Manager

After you've created a resource manager, you can pull out nested resources by name using the GetObject method, casting to the appropriate type. However, if you're using the .resx file for string resources, you use the GetString method instead. This method performs the cast to the System.String type for you:

```
// MainForm.cs
namespace ResourcesSample {
  partial class MainForm : Form {
    public MainForm() {
      ...
      // Load ResourcesSample.MainForm.resources from MainForm.resx
      ResourceManager resman = new ResourceManager(this.GetType());

      // Access the MyString string resource from the ResourceManager
      // (these two techniques are equivalent for strings)
      string s1 = (string)resman.GetObject("MyString");
      string s2 = resman.GetString("MyString");
    }
  }
}
```

The resource manager acts as a logical wrapper around a resource reader, exposing the nested resources by name, as shown in Figure 13.14.

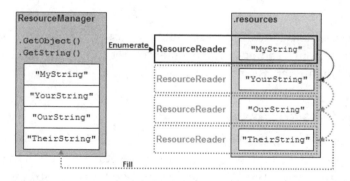

Figure 13.14   Logical View of the Way ResourceManager Uses ResourceReader

Again, because the naming scheme for embedded resources is somewhat obscured, Figure 13.15 summarizes how VS05 settings influence the names used with ResourceManager.

Figure 13.15   Resource Naming and ResourceManager

Using a resource manager directly, especially one associated with a specific type, is a useful thing to do although somewhat labor-intensive. Fortunately, VS05 incorporates special support that can alleviate the need for such coding.

Strongly Typed Resource Classes

The resource manager simplifies life in the resources world somewhat by providing the weakly typed GetObject method, which returns any resource, although the onus is on you to cast the data to the correct type. Even more simplified is the GetString method, which returns a strongly typed resource value, albeit only for strings.

Neither technique, however, provides the simple and complete solution that developers require: the ability to access any resource in a strongly typed fashion. The answer to this problem is provided by VS05 and a custom tool, ResXFileCodeGenerator, shown in Figure 13.16.

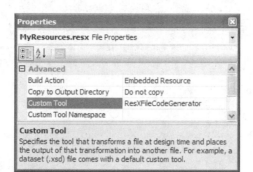

Figure 13.16   The ResXFileCodeGenerator Custom Tool

When a .resx file is saved, VS05 applies the custom tool to the .resx file, generating a corresponding .Designer.cs file, as shown in Figure 13.17.

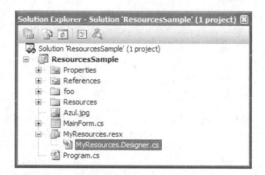

Figure 13.17   A .Designer.cs Code File Associated with a .resx File After Project Compilation

The .Designer.cs file exposes a class with the same name as the .resx file; the class is located within a namespace that corresponds to *defaultNamespace.projectPath*. For example, the following code shows a slightly abridged version of what is generated for My-Resources.resx when resources are absent:

```
namespace ResourcesSample {
    /// <summary>
    ///    A strongly typed resource class, for looking up localized
    ///    strings, etc.
    /// </summary>
    // This class was autogenerated by the StronglyTypedResourceBuilder
    // class via a tool like ResGen or Visual Studio.
    // To add or remove a member, edit your .resx file and then rerun ResGen
```

```
// with the /str option, or rebuild your VS project.
internal class MyResources {
  static global::System.Resources.ResourceManager resourceMan;
  static global::System.Globalization.CultureInfo resourceCulture;

  internal MyResources() {}

  /// <summary>
  ///   Returns the cached ResourceManager instance used by this
  ///   class.
  /// </summary>
  internal static global::
    System.Resources.ResourceManager ResourceManager {
    get {
      if( (resourceMan == null) ) {
        global::System.Resources.ResourceManager temp =
          new global::System.Resources.ResourceManager(
            "ResourcesSample.MyResources",
            typeof(MyResources).Assembly);
        resourceMan = temp;
      }
      return resourceMan;
    }
  }

  /// <summary>
  ///   Overrides the current thread's CurrentUICulture property for
  ///   all resource lookups using this strongly typed resource class.
  /// </summary>
  internal static global::System.Globalization.CultureInfo Culture {
    get { return resourceCulture; }
    set { resourceCulture = value; }
  }
}
}
```

There are two key features of the MyResources type. First, it provides static access to a ResourceManager via the like-named ResourceManager property, which relieves you of the need to write the creation logic we saw earlier. Second, static access to localization information is exposed from a CultureInfo object via the Culture property (localization is discussed extensively later in this chapter).

Although these helper properties are useful in their own right, the generated .Designer.cs file becomes much more interesting when resources are added to it. The following shows how MyResources.Designer.cs exposes a string, an icon, an image, a sound, and a text file resource:

```
using System.Drawing;
using System.IO;
...
namespace ResourcesSample {
  internal class MyResources {

    ...
    internal static Icon MyIcon { get { ... } }
    internal static Bitmap MyImage { get { ... } }
    internal static UnmanagedMemoryStream MySound { get { ... } }
    internal static string MyString { get { ... } }
    internal static string MyTextFile { get { ... }

  }
}
```

Each resource is exposed as a strongly typed, static, read-only property. The beauty of this implementation is that developers now need only write a single line of code to access any single resource:[5]

```
// MainForm.cs
namespace ResourcesSample {
  partial class MainForm : Form {
    public MainForm() {
      ...
      // Access strongly typed resources from MyResources.resx
      string myString = MyResources.MyString;
      Icon myIcon = MyResources.MyIcon;
      Image myImage = MyResources.MyImage;
      UnmanagedMemoryStream mySound = MyResources.MySound;
      string myTextFile = MyResources.MyTextFile;
    }
    ...
  }
}
```

Internally, each property exposed by the designer-generated resources class uses its internally managed ResourceManager object in much the same fashion as you would:

```
using System.Drawing;
...
namespace ResourcesSample {
  internal class MyResources {

    ...
    static global::System.Globalization.CultureInfo resourceCulture;

    ...
```

---

[5] A great benefit of writing code against strongly typed implementations is, of course, that such code can be checked for errors at compile time.

```
    internal static Icon MyIcon {
      get {
        return ((Icon)
          (ResourceManager.GetObject("MyIcon", resourceCulture)));
      }
    }
  }
}
```

Each call to ResourceManager passes information about the current UI culture, a topic that we cover shortly. For now, however, it's enough to know that this means your resources are geared for internationalization support.

Designer Resources

So far, you've seen how to manually create and manage .resx files for VS05 projects. VS05 and the Windows Forms Designer also do a variety of additional things with .resx files, something we look at now.

Default Project Resources

First and foremost, VS05 manages projectwide resources for you. You can view and manage these resources from the Resources Editor, which is embedded in the Resources tab of your project's property pages, as shown in Figure 13.18.

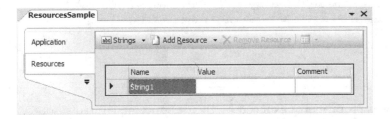

Figure 13.18   Editing Projectwide Resources with the Resources Editor

Because Resources.resx is really managed from your project's property pages, VS05 stores it in your project's Properties folder. And, as with the .resx files you add to your project, the custom ResXFileCodeGenerator tool is automatically applied to generate Resources.Designer.cs, a strongly typed class abstraction of the Resources.resx file:

```
namespace ResourcesSample.Properties {
  ...
  internal class Resources {
    ...
    internal static global::
      System.Resources.ResourceManager ResourceManager {
      get { ... }
    }

    internal static global::System.Globalization.CultureInfo Culture {
      get { ... }
      set { ... }
    }
  }
}
```

Given the location of the Resource.resx file, the generated Resources class resides in the ResourcesSample.Properties namespace. Any resources you add to Resource.resx are, of course, accessible through a strongly typed and static property, so you can use the following code with them:

```
MessageBox.Show(Properties.Resources.MyString);
```

As a rule of thumb, resources that are shared across more than one of an assembly's types should be placed in Resources.resx.

Automatic Resource Association

If your project has a form and if you open the VS05 Solution Explorer before pressing the Show All Files button, you'll see that your form has a corresponding .resx file without your having to do anything. This keeps resources associated with certain properties of the form, such as BackgroundImage and Icon. To assist with the setting of either of these properties, the Properties window opens the Select Resource UITypeEditor, which allows you to choose an appropriate image resource from one of several locations, as shown in Figure 13.19.[6]

[6] UITypeEditors are covered in Chapter 11: Design-Time Integration: The Properties Window.

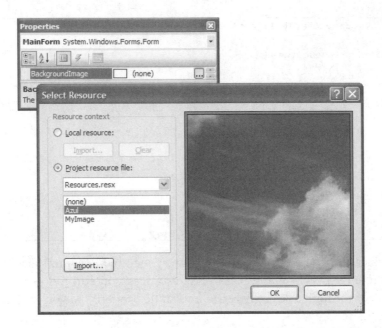

Figure 13.19   Adding Resources with the Select Resource UITypeEditor

The Select Resource UITypeEditor allows you to import and store your image resources in one of two ways: as a local resource or as a project .resx. For a form, the local resource is embedded into the .resx file that's automatically created by the Windows Forms Designer and associated with the form. If you choose this option, you can import an image resource straight into the form's .resx file, or you can use an image resource that's already located in any other .resx files in the project not associated with forms. If the image resource you want hasn't been imported and if you want to share it among more than one type, you can also import the desired image resource straight into Resources.resx before selecting it.

If you import an image resource straight into a form's .resx file, you get what is shown in Figure 13.20.

Figure 13.20   Image Resource Imported as a Local Resource into a Form's .resx

In particular, the Windows Forms Designer uses a special naming convention to distinguish all the resources that it's managing:

```
$this.PropertyName
```

If you'd like to add your own per-component typed resources to a .resx, use a leading dollar sign, or some other character that's illegal for use as a field name, and avoid the "$this" prefix (and the ">>" prefix, as you'll see shortly). For example, the following is suitable:

```
$mine.ResourceName
```

However, because the implementation of the Windows Forms Designer could change, adding your own .resx to the project is the surest way of maintaining custom resources outside the influence of the Designer.

If an image resource is added to a Windows Forms Designer-managed .resx, the Windows Forms Designer generates code into InitializeComponent to load a resource manager and populate the form's property from the Windows Forms Designer-managed .resx:

```
// MainForm.Designer.cs
using System.ComponentModel;
using System.Windows.Forms;
...
partial class MainForm {
  ...
  void InitializeComponent() {
    ...
    ComponentResourceManager resources =
      new ComponentResourceManager(typeof(MainForm));
    ...
    // MainForm
    this.BackgroundImage =
      ((System.Drawing.Image)
        (resources.GetObject("$this.BackgroundImage")));
    ...
  }
  ...
}
```

The reason that a resource manager is used, rather than a strongly typed class, is that the latter hasn't been generated. By default, Windows Forms Designer-managed .resx files associated with forms are not set with the custom ResXFileCodeGenerator tool, presumably to avoid name collisions, as you saw earlier. However, if an image resource you assigned to a property comes from a non-Windows Forms Designer-managed .resx file, such as

Properties Resources.resx, a strongly typed class is generated, and the Windows Forms Designer generates the following, more compact, alternative code to InitializeComponent:

```
// MainForm.Designer.cs
using System.ComponentModel;
using System.Windows.Forms;
...
partial class MainForm {
  ...
  void InitializeComponent() {
    ...
    // MainForm
    this.BackgroundImage = ResourcesSample.Properties.Resources.Azul;
    ...
  }
  ...
}
```

Embedding Native Resources

All the resources we've talked about so far are managed, and VS05 provides great support for them. Unfortunately, except for a single icon and version information, VS05 projects don't support the addition of native resources. All files marked as Embedded Resource or pulled into a .resx file are managed resources. This makes them unavailable for use by native components, such as the COM-based DirectX API. To support some interop scenarios, you need to use the /win32resource compiler command line switch, which can't be used from within VS05 builds, or you need to use a third-party tool that adds unmanaged resources after a compile.[7] At the time of this writing, Microsoft supplies no tools that provide this functionality.[8]

Application Internationalization

Throughout this chapter, we've come back repeatedly to the workhorse of the resources world, the ResourceManager class. This situation is no different when you talk about

---

[7] This chapter's EmbeddingUnmanagedResourcesSample includes a tool from Peter Chiu called ntcopyres.exe that adds unmanaged resources to a managed assembly. It was obtained from http://www.codeguru.com/cpp_mfc/rsrc-simple.html (http://tinysells.com/23) and is executed from a post-build step on the C# project.

[8] One problem with adding the native resources after a build is that if you've already signed it with a strong name key, the additional resources will screw up the hash of the file.

providing support for application internationalization (i18n).[9] *Globalization* is the act of creating an application that will execute across multiple cultures without the need for recompilation. *Localization* is the act of providing one or more sets of culture- and location-specific data over which a globalized application operates. Together, these two concepts are often joined under the umbrella term: *internationalization*.[10] Figure 13.21 illustrates.

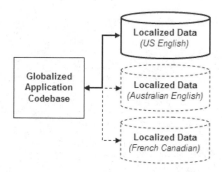

Figure 13.21   Localized Data Sets

A globalized application might be one that uses code to format currency or dates according to the current locale, as shown in Figure 13.22.

Culture English Name	Name	Currency	Date
English	en		
English (Australia)	en-AU	$4.52	26/11/2005
English (Belize)	en-BZ	BZ$4.52	26/11/2005
English (Canada)	en-CA	$4.52	26/11/2005
English (Caribbean)	en-CB	$4.52	11/26/2005
English (Ireland)	en-IE	€4.52	26/11/2005
English (Jamaica)	en-JM	J$4.52	26/11/2005
English (New Zealand)	en-NZ	$4.52	26/11/2005
English (Republic of the Philippines)	en-PH	Php4.52	11/26/2005
English (South Africa)	en-ZA	R 4.52	2005/11/26
English (Trinidad and Tobago)	en-TT	TT$4.52	26/11/2005
English (United Kingdom)	en-GB	£4.52	26/11/2005
English (United States)	en-US	$4.52	11/26/2005
English (Zimbabwe)	en-ZW	Z$4.52	11/26/2005

Figure 13.22   Localized Currencies and Dates

This code requires special knowledge of available cultures in .NET.

[9] The i18n abbreviation came from the need to spell out *internationalization* so often that the middle 18 letters were replaced with the number 18. Similarly, *globalization* and *localization* become g11n and l10n, respectively. In this same spirit, I plan to switch from *abbreviation* to "a10n" any day now.

[10] Further information on internationalization can be found at http://msdn.microsoft.com/library/default.asp?url=/library/en-us/vbcon/html/vboriInternationalization.asp (http://tinysells.com/24).

Culture Information

I generated the currencies and dates in Figure 13.22 by enumerating all the cultures that .NET knows about (centralized in the System.Globalization namespace) and using the information about each culture to provide formatting information:

```
// MainForm.cs
using System.Globalization;
...
partial class MainForm : Form {
  ...
  void MainForm_Load(object sender, EventArgs e) {

    // Get example values
    double amount = 4.52;
    DateTime date = DateTime.Now;

    // Show localized versions of the example values
    foreach( CultureInfo info in
            CultureInfo.GetCultures(CultureTypes.AllCultures) ) {
      ListViewItem item = listView.Items.Add(info.EnglishName);
      item.SubItems.Add(info.Name);
      if( !info.IsNeutralCulture ) {
        item.SubItems.Add(amount.ToString("C", info.NumberFormat));
        item.SubItems.Add(date.ToString("d", info.DateTimeFormat));
      }
    }
  }
}
```

This code enumerates all known cultures, pulling out the name, the number-formatting information, and the date-formatting information; the latter two are passed to the ToString function to govern formatting. The intrinsic ToString implementations format strings by using the culture stored in the CurrentCulture property of the current thread (available via System.Threading.Thread.CurrentThread). The CurrentCulture property on the System.Windows.Forms.Application class is a wrapper around the CurrentCulture property of the current thread, so either can be used to test your programs in alternative cultures:

```
void testCulturesButton_Click(object sender, EventArgs e) {
    double amount = 4.52;

    // Show currency using default culture
    MessageBox.Show(amount.ToString("C"),
      Application.CurrentCulture.EnglishName);
```

```
  // Change current culture (one way)
  Application.CurrentCulture = new CultureInfo("fr-CA");

  // Change current culture (another way)
  System.Threading.Thread.CurrentThread.CurrentCulture =
    new CultureInfo("fr-CA");

  // Show currency in current culture (Canadian French)
  MessageBox.Show(amount.ToString("C"),
    Application.CurrentCulture.EnglishName);
}
```

By default, the current culture is whatever the user has set on their machine. Changing it requires an instance of the CultureInfo object, which is most easily constructed with a culture name. A *culture name* is composed of unique identifiers of a language and a country and is formatted this way:

```
twoLetterLanguageId-twoLetterCountryId
```

For example, U.S. English is "en-US," and Australian English is "en-AU."[11]

Resource Localization

Thread.CurrentCulture exposes a CultureInfo object that provides access to localization data—including date, time, and formatting—for the current region.[12] But what about localization data that is application specific, such as control text? .NET supports application-specific localization via culture-specific resource assemblies deployed in satellite assemblies. *Satellite assemblies* are separate assemblies that can be found near the location of the *main assembly,* which is the assembly containing the code for the localized forms.

The resources embedded in the main assembly are considered *culture neutral* in that they aren't specialized for any culture. *Culture-specific* resources, in contrast, are embedded into a project on a per-form basis, with each form being responsible for one or more sets of culture- and language-specific localized data sets, as well as a culture-neutral data set.

To support form localization, each form has a Localizable property that can be changed from the default value of false to true. When the Localizable property is false, a form doesn't have any entries in its .resx file. When the Localizable property is set to true, a form's .resx file expands to hold the three entries shown in Figure 13.23.

---

[11] The language/country naming convention is dictated by two ISO standards: ISO 639, http://en.wikipedia.org/wiki/ISO_639 (http://tinysells.com/25), and ISO 3166, http://en.wikipedia.org/wiki/ISO_3166 (http://tinysells.com/26).

[12] In Windows XP, the current region and date, time, and currency formatting are set from the Regional and Language Options control panel.

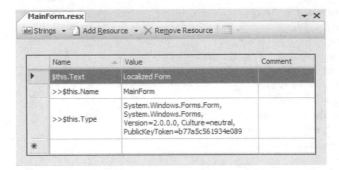

Figure 13.23   Default Resource Entries for an Empty Form

Resource entries that are localizable are given resource names in the following format:

```
$this.FormProperty
```

As you can see in Figure 13.23, then, only Form.Text is localized by default. The remaining entries, prefixed by ">>," are form properties that aren't localizable.

As you saw earlier, the localizable form properties are set from the .resx file during form initialization:

```
// MainForm.Designer.cs
using System.ComponentModel;
...
partial class MainForm {
  ...
  void InitializeComponent() {
    ...
    ComponentResourceManager resources =
      new ComponentResourceManager(typeof(LocalizedFormSampleForm));
    ...
    // MainForm
    resources.ApplyResources(this, "$this");
    ...
  }
}
```

InitializeComponent uses ComponentResourceManager (from the System.Component-Model namespace) and its ApplyResources method to enumerate the underlying form resources and set their equivalent properties on the form.

Although resource data entries are automatically created for three localizable form properties, additional form properties also become localized when you edit them in the Windows Forms Designer. But, not all form properties can be localized, and unfortunately neither IntelliSense nor the SDK documentation has an immediately obvious technique for determining property localizability. However, the implementations of localizable form properties are adorned with the Localizable from attribute, with its IsLocalizable property set to true. This information can be discovered using reflection, eliciting the following localizable form properties:[13]

- AccessibleDescription (String)
- AccessibleName (String)
- Anchor (AnchorStyles)
- AutoScaleBaseSize (Size)
- AutoScaleDimensions (SizeF)
- AutoScroll (Boolean)
- AutoScrollMargin (Size)
- AutoScrollMinSize (Size)
- AutoSize (Boolean)
- AutoSizeMode (AutoSizeMode)
- BackgroundImage (Image)
- BackgroundImageLayout (ImageLayout)
- ClientSize (Size)
- Dock (DockStyle)
- Enabled (Boolean)

- Font (Font)
- Icon (Icon)
- ImeMode (ImeMode)
- Location (Point)
- Margin (Padding)
- MaximumSize (Size)
- MinimumSize (Size)
- Padding (Padding)
- RightToLeft (RightToLeft)
- RightToLeftLayout (Boolean)
- Size (Size)
- StartPosition (FormStartPosition)
- TabIndex (Int32)
- Text (String)
- Visible (Boolean)

Additionally, you can use the Windows Resource Localization Editor tool, covered shortly, to quickly identify localizable properties.

It's the act of localizing a form that results in the InitializeComponent method probing for satellite resources, specifically for any property that could be culture specific. You create a culture-specific satellite resource when you choose a culture from a form's Language property in the Properties window, as shown in Figure 13.24.

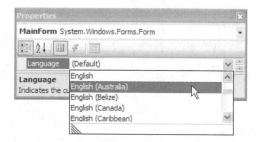

Figure 13.24   Choosing a Culture in the Properties Window

[13] Christophe Nasarre very kindly provided the code sample to find localizable form properties, a version of which (LocalizableFormPropertyDiscoverer) is part of the samples for this chapter.

When a culture is chosen, you add culture-specific values by setting the desired form properties. For each culture you choose, a corresponding .resx file containing culture-specific data is created and associated with the form (when the culture-specific data is provided and differs from the default values). Figure 13.25 shows a form in Solution Explorer after the developer has chosen to support several languages—some country specific and others country neutral.

Figure 13.25   One Form with Localization Information for Several Cultures

When the project is built, all of the form's culture-specific resources are bundled into a satellite assembly, one per culture, and placed into the appropriately named folder, as shown in Figure 13.26.

Figure 13.26   Use of Appropriately Named Folders to Store Satellite Assemblies

The folders and satellite assemblies are named so that the resource manager can find the culture-specific resources it's probing for:

```
LocalizedFormSample.exe
en\LocalizedFormSample.resources.dll
en-US\LocalizedFormSample.resources.dll
fr\LocalizedFormSample.resources.dll
fr-CA\LocalizedFormSample.resources.dll
```

Notice that the main application is at the top level, containing the culture-neutral resources, and the culture-specific resource assemblies are in subfolders named after the culture. Notice also that VS05 has chosen the names of the subfolders and satellite assemblies that the resource manager looks for first (as shown in Table 13.1 later in this chapter), saving probing time.

The presence of a new satellite assembly in the file system in a place that the resource manager can find it is the only thing required to localize an assembly's form for a new culture. When a localized form is loaded, the resource manager finds the new satellite assembly and loads the resources from it as appropriate, without the need to recompile the main assembly itself. This provides *no-compile deployment* for localized resources.

Resource Localization for Nondevelopers

VS05 is a handy tool for resource localization, but it's not something you want to force non-developers to use. Luckily, after you set the Localizable property to true for each localizable form and rebuild your component, your user can localize a set of forms in an assembly without further use of VS05.

To allow nondevelopers to localize resources, the .NET Framework SDK ships with a tool called Windows Resource Localization Editor (winres.exe).[14] One way to use it is to open a culture-neutral .resx file for a localizable form—that is, a form with the Language property set to (Default). After you've loaded the .resx file, you're presented with a miniature version of the VS05 Forms Designer, which you can use to set culture-specific resource information, as shown in Figure 13.27.

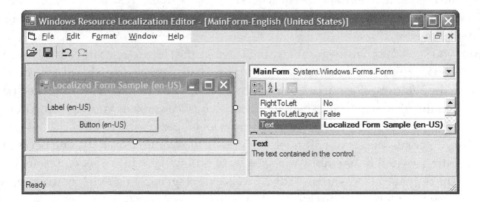

Figure 13.27   Localizing a Form Using winres.exe

Before you make any changes, I recommend choosing File | Save As, which opens the Select Culture dialog, where you can choose a culture and a file mode, both shown in Figure 13.28.

---

[14] Another advantage of using winres.exe is that the Properties window for each edited form contains only properties that can be localized.

Figure 13.28   Saving a Localized Form

The culture is used to format a culture-specific name for the .resx file. For example, MainForm.resx is saved as MainForm.en-US.resx for the U.S. English culture, just as VS05 does it. The file mode determines what is persisted to localized .resx files; Visual Studio file mode (VSFM) ensures that only resource deltas (differences) are persisted, something that can save quite a bit of space.

After you save the culture-specific .resx file, make the culture-specific changes and save again. Because both culture-neutral and culture-specific .resx files can be edited equally in VS05 and the Windows Resource Localization Editor, you can also create culture-specific .resx files in the former and edit them in the latter, or vice versa as you've seen. Thus, you can choose a model that works best for your nondevelopers.

Next, you create the set of culture-specific .resx files for an assembly, one per form, to use in creating a satellite assembly. You start by bundling them into a set of .resources files by using the resgen.exe tool shown earlier. To execute resgen.exe on more than one .resx file at a time, use the /compile switch:

```
C:/> resgen.exe /compile MainForm.en-US.resx OtherForm.en-US.resx ...
```

Running resgen.exe in this manner produces multiple .resources files, one per .resx file. After you have the .resources files for all the localized forms for a particular culture, you can bundle them into a single resource assembly by using al.exe, the assembly linker command line tool:

```
C:/> al.exe /out:en-US\WinResLocalizedFormSample.resources.dll
/culture:en-US
/embedresource:LocalizedForm1.en-
US.resources,WinResLocalizedFormSample.LocalizedForm1.en-US.resources
/embedresource:LocalizedForm2.en-
US.resources,WinResLocalizedFormSample.LocalizedForm2.en-US.resources
...
```

The assembly linker tool has all kinds of uses in .NET. In this case, we're using it to bundle a number of .resources files into a single satellite assembly. The /out argument determines the file path and the name of the produced assembly. Make sure that the file path exists, and pick one of the file names that the resource manager will probe for (as shown later in Table 13.1).

The /culture argument determines the culture of the resource assembly and must match the culture name for the resources you're building. The /embedresource arguments provide the .resources files along with the *alternative names* to match the names that the resource manager will look for. By default, al.exe bundles each resource into a named container based on the file name. However, to match what the resource manager is looking for, you must use the alternative name syntax to prepend the resource namespace.

Again, ildasm is a useful tool for making sure that you have things right when it comes to building satellite resources. Figure 13.29 shows the result of running ildasm on WinResLocalizedFormSample.resources.dll, which was produced by the earlier call to al.exe.

```
// Metadata version: v2.0.50727
.assembly WinResLocalizedFormSample.resources
{
  .hash algorithm 0x00008004
  .ver 0:0:0:0
}
.mresource public 'WinResLocalizedFormSample.LocalizedForm1.en-US.resources'
{
  // Offset: 0x00000000 Length: 0x00000362
}
.mresource public 'WinResLocalizedFormSample.LocalizedForm2.en-US.resources'
{
  // Offset: 0x00000368 Length: 0x0000028E
}
.module WinResLocalizedFormSample.Resources.dll
```

Figure 13.29   ildasm Showing a Culture-Specific Resource Satellite Assembly

Figure 13.29 shows two localized forms, one for each of the .resources files passed to the al.exe file. In addition, notice that the locale has been set to en-US in the .assembly block. This locale setting is reserved for resource-only satellite assemblies and is used by the resource manager to confirm that the loaded resources match the folder and assembly name used to find the satellite assembly.

Resource Probing

After you create localized resources and store them in either the main assembly (culture-neutral resources) or satellite assemblies (culture-specific resources), an application needs a way to find the appropriate localization data.

As you saw earlier, Thread.CurrentCulture provides access to localization data that's stored on a per-system basis. For per-form localization, the resource manager uses the CurrentUICulture property of the current thread to determine which culture's resources to load. When the resource manager needs its first resource, it *probes* the file system for a satellite assembly that contains the appropriate culture-specific resource.

Based on the assembly name of the type it's loaded with, the ResourceManager component looks in 16 places for the assembly, specifically targeting executables (.exes) and libraries (.dlls). It probes satellite assemblies first for country- and language-specific resources and then for country-neutral and language-specific resources, before falling back on the culture-neutral resources bundled with the calling assembly. Assuming an assembly name of LocalizedDataSample, Table 13.1 shows the relative paths that the resource manager probes looking for localized resources.

Table 13.1 Resource Manager Probing for Localized Resources

Relative Probed Assembly Name
Country- and Language-Specific Probing
1. en-US/**LocalizedDataSample**.resources.DLL
2. en-US/**LocalizedDataSample**.resources/**LocalizedDataSample**.resources.DLL
3. bin/en-US/**LocalizedDataSample**.resources.DLL
4. bin/en-US/**LocalizedDataSample**.resources/**LocalizedDataSample**.resources.DLL
5. en-US/**LocalizedDataSample**.resources.EXE
6. en-US/**LocalizedDataSample**.resources/**LocalizedDataSample**.resources.EXE
7. bin/en-US/**LocalizedDataSample**.resources.EXE
8. bin/en-US/**LocalizedDataSample**.resources/**LocalizedDataSample**.resources.EXE

Table 13.1   Resource Manager Probing for Localized Resources (Continued)

Country-Neutral and Language-Specific Probing
9. en/**LocalizedDataSample**.resources.**DLL**
10. en/**LocalizedDataSample**.resources/**LocalizedDataSample**.resources.**DLL**
11. bin/en/**LocalizedDataSample**.resources.**DLL**
12. bin/en/**LocalizedDataSample**.resources/**LocalizedDataSample**.resources.**DLL**
13. en/**LocalizedDataSample**.resources.**EXE**
14. en/**LocalizedDataSample**.resources/**LocalizedDataSample**.resources.**EXE**
15. bin/en/**LocalizedDataSample**.resources.**EXE**
16. bin/en/**LocalizedDataSample**.resources/**LocalizedDataSample**.resources.**EXE**

When the main assembly code also contains the culture-specific resources, you can avoid unnecessary resource probing by marking the main assembly as culture-specific; to do this, you apply the NeutralResourcesLanguage attribute (from the System.Resources namespace) to the assembly as a whole.[15] The following is an example of marking an assembly's resources as country- and language-specific:

```
using System.Resources;
...
// Mark all resources in this assembly as U.S. English.
// No probing will be done in the en-US culture.
[assembly: NeutralResourcesLanguage("en-US")]
```

The following is an example of marking an assembly's resources as country-neutral and language-specific:

```
using System.Resources;
...
// Mark all resources in this assembly as country-neutral English.
// Probing will be done for country-specific resources but
// will stop when country-neutral resources are needed.
[assembly: NeutralResourcesLanguage("en")]
```

You can circumvent the probing process using the NeutralResourcesLanguage attribute, but you need to rely on the resource manager to decide which set of resource data to rely on when resources exist for multiple languages for a specific culture.

---

[15] The VS05-generated AssemblyInfo.cs file is a handy place to put assembly-level attributes.

Resource Resolution

When multiple resources match the current culture, the resource manager must choose among them. For example, if an application is running under the fr-CA culture, a resource with the same name can be present in an fr-CA satellite assembly, in an fr satellite assembly, and in the main assembly itself. When multiple assemblies can contain a resource, the resource manager looks first in the most specific assembly, that is, the culture-specific assembly. If that's not present, the language-specific assembly is checked, and finally the culture-neutral resources.

For example, imagine a form that has three resource-specific Text properties: one for a Label control, one for a Button control, and one for the Form itself. Imagine further that there are two satellite assemblies—one for fr-CA and one for fr—along with the neutral resources bundled into the form's assembly. Figure 13.30 shows how the resource manager resolves the resources while running in the en-US culture.

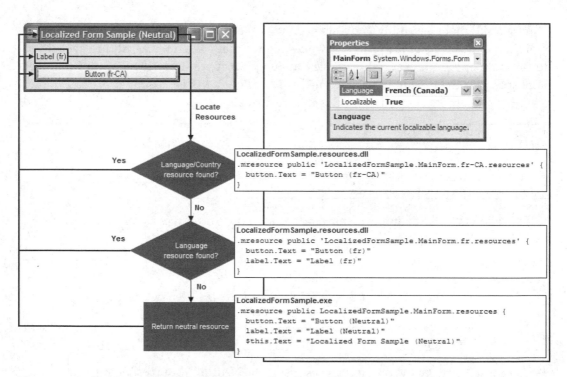

Figure 13.30   The Resource Manager's Resource Resolution Algorithm

Remember that the resource manager always looks for the most specific resource it can find. So even though there are three instances of the button's Text property, the most culture-specific resource in the fr-CA assembly "overrides" the other two. Similarly, the language-specific resource for the label is pulled from the fr assembly only because it's not present in the fr-CA assembly. Finally, the culture-neutral resource is pulled from the main assembly for the form's Text property when it's not found in the satellite assemblies. This resolution algorithm enables resources that are shared between all cultures to be set in the culture-neutral resources, leaving the culture-specific resources for overriding only the things that are culture specific.

However, resolving resources in less-culture-specific assemblies works only when a resource is missing from the more-culture-specific assembly. Both VS05 and WinRes are smart about putting only those properties that have changed into a more-culture-specific assembly.

Testing Resource Resolution

To test that resource resolution is working the way you think it should, you can manually set the CurrentUICulture property of the current thread:

```
// Program.cs
using System.Threading;
...
[STAThread]
static void Main() {
  ...
  // Test localized resources under fr-CA culture
  Thread.CurrentThread.CurrentUICulture = new CultureInfo("fr-CA");

  Application.Run(new MainForm());
}
```

CurrentUICulture defaults to the current culture setting of Windows itself, and this is why you don't need to set it unless you want a culture other than the current one. Whether you use the current Windows culture or some alternative culture, the culture used by the resource manager is the value of CurrentUICulture at the time the ApplyResources method is invoked for a form or control. As a rule of thumb for ensuring that the desired culture takes effect, set CurrentUICulture before the call to InitializeComponent in places like the application's entry point.

Input Language

Closely related to a thread's current culture is the *input language* to which the keyboard is currently mapped. The input language determines which keys map to which characters. Input language support is exposed by the .NET Framework as the InputLanguage type, which offers a variety of support for inspecting and changing culture and language information:

```
namespace System.Windows.Forms {
  sealed class InputLanguage {
    // Properties
    public CultureInfo Culture { get; }
    public static InputLanguage CurrentInputLanguage { get; set; }
    public static InputLanguage DefaultInputLanguage { get; }
    public static
       InputLanguageCollection InstalledInputLanguages { get; }
    public string LayoutName { get; }

    // Methods
    public static InputLanguage FromCulture(CultureInfo culture);
  }
}
```

For example, to enumerate the list of installed layouts, you use the InputLanguage type's InstalledInputLanguages property:

```
void listInputLanguagesButton_Click(
  object sender, EventArgs e) {
  foreach( InputLanguage lng in
    InputLanguage.InstalledInputLanguages ) {
    string language = lng.LayoutName + " [" + lng.Culture + "]";
    this.inputLanguagesList.Items.Add(language);
  }
}
```

Figure 13.31 shows the result of executing this code on a computer with three input languages, including U.S. English, Australian English, and Canadian French.

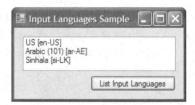

Figure 13.31   Discovering a Computer's Input Languages

As a further means of testing your application in alternative cultures, the Windows Forms Application class supports switchable input languages. You can change the current input language by setting one of the installed input languages to either of two properties of the InputLanguage class (which is also wrapped by the Application.CurrentInput-Language property):

```
// Change input language to Australian English
InputLanguage lng = InputLanguage.FromCulture(new CultureInfo("en-AU"));
Application.CurrentInputLanguage = lng; // one way
InputLanguage.CurrentInputLanguage = lng; // another way
```

The default system input language is available via the DefaultInputLanguage property of the InputLanguage class, should you need to reinstate it:

```
// Reinstate default
Application.CurrentInputLanguage = InputLanguage.DefaultInputLanguage;
```

.NET offers various input language support features that you should become familiar with when globalizing your applications.

Reading Direction

One feature that internationalized applications may need is the ability to support both right-to-left and left-to-right reading order. You can toggle all the text on a form between left and right alignments, including the form's caption and text on child controls, by toggling the RightToLeft property:

```
partial class MainForm : Form {
  void ltrRadioButton_CheckedChanged(object sender, EventArgs e) {
    // For text
    this.RightToLeft = RightToLeft.No;
  }
  void rtlRadioButton_CheckedChanged(object sender, EventArgs e) {
    // For text
    this.RightToLeft = RightToLeft.Yes;
  }
}
```

Figure 13.32 illustrates the effect of toggling the RightToLeft property.

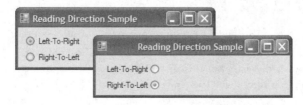

Figure 13.32   Toggling the Form's RightToLeft Property

Unfortunately, even though the text is swapped between left- and right-aligned, you can see that the controls hosted by the form aren't themselves changing alignment, just as the form's adornments remain where they are.[16] What we really need to do is swap the whole UI between left-to-right and right-to-left layout. We can do that by toggling a form's Right-ToLeftLayout property:

new

```
partial class MainForm : Form {
    void ltrRadioButton_CheckedChanged(object sender, EventArgs e) {
        // For text
        this.RightToLeft = RightToLeft.No;
    }
    void rtlRadioButton_CheckedChanged(object sender, EventArgs e) {
        // For text
        this.RightToLeft = RightToLeft.Yes;
    }
    void rtlLayoutCheckBox_CheckedChanged(object sender, EventArgs e) {
        this.RightToLeftLayout = this.rtlLayoutCheckBox.Checked;
    }
}
```

Toggling RightToLeftLayout yields the behavior illustrated in Figure 13.33.

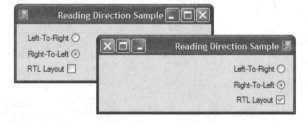

Figure 13.33　Toggling the Form's RightToLeftLayout Property

The best thing about both properties is that they are localizable, so, for example, you could ensure that all English-derived languages are laid out left-to-right and that all Arabic-derived languages are laid out right-to-left, changing the values of RightToLeft and Right-ToLeftLayout as necessary between languages.[17]

---

[16] The adornments are the system menu and the minimize, maximize, and close buttons.

[17] As you saw in Chapter 6: Drawing Text, painting complex scripts can be problematic with GDI+. See http://www.microsoft.com/middleeast/msdn/visualstudio2005.aspx (http://tinysells.com/27) for more information on the finer points of right-to-left text rendering.

Where Are We?

Resources are a great way to bundle arbitrary data, both untyped (in manifest resources) and typed (in .resources resources). VS05 provides extensive support for embedding both kinds of resources, even providing them on a per-component basis or, for even more usability, as strongly typed properties. And for forms that need to support internationalization, VS05 handles that, too, although WinRes is a better choice when nondevelopers are doing specific localization.

14

Applications

APPLICATIONS HAVE SPECIAL SUPPORT in Windows Forms. For starters, you can manage and tailor your application's lifetime, and, when the work flow is disrupted by an unhandled exception, you can choose from several methods of response. Then, there are several application models that you can employ, including Single Document Interface (SDI) and Multiple Document Interface (MDI) applications, each of which can support either multiple-instance or single-instance mode, the former the VS05 default and the latter requiring special consideration. All applications, however, can discover and use a wide variety of information about the system and environment they execute in.

This chapter focuses on these topics in depth, and starts by defining what an application actually is.

Applications

An *application* is anything with an .exe extension that can be started from the Windows shell. However, applications are also provided for directly in Windows Forms by the Application class:

```
namespace System.Windows.Forms {
    sealed class Application {

        // Properties
        public static bool AllowQuit { get; }
        public static string CommonAppDataPath { get; }
        public static RegistryKey CommonAppDataRegistry { get; }
        public static string CompanyName { get; }
        public static CultureInfo CurrentCulture { get; set; }
        public static InputLanguage CurrentInputLanguage { get; set; }
        public static string ExecutablePath { get; }
        public static string LocalUserAppDataPath { get; }
        public static bool MessageLoop { get; }
```

```
        public static FormCollection OpenForms { get; } // New
        public static string ProductName { get; }
        public static string ProductVersion { get; }
        public static bool RenderWithVisualStyles { get; } // New
        public static string SafeTopLevelCaptionFormat { get; set; }
        public static string StartupPath { get; }
        public static string UserAppDataPath { get; }
        public static RegistryKey UserAppDataRegistry { get; }
        public static bool UseWaitCursor { get; set; } // New
        public static VisualStyleState VisualStyleState { get; set; } // New

        // Methods
        public static void AddMessageFilter(IMessageFilter value);
        public static void DoEvents();
        public static void EnableVisualStyles();
        public static void Exit();
        public static void Exit(CancelEventArgs e); // New
        public static void ExitThread();
        public static bool FilterMessage(ref Message message); // New
        public static ApartmentState OleRequired();
        public static void OnThreadException(Exception t);
        public static void RaiseIdle(EventArgs e); // New
        public static void RegisterMessageLoop(
          MessageLoopCallback callback); // New
        public static void RemoveMessageFilter(IMessageFilter value);
        public static void Restart(); // New
        public static void Run();
        public static void Run(ApplicationContext context);
        public static void Run(Form mainForm);
        public static void SetCompatibleTextRenderingDefault(
          bool defaultValue); // New
        public static bool SetSuspendState(
          PowerState state, bool force, bool disableWakeEvent); // New
        public static void SetUnhandledExceptionMode(
          UnhandledExceptionMode mode); // New
        public static void SetUnhandledExceptionMode(
          UnhandledExceptionMode mode, bool threadScope); // New
        public static void UnregisterMessageLoop();// New

        // Events
        public static event EventHandler ApplicationExit;
        public static event EventHandler EnterThreadModal; // New
        public static event EventHandler Idle;
        public static event EventHandler LeaveThreadModal; // New
        public static event ThreadExceptionEventHandler ThreadException;
        public static event EventHandler ThreadExit;
    }
  }
```

Notice that all the members of the Application class are static. Although there is per-application state in Windows Forms, there is no instance of an Application class. Instead, the Application class is a scoping mechanism for exposing the various services that the class provides, including control of application lifetime and support for message handling.

Application Lifetime

A Windows Forms application starts when the Main method is called. However, to initialize a Windows Forms application fully and start it routing Windows Forms events, you need to invoke Application.Run in one of three ways.

The first is simply to call Run with no arguments. This approach is useful only if other means have already been used to show an initial UI:

```
// Program.cs
static class Program {

  [STAThread]
  static void Main() {
    ...
    // Create and show the main form modelessly
    MainForm form = new MainForm();
    form.Show();

    // Run the application
    Application.Run();
  }
}
```

When you call Run with no arguments, the application runs until explicitly told to stop, even when all its forms are closed. This puts the burden on some part of the application to call the Application class Exit method, typically when the main application form is closing:

```
// MainForm.cs
partial class MainForm : Form {
  ...
  void MainForm_FormClosed(object sender, FormClosedEventArgs e) {
    // Close the application when the main form goes away
    // Only for use when Application.Run is called without
    // any arguments
    Application.Exit();
  }
  ...
}
```

Typically, you call Application.Run without any arguments only when the application needs a secondary UI thread. A *UI thread* is one that calls Application.Run and can process the events that drive a Windows application. Because a vast majority of applications contain a single UI thread and because most of them have a *main form* that, when closed, causes the application to exit, another overload of the Run method is used far more often. This overload of Run takes as an argument a reference to the form designated as the main form. When Run is called in this way, it shows the main form and doesn't return until the main form closes:

```
// Program.cs
static class Program {

  [STAThread]
  static void Main() {
    ...
    // Create the main form
    MainForm form = new MainForm();

    // Run the application until the main form is closed
    Application.Run(form);
  }
}
```

In this case, there is no need for explicit code to exit the application. Instead, Application watches for the main form to close before exiting.

Application Context

Internally, the Run method creates an instance of the ApplicationContext class. ApplicationContext detects main form closure and exits the application as appropriate:

```
namespace System.Windows.Forms {
  class ApplicationContext {

    // Constructors
    public ApplicationContext();
    public ApplicationContext(Form mainForm);

    // Properties
    public Form MainForm { get; set; }
    public object Tag { get; set; } // New

    // Events
    public event EventHandler ThreadExit;

    // Methods
    public void ExitThread();
    protected virtual void ExitThreadCore();
    protected virtual void OnMainFormClosed(object sender, EventArgs e);
  }
}
```

In fact, the Run method allows you to pass an ApplicationContext yourself:

```
// Program.cs
static class Program {

  [STAThread]
  static void Main() {
    ...
    // Run the application with a context
    ApplicationContext ctx = new ApplicationContext(new MainForm());
    Application.Run(ctx);

  }
}
```

This is useful if you'd like to derive from the ApplicationContext class and provide your own custom context:

```
// TimedApplicationContext.cs
class TimedApplicationContext : ApplicationContext {

  Timer timer = new Timer();

  public TimedApplicationContext(Form mainForm) : base(mainForm) {
    timer.Tick += timer_Tick;
    timer.Interval = 5000; // 5 seconds
    timer.Enabled = true;
  }

  void timer_Tick(object sender, EventArgs e) {
    timer.Enabled = false;
    timer.Dispose();

    DialogResult res =
      MessageBox.Show(
        "OK to charge your credit card?",
        "Time's Up!",
        MessageBoxButtons.YesNo);

    if( res == DialogResult.No ) {
      // See ya...
      this.MainForm.Close();
    }
  }
}

// Program.cs
static class Program {
```

```
[STAThread]
static void Main() {
  ...
  // Run the application with a custom context
  TimedApplicationContext ctx =
    new TimedApplicationContext(new MainForm());
  Application.Run(ctx);
}
}
```

This custom context class waits for five seconds after an application has started and then asks to charge the user's credit card. If the answer is no, the main form of the application is closed (available from the MainForm property of the base ApplicationContext class), causing the application to exit.

You might also encounter situations when you'd like to stop the application from exiting when the main form goes away, such as an application that's serving .NET remoting clients and needs to stick around even if the user has closed the main form.[1] In these situations, you override the OnMainFormClosed method from the ApplicationContext base class:

```
// RemotingServerApplicationContext.cs
class RemotingServerApplicationContext : ApplicationContext {

  public RemotingServerApplicationContext(Form mainForm) :
    base(mainForm) {}

  protected override void OnMainFormClosed(object sender, EventArgs e) {
    // Don't let base class exit application
    if( this.IsServicingRemotingClient() ) return;

    // Let base class exit application
    base.OnMainFormClosed(sender, e);
  }

  protected bool IsServicingRemotingClient() {...}
}
```

When all the .NET remoting clients have exited, you must make sure that Application.Exit is called, in this case by calling the base ApplicationContext class's OnMainFormClosed method.

---

[1] .NET remoting is a technology that allows objects to talk to each other across application and machine boundaries. Remoting is beyond the scope of this book but is covered very nicely in Ingo Rammer's book *Advanced .NET Remoting* (APress, 2002).

Application Events

During the lifetime of an application, several key application events—Idle, ThreadExit, and ApplicationExit—are fired by the Application object. You can subscribe to application events at any time, but it's most common to do it in the Main function:

```
// Program.cs
static class Program {

  [STAThread]
  static void Main() {
    ...
    Application.Idle += App_Idle;
    Application.ThreadExit += App_ThreadExit;
    Application.ApplicationExit += App_ApplicationExit;

    // Run the application
    Application.Run(new MainForm());
  }

  static void App_Idle(object sender, EventArgs e) {...}
  static void App_ThreadExit(object sender, EventArgs e) {...}
  static void App_ApplicationExit(object sender, EventArgs e) {...}
}
```

The Idle event happens when a series of events have been dispatched to event handlers and no more events are waiting to be processed. The Idle event can sometimes be used to perform concurrent processing in tiny chunks, but it's much more convenient and robust to use worker threads for those kinds of activities. This technique is covered in Chapter 18: Multithreaded User Interfaces.

When a UI thread is about to exit, it receives a notification via the ThreadExit event. When the last UI thread goes away, the application's ApplicationExit event is fired.

UI Thread Exceptions

One other application-level event that is fired as necessary by the Application object is the ThreadException event. This event is fired when a UI thread causes an exception to be thrown. This one is so important that Windows Forms provides a default handler if you don't.

The typical .NET unhandled-exception behavior on a user's machine yields a dialog, as shown in Figure 14.1.[2]

---

[2] A developer's machine is likely to have VS05 installed, and VS05 provides a much more detailed, developer-oriented dialog.

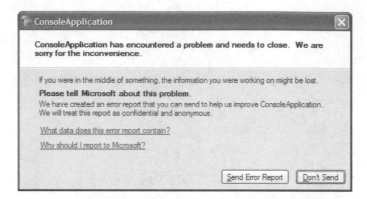

Figure 14.1   Default .NET Unhandled-Exception Dialog

This kind of exception handling tends to make users unhappy. This dialog isn't necessarily explicit about what actually happened, even if you view the data in the error report. And worse, there is no way to continue the application to attempt to save the data being worked on at the moment. On the other hand, a Windows Forms application that experiences an unhandled exception during the processing of an event shows a more specialized default dialog like the one in Figure 14.2.

Figure 14.2   Default Windows Forms Unhandled-Exception Dialog

This dialog is the ThreadExceptionDialog (from the System.Windows.Forms namespace), and it looks functionally the same as the one in Figure 14.1, with one important difference: The Windows Forms version has a Continue button. What's happening is that Windows Forms itself catches exceptions thrown by event handlers; in this way, even if that event handler caused an exception—for example, if a file couldn't be opened or there was a security violation—the user is allowed to continue running the application with the hope that saving will work, even if nothing else does. This safety net makes Windows Forms applications more robust in the face of even unhandled exceptions than Windows applications of old.

However, if an unhandled exception is caught, the application could be in an inconsistent state, so it's best to encourage your users to save their files and restart the application. To implement this, you replace the Windows Forms unhandled-exception dialog with an application-specific dialog by handling the application's thread exception event:

```
// Program.cs
static class Program {

  [STAThread]
  static void Main() {
    // Handle unhandled thread exceptions
    Application.ThreadException += App_ThreadException;
    ...
    // Run the application
    Application.Run(new MainForm());
  }

  static void App_ThreadException(
    object sender, ThreadExceptionEventArgs e) {
    // Does user want to save or quit?
    string msg =
      "A problem has occurred in this application:\r\n\r\n" +
      "\t" + e.Exception.Message + "\r\n\r\n" +
      "Would you like to continue the application so that\r\n" +
      "you can save your work?";
    DialogResult res = MessageBox.Show(
      msg,
      "Unexpected Error",
      MessageBoxButtons.YesNo);
    ...
  }
}
```

Notice that the thread exception handler takes a ThreadExceptionEventArgs object, which includes the exception that was thrown. This is handy if you want to tell the user what happened, as shown in Figure 14.3.

Figure 14.3 Custom Unhandled-Exception Dialog

If the user wants to return to the application to save work, all you need to do is return from the ThreadException event handler. If, on the other hand, the user decides not to continue with the application, calling Application.Exit shuts down the application. Both are shown here:

```
// Program.cs
static class Program {
  ...
  static void App_ThreadException(
    object sender, ThreadExceptionEventArgs e) {
    ...
    // Save or quit
    DialogResult res = MessageBox.Show(...);

    // If save: returning to continue the application and allow saving
    if( res == DialogResult.Yes ) return;

    // If quit: shut 'er down, Clancy, she's a'pumpin' mud!
    Application.Exit();
  }
}
```

Handling exceptions in this way gives users a way to make decisions about how an application will shut down, if at all, in the event of an exception. However, if it doesn't make sense for users to be involved in unhandled exceptions, you can make sure that the Thread-Exception event is never fired. Call Application.SetUnhandledExceptionMode:

```
Application.SetUnhandledExceptionMode(
  UnhandledExceptionMode.ThrowException);
```

Although it's not obvious from the enumeration value's name, this code actually prevents ThreadException from being fired. Instead, it dumps the user straight out of the application before displaying the .NET unhandled-exception dialog from Figure 14.1:

```
namespace System.Windows.Forms {
  enum UnhandledExceptionMode {
    Automatic = 0, // default
    ThrowException = 1, // Never fire Application.ThreadException
    CatchException = 2, // Always fire Application.ThreadException
  }
}
```

In general, the behavior exhibited by UnhandledExceptionMode.ThrowException isn't the most user friendly, or informative, when something catastrophic happens. Instead, it's much better to involve users in deciding how an application shuts down.

Going the other way, you can also use command line arguments to let users make decisions about how they want their application to start up.

Passing Command Line Arguments

Command line arguments allow users to determine an application's initial state and operational behavior when launched.[3] Before command line arguments can be processed to express a user's wishes, they need to be accessed. To do this, you change your application's entry point method, Main, to accept a string array to contain all the passed arguments:

```
// Program.cs
static class Program {
  [STAThread]
  static void Main(string[] args) {
    ...
  }
}
```

.NET constructs the string array by parsing the command line string, which means extracting substrings, delimited by spaces, and placing each substring into an element of the array. Command line syntax, which dictates which command line arguments your application can process and the format they should be entered in, is left up to you. Here is one simple approach:

```
// Program.cs
static class Program {
  [STAThread]
  static void Main(string[] args) {
    ...
    bool flag = false;
    string name = "";
    int number = 0;

    // *Very* simple command line parsing
    for( int i = 0; i != args.Length; ++i ) {
      switch( args[i] ) {
        case "/flag": flag = true; break;
        case "/name": name = args[++i]; break;
        case "/number": number = int.Parse(args[++i]); break;
        default: MessageBox.Show("Invalid args!"); return;
      }
    }
    ...
  }
}
```

[3] Application and user settings are another mechanism for doing so, and they are covered in Chapter 15: Settings.

If your static Main method isn't where you want to handle the command line arguments for your application session, GetCommandLineArgs can come in handy for retrieving the command line arguments for the current application session:[4]

```
// Program.cs
static class Program {
  [STAThread]
  static void Main() {
    ...
    string[] args = Environment.GetCommandLineArgs();

    // *Very* simple command line parsing
    // Note: Starting at item [1] because args item [0] is exe path
    for( int i = 1; i != args.Length; ++i ) {
      ...
    }
    ...
  }
}
```

You can see that GetCommandLineArgs always returns a string array with at least one item: the executable path.

Processing command line arguments is relatively straightforward, although special types of applications, known as single-instance applications, need to process command line arguments in special ways.

Single-Instance Applications

By default, each EXE is an application that has an independent lifetime, even if multiple instances of the same application are running at the same time. However, it's common to want to limit an EXE to a single instance, whether it's an SDI application with a single top-level window, an MDI application, or an SDI application with multiple top-level windows. All these kinds of applications require that another instance detect the initial instance and then cut its own lifetime short.

Single-Instance Detection and Management

You could build a custom single-instance application using custom code that incorporates threading and .NET remoting. However, the VB.NET runtime library, Microsoft. VisualBasic.dll, contains a class that provides such an implementation for you: WindowsFormsApplicationBase, located in the Microsoft.VisualBasic.ApplicationServices

---

[4] If you want to see more robust command line parsing support, see the Genghis class library, which is available at http://www.genghisgroup.com (http://tinysells.com/8).

namespace.[5] WindowsFormsApplicationBase does not inherit from the Application class in System.Windows.Forms, but WindowsFormsApplicationBase is designed to replace the use of the Application class to run and manage an application's lifetime, as you'll see shortly.

If you are using C#, you add a reference to this assembly by right-clicking the project and selecting Add Reference from the context menu. From the .NET tab of the subsequently loaded Add Reference dialog, select Microsoft.VisualBasic.dll. When this DLL is referenced, you derive from WindowsFormsApplicationBase before extending your custom class with support for single-instance applications and passing command line arguments:

```
// SingleInstanceApplication.cs
using Microsoft.VisualBasic.ApplicationServices;
...
class SingleInstanceApplication : WindowsFormsApplicationBase {...}
```

Next, you configure SingleInstanceApplication to support single-instance applications. Set the SingleInstanceApplication class's IsSingleInstance property (implemented by the base WindowsFormsApplicationBase class) to true:

```
// SingleInstanceApplication.cs
class SingleInstanceApplication : WindowsFormsApplicationBase {

  // Must call base constructor to ensure correct initial
  // WindowsFormsApplicationBase configuration
  public SingleInstanceApplication() {

    // This ensures the underlying single-SDI framework is employed,
    // and OnStartupNextInstance is fired
    this.IsSingleInstance = true;
  }
}
```

IsSingleInstance is false by default, and the constructor is a great place to change this situation. To incorporate this into your application, replace the standard application start-up logic from your application's entry point. Then, use the following code to create an instance of your custom WindowsFormsApplicationBase type:

```
// Program.cs
static class Program {
```

---

[5] It's difficult to determine why this nice feature wasn't folded into the .NET Framework, which would explicitly expose it to all languages. However, Microsoft.VisualBasic.dll ships with the .NET Framework, so it's available to any .NET language, in spite of its name.

```
  [STAThread]
  static void Main(string[] args) {
    Application.EnableVisualStyles();
    SingleInstanceApplication application =
      new SingleInstanceApplication();
    application.Run(args);
  }
}
```

WindowsFormsApplicationBase exposes the Run method—the Application.Run method analog—which you invoke to open the main application form. Additionally, Windows-FormsApplicationBase.Run expects a string array containing command line arguments; passing null causes an exception to be thrown.

To specify which form is the main application form, you override WindowsForms-ApplicationBase.OnCreateMainForm and set WindowsFormsApplicationBase.MainForm appropriately:

```
// SingleInstanceApplication.cs
class SingleInstanceApplication : WindowsFormsApplicationBase {
  ...
  protected override void OnCreateMainForm() {
    this.MainForm = new MainForm();
  }
}
```

As a final flourish, you can expose your custom WindowsFormsApplicationBase type via a static instantiation-helper method and thereby cut down on client code:

```
// SingleInstanceApplication.cs
class SingleInstanceApplication : WindowsFormsApplicationBase {

  static SingleInstanceApplication application;
  internal static SingleInstanceApplication Application {
    get {
      if( application == null ) {
        application = new SingleInstanceApplication();
      }
      return application;
    }
  }
  ...
}

// Program.cs
static class Program {
  ...
```

```
[STAThread]
static void Main(string[] args) {
  Application.EnableVisualStyles();
  SingleInstanceApplication.Application.Run(args);
}
}
```

The effect of SingleInstanceApplication is to restrict an application to only one instance, no matter how many times it is executed. This single-instance scheme works fine as is, but it works better when the first instance of the application has a need to get command line arguments from any subsequent instances. Multiple-SDI and single-MDI applications are examples of applications that use this kind of processing.

Multiple-SDI Applications

A *multiple-SDI* application has multiple windows for content, although each window is a top-level window. Internet Explorer and Office 2003 are popular examples of multiple-SDI applications.[6] Figure 14.4 shows an example of a multiple-SDI application.

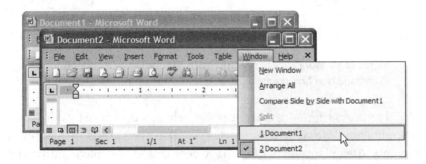

Figure 14.4   A Sample Multiple-SDI Application

A multiple-SDI application typically has the following features:

- A single instance of the application is running.
- Multiple top-level windows are running independently of each other.
- It doesn't reopen files that are currently loaded.
- When the last window goes away, the application does, too.
- A Window menu allows a user to see and select from the currently available windows.

[6] Internet Explorer can be configured to show each top-level window in its own process, making it an SDI application, or to share all windows in a single process, making it a multiple-SDI application.

When a document is created or opened, it is loaded into a new window each time, whether the file was requested via the menu system or the command line. The first time the application is called, the first new instance of the top-level form is created and set as the main application form instance; if a file was requested, it is also opened by the form.

Subsequent requests to the application are routed to the custom WindowsForms-ApplicationBase object located in the already-running application instance. Each request is handled to create a new form and build up the appropriate menu structures to support navigation between top-level instances, as well as opening and closing existing top-level instances. Figure 14.5 illustrates the work flow.

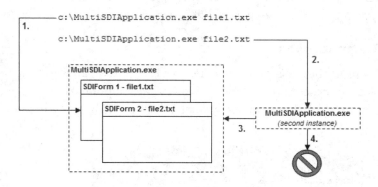

Figure 14.5   Work Flow of a Multiple-SDI Application with Support for Command Line Argument Passing

Multiple SDI requires single-instance support, which we acquire by deriving from WindowsFormsApplicationBase, as you saw earlier. We also need to ensure that the application stops running only after all top-level forms have been closed. We make the appropriate configurations from the constructor of the custom WindowsFormsApplicationBase class:

```
// MultiSDIApplication.cs
class MultiSDIApplication : WindowsFormsApplicationBase {

  static MultiSDIApplication application;
  internal static MultiSDIApplication Application {
    get {
      if( application == null ) {
        application = new MultiSDIApplication();
      }
      return application;
    }
  }
  public MultiSDIApplication() {
```

```
    // This ensures the underlying single-SDI framework is employed,
    // and OnStartupNextInstance is fired
    this.IsSingleInstance = true;

    // Needed for multiple SDI because no form is the main form
    this.ShutdownStyle = ShutdownMode.AfterAllFormsClose;
  }
}
```

By default, the ShutdownStyle for a WindowsFormsApplicationBase object is After-MainFormCloses, which refers to the form specified as the main form. However, with a multiple-instance SDI application, no form is the main form; therefore, no matter which form was created first, we want the application to close only after the last remaining top-level form is closed, and hence the need to explicitly set ShutdownStyle to AfterAllFormsClose.

Next, MultiSDIApplication must handle the first execution of the application. It does this by overriding OnCreateMainForm to create a new TopLevelForm object:

```
// MultiSDIApplication.cs
class MultiSDIApplication : WindowsFormsApplicationBase {
  ...
  public MultiSDIApplication() {...}

  // Create first top-level form
  protected override void OnCreateMainForm() {
    this.MainForm = this.CreateTopLevelWindow(this.CommandLineArgs);
  }

  TopLevelForm CreateTopLevelWindow(
    ReadOnlyCollection<string> args) {
    // Get file name, if provided
    string fileName = (args.Count > 0 ? args[0] : null);

    // Create a new top-level form
    return TopLevelForm.CreateTopLevelWindow(fileName);
  }
}
```

In this code, if a file argument was passed, a request is made to the main form to open it. Because all forms in a multiple-instance SDI application are top-level, however, no form is actually the main form. However, we must specify one if we override OnCreateMainForm, which helps later when the application needs to know which of the top-level forms is the active form. OnCreateMainForm passes the command line args—supplied by WindowsFormsApplicationBase.CommandLineArgs—to the helper Create TopLevel-Window method, which parses the args for a file name, passing whatever it finds to the static CreateTopLevelWindow method that's implemented by TopLevelForm. CreateTopLevel Window is static because no specific form instance is responsible for creating another form.

To cope with subsequent requests to launch the application, we again override OnStartup NextInstance:

```
// MultiSDIApplication.cs
class MultiSDIApplication : WindowsFormsApplicationBase {
  ...
  public MultiSDIApplication() {...}

  // Create first top-level form
  protected override void OnCreateMainForm() {...}

  // Create subsequent top-level form
  protected override void OnStartupNextInstance(
    StartupNextInstanceEventArgs e) {
    this.CreateTopLevelWindow(e.CommandLine);
  }

  TopLevelForm CreateTopLevelWindow(
    ReadOnlyCollection<string> args) {...}
}
```

Here, the helper CreateTopLevelWindow is again passed command line arguments and called upon to create a new top-level window, opening a file if necessary.

Multiple-instance SDI applications also allow files to be opened from existing top-level forms via the File | Open menu, something we implement using the same static Create TopLevelWindow method to open files from the command line:

```
// TopLevelForm.cs
partial class TopLevelForm : Form {
  ...
  string fileName;
  ...
  public static TopLevelForm CreateTopLevelWindow(string fileName) {
    // Detect whether file is already open
    if( !string.IsNullOrEmpty(fileName) ) {
      foreach( TopLevelForm openForm in Application.OpenForms ) {
        if( string.Compare(openForm.FileName, fileName, true) == 0 ) {
          // Bring form to top
          openForm.Activate();
          return openForm;
        }
      }
    }

    // Create new top-level form and open file
    TopLevelForm form = new TopLevelForm();
    form.OpenFile(fileName);
    form.Show();
```

```
    // Bring form to top
    openForm.Activate();
    return form;
  }

  void openToolStripMenuItem_Click(object sender, EventArgs e) {
    // Open new window
    if( this.openFileDialog.ShowDialog() == DialogResult.OK ) {
      TopLevelForm.CreateTopLevelWindow(this.openFileDialog.FileName);
    }
  }
  ...
  void OpenFile(string fileName) {
    this.fileName = fileName;
    using( StreamReader reader = new StreamReader(fileName) ) {
      textBox.Text = reader.ReadToEnd();
    }
    this.Text = this.Text + " (" + this.fileName + ")";
  }

  string FileName {
    get { return this.fileName; }
  }
}
```

CreateTopLevelWindow contains the code to check whether the desired file is already opened and, if it is, to bring the top-level window that contains it to the foreground; otherwise, the file is opened into a new top-level window.

Multiple-instance SDI applications also typically allow the creation of new files from the command line or from the File | New Window menu of a currently open top-level form. We tweak the OpenFile method to not open a file if null or if an empty string was passed as the file name:

```
// TopLevelForm.cs
partial class TopLevelForm : Form {
  ...
  static int formCount = 0;

  public TopLevelForm() {
    InitializeComponent();

    // Set form count
    ++formCount;
    this.Text += ": " + formCount.ToString();
  }
  ...
  public static TopLevelForm CreateTopLevelWindow(string fileName) {
    ...
```

```
      // Create new top-level form and open file
      TopLevelForm form = new TopLevelForm();
      form.OpenFile(fileName);
      form.Show();
      ...
    }

    void newWindowToolStripMenuItem_Click(
      object sender, EventArgs e) {
      // Open new window
      TopLevelForm.CreateTopLevelWindow(null);
    }
    ...
    void OpenFile(string fileName) {
      this.fileName = fileName;
      if( !string.IsNullOrEmpty(fileName) ) {
        using( StreamReader reader = new StreamReader(fileName) ) {
          textBox.Text = reader.ReadToEnd();
        }
      }
      else this.fileName = "Untitled" + formCount.ToString();
      this.Text = this.Text + " (" + this.fileName + ")";
    }
    ...
}
```

Because a new file doesn't have a name, the top-level form gives it one; the standard naming convention for a new file is the concatenation of some default text with a version number. In this example, we use a combination of "Untitled" and an incremental count of the number of opened top-level forms, for uniqueness.

As mentioned before, a multiple-SDI application should implement a menu that allows users to navigate between open top-level forms as this is easier when files have unique names. MultiSDIApplication is an appropriate location for this logic because it manages the application:

```
// MultiSDIApplication.cs
class MultiSDIApplication : WindowsFormsApplicationBase {
  ...
  public void AddTopLevelForm(Form form) {

    // Add form to collection of forms and
    // watch for it to activate and close
    form.Activated += Form_Activated;
    form.FormClosed += Form_FormClosed;
```

```
      // Set initial top-level form to activate
      if( this.OpenForms.Count == 1 ) this.MainForm = form;
    }

  void Form_Activated(object sender, EventArgs e) {
      // Set the currently active form
      this.MainForm = (Form)sender;
    }

  void Form_ FormClosed(object sender, FormClosedEventArgs e) {
      // Set a new "main" if necessary
      if( ((Form)sender == this.MainForm) &&
          (this.OpenForms.Count > 0) ) {
        this.MainForm = (Form)this.OpenForms[0];
      }

      form.Activated -= Form_Activated;
      form.FormClosed -= Form_FormClosed;
    }
  }
```

The MultiSDIApplication class uses the AddTopLevelForm method to keep track of a list of top-level forms as they are added. Each new form is kept in a collection and is watched for Activated and FormClosed events. When a top-level form is activated, it becomes the new "main" form, which is the one whose closure is detected by the base ApplicationContext class. When a top-level form closes, it's removed from the list. If the closed form was the main form, another form is promoted to that lofty position. When the last form goes away, the base ApplicationContext class notices and exits the application.

To keep the context up-to-date with the current list of top-level forms, the custom context watches for the Closed event on all forms. In addition, the custom context needs to be notified when a new top-level form has come into existence, a task that is best handled by the new form itself:

```
// TopLevelForm.cs
partial class TopLevelForm : Form {
  ...
  public TopLevelForm() {
    ...
    // Add new top-level form to the application context
    MultiSDIApplication.Application.AddTopLevelForm(this);
    ...
  }
  ...
}
```

The only remaining task is to designate and populate the Window menu with one menu item for each top-level form. The forms themselves can do this by handling the Drop-DownOpening event on the ToolStripMenuItem's Window object, using that opportunity to build the list of submenu items based on the names of all the forms. However, this code is boilerplate, so it's a good candidate to be handled by MultiSDIApplication on behalf of all top-level windows, from the AddWindowMenu method:

```
// MultiSDIApplication.cs
class MultiSDIApplication : WindowsFormsApplicationBase {
  ...
  public void AddWindowMenu(ToolStripMenuItem windowMenu) {
    // Handle tool strip menu item's drop-down opening event
    windowMenu.DropDownOpening += windowMenu_DropDownOpening;
  }
}
```

Each top-level form with a Window menu can add it to the context, along with itself, when it's created:

```
// TopLevelForm.cs
partial class TopLevelForm : Form {
  ...
  public TopLevelForm() {
    ...
    // Add Window ToolStripMenuItem to the application context
    MultiSDIApplication.Application.AddWindowMenu(
      this.windowToolStripMenuItem);
    ...
  }
  ...
}
```

Now, when the Window menu is shown on any top-level window, the Drop-DownOpening event fires. This constructs a new menu showing the currently open top-level forms during the time gap between mouse click and menu display:

```
// MultiSDIApplication.cs
class MultiSDIApplication : WindowsFormsApplicationBase {
  ...
  void windowMenu_DropDownOpening(object sender, EventArgs e) {
    ToolStripMenuItem menu = (ToolStripMenuItem)sender;

    // Clear current menu
    if( menu.DropDownItems.Count > 0 ) {
      menu.DropDown.Dispose();
    }
    menu.DropDown = new ToolStripDropDown();
```

```
    // Populate menu with one item for each open top-level form
    foreach( Form form in this.OpenForms ) {
      ToolStripMenuItem item = new ToolStripMenuItem();
      item.Text = form.Text;
      item.Tag = form;
      menu.DropDownItems.Add(item);
      item.Click += WindowMenuItem_Click;

      // Check menu item that represents currently active window
      if( form == this.MainForm ) item.Checked = true;
    }
  }
}
```

As each menu item is added to the Window menu, a handler is added to the Click event so that the appropriate form can be activated when it's selected. The form associated with the ToolStripMenuItem's Tag property is extracted and activated:

```
// MultiSDIApplication.cs
class MultiSDIApplication : WindowsFormsApplicationBase {
  ...
  void WindowMenuItem_Click(object sender, EventArgs e) {
    // Activate top-level form based on selection
    ((Form)((ToolStripMenuItem)sender).Tag).Activate();
  }
  ...
}
```

That's it. The extensible lifetime management of Windows Forms applications via a custom application context, along with a helper to find and activate application instances already running, provides all the help we need to build a multiple-SDI application in only a few lines of code. The result is shown in Figure 14.6.

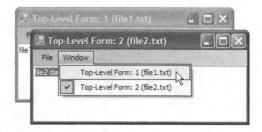

Figure 14.6   Multiple-Instance SDI Application in Action

Multiple-SDI applications share much in common with MDI applications, although each document in an MDI application is loaded into a child window rather than a new main window. The key similarities include the requirement for MDI applications to be managed from a single executable and the ability to handle command line parameters.

Single-MDI Applications

Consider an MDI application like Microsoft Excel; files opened from the file system (by double-clicking) are all opened as separate child windows within the parent Excel window.[7] For the first instance of an MDI application to open a new child window to display the file that was passed to the second instance of the application, the second instance must be able to communicate with the initial instance.

A single-MDI application exhibits the characteristics we described in Chapter 2: Forms, as well as the following features:

- A single instance of the application is running.
- Multiple MDI child windows are running within the same MDI parent window.
- Currently opened files are not reopened.
- When the last MDI child window goes away, the application remains.
- When the MDI parent window goes away, the application exits.
- A Window menu allows a user to see and select from the currently available windows.

The work flow for a single-MDI application ensures that a new MDI child form is opened each time the application is called, whether or not a file was requested for opening.

The first time the application is called, the MDI parent is created and set as the main application form instance; if a file was requested, it is also opened into a new MDI child form. Subsequent requests to the application are routed through the MDI parent form to create a new MDI child form and build up the appropriate menu structures to support navigation between top-level instances, as well as opening and closing existing top-level instances. Figure 14.7 illustrates the work flow.

---

[7] The fundamentals of building an MDI application in Windows Forms are described in Chapter 2: Forms.

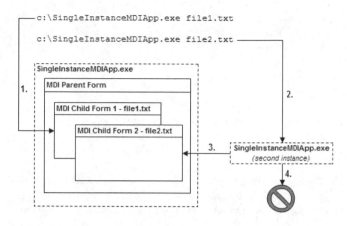

Figure 14.7   Work Flow of a Single-MDI Application with Support
for Passing Command Line Arguments

With WindowsFormsApplicationBase ensuring that only one instance of the application
executes, we need to handle two specific scenarios: first, when arguments are passed from
the command line directly when the first instance loads and, second, when the first instance
is passed command line arguments from a second instance.

Handling the first scenario requires a main application form that's an MDI parent and
can open a new or existing file into an MDI child form:

```
// MDIParentForm.cs
partial class MDIParentForm : Form {
  ...
  // This is necessary to bring the MDI parent window to the front,
  // because Activate and BringToFront don't seem to have any effect.
  [DllImport("user32.dll")]
  static extern bool SetForegroundWindow(IntPtr hWnd);

  public void CreateMDIChildWindow(string fileName) {

    SetForegroundWindow(this.Handle);

    // Detect whether file is already open
    if( !string.IsNullOrEmpty(fileName) ) {
      foreach( MDIChildForm openForm in this.MdiChildren ) {
        if( string.Compare(openForm.FileName, fileName, true) == 0 ) {
          openForm.Activate();
          return;
        }
      }
    }
```

```
    // If file not open, open it
    MDIChildForm form = new MDIChildForm();
    form.OpenFile(fileName);
    form.MdiParent = this;
    form.Show();
  }

  void newToolStripMenuItem_Click(object sender, EventArgs e) {
    this.CreateMDIChildWindow(null);
  }

  void openToolStripMenuItem_Click(object sender, EventArgs e) {
    if( this.openFileDialog.ShowDialog() == DialogResult.OK ) {
      this.CreateMDIChildWindow(this.openFileDialog.FileName);
    }
  }
  ...
}
```

This code allows users to open a file using a menu strip item, and it lays the foundation for opening a file from the command line, including preventing the reopening of an already open file. We continue using WindowsFormsApplicationBase to achieve this, updating the earlier sample to acquire the command line arguments and pass them to the application main form's CreateMDIChildWindow method to open a file:

```
// SingleMDIApplication.cs
class SingleMDIApplication : WindowsFormsApplicationBase {

  static SingleMDIApplication application;
  internal static SingleMDIApplication Application {
    get {
      if( application == null ) {
        application = new SingleMDIApplication();
      }
      return application;
    }
  }

  public SingleMDIApplication() {
    // This ensures the underlying single-SDI framework is employed,
    // and OnStartupNextInstance is fired
    this.IsSingleInstance = true;
  }

  // Load MDI parent form and first MDI child form
  protected override void OnCreateMainForm() {
```

```
      this.MainForm = new MDIParentForm();
      this.CreateMDIChildWindow(this.CommandLineArgs);
   }

   void CreateMDIChildWindow(ReadOnlyCollection<string> args) {
      // Get file name, if provided
      string fileName = (args.Count > 0 ? args[0] : null);

      // Ask MDI parent to create a new MDI child
      // and open file
      ((MDIParentForm)this.MainForm).CreateMDIChildWindow(fileName);
   }
}
```

During construction, we specify that this application is a single-instance application. Unlike with multiple-SDI applications, however, we don't need to set the ShutdownStyle property because its value defaults to AfterMainFormCloses—exactly what is needed for an MDI application.

OnCreateMainForm creates the MDI parent form and sets it as the application's main form and the one responsible for creating MDI child windows. Then, the command line arguments are passed to the helper CreateMDIChildWindow method, which parses them for a file name. Either a file name or null is passed to the MDI parent form's version of CreateMDIChildWindow, which creates the new MDI child window, into which it loads a file; then CreateMDIChildWindow establishes the MDI parent-child relationship and shows the requested file. CreateMDIChildWindow also activates the MDI parent form to bring the application to the foreground.

In the second scenario, the desired processing is for the command line arguments to be passed from the second instance to the first, to which the first instance responds by processing the command line arguments and, if required, creating a new MDI child form. WindowsFormsApplicationBase handles the underlying mechanics of passing arguments from the second instance to the first, but it is up to you to process the command line arguments accordingly. You can achieve this by overriding WindowsFormsApplicationBase.OnStartup-NextInstance, which passes the command line arguments via the CommandLine property of a StartupNextInstanceEventArgs object. The following code shows the OnStartupNextInstance override implementation:

```
// SingleMDIApplication.cs
class SingleMDIApplication : WindowsFormsApplicationBase {
   ...
   // Must call base constructor to ensure correct initial
   // WindowsFormsApplicationBase configuration
   public SingleMDIApplication() {...}
```

```
// Load MDI parent form and first MDI child form
protected override void OnCreateMainForm() {...}

// Load subsequent MDI child form
protected override void OnStartupNextInstance(
  StartupNextInstanceEventArgs e) {
  this.CreateMDIChildWindow (e.CommandLine);
}

void CreateMDIChildWindow(ReadOnlyCollection<string> args) {...}
}
```

As you can see, centralizing CreateMDIChildWindow into a single helper method greatly simplifies the implementation of OnStartupNextInstance.

That's the complete solution, so let's look at how it operates. Suppose we start the application for the first time by executing the following statement from the command line:

```
C:\SingleInstanceSample.exe C:\file1.txt
```

The result is to load the application, configure the single-instance command line argument (passing support from our derivation of WindowsFormsApplicationBase), load the main MDI parent form, and, finally, open an MDI child form, displaying the file specified from the command line arguments. Figure 14.8 illustrates the result.

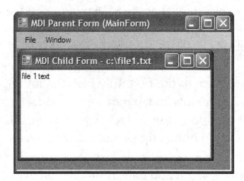

Figure 14.8   Result of Creating a First Instance of a Single-Instance Application

Now, consider the next statement being called while the first instance is still executing:

```
C:\SingleInstanceSample.exe C:\file2.txt
```

This time, a second instance of the application is created, but—thanks to SingleMDI-Application, our WindowsFormsApplicationBase derivation—the second instance passes its command line arguments to the first instance before closing itself down. The first instance processes the incoming command line arguments from OnStartupNextInstance, requesting the MDI parent form to open a new MDI child and display the specified file. The result is shown in Figure 14.9.

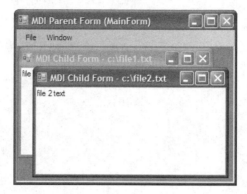

Figure 14.9   Result of Creating a Second Instance of a Single-Instance Application

Although it would be difficult to code single-instance applications such as single MDI and multiple SDI by hand, the presence of support in the Visual Basic runtime assembly makes life a lot easier. This is one of the strengths of Windows Forms; unlike forms packages of old, Windows Forms is only one part of a much larger, integrated whole. When its windowing classes don't meet your needs, you still have all the rest of the .NET Framework Class Library to fall back on.

Where Are We?

The seemingly simple application architecture in Windows Forms and .NET provides some useful capabilities, including tailored lifetime support and support for building SDI and MDI applications, whether multiple or single-instance.

15

Settings

S OME WINDOWS FORMS APPLICATIONS can happily operate in a microcosm, but most real-world applications rely on information from the environment around them. This information can come from many sources and is dictated by an application, its users, and even the machine on which an application executes.

.NET provides several specialized classes that applications can use to inspect their operational environment, as well as a comprehensive system for managing application- and user-specific settings. There are several additional options along these lines, including environment variables, command line arguments, .config files, the Registry, and special folders.

The Application Environment

During its lifetime, an application runs in a certain environment composed of networks, servers, operating systems, and users. Information about the myriad aspects of this environment is exposed from a combination of compile-time and run-time settings provided by the .NET Framework and Windows.

Compile-Time Settings

Assemblies can provide metadata about themselves to the environment, including common details like company name, product name, and version. You edit this information in VS05 by right-clicking your project and choosing Properties | Application | Assembly Information, opening the dialog shown in Figure 15.1.

Figure 15.1   Editing Assembly Information

These values are stored in assembly-wide attributes located in a wizard-generated file called AssemblyInfo.cs (in a Windows Forms project's Properties folder):

```
// Properties\AssemblyInfo.cs
using System.Reflection;
using System.Runtime.CompilerServices;
using System.Runtime.InteropServices;
...
[assembly: AssemblyTitle("CompileTimeSettingsSample Title")]
[assembly: AssemblyDescription("CompileTimeSettingsSample Description")]
[assembly: AssemblyCompany("CompileTimeSettingsSample Company")]
[assembly: AssemblyProduct("CompileTimeSettingsSample Product")]
[assembly: AssemblyCopyright("CompileTimeSettingsSample Copyright")]
[assembly: AssemblyTrademark("CompileTimeSettingsSample Trademark")]
[assembly: ComVisible(true)]
[assembly: Guid("fea43d77-40e1-40cf-9367-768ef5bf26d1")]
[assembly: AssemblyVersion("1.0.0.0")]
[assembly: AssemblyFileVersion("1.0.0.0")]
[assembly: NeutralResourcesLanguage("en-AU")]
```

The Assembly*Xxx* attributes are bundled into the Win32 version information for the assembly, as shown by the Version property page of Explorer's file property dialog in Figure 15.2.

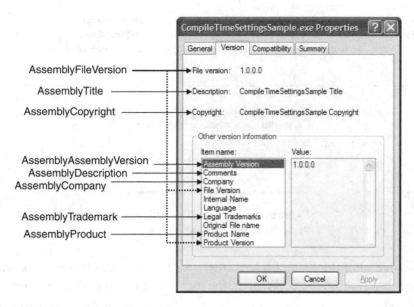

Figure 15.2   Viewing Assembly Details

Internal Name, Original File Name, and Language are beyond the reach of .NET, although Internal Name and Original File Name resolve to *ApplicationName*.exe.

The company name, product name, and product version values stored in the Assembly*Xxx* attributes are also available in the Application class via three static properties:

```
namespace System.Windows.Forms {
  sealed class Application {
    ...
    // Compile-Time Settings
    public static string CompanyName { get; } // AssemblyCompany
    public static string ProductName { get; } // AssemblyProduct
    public static string ProductVersion { get; } // AssemblyFileVersion
    ...
  }
}
```

You can retrieve the data shown in Figure 15.3 from these properties by using the following code:

```
// MainForm.cs
partial class MainForm : Form {
  public MainForm() {
    ...
```

```
      this.companyNameTextBox.Text = Application.CompanyName;
      this.productNameTextBox.Text = Application.ProductName;
      this.productVersionTextBox.Text = Application.ProductVersion;
    }
  }
```

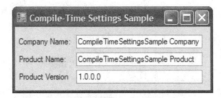

**Figure 15.3   Assembly*Xxx* Attributes
Provided by the Application Class**

Because several of the Assembly*Xxx* attributes aren't available from Application, you need to use other techniques to get them, the most common of which relies on reflection:[1]

```
using System.Reflection;
...
string AssemblyDescription() {
  // Get all Description attributes on this assembly
  object[] attributes =
    Assembly.GetExecutingAssembly().GetCustomAttributes(
      typeof(AssemblyDescriptionAttribute),
      false);

  // If there aren't any Description attributes, return empty string
  if( attributes.Length == 0 ) return "";

  // If there are Description attributes, return the first
  return ((AssemblyDescriptionAttribute)attributes[0]).Description;
}
```

Run-Time Settings

Compile-time settings represent a group of settings that never change after an assembly is deployed to the environment. However, there are many environmental factors that can change for a deployed assembly, and consequently they can't be compiled into an application. Instead, an application must dynamically retrieve them at run time, and there are several classes in the .NET Framework that provide this support.

---

[1] VS05 includes an About Box project wizard that generates code in exactly this fashion.

Application

Our old friend, the Application class, exposes several such run-time environment settings that generally pertain to what can change about the application itself, within the context of its environment:

```
namespace System.Windows.Forms {
  sealed class Application {
    ...
    // Run-Time Settings
    public static string CommonAppDataPath { get; }
    public static RegistryKey CommonAppDataRegistry { get; }
    public static CultureInfo CurrentCulture { get; set; }
    public static InputLanguage CurrentInputLanguage { get; set; }
    public static string ExecutablePath { get; }
    public static string LocalUserAppDataPath { get; }
    public static FormCollection OpenForms { get; } // New
    public static string SafeTopLevelCaptionFormat { get; set; }
    public static string StartupPath { get; }
    public static string UserAppDataPath { get; }
    public static RegistryKey UserAppDataRegistry { get; }
    ...
  }
}
```

This information is shown in Figure 15.4.

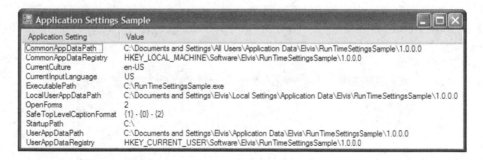

Figure 15.4   Run-Time Settings Exposed by the Application Class

Environment

If you want more environment settings, such as the environment variables or the command line string, you can get them from the Environment object:

updated

```
namespace System {
  static class Environment {
    ...
    // Properties
    public static string CommandLine { get; }
    public static string CurrentDirectory { get; set; }
    public static bool HasShutdownStarted { get; }
    public static string MachineName { get; }
    public static string NewLine { get; }
    public static OperatingSystem OSVersion { get; }
    public static int ProcessorCount { get; } // New
    public static string StackTrace { get; }
    public static string SystemDirectory { get; }
    public static int TickCount { get; }
    public static string UserDomainName { get; }
    public static bool UserInteractive { get; }
    public static string UserName { get; }
    public static Version Version { get; }
    public static long WorkingSet { get; }
    ...
  }
  ...
}
```

The Environment class affords your application the insight garnered by the sample in Figure 15.5.

Figure 15.5 Run-Time Settings Exposed by the Environment Class

Environment implements several methods that allow you to inspect and update a few additional environmental settings:

```
namespace System.Windows.Forms {
  static class Environment {
    ...
    // Methods
    public static string ExpandEnvironmentVariables(string name);
    public static string[] GetCommandLineArgs();
    public static string GetEnvironmentVariable(string variable);
    public static string GetEnvironmentVariable(
      string variable, EnvironmentVariableTarget target); // New
    public static IDictionary GetEnvironmentVariables();
    public static IDictionary GetEnvironmentVariables(
      EnvironmentVariableTarget target); // New
    public static string GetFolderPath(SpecialFolder folder);
    public static string[] GetLogicalDrives();
    public static void SetEnvironmentVariable(
      string variable, string value); // New
    public static void SetEnvironmentVariable(
      string variable, string value,
      EnvironmentVariableTarget target); // New
    ...
  }
}
```

Several methods are included for dealing with environment variables and for discovering the logical drives mounted on the current machine. GetFolderPath returns the path to one of a variety of special folders, which are discussed later in this chapter. You saw the use of GetCommandLineArgs in Chapter 14: Applications.

SystemInformation

If you need run-time access to shell settings, System.Windows.Forms.SystemInformation is for you. SystemInformation exposes more than 100 settings that encompass a wide variety of areas of the environment, from the mouse, keyboard, and monitor configuration, to a myriad of UI element settings and dimensions. Most are settings that an application might need to adapt to; for example, applications that support mouse wheel scrolling need to check whether the machine on which they are executing actually has a mouse with a mouse wheel.

Although there are too many settings to show all of them here, the following subset should provide a taste of the kind of information available from SystemInformation:

```
namespace System.Windows.Forms {
  class SystemInformation {
    // Selection of settings on offer
    public static BootMode BootMode { get; }
    public static Size Border3DSize { get; }
    public static Size BorderSize { get; }
    public static int CaretBlinkTime { get; }
    public static Size CursorSize { get; }
    public static int DoubleClickTime { get; }
    public static bool DragFullWindows { get; }
    public static int FontSmoothingType { get; }
    public static int IconHorizontalSpacing { get; }
    public static int IconVerticalSpacing { get; }
    public static int KeyboardDelay { get; }
    public static int KeyboardSpeed { get; }
    public static Font MenuFont { get; }
    public static int MenuHeight { get; }
    public static int MenuShowDelay { get; }
    public static int MonitorCount { get; }
    public static int MouseSpeed { get; }
    public static bool MouseWheelPresent { get; }
    public static bool PenWindows { get; }
    public static PowerStatus PowerStatus { get; }
    public static ScreenOrientation ScreenOrientation { get; }
    public static Rectangle WorkingArea { get; }
    ...
  }
}
```

Screen

One special subset of system information pertains to the screen, and is encapsulated by the appropriately named Screen class:

```
namespace System.Windows.Forms {
  class Screen {
    // Methods
    public static Screen FromControl(Control control);
    public static Screen FromHandle(IntPtr hwnd);
    public static Screen FromPoint(Point point);
    public static Screen FromRectangle(Rectangle rect);
    public static Rectangle GetBounds(Point pt);
    public static Rectangle GetBounds(Rectangle rect);
    public static Rectangle GetBounds(Control ctl);
```

```
    public static Rectangle GetWorkingArea(Point pt);
    public static Rectangle GetWorkingArea(Rectangle rect);
    public static Rectangle GetWorkingArea(Control ctl);

    // Properties
    public static Screen[] AllScreens { get; }
    public int BitsPerPixel { get; }
    public Rectangle Bounds { get; }
    public string DeviceName { get; }
    public bool Primary { get; }
    public static Screen PrimaryScreen { get; }
    public Rectangle WorkingArea { get; }
  }
}
```

Screen is designed to provide information about one or more screens that are connected to the computer. You can use Screen to acquire either a screen or an area of a screen using one of several methods.

Figure 15.6 shows the properties for the main screen, as determined by the Primary-Screen property.

Figure 15.6   Details Pertaining to the Primary Screen

SystemEvents

If your application depends on system or screen information to execute or render, it needs to detect when any changes to such information occur to dynamically refresh itself if required. For this, we have the SystemEvents class:

```
namespace Microsoft.Win32 {
  sealed class SystemEvents {
    // Events
    public static event EventHandler DisplaySettingsChanged;
    public static event EventHandler DisplaySettingsChanging;
    public static event EventHandler EventsThreadShutdown;
    public static event EventHandler InstalledFontsChanged;
```

```
      public static event EventHandler PaletteChanged;
      public static event PowerModeChangedEventHandler PowerModeChanged;
      public static event SessionEndedEventHandler SessionEnded;
      public static event SessionEndingEventHandler SessionEnding;
      public static event SessionSwitchEventHandler SessionSwitch;
      public static event EventHandler TimeChanged;
      public static event TimerElapsedEventHandler TimerElapsed;
      public static event
        UserPreferenceChangedEventHandler UserPreferenceChanged;
      public static event
        UserPreferenceChangingEventHandler UserPreferenceChanging;
      ...
   }
}
```

The SystemEvents class provides a variety of notifications that it broadcasts when interesting system events take place, including low memory warnings for notebooks, various moments in the life of a shell session, and user changes made to system preferences and display settings specifically. The following example detects system preference and display settings changes:

```csharp
// MainForm.cs
using Microsoft.Win32;
...
partial class MainForm : Form {
  public MainForm() {
    InitializeComponent();

    SystemEvents.UserPreferenceChanged +=
      SystemEvents_UserPreferenceChanged;
    SystemEvents.DisplaySettingsChanged +=
      SystemEvents_DisplaySettingsChanged;
  }

  void SystemEvents_UserPreferenceChanged(
    object sender, UserPreferenceChangedEventArgs e) {
    // Handle user system setting change
    MessageBox.Show(
      "User Preference Changed: " + e.Category.ToString());
  }

  void SystemEvents_DisplaySettingsChanged(
    object sender, EventArgs e) {
    // Handle user system setting change
    MessageBox.Show("Display Settings Changed");
  }
}
```

The DisplaySettingsChanged event handler isn't passed any useful arguments to describe the type of change, but the UserPreferenceChanged event handler is passed change information stored in the Category property of UserPreferenceChangedEventArgs. Category is of type UserPreferenceCategory, an enumeration that has the following, somewhat coarse-grained, values:

```
namespace Microsoft.Win32 {
  enum UserPreferenceCategory {
    Accessibility = 1,
    Color = 2,
    Desktop = 3,
    General = 4,
    Icon = 5,
    Keyboard = 6,
    Menu = 7,
    Mouse = 8,
    Policy = 9,
    Power = 10,
    Screensaver = 11,
    Window = 12,
    Locale = 13,
    VisualStyle = 14,
  }
}
```

Collectively, the Application, Environment, SystemInformation, Screen, and System-Events classes offer a wide variety of environmental information and notifications that Windows Forms applications may need access to, and these classes can almost always save you the effort of writing the code to find it yourself.

Application, User, and Roaming-User Settings

Although applications can acquire any number of environmental settings, there are two basic groups of settings that the environment can't provide. First, there are *application settings*, which are settings that are shared between all users of an application on a machine; an example is the list of the folders that contain the assemblies to show in the VS05 Add Reference dialog. Second, there are *user settings*, which are specific to both an application and a user, such as Minesweeper high scores or almost anything you'll find in the Tools | Options dialog.

Additionally, there is a special variation of user settings for roaming users; both application and user settings are specific to a machine, but *roaming-user settings* are machine-independent user settings. For example, if Minesweeper high scores were roaming, they'd be available to a specific user no matter what computer the user was logged in to.[2] Roaming-user settings are good for things that don't depend on a machine, such as a list of color preferences, but not for things that are dependent on a current machine's configuration, such as a window location.[3] Roaming-user settings presuppose that the machine is properly configured to support roaming. Otherwise, roaming-user settings are equivalent to nonroaming-user settings.

The .NET Framework and VS05 provide comprehensive support for creating and managing application, user, and roaming-user settings, all of which are built on a fundamental unit of information: the setting.

What Is a Setting?

A *setting* is comprised of four pieces of information: name, type, value, and scope. The *name* is a string value that uniquely identifies each setting. The *type* defines the sort of value a setting is and can be a simple type, a complex type, a user-defined type, or an enumeration. The *value* must be a valid string representation of the selected type. The *scope* is used to differentiate whether a setting is an application or user setting; scope is a key factor in several scenarios discussed throughout this chapter, including whether settings support roaming.

Settings Files

One or more settings are stored together in a *settings file*, which is a file with the .settings extension. By default, VS05 automatically creates a settings file for you when the Windows Application project template is run. The settings file is called Settings.settings and is located in the project's Properties folder, as shown in Figure 15.7.

Figure 15.7   The VS05 Windows Application Wizard-Generated settings File

[2] Roaming user settings depend on specific Windows domain network settings being enabled.

[3] For example, if a user moved an application window to a second monitor on one machine and then "roamed" to another machine that didn't support two monitors, the user wouldn't be able to see the application because the window location setting would position it off the first screen.

Note that you can manually add settings files to your projects by right-clicking your project in Solution Explorer and clicking Add | New Item | Settings File. However, one settings file has always been plenty for me, so the rest of this chapter discusses settings from the default settings file point of view, which applies equally to manually created settings files.

By default, a new settings file contains six lines of XML, including namespace information. A settings file with two settings—HighScore and AssemblyPaths—is shown here:[4]

```
<?xml version='1.0' encoding='utf-8'?>
<SettingsFile ...>
  ...
  <Settings>
    <Setting Name="HighScore" ...>
      <Value...>0</Value>
    </Setting>
    <Setting Name="AssemblyPaths"...>
      <Value...>c:\windows\microsoft.net</Value>
    </Setting>
  </Settings>
</SettingsFile>
```

As with .resx files (discussed in Chapter 13: Resources), the XML format of the settings file is optimized more for persistence than for editing by hand. VS05 provides a rich Settings Editor UI to help you manage settings files with aplomb.

Managing Settings

The Settings Editor, shown in Figure 15.8, is opened when you double-click a settings file in Solution Explorer.[5]

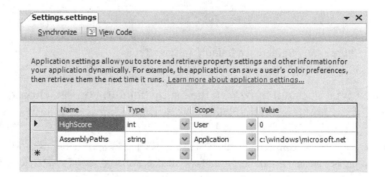

Figure 15.8   VS05 Settings Designer

---

[4] To view the XML for a settings file, right-click it in Solution Explorer and choose Open With | XML Editor.

[5] You can edit the default project settings file from the Settings tab of your project's property pages, although this way you'll have less UI real estate to play with.

You use the Settings Designer grid like any other grid to create, navigate, select, and delete settings. Additionally, you can use the Properties window to configure the name, scope, and value of existing settings; you can specify type only from the settings grid.

Editing Settings

Each setting property captures a different piece of information, so editing differs from one property to the next.

Name

Because a setting's Name property is a string value, you can simply type it into the cell directly.

Type

Type, on the other hand, must be selected from a drop-down list of items that, by default, includes a variety of common simple and complex types. It also includes two special settings types—database connections and web service URLs—which require specialized storage considerations that are provided by the settings system.[6] All these options are shown in Figure 15.9.

Figure 15.9   Selecting a Default Settings Type

If the required type does not appear in the list by default, you can choose one by clicking the Browse list option to open the Select a Type dialog shown in Figure 15.10.

[6] When you create a new database connection in the Data Sources window and choose to save the connection string, it's stored in a project-managed settings file and specified as a special setting. Web references are automatically added to the project-managed settings file with the same specification.

Figure 15.10   Selecting a Nondefault Settings Type

The only items that appear in this list are .NET Framework types that can be serialized, whether by TypeConverter (by converting to and from a string) or with the XmlSerializer.[7] Note that you can also add custom types of your own by entering their fully qualified names into the Selected Type text box, although they'll need a TypeConverter just as the .NET Framework types do.[8] When selected, the chosen settings type is added to the type drop-down list as a default list item and remains there until VS05 is closed.

Scope

The Scope drop-down list has two options: Application and User. *Application* settings are read-only and are used to store permanent settings values. *User* settings are read-write and store values that can be changed by users as required; the value you specify for a user setting becomes its default value. Both application settings and user settings are used in a variety of ways that are covered in more detail throughout the remainder of this chapter.

Value

In most situations, editing a value in the Settings Designer is the same as editing a value in the Properties window. Specifically, if the type of the setting you specified is associated with a type converter, you can provide a string value that can be converted to the desired type because settings values are stored as strings.[9] Additionally, if the settings type has a UI type

---

[7] Thanks to Raghavendra Prabhu from Microsoft for this information.

[8] Type converters are the conversion workhorses of the .NET Framework, and they know how to convert a value of one type into the value of another. The Properties window relies heavily on type converters; see Chapter 11: Design-Time Integration: The Properties Window for more information.

[9] Type converters are used by the Properties window to facilitate conversion between a type and an equivalent string representation of the type. Further detailed discussion can be found in Chapter 11.

editor associated with it, such as the System.Drawing.Font type, you can use a full-featured dialog to construct the value and return a suitable string representation, as illustrated in Figure 15.11.[10]

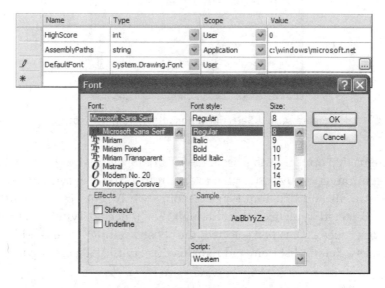

Figure 15.11   Using a UI Type Editor to Edit a Settings Value

If the settings type is an enumeration, you can select its value from a drop-down list of items, one for each value of the enumeration, as illustrated in Figure 15.12.

Name	Type	Scope	Value
HighScore	int	User	0
AssemblyPaths	string	Application	c:\windows\microsoft.net
DefaultFont	System.Drawing.Font	User	Microsoft Sans Serif, 8.25pt
DefaultWindowState	System.Windows.Forms.FormWindowState	Application	Normal
			Normal / Minimized / Maximized

Figure 15.12   Editing a Complex Type Value in the Settings Designer

In some situations, a setting's type simply doesn't provide enhanced Properties window-style editing support. In these cases, the settings system uses XML serialization to store the type, but only if the type supports XML serialization.

---

[10] UI type editors are visual aids for simplifying the value of a complex property used by the Properties window. A complete discussion is given in Chapter 11.

The following code shows how the Settings Designer persists a settings configuration to the settings file:

```xml
<?xml version='1.0' encoding='utf-8'?>
<SettingsFile ...>
  ...
  <Settings>
    <Setting
      Name="HighScore"
      Type="System.Int32"
      Scope="User">
      <Value...>0</Value>
    </Setting>
    <Setting
      Name="AssemblyPaths"
      Type="System.String"
      Scope="Application">
      <Value ...>c:\windows\microsoft.net</Value>
    </Setting>
    <Setting
      Name="DefaultFont"
      Type="System.Drawing.Font"
      Scope="User">
      <Value ...>Microsoft Sans Serif, 8.25pt</Value>
    <Setting
      Name="DefaultWindowState"
      Type="System.Windows.Forms.FormWindowState"
      Scope="Application">
      <Value ...>Normal</Value>
  </Settings>
</SettingsFile>
```

Note that FontConverter and EnumConverter—the type converters used by the Settings Editor to help out with Font type and FormWindowState type settings, respectively—are used to persist values for the DefaultFont and DefaultWindowState settings as strings.

After you've configured the settings for your application, you need to make them available to your application for debugging and deployment. For this, we have a special file known as the application configuration file.

Application Configuration Files

When a project is compiled, VS05 stores the configured settings and values in app.config, which is automatically created by VS05 and added to the project root. A project with one application setting and one user setting, app.config would look like this:

```
<?xml version="1.0" encoding="utf-8" ?>
<configuration>
  <configSections>
    <sectionGroup name="userSettings"...>
      <section name="ApplicationSettingsSample.Properties.Settings".../>
    </sectionGroup>
    <sectionGroup name="applicationSettings"...>
      <section name="ApplicationSettingsSample.Properties.Settings".../>
    </sectionGroup>
  </configSections>
  <userSettings>
    <ApplicationSettingsSample.Properties.Settings>
      <setting name="HighScore" serializeAs="String">
        <value>0</value>
      </setting>
    </ApplicationSettingsSample.Properties.Settings>
  </userSettings>
  <applicationSettings>
    <ApplicationSettingsSample.Properties.Settings>
      <setting name="AssemblyPaths" serializeAs="String">
        <value>c:\windows\microsoft.net</value>
      </setting>
    </ApplicationSettingsSample.Properties.Settings>
  </applicationSettings>
</configuration>
```

In app.config, user and application settings are grouped by the userSettings and applicationSettings section groups. Within those section groups, the settings and their values are stored in a section whose name conforms to the following convention:

```
Namespace.SettingsFileName
```

Because the settings and values are grouped by their settings files, app.config can manage all settings and values stored in settings files across your project. This situation might occur when your application has so many settings that it is far easier to manage them by splitting them across several smaller settings files, while still requiring them to be merged into app.config:

```
<?xml version="1.0" encoding="utf-8" ?>
<configuration>
  <configSections>
    <sectionGroup name="userSettings"...>
      <section name="ApplicationSettingsSample.MyOtherSettings".../>
      <section name="ApplicationSettingsSample.Properties.Settings".../>
```

```
    </sectionGroup>
    <sectionGroup name="applicationSettings"...>
      <section name="ApplicationSettingsSample.MyOtherSettings".../>
      <section name="ApplicationSettingsSample.Properties.Settings".../>
    </sectionGroup>
  </configSections>
  <userSettings>
    <ApplicationSettingsSample.MyOtherSettings>
      ...
    </ApplicationSettingsSample.MyOtherSettings>
    <ApplicationSettingsSample.Properties.Settings>
      ...
    </ApplicationSettingsSample.Properties.Settings>
  </userSettings>
  <applicationSettings>
    <ApplicationSettingsSample.MyOtherSettings>
      ...
    </ApplicationSettingsSample.MyOtherSettings>
    <ApplicationSettingsSample.Properties.Settings>
      ...
    </ApplicationSettingsSample.Properties.Settings>
  </applicationSettings>
</configuration>
```

The app.config file is really managed by VS05 to represent the current settings for a project. Before you execute an application—under the auspices of VS05 or from a client-installed location—the settings in app.config need to be deployed with the application executable.

Therefore, when a project is compiled, VS05 creates a file called *app*.exe.config, where *app* is the name of the generated application. The *app*.exe.config file is an exact copy of the app.config file that's generated to the same folder as all the other project compilation output, including the application assembly. As such, *app*.exe.config contains all application and user settings for all settings files in a project. When an application is deployed, its *app*.exe.config file could reside in one of several locations that depend on how the user configured things and how the application was installed.

For locally installed applications, *app*.exe.config is located in the same folder as the assembly. For ClickOnce-deployed applications, *app*.exe.config is stored in the following location:

```
%SystemDrive%\Documents and Settings\UserName\Local
Settings\Apps\HashedPath\
```

For roaming profiles, *app*.exe.config is installed here:

```
%SystemDrive%\Documents and Settings\UserName\Local
Settings\Application Data\ProductName\HashedPath
```

The application- and user-scoped settings contained within *app*.exe.config are considered the default values for an application's lifetime.

The Configuration Manager

After settings are deployed, they need to be pulled from *app*.exe.config into the application for use. Some of those settings—user-scoped settings—are expected to change and may need to be written to disk. Manually writing the code to open, navigate, read, write, and close the XML-encoded *app*.exe.config file is nontrivial. Instead, the ConfigurationManager class and its friends in System.Configuration, wrap this raw XML processing into a settings-oriented abstraction.

You use ConfigurationManager to open a .config file by calling its OpenExeConfiguration method, which returns a Configuration class that wraps the actual .config file:

```
// ConfigurationManagerForm
partial class ConfigurationManagerForm : Form {

  Configuration configuration;

  public ConfigurationManagerForm() {
    InitializeComponent();

    // Open .config file (current local userSettings)
    this.configuration = ConfigurationManager.OpenExeConfiguration(
      ConfigurationUserLevel.PerUserRoamingAndLocal);
  }
}
```

OpenExeConfiguration accepts a ConfigurationUserLevel argument, which specifies the kind of settings to load:

```
namespace System.Configuration {
  enum ConfigurationUserLevel {
    None = 0, // Open application settings
    PerUserRoaming = 10, // Open user settings (Roaming)
    PerUserRoamingAndLocal = 20 // Open user settings (Local)
  }
}
```

In our example, we're opening the local user settings.

Reading Settings

The in-memory .config file wrapped by the Configuration object is structured in section groups, sections, and settings to represent the file structure naturally. For example, the HighScore setting is located in the "ApplicationSettingsSample.Properties.Settings" section of the "userSettings" section group:

```xml
<?xml version="1.0" encoding="utf-8" ?>
<configuration>
  ...
  <userSettings> <!-- Section Group -->
    <ApplicationSettingsSample.Properties.Settings> <!-- Section -->
      <setting name="HighScore" serializeAs="String">
        <value>0</value>
      </setting>
      ...
    </ApplicationSettingsSample.Properties.Settings>
  </userSettings>
  ...
</configuration>
```

Consequently, we need to navigate through these elements to find the appropriate setting. The following code uses the ConfigurationSectionGroup, ClientSettingsSection, and SettingElement objects to do just that:

```csharp
// ConfigurationManagerForm.cs
partial class ConfigurationManagerForm : Form {
  ...
  public ConfigurationManagerForm() {
    ...
    // Read a setting from the config file
    string setting =
      this.ReadSetting(
        "userSettings",
        "ApplicationSettingsSample.Properties.Settings",
        "HighScore");
    MessageBox.Show(setting);
  }

  string ReadSetting(
    string sectionGroupName,
    string sectionName,
    string settingName) {

    // Get sectionGroup
    ConfigurationSectionGroup sectionGroup =
      this.configuration.GetSectionGroup(sectionGroupName);
```

```
      // Get section
      ClientSettingsSection section =
        (ClientSettingsSection)sectionGroup.Sections.Get(sectionName);
      // Get setting
      SettingElement setting = section.Settings.Get(settingName);
      // Read setting value
      return setting.Value.ValueXml.InnerText;
    }
  }
```

As we know, user settings are read-write, so we need to write them back to disk so that the updated value is available during the new application session.

Writing Settings

Writing a setting back to disk uses the same technique to find a setting, although this time you're setting the value instead of reading it:

```
// ConfigurationManagerForm
partial class ConfigurationManagerForm : Form {
  ...
  public ConfigurationManagerForm() {
    ...
    // Write a setting to the config file
    this.WriteSetting(
      "userSettings",
      "ApplicationSettingsSample.Properties.Settings",
      "HighScore",
      "200");
  }
  ...
  void WriteSetting(
    string sectionGroupName,
    string sectionName,
    string settingName,
    string newSettingValue) {

    // Get sectionGroup
    ConfigurationSectionGroup sectionGroup =
      this.configuration.GetSectionGroup(sectionGroupName);
    // Get section
    ClientSettingsSection section =
      (ClientSettingsSection)sectionGroup.Sections.Get(sectionName);
    // Get setting
    SettingElement setting = section.Settings.Get(settingName);
    // Writing a setting value
    setting.Value.ValueXml.InnerText = newSettingValue;
  }
}
```

However, this step goes only as far as writing the value to the in-memory .config file available from the Configuration object. To persist it to disk, we take the additional step of calling the Configuration object's Save method:

```
// ConfigurationManagerForm
partial class ConfigurationManagerForm : Form {
  ...
  public ConfigurationManagerForm() {
    ...
    // Write a setting to the config file
    this.WriteSetting(
      "userSettings",
      "ApplicationSettingsSample.Properties.Settings",
      "HighScore",
      "200");

    // Save all settings
    this.configuration.Save(ConfigurationSaveMode.Full, true);
  }
  ...
}
```

This use of the Save method ensures that the entire configuration file is written back to disk.

User Configuration Files

All settings deployed with the *app*.exe.config file, including both user settings and application settings, are considered *read-only*. It's this characteristic that turns application settings into permanent settings and turns user settings into default settings.

As we know, however, user settings are designed to allow users to change them. Because the default user settings deployed with *app*.exe.config are effectively read-only, the settings system creates a new file, user.config, to store any user settings whose values differ from their defaults stored in *app*.exe.config.

The user.config file is located in one of four special Windows-compliant folders, depending on where the application was executed from. Settings saved from an application run from within VS05 are stored in the following folder:

```
%SystemDrive%\Documents and Settings\UserName\Local Settings\Application.
Data\UserName\ApplicationName.vshost.exe_StrongNameHash\AssemblyVersionNumber
```

If settings are saved from a locally installed application, user.config ends up in this folder:

```
%SystemDrive%\Documents and Settings\UserName\Local Settings\Application
Data\ProductName\ApplicationName.exe_Url_UrlHash\AssemblyVersionNumber
```

If settings are saved from an application deployed via ClickOnce, you'll find user. config here:

```
%SystemDrive%\Documents and Settings\UserName\Local
Settings\Apps\Data\HashedPath\Data\ProductVersion
```

Finally, if roaming profiles are enabled for the current user—whether or not settings are being saved from a locally installed or ClickOnce-deployed application—user.config is placed here:

```
%SystemDrive%\Documents and Settings\UserName\Local
Settings\Application Data\ProductName\HashedPath
```

So, when our code wrote the local user settings, a user.config was created and stored in the locally installed user.config location, containing only the user settings:

```xml
<?xml version="1.0" encoding="utf-8"?>
<configuration>
  <userSettings>
    <ApplicationSettingsSample.MyOtherSettings />
    <ApplicationSettingsSample.Properties.Settings>
      <setting name="HighScore" serializeAs="String">
        <value>200</value>
      </setting>
    </ApplicationSettingsSample.Properties.Settings>
  </userSettings>
</configuration>
```

Unmodified user settings are copied from the defaults located in *app*.exe.config, whereas modified settings are updated with the new values. In addition to logically separating application settings from user settings, the division enables a wide variety of additional settings-oriented scenarios for rollback and migration of settings.

During development, you may find that multiple user.config files are created—for example, as a result of versioning changes. This can lead to weird issues derived from a lack of synchronicity between the settings your application expects and those that are actually stored in user.config. The Settings Editor provides the Synchronize button, shown in Figure 15.13, to quickly remove all user.config files for a current application from all possible paths.

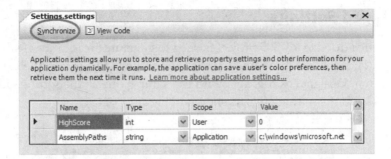

Figure 15.13   Synchronize Button to Clean All user.config Files

Note that it is possible to write the following code to specifically update *app*.exe.config:

```
// ConfigurationManagerForm
partial class ConfigurationManagerForm : Form {
  ...
  public ConfigurationManagerForm() {

    // BAD - writing to app.exe.config violates
    // the spirit of read-only application settings
    this.configuration = ConfigurationManager.OpenExeConfiguration(
      ConfigurationUserLevel.None);

    // Write a setting to the config file
    this.WriteSetting(
      "applicationSettings",
      "SettingsSample.Properties.Settings",
      "AssemblyPaths",
      "naughtyValue");

    // Save updated settings
    this.configuration.Save(ConfigurationSaveMode.Full, true);
  ...
}
```

Writing to the app.config file circumvents the philosophy and practice of the settings system, which treats the app.config file as read-only and stores the changed user settings in the user.config file. This philosophy is practiced in a much simpler and safer way provided by VS05 to deal with settings of all kinds: strongly typed settings.

Strongly Typed Settings

Every settings file added to a VS05 project is used to generate an additional strongly typed settings class.[11] The class has the same name as the settings file, minus the extension. The class is stored in a .Designer.cs file, also with the same name as the settings file, which is then associated with the settings file, as shown in Figure 15.14.

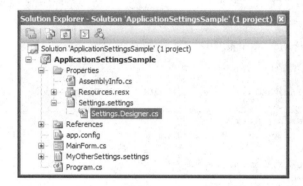

Figure 15.14   The Designer-Generated Settings Class File

Here are the relevant elements of the generated class implementation created for the VS05 default settings file, which is generated to Settings.Designer.cs:

```csharp
// Settings.Designer.cs
using System.Configuration;
using System.Runtime.CompilerServices;
...
namespace ApplicationSettingsSample.Properties {

  [global::CompilerGenerated()]
  internal sealed partial class Settings :
    global::ApplicationSettingsBase {

    static Settings defaultInstance = new Settings();
    public static Settings Default {
      get { return defaultInstance; }
    }
    ...
    [global::UserScopedSetting()]
    [global::DefaultSettingValue("0")]
    public int HighScore {
```

[11] The strongly typed settings class is generated by the SettingsSingleFileGenerator custom tool, which is associated with settings files by default.

```
      get { return ((int)(this["HighScore"])); }
      set { this["HighScore"] = value; }
   }
   ...
   [global::ApplicationScopedSetting()]
   [global::DefaultSettingValue("c:\\...\\microsoft.net")]
   public string AssemblyPaths {
      get { return ((string)(this["AssemblyPaths"])); }
   }
 }
}
```

The Settings class derives from ApplicationSettingsBase, which is the workhorse of the settings system. ApplicationSettingsBase exposes the vast majority of the settings functionality you'll need through a relatively simple interface. ApplicationSettingsBase is the functional tip of the settings iceberg; it not only encompasses the basic read and write operations but also extends them with a variety of higher-level operations to handle a variety of settings scenarios. Additionally, ApplicationSettingsBase takes care of safely ensuring that the right settings are written to the right .config files.

Additionally, Settings derives from ApplicationSettingsBase and extends it by exposing settings as strongly typed properties. Our example shows both the HighScore and the AssemblyPaths settings as having been generated as strongly typed properties of the same name, each adorned with two attributes: *Xxx*ScopedSetting and DefaultSettingValue.

Because the HighScore setting has a user scope, its property implementation includes both get and set accessors and is adorned with the UserScopedSetting attribute. On the other hand, the AssemblyPaths setting has an application scope, and this causes its property implementation to include only a get accessor; AssemblyPaths is augmented with the ApplicationScopedSetting attribute. Ultimately, these attributes are used by ApplicationSettingsBase and the settings system to determine which settings can be written and where they can be written to.

The DefaultSettingValue attribute that's applied to both properties represents the value you entered into the Value column of the settings grid on the Settings Editor, and this attribute is used to support several settings rollback scenarios, as you'll soon see.

The generated Settings class also implements a helper method that provides access to a statically managed instance of itself. All generated settings classes reside in a namespace that matches the class's location in the project folder hierarchy. For example, the VS05 default Settings class resides in the following namespace: *DefaultNameSpace*.Properties. A generated class for a settings file located in the project root resides in the following namespace: *DefaultNameSpace*.

Although not configurable from the Settings Editor, the generated values for both the namespace and the class name are also stored in the settings file in the GeneratedClass-Namespace and GeneratedClassName attributes:

```
<?xml version='1.0' encoding='utf-8'?>
<SettingsFile
   ...
   GeneratedClassNamespace="ApplicationSettingsSample.Properties"
   GeneratedClassName="Settings">
   ...
</SettingsFile>
```

We have quite a flexible system for configuring application, user, and roaming-user settings, leaving you with a nicely generated strongly typed settings class. Now it's time to unleash the beast.

Using Strongly Typed Settings

Thanks in large part to its ApplicationSettingsBase ancestor, the strongly typed class that's generated by the Designer for your settings files dramatically simplifies reading and writing settings, rollback, and migration. Let's take a look.

Using the Settings Class

To use the strongly typed settings properties, you first instantiate the desired settings class:

```
// MainForm.cs
partial class MainForm : Form {
  ...
  ApplicationSettingsSample.Properties.Settings settings =
    new ApplicationSettingsSample.Properties.Settings();

  void getSettingsButton_Click(object sender, EventArgs e) {
    int highScore = this.settings.HighScore;
    string assemblyPaths = this.settings.1AssemblyPaths;
  }
}
```

This technique puts the onus on you to manage the lifetime of the Settings object instance and to make sure that all the forms and classes in your application have access to it. In trivial scenarios, this may be fine, but for more complex situations, you'll want to rely on the statically managed instance exposed by the generated settings class, as you saw earlier:

```
// Settings.Designer.cs
namespace ApplicationSettingsSample.Properties {

  [global::CompilerGenerated()]
  internal sealed partial class Settings :
    global::ApplicationSettingsBase {

    static Settings defaultInstance = new Settings();
    public static Settings Default {
      get { return defaultInstance; }
    }
    ...
  }
}
```

In this example, the statically managed Settings instance is created before it's requested and subsequently is retained in memory until the application session ends. The benefit for you is less worry and less code:

```
// MainForm.cs
partial class MainForm : Form {
  ...
  void getSettingsButton_Click(object sender, EventArgs e) {
    int highScore = Properties.Settings.Default.HighScore;
    string assemblyPaths = Properties.Settings.Default.AssemblyPaths;
  }
}
```

Loading and Inspecting Settings

At some point before you use your first setting in client code, you'll likely want your settings loaded. In your favor, loading settings from the .config file requires no client code; the first time you inspect or update a property on the Settings class, it automatically loads all your settings into memory:

```
// MainForm.cs
partial class MainForm : Form {
  ...
  void getSettingsButton_Click(object sender, EventArgs e) {
    // No settings are loaded yet
    int highScore = Properties.Settings.Default.HighScore;
    // All settings are now loaded (caused by previous line)
    ...
  }
}
```

If you have client code that is dependent on when settings are loaded, you can handle the SettingsLoaded event exposed by the Settings class:

```
// MainForm.cs
using System.Configuration;
...
partial class MainForm : Form {
  ...
  public MainForm() {
    ...
    Properties.Settings.Default.SettingsLoaded +=
      DefaultSettings_SettingsLoaded;
  }
  ...
  void DefaultSettings_SettingsLoaded(
    object sender, SettingsLoadedEventArgs e) {
    MessageBox.Show("Settings loaded by " + e.Provider.Name);
  }
}
```

The SettingsLoaded event handler accepts a SettingsLoadedEventArgs argument whose single interesting property is Provider, which returns an instance of a settings provider.

Settings Providers

ApplicationSettingsBase uses a *settings provider* to manage the reading and writing of a setting to a data store, two tasks that are embodied by the SettingsProvider class:

```
namespace System.Configuration {
  class SettingsLoadedEventArgs : EventArgs {
    public SettingsProvider Provider { get; }
  }
}
```

By default, ApplicationSettingsBase uses LocalFileSettingsProvider, which manages settings persistence in .config files, as shown in Figure 15.15.

Figure 15.15　SettingsLoaded Event and SettingsLoadedEventArgs in Action

The reason to abstract away the actual persistence part of the settings process is to support the creation of multiple settings providers, each capable of persisting settings to different data stores, such as the Registry, databases, and even web services.[12] It is possible for one settings file to use settings that are managed by more than one provider, and hence the provider distinction made by SettingsLoadedEventArgs.

Updating Settings

Whereas all settings can be inspected for their values, only user-scoped settings can be updated programmatically. This is as simple as setting a property value because they are exposed as strongly typed properties:

```
Properties.Settings.Default.HighScore =
  int.Parse(this.settingsTextBox.Text);
```

A user setting may be updated directly from user input via a Windows Form, in which case you can validate the data at the point of entry. However, some user settings may be set by other means, in which case you need another validation mechanism. This is provided by the SettingChanging event, which is exposed by the Settings class. The SettingChanging event handler is passed a SettingChangingEventArgs type:

```
// UpdateSettingForm.cs
partial class UpdateSettingForm : Form {
  public UpdateSettingForm() {
    ...
    // Handle SettingChanging event
    Properties.Settings.Default.SettingChanging +=
      DefaultSettings_SettingChanging;
    ...
  }

  void updateSettingButton_Click(object sender, EventArgs e) {
    // Attempt to set value
    // Note: when the property is set, the SettingChanging
    //       event is fired
    Properties.Settings.Default.HighScore =
      int.Parse(this.settingTextBox.Text);
  }
```

---

[12] Discussion of how to create setting providers can be found at MSDN Online, at http://msdn2.microsoft.com/en-us/library/8eyb2ct1.aspx (http://tinysells.com/28).

```
    void DefaultSettings_SettingChanging(object sender,
      SettingChangingEventArgs e) {
      // Validate HighScore
      if( e.SettingName == "HighScore" ) {
        if( ((int)e.NewValue) < 0 ) {
          MessageBox.Show("HighScore can't be less than 0.");
          e.Cancel = true;
        }
      }
    }
  }
}
```

SettingChangingEventArgs provides the desired new value in the NewValue property. Additionally, it provides information about the setting that you need in order to determine which setting is about to be changed. Also, because SettingChangingEventArgs derives from CancelEventArgs, you can set its Cancel property to true to prevent an update of the setting if the new value is invalid.

Note that the Cancel property is false by default, so you need to set it to true to prevent the invalid setting value from being applied. Figure 15.16 shows the result.

Figure 15.16   Validating a Settings Change

If you need to respond to a successful settings update, you can handle the Property-Changed event fired by the settings class. The passed PropertyChangedEventArgs simply details which setting was changed.

Saving Settings

When user settings change, your user will want them to be saved. All updates to user settings are retained in memory until the Save method exposed by the settings class is invoked, which results in the modified values being persisted back to user.config.

```
// MainForm.cs
partial class MainForm : Form {
  ...
  public MainForm() {
    ...
    Properties.Settings.Default.SettingsSaving +=
      DefaultSettings_SettingsSaving;
    ...
  }
  ...
  void MainForm_FormClosing(object sender, FormClosingEventArgs e) {
    Properties.Settings.Default.Save();
  }

  void DefaultSettings_SettingsSaving(object sender, CancelEventArgs e) {
    // Ask whether user really wants to save changed settings
    DialogResult result =
      MessageBox.Show(
        "Save Settings before application shutdown?",
        Application.ProductName,
        MessageBoxButtons.YesNo,
        MessageBoxIcon.Question);
    e.Cancel = (result == DialogResult.No);
  }
}
```

The SettingsSaving handler is passed a CancelEventArgs whose Cancel property you set to true to prevent settings persistence. The next section covers what happens when changed settings are persisted.

Rolling Back Settings

Because settings can be updated and saved, there needs to be some recourse for users when new settings go awry. The settings system supports rolling back settings updates, and dealing with a total loss of the settings file.

Rolling Back to Last Saved Settings

User settings are for users to change and use, to personalize an application to serve their visual and functional needs. Allowing users to update settings, however, means that things can turn pear-shaped. For example, a user might try out a new color scheme that, in the end, simply goes wrong. Even worse, the color scheme may be composed of so many colors that users can't easily recall the original colors.

The settings system provides a simple mechanism by which you can allow users to refresh the current settings using the last saved settings values. This entails calling a single method, Reload, implemented by the Settings class:

```
void saveRollbackToolStripMenuItem_Click(object sender, EventArgs e) {

  // Roll back to last saved settings
  Properties.Settings.Default.Reload();

  // Retrieve
  this.userSettingTextBox.Text =
    Properties.Settings.Default.userSettingv1;
}
```

Because settings are cached in memory by the Settings class, the Reload method simply refreshes the cache from user.config or *app*.exe.config, depending on whether user settings have been previously updated.

Rolling Back to Original Settings

In more extreme scenarios, users may want to start with a clean slate and roll their settings back to their default values when the application was installed. In these cases, it is possible that settings have been repeatedly updated and saved many times since installation, removing all likelihood that anyone remembers the defaults. You can use the Reset method, implemented by Settings, to let users roll their settings back to installation defaults:

```
void installRollbackToolStripMenuItem_Click(
    object sender, EventArgs e) {

  // Roll back to original settings
  Properties.Settings.Default.Reset();

  // Retrieve
  this.userSettingTextBox.Text =
    Properties.Settings.Default.userSettingv1;
}
```

Reset causes the settings system to pull settings values out of the *app*.exe.config file, and these values also happen to be the values you entered into the Settings Editor. If user.config happens to be deleted, an application automatically reverts to the settings values contained in *app*.exe.config, just as if the Reset method had been called.

Dealing with .config File Deletion

As you've just seen, there's a lot of dependency on *app*.exe.config. Of course, it is also an obvious point of failure; what happens if the *app*.exe.config file itself is deleted?

The settings system incorporates an additional layer of redundancy that ultimately provides a solid backup for the *app*.exe.config file: The value you enter for a setting when creating or editing it is considered its default value, which, by default, is added to a project's compiled assembly.[13] The happy result is that if *app*.exe.config is missing a setting or missing completely, the settings system pulls default values directly from code.

Through the combination of user.config files, *app*.exe.config files, and compiled settings and values, .NET's settings system provides highly redundant support for rolling settings values back to previous versions.

Migrating Settings

Settings rollback is only half the story. When a new version of an application is released, it can be useful to automatically migrate user-changed settings from the old version to save them the effort of manually changing the default settings deployed with the new version. .NET offers the ability to migrate settings from the previous version of an application to a new one, using either batch or selective migration as required.

Determining When to Migrate Settings

Before a user's settings can be migrated, however, you must determine whether settings need to be migrated. Unfortunately, the settings system lacks a native mechanism for reporting whether settings need to be migrated, so you have to roll your own.

A simple solution relies on the use of an additional Boolean flag setting that defaults to true and signals the new version to migrate settings from the previous version, if there was one. After a migration has occurred, the flag should be set to false to prevent further migration attempts. Even though the flag represents a setting that is used by the application only, it needs to be changed and must, therefore, be a user-scoped setting because it needs to be set to false after migration. Figure 15.17 shows the new setting, UpgradeRequired.

---

[13] Whether setting and its value are included in the compiled output depends on there being a default value and on the GenerateDefaultValueInCode property being set to true. You can use the Settings Editor to set GenerateDefaultValueInCode from the Properties window for each setting, as discussed later in this chapter.

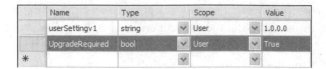

Name	Type		Scope		Value
userSettingv1	string	⌄	User	⌄	1.0.0.0
UpgradeRequired	bool	⌄	User	⌄	True
*		⌄		⌄	

Figure 15.17   UpgradeRequired Migration Flag

Next, you write the code to use the UpgradeRequired setting as just discussed. A good location for this code is an application's Main method:[14]

```
// Program.cs
static class Program {
  ...
  [STAThread]
  static void Main() {
    Application.EnableVisualStyles();

    // Check whether upgrade required
    if( Properties.Settings.Default.UpgradeRequired ) {

      // Upgrade settings
      ...

      // Prevent further upgrades
      Properties.Settings.Default.UpgradeRequired = false;
      Properties.Settings.Default.Save();
    }

    Application.Run(new MainForm());
  }
}
```

With the upgrade required detection in place, we can employ one of two types of settings migration techniques.

Migrating Settings Values in Bulk

If a new version of an application contains few or no changes in the settings it uses, or if the user simply doesn't need to participate in the process, you call the Upgrade method to migrate all settings values from the previous application version in one step:

[14] The UpgradeRequired trick was posted to Chris Sells's web site by the very wily Raghavendra Prabhu at http://www.sellsbrothers.com/news/showTopic.aspx?ixTopic=1537 (http://tinysells.com/29).

```
// Check whether upgrade required
if( Properties.Settings.Default.UpgradeRequired ) {

    // Bulk migrate settings from previous version
    Properties.Settings.Default.Upgrade();
    Properties.Settings.Default.Reload();

    // Prevent further upgrades
    Properties.Settings.Default.UpgradeRequired = false;
    Properties.Settings.Default.Save();
}
```

Upgrade copies all settings from the previous application version's user.config file and creates a new user.config under a folder for the new application version. Settings from the old version that do not appear in the new version are dropped because they need to be reloaded from the new user.config file, and hence the call to reload.

One problem that upgrades might encounter is a missing user.config from the previous application's version, a file that Upgrade depends on. Although it's unlikely, this file may have been deleted or uninstalled. The Upgrade method throws a ConfigurationSettings-Exception if it can't find a previous version:

```
// Program.cs
static class Program {
  ...
  [STAThread]
  static void Main() {
    Application.EnableVisualStyles();

    try {
      // Check whether upgrade required
      if( Properties.Settings.Default.UpgradeRequired ) {...}
    }
    catch( Exception ex ) {
      string msg =
        string.Format("{0}\n\nTry again next time?", ex.Message);
      DialogResult result =
        MessageBox.Show(
          msg,
          Application.ProductName,
          MessageBoxButtons.YesNo,
          MessageBoxIcon.Warning);
      if( result == DialogResult.No ) {
        // Prevent further upgrades
        Properties.Settings.Default.UpgradeRequired = false;
        Properties.Settings.Default.Save();
```

```
          }
        }
      }

      Application.SetCompatibleTextRenderingDefault(false);
      Application.Run(new MainForm());
    }
    ...
  }
```

When the settings upgrade can't take place, the sample code gives the user the option to prevent further upgrades or to try to upgrade the next time the application executes.

Your application can take many approaches to handling a missing user.config file, but depending on application, business, user, and deployment requirements, this sample gives users two options: They can continue using the application and forget any further upgrade attempts or they can continue but try to upgrade the next time the application executes.

Migrating Settings Values Selectively

Sometimes, the differences between the settings used by two versions might be nontrivial and only a few settings remain the same. Alternatively, you might like to give users the opportunity to choose which settings values to migrate from a previous application version. Either requirement would benefit from a selective style of migration, and the GetPreviousVersion method of the Settings class nicely provides this option. GetPreviousVersion simply retrieves the value of a specified setting from the previous version.

This sample uses a batch migration approach to manage the entire upgrade process, albeit selective in this instance:

```
// Program.cs
static class Program {
  ...
  [STAThread]
  static void Main() {
    Application.EnableVisualStyles();

    // Check whether upgrade required
    if( Properties.Settings.Default.UpgradeRequired ) {

      // Selectively migrate settings from previous version
      string oldValue = (string)
        Properties.Settings.Default.GetPreviousVersion("userSetting");
      Properties.Settings.Default.userSettingv1 = oldValue;

      // Upgrade and prevent further attempts
      Properties.Settings.Default.UpgradeRequired = false;
```

```
        Properties.Settings.Default.Save();
    }

    Application.Run(new MainForm());
  }
}
```

When using the GetPreviousVersion method, you should consider two things. First, GetPreviousVersion returns an object, so you must always cast the result to the target setting's type. Second, GetPreviousVersion returns a return null if a previous version of the setting does not exist.

Designer Settings

To this point, we've used the Settings Designer to manage settings configuration. However, VS05, the Settings Designer, and the Windows Forms Designer offer several other designer features to simplify settings development.[15]

Properties Window Configuration

In addition to allowing configuration of the four basic setting elements—name, type, scope, and value—the Settings Editor offers four additional configurations through the Properties window (shown in Figure 15.18 for the HighScore setting) that you can use to edit individual settings, including Description, GenerateDefaultValueInCode, Provider, and Roaming.

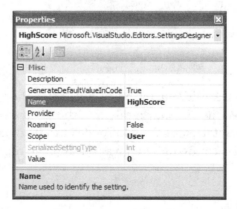

Figure 15.18   Editing a Setting in the Properties Window

---

[15] Tool strip controls also offer the ability to persist layout-oriented settings at run time, a feature discussed in Chapter 4: Layout.

Description allows you to provide expressive text for your setting, which is then displayed via IntelliSense as you code against the generated settings class's property. *GenerateDefaultValueInCode* is a Boolean (true by default) that specifies whether the associated setting has a default value that is used in lieu of one being provided by developers or users; this property comes in handy in certain versioning scenarios described earlier in this chapter. As already mentioned, settings providers can be associated with your settings, and you set the *Provider* property to make that association. Finally, you use the *Roaming* property to specify whether a user setting supports roaming users. Because users, rather than applications, roam, the Roaming property is disabled for application settings.

These configurations are applied to each setting as attributes adorning the strongly typed properties in the generated settings class:

```
// Properties/Settings.Designer.cs
using System.Configuration;
...
namespace AppSettingsProvider.Properties {
  ...
  internal sealed partial class Settings :
    global::ApplicationSettingsBase {
    ...
    [global::SettingsDescription("HighScore description.")]
      [global::DefaultSettingValue("0")]
    [global::SettingsProvider("WebServiceProvider")]
    [global::SettingsManageability(
      global::SettingsManageability.Roaming)]
    [global::UserScopedSetting()]
    public int HighScore {
      get { return ((int)(this["HighScore"])); }
      set { this["HighScore"] = value; }
    }
  ...
  }
}
```

Note that if GenerateDefaultValueInCode is false, then the DefaultSettingValue attribute isn't applied. However, as you may recall from the discussion of settings rollback, you should really keep GenerateDefaultValueInCode set to its default of true to ensure that users can recover if all the .config files for an application go missing.

Property Binding

Settings are also integrated into the Properties window of the Windows Forms Designer, allowing you to use data binding to bind form, control, and component properties directly to settings. Data binding is a technology by which the property of some control has a synchronization relationship with the property of some data object.[16] For example, if your application supports user themes, you might like to give users the option of choosing their own background color for a form. Data binding allows the form's background color to be stored in a setting that is automatically retrieved and applied to the BackColor property of the form the next time it is opened, as well as automatically synchronizing its value back to the setting whenever the user changes it. For this reason, Form.BackColor makes a perfect candidate for property binding.

To bind the BackColor property of a form to a setting exposed as a property from the Settings class, you bring up the form's Properties window and press the ellipses ("...") button under (ApplicationSettings) | (PropertyBinding), as shown in Figure 15.19.

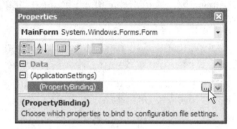

Figure 15.19   Property Binding in the Properties Window

In the Application Settings dialog, click the drop-down list of the BackColor property, shown in Figure 15.20.

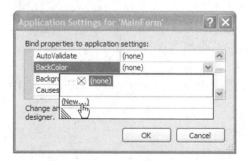

Figure 15.20   Creating a New Setting to Bind To

---

[16] This special relationship keeps the value of the property on both ends of the relationship in sync. If you need more information, Chapter 16: Data Binding Basics and Chapter 17: Applied Data Binding delve deep into data binding.

The list shown in Figure 15.20 allows you to select a setting to bind to. If none is present, you can click the New link to create a new setting to bind to. This action opens the New Application Setting dialog, shown in Figure 15.21.

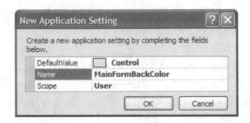

Figure 15.21   New Application Setting Dialog

Figure 15.21 shows the configuration of the new setting to capture BackgroundColor, and, like all bound properties, it requires a default value, a name, and a scope. In this case, the MainFormBackColor setting should be user-scoped because it can change from one application session to the next. Note that you don't have a choice as to which settings file the new setting is added to; you can bind properties only to settings stored in the project default Settings.settings file.

When you click OK, several things happen. First, a new setting is added to the project's default Settings.settings file, shown in Figure 15.22 in the Settings Designer.

	Name	Type	Scope	Value
▶	MainFormBackColor	System.Drawing.Color ⌄	User ⌄	☐ Control
✳		⌄	⌄	

Figure 15.22   New Setting Created

Second, the Settings class is updated to implement a new, strongly typed property:

```
// Properties/Settings.Designer.cs
using System.Configuration;
...
namespace ApplicationSettingsSample.Properties {
  ...
  sealed partial class Settings : ApplicationSettingsBase {
    ...
    [global::UserScopedSetting()]
    [global::DefaultSettingValue("Control")]
    public global::Color MainFormBackColor {
```

```
      get {...}
      set {...}
    }
  }
  ...
}
```

Third, it's to this strongly typed property that the form's BackColor property is now bound, as configured in InitializeComponent:

```
// MainForm.Designer.cs
partial class MainForm {
  ...
  void InitializeComponent() {
    ...
    // MainForm
    this.DataBindings.Add(
      new Binding(
        "BackColor",
        Properties.Settings.Default,
        "MainFormBackColor",
        true,
        DataSourceUpdateMode.OnPropertyChanged));
    ...
  }
}
```

The Binding object binds the form's BackColor property to Properties.Settings' Main-FormBackColor property, ensuring that both property values are kept in sync.

Finally, the Properties window displays a cute icon in the BackColor property item for the form, a visual cue that it is now bound, as shown in Figure 15.23.

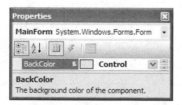

Figure 15.23   BackColor Property Binding Indicator

This icon also indicates that the default value of the setting to which a property is bound is changed automatically whenever the property is changed from the Properties window.

To provide easy access to the bound property, notice that the bound property also appears in the Properties window's (ApplicationSettings) | (PropertyBinding) list, shown as bound in Figure 15.24.

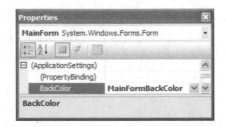

Figure 15.24   BackColor Bound Property

What's nice about having a property bound to a setting is that when the form's Back-Color is changed (perhaps via the Options dialog), its value is automatically copied to the Settings class's MainFormBackColor property.

In this example, we're remembering the BackColor property, although you could pick any property you like. Sometimes, however, you'll find that you can't bind all the form properties you'd like to application or user settings.

Persisting Form State, Size, and Position

Although you can bind a form's BackColor to a setting, you can't bind WindowState, Size, and Location. The problem is that when a form is minimized, the location is set to the following:

```
Point hiddenLocation = new Point(-32000, -32000);
```

So if you bind Form.Size to a setting, this size is retrieved when the form is next normalized, thereby making it disappear off the edge of the screen. To solve this problem requires custom code. The following code replicates the experience provided by Office 2003 applications, whose main windows always open normalized or maximized:

```
// MainForm.cs
partial class MainForm : Form {
  public MainForm() {
    InitializeComponent();

    // Take over initial resizing
    this.StartPosition = FormStartPosition.Manual;
```

```
  // Resize
  this.Location = FormSettings.Default.MainFormLocation;
  this.Size = FormSettings.Default.MainFormSize;
  this.WindowState = FormSettings.Default.MainFormWindowState;
}

void MainForm_FormClosing(object sender, FormClosingEventArgs e) {

  // Store location and size data, using RestoreBounds to remember
  // normal position if minimized or maximized
  if( this.WindowState == FormWindowState.Normal ) {
    Properties.Settings.Default.MainFormLocation = this.Location;
    Properties.Settings.Default.MainFormSize = this.Size;
  }
  else {
    Properties.Settings.Default.MainFormLocation =
      this.RestoreBounds.Location;
    Properties.Settings.Default.MainFormSize =
      this.RestoreBounds.Size;
  }
  Properties.Settings.Default.MainFormWindowState = this.WindowState;

  FormSettings.Default.Save();
}
}
```

Here, we operate over three settings—MainFormLocation, MainFormSize, and Main-FormWindowState—which are located in a separate settings file: FormSettings.settings. When the form is loaded, it is instructed to yield start position handling to code, which is the subsequent code to load the settings and apply them to the form.

When the form closes down, it saves the values. If the form is maximized or minimized, we need to use size and location data from the RestoreBounds property so that the form knows where to restore to from the Maximized state in the next session, or we can automatically restore it as we turn a minimized form into a normalized form next load, à la Word. If the form is currently normalized, we simply use the location and size data stored in the Bounds property. You also need to remember the size and position of a UI element when your application has tool strips.

Support for Automatic Tool Strip Layout

Recall from Chapter 4 that tool strip controls can be dragged around the edges of a form at run time. Consequently, your application should remember those details and apply them the next time it runs to ensure that its tool strips are laid out as the user expects.

Rather than having to write a bunch of code as we did for form size and position, we can lean on the ToolStripManager class (from System.Windows.Forms), which has that support built in:

```
// MainForm.cs
public partial class MainForm : Form {
   public MainForm() {
      InitializeComponent();

      ToolStripManager.LoadSettings(this);
   }

   void MainForm_FormClosing(object sender, FormClosingEventArgs e) {
      ToolStripManager.SaveSettings(this);
   }
}
```

ToolStripManager offers two static methods—LoadSettings and SaveSettings—to persist tool strip settings across application settings by leveraging the settings system. Both methods are passed the form to provide a unique name for the section in user.config, to which the settings are persisted. For MainForm, it looks like this:

```
// user.config
<?xml version="1.0" encoding="utf-8"?>
<configuration>
  <configSections> ... </configSections>
  <userSettings>
    <System.Windows.Forms.ToolStripSettings.
     ToolStripManagerSample.MainForm.toolStrip>
    <setting name="IsDefault" serializeAs="String">
      <value>False</value>
    </setting>
    <setting name="Name" serializeAs="String">
      <value>toolStrip1</value>
    </setting>
    <setting name="Size" serializeAs="String">
      <value>208, 25</value>
    </setting>
    <setting name="Location" serializeAs="String">
      <value>36, 0</value>
    </setting>
    <setting name="Visible" serializeAs="String">
      <value>True</value>
    </setting>
```

```
        <setting name="ItemOrder" serializeAs="String">
          <value>newToolStripButton, ... rest of toolstrip items </value>
        </setting>
        <setting name="ToolStripPanelName" serializeAs="String">
          <value>toolStripContainer1.Bottom</value>
        </setting>
      </System.Windows.Forms.ToolStripSettings.
        ToolStripManagerSample.MainForm.toolStrip>

      </System.Windows.Forms.ToolStripSettings.
        ToolStripManagerSample.MainForm.menuStrip>
        ...
      </System.Windows.Forms.ToolStripSettings.
        ToolStripManagerSample.MainForm.menuStrip>
    </userSettings>
  </configuration>
```

As you can see, ToolStripManager stores the size, location, visibility, and order of tool strip items for each tool strip it finds on a form. Although it certainly makes life easier, it doesn't correctly restore tool strip settings in some scenarios, particularly when several tool strips are positioned on the same row. In those cases, you can revert to manually managing your own settings.

Alternative Storage for Settings

The settings system offered by Windows Forms is comprehensive, but there are alternative data stores you may need to consider, including the Registry and special folders.

The Registry

The Registry was the place to keep read-write application and roaming-user settings from Windows 3.1 through Windows NT (it has fallen out of favor in more recent versions of Windows). The Registry is a hierarchical machinewide storage of arbitrary name/value pairs split into application and roaming-user localities based on the path to the value. The Registry Editor (regedit.exe) is a built-in tool for setting and updating Registry values, as shown in Figure 15.25.[17]

---

[17] Be careful when editing Registry values. You're working on live data that's used by the entire system. One wrong move and you're reinstalling the OS; there's no Undo!

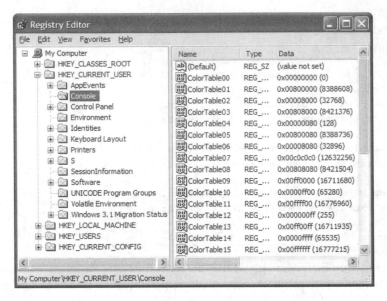

Figure 15.25 The Registry Editor

The Registry is used a lot by Win32 applications, including the Explorer shell, so you can find yourself reading and writing Registry values whether you use it to store your own application's settings.

The Registry is composed of several special top-level folders known as *hive keys*, each of which has a well-known name and provides access to a broad category of settings. The Registry class (from the Microsoft.Win32 namespace) exposes a one-to-one mapping of properties to these hive keys, as listed in Table 15.1.

Table 15.1 Registry Properties and Hive Key Names

Registry Class Static Property	Registry Hive Key Name
Registry.ClassesRoot	HKEY_CLASSES_ROOT
Registry.CurrentConfig	HKEY_CURRENT_CONFIG
Registry.CurrentUser	HKEY_CURRENT_USER
Registry.DynData	HKEY_DYN_DATA*
Registry.LocalMachine	HKEY_LOCAL_MACHINE
Registry.PerformanceData	HKEY_PERFORMANCE_DATA
Registry.Users	HKEY_USERS

* Win9x only

It's beneath the following recommended Registry path that Microsoft recommends storing user settings, under HKEY_CURRENT_USER:

```
HKEY_CURRENT_USER\Software\companyName\productName\productVersion
```

A path like this is known as a *subkey* in Registry parlance, and the following is an example:

```
HKEY_CURRENT_USER\Software\elvis\RegistrySample\1.0.0.0
```

Coincidentally, the variable values are exactly the same values provided by Application.CompanyName, Application.ProductName, and Application.Version, so you can construct a top-level key name using the following:

```
string key =
    string.Format(
      @"Software\{0}\{1}\{2}",
      Application.CompanyName,
      Application.ProductName,
      Application.ProductVersion);
```

Whereas keys are like folders, any hive key or subkey in the Registry is a container for one or more named values, with a name of null denoting the *default value* of a key. These values can be of several types, including string, unsigned integer, and arbitrary bytes. Although you should avoid using the Registry for application settings in general, one very good reason to use it is to enable tight shell integration for your Windows Forms applications, a topic discussed in Appendix F: Document Management.

Special Folders

Special folders are folders that Windows designates as having a special purpose. For example, the folder where programs are installed by default is a special folder:

```
// Generally "C:\Program Files"
string programFiles =
    Environment.GetFolderPath(Environment.SpecialFolder.ProgramFiles);
```

There are three special folders for settings: one each for the application, user, and roaming-user localities. You are better off accessing these locations through the special folders than by hard-coded paths because localized versions of Windows might change the names of the actual folders. Table 15.2 shows them, along with some sample paths running on Windows XP.

Table 15.2 Settings-Oriented Special Folders, Locality, and Examples

SpecialFolder Enum Value	Locality	Example Path
CommonApplicationData	Application	C:\Documents and Settings\All Users\ Application Data
LocalApplicationData	User	C:\Documents and Settings\<user>\ Local Settings\Application Data
ApplicationData	Roaming user	C:\Documents and Settings\<user>\ Application Data

The special folder serves as the top-level folder in the folder under which applications can store application, user, and roaming-user settings (just as Registry.LocalMachine and Registry.CurrentUser serve as the top level for application and roaming-user settings). Under that folder, an application is expected to construct a subfolder to avoid colliding with other applications or even versions of itself. The subfolder name has the following format:

```
specialFolder\companyName\productName\productVersion
```

For example:

```
C:\Documents and Settings\elvis\Local Settings\Application Data\Sells Brothers,
Inc.\My Settings Test\1.0.1124.33519
```

And just as the Application object provides shortcut access to Registry keys via properties, it also provides shortcut access to prefabricated folder names and precreated folders via the CommonAppDataPath, LocalUserAppDataPath, and UserAppDataPath properties.[18]

Where Are We?

The core of the environmental settings you'll likely need is broadly provided by four classes: Application, Environment, SystemInformation, and Screen. When system information is changed, the SystemEvents class offers a variety of events that are fired for interesting system occurrences, such as updates to user preferences and display settings.

For more specific application and user settings, you can lean on the .NET settings system, which provides comprehensive support for the creation, deployment, reading from, writing to, rollback, and migration of settings. Additionally, VS05 and the Windows Forms Designer are integrated with the settings system to allow simplified design-time management, along with the production of strongly typed settings wrapper classes. Although the settings system is rich, you may need to lean on the Registry and special folders in some situations.

---

[18] The user.config file is saved to the path stored in LocalUserAppDataPath.

16
Data Binding Basics

MUCH OF WHAT WINDOWS FORMS APPLICATIONS do is to provide users with a nice way to work with data. Much of the data that users work with resides in a wide variety of data stores, commonly databases and file systems. The equally wide variety of technologies to expose data includes ADO.NET, native data access APIs, custom objects, and even web services. It's the job of Windows Forms applications to interact with these data sources to read data from a data store, present it, provide a way to edit it, and write any changes back to the data store.

In the face of so many data stores and data access APIs, Windows Forms simplifies life with the concept of a data source. This abstraction enables Windows Forms to treat disparate data stores and access technologies in a unified, consistent way. The data source is also the cornerstone of a rich technology whose sole purpose is to simplify the integration of Windows Forms applications with data. This technology is known as data binding.

The Land before Data Binding

Logically, *data binding* is the association of object properties with control properties, facilitated by a data binding engine. Conceivably, you could create a data binding engine using your own code. For example, consider the following RaceCarDriver class:

```
// RaceCarDriver.cs
class RaceCarDriver {

  string name;
  int wins;

  public RaceCarDriver(string name, int wins) {
    this.name = name;
    this.wins = wins;
  }
```

```
  public string Name {
    get { return this.name; }
    set { this.name = value; }
  }

  public int Wins {
    get { return this.wins; }
    set { this.wins = value; }
  }
}
```

The idea is to allow editing of the RaceCarDriver object's properties via two text box controls on the form. To do that, we need to maintain synchronicity between the values of the Text properties of both text controls and the Name and Wins properties of the RaceCarDriver object.

First, we copy the RaceCarDriver object's initial state to the text box controls:

```
// TheLandBeforeDataBindingForm.cs
partial class TheLandBeforeDataBindingForm : Form {

  RaceCarDriver raceCarDriver = new RaceCarDriver("M Schumacher", 500);

  public TheLandBeforeDataBindingForm() {
    InitializeComponent();

    // Copy initial RaceCarDriver state to text box controls
    this.nameTextBox.Text = this.raceCarDriver.Name;
    this.winsTextBox.Text = this.raceCarDriver.Wins.ToString();
  }
}
```

Because TextBox.Text is a string and RaceCarDriver.Wins is an integer, we must also coerce the Wins data from an integer to a string. The RaceCarDriver object's initial values are displayed, as shown in Figure 16.1.

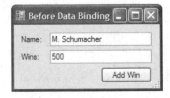

Figure 16.1 Text Boxes Displaying Initial RaceCarDriver Object State

Second, because it's possible to change the text box values after they're loaded, we need to notice when those changes are made and copy the new values back to the RaceCarDriver object. Because we're using text box controls, we can notice the changes via the TextChanged event:

```
// TheLandBeforeDataBindingForm.cs
partial class TheLandBeforeDataBindingForm : Form {
  ...
  public TheLandBeforeDataBindingForm() {
    ...
    // Detect changes to text box controls
    this.nameTextBox.TextChanged += this.nameTextBox_TextChanged;
    this.winsTextBox.TextChanged += this.winsTextBox_TextChanged;
  }

  void nameTextBox_TextChanged(object sender, EventArgs e) {
    this.raceCarDriver.Name = this.nameTextBox.Text;
  }

  void winsTextBox_TextChanged(object sender, EventArgs e) {
    this.raceCarDriver.Wins = int.Parse(this.winsTextBox.Text);
  }
}
```

This step also requires coercing the Wins data, this time from a string to an integer, as the data is copied from the text box to the RaceCarDriver object.

Now, consider the following scenario, in which the RaceCarDriver object is changed directly:

```
// TheLandBeforeDataBindingForm.cs
partial class TheLandBeforeDataBindingForm : Form {
  ...
  void addWinButton_Click(object sender, EventArgs e) {
    ++this.raceCarDriver.Wins;
    // Don't forget to update the Wins text box!
    this.winsTextBox.Text = raceCarDriver.Wins.ToString();
  }
}
```

In this example, we manually update our view of the object's state in the text boxes whenever the RaceCarDriver object's state is changed. Unfortunately, that doesn't work if the RaceCarDriver object's state is changed by the object itself or by other code that doesn't know about the text boxes. To combat this problem, we update the Text property's value on the relevant text box controls in the event that the RaceCarDriver object's state changes.

The preferred way to do this is for a type to implement INotifyPropertyChanged (from the System.ComponentModel namespace):[1]

```
// RaceCarDriver.cs
class RaceCarDriver : INotifyPropertyChanged {
  ...
  public event PropertyChangedEventHandler PropertyChanged;

  public string Name {
    get { return this.name; }
    set {
      this.name = value;
      this.OnPropertyChanged("Name");
    }
  }

  public int Wins {
    get { return this.wins; }
    set {
      this.wins = value;
      this.OnPropertyChanged("Wins");
    }
  }

  // Helper
  void OnPropertyChanged(string propertyName) {
    if( this.PropertyChanged != null ) {
      this.PropertyChanged(
        this,
        new PropertyChangedEventArgs(propertyName));
    }
  }
}
```

The PropertyChanged event is passed a PropertyChangedEventArgs object through which you specify which property changed. The form then handles the PropertyChanged event to update the text boxes without building internal knowledge of how a RaceCarDriver object manages its state or when it is changed by a third party beyond our control:

```
// TheLandBeforeDataBindingForm.cs
partial class TheLandBeforeDataBindingForm : Form {
  ...
  public TheLandBeforeDataBindingForm() {
    ...
```

[1] .NET also supports change notification through the implementation of *PropertyName*Changed events, although this technique doesn't scale as well as implementing INotifyPropertyChanged.

```
      // Detect changes to text box controls
      this.nameTextBox.TextChanged += this.nameTextBox_TextChanged;
      this.winsTextBox.TextChanged += this.winsTextBox_TextChanged;

      // Detect changes to RaceCarDriver object
      this.raceCarDriver.PropertyChanged += raceCarDriver_PropertyChanged;
   }
   ...
   void nameTextBox_TextChanged(object sender, EventArgs e) {
      this.raceCarDriver.Name = this.nameTextBox.Text;
   }
   void winsTextBox_TextChanged(object sender, EventArgs e) {
      this.raceCarDriver.Wins = int.Parse(this.winsTextBox.Text);
   }

   void raceCarDriver_PropertyChanged(
      object sender, PropertyChangedEventArgs e) {
      switch( e.PropertyName ) {
        case "Name":
          this.nameTextBox.Text = this.raceCarDriver.Name;
          break;
        case "Wins":
          this.winsTextBox.Text = this.raceCarDriver.Wins.ToString();
          break;
      }
   }
}
```

Now, when the Add Win button is pressed, we simply increase the RaceCarDriver object's Wins property:

```
// TheLandBeforeDataBindingForm.cs
partial class TheLandBeforeDataBindingForm : Form {
   ...
   void addWinButton_Click(object sender, EventArgs e) {
      // Causes the RaceCarDriver object's WinsChanged event to fire,
      // which is used to keep the Wins text box up-to-date
      ++this.raceCarDriver.Wins;
   }
   ...
}
```

In turn, this fires the PropertyChanged event, which is finally caught by the form to update its Wins text box.

At this point, we've written code that synchronizes and converts data between the text boxes and the RaceCarDriver object bidirectionally, both initially and in the face of subsequent changes on either side of the relationship, as illustrated in Figure 16.2.

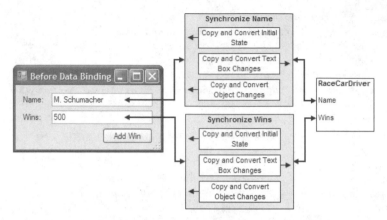

Figure 16.2   Text Box Controls Bidirectionally Synchronized with a RaceCarDriver Object

In this way, we have logically *bound* the Text properties of the Name and Wins text boxes to the Name and Wins properties of the RaceCarDriver object, as illustrated in Figure 16.3.

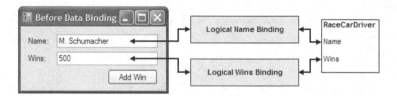

Figure 16.3   Text Box Controls Logically Bound to a RaceCarDriver Object

Unfortunately, we have spent quite a lot of time writing our binding code, and the result requires intimate knowledge of RaceCarDriver. What we need is a generic way to bind any controls to any type of object, which automatically handles both bidirectional synchronization and data conversion.

Happily for all, the data binding engine that's built right into Windows Forms provides exactly this support.

Simple Data Binding and Item Data Sources

The fundamental building block of the Windows Forms data binding engine is the Binding object, which binds control properties to object properties:

```
// RaceCarDriver.cs
class RaceCarDriver {...}

// SimpleBindingAndItemDataSources.cs
partial class SimpleBindingAndItemDataSources : Form {
```

```
        RaceCarDriver raceCarDriver = new RaceCarDriver("M. Schumacher", 500);

    public SimpleBindingAndItemDataSources() {
        InitializeComponent();

        // Bind the Name and Wins properties to the Name and Wins text boxes
        Binding nameBinding =
            new Binding("Text", this.raceCarDriver, "Name", true);
        this.nameTextBox.DataBindings.Add(nameBinding);
        Binding winsBinding =
            new Binding("Text", this.raceCarDriver, "Wins", true);
        this.winsTextBox.DataBindings.Add(winsBinding);
    }

    void addWinButton_Click(object sender, EventArgs e) {
        // Causes the RaceCarDriver object's PropertyChanged event to fire,
        // which is used to keep the Wins text box up-to-date
        ++this.raceCarDriver.Wins;
    }
}
```

Two interesting things are going on in this code. First, two Binding objects are created, each requiring four parameters: the name of the property on the control to set (name-TextBox.Text and winsTextBox.Text); the object that exposes the property (raceCarDriver); the name of the property to which to bind (raceCarDriver.Name and raceCarDriver.Wins); and whether to enable automatic formatting.[2]

As a simplification, it is possible to use an overload of the Bindings collection's Add method to pass the binding values directly:

```
// SimpleBindingAndItemDataSources.cs
partial class SimpleBindingAndItemDataSources : Form {
    ...
    public RaceCarDriverForm() {
        ...
        // Bind the Name and Wins properties to the Name and Wins text boxes
        this.nameTextBox.DataBindings.Add(
            "Text", this.raceCarDriver, "Name");
        this.winsTextBox.DataBindings.Add(
            "Text", this.raceCarDriver, "Wins");
    }
    ...
}
```

[2] Although you always pass true as the last argument when creating a Binding object, formatting itself is discussed in Chapter 17: Applied Data Binding. Second, each binding object is inserted into the Bindings collection of the appropriate text box control, thereby establishing the binding.

Whichever technique is used, two things happen when a binding is added. First, the data binding engine automatically populates the control's property with the value of the object's property, just as if we'd set nameTextBox.Text to raceCarDriver.Name manually. Any required data conversion occurs automatically (more on that in Chapter 17). Because the initialization is automatic, there is no need to manually set the initial content, and this is why there is no code to do so in the form's constructor.

Second, after initialization, the data binding engine takes care of synchronization between the control and the raceCarDriver object's properties. To ensure that changes are replicated from the object to the control, the binding engine looks for the INotifyProperty-Changed.PropertyChanged event when a Binding object is added to a control. If this event is found, the binding subscribes to it and, when it's fired, copies the new object property value to the bound control property. Consequently, we need not write any code to update the Wins text box when the Wins property is updated via the Add Win button's Click event handler.

Whenever you bind a control's property to an object's property, it is called *simple binding*. Most control properties (for example, Color, BackgroundImage) can be bound in this way and can be kept synchronized with public properties on any object. A simple binding is *two-way* only if the object fires an INotifyPropertyChanged.PropertyChanged event (or a *PropertyName*Changed event) and if the public property is read-write (implements both get and set accessors). Further, in data binding parlance, a bound object like RaceCarDriver is known as an *item data source* because its data is located in a single item. However, if the data we want to bind to is located in a collection of items, we need a list data source.

Simple Binding and List Data Sources

A *list data source* is exactly what it sounds like: a collection of homogenous objects to be used as data in a binding operation. The minimum implementation that is considered a list data source by the Windows Forms binding engine is a class that implements the IList interface (from System.Collections). For convenience, you can use the generic IList implementation, List<T>, located in System.Collections.Generic, which is a strongly typed implementation of IList. For example, you could use List<T> to create a list of RaceCarDriver objects:

```
// SimpleBindingAndListDataSourcesForm.cs
partial class SimpleBindingAndListDataSourcesForm : Form {

  // Create strongly typed list data source
  List<RaceCarDriver> raceCarDrivers = new List<RaceCarDriver>();
```

```
    public SimpleBindingAndListDataSourcesForm() {
      InitializeComponent();
      // Populate list data source with data items
      this.raceCarDrivers.Add(new RaceCarDriver("M. Schumacher", 500));
      this.raceCarDrivers.Add(new RaceCarDriver("A. Senna", 1000));
      this.raceCarDrivers.Add(new RaceCarDriver("A. Prost", 400));
    }
  }
```

As you can see in this code, a list data source contains one or more item data sources (items). Although the items are contained within the list data source, we can still bind them to our Name and Wins text boxes:

```
  // SimpleBindingAndListDataSourcesForm.cs
  partial class SimpleBindingAndListDataSourcesForm : Form {
    ...
    public SimpleBindingAndListDataSourcesForm() {
      ...
      // Bind the Name and Wins properties to the Name and Wins text boxes
      this.nameTextBox.DataBindings.Add(
        "Text", this.raceCarDrivers, "Name");
      this.winsTextBox.DataBindings.Add(
        "Text", this.raceCarDrivers, "Wins");
    }
  }
```

This code should look familiar because it's almost exactly the same code used to bind our controls to an item data source. The only difference is in the object we specify as the data source; this time it's a list data source. When you simple-bind to a list data source like this, the controls default their values to the properties on the first item in the list, as Figure 16.4 demonstrates.

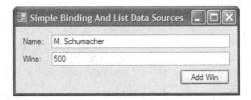

Figure 16.4   Controls Bound to a List Data Source and Displaying the First Item in the List

However, because TextBox controls support only simple binding, we can display the data for only one RaceCarDriver object at a time. To show more RaceCarDriver items, we need to add support to the form to navigate between them, as shown in Figure 16.5.

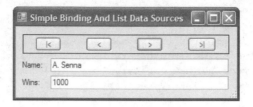

Figure 16.5   Navigating the Items in a Bound List Data Source

Navigation means changing the current item to another item in the list. The *current* item is special because it's managed by a special object known as a *binding manager*. Binding managers have the responsibility of managing a set of bindings for a particular data source and come in two flavors: property managers and currency managers. A *property manager* is an instance of the PropertyManager class and is created for an item data source. A *currency manager* is an instance of the CurrencyManager class and is created for a list data source. Both of these are implementations of the abstract base class BindingManagerBase:

```
namespace System.Windows.Forms {
    abstract class BindingManagerBase {

        // Constructor
        public BindingManagerBase();

        // Properties
        public BindingsCollection Bindings { get; }
        public abstract int Count { get; }
        public abstract object Current { get; }
        public bool IsBindingSuspended { get; } // New
        public abstract int Position { get; set; }

        // Methods
        public abstract void AddNew();
        public abstract void CancelCurrentEdit();
        public abstract void EndCurrentEdit();
        public virtual PropertyDescriptorCollection GetItemProperties();
        public abstract void RemoveAt(int index);
        public abstract void ResumeBinding();
        public abstract void SuspendBinding();

        // Events
        public event BindingCompleteEventHandler BindingComplete; // New
        public event EventHandler CurrentChanged;
        public event EventHandler CurrentItemChanged; // New
        public event BindingManagerDataErrorEventHandler DataError; // New
        public event EventHandler PositionChanged;
    }
```

updated

```
...
  class PropertyManager : BindingManagerBase {...}
  class CurrencyManager : BindingManagerBase {...}
}
```

One of the jobs of a binding manager (both property manager and currency manager) is to keep track of the location of the current object, a task known as *currency* management. The current location is available from the binding manager's Position property. The Position property is always zero for a property manager, however, because it only manages a data source with a single item, as shown in Figure 16.6.

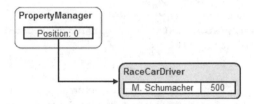

Figure 16.6   A Property Manager Maintaining Currency on an Item Data Source

For a currency manager, however, the position is an index into the list of items in the list data source, as shown in Figure 16.7.

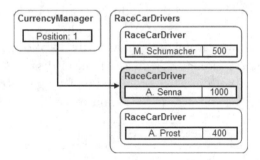

Figure 16.7   A Currency Manager Maintaining Currency on a List Data Source

To implement navigation for a list data source—doing so for an item data source doesn't make sense—you acquire the BindingManager for the desired data source and use it to change the binding manager's position as appropriate:

```
// SimpleBindingAndListDataSourcesForm.cs
partial class SimpleBindingAndListDataSourcesForm : Form {
  ...
```

```
BindingManagerBase BindingManager {
  get { return this.BindingContext[this.raceCarDrivers]; }
}

void moveFirstButton_Click(object sender, EventArgs e) {
  this.BindingManager.Position = 0;
}

void movePreviousButton_Click(object sender, EventArgs e) {
  // No need to worry about being < 0
  --this.BindingManager.Position;
}

void moveNextButton_Click(object sender, EventArgs e) {
  // No need to worry about being > BindingManager.Count
  ++this.BindingManager.Position;
}

void moveLastButton_Click(object sender, EventArgs e) {
  this.BindingManager.Position = this.BindingManager.Count - 1;
}
}
```

Here, the code implements a property that provides access to the binding manager for the RaceCarDriver's list data source to which the Text properties of the Name and Wins text boxes are bound. Then, the code simply updates the binding manager's position as appropriate. The change in position causes the bindings of all bound controls to update to the new current object.

As a useful visual aid, we can relay to the user the location of the current item with respect to the total number of items, as well as enable or disable the move buttons as we reach either end of the list. Both functions rely on displaying the BindingManager's Position and Count properties when the form loads and when the current item changes:

```
// SimpleBindingAndListDataSourcesForm.cs
partial class SimpleBindingAndListDataSourcesForm : Form {
  ...
  public SimpleBindingAndListDataSourcesForm() {
    ...
    RefreshItems();
  }
  ...
  void moveFirstButton_Click(object sender, EventArgs e) {
    this.BindingManager.Position = 0;
    RefreshItems();
  }
}
```

```
void movePreviousButton_Click(object sender, EventArgs e) {
  // No need to worry about being < 0
  --this.BindingManager.Position;
  RefreshItems();
}

void moveNextButton_Click(object sender, EventArgs e) {
  // No need to worry about being > BindingManager.Count
  ++this.BindingManager.Position;
  RefreshItems();
}

void moveLastButton_Click(object sender, EventArgs e) {
  this.BindingManager.Position = this.BindingManager.Count - 1;
  RefreshItems();
}
...
void RefreshItems() {
  int count = this.BindingManager.Count;
  int position = this.BindingManager.Position + 1;

  // Update count and position text
  this.countLabel.Text = count.ToString();
  this.positionLabel.Text = position.ToString();

  // Enable or disable move buttons
  this.moveFirstButton.Enabled = (position > 1);
  this.movePreviousButton.Enabled = (position > 1);
  this.moveNextButton.Enabled = (position < count);
  this.moveLastButton.Enabled = (position < count);
}
}
```

The result is shown in Figure 16.8.

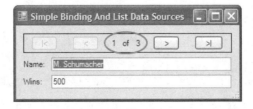

Figure 16.8   Displaying Position and Count

Although simple binding works just fine for list data sources, it's quite likely you'll want to use list data sources with controls that can show more than one object at a time, such as ListBox and DataGridView. For this, we have complex binding.

Complex Binding and List Data Sources

Whereas simple binding to list data sources binds a control property to a property on the current object of a list data source, *complex binding* binds a control property to an entire list data source. The "complex" in complex binding refers to the additional support that's built into controls themselves to operate over and render list data.

For example, when you bind a ListBox control to a list data source, the ListBox automatically hooks up the relevant bindings and adds each object in the list data source to its list of items to display:

```csharp
// ComplexBindingListBoxForm.cs
partial class ComplexBindingListBoxForm: Form {

  // Create strongly typed list data source
  List<RaceCarDriver> raceCarDrivers = new List<RaceCarDriver>();

  public ComplexBindingListBoxForm () {

    // Populate list data source with data items
    this.raceCarDrivers.Add(new RaceCarDriver("M. Schumacher", 500));
    this.raceCarDrivers.Add(new RaceCarDriver("A. Senna", 1000));
    this.raceCarDrivers.Add(new RaceCarDriver("A. Prost", 400));

    // Simple-bind the Name and Wins properties to the Name and
    // Wins text boxes. Keeps the RaceCarDriver object up-to-date as
    // user enters data
    this.nameTextBox.DataBindings.Add(
      "Text", this.raceCarDrivers, "Name");
    this.winsTextBox.DataBindings.Add(
      "Text", this.raceCarDrivers, "Wins");

    // Complex-bind list box to RaceCarDriver's list data source
    this.raceCarDriversListBox.DataSource = this.raceCarDrivers;
    // Specify the property whose value will appear in the list box
    // for each item in the list data source
    this.raceCarDriversListBox.DisplayMember = "Name";
    ...
  }
  ...
  // Navigation code
  ...
}
```

There are three interesting aspects to this code. First, the list box is bound to the list data source via the list box's DataSource property. Complex controls usually expose DataSource to consume list data sources. Second, the list box's DisplayMember property is set to specify which property of the contained objects provides the value that's displayed in the list; by default, this value is retrieved from the ToString property of each contained object, but list box controls allow customization via the DisplayMember property.

Third, all three controls are bound to the same list data source, and this means that they share the same binding manager by default and, therefore, share the same idea of which object is current, as Figure 16.9 demonstrates.

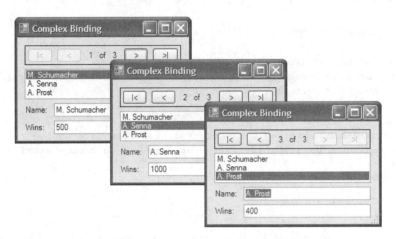

Figure 16.9   Complex-Bound ListBox and Simple-Bound TextBox Controls Sharing the Same Current Object

At this point, our sample UI supports navigating through a list of RaceCarDriver objects. It doesn't, however, support the addition of new RaceCarDriver objects, or even the deletion of existing ones. We could either update our UI to provide these abilities or use a DataGridView control, which has this additional support built in. The updated form would look like Figure 16.10.

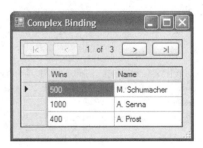

Figure 16.10   DataGridView Complex-Bound to RaceCarDriver's List Data Source

With a DataGridView dropped onto a form at design time, the form shown in Figure 16.10 is enabled with the following code:

```
// ComplexBindingDataGridViewForm.cs
public partial class ComplexBindingDataGridViewForm : Form {

  // Create strongly typed list data source
  List<RaceCarDriver> raceCarDrivers = new List<RaceCarDriver>();

  public ComplexBindingDataGridViewForm() {

    // Populate list data source with data items
    this.raceCarDrivers.Add(new RaceCarDriver("M. Schumacher", 500));
    this.raceCarDrivers.Add(new RaceCarDriver("A. Senna", 1000));
    this.raceCarDrivers.Add(new RaceCarDriver("A. Prost", 400));

    // Complex-bind list box to RaceCarDriver's list data source
    this.racingCarDriversDataGridView.DataSource = this.raceCarDrivers;
  }
  // Navigation code
  ...
}
```

As you can see, the code is slightly slimmer, but we have gained some additional support: First, the DataGridView can peer into a list data source to determine the type of items it contains and, for each public property, dynamically create a column on our behalf. Second, the DataGridView lets us edit items in-place, including support for adding and deleting items.

```
void addButton_Click(object sender, EventArgs e) {
  // Add item to list data source directly
  RaceCarDriver raceCarDriver = new RaceCarDriver("Nelson Piquet", 300);
  this.raceCarDrivers.Add(raceCarDriver);

  // Select new item
  this.BindingManager.Position = this.BindingManager.Count - 1;
}

private void deleteButton_Click(object sender, EventArgs e) {
  // Remove item from list data source directly
  this.raceCarDrivers.Remove(
    (RaceCarDriver)this.BindingManager.Current);
}
```

Unfortunately, this code has no immediate visual effect: DataGridView neither displays the newly added RaceCarDriver object nor shows the effects of its removal.[3] Figure 16.11 illustrates.

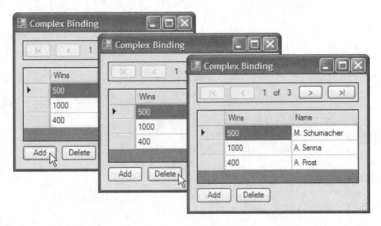

Figure 16.11   DataGridView Not Automatically Reflecting List Data Source Changes

The reason is that a list data source of type List<T> doesn't provide notification of actions taken against its list items, such as adding, updating, and deleting, and thus the data binding engine doesn't see them. Therefore, just as item data sources need to implement a communications protocol to notify simple-bound controls of change, list data sources need to implement a communications protocol to let both simple-bound and complex-bound clients know about both list and item changes.

This protocol is embodied by the IBindingList interface.

IBindingList

The minimum level of usable data binding functionality for list data sources really comprises all that we've seen so far:

- Support for both simple and complex binding models
- The ability to add, update, and delete items on both bound controls and list data sources
- The issuing of list and list item change notifications

---

[3] Actually, these changes are visible when DataGridView is forced to repaint its UI in response to the cursor moving over a cell or a call to the Refresh method. However, these techniques are suboptimal.

This and other related functionality is encapsulated by the IBindingList data binding interface:

```
namespace System.ComponentModel {
   interface IBindingList : IList, ... {

      // List management
      bool AllowEdit { get; set; }
      bool AllowNew { get; set;  }
      bool AllowRemove { get; set; }
      object AddNew();

      // List change notification
      bool SupportsChangeNotification { get; }
      event ListChangedEventHandler ListChanged;

      // Sorting
      bool SupportsSorting { get; }
      ... // Rest of sorting members elided

      // Searching
      bool SupportsSearching { get; }
      ... // Rest of searching members elided
   }
}
```

IBindingList is a well-known data binding infrastructure contract that extends IList with data-binding-specific functionality for list data sources. IBindingList implementations must support the list management members of the interface to let users add, update, and delete list data source items (via AllowEdit, AllowNew, and AllowRemove) and to provide a hook into the item adding process with AddNew. List change notification, sorting, and searching, unlike list management, can be optionally implemented, a fact that's advertised by SupportsChangeNotification, SupportsSorting, and SupportsSearching, respectively.

If list change notification is supported, bound controls can subscribe to the ListChanged event to notice when items are added, updated, or removed and thereby keep their displayed data synchronized with the list data source. If sorting or searching is provided, bound controls like DataGridView can tailor their UIs with additional elements to provide a mechanism for users to exercise these capabilities;[4] DataGridView enables sorting via column header clicking, and it paints a special arrow glyph in the sorted column to indicate sort order.

---

[4] Using searching and sorting is shown in Chapter 17. While it's beyond the scope of this book to discuss how to implement sorting and searching custom data sources, it's nicely covered in Brian Noyes's book *Data Binding with Windows Forms 2.0 : Programming Smart Client Data Applications with .NET* (Addison-Wesley, 2006).

IBindingList is the interface you implement to add list management and list change notification to your list data sources, which might themselves implement IEnumerable, ICollection, and IList. Unfortunately, this is a nontrivial exercise. Fortunately, it's also an unnecessary exercise because BindingList<T> implements these elements of IBindingList for you.

BindingList<T>

BindingList<T>, from the System.ComponentModel namespace, is a generic implementation of IBindingList:

```
class BindingList<T> : IBindingList, ... {...}
```

BindingList<T> nicely implements the list management (AllowEdit, AllowNew, AllowRemove, and AddNew) and change notification (SupportsChangeNotification, ListChanged) functional subsets of IBindingList.[5] And because it's generic, it can turn any type into a strongly typed list data source with data-binding-savvy list management and change notification using something like the following code:

```
// ComplexBindingDataGridViewForm.cs
partial class ComplexBindingDataGridViewForm : Form {

  // Create strongly typed list data source with list management
  // and change notification
  BindingList<RaceCarDriver> raceCarDrivers =
    new BindingList<RaceCarDriver>();

  public ComplexBindingDataGridViewForm() {
    InitializeComponent();

    // Populate list data source with data items
    this.raceCarDrivers.Add(new RaceCarDriver("M. Schumacher", 500));
    this.raceCarDrivers.Add(new RaceCarDriver("A. Senna", 1000));
    this.raceCarDrivers.Add(new RaceCarDriver("A. Prost", 400));

    this.racingCarDriversDataGridView.DataSource = this.raceCarDrivers;
    ...
  }
  ...
}
```

---

[5] Note that BindingList<T> does not implement the sorting and searching functional subsets of IBindingList. *Data Binding with Windows Forms 2.0* (Addison-Wesley) by Brian Noyes has the answers.

Two-Way List Change Synchronization

Figure 16.12 illustrates BindingList<T>'s automatic support for broadcasting list change notifications when an item is added or deleted directly to or from the list.

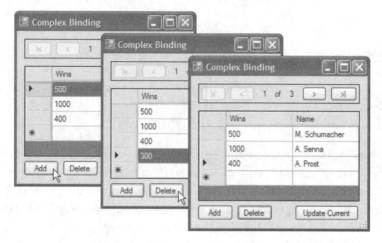

Figure 16.12   DataGridView Automatically Reflecting List Data Source Changes Via BindingList<T>

You can see that when the Add button is clicked to add a new RaceCarDriver instance to the list data source, the change is broadcast to all bound controls (in this case, DataGridView). When DataGridView receives the notification, it repaints its UI to show the change. The same applies when an item is deleted from the list data source.

Just as both of these notifications are broadcast when the list data source is changed, BindingList<T> broadcasts similar notifications when the values of an individual item it contains are updated. Further, data binding notifications work both ways; as changes are made to cells in DataGridView or as rows are added to or removed from DataGridView, DataGridView notifies the list data source to reflect those changes. BindingList<T> responds to both DataGridView operations, but we can't add new items until we go one step further.

When a new row is added to DataGridView, no values are added to the row because the user obviously hasn't had the opportunity to enter them. Consequently, DataGridView relies on the item type of the list data source to provide the default state, which is used to populate the new row. We instantiate the item type using the default constructor. If the item type implements a default constructor, DataGridView automatically supports adding a new row; in contrast, if the default constructor is not implemented—as is the case with RaceCarDriver—then DataGridView disables this capability (although DataGridView supports the ability to delete rows in either case).

Solving this problem is simple: We make sure that our item type implements the *default constructor* (a constructor that takes no parameters):

```
// RaceCarDriver.cs
class RaceCarDriver {
  ...
  // Needed so DGV can add new rows
  public RaceCarDriver() {
    // Provide default values, if needed
    ...
  }

  public RaceCarDriver(string name, int wins) {
    this.name = name;
    this.wins = wins;
  }
  ...
}
```

After the default constructor has been added to the RaceCarDriver class, new items can be added via DataGridView, as shown in Figure 16.13.

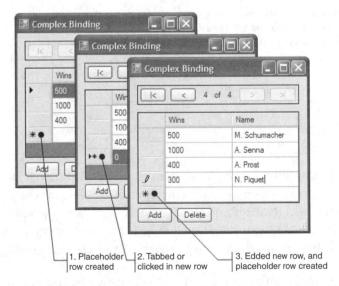

1. Placeholder row created   2. Tabbed or clicked in new row   3. Edded new row, and placeholder row created

Figure 16.13   Visually Adding New List Data Source Items via DataGridView

You can see how DataGridView takes advantage of the data source. First, DataGridView determines whether the bound list data source allows the addition of new items; to do that,

DataGridView inspects its Boolean IBindingList.AllowNew property. In the case of Bind-ingList<T>, AllowNew returns true if the type T has a default constructor, or false other-wise. If AllNew returns true, DataGridView adds the placeholder row.

Second, DataGridView calls IBindingList.AddNew to create a new RaceCarDriver object when a placeholder row is selected (by tabbing or mouse clicking) and adds it to the list.[6]

Third, DataGridView adds a new placeholder row when the new RaceCarDriver object is edited.

Two-Way Item Change Synchronization

When the values in a DataGridView row are changed, DataGridView automatically repli-cates the changes to the bound list data source. Similarly, when changes are made to an item in the list data source of BindingList<T>, an item change notification is broadcast to all bound controls.

For example, consider the following code, which increments the number of wins for the currently selected race car driver in the list data source:

```
// ComplexBindingDataGridViewForm.cs
partial class ComplexBindingDataGridViewForm : Form {
  ...
  void updateCurrentButton_Click(object sender, EventArgs e) {
    int current = this.BindingManager.Position;
    ++((RaceCarDriver)this.raceCarDrivers[current]).Wins;
  }
  ...
  BindingManagerBase BindingManager {
    get { return this.BindingContext[this.raceCarDrivers]; }
  }
  ...
}
```

By default, BindingList<T> broadcasts item change notifications. However, DataGrid-View visually reflects changes only to the current item—unless the changed item in the list data source implements INotifyPropertyChange. In this case, DataGridView reflects the changes appropriately. If INotifyPropertyChange is not implemented, and if an item other than the current item is changed, those changes aren't reflected in bound controls unless the

---

[6] You can derive from BindingList<T> to override AddNew and AllowNew to allow the creation of default item instances irrespective of whether the item type implements a default constructor. This technique can be handy when you don't control the item type you are working with—for example, if it is provided by a web service.

controls are repainted.[7] As you would expect, the same applies to simple-bound UIs, but that is not important because you can't see anything other than the current row.

The BindingSource Component

BindingList<T> allows us to use almost any class to create a data-binding-savvy strongly typed list data source. However, some item classes come already associated with their own collection classes. Although any collection class that implements IList can be used as a list data source, you don't get full-flavor data binding if you don't implement IBindingList— namely, support for two-way list and item change notification.

To gain this support and to avoid the highly involved implementation of IBindingList ourselves, we'd love to be able to "upgrade" an existing IList implementation to IBindingList. The class that performs this upgrade for you is BindingSource.

The BindingSource component (from System.Windows.Forms) consumes either item types or list types and exposes them as IBindingList implementations. As you'll see throughout this chapter and well into the next, BindingSource gives you an enormous amount of data binding ability, both in code and via designers. All this ability hinges on BindingSource acting as an IBindingList implementation for types that don't implement IBindingList themselves.

Turning an Item Type into a List Data Source

To turn a less-than-IBindingList type into an IBindingList type, you might consider trying something like this:

```
// BindingSourceForm.cs
partial class BindingSourceForm : Form {

  // Create strongly typed list data source
  List<RaceCarDriver> raceCarDrivers = new List<RaceCarDriver>();

  // Create a BindingSource
  BindingSource raceCarDriversBS = new BindingSource();

  public BindingSourceForm() {
    InitializeComponent();
```

[7] If you need changes to list data source items to be reflected automatically, current or otherwise, Brian Noyes provides an implementation in his book.

```
        // Populate list data source with data items
        this.raceCarDrivers.Add(new RaceCarDriver("M. Schumacher", 500));
        this.raceCarDrivers.Add(new RaceCarDriver("A. Senna", 1000));
        this.raceCarDrivers.Add(new RaceCarDriver("A. Prost", 400));

        // This code augments the List<RaceCarDriver> with IBindingList
        // list management and change notification capabilities
        // but only when used via the BindingSource
        this.raceCarDriversBS.DataSource = this.raceCarDrivers;
        ...
    }
    ...
}
```

This code augments a List<T> instance with IBindingList list management and change notification support via the BindingSource.

After the binding is established, you programmatically add and delete items via BindingSource for the IBindingList list support to work, because that's where the list change notification logic is located:

```
// Add items to binding source - GOOD
this.raceCarDriversBS.Add(new RaceCarDriver("M. Schumacher", 500));
```

If you programmatically add items via the original list, such as our raceCarDrivers object, change notification does not work:

```
// Add items to list data source directly - BAD
this.raceCarDrivers.Add(new RaceCarDriver("M. Schumacher", 500));
```

To avoid providing two unequal APIs to your list data—one with data change notifications and one without—you can turn over storage responsibilities completely to BindingSource. To specify that BindingSource should be responsible for the list-based storage of your item data type, you seed the DataSource property with the type of the item data type:

```
// BindingSourceForm.cs
partial class BindingSourceForm : Form {
  ...
  // Create a BindingSource
  BindingSource raceCarDriversBS = new BindingSource();

  public BindingSourceForm() {
    InitializeComponent();
    ...
    // This will allow BindingSource to act as a list data source
    // that operates over the RaceCarDriver item
```

```
        this.raceCarDriversBS.DataSource = typeof(RaceCarDriver);
        ...
    }
    ...
}
```

Internally, BindingSource instantiates BindingList<T> to operate over the designated type and provide IBindingList services. The result is that BindingSource now both provides and manages the storage of a list data source that operates over the desired type. To access the storage provided by BindingSource, you use the List property, which is of type IList:

```
IList bindingSourceStorage = this.raceCarDriversBS.List;
```

In addition to providing storage based on the type of the item data, you get the same behavior from BindingSource if you provide a list data source of a type that doesn't implement IBindingList:

```
// BindingSourceForm.cs
partial class BindingSourceForm : Form {
    ...
  // Create a BindingSource
  BindingSource raceCarDriversBS = new BindingSource();

  public BindingSourceForm() {
    InitializeComponent();
    ...
    // This will allow BindingSource to act as a list data source
    // that operates over the RaceCarDriver item
    this.raceCarDriversBS.DataSource = typeof(RaceCarDriver);
    ...
  }
  ...
}
```

In this case, BindingSource inspects the list type and extracts the item type over which it operates, using BindingsList<T> for storage as before.

Using BindingSource at Design Time

The act of using either an item or a list data type to indicate storage requirements to the BindingSource is known as *shaping*. The idea is that the type of the item provides the shape of the data being bound to, and this shape is used at design time to provide a list of item data properties that support binding for any particular type.

Shaping is combined with component-based interaction to provide a consistent design-time binding experience no matter what kind of data you're binding to. This allows BindingSource to project any data source onto a form's design surface and, even better, allows controls to bind directly against the BindingSource itself, thereby allowing you to shape a data-bound UI against any data source, whether or not that data source is a component (most data sources aren't) and whether or not that data source implements IBindingList (most data sources don't).

To expose any CLR object or list as a data source, you drag a BindingSource from the Data tab of the Toolbox and drop it onto a design surface, as shown in Figure 16.14.

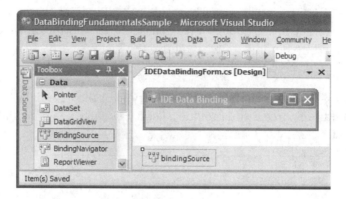

Figure 16.14   The BindingSource Design-Time Component

When on the design surface, a BindingSource component opens a Pandora's Box of design-time fun for declaratively configuring bound UIs.

Design-Time Data Sources

 You use VS05's Data Sources window to identify and create data sources for a project. You open the Data Sources window, shown in Figure 16.15, by choosing Data | Show Data Sources from the VS05 main menu.

Figure 16.15   Data Sources Window in VS05

When a project has no data sources, the Data Sources window displays a comment to make sure you know about it, and it gives you two mechanisms for adding a new one: the Add New Data Source link label or its tool strip button counterpart.[8] Either way opens the Data Source Configuration Wizard, shown in Figure 16.16.

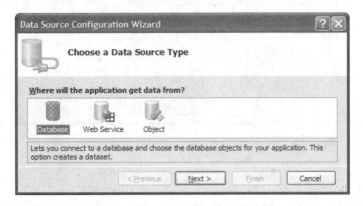

Figure 16.16   Data Source Configuration Wizard

Here, you create a data source to encapsulate data stored in a database, a web service, or a .NET type.

Databases

Arguably the most common location of data is within a database and, therefore, is the most common data to expose as a data source for data binding. Visual Studio has always provided the means to encapsulate data located in databases using typed data sets. A *typed data set* is a class that contains one or more database tables, views, stored procedures, and functions, each of which is exposed as a strongly typed .NET class. Each of these needs to be loaded with data from the database and, in some cases, needs to update the database with any changes. This work is performed by a *typed table adapter*. VS05 automatically creates one for each database object exposed from a typed data set.

To use the Data Source Configuration Wizard to facilitate the creation of typed data sets and table adapters, you choose the Database option, as shown in Figure 16.16. This process revolves around selecting one or more tables, stored procedures, or views that will supply the data you require. The next step is to identify the desired database by choosing a database connection, shown in Figure 16.17.

[8] You can also add a data source to your project by clicking Data | Add New Data.

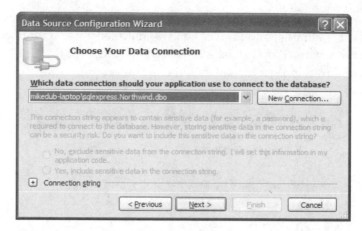

Figure 16.17 Choosing a Data Connection

Although supplying a connection string at design time helps our data binding config-uration, we'll need the same connection string at run time. Consequently, the Data Source Configuration Wizard next asks you whether you want the database connection to be stored as an application setting, as shown in Figure 16.18.[9]

Figure 16.18 Persisting a Data Connection as an Application Setting

If you choose yes, the setting shown in Figure 16.19 is added to your application-wide settings.

[9] By splitting out the connection string as an application setting, you can easily change it so that applications can use different database servers as dictated by deployment. See Chapter 15: Settings for more information on application settings and how they're used.

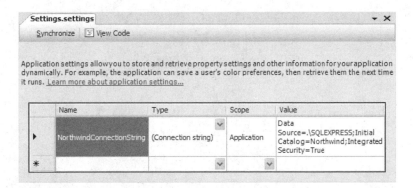

Figure 16.19   Storing the Database Connection String as an Application Setting

With your database connection string in hand, the Data Source Configuration Wizard can interrogate the desired database for all database objects that expose data. If the database is SQL Server, this includes tables, views, stored procedures, and functions, as shown in Figure 16.20.

Figure 16.20   Choosing Database Objects

After you choose the desired database objects and specify the name of the generated typed data set, you click the Finish button to complete the process. This creates the typed data set with the name you specified as an .xsd file added to your VS05 project root, as shown in Figure 16.21.[10]

---

[10] Typed data sets are a world unto themselves, and further exploration is beyond the scope of this book.

Figure 16.21   A Generated Typed Data Set with a Single Table and Corresponding Typed Table Adapter

Any typed data set (.xsd) is automatically detected by VS05—whether it was produced via the Data Source Configuration Wizard or added manually—and is listed in the Data Sources window, as shown in Figure 16.22.

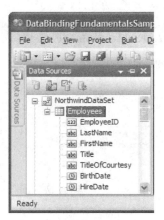

Figure 16.22   The Generated Typed Data Set as a Data Source

In Figure 16.22, you can see the new Northwind typed data set, which includes the Employees table. Each field in the table is displayed with an icon that hints at the type of data it represents. Additionally, the middle two tool strip buttons are enabled (they weren't in Figure 16.15). With these two new buttons, the Data Sources window tool strip allows you to edit and reconfigure the typed data set.[11]

---

[11] When reconfiguring your database data source, the Data Source Configuration Wizard isn't comprehensive: It highlights column name changes for you, but it doesn't highlight columns whose data types, default values, and nullability have been changed.

Web Services

As you know, data sources are simply instances of item or list types. In the case of a database, each table is a list data source. On the other hand, to bind to data exposed via a web service means binding to a type exposed by that service.[12] The purpose of the Data Source Configuration Wizard, with respect to web services, is to turn types exposed from a web service into .NET-specific data sources against which you can bind.

To create a data source for a web service-exposed type, you begin by selecting the Web Service option when you open the Data Source Configuration Wizard, which then opens the Add Web Reference dialog to allow you to locate the desired web service, as shown in Figure 16.23.[13]

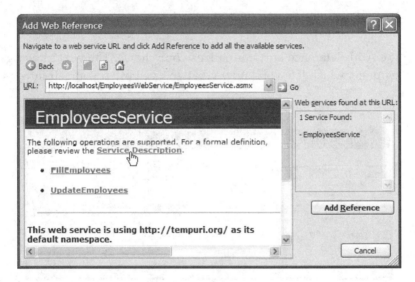

Figure 16.23   Choosing a Web Service That Exposes the Type You Want to Turn into a Data Source

You need to choose a web service that implements web methods that return item or list data source objects. To complete the process, you select the web service's service description, shown in Figure 16.24. This indicates the Web Services Description Language (WSDL) document that enables VS05 to generate a .NET class that maps to the web service.[14]

---

[12] Typically, web services that expose types you'd like to bind to expose the necessary web methods to retrieve instances of those types and to update the state of those instances.

[13] The Add Web Reference dialog is also displayed when you add a web reference to your project.

[14] WSDL is an XML format for describing web service end points. See http://www.w3.org/TR/wsdl (http://tinysells.com/37).

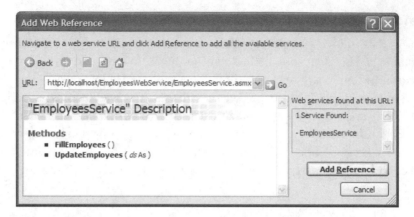

Figure 16.24   Selecting the WSDL Web Service Description

Clicking the Add Reference button finalizes your choice. The wizard navigates to the final summary page, which lets you know what you've gotten yourself into, as shown in Figure 16.25.

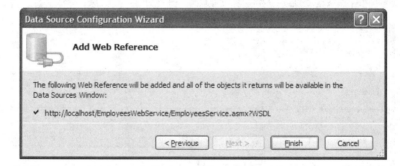

Figure 16.25   Confirming the Addition of the Specified Web Service to Your Project

When you click Finish, the web reference is added to your project, and all types from the web service that expose public properties are automatically listed in the Data Sources window, as shown in Figure 16.26.[15]

---

[15] See Chapter 18: Multithreaded User Interfaces for further discussion of VS05's web service support.

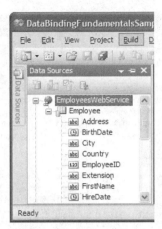

**Figure 16.26   Web Service Data Sources
Available from the Data Sources Window**

As with typed data sets, web references added using either the Data Source Configuration Wizard or manually are listed automatically in the Data Sources window.

The example in Figure 16.26 shows that the Employees web service we referenced operates over a typed data set for the Northwind database and, consequently, has re-created a familiar-looking data source. However, you can import any type exposed from any web service described with WSDL anywhere in the world.

Objects

Any typed data sets and public types exposed from referenced web services are automatically turned into data sources, but not all other types visible to your project are. The reason is that any object with public properties can conceivably become a data source, so automatically turning them into data sources would become quite unwieldy. To avoid this problem, VS05 supports a model that requires you to *opt-in* local and referenced .NET types as data sources.[16]

To turn one of these types into a data source, choose Object when you open the Data Source Configuration Wizard. The wizard navigates to a page from which you can choose the desired type, as shown in Figure 16.27.

---

[16] It is possible to opt-in COM components as data sources, although it is not as robust an option as using native .NET types. Be sure to test this choice rigorously.

Figure 16.27   Object Data Sources Available from the Current Project

The Data Source Configuration Wizard scans the entire project for possible types, including forms, typed data sets, and web services, all grouped by namespace. With a click of the check box, you can show or hide any types in referenced assemblies that begin with "Microsoft" or "System." Notice in Figure 16.27 that the text box beneath the object list displays a description of the selected object. This description is derived from the XML summary comment at the top of the class:

```
/// <summary>
/// RaceCarDriver stores information about a Formula 1 race car driver.
/// </summary>
class RaceCarDriver : INotifyPropertyChanged {...}
```

When you've picked the desired type, click Finish to turn it into a data source. As with data sources for databases and web services, an object data source appears in the Data Sources window, as shown in Figure 16.28.

Figure 16.28   Object Data Source Added to the Data Sources Window

If the desired type is not located in your project, you reference it by clicking the Add Reference button in the Data Source Configuration Wizard (Figure 16.27). This opens VS05's standard Add Reference dialog, shown in Figure 16.29.

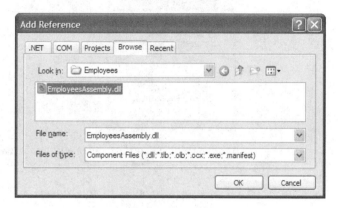

Figure 16.29   Referencing a .NET Assembly

Here, you can reference .NET assemblies located in the assembly cache, a project, the file system, or the list of most recently referenced assemblies. When you make your choice and click OK, the Data Source Configuration Wizard assembly list is updated with your selection, allowing you to then find the type from which you want a data source to be composed. An example is the Employee type, located in the EmployeesAssembly, as shown in Figure 16.30.

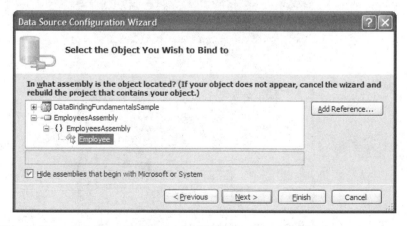

Figure 16.30   Selecting the Employee .NET Type to Be Turned into a Data Source

When you select your type and click Finish, the new data source is available in the Data Sources window, as shown in Figure 16.31.

Figure 16.31   Data Source Based on a .NET Type Located in a Different Assembly

Notice that data sources based on types located in referenced .NET assemblies are categorized by namespace.

Configuring the BindingSource

After you've designated a type as a data source and you've dropped a BindingSource component onto your form, you reference the former from the latter to enable data binding against the BindingSource. This involves setting the BindingSource component's Data-Source property with the desired data source, as shown in Figure 16.32.

Figure 16.32   Configuring the BindingSource with a Data Source

All currently identified data sources are listed in the DataSource property's drop-down, under Other Data Sources | Project Data Sources. Note that you also have the option to add a new data source to your project, if you haven't already, using the Data Source Configuration Wizard.

In this example, the selected data source is represented in the Properties window, as shown in Figure 16.33.

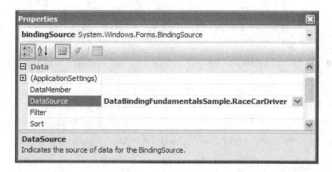

Figure 16.33   BindingSource with a Configured Data Source

The following code is generated by the Windows Forms Designer when a data source is hooked up to a BindingSource from the Properties window (it should seem familiar):

```
// IDEDataBindingForm.Designer.cs
partial class IDEDataBindingForm {
  ...
  BindingSource bindingSource;
  ...
  void InitializeComponent() {
    ...
    this.bindingSource = new BindingSource(this.components);
    ...
    // bindingSource
    this.bindingSource.DataSource =
      typeof(DataBindingFundamentalsSample.RaceCarDriver);
    ...
  }
}
```

For data sources that aren't containers for other data sources (such as typed data sets), you need only set the DataSource property. However, for those that are containers, you also need to identify the contained data source you'd like to bind to. Contained data sources are known as *data members* and are referenced from the BindingSource component's aptly named DataMember property. Use the Properties window, as shown in Figure 16.34.

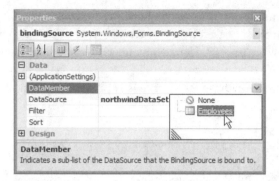

Figure 16.34   BindingSource with a Configured Data Source and Data Member

The Properties window is smart enough to inspect the data source for all possible data members and, as you can see in Figure 16.33, list them for your selection. The Windows Forms Designer-generated code to reflect your selection is shown here:

```
// IDEDataBindingForm.Designer.cs
partial class IDEDataBindingForm {
  ...
  void InitializeComponent() {
    this.components = new System.ComponentModel.Container();
    this.bindingSource = new BindingSource(this.components);
    this.northwindDataSet = new NorthwindDataSet();
    this.employeesTableAdapter = new EmployeesTableAdapter();
    ...
    // bindingSource
    this.bindingSource.DataMember = "Employees";
    this.bindingSource.DataSource = this.northwindDataSet;
    ...
    // northwindDataSet
    this.northwindDataSet.DataSetName = "NorthwindDataSet";
    ...
    // employeesTableAdapter
    this.employeesTableAdapter.ClearBeforeFill = true;
    ...
  }
  ...
  IContainer components = null;
  BindingSource bindingSource;
  NorthwindDataSet northwindDataSet;
  EmployeesTableAdapter employeesTableAdapter;
}
```

As you can see, the BindingSource component's DataSource and DataMember properties are set as expected. Perhaps unexpectedly, however, the Windows Forms Designer has taken the liberty of adding the NorthwindDataSet component to the form, referencing it directly from the DataSource property and eschewing the special *typeof* syntax. This special behavior is covered in Chapter 17.

An EmployeesTableAdapter component has also been added to the form. When a data member is selected for a data source that's a typed data set, the Windows Forms Designer is smart enough to find a corresponding typed table adapter, if one exists, and drop it onto the form. Typed table adapters are also components, and their primary role is to facilitate data persistence for the database object that's represented by the data member.

Data Source Persistence

In most cases, data sources need to be filled, at least initially, with data from a data store. For typed data sets, the role of managing persistence is delegated to typed table adapters, one of which is created for each data member in a typed data set. When you use the Properties window to configure a BindingSource component's DataSource and DataMember properties, the Windows Forms Designer not only adds both typed data sets and typed table adapters to a form, but it also generates the following code to load the typed data set with data from the database:

```
// IDEDataBindingForm.cs
partial class IDEDataBindingForm : Form {
  . . .
  void IDEDataBindingForm_Load(object sender, EventArgs e) {
    // TODO: This line of code loads data into the
    // 'northwindDataSet.Employees' table. You can move
    // or remove it, as needed.
    this.employeesTableAdapter.Fill(this.northwindDataSet.Employees);
  }
}
```

In this code, the typed table adapter loads data into the Northwind typed data set's Employees table by invoking the former's Fill method. Details of the database connections and commands are handled internally by both the typed data set and the table adapter. In fact, if you saved the database connection string as an application setting, the typed table adapter interrogates the setting directly.

Although the code to load a typed data set is generated for you, you're on your own if you need to update the data store with any changes. The typed table adapter exposes the Update method for just this purpose:

```
// IDEDataBindingForm.cs
public partial class IDEDataBindingForm : Form {
  ...
  void IDEDataBindingForm_Load(object sender, EventArgs e) {
    // TODO: This line of code loads data into the
    // 'northwindDataSet.Employees' table. You can move
    // or remove it, as needed.
    this.employeesTableAdapter.Fill(this.northwindDataSet.Employees);
  }

  void IDEDataBindingForm_FormClosing(
    object sender, FormClosingEventArgs e) {
    // Save updates back to the Northwind database's Employees table
    this.employeesTableAdapter.Update(this.northwindDataSet.Employees);
  }
}
```

It's easy for the Windows Forms Designer, typed data sets, and table adapters to provide a persistence framework because they all leverage ADO.NET, which provides a consistent, reliable model for doing so. Unfortunately, the same is not true for data sources created from types located in web services or assemblies. In these situations, you need to manually write the code to load and save data.

Whether you can load data into or save data from a data source, however, the simple act of specifying a BindingSource component's DataSource (and, if required, DataMember) properties does allow you to declaratively bind your UI.

Binding UI Elements in the Designer

A BindingSource that is bound to an underlying data source can do wonderful things; part of BindingSource's magic lies in its ability to use reflection to inspect its data source for data members and data properties that controls will want to bind to. The BindingSource then makes those available in such a way that controls that attempt to bind to it have access to both data members and data properties as if the BindingSource were the data source to which the BindingSource is bound. This trick makes it easy to declaratively construct bound UIs in the Windows Forms Designer.

BindingSource as a Bindable List Data Source

Consider a form with a BindingSource component whose data source and data member properties refer to the Northwind Employees data source, as shown in Figure 16.35.

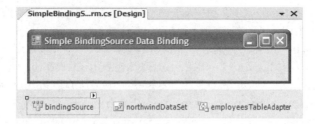

Figure 16.35   Form with BindingSource Hooked Up to a
Typed Data Set and a Typed Table Adapter

A BindingSource that's bound to a data source is in a perfect position to allow you to
build your bound UI.

Simple Binding to a List Data Source Exposed by a BindingSource

To simple-bind controls to a BindingSource visually, you use the Properties window and its
Data | (DataBindings) category, shown in Figure 16.36, which are designed to facilitate this
endeavor.

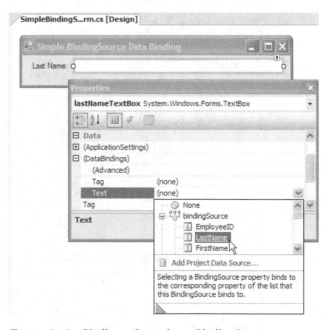

Figure 16.36   Binding a Control to a BindingSource

Figure 16.36 shows the use of the Properties window to bind the last name text box control's Text property to the LastName property that's exposed by the BindingSource on behalf of the Northwind.Employees list data source.

For text box controls, Tag and Text properties are considered the two most likely to be bound, and thus they appear as subproperties beneath Data | (DataBindings). To bind them to the desired data source property, you open the drop-down list, expand the Binding-Source entry to reveal the list of properties that can be bound to, and select the desired property—in this case, LastName.

For properties on controls that don't have simple binding shortcuts, never fear, because you can configure them via the Formatting and Advanced Binding dialog, shown in Figure 16.37, which is opened from Data | (DataBindings) | (Advanced).

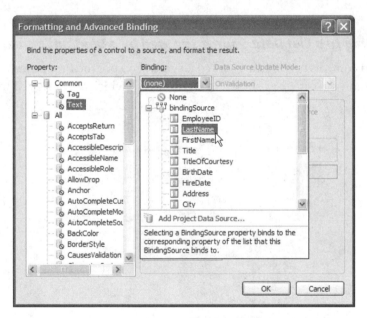

Figure 16.37   Configuring a Simple Binding Using the Formatting and Advanced Binding Dialog

When this dialog opens, you use the same technique to simple-bind a control property by opening the Binding drop-down list and selecting the required property from the BindingSource.

Whether by shortcut or by dialog, the Properties window provides two visual clues as to which property is bound and to which data source property it is bound, as illustrated in Figure 16.38.

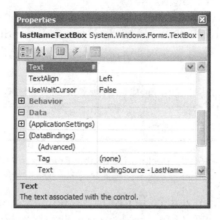

Figure 16.38   The Text Property of the Name Text Box Bound to the
BindingSource's Name Property

The shortcut Text subproperty shows itself as bound by displaying the BindingSource and the property to which it's bound. Additionally, the actual Text property now contains a small icon to reveal its bound status. The Windows Forms Designer generates the following code to InitializeComponent to create this binding:

```
// SimpleBindingSourceDataBindingForm.Designer.cs
partial class SimpleBindingSourceDataBindingForm {
  ...
  void InitializeComponent() {
    this.employeesBindingSource = new BindingSource(this.components);
    this.lastNameTextBox = new TextBox();
    ...
    // bindingSource
    this.employeesBindingSource.DataMember = "Employees";
    this.employeesBindingSource.DataSource = this.northwindDataSet;
    ...
    // lastNameTextBox
    this.lastNameTextBox.DataBindings.Add(
      new Binding(
        "Text", this.employeesBindingSource, "LastName", true));
    ...
  }
  BindingSource employeesBindingSource;
  TextBox lastNameTextBox;
  ...
}
```

If all the controls on a form are simple-bound to a BindingSource like this and if you've loaded the data source, then all you need to do is run it. Everything just works, as demonstrated in Figure 16.39.

Figure 16.39   Declarative Simple Binding in Action

To this point, we've written zero code to add a BindingSource to a form, configure it to reference a typed data set list data source, load it with data, simple-bind a control's property to it, and run it. Complex binding with a BindingSource component to a typed data set is an equally code-free experience.

Complex Binding to a List Data Source Exposed by a BindingSource

To complex-bind a control like DataGridView to a BindingSource, we again use the Properties window, although this time we set the DataGridView's DataSource property, as shown in Figure 16.40.[17]

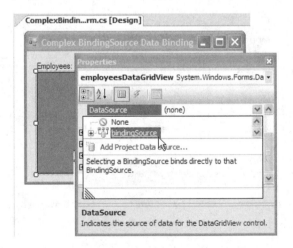

Figure 16.40   Binding a DataGridView to a BindingSource

---

[17] Alternatively, you can use DataGridView's smart tag.

The result of making this selection is generated to InitializeComponent by the Windows Forms Designer:

```
// ComplexBindingSourceDataBindingForm.Designer.cs
partial class ComplexBindingSourceDataBindingForm {
  void InitializeComponent() {
    ...
    this.employeesBindingSource = new BindingSource(this.components);
    this.employeesDataGridView = new DataGridView();
    this.employeeIDDataGridViewTextBoxColumn =
      new DataGridViewTextBoxColumn();
    this.lastNameDataGridViewTextBoxColumn =
      new DataGridViewTextBoxColumn();
    ...
    // bindingSource
    this.employeesBindingSource.DataMember = "Employees";
    this.employeesBindingSource.DataSource = this.northwindDataSet;
    ...
    // employeesDataGridView
    this.employeesDataGridView.Columns.AddRange(
      new DataGridViewColumn[] {
        this.employeeIDDataGridViewTextBoxColumn,
        this.lastNameDataGridViewTextBoxColumn,
        ...
      });
    this.employeesDataGridView.DataSource = this.employeesBindingSource;
    ...
    // employeeIDDataGridViewTextBoxColumn
    this.employeeIDDataGridViewTextBoxColumn.DataPropertyName =
      "EmployeeID";
    ...
    // lastNameDataGridViewTextBoxColumn
    this.lastNameDataGridViewTextBoxColumn.DataPropertyName =
      "LastName";
    ...
  }
  ...
  BindingSource employeesBindingSource;
  DataGridView employeesDataGridView;
  DataGridViewTextBoxColumn employeeIDDataGridViewTextBoxColumn;
  DataGridViewTextBoxColumn lastNameDataGridViewTextBoxColumn;
  ...
}
```

When the BindingSource is set with both a data source and a data member, it exposes the data member as a data source in its own right. Consequently, only the DataGridView control's DataSource property needs to be set to the BindingSource.

When the DataGridView control's DataSource property is set, it uses reflection to inspect the BindingSource for the list of properties on the data member that it can be bound to. For each property it finds, a DataGridViewColumn is created and bound to it; just as a BindingSource shapes itself to the data source to which it's bound, the DataGridView shapes its UI to the BindingSource to which it's bound. Additionally, each DataGridView-Column is given a name that reflects the property to which it's bound, saving you the effort.

If you need to reconfigure the DataGridView's default column ordering from the BindingSource, you can use DataGridView's Edit Columns command via the Properties window or smart tag, as shown in Figure 16.41.

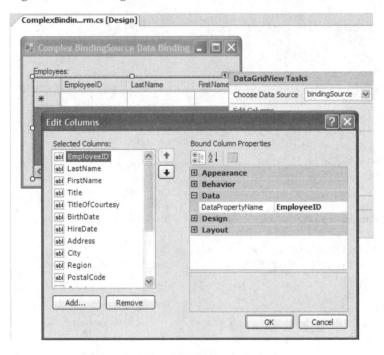

Figure 16.41   Declarative Complex Binding in Action

Without using any of the DataGridView's configuration support—the same as if you bind a DataGridView to a BindingSource at run time—you end up with something like Figure 16.42.

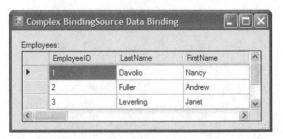

Figure 16.42   Declarative Complex Binding in Action

As with simple binding against a BindingSource component, you can rely completely on the Windows Forms Designer to drop a BindingSource component onto a form, bind it to a typed data set list data source, load it with data, bind a complex-bound control like a DataGridView to it, configure the control around it, and run the application.

Creating a BindingSource Component Implicitly

To this point, we've established simple-bound and complex-bound UIs by explicitly dropping a BindingSource onto a form and binding it to a data source before binding the controls to the BindingSource. To save you time, the Windows Forms Designer offers a mechanism by which you can achieve the same results by implicitly creating a BindingSource component that's bound to the required data source.

All you do is shortcut the BindingSource step by dropping a control onto a form and binding it directly to one of the data sources listed in the Properties window under Data | DataSource | Other Data Sources | Project Data Sources. This list contains the same data sources as the Data Sources window. Figure 16.43 illustrates this for simple binding, and Figure 16.44 does the same for complex binding.

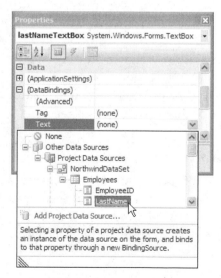

Figure 16.43   Implicitly Creating a Binding Source Component for Simple Binding

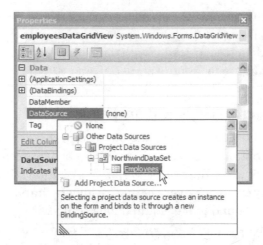

Figure 16.44 Implicitly Creating a Binding Source Component
for Complex Binding

In either case, the Windows Forms Designer creates a BindingSource that's bound to the selected data source and adds it to the form before establishing the specified simple or complex binding for you. When the BindingSource is added to the form, you can explicitly bind against it as before.

In general, the Windows Forms Designer prevents you from declaratively binding a control to a data source directly; the Windows Forms Designer always makes sure that a BindingSource component is in place between bound controls and a data source.[18] One good reason to do this is to simplify currency management.

Simple Currency Management

Recall from earlier in this chapter that we had to acquire a data source's binding manager before writing the code to change the current item in a list data source. As it turns out, the BindingSource is also a currency manager for the data source that it's bound to.[19] As you would expect, all simple and complex bound controls stay in sync, as shown in Figure 16.45.

---

[18] You can write your own code to bind a control directly to the data source, although doing so means you circumvent the consistent client coding model enabled by the BindingSource component.

[19] Specifically, BindingSource implements ICurrencyManager.

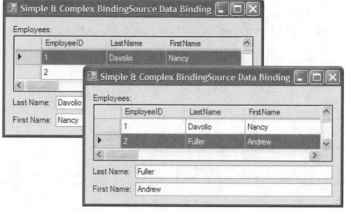

Figure 16.45   Declarative Simple and Complex Binding with Currency

On top of that, if you need to implement a VCR-type control to navigate the items in a data source, you don't have to acquire a BindingManager and you don't have to manually create your own navigation methods. Instead, you simply rely on the BindingSource to manage currency and use its currency-oriented methods as required:

```csharp
// SimpleComplexBindingSourceDataBindingForm.cs
SimpleComplexBindingSourceDataBindingForm : Form {
  ...
  void SimpleComplexBindingSourceDataBindingForm_Load(
    object sender, EventArgs e) {
    ...
    RefreshItems();
  }

  void moveFirstButton_Click(object sender, EventArgs e) {
    this.employeesBindingSource.MoveFirst();
    RefreshItems();
  }
  void movePreviousButton_Click(object sender, EventArgs e) {
    this.employeesBindingSource.MovePrevious();
    RefreshItems();
  }
  void moveNextButton_Click(object sender, EventArgs e) {
    this.employeesBindingSource.MoveNext();
    RefreshItems();
  }
  void moveLastButton_Click(object sender, EventArgs e) {
    this.employeesBindingSource.MoveLast();
    RefreshItems();
  }
```

```
void RefreshItems() {
  int count = this.employeesBindingSource.Count;
  int position = this.employeesBindingSource.Position + 1;

  // Update count and position text
  this.countLabel.Text = count.ToString();
  this.positionLabel.Text = position.ToString();

  // Enable or disable move buttons
  this.moveFirstButton.Enabled = (position > 1);
  this.movePreviousButton.Enabled = (position > 1);
  this.moveNextButton.Enabled = (position < count);
  this.moveLastButton.Enabled = (position < count);
  }
}
```

However, you can avoid writing this code by using the BindingNavigator component.

The BindingNavigator

.NET provides the BindingNavigator component to visually encapsulate navigation for you. BindingNavigator is a VCR-style tool strip control that binds to the same binding source to which your other simple-bound (and complex-bound) controls bind to provide navigation, as shown in Figure 16.46.

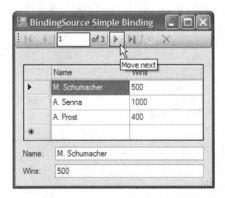

Figure 16.46   BindingNavigator in Action

To use a BindingNavigator, you drop one onto the form from the Toolbox's Data tab. BindingNavigator is automatically configured to dock to the top of the form and contain all the tool strip items you see in Figure 16.46. You also specify BindingNavigator's data source by setting its DataSource property, most easily from the Properties window, as shown in Figure 16.47.

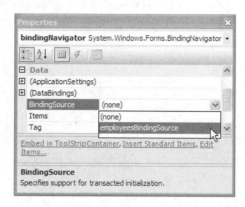

Figure 16.47   BindingNavigator in Action

Selecting the BindingSource for a BindingNavigator from the Properties window generates the following code:

```
// SimpleComplexBindingSourceDataBindingForm.cs
partial class SimpleComplexBindingSourceDataBindingForm {
  ...
  void InitializeComponent() {
    ...
    this.employeesBindingSource = new BindingSource(this.components);
    this.bindingNavigator = new BindingNavigator(this.components);
    // BindingNavigator tool strip button items for
    // navigation, position, and count
    ...
    // employeesBindingSource
    this.employeesBindingSource.DataMember = "Employees";
    this.employeesBindingSource.DataSource = this.northwindDataSet;
    ...
    // bindingNavigator
    this.bindingNavigator.BindingSource = this.employeesBindingSource;
    ...
  }
  ...
  BindingSource employeesBindingSource;
  BindingNavigator bindingNavigator;
  ...
}
```

By default, the tool strip items that appear on the BindingNavigator implement the code that calls the necessary methods on the BindingSource to perform the appropriate actions. For navigation, this includes calling MoveFirst, MovePrevious, MoveNext, and MoveLast. To add and remove items to and from the BindingSource, this includes calling AddNew and RemoveCurrent. To display the position and total item count, this includes handling whenever the current item or list in general changes, and inspecting and displaying the Position and Count properties each time. All tool strip items on the BindingNavigator enable or disable as appropriate.

Where Are We?

In this chapter, we've covered the fundamental elements of data binding in Windows Forms. We started by looking at the underlying mechanics and how they can be used to build a list data source that supports basic data binding functionality, such as bidirectional synchronization and data conversion between a data source and a bound control, as well as currency, navigation, list management, and item, list, and list item change notification. Windows Forms provides the BindingSource component, which can consume a simple type and provide all these features for you and save significant effort. Thanks to its ability to provide shape information about items contained in list data sources, and because it's a design-time component, BindingSource can be dropped onto a form and used to construct a data-bound UI declaratively, in conjunction with the Data Sources window.

In the next chapter, we see how these fundamental elements to support drag-and-drop data binding, and we address complex real-world data binding scenarios, including formatting and parsing data as it's synchronized between bound controls and data sources, sorting, searching, and filtering, and building common data-bound UIs such as master-details UIs.

17
Applied Data Binding

I N CHAPTER 16: DATA BINDING BASICS, you saw the fundamental elements of the Windows Forms data binding system, including bidirectional synchronization, data conversion between bound clients and data sources, currency management, item and list change notification, the BindingSource component, and a slew of Windows Forms Designer support for automatically generating data-bound UIs. This isn't the end of the data binding story. You can extend these elements and use them in numerous ways to support a wide variety of real-world data binding situations.

Drag-and-Drop Data Binding

Chapter 16 looked at a variety of visual techniques for composing a bound UI. But in the data binding world, there's visual, and then there's visual; the Data Sources window not only manages data sources, but also helps minimize the time it takes to construct a bound UI. That's because it allows you to drag data sources and drop them onto a form, as shown in Figure 17.1.

When a data source is dropped onto the form, the Windows Forms Designer automatically generates a bound UI comprising two things: a BindingSource component to represent the data source; and one or more controls bound to the BindingSource for viewing, editing, and navigating the data source.[1] The kind of UI that is generated depends on your choice, which you specify from the drop-down menu for the data source in the Data Sources window, as shown in Figure 17.2.

---

[1] Note that the generated controls are positioned left-to-right, top-to-bottom starting from where the mouse hot spot is when a data source is dropped onto a form.

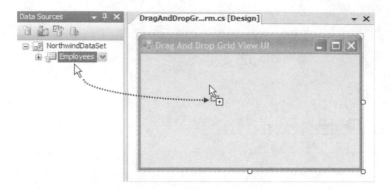

Figure 17.1   Drag-and-Drop Data Binding

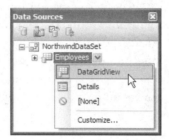

Figure 17.2   Configuring the UI to Be Generated
When a Data Source Is Dragged and Dropped

The default option is DataGridView, with Details as the only other draggable option. If you don't want a data source to be dragged onto a form, you choose [None]. To change the default option, add options, or remove options, you click Customize to open the Options dialog.[2] In most cases, however, you'll likely be concerned with either the DataGridView or the Details option.

DataGridView Bound UIs

The DataGridView UI is the default option for generating a complex-bound UI, as shown in Figure 17.3.

The result is a form that comprises two elements. The first is a BindingSource that's bound to the data source you dragged from the Data Sources window (in this case a typed data set, and hence the additional typed data set and table adapters). The second is a

---

[2] Data UI customization is also available from Tools | Options | Windows Forms Designer | Data UI Customization.

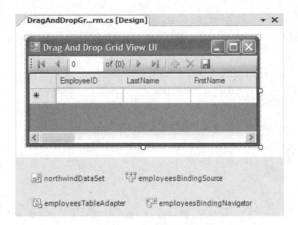

Figure 17.3 Drag-and-Drop DataGridView UI

DataGridView and BindingNavigator, both bound to the BindingSource component.[3] Additionally, the Windows Forms Designer creates reasonable default names for each generated component or control it adds to the form.[4] All you need to do is configure the final layout of the DataGridView UI.

When you create a DataGridView UI by dragging and dropping a data source that exposes a typed data set, the Windows Forms Designer generates the code to load the typed data set and also generates the code to save changes made from the UI:

```
// DragAndDropGridViewForm.cs
DragAndDropGridViewForm : Form {
  ...
  void DragAndDropGridViewForm_Load(object sender, EventArgs e) {
    // TODO: This line of code loads data into the
    // 'NorthwindDataSet.Employees' table. You can move
    // or remove it, as needed.
    this.employeesTableAdapter.Fill(this.NorthwindDataSet.Employees);
  }

  void employeesBindingNavigatorSaveItem_Click(
    object sender, EventArgs e) {
    this.Validate();
    this.employeesBindingSource.EndEdit();
    this.employeesTableAdapter.Update(this.NorthwindDataSet.Employees);
  }
}
```

[3] The generated BindingNavigator includes an additional Save button, which is enabled only when a database data source is dropped onto a form. Also added to the form is code to save changes to bound data sources.

[4] Unfortunately, this handiwork doesn't extend to the naming of each column generated for DataGridView.

The save code is deployed in the event handler for BindingNavigator's Save button. When a BindingSource exposes a typed data set, the Save button is enabled by default; otherwise it's disabled. The save code also does its best to ensure that the data is in a consistent state by validating the form and its controls and ending editing of the current item. Then, it calls the typed table adapter's Update method to save changes back to the database.

The same code is generated for BindingSource components that expose typed data sets when you build a Details UI.

Details Bound UIs

When the Windows Forms Designer generates a Details UI, it creates labels and simple-bound controls for each of the data source's properties, as shown in Figure 17.4.

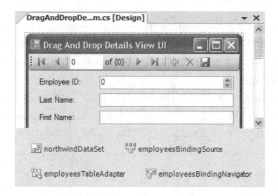

Figure 17.4   Drag-and-Drop Details View UI

As before, the Windows Forms Designer generates a nice set of control names and label text for you. However, it's a little trickier to create a useful default for the generated layout, given the complexities of UI layout and design, so you're very likely to finagle the form's final appearance.

The Windows Forms Designer makes educated guesses as to the type of control that is generated for each data source property. If you're not satisfied, you can override those guesses by configuring each property in the Data Sources window, as shown in Figure 17.5.

When any of these controls is dropped onto a form, it is simple-bound to the data source property it was dragged from. Specifically, the TextBox, ComboBox, Label, and LinkLabel controls are bound by their Text properties, and the ListBox is bound by its SelectedItem property. The ListBox and ComboBox options provide support for lookups, which are discussed later in this chapter. You can alter the options in this list in the Options dialog by clicking Customize.

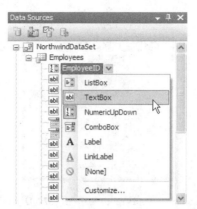

Figure 17.5   Configuring the Controls to Be
Generated When Data Source Properties Are
Dragged and Dropped

Drag-and-drop data binding support doesn't end here. You can actually drag your UI from the Data Sources window in a field-by-field manner. If you prefer this finer-grained approach to building your UI, you'll be happy to discover that the data bindings and nice names are still created automatically to save you the effort. Also, if your UI has already been laid out in preparation for binding or if you wish to change the binding of a specific control, you can connect the dots by dragging data source fields directly onto existing controls. The Windows Forms Designer ensures that the resulting binding is created.

Fundamentals of Data-Bound UIs

Data binding is designed to make your life easier when it comes to building UIs. Standing on the shoulders of data binding and related designer support are two core styles of UI that you can use in their entirety or mix and match to build other styles of UI. These are commonly referred to as item UIs and list UIs.

Item UIs

When users need the most intuitive and informative experience possible, you should consider using an item UI. *Item UIs* display one data item at a time, whether from an item or list data source, and are composed using the standard form and control support you've seen throughout this book. To create an item UI, we choose the Details option for the data source from the Data Sources window, as shown in Figure 17.6.

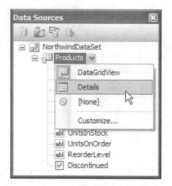

Figure 17.6   Creating an Item UI for a Data Source

For any data source with a nontrivial number of properties, such as the Northwind database's Products table, the generated UI is quite plain, as illustrated in Figure 17.7.

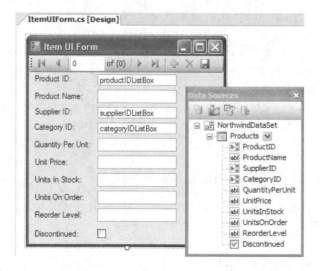

Figure 17.7   Default Details View UI for the Products Table

But consider that the whole UI is nicely bound, and it automatically loads and saves itself. Additionally, Windows Forms has a rich set of controls and layout support that allow us to easily transform the generated original into something a little more like the UI users expect, as shown in Figure 17.8.

Straightaway, you can see the whole form at once, and the large number of controls has been categorized into two tabs using a tab control. This should help users locate data quickly. Furthermore, key information—the Product ID (top left) and the Product Name (top right)—is called out using two label controls. Because the Windows Forms control and component suite is rich, there are many directions you can take a UI, although this demonstrates the basic principle.

Figure 17.8   Designed Item UI

The UI is nicely laid out and functional, in a broad sense, but data binding also comes to the rescue when you face other problems.

Formatting and Parsing

One of the problems with using drag-and-drop data sources is that the Windows Forms Designer has no idea how you want your data properties to be formatted, beyond the default formatting applied by bound controls. Controls like DateTimePicker allow you to specify a data format and take care of converting between what is displayed and what is stored, the latter typically being the property that's bound to the data source. Controls like Label, however, offer no such support.

Consider the Product ID in our example, which is displayed in its raw integer format. Unfortunately, this format probably doesn't comply with the crazy types of formats that the accounting department is likely to come up with, which probably look more like "#0-00-00."

To change the displayed format of a data source's property, you need the Formatting and Advanced Binding dialog, shown in Figure 17.9. You open it by selecting the bound control and then (DataBindings) | (Advanced) from the Properties window.[5]

In the formatting group box on this dialog, you can specify no formatting, formatting for well-known types, or custom formatting. The latter is useful when you need to mix and match formatting and alphanumeric characters in ways that aren't supported by the other options. Whichever option you choose, a sample output is displayed. Additionally, you can specify what to display in the event that the data source's property is null.

[5] You can also create and manage simple bindings as you saw in Chapter 16.

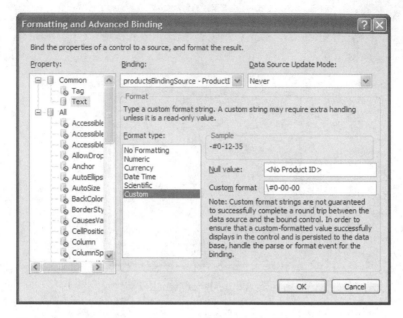

Figure 17.9　Specifying a Format for a Simple Binding

When you click OK, the Windows Forms Designer updates the simple-binding code it generates into InitializeComponent. The updated code uses an overload of the Binding object's constructor that accepts a Boolean to specify whether formatting is enabled (true by default) and both a null value and a format string:

```
// ItemUIForm.Designer.cs
partial class ItemUIForm {
  ...
  void InitializeComponent() {
    ...
    this.productIDLabel.DataBindings.Add(
      new Binding(
        "Text", // Bound property
        this.productsBindingSource, // Data source
        "ProductID", // Data source property
        true, // Formatting enabled?
        DataSourceUpdateMode.Never, // Label is read-only, so no updates
        "<No Product ID>", // Null value
        "\\#0-00-00"));// Format string
    ...
  }
  ...
}
```

The result is shown in Figure 17.10.

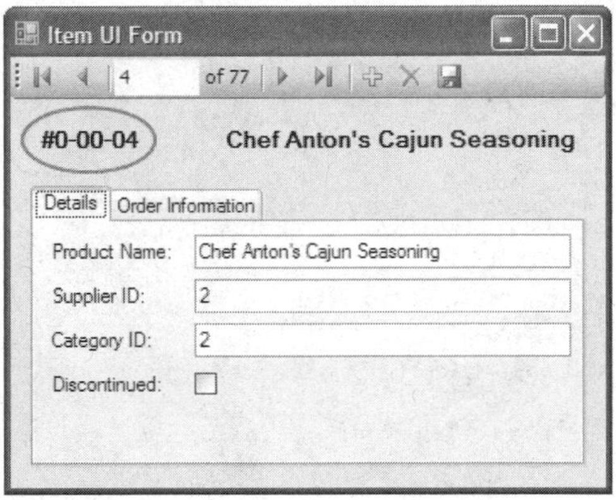

Figure 17.10   Format String Applied to Product ID

Formatting the Product ID declaratively is easy, because it is exposed from the data source as a simple type and is displayed via a read-only label. In some scenarios, however, your data format may be more complex than you can process with a simple formatting string.

For example, consider the UnitPrice property of the Products data source. Depending on which currency you are dealing with, this property may be equal in worth to bananas and formatted accordingly:

```
// ItemUIForm.Designer.cs
partial class ItemUIForm {
  ...
  void InitializeComponent() {
    ...
    this.unitPriceTextBox.DataBindings.Add(
      new Binding(
        "Text",
        this.productsBindingSource,
        "UnitPrice",
        true,
        DataSourceUpdateMode.OnValidation,
        "No Bananas", // Null value
        "0.00 Bananas")); // Format string
    ...
  }
  ...
}
```

This yields Figure 17.11.

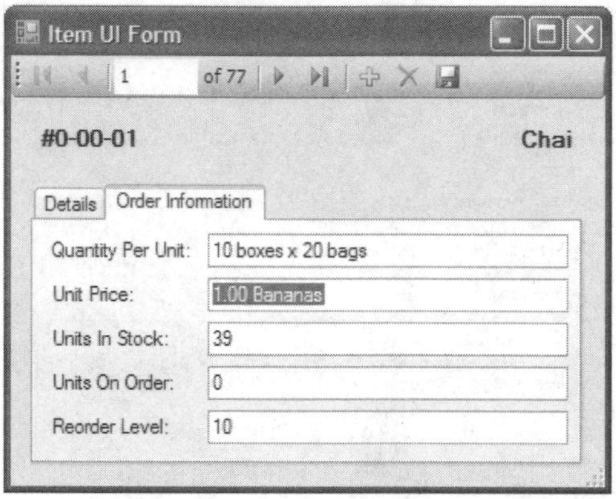

Figure 17.11   Format String Applied to UnitPrice

Figure 17.11 shows the problem: UnitPrice is displaying the current value as a plural (Bananas), even though it should be singular (Banana).

Because formatting support available from the Formatting and Advanced Binding dialog doesn't support the degree of complexity we're after, we need to write our own code. This task is made easier if we handle Format, a special event implemented by the Binding object for this purpose. The Format event is fired while data is being shuttled from the data source to the bound control, and it's at this moment and from this event that we execute our custom formatting code to ensure that UnitPrice is either singular or plural as required. Specifically, we register and handle the Format event for the UnitPrice text box's bound Text property:

```
// ItemUIForm.cs
partial class ItemUIForm : Form {
  public ItemUIForm() {
    InitializeComponent();

    this.unitPriceTextBox.DataBindings["Text"].Format +=
      unitPriceTextBox_Format;
  }

  void unitPriceTextBox_Format(object sender, ConvertEventArgs e) {
    // Bail if data source's property is null
    if( e.Value == DBNull.Value ) return;

    // Format data source value and concatenate with " Banana"
    // and pluralize if necessary
    string unitPrice = string.Format("{0:0.00 Banana}", e.Value);
```

```
      if( (decimal)e.Value != 1 ) unitPrice += "s";
      e.Value = unitPrice;
   }
   ...
}
```

The Format event handler is passed ConvertEventArgs, which allows you to alter the value pulled from the data source if needed.[6] In this case, we check to see what the Unit-Price value is and pluralize if appropriate, as shown in Figure 17.12.

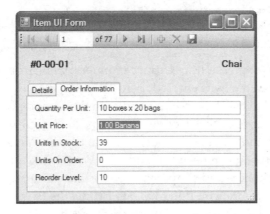

Figure 17.12   Custom Formatting to Display Plurals Correctly

If you do apply a custom format using the Advanced Formatting and Binding dialog, the Formatting and Advanced Binding dialog shown earlier in Figure 17.9 warns you of the potential for data conversion issues.

As long as users enter a value that .NET can convert to the list data source property's type, such as a decimal for UnitPrice, the entered value is converted when data binding copies it to the list data source. However, if the value can't be converted to the underlying data source's type, the data is considered invalid. To cope with this, we transform the entered value into a type that matches the type of the data source property on its way back to the data source. For this, we have the Parse event:

```
// ItemUIForm.cs
using System.Text.RegularExpressions;
...
partial class ItemUIForm : Form {
  public ItemUIForm() {
    ...
```

---

[6] If you'd like to use the format string you entered via the Advanced Formatting and Binding dialog, you can cast the sender argument to a Binding class and retrieve the format string from the FormatString property.

```
        this.unitPriceTextBox.DataBindings["Text"].Parse +=
          unitPriceTextBox_Parse;
    }
    ...
    void unitPriceTextBox_Parse(object sender, ConvertEventArgs e) {
      // Bail if value not entered
      if( string.IsNullOrEmpty((string)e.Value) ) return;

      // Extract first number from value and convert to decimal
      string unitPrice = (string)e.Value;
      Match match = Regex.Match(unitPrice, @"\d+(.\d{1,2})?");
      e.Value = decimal.Parse(match.Value);
    }
}
```

Here we use regular expressions to extract a numeric value from the value entered into the unit price text box, if one was entered, before sending it back to the data source. The entered value is passed to the Parse event handler in the second argument, which, as with the Format event handler, is of type ConvertEventArgs.

You don't need to handle the Format event to handle the Parse event; if a custom format is simple enough that it can be specified in the Formatting and Advanced DataBinding dialog, you can set it there and simply handle the Parse event on the way for the return trip, as required. Furthermore, you don't have to handle the Parse event for read-only values because the only values that need parsing are those that users can change.

If your data source is created from a custom type, you can bundle formatting and parsing functionality into the type itself by using a custom type converter, which is discussed later in this chapter.

Validation

Before data is parsed and sent back to the data source, it should be validated to ensure it's of a certain type, in a certain range and, possibly, formatted in a certain way. To provide this certainty, your form should be validating itself using the techniques described in Chapter 3: Dialogs. You also need to make sure that the data source is not updated until the control's value has been validated.

When a data source is updated is determined by the Binding object's DataSourceUpdateMode property, which can be one of three possible DataSourceUpdateMode enumeration values:

```
enum DataSourceUpdateMode {
    Never = 2, // Never update
    OnPropertyChanged = 1, // Update when control property changes
    OnValidation = 0 // Update after control Validated is fired (Default)
}
```

By default, this property is set to OnValidation, which means that the data source is only updated after a bound control's validated event is raised.[7] You can set the DataSource-UpdateMode to be OnPropertyChanged to eschew validation and update as soon as the bound control property is changed, or you can set it to None to prevent any data source updates at all.

DataSourceUpdateMode can be configured declaratively from the Formatting and Advanced Binding dialog for the binding, as shown in Figure 17.13.

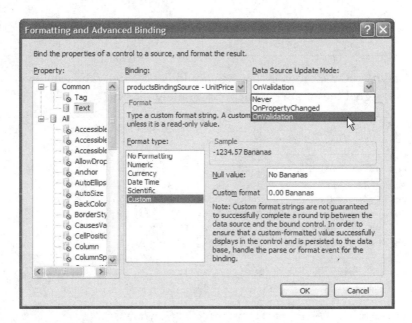

Figure 17.13 Setting a Binding's Data Source Update Mode

Whichever value you specify, the Windows Forms Designer generates the code that passes the DataSourceUpdateMode value to the appropriate Binding object's constructor:

```
// ItemUIForm.Designer.cs
partial class ItemUIForm {
  ...
  void InitializeComponent() {
    ...
```

[7] In conjunction with form validation techniques (like those we saw in Chapter 3), this generally allows you to create a bound form that doesn't force users to remain in a control until it's valid. For custom business objects that raise their own exceptions, you may need to employ a little more effort, as outlined here: http://msdn2.microsoft.com/en-us/library/k26k86tb.aspx (http://tinysells.com/37).

```
      this.unitPriceTextBox.DataBindings.Add(
        new Binding(
          "Text",
          this.productsBindingSource,
          "UnitPrice",
          true,
          DataSourceUpdateMode.OnValidation,
          "No Bananas",
          "0.00 Bananas"));
      ...
    }
    ...
}
```

Choosing OnValidation means that we should handle the Validating event and, if the data is invalid, signal the Parsing event appropriately, like so:

```
// ItemUIForm.cs
using System.Text.RegularExpressions;
...
partial class ItemUIForm : Form {
  ...
  void unitPriceTextBox_Validating(object sender, CancelEventArgs e) {
    // Check if unit price is a number
    string unitPrice = this.unitPriceTextBox.Text;
    Match match = Regex.Match(unitPrice, @"\d+(.\d{1,2})?");

    // If not correctly formatted, show error
    string message = null;
    decimal result;
    if (!decimal.TryParse(match.Value, out result)) {
      message = "Unit Price must be in this format: 0.00 Bananas";
      e.Cancel = true;
    }
    this.errorProvider.SetError(this.unitPriceTextBox, message);
  }

  void unitPriceTextBox_Parse(object sender, ConvertEventArgs e) {
    // Bail if value is invalid
    if (this.errorProvider.GetError(this.unitPriceTextBox) != "") {
      return;
    }

    // Extract first number from value and convert to decimal
    string unitPrice = (string)e.Value;
    Match match = Regex.Match(unitPrice, @"\d+(.\d{1,2})?");
    e.Value = decimal.Parse(match.Value);
  }
}
```

Entering data into text boxes should be a free-form experience, which is why validation is absolutely required when you use them, although you may also consider masked text boxes as a way to ensure data is entered in a specific format. However, if a data source property can only be one of several values, you can use lookup lists in the UI to allow the user to choose just those values.

Lookups

Where specific values are required, as compared with specifically formatted values, drop-down lists of valid options come in handy. For example, the Products table has a SupplierID field that accepts a number that uniquely identifies the supplier of a particular product. The trouble is that unless users have savant talents, they are unlikely to remember numeric identifiers for all possible suppliers. We can help by displaying human-readable supplier names and converting the selected one into a number that can be stored in the underlying data source; the result is commonly known as a *lookup.*

To create a lookup, we first need a data source. Northwind comes complete with a Suppliers table, so we simply use the Data Source Configuration Wizard to turn the table into a data source, as shown in Figure 17.14.

Figure 17.14   Suppliers Data Source

The Product table's SupplierID column is a foreign key to the Suppliers table, as reflected by the Suppliers data source. Thus, we can leverage the relationship to display the human-readable Suppliers.CompanyName field while actually storing Suppliers.SupplierID. We begin by dropping a BindingSource component onto a form and setting its DataSource property to the Suppliers data source. A typed data set for the Northwind data source already exists on the form, but configuring BindingSource adds a Suppliers table adapter to the form, and the table adapter fills the Northwind data source's Suppliers data member. The result is shown in Figure 17.15.

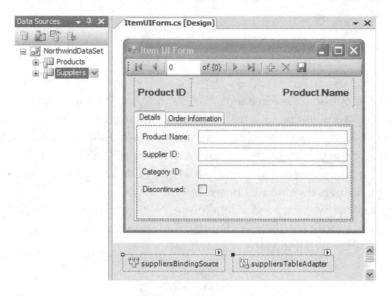

Figure 17.15   Creating the BindingSource

By now, you should be familiar with the code generated by the Windows Forms Designer to hook the BindingSource to a data source and automatically fill it with data from the database:

```
// ItemUIForm.Designer.cs
partial class ItemUIForm {
  ...
  void InitializeComponent() {
    ...
    // SuppliersBindingSource
    this.SuppliersBindingSource.DataMember = "Suppliers";
    this.SuppliersBindingSource.DataSource = this.NorthwindDataSet;
    ...
  }
}

// ItemUIForm.cs
partial class ItemUIForm : Form {
  ...
```

```
void ItemUIForm_Load(object sender, EventArgs e) {
    // TODO: This line of code loads data into the
    // 'NorthwindDataSet.Suppliers' table. You can move
    // or remove it, as needed.
    this.suppliersTableAdapter.Fill(this.NorthwindDataSet.Suppliers);
    ...
    }
  ...
}
```

Because a combo box control is a great way to present a list of options, we first replace the default drag-and-drop text box with a combo box. To then turn the combo box into a lookup, we perform the following steps, using the combo box Properties window or smart tag:

1. Set the DataSource property to the lookup BindingSource (SuppliersBindingSource).
2. Set DisplayMember to the property on the lookup BindingSource whose value is displayed in the combo box (SuppliersBindingSource.CompanyName).
3. Set ValueMember to the property on the lookup BindingSource whose value is used to update the bound property value (SuppliersBindingSource.SupplierID).

As a shortcut, you can drag the data source (Suppliers) from the Data Sources window directly onto the combo box; the Windows Forms Designer ensures that the combo box is configured to be filled appropriately, starting with setting the combo box control's Data-Source property. Further, the ValueMember field is set to the first field in the data source that's part of a primary key, or, if no primary key exists, the first field is used. Display-Member is automatically configured to be the first string field that's not part of the primary key; otherwise, it is set to the first field of any type that's not part of the primary key or, failing that, the first column if no primary key exists.

The Windows Forms Designer leaves one real step for us, which is to bind the SelectedValue property to the desired property on the data BindingSource whose value will be updated when an item is selected in the combo box (productsBindingSource.SupplierID).[8]

---

[8] If you configure the field of one data source in the Data Sources window to be a combo box, drag it onto a form, and then drag another data source onto the generated combo box to create the lookup binding configuration. The Windows Forms Designer sets SelectedValue to the same field to which the combo box's Text property is bound.

The combo box's smart tag in Figure 17.16 shows the resulting configuration.

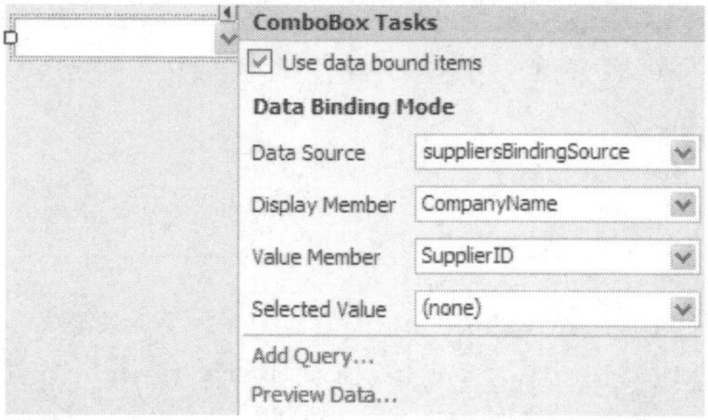

Figure 17.16   Turning a Combo Box into a Lookup

Note that if the Windows Forms Designer's defaults for DisplayMember and Value-Member are not to your liking, you can change them from the smart tag or Properties window for the combo box. To do that, you select the desired field from the respective drop-down lists.

The Windows Forms Designer produces the following code to hook up the bindings as specified:

```
// ItemUIForm.Designer.cs
partial class ItemUIForm {
  ...
  void InitializeComponent() {
    ...
    // productsBindingSource
    this.productsBindingSource.DataMember = "Products";
    this.productsBindingSource.DataSource = this.NorthwindDataSet;
    ...
    // SuppliersBindingSource
    this.SuppliersBindingSource.DataMember = "Suppliers";
    this.SuppliersBindingSource.DataSource = this.NorthwindDataSet;
    ...
    // suppliersComboBox
    this.suppliersComboBox.DataBindings.Add(
      new Binding(
        "SelectedValue", // Bound property
        this.productsBindingSource, // Data source
        "SupplierID", // Data source property
        true)); // Formatting enabled?
    this.suppliersComboBox.DataSource = this.SuppliersBindingSource;
    this.suppliersComboBox.DisplayMember = "CompanyName";
    this.suppliersComboBox.ValueMember = "SupplierID";
    ...
  }
}
```

Figure 17.17 illustrates the binding relationships between the combo box and the products binding source, the source of the actual data.

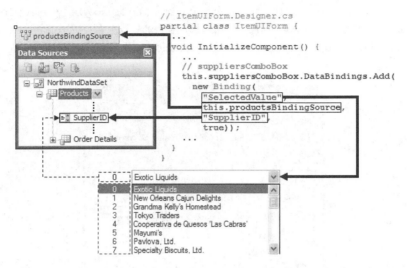

Figure 17.17   Turning a Combo Box into a Lookup: Binding to the Actual Data

Figure 17.18 illustrates the binding relationships between the combo box and the suppliers binding source, the source of the lookup data.

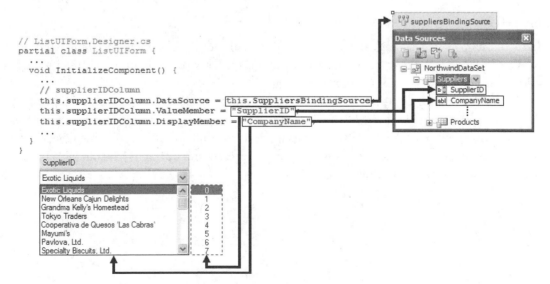

Figure 17.18   Turning a Combo Box into a Lookup: Binding to Lookup Data

Note that binding the combo box's SelectedValue property to the Country property on the Suppliers BindingSource has the added advantage of making sure that only legal values—those sourced from LookupItem.Value—set the bound property value. On that note, you might also consider setting the combo box control's DropDownStyle property to Drop-DownList to prevent user entry in the combo box's text box.

Figure 17.19 shows the combo box lookup in action.

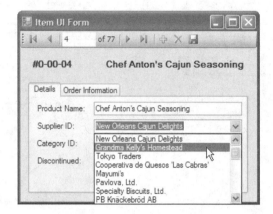

Figure 17.19   ComboBox Lookup Table in Action

Controls that provide lookup support include ComboBox and ListBox.

List UIs

Item UIs, as you've just seen, allow you to present complex data with a consistent Windows user experience by leveraging all that Windows Forms has to offer. By their nature, item UIs allow you to focus on a single record at a time.

However, if your UI needs to support mass data entry, such as maintaining a product list, you should consider a *list UI*, a UI style that's designed around a grid style of control to maximize keyboard use for efficient navigation and data entry. Recall from Chapter 16 that the default Data Sources window drag-and-drop binding option is to establish a bound list UI, as shown in Figure 17.20.

Figure 17.20   Specifying a Data Source to be List View

After dragging the data source onto a form, and with a bit of layout jiggling, you end up with the form shown in Figure 17.21.

	ProductName	SupplierID	CategoryID	QuantityPerUnit	UnitPrice	UnitsInStock	UnitsOnOrder	ReorderLevel	Discontinued
▶	Chai	1	1	10 boxes x 20 bags	18.0000	39	0	10	☐
	Chang	1	1	24 - 12 oz bottles	19.0000	17	40	25	☐
	Aniseed Syrup	1	2	12 - 550 ml bottles	10.0000	13	70	25	☐
	Chef Anton's Cajun Seasoning	2	2	48 - 6 oz jars	22.0000	53	0	0	☐
	Chef Anton's Gumbo Mix	2	2	36 boxes	21.3500	0	0	0	☑
	Grandma's Boysenberry Spread	3	2	12 - 8 oz jars	25.0000	120	0	25	☐

Figure 17.21   Products List UI Form

This form is wide, but users can quickly navigate through the various columns, enter new rows, and change values, all without leaving the keyboard.

A side effect of using the list UI model is that you can't leverage standard Windows Forms support for formatting, parsing, validation, and lookups. Fortunately, DataGridView offers alternative support for all these features.

Formatting and Parsing

You can declaratively set the format of any field by configuring the DataGridView column that's bound to the desired data source property. The easiest way to configure the format is to select DataGridView in the Windows Forms Designer, open its smart tag, and choose Edit Columns | *DesiredColumnName* | DefaultCellStyle to open the CellStyle Builder dialog. This dialog allows you to specify a variety of column-specific information, including entering a format string straight into the Format property. Or you can use the Format String dialog, shown in Figure 17.22, which you open using the Format property's ellipses button.

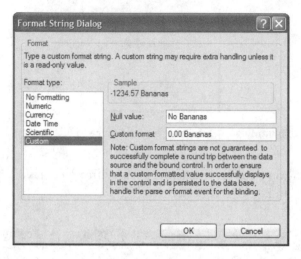

Figure 17.22   Format String Dialog for DataGridView Column Formatting

As with the Formatting and Advanced Bindings dialog you saw earlier, you can provide a string to be displayed if the data source property is null and select from a range of off-the-shelf formatting choices. Additionally, you can specify both a custom format and a null value.

Your null value and formatting choices are applied by the Windows Forms Designer to InitializeComponent:

```
// ListUIForm.Designer.cs
partial class ListUIForm {
  ...
  void InitializeComponent() {
    ...
    // unitPriceColumn
    this.unitPriceColumn.DataPropertyName = "UnitPrice";
    unitPriceColumnCellStyle.Format = "$0.00 Bananas";
    unitPriceColumnCellStyle.NullValue = "No Bananas";
    this.unitPriceColumn.DefaultCellStyle =
      unitPriceColumnCellStyle;
    this.unitPriceColumn.HeaderText = "UnitPrice";
    this.unitPriceColumn.Name = "UnitPrice";
    ...
  }
}
```

DataGridView column style and formatting are specified with a special DataGridView-CellStyle object that's attached to the DataGridView column. In this case, both the format string and the null value are stored in DataGridViewCellStyle's Format and NullValue properties, respectively.

As with item UI formatting, you need to consider taking over when the approach specified by the Windows Forms Designer doesn't handle unusual situations. Recall our example that formatted the UnitPrice as bananas and correctly pluralized it. To apply the same thing to a bound DataGridView column, you handle DataGridView's CellFormatting event:

```
// ListUIForm.cs
partial class ListUIForm : Form {
  ...
  void productsDataGridView_CellFormatting(
    object sender, DataGridViewCellFormattingEventArgs e) {

    // Don't format if value is null
    if( e.Value == null ) return;

    // Get DataGridView column
    DataGridViewColumn clm =
      this.productsDataGridView.Columns[e.ColumnIndex];

    // If unit price column
    if( clm.DataPropertyName == "UnitPrice" ) {

      // Format data source value and concatenate with " Banana"
      // and pluralize if necessary
      string unitPrice = string.Format("{0:0.00 Banana}", e.Value);
      if( (decimal)e.Value != 1 ) unitPrice += "s";
      e.Value = unitPrice;

      // Signal that we've formatted this value
      e.FormattingApplied = true;
    }
  }
}
```

CellFormatting is passed a DataGridViewCellFormattingEventArgs object, which exposes the ColumnIndex property that identifies the column in which data was entered. Because the format is the same for all the cells in a column, you can use ColumnIndex to determine which format needs to be applied to which column, if at all. If it turns out to be the right column, you can format that value as necessary and pass it to the cell via Data-GridViewCellFormattingEventArgs.Value.[9]

---

[9] You can also get the format string from the sender argument by casting it to a DataGridView and retrieving it from DefaultCellStyle.Format for the column you're interested in.

Additionally, you need to set DataGridViewCellFormattingEventArgs.Formatting-Applied to prevent any further formatting. If you set this property to false, the default format string overrides your programmatic efforts. Figure 17.23 shows the results of our custom formatting code.

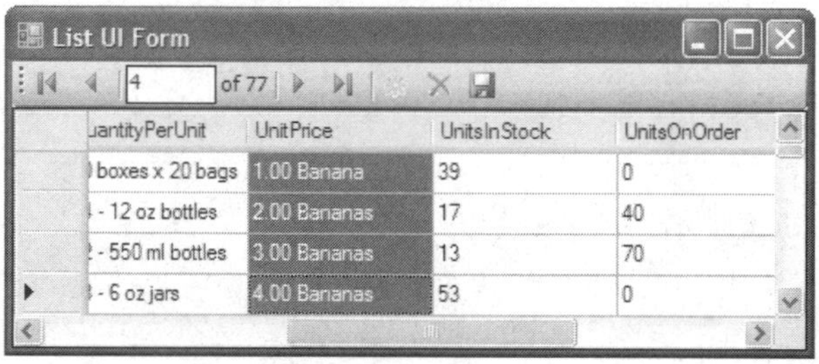

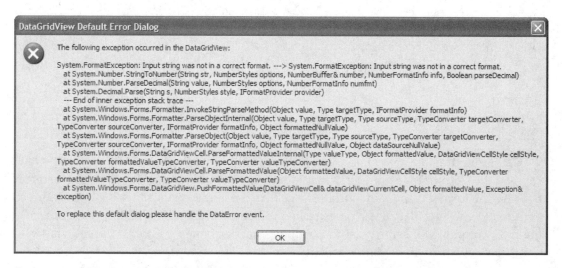

Figure 17.23   Custom Formatting to Display Plurals Correctly

If you do use a custom format, the Format String dialog from Figure 17.22 warns you of the potential data-conversion issues. As long as the user enters either a raw integer or a decimal value for the Unit Price (or any value that conforms to the format), the entered value is nicely converted to the underlying data source's decimal type when the value of the data grid view column cell is copied to it.

However, if the value cannot be converted to the underlying data source's type, you receive a truly gruesome exception shown in Figure 17.24.

Figure 17.24   The Exception That's Displayed When Unconvertible Data Is Entered

This error is likely because users will try to enter a value that looks like the formatted value rather than a value that needs to be converted. In this sense, formatting seems counterintuitive, but, as with item UIs, you can increase intuitiveness by using CellParsing, DataGridView's version of Binding.Parsing.

```csharp
// ListUIForm.cs
partial class ListUIForm : Form {
  ...
  void productsDataGridView_CellParsing(
    object sender, DataGridViewCellParsingEventArgs e) {

    // Get DataGridView column
    DataGridViewColumn clm =
      this.productsDataGridView.Columns[e.ColumnIndex];

    // If unit price column
    if( clm.DataPropertyName == "UnitPrice" ) {

      // Extract first number from value and convert to decimal
      string unitPrice = (string)e.Value;
      Match match = Regex.Match(unitPrice, @"\d+(.\d{1,2})?");
      e.Value = decimal.Parse(match.Value);

      // Signal that we've parsed this value
      e.ParsingApplied = true;
    }
  }
  ...
}
```

A DataGridViewCellParsingEventArgs object is passed to CellParsing to help you determine whether the value is from a column that you are trying to parse. If the correct column is found, you parse the value entered into DataGridView's cell—in this case, the first numeric value in the user-provided value—and convert it to the data source property's decimal type. You also signal that you've parsed the value by setting the ParsingApplied property of the DataGridViewCellParsingEventArgs object to true, because it's false by default. If you don't set this property to true, DataGridView treats the value as unparsed even if you parsed it, and the exception is raised.

As with any custom parsing, it helps to ensure that the value being parsed is something we can actually parse. This is where validation comes into play.

Validation

DataGridView fires the CellValidating event, which you can handle to validate a cell before it is parsed:

```
// ListUIForm.cs
partial class ListUIForm : Form {
  ...
  void productsDataGridView_CellValidating(
    object sender, DataGridViewCellValidatingEventArgs e) {

    // Don't format if value is null
    if( e.FormattedValue == null ) return;

    // Get DataGridView column
    DataGridViewColumn clm =
      this.productsDataGridView.Columns[e.ColumnIndex];

    // If unit price column
    if( clm.DataPropertyName == "UnitPrice" ) {

      string unitPrice = (string)e.FormattedValue;

      // Check whether unitPrice is a number
      Match match = Regex.Match(unitPrice, @"\d+(.\d{1,2})?");

      // If not correctly formatted, show error and
      // prevent focus leaving cell
      decimal result;
      if( !decimal.TryParse(match.Value, out result) ) {
        MessageBox.Show(
          "Unit Price must be in this format: 0.00 Bananas");
        e.Cancel = true;
      }
    }
  }
}
```

As with most DataGridViewCell*Xxx* events, the CellValidating event handler is passed an argument that exposes a ColumnIndex for column identification, this time via a DataGridViewCellValidatingEventArgs object. This example uses regular expression to check the formatting. If the formatting is invalid, we let the user know and set the DataGridViewCellValidatingEventArgs object's Cancel property to true, indicating that the cell value is invalid. This also prevents the user from leaving the cell, and avoid displaying the ghastly exception dialog.

Lookups

As with item UIs, one way to ensure that users provide the right data is to give them a list of options using a lookup. Again, human-readable text is easier for users to deal with than raw numeric identifiers like Supplier ID.

The first step in creating a lookup column for a DataGridView is to ensure that the desired lookup column is of type DataGridViewComboBoxColumn. You specify this in DataGridView's Edit Columns dialog, shown in Figure 17.25, which you open via DataGridView's smart tag.

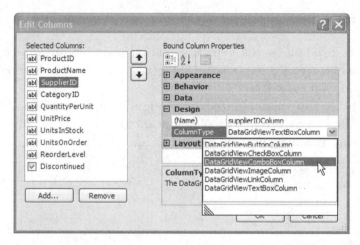

Figure 17.25   Replacing DataGridViewTextBoxColumn with DataGridViewComboBoxColumn

You next set the desired column's ColumnType property to DataGridViewComboBox-Column. Then, you configure the column much as you did when establishing lookups for item UIs: You specify a lookup BindingSource (Suppliers), a display member, and a value member, as shown in Figure 17.26.[10]

---

[10] The data property name is configured by the Windows Forms Designer when you drag and drop a DataGridView data source onto a form.

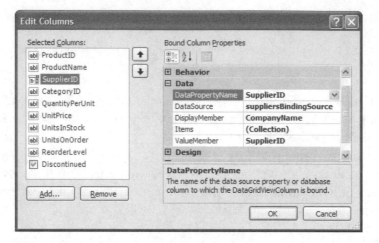

Figure 17.26 Configuring the ComboBox to Be a Lookup

When you create a DataSource, you can either choose a BindingSource that's already on the form or refer to a project data source. In the latter case, the Windows Forms Designer creates the BindingSource for you.

When you click OK to commit the lookup configuration, the Windows Forms Designer generates the following code to InitializeComponent to make sure that the data grid view column and lookup BindingSource are hooked up appropriately:

```
// ListUIForm.Designer.cs
partial class ListUIForm {
  ...
  void InitializeComponent() {
    ...
    // NorthwindDataSet
    this.NorthwindDataSet.DataSetName = "NorthwindDataSet";
    ...
    // suppliersBindingSource
    this.suppliersBindingSource.DataMember = "Suppliers";
    this.suppliersBindingSource.DataSource = this.NorthwindDataSet;
    ...
    // productsDataGridView
    this.productsDataGridView.DataSource = this.productsBindingSource;
    this.productsDataGridView.Columns.Add(this.supplierIDColumn);
    ...
    // supplierIDColumn
    this.supplierIDColumn.DataSource = this.suppliersBindingSource;
    this.supplierIDColumn.DataPropertyName = "SupplierID";
    this.supplierIDColumn.DisplayMember = "CompanyName";
    this.supplierIDColumn.ValueMember = "SupplierID";
    ...
  }
}
```

Figure 17.27 shows how the generated code binds the DataGridView to the products binding source, with the SupplierID DataGridView column bound to the SupplierID data source property.

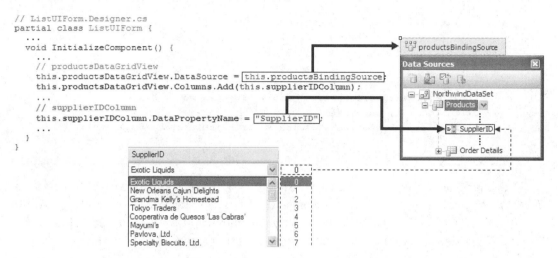

Figure 17.27 Turning a DataGridView Combo Box Column into a Lookup: Binding to the Actual Data

Figure 17.28 illustrates the binding relationships between the SupplierID combo box column and the suppliers binding source, the lookup data source.

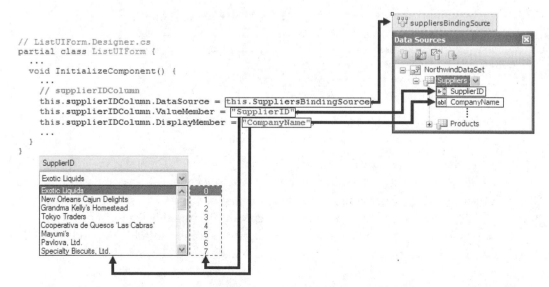

Figure 17.28 Turning a DataGridView Combo Box Column into a Lookup: Binding to Lookup Data

Additionally, if the data source is a typed data set, the typed table adapter for the data source is also placed onto a form. Code is injected into your form's Load event to populate the data source—and, implicitly, the bound drop-downs—from the database.

```
// ListUIForm.Designer.cs
partial class ListUIForm : Form {
  ...
  void ListUIForm_Load(object sender, EventArgs e) {
    ...
    // TODO: This line of code loads data into the
    // 'NorthwindDataSet.Suppliers' table. You can move,
    // or remove, it, as needed.
    this.suppliersTableAdapter.Fill(this.NorthwindDataSet.Suppliers);
  }
}
```

However, because we've configured the column to be a read-only lookup, the Windows Forms Designer is smart enough not to generate the code to update the data source. Additionally, the DataGridView is smart enough to use the drop-down's selected value, specified by ValueMember, as the bound property value that's passed back to the data source.

Figure 17.29 shows a lookup in operation.

Figure 17.29   A Fully Operational DataGridView Column Lookup

Unlike item UI lookups built from the ComboBox control, DataGridViewComboBox-Column doesn't support text editing, whether you select its display style to be Drop-DownButton (the default) or ComboBox. This means that users can select data only from the lookup. You can also specify a display style as None, hiding the drop-down button until the column is edited. When a DataGridView column becomes editable depends on Data-GridView's EditMode property, which is of type DataGridViewEditMode:

```
namespace System.Windows.Forms {
  enum DataGridViewEditMode {
    EditOnEnter = 0,
    EditOnF2 = 3,
    EditOnKeystroke = 1,
    EditOnKeystrokeOrF2 = 2, // Default
    EditProgrammatically = 4
  }
}
```

You'll likely be happy with the default, although you may need to use visual aids or thorough help documentation to ensure that your users are aware of the less obvious F2 option.

Data Views

Much of the process of creating item and list UIs revolves around displaying and massaging data for usability. For example, formatting and parsing allow us to transform data as it's shuttled between a data source and a bound control. With regard to list data sources, users are accustomed to transforming the data as it appears in the UI, most often to facilitate the location of specific data items.

The most common style of transformation is *sorting*, which allows users to find specific data in a list based on order. Instead of looking through all the items in a list, users might prefer *filtering* the items that don't match certain criteria in order to focus on the subset of items that do. Although not a transformation, *searching* is the most immediate way to find a specific data item.

In the data binding world, these features are provided by a *data view*, a special class that provides custom views of list data sources. To provide these features, data view classes implement two data binding interfaces: IBindingList and IBindingListView. As you saw in Chapter 16, IBindingList not only provides list management and change notification using BindingList<T>, but it also allows classes to implement single-column sorting and searching in a well-known data binding fashion. Similarly, IBindingListView is used to provide multiple-column sorting and filtering support.

BindingSource exposes both interfaces for complex bound controls to use, and it exposes simplified methods for sorting, filtering, and searching.

Sorting

Data can be sorted through one or more columns in either ascending or descending order. Setting the sort criteria is a simple matter of setting the Sort string property on the BindingSource that encapsulates the data view:

```
// DataViewForm.cs
partial class DataViewForm : Form {
  ...
  void sortButton_Click(object sender, EventArgs e) {
    string sortCriteria = this.sortCriteriaTextBox.Text;
    this.customersBindingSource.Sort = sortCriteria;
  }
}
```

The sort criteria string is parsed to the following format:

DataSourcePropertyName [ASC|DESC][, *DataSourcePropertyName* [ASC|DESC]]*

Figure 17.30 illustrates the effects of sorting in this way.

Figure 17.30   Creating a Sorted View

If you need to return the data view to its presorted order, you invoke Binding-Source.RemoveSort:

```
// DataViewForm.cs
partial class DataViewForm : Form {
  ...
  void removeSortButton_Click(object sender, EventArgs e) {
    this.customersBindingSource.RemoveSort();
  }
}
```

Note that by sorting the BindingSource component, you are changing the underlying list data source in a way that affects all controls bound to the BindingSource. When such a change occurs, list data sources are required to issue a list change notification, ensuring that all simple-bound and complex-bound controls automatically update themselves visually to reflect the change.

This is why the DataGridView appears re-sorted, even though it didn't initiate the sort itself. And, this is also why the DataGridView doesn't display sort chevrons in the column headers to indicate the current sort orders; full-list change notifications don't broadcast that it is specifically a sort operation that initiated them, so the DataGridView, and other bound controls, can refresh only the list items. Even so, no control provides enough UI to initiate and show multiple column sorting, as per our example. The native UI is single-column sorting provided by the DataGridView, which users access by left-clicking column headers. This sort is indicated visually with a sort chevron, as shown in Figure 17.31.[11]

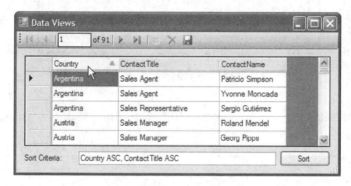

Figure 17.31 Single-Column Sorting Natively Supported by DataGridView

Although DataGridView does provide UI support for single-column sorting; no native Windows Forms control provides a UI for either filtering or searching, discussed next.

Filtering

Filtering is the ability to reduce the visible data to the set of items that meet specific criteria. In lieu of native UI support, you need to provide a way for users to specify filter criteria and apply it to the data source. The BindingSource component's Filter property enables the latter, and you collect the filter string via a text box to do the former:

```
// DataViewForm.cs
partial class DataViewForm : Form {
  ...
  void filterButton_Click(object sender, EventArgs e) {
    string filterCriteria = this.filterCriteriaTextBox.Text;
    this.customersBindingSource.Filter = filterCriteria;
  }
}
```

[11] IBindingList implements single-column sorting, whereas IBindingListView implements single- and multiple-column sorting. Internally, DataGridView knows only about IBindingList sorting, whereas BindingSource can handle both, depending on what the underlying list data source implements. Consequently, the lowest common denominator is IBindingList single-column sorting.

As with sorting, a list change notification is issued from the data source when Filter is set, thereby ensuring that all bound clients update themselves visually, as with the Data-GridView shown in Figure 17.32.

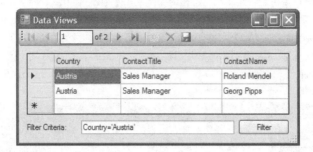

Figure 17.32   Creating a Filtered View

To remove the filtered view to display all items in the list data source, you call Bind-ingSource.RemoveFilter:

```
// DataViewForm.cs
partial class DataViewForm : Form {
  ...
  void removeFilterButton_Click(object sender, EventArgs e) {
    this.customersBindingSource.RemoveFilter();
  }
}
```

Note that if you add a new item, via the UI, that doesn't match the filter criteria, it is added to the list data source and removed from the filtered view. You can also sort a filtered view and filter a sorted view if needed.

Searching

Searching uses specific criteria to find a particular item but doesn't change the list itself. Consequently, you can search sorted and filtered views. Again, none of the Windows Forms controls provides a UI to enable searching. Instead, you need to build a UI that harvests two values from the user: the column to be searched, and the value searched for in that column, before these are passed as arguments to the BindingSource component's Find method:

```
// DataViewForm.cs
partial class DataViewForm : Form {
  ...
  void searchButton_Click(object sender, EventArgs e) {
```

```
        // Get search criteria
        string searchColumn = this.searchColumnTextBox.Text;
        string searchValue = this.searchValueTextBox.Text;

        // Execute search
        int index =
          this.customersBindingSource.Find(searchColumn, searchValue);

        // Select row
        this.customersBindingSource.Position = index;
    }
}
```

The Find method returns the index of the first item it finds whose property value (specified by the search column) matches the search value. A search doesn't cause a full-list change notification to be issued from the list data source, because the list hasn't changed. Thus, you need to select the found item manually in a way that ensures that all bound controls point to it. This is why we set the BindingSource component's Position property, which changes the current item in the list data source and consequently causes the DataGridView to change its selected row, as illustrated in Figure 17.33.

Figure 17.33   Searching a View

BindingSource.Find can return only a single index, and this is consistent with its behavior of returning the index to the first row that's found. For example, if the search were run again, the same item would be found, not the next item that matches the criteria. BindingSource.Find does not implicitly support FindNext.

Checking for View Support

Typed data sets support simple and advanced sorting, searching, and filtering, but not all item types completely implement IBindingList and IBindingListView. Both interfaces offer methods for checking whether those features are supported: IBindingList.SupportsSearching, IBindingList.SupportSearching, IBindingListView.SupportsAdvancedSearching, and IBindingListView.SupportsFiltering. Instead of attempting to acquire references to those interfaces on a data source, you can use the BindingSource component's helper methods:

```
// DataViewForm.cs
public partial class DataViewForm : Form {
  ...
  void DataViewForm_Load(object sender, EventArgs e) {
    ...
    this.sortButton.Enabled =
      this.customersBindingSource.SupportsSorting |
      this.customersBindingSource.SupportsAdvancedSorting;
    this.searchButton.Enabled =
      this.customersBindingSource.SupportsSearching;
    this.filterButton.Enabled =
      this.customersBindingSource.SupportsFiltering;
  }
```

Data views, item UIs, and list UIs form the basic UI models that allow you to build a variety of real-world data-bound UIs.

Real-World Data-Bound UIs

You can pull together the fundamental elements of data binding in many ways to enable a variety of common, real-world data presentation and editing scenarios. To do this, you can use additional controls in a variety of layouts to simplify the listing and editing of data in specific situations. Master-details UIs are one well-known technique for doing so, but alternatives like list-edit and hierarchical UIs are equally useful, depending on the situation.

Master-Details UIs

Earlier, we used filtering to display only a subset of list data source items, rather than all items, based on certain filter criteria. Another way to filter list data source items is to use values from one data source to determine which values are available from another data source. The type of UI designed to support this is known as a *master-details* UI, and it is the most common model for presenting parent-child (one-to-many) relationships between data sources.[12] Figure 17.34 shows the fundamental breakdown of master and item UI controls on a master-details UI, which shows product data being filtered by suppliers.

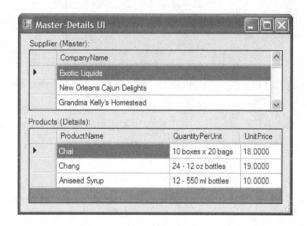

Figure 17.34   A Master-Details UI

Because the master component of a master-details UI focuses on one item at a time, the UI can be either item-style or list-style. If the master is an item UI, you must give users a way to navigate the list of items. The details component, however, is typically a list UI because it's the "many" part of the one-to-many relationship.

Figure 17.35 illustrates how navigating between the master data UI filters the data that's displayed on the details data UI on a per-supplier basis.

---

[12] Note that the "details" in master-details doesn't dictate that the child controls should be displayed in Details view. Instead, it refers to the display of one or more rows of detailed data that relates to another row. "Parent-child" is the more accurate moniker, although "master-details" is more widely used.

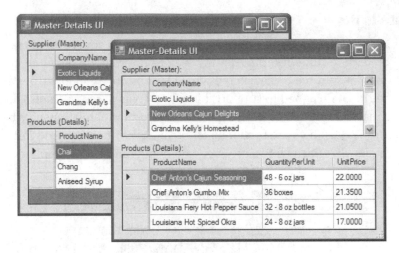

Figure 17.35   Filtering One Set of Data Based on Another Set of Data

To establish a master-details UI, we use data binding to bind to a relation so that as master item selection changes, the details UI is automatically populated with only the related details rows.

For example, the typed data set that contains both the Suppliers and the Products data tables also establishes a one-to-many relationship between the two, as shown in Figure 17.36.

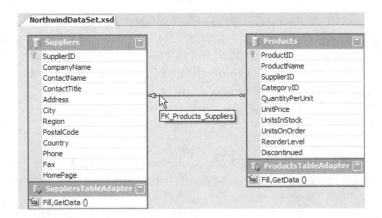

Figure 17.36   Relationship Between the Suppliers Table, the Products Table, and FK_Products_Suppliers

To build a master-details form based on this relationship, you first add controls to display the master Suppliers data. The easiest technique is to create the Suppliers data source and drag it from the Data Sources window onto the form. This action creates the usual data binding suspects, including a BindingSource that is bound to the Northwind data source's Suppliers data member.

Next, you add the controls to display the child Products data. This requires you to create a new BindingSource component that provides the child items as determined by the relationship, and this means binding to the relationship itself. In Windows Forms data binding, a typed data set relationship is a bindable member of the parent table (in this case, Suppliers). Therefore, we set the details BindingSource component's DataSource and DataMember properties to the Suppliers BindingSource and the Suppliers FK_Products_Suppliers members, respectively, as shown in Figure 17.37.

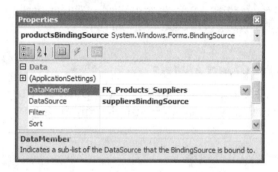

Figure 17.37   Creating the Details BindingSource,
Bound to the Master BindingSource

Binding the details BindingSource directly to the master BindingSource in this way ensures that the same binding manager is used, thus correctly synchronizing master-details data. Consequently, when you bind your item UI controls to the new details BindingSource, the child items are updated as the parent items are navigated by the master UI controls, as you saw in Figure 17.35.

The Data Sources window happens to provide a shortcut technique that automatically allows you to add a complete item UI, complete with data binding bits. Whenever it sees a relationship between two data sources, it adds a relationship property to the parent data source, as shown in Figure 17.38.

When you drag the relationship onto a form, the Windows Forms Designer automatically hooks up all the pieces that we just did manually. Also, when you drag a parent data source that contains a relationship onto a form, the relationship is not dropped; that's left for you to do using the techniques just described.

Figure 17.38   Data Sources Window Automatically
Displaying Data Source Relationships

Master-Details UIs for Object Models

Master-details data binding also works for another popular way to represent one-to-many
data: object models. For example, consider the following type:

```csharp
// Races.cs
class Races : BindingList<Race> { }

// Race.cs
class Race {
  ...
  RaceCarDrivers drivers = new RaceCarDrivers();
  public RaceCarDrivers Drivers {
    get {...}
    set {...}
  }
  ...
}

// RaceCarDrivers.cs
class RaceCarDrivers : BindingList<RaceCarDriver>, ... { }

// RaceCarDriver.cs
class RaceCarDriver : INotifyPropertyChanged, ... {
  ...
  public int Wins {
```

```
      get {...}
      set {...}
    }

    public string Name {
      get {...}
      set {...}
    }
    ...
  }
```

If you were to create a data source for the Races type, you would also see the Drivers property as a relationship, as shown in Figure 17.39.

Figure 17.39   Object List Data Source Relationships

To build the UI, you first drag and drop the Races data source onto the form as an item UI. The Windows Forms Designer then generates the appropriate master bindings:

```
// MasterDetailsRacesDriversForm.Designer.cs
partial class MasterDetailsRacesDriversForm {
  void InitializeComponent() {
    ...
    this.racesBindingSource = new BindingSource(this.components);
    this.racesBindingNavigator = new BindingNavigator(this.components);
    this.dateDateTimePicker = new DateTimePicker();
    this.trackTextBox = new System.Windows.Forms.TextBox();
    ...
    // racesBindingSource
    this.racesBindingSource.DataSource = typeof(Race);

    // racesBindingNavigator
    this.racesBindingNavigator.BindingSource =
      this.racesBindingSource;

    // dateDateTimePicker
    this.dateDateTimePicker.DataBindings.Add(
```

```
          new Binding("Value", this.racesBindingSource, "Date", true));

      // trackTextBox
      this.trackTextBox.DataBindings.Add(new
        Binding("Text", this.racesBindingSource, "Track", true));
      ...
    }
    BindingSource racesBindingSource;
    BindingNavigator racesBindingNavigator;
    DateTimePicker dateDateTimePicker;
    TextBox trackTextBox;
}
```

Second, you drag the Drivers data source as a list UI, and that nicely establishes the necessary binding pieces to enable the details side of the relationship:

```
// MasterDetailsRacesDriversForm.Designer.cs
partial class MasterDetailsRacesDriversForm {
  ...
  void InitializeComponent() {
    ...
    this.driversBindingSource = new BindingSource(this.components);
    this.driversDataGridView = new DataGridView();
    ...
    // driversBindingSource
    this.driversBindingSource.DataMember = "Drivers";
    this.driversBindingSource.DataSource = this.racesBindingSource;
    ...
    // driversDataGridView
    this.driversDataGridView.DataSource = this.driversBindingSource;
    ...
  }
  ...
  BindingSource driversBindingSource;
  DataGridView driversDataGridView;
}
```

Figure 17.40 shows the object data source master-details form at run time.

Master-details UIs provide a good way to present data from related data sources in an easy-to-view layout, and the Windows Forms Designer makes it easy to create them.

List-Item UIs

Whereas master-details UIs employ both item and list UI elements visually to concatenate data from two data sources, list-item UIs use both item and list UI elements to enhance the display of a large amount of data for a single data source.

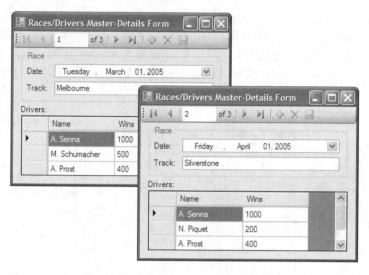

Figure 17.40   Master-Details UI for an Object Model

For example, consider the Employees table, which has 18 columns; this is simply too much data to display because some users will quickly get lost. One technique for creating a more usable experience in this situation is to spread the listing and editing of data across two forms. This technique takes advantage of controls like DataGridView to provide a sortable, filterable UI to simplify both general browsing and targeted searching for specific data, giving users a separate details view UI for adding and editing data items.

To help users find an item, you create a list UI that allows them to view all the data and easily find the specific record they want to edit. A sample form is shown in Figure 17.41.

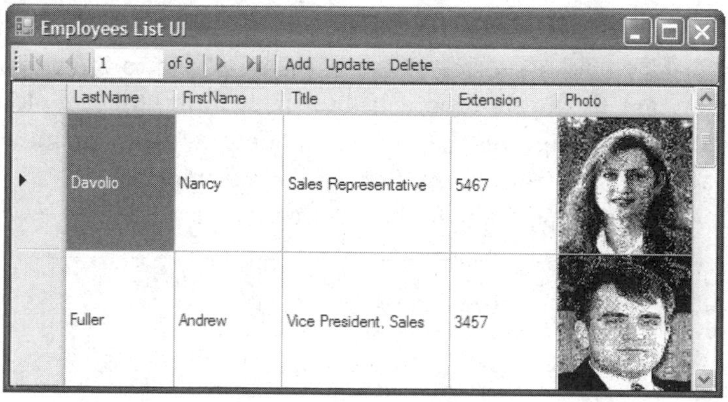

Figure 17.41   Employees (Sporting 1980s Hairstyles) List Form (See Plate 4)

This employees list UI uses a DataGridView to optimize data presentation for browsing by displaying only key, relevant data fields from DataGridView. Users can sort, search, and filter these fields as long as the list data source supports such functionality.

To let users edit an item, you create a details-style UI, like the one shown in Figure 17.42, providing a rich editing experience.

Figure 17.42   Employees Edit Form

This employee item details-view UI is optimized for adding and updating data by using Windows Forms controls and layout to achieve maximum visual benefit.

Because of data binding, it's easy to build both view and edit forms. However, we still need to add the code that integrates the two, allowing users to add new items and update or delete existing items.

Adding a New Item

To let users add a new employee item, we open the edit form to collect the new employee data and pass it back to the list form, where it can be added to the employees list data source. We don't want to shuttle around a bunch of individual employee properties. Instead, we use a class that captures the entire set of employee information at once.

This class, DataRowView, is the item over which the employees list data source operates. To create one, we add a new row to the BindingSource:

```
// EmployeesListForm.cs
partial class EmployeesListForm : Form {
  ...
  void addToolStripButton_Click(object sender, EventArgs e) {
    // Create new item
    object item = this.NorthwindDataSet.Employees.DefaultView.AddNew();
```

```
    // Pass new item to edit form
    ...
  }
}
```

Rather than try to extract the current item as a DataRowView specifically—something that would require extra code—we simply extract it as an object. We then send this to the add form, where its values are filled and returned to the employees list form and incorporated into the newly added row:

```
// EmployeesListForm.cs
partial class EmployeesListForm : Form {
  ...
  void addToolStripButton_Click(object sender, EventArgs e) {
    // Create new item
    object item = this.NorthwindDataSet.Employees.DefaultView.AddNew();

    // Pass new item to edit form
    EmployeeItemForm dlg = new EmployeeItemForm(item);
    if( dlg.ShowDialog() == DialogResult.OK ) {
      // Reset to reflect changes automatically
      this.employeesBindingSource.ResetCurrentItem();
    }
  }
}

// EmployeeItemForm.cs
partial class EmployeeItemForm : Form {
  ...
  public EmployeesEditForm(object item) : {...}
  ...
}
```

The trick is to populate the edit form's controls with the data from the passed list data source item. With data binding, this is no problem. We simply shape the form at design time by dropping the employees data source on the form, configured as "Details." Then, at run time, we set the BindingSource component's DataSource property with the item instance:

```
// EmployeesEditForm.cs
partial class EmployeesEditForm : Form {
  ...
  public EmployeeItemForm(object item) {

    // Check that item is a DataRowView for an EmployeesRow
    if( (item is DataRowView) &&
        (((DataRowView)item).Row is NorthwindDataSet.EmployeesRow) ) {
```

```
          InitializeComponent();

            // Acquire employee list data source item
            this.employeesBindingSource.DataSource = item;
        }
        else throw new ArgumentException("Incorrect type");
    }
    ...
}
```

This code ensures that the new item that was passed is a DataRowView for an Employ-eesRow, which is what the employees BindingSource of the employees list UI operates over. If the new item proves to be valid, it is fed into the BindingSource, effectively turning it into an item data source. One benefit of this technique is that it frees you from worrying about currency, leaving you to simply refer to the data source and streamlining the code.

Now users can provide the details and press either OK or Cancel to commit or cancel the new item. By default, each time a control's bound property value is validated, it is auto-matically copied back to the data source. This is why we don't need to manually commit those changes when the OK button is clicked.

However, we need to roll back the changes when users click Cancel or close the form by clicking the close box or from the system menu. To roll back the changes, we invoke the BindingSource component's CancelEdit method from the FormClosing event handler:

```
// EmployeesEditForm.cs
partial class EmployeesEditForm : Form {
    ...
    void EmployeeItemForm_FormClosing(
        object sender, FormClosingEventArgs e) {
        // Cancel edit if Cancel button is pressed or form is closed from
        // either the system menu or close box
        if( (e.CloseReason == CloseReason.UserClosing) ||
            (this.DialogResult == DialogResult.Cancel) ) {
            this.employeesBindingSource.CancelEdit();
        }
    }
}
```

BindingSource.EndEdit ensures that all changes are committed to the current data item, which, in this case, is the only data item. And, as you would expect, BindingSource.Can-celEdit rolls back any changes.[13]

---

[13] BindingSource.CancelEdit internally invokes a method of the same name on DataRowView, which is part of its IEditableObject implementation to support committing or rolling back changes. A discussion of IEditableObject is beyond the scope of this book, but Rockford Lhotka provides insight here: http://msdn.microsoft.com/library/en-us/dnadvnet/html/vbnet02252003.asp (http://tinysells.com/37).

Updating an Item

Updating an item turns out to be quite similar to adding an item because both actions pass a reference to the current item, although adding creates a new item as well. The code on the edit form doesn't need to change, and the changes on the view form are minimal:

```
// EmployeesViewForm.cs
class EmployeesViewForm : Form {
  ...
  void addToolStripButton_Click(object sender, EventArgs e) {
    this.EditEmployee(this.employeesBindingSource.AddNew());
  }

  void updateToolStripButton_Click(object sender, EventArgs e) {
    this.EditEmployee((DataRowView)this.employeesBindingSource.Current);
  }

  void EditEmployee(DataRowView item) {
    // Pass to child employee details form
    EmployeesEditForm dlg = new EmployeesEditForm(item);
    if( dlg.ShowDialog() == DialogResult.OK ) {
      // Reset to reflect changes automatically
      this.employeesBindingSource.ResetCurrentItem();
    }
  }
  ...
}
```

Notice that we reset the current item when the edit form returns, thus making sure that the changes are picked up; changes to the current item were made while under the control of the employee item UI BindingSource and consequently are not picked up by the employees list UI BindingSource, so we give the latter a helping hand.

Deleting an Item

To support updating, we don't need to make any changes to the child form. The same thing is true when we're supporting deletion, because this activity occurs on the list form in a list-view UI. Instead, we operate directly against the parent form's BindingSource, asking the standard warning question before deleting:

```
// EmployeesViewForm.cs
class EmployeesViewForm : Form {
  ...
  void deleteToolStripButton_Click(object sender, EventArgs e) {
    DialogResult result =
      MessageBox.Show(
```

```
            "Delete current row?",
            Application.ProductName,
            MessageBoxButtons.YesNo,
            MessageBoxIcon.Warning);
        if( result == DialogResult.Yes ) {
          this.employeesBindingSource.RemoveCurrent();
        }
      }
    }
  }
```

Data binding plays a key role in simplifying the creation of the basic infrastructure to support a UI that allows viewing and editing of data. Although you can add all manner of visual accoutrements to support the standard Add, Update, and Delete operations, the core logic is relatively simple.

Hierarchical UIs

Some data can be stored in hierarchies that are often more than two levels deep. In the Northwind database, one such hierarchy is Customers to Orders to Order Details. Users might need to quickly navigate between all three levels of data, and that is certainly easier than opening multiple forms.

However, you can't readily use the master-details technique to present three or more levels of data; there's no limit to the number of BindingSource components you can link through Binding, but form space is finite. Instead, you want a control that has built-in support for tree-style navigation. Believe it or not, this is a good reason to use the DataGrid control instead of DataGridView. DataGrid supports multilevel list data source navigation, whereas DataGridView does not.[14]

To use DataGrid hierarchically, you do three things. First, you create the data source that contains the multilevel hierarchy you want. Second, you configure the Data Sources window to create a DataGrid UI, rather than a DataGridView UI, when it's dragged and dropped, as shown in Figure 17.43.

Third, you add the code to load the child list data sources (in this case, tables) with data, because dragging and dropping from the Data Sources window creates only enough data binding and Designer-generated code to load the topmost parent object in the hierarchy. So even though the typed data set provides all the tables you need, you must fill them.

---

[14] Tree-style navigation support for bound data would be a good reason to use the Windows Forms TreeView control, except that it doesn't support data binding.

Figure 17.43   Specifying a List Data
Source to Create a DataGrid

To do that, you drag additional table adapters for each child table from the topmost tab in the Toolbox onto the form and write the appropriate client code to fill the tables:

```
// HierarchicalDataForm.cs
partial class HierarchicalDataForm : Form {
  ...
  void HierarchicalDataForm_Load(object sender, EventArgs e) {
    // TODO: This line of code loads data into the
    // 'NorthwindDataSet.Customers' table. You can move
    // or remove it, as needed.
    this.customersTableAdapter.Fill(this.NorthwindDataSet.Customers);

    // Load child table data
    this.ordersTableAdapter.Fill(
      this.NorthwindDataSet.Orders);
    this.order_DetailsTableAdapter.Fill(
      this.NorthwindDataSet.Order_Details);
  }
}
```

Then, at run time, the DataGrid allows users to navigate the hierarchical data, as shown in Figure 17.44.

In Figure 17.44, you can see that DataGrid displays a hyperlink that, when clicked, navigates to the next level down in the hierarchy. Because the data source is a typed data set, these links are sourced from the foreign keys that enable the one-to-many relationships between the data tables. As you navigate down through successive child rows, a row for each parent is added to only the title bar, giving quick access to its data without the need to navigate back to it. DataGrid also provides navigation support, in the form of two buttons at the top right of the DataGrid's UI. The back arrow allows users to navigate back to the parent rows, and the other button allows them to hide or show the parent rows (showing is the default).

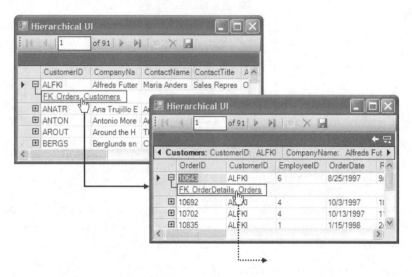

Figure 17.44   Navigating a Hierarchical Data Source

DataGrid has effectively been superceded by DataGridView as a general-purpose grid control, but DataGrid still offers excellent support for navigating hierarchical data sources, a feature you may not be interested in writing yourself.

Multiple Data Contexts

Often, UIs contain two or more fields that capture the same type of data. For example, in credit card billing, it is common to collect both billing address and delivery address details. Each address requires a State value, which could be selected from a combo box lookup. Even better, you could load your list of States once—perhaps by filling a typed data set via a typed table adapter—and then share the data among both lookups.

With that in mind, you might be tempted to bind both lookups to a single State BindingSource (bound to a typed data set), as shown in Figure 17.45.

The problem with this design is that it ensures that the values in both lookups remain synchronized, because they are looking at the same binding; as you may recall from Chapter 16, a BindingSource component is also a currency manager, a special type of binding manager for list data sources, and is why both lookups point to the same current BindingSource item. If you need to provide two or more independent views of the same data, however, you need only provide two or more BindingSources exposing the same list of data, as shown in Figure 17.46.

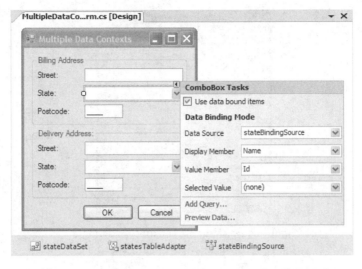

Figure 17.45   Binding Multiple Lookups to a Single BindingSource

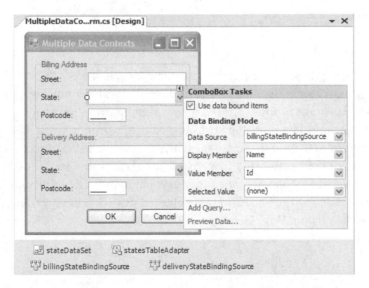

Figure 17.46   Binding Multiple Lookups to Multiple BindingSources

In this design, each BindingSource is bound to the same typed data set and subsequently to the same, single set of State data. However, each BindingSource provides its own currency management for that data, including determining which item is current, independently of any other BindingSource. Consequently, although each lookup is basically filled from the same data, the values are never synchronized with each other at the binding level, as shown in Figure 17.47.

**Figure 17.47   Multiple Lookups for a Single
Data Source via Multiple BindingSources**

Note that even though the values chosen by a user might be the same, the lookups aren't synchronized.

Type Converters

When a custom list data source class uses simple types, it is easy to convert them to and from strings. This isn't an issue when the bound property of a control is a string type, such as TextBox.Text. However, binding simple types to string properties isn't always what you want to do. For example, you may need to bind a control's property to a custom data type—rather than a simple data type like integer or string—on the data source. For that to work, not only must the data be converted to a string, but also it must be converted back from a string to the custom data type; otherwise, any user changes made to the bound control will be lost. Consider updating the RaceCarDriver class to store first, second, and third positions as a property of the custom Positions type:

```csharp
// RaceCarDriver.cs
class RaceCarDriver : INotifyPropertyChanged, ... {
  ...
  Positions positions;
  ...
  public Positions Positions {
    get {...}
    set {...}
  }
}

// Positions.cs
```

```
class Positions {

  int firsts;
  int seconds;
  int thirds;

  public Positions() { }
  public Positions(int firsts, int seconds, int thirds) {
    this.firsts = firsts;
    this.seconds = seconds;
    this.thirds = thirds;
  }

  public int Firsts {
    get {...}
    set {...}
  }
  public int Seconds {
    get {...}
    set {...}
  }
  public int Thirds {
    get {...}
    set {...}
  }
}
```

By default, this binding shows the name of the type instead of a meaningful value, as shown in Figure 17.48.

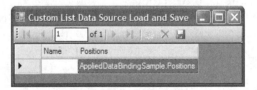

Figure 17.48   Binding to a Custom Item Data Source with No Conversion to String

To get the string value to set as the Text property, the binding falls back on the ToString method of the custom Positions class, which defaults in the Object base class's implementation to returning the name of the type. Overriding the ToString method of the Positions class solves the display problem, as shown in Figure 17.49:

```
// Positions.cs
class Positions {
  ...
  public override string ToString() {
    return string.Format(
      "{0}-{1}-{2}", this.firsts, this.seconds, this.thirds);
  }
}
```

Figure 17.49   Binding to a Custom Item Data Source with a Conversion to String

However, implementing ToString fixes only half of the conversion problem: The Positions column is read-only. This is because data binding and the DataGridView can't find an implementation that allows them to convert a value from the user's input to the Positions type.

Instead, you need a custom type converter, as discussed in Chapter 11: Design-Time Integration: The Properties Window. To support conversion between a string (to display the DataGridView) and a Position object (the item in the data source), we derive a class from TypeConverter and implement the following virtual methods: CanConvertFrom, CanConvertTo, ConvertFrom, and ConvertTo.

First, we implement CanConvertTo and ConvertTo to enable conversion from a Positions type to a string:

```
// PositionsConverter.cs
class PositionsConverter : ExpandableObjectConverter {
  public override bool CanConvertTo(
    ITypeDescriptorContext context, Type destinationType) {
    // We can convert from a Positions type to a string
    return( destinationType == typeof(string) );
  }
  ...
  public override object ConvertTo(
    ITypeDescriptorContext context, CultureInfo culture,
    object value, Type destinationType) {

    // If source value is a Positions type
    if( value is Positions ) {
```

```
    // Convert to string
    if( (destinationType == typeof(string)) ) {
      Positions Positions = (Positions)value;
      return string.Format(
        "{0}-{1}-{2}",
        Positions.Firsts,
        Positions.Seconds,
        Positions.Thirds);
    }
  }

  // Base ConvertTo if neither string nor InstanceDescriptor required
  return base.ConvertTo(context, culture, value, destinationType);
  }
}
```

Second, we convert a string back to a Positions type:

```
// PositionsConverter.cs
class PositionsConverter : ExpandableObjectConverter {
  ...
  public override bool CanConvertFrom(
    ITypeDescriptorContext context, Type sourceType) {
    // We can convert from a string to a Positions type
    if( sourceType == typeof(string) ) { return true; }
    return base.CanConvertFrom(context, sourceType);
  }

  public override object ConvertFrom(
    ITypeDescriptorContext context, CultureInfo info, object value) {

    // If converting from a string
    if( value is string ) {
      // Build a Positions type
      try {
        // Get Positions properties
        string propertyList = (string)value;
        string[] properties = propertyList.Split('-');
        return new Positions(
          int.Parse(properties[0]),
          int.Parse(properties[1]),
          int.Parse(properties[2]));
      }
      catch { }
      throw new ArgumentException("The arguments were not valid.");
    }
    return base.ConvertFrom(context, info, value);
  }
}
```

Associating the type converter with the type is a matter of applying the TypeConverter attribute:

```
// Positions.cs
[TypeConverter(typeof(PositionsConverter))]
class Positions {...}
```

Now, instead of using the ToString method to get the Positions string to display in the bound control, the binding uses the PositionsConverter class's CanConvertTo and ConvertTo methods. Similarly, when new data is available, the binding uses the CanConvertFrom and ConvertFrom methods.

Note that if you don't control the data source, you can't use this technique to provide automatic type conversion between bound control property and data source property. However, you can fall back on the Binding object's Format and Parse events, or DataGridView's CellFormatting and CellParsing events, all of which you saw earlier in this chapter. Alternatively, you can use a custom type converter from these events and thus support at least a modicum of conversion reusability.

Where Are We?

The data binding infrastructure, revolving around the BindingSource component and extensive Windows Forms Designer data binding support, facilitates the development of Windows Forms applications to deal with a broad variety of data-bound applications. This includes the use of custom formatting and parsing, as well as type converters, to enable dynamic data binding conversion for complex scenarios or when custom types are used. Additionally, you can mix and match the various data binding elements in several ways to enable common data-bound UIs, including master-details, list-view, and hierarchical models.

18

Multithreaded User Interfaces

W INDOWS FORMS APPLICATIONS often need to support long-running operations, such as an intensive calculation or a call to a web service. In those cases, it's important to run the operation so that the application continues to interact with the user without freezing, while still allowing the user to see the progress of the operation and even to cancel it.

Before we get started, I should mention that this chapter discusses the issues surrounding multithreaded user interfaces only. This simplifies the discussion and covers the information you need most of the time when handling long-running operations in a Windows Forms application. For more details about threading specifics in .NET—including the details of the Thread class, thread pooling, locking, synchronization, race conditions, and deadlocks—you should turn to your favorite low-level .NET book.

Long-Running Operations

Imagine that the value of pi in System.Math.PI, at only 20 digits, just isn't precise enough for you. In that case, you may find yourself writing an application like the one in Figure 18.1 to calculate pi to an arbitrary number of digits.

This program takes as input the number of digits of pi to calculate and, when the Calculate button is pressed, shows the progress as the calculation happens.

Progress Indication

Although some applications don't need to calculate the digits of pi, many kinds of applications need to perform long-running operations, whether it's printing, making a web service call, or calculating the interest earnings of a certain multibillionaire in the Pacific Northwest. Users are generally content to wait for such things as long as they can see that progress is being made. That's why even our simple pi application has a progress bar.

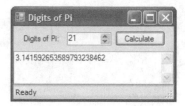

Figure 18.1   Digits of Pi Application

The algorithm to calculate pi calculates 9 digits at a time. As each new set of digits is available, the application updates the text and the progress bar. For example, Figure 18.2 shows progress on the way to calculating 1,000 digits of pi (if 21 digits are good, then 1,000 must be better).

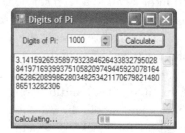

Figure 18.2   Calculating Pi to 1,000 Digits

The following shows how the UI is updated as the digits of pi are calculated:

```
// SyncCalcPiForm.cs
partial class SyncCalcPiForm : Form {
  ...
  void ShowProgress(string pi, int totalDigits, int digitsSoFar) {
    // Display progress in UI
    this.resultsTextBox.Text = pi;
    this.calcToolStripProgressBar.Maximum = totalDigits;
    this.calcToolStripProgressBar.Value = digitsSoFar;

    if( digitsSoFar == totalDigits ) {
      // Reset progress UI
      this.calcToolStripStatusLabel.Text = "Ready";
      this.calcToolStripProgressBar.Visible = false;
    }

    // Force UI update to reflect calculation progress
    this.Refresh();
  }
```

```
void CalcPi(int digits) {
  StringBuilder pi = new StringBuilder("3", digits + 2);

  // Show initial progress
  ShowProgress(pi.ToString(), digits, 0);

  if( digits > 0 ) {
    pi.Append(".");

    for( int i = 0; i < digits; i += 9 ) {
      int nineDigits = NineDigitsOfPi.StartingAt(i + 1);
      int digitCount = Math.Min(digits - i, 9);
      string ds = string.Format("{0:D9}", nineDigits);
      pi.Append(ds.Substring(0, digitCount));

      // Show continuing progress
      ShowProgress(pi.ToString(), digits, i + digitCount);
    }
  }
}

void calcButton_Click(object sender, EventArgs e) {
  // Set calculating UI
  this.calcToolStripProgressBar.Visible = true;
  this.calcToolStripStatusLabel.Text = "Calculating...";

  // Calculate pi to the number of digits in the up-down control
  // (need to convert up-down control's decimal Value to an integer)
  CalcPi((int)this.decimalPlacesNumericUpDown.Value);
}
}
```

This implementation works just fine for a small number of digits. But suppose that, in the middle of calculating pi to a large number of digits, the user switches away from the application and then returns, as shown in Figure 18.3.

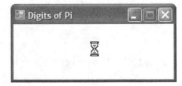

Figure 18.3   No Paint for You!

The problem is that the application has a single thread of execution (this kind of application is often called a single-threaded application). Consequently, while the thread is calculating pi, it can't also be drawing the UI in response to system paint requests. This didn't happen before the user switched the application to the background, because the call to the form's Refresh method forces an immediate repaint. However, after the user puts the application into the background and then the foreground again, the system requests the main form to repaint its entire client area, and that means processing the Paint event. Because no other event can be processed until the application returns from the Click event on the Calculate button, the user doesn't see any display of progress until all the digits of pi are calculated.

The same problem prevents the client area from processing events related to user input via, for example, the mouse or keyboard. In these situations, if users try repeatedly to click in the results text box or resize the form with the status strip's size grip, the UI locks up and adds the infamous "(Not Responding)" message to the application's title bar, as shown in Figure 18.4.

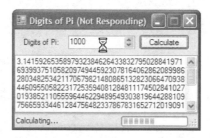

Figure 18.4   No User Input for You!

The user's only options are either to wait until the Click button event returns or to use the system-managed control box to close the application immediately. To avoid these issues, this application needs a way to free the UI thread to do UI work and handle the long-running pi calculation in the background. For this, it needs another thread of execution.

Asynchronous Operations

A *thread of execution* (often simply called a *thread*) is a series of instructions and a call stack that operate independently of the other threads in the application or those in any other application. In every version of Windows since Windows 95, Windows schedules each thread transparently so that a programmer can write a thread almost (but not quite) as if it were the only thing happening on the system.

Starting a thread is an *asynchronous operation* in that the current thread of execution continues, executing independently of the new thread. In .NET, you start a new thread of execution by creating a Thread object from the System.Threading namespace, passing a delegate as the constructor parameter, and invoking the Start method:[1]

```
// AsyncCalcPiForm.cs
using System.Threading;
...
partial class AsyncCalcPiForm  : Form {
  ...
  void CalcPi(int digits) {...}

  void calcButton_Click(object sender, EventArgs e) {
    // Set calculating UI
    this.calcToolStripProgressBar.Visible = true;
    this.calcToolStripStatusLabel.Text = "Calculating...";

    // Start pi calculation on new thread of execution
    Thread piThread = new Thread(CalcPiThreadStart);
    piThread.Start((int)this.decimalPlacesNumericUpDown.Value);
  }

  void CalcPiThreadStart(object digits) {
    // Convert thread start parameter to int
    CalcPi((int)digits);
  }
}
```

This code creates a new thread and begins execution of the thread when the thread Start method is called. Now, instead of waiting for CalcPi to finish before returning from the button Click event, the UI thread spawns a *worker thread* before immediately returning to the UI thread and allowing it to continue user interaction duties. Figure 18.5 shows the two threads doing their separate jobs.

---

[1] You can read more about delegates in Appendix C: Delegates and Events.

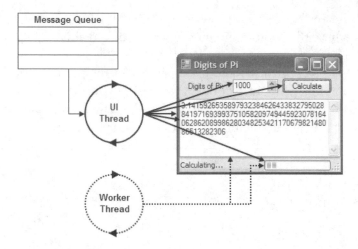

Figure 18.5   Naïve Multithreading

Spawning a worker thread to calculate pi leaves the UI thread free to handle events (which Windows Forms creates and fires as it takes messages off the Windows message queue). When the worker thread has more digits of pi to share with the user, it directly sets the values of the text box and the progress bar controls.

Unfortunately, such direct manipulation of controls from the worker thread is a no-no. Luckily, when you execute your application under the debugger, you'll see an Invalid-OperationException thrown, as shown in Figure 18.6.[2]

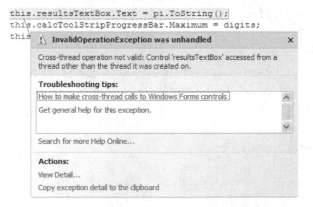

Figure 18.6   Illegal Cross-Thread Operation Detected
and InvalidOperationException Raised

---

[2] Throwing InvalidOperationException is the default. You can set the static Control.CheckForIllegalCross-ThreadCalls property to false to prevent the InvalidOperationException, although I don't advise it. Also, note that InvalidOperationExceptions are raised only when the app is executing from within the debugger. No exception is raised when your application executes outside a debugger, so you must be vigilant during development.

Because we start the CalcPi method on a worker thread, when CalcPi calls the Show-Progress method, ShowProgress accesses the text box and progress bar controls from the worker thread, even though those controls were created on the UI thread. This violates a key requirement that's been present since Windows first got support for threads:

Thou shalt operate on a window only from its creating thread.

In fact, the Windows Forms documentation is clear on this point:

There are four methods on a control that are safe to call from any thread: Invoke, BeginInvoke, EndInvoke, and CreateGraphics. For all other method calls, you should use one of the invoke methods to marshal the call to the control's thread.[3]

When the CalcPi method calls the ShowProgress method, it accesses controls created by the UI thread. When the application is executing under the debugger, this causes an InvalidOperationException to be thrown on the first line of the following code:

```
void ShowProgress(string pi, int totalDigits, int digitsSoFar) {
    // Display progress in UI
    this.resultsTextBox.Text = pi; // Can't call from worker thread!
    ...
}
```

This code is in clear violation.

Safety and Multithreading

Luckily, long-running operations are common in Windows applications. Through the use of custom delegates, applications can take advantage of specific Windows Forms features to ensure that worker threads communicate with the UI thread safely.

Multithreading with Custom Delegates

Recall that the CalcPi application starts a worker thread by passing an object argument to CalcPiThreadStart, the worker thread's entry point:

```
void calcButton_Click(object sender, EventArgs e) {
    ...
    // Start pi calculation on new thread of execution
```

[3] See http://msdn.microsoft.com/library/default.asp?url=/library/en-us/cpref/html/frlrfSystemWindows-FormsControlClassTopic.asp (http://tinysells.com/42). It is actually possible for CreateGraphics to cause a control to be created on the wrong thread; when CreateGraphics is called from a worker thread on a control that hasn't yet had its HWND created, the act of accessing the control's Handle property (used internally by Create-Graphics) causes the control's HWND to be created. The Graphics object is just fine, but the control's window has been created on the worker thread and cannot be of use from the UI thread. Because accessing the Handle property of a control creates the HWND, you can use that to force its creation on the UI thread. You can also check whether the HWND was created via the IsHandleCreated property from the worker thread.

```
    Thread piThread = new Thread(CalcPiThreadStart);
    piThread.Start((int)this.decimalPlacesNumericUpDown.Value);
}

void CalcPiThreadStart(object digits) {
    // Convert thread start parameter to int
    CalcPi((int)digits);
}
```

When the thread start method is called on the worker thread, we simply cast the object parameter to an integer and pass it to the real CalcPi method. Because you can't pass strongly typed arguments to the CalcPiThreadStart method, you might prefer to use custom delegates for spawning threads. Additionally, asynchronously executed delegates are processed on threads allocated from the per-process thread pool, an approach that scales better than creating a new thread for each of a large number of asynchronous operations.

Here's how to declare a custom delegate suitable for calling CalcPi:

```
delegate void CalcPiDelegate(int digits);
```

After the custom delegate has been defined, the following code creates an instance of the delegate to call the CalcPi method synchronously:

```
void calcButton_Click(object sender, EventArgs e) {
    ...

    // Begin calculating pi synchronously
    CalcPiDelegate calcPi = new CalcPiDelegate(CalcPi);
    calcPi((int)this.decimalPlacesNumericUpDown.Value);
}
```

Because calling CalcPi synchronously causes our UI to freeze (remember how we got into this discussion in the first place?), we need to call CalcPi asynchronously. Before we do that, however, we need to explain a bit more about how delegates work. The CalcPi-Delegate declaration implicitly declares a new class derived from MulticastDelegate (from the System namespace), which has three methods: Invoke, BeginInvoke, and EndInvoke:

```
namespace System {
    ...
    class CalcPiDelegate : MulticastDelegate {
      public void Invoke(int digits);

      public void BeginInvoke(
        int digits, AsyncCallback callback, object asyncState);

      public void EndInvoke(IAsyncResult result);
    }
    ...
}
```

When the application created an instance of CalcPiDelegate and called it like a method, it was actually calling the Invoke method, which turned around and synchronously called the CalcPi method on the same thread. BeginInvoke and EndInvoke, however, are the pair of methods that allows asynchronous invocation of a method on a new thread for a per-process pool of threads.

To have the CalcPi method called on another thread—the aforementioned worker thread—the application uses BeginInvoke:

```
delegate void CalcPiDelegate(int digits);

void calcButton_Click(object sender, EventArgs e) {
  ...
  // Begin calculating pi asynchronously
  CalcPiDelegate calcPi = new CalcPiDelegate(CalcPi);
  calcPi.BeginInvoke(
    (int)this.decimalPlacesNumericUpDown.Value, // CalcPi argument
    EndCalcPi, // Called when CalcPi completes
    calcPi); // EndCalcPi argument (indirectly)
}
```

When we call BeginInvoke on our CalcPiDelegate, the first argument is always the argument to our CalcPi method. This causes a thread from the thread pool to act as our worker thread, calling CalcPi and then returning the thread to the pool when CalcPi returns. But how will we know when CalcPi has finished executing? In our example, we're getting progress indicators, but what if there's an exception on the worker thread? Also, what if CalcPi returned something other than void? How would we get those results?

To answer these questions, we make sure that the last two arguments to our custom delegate's BeginInvoke method are a delegate to call and an object to pass it when our custom delegate has completed:

```
void EndCalcPi(IAsyncResult result) {
  // Harvest results, handle exceptions, and clean up resources
  try {
    CalcPiDelegate calcPi = (CalcPiDelegate)result.AsyncState;
    calcPi.EndInvoke(result);
  }
  catch( Exception ex ) {
    // EndCalcPi executed on worker thread
    ShowProgress(ex.Message, 0, 0); // ERR!
  }
}
```

It's certainly possible to write code that never calls EndInvoke, but failing to call End-Invoke causes resources to stick around a lot longer than they should. Also, it's by calling

EndInvoke that you can access any results or exceptions from our delegate executing on our worker thread. However, if there is a result or an exception, you should take care not to report it directly to the UI, as I've done here. EndCalcPi is called on a worker thread and not on a UI thread, so you must use the techniques I'm about to show you for that, too.

Detecting UI Access on Worker Threads

At this point, the CalcPi application side of things nicely kicks off the calculation of pi asynchronously, passing in our typed arguments and using a thread from the thread pool. However, the code running on a worker thread is still setting controls created on the UI thread, and that, as you know, is illegal.

Luckily, Windows Forms provides the necessary additional support for long-running operations natively: Each UI class in Windows Forms—meaning every class that ultimately derives from System.Windows.Forms.Control—has a property that you can use to find out whether it's safe to act on the control from the current thread. The property, InvokeRequired, returns true if the calling thread needs to pass control to the UI thread before calling a method on the control. A simple Assert in the ShowProgress method would have immediately shown the error in our sample application:

```
using System.Diagnostics;
...
void ShowProgress(string pi, int totalDigits, int digitsSoFar) {
  // Make sure we're on the UI thread
  Debug.Assert(this.InvokeRequired == false);
  ...
}
```

Because the worker thread is not allowed to show progress directly, we need to pass control from the worker thread back to the UI thread. From the names of the first three methods that are safe to call from any thread—Invoke, BeginInvoke, and EndInvoke—it should be clear that you need another custom delegate to pass control appropriately. Using the same techniques to create and use the CalcPiDelegate to communicate from the UI thread to the worker thread, we can just as easily create a custom delegate on the worker thread and execute it on the UI thread, giving us safe, single-threaded access to UI objects.

Synchronous Callbacks

Asynchronous operations, such as the call to a delegate's BeginInvoke method, return immediately, so they are *nonblocking*. This means that the thread isn't blocked waiting for the method to complete. Synchronous operations, on the other hand, are *blocking*, because they do cause the calling thread to block until the method returns.

Depending on the blocking behavior you're interested in, you can call either Invoke or BeginInvoke on a control when calling into the UI thread:

```
namespace System.Windows.Forms {
  class Control : ... {
    public object Invoke(Delegate method);
    public virtual object Invoke(Delegate method, object[] args);
    public IAsyncResult BeginInvoke(Delegate method);
    public virtual IAsyncResult BeginInvoke(
      Delegate method, object[] args);
    public virtual object EndInvoke(IAsyncResult asyncResult);
    ...
  }
}
```

Control.Invoke blocks until the UI thread has processed the request. The request is processed by putting a message on the UI thread's message queue and executing the message handler like any other message (in this case, the event handler calls our delegate). Because Invoke takes a Delegate argument, which is the base class for all delegates, it can form a call to any method, using the optional array of objects as arguments and returning an object as the return value for the called method. Using Control.Invoke looks like this:

```
void ShowProgress(string pi, int totalDigits, int digitsSoFar) {
  // Make sure we're on the UI thread
  Debug.Assert(this.InvokeRequired == false);

  ...

  // No need to force UI update when calculating asynchronously
  //this.Refresh();
}

delegate void ShowProgressDelegate(
  string pi, int totalDigits, int digitsSoFar);

void CalcPi(int digits) {
  StringBuilder pi = new StringBuilder("3", digits + 2);

  // Get ready to show progress
  ShowProgressDelegate showProgress =
    new ShowProgressDelegate(ShowProgress);

  // Show initial progress
  this.Invoke(
    showProgress,
```

```
      new object[] { pi.ToString(), digits, 0 });

  if( digits > 0 ) {
    pi.Append(".");

    for( int i = 0; i < digits; i += 9 ) {
      ...

      // Show continuing progress
      this.Invoke(
        showProgress,
        new object[] { pi.ToString(), digits, i + digitCount });
    }
  }
}
```

Notice the declaration of a new delegate, ShowProgressDelegate. This delegate matches the signature of the ShowProgress method we'd like invoked on the UI thread. Because ShowProgress takes three arguments, the code uses an overload to Invoke that takes an array of objects to form the arguments to the ShowProgress method.

The entire process has the UI thread using a delegate that calls Delegate.BeginInvoke to spawn a worker thread, and the worker thread using Control.Invoke to pass control back to the UI thread when the progress controls need updating. Figure 18.7 shows our safe multithreading architecture.

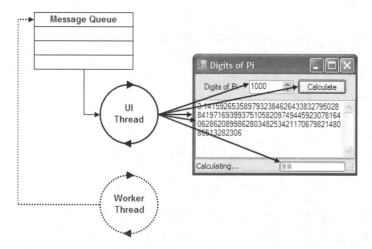

Figure 18.7 Safe Multithreading

You can see that when the worker thread calls Invoke, the request is placed onto the message queue, thereby allowing the UI thread to retrieve the progress data and safely update the controls appropriately.

Asynchronous Callbacks

Our use of the synchronous call to Control.Invoke works just fine, but it gives us more than we need. The worker thread doesn't get any output or return values from the UI thread when calling through ShowProgressDelegate. By calling Invoke, we force the worker thread to wait for the UI thread, blocking the worker thread from continuing its calculations. This is a job tailor-made for the asynchronous Control.BeginInvoke method:

```
using System.Threading;
...
void CalcPi(int digits) {
  StringBuilder pi = new StringBuilder("3", digits + 2);

  // Get ready to show progress
  ShowProgressDelegate showProgress =
    new ShowProgressDelegate(ShowProgress);

  // Show initial progress asynchronously
  this.BeginInvoke(
    showProgress,
    new object[] { pi.ToString(), digits, 0 });

  if( digits > 0 ) {
    pi.Append(".");

    for( int i = 0; i < digits; i += 9 ) {
      ...
      // Show continuing progress asynchronously
      this.BeginInvoke(
        showProgress,
        new object[] { pi.ToString(), digits, i + digitCount });
    }
  }
}
```

The only difference in this code is the call to BeginInvoke (instead of Invoke) to asynchronously kick off the delegate.

Unlike our custom delegate's BeginInvoke, which we needed to match to a corresponding EndInvoke, there is no call to EndInvoke here. It's true that you should always call a delegate's EndInvoke after a call to a delegate's BeginInvoke, but in this case, we call Control.BeginInvoke, passing a delegate to call on the UI thread. It's completely safe to call

Control.BeginInvoke without ever calling Control.EndInvoke, because it doesn't create the same resources associated with a delegate's BeginInvoke call.[4]

Even if you do want the results from a call to Control.BeginInvoke, there's no way to pass a callback, so you need to use the IAsyncResult implementation as returned from Control.BeginInvoke. You keep checking the IsCompleted property for true during your other worker thread processing before calling Control.EndInvoke to harvest the result. This is such a pain that, if you want results from the call to the UI thread, I suggest that the worker thread use Control.Invoke instead.

Simplified Multithreading

To establish safe, asynchronous, long-running operations with progress reports, you first need to create a delegate for your long-running operation and execute it asynchronously with a call to BeginInvoke, making sure to always call EndInvoke. Second, you use Control.BeginInvoke to update the UI thread from the worker thread with progress visuals. Unfortunately, this technique takes a nontrivial amount of effort.

Fortunately, you can simplify things by using the BackgroundWorker component from the System.ComponentModel namespace. BackgroundWorker builds on the mechanisms I've shown you but gathers them into a component that you can drop onto a form and configure declaratively, as shown in Figure 18.8.

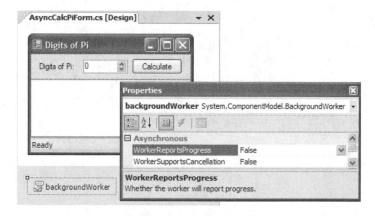

Figure 18.8   The BackgroundWorker Component

---

[4] Chris Brumme discusses both the need for a call to a delegate's EndInvoke and the optionality of a call to Control.EndInvoke at http://blogs.msdn.com/cbrumme/archive/2003/05/06/51385.aspx (http://tinysells.com/43).

This humble component provides the necessary thread communication infrastructure for you, leaving you to configure it and incorporate only the code you need to solve the functional problem at hand.

Initiating a Worker Thread

After you have placed a BackgroundWorker component on your form, you initiate the worker thread by calling BackgroundWorker's RunWorkerAsync method from the Calculate button's Click event handler:

```
// AsyncCalcPiForm.cs
partial class AsyncCalcPiForm : Form {
  ...
  void calcButton_Click(object sender, EventArgs e) {
    ...

    // Initiate asynchronous pi calculation on worker thread
    this.backgroundWorker.RunWorkerAsync(
      (int)this.decimalPlacesNumericUpDown.Value);
  }
}
```

RunWorkerAsync instructs BackgroundWorker to create the desired worker thread and begin executing on it. RunWorkerAsync accepts a single object argument, which is dutifully passed to the worker thread and should be used to pass any information that your worker thread code might need. Because the argument is an object, you can pass either a single value, such as the digit's integer value, or a custom type that packages several pieces of information into on object.

Executing from the Worker Thread

BackgroundWorker provides the DoWork event that you handle to process your long-running operation on a worker thread from the thread pool. DoWork is Background-Worker's default event, and this means that you double-click BackgroundWorker to have the Windows Forms Designer automatically create a handler and register it:

```
// AsyncCalcPiForm.Designer.cs
partial class AsyncCalcPiForm {
  ...
  System.ComponentModel.BackgroundWorker backgroundWorker;
  ...
  void InitializeComponent() {
    ...
    this.backgroundWorker =
```

```
      new System.ComponentModel.BackgroundWorker();
    ...
    // backgroundWorker
    this.backgroundWorker.DoWork += this.backgroundWorker_DoWork;
    ...
  }
}

// AsyncCalcPiForm.cs
partial class AsyncCalcPiForm : Form {
  ...
  // Executed on a worker thread from the thread pool
  void backgroundWorker_DoWork(object sender, DoWorkEventArgs e) {
    ...
  }
}
```

Don't forget that any code that you place within the DoWork event handler is executing from the worker thread and, therefore, must not manipulate controls created on the UI thread. DoWork provides DoWorkEventArgs (from the System.ComponentModel namespace), which, among other things, is the receptacle for data passed from the UI thread to the worker thread. To pull the object passed to RunWorkerAsync, you use the DoWorkEventArgs object's Argument property:

```
// AsyncCalcPiForm.cs
partial class AsyncCalcPiForm : Form {
  ...
  void calcButton_Click(object sender, EventArgs e) {
    ...
    // Begin calculating pi asynchronously
    this.backgroundWorker.RunWorkerAsync(
      (int)this.decimalPlacesNumericUpDown.Value);
  }

  void backgroundWorker_DoWork(object sender, DoWorkEventArgs e) {
    CalcPi((int)e.Argument);
  }
}
```

When we have acquired the desired number of digits, the rest of the pi calculation can proceed on a worker thread from the pool until completion, at which time Background-Worker returns from DoWork and the worker thread is returned to the pool.

Reporting Progress

Our use of BackgroundWorker so far shows how we can rid ourselves of the custom delegate we introduced earlier to start our worker thread but still use a thread from the thread pool.

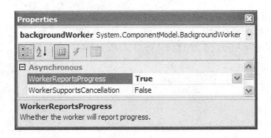

Similarly, BackgroundWorker also provides a simplified communication protocol for reporting progress from the worker thread back to the UI thread. However, the communication infrastructure for reporting progress isn't enabled by default, so you must enable it by setting the BackgroundWorker object's WorkerReportsProgress property to true. For this, you can use the Properties window, as illustrated in Figure 18.9.

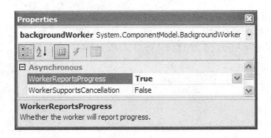

Figure 18.9   Enabling BackgroundWorker to Report Progress

Failure to set WorkerReportsProgress to true causes an InvalidOperationException if progress is reported from the worker thread. If the exception is not handled, any exception on the worker thread started by BackgroundWorker causes the application to abruptly hang for no apparent reason (you'll see how to handle worker thread exceptions shortly).

To report progress from the worker thread, you call the BackgroundWorker object's ReportProgress method in one of two ways. First, you can simply pass an integer value that represents the background operation's percentage of completion:

```
// Report progress percentage
this.backgroundWorker.ReportProgress(progressPercentage);
```

Alternatively, you can use a ReportProgress overload to pass an additional object containing any kind of progress information that needs to be relayed to the UI thread. With regard to calculating pi, we use this technique to bundle the arguments to call Show-Progress:

```
class AsyncCalcPiForm : Form {
  ...
  class CalcPiUserState {
    public readonly string Pi;
    public readonly int TotalDigits;
    public readonly int DigitsSoFar;

    public CalcPiUserState(
      string pi, int totalDigits, int digitsSoFar) {

      this.Pi = pi;
```

```
      this.TotalDigits = totalDigits;
      this.DigitsSoFar = digitsSoFar;
    }
  }

void CalcPi(int digits) {
  StringBuilder pi = new StringBuilder("3", digits + 2);

  // Report initial progress
  this.backgroundWorker.ReportProgress(0,
    new CalcPiUserState(pi.ToString(), digits, 0));

  if( digits > 0 ) {
    pi.Append(".");

    for( int i = 0; i < digits; i += 9 ) {
      ...

      // Report continuing progress
      this.backgroundWorker.ReportProgress(0,
        new CalcPiUserState(pi.ToString(), digits, i + digitCount));
    }
  }
}
```

In our example, we've updated CalcPi to use the BackgroundWorker component's
ReportProgress method (instead of Control.BeginInvoke) to transition from the worker
thread to the UI thread. ShowProgress is perfectly capable of calculating the progress percentage on its own, so we eschew this argument to ReportProgress in favor of an instance
of a new custom type called CalcPiUserState. BackgroundWorker packages the arguments
passed to ReportProgress and passes them back to the UI thread. You can access them and
respond accordingly by handling BackgroundWorker's ProgressChanged event:

```
// AsyncCalcPiForm.Designer.cs
partial class AsyncCalcPiForm {
  ...
  System.ComponentModel.BackgroundWorker backgroundWorker;
  ...
  void InitializeComponent() {
    ...
    this.backgroundWorker =
      new System.ComponentModel.BackgroundWorker();
    ...
    // backgroundWorker
    this.backgroundWorker.ProgressChanged +=
      backgroundWorker_ProgressChanged;
    ...
```

```
  }
}

// AsyncCalcPiForm.cs
partial class AsyncCalcPiForm : Form {
  ...
  void ShowProgress(string pi, int totalDigits, int digitsSoFar) {
    ...
  }

  void backgroundWorker_ProgressChanged(
    object sender, ProgressChangedEventArgs e) {

    // Show progress
    CalcPiUserState progress = (CalcPiUserState)e.UserState;
    ShowProgress(
      progress.Pi, progress.TotalDigits, progress.DigitsSoFar);
  }
}
```

The results of bringing a BackgroundWorker into things are shown in Figure 18.10.

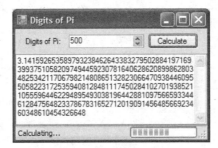

**Figure 18.10 Safely Displaying
Progress Information on the UI Thread**

At this point, we've replaced two things—our use of a custom delegate to start a worker thread and our use of a custom delegate to communicate progress to the UI thread—with two event handlers provided by the BackgroundWorker component, simplifying our code to the following:

```
partial class AsyncCalcPiForm : Form {
  public AsyncCalcPiForm() {
    InitializeComponent();
  }

  void ShowProgress(string pi, int totalDigits, int digitsSoFar) {
```

```csharp
    // Make sure we're on the UI thread
    Debug.Assert(this.InvokeRequired == false);
    if(this.InvokeRequired == true ) throw new Exception("Doh!");

    // Display progress in UI
    this.resultsTextBox.Text = pi;
    this.calcToolStripProgressBar.Maximum = totalDigits;
    this.calcToolStripProgressBar.Value = digitsSoFar;

    if( digitsSoFar == totalDigits ) {
      // Reset progress UI
      this.calcToolStripStatusLabel.Text = "Ready";
      this.calcToolStripProgressBar.Visible = false;
    }
  }

class CalcPiUserState {
  public readonly string Pi;
  public readonly int TotalDigits;
  public readonly int DigitsSoFar;

  public CalcPiUserState(
    string pi, int totalDigits, int digitsSoFar) {

    this.Pi = pi;
    this.TotalDigits = totalDigits;
    this.DigitsSoFar = digitsSoFar;
  }
}

void CalcPi(int digits) {
  StringBuilder pi = new StringBuilder("3", digits + 2);

  // Report initial progress
  this.backgroundWorker.ReportProgress(0,
    new CalcPiUserState(pi.ToString(), digits, 0));

  if( digits > 0 ) {
    pi.Append(".");

    for( int i = 0; i < digits; i += 9 ) {
      int nineDigits = NineDigitsOfPi.StartingAt(i + 1);
      int digitCount = Math.Min(digits - i, 9);
      string ds = string.Format("{0:D9}", nineDigits);
      pi.Append(ds.Substring(0, digitCount));

      // Report continuing progress
      this.backgroundWorker.ReportProgress(0,
```

```
            new CalcPiUserState(pi.ToString(), digits, i + digitCount));
      }
    }
  }

  void calcButton_Click(object sender, EventArgs e) {
    // Set calculating UI
    this.calcToolStripProgressBar.Visible = true;
    this.calcToolStripStatusLabel.Text = "Calculating...";

    // Begin calculating pi asynchronously
    this.backgroundWorker.RunWorkerAsync(
      (int)this.decimalPlacesNumericUpDown.Value);
  }

  void backgroundWorker_DoWork(object sender, DoWorkEventArgs e) {
    CalcPi((int)e.Argument);
  }

  void backgroundWorker_ProgressChanged(
    object sender, ProgressChangedEventArgs e) {

    // Show progress
    CalcPiUserState progress = (CalcPiUserState)e.UserState;
    ShowProgress(
      progress.Pi, progress.TotalDigits, progress.DigitsSoFar);
  }
}
```

When the number of digits calculated equals the requested number of digits to be calculated in ShowProgress, we intuit that our long-running operation is complete and reset the UI appropriately. However, we'd like to be able to know when DoWork is completed more generally, as we did in the asynchronous delegate case earlier. Further, we'd like the notification of completion to occur on the UI thread to avoid the need to transition manually, as we had to do before.

Completion

When a BackgroundWorker-managed worker thread completes, BackgroundWorker fires the RunWorkerCompleted event. This allows us to refactor our ShowProgress method and let RunWorkerCompleted reset the status strip progress bar state:

```
void ShowProgress(string pi, int totalDigits, int digitsSoFar) {
  // Make sure we're on the UI thread
  Debug.Assert(this.InvokeRequired == false);
  if(this.InvokeRequired == true ) throw new Exception("Doh!");
```

```
    // Display progress in UI
    this.resultsTextBox.Text = pi;
    this.calcToolStripProgressBar.Maximum = totalDigits;
    this.calcToolStripProgressBar.Value = digitsSoFar;

    // No need to check for digitsSoFar == totalDigits
  }

void backgroundWorker_RunWorkerCompleted(
  object sender, RunWorkerCompletedEventArgs e) {

  // Reset progress UI
  this.calcToolStripStatusLabel.Text = "Ready";
  this.calcToolStripProgressBar.Visible = false;
}
```

This is the simplest possible completion logic you'll find. A more complex scenario might require you to pass some information from the DoWork event at the end of background operation processing. For example, the pi calculator might want to know the calculation's elapsed time. To do this requires calculating it from the DoWork method and returning it to the RunWorkerCompleted event handler. DoWork's DoWorkEventArgs exposes a Result property that you can set to return a value from the worker thread when complete:

```
void backgroundWorker_DoWork(object sender, DoWorkEventArgs e) {
  // Track start time
  DateTime start = DateTime.Now;

  CalcPi((int)e.Argument);

  // Return elapsed time
  DateTime end = DateTime.Now;
  TimeSpan elapsed = end - start;
  e.Result = elapsed;
}
```

The returned value can be accessed from the suitably named Result property exposed by the RunWorkerCompletedEventArgs object passed to RunWorkerCompleted:

```
void backgroundWorker_RunWorkerCompleted(
  object sender, RunWorkerCompletedEventArgs e) {
  ...

  // Show elapsed time
  TimeSpan elapsed = (TimeSpan)e.Result;
  MessageBox.Show("Elapsed: " + elapsed.ToString());
}
```

Figure 18.11 shows the result.

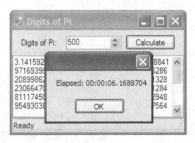

Figure 18.11   Result of Passing a Result Value from DoWork to RunWorkerCompleted

All's well that ends well. Well, almost. Not every background operation ends nicely. For example, it is possible that DoWork will throw an exception and end prematurely. In these cases, you won't notice unless you handle the RunWorkerCompleted event and inspect the Result property of RunWorkerCompletedEventArgs. If you don't wrap the access to the Result property in a try-catch handler, your users will see something like Figure 18.12 in the event of an exception on the worker thread.

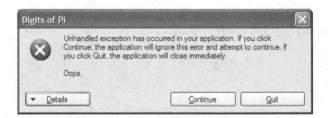

Figure 18.12   Exception Raised from the RunWorker-Completed Event Handler

One good reason to handle the RunWorkerCompleted event is to check for and respond appropriately to exceptions raised on the worker thread. In fact, if you'd like to catch the exception on the UI thread thrown from the worker thread, you should wrap your access to the Result property of the RunWorkerCompletedEventArgs in a try-catch block. If you prefer to avoid the exception altogether or if you just don't need anything from the Result property, RunWorkerEventArgs provides an Error property:

```
void backgroundWorker_RunWorkerCompleted(
    object sender, RunWorkerCompletedEventArgs e) {
    // Was there an error?
```

```
if( e.Error != null ) {
  this.resultsTextBox.Text = e.Error.Message;
  return;
}
...
}
```

Figure 18.13 illustrates a more graceful result.

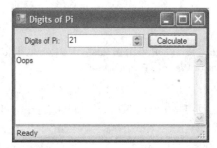

Figure 18.13   Result of Nicely Handling an Exception in DoWork

Cancellation

In the case of an exception on the worker thread, our pi calculation will be prematurely aborted. However, what if the user wants to cancel it? Maybe the user only wants 100,000 digits after mistakenly asking for 100,001. Figure 18.14 shows an updated CalcPi UI that allows cancellation.

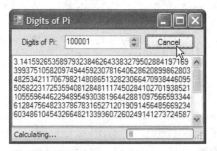

Figure 18.14   Letting the User Cancel a Long-Running Operation

Implementing cancellation for a long-running operation is a multistep process. First, we provide a UI so that users can cancel the operation. In this case, the Calculate button changes to a Cancel button after the calculation begins. Another popular choice is to open a separate progress dialog to display current progress details, typically via a progress bar that shows the percentage of completed work, and a Cancel button.

Second, if the user decides to cancel, the UI should be disabled for the short amount of time that elapses between the time that the UI thread knows the worker thread should stop and the time that the worker thread itself knows and has a chance to stop. If this period of time is ignored, it's possible that the user could start another operation before the first worker thread stops sending progress, making it the job of the UI thread to figure out whether it's getting progress from the new worker thread or the old worker thread that's supposed to be shutting down.

Luckily, BackgroundWorker itself provides all the information we need to implement our cancellation UI:

```
void calcButton_Click(object sender, EventArgs e) {
  // Don't process if cancel request pending
  // (Should not be called, because we disabled the button...)
  if( this.backgroundWorker.CancellationPending ) return;

  // If worker thread currently executing, cancel it
  if( this.backgroundWorker.IsBusy ) {
    this.calcButton.Enabled = false;
    this.backgroundWorker.CancelAsync();
    return;
  }

  // Set calculating UI
  this.calcButton.Text = "Cancel";
  this.calcToolStripProgressBar.Visible = true;
  this.calcToolStripStatusLabel.Text = "Calculating...";

  // Begin calculating pi asynchronously
  this.backgroundWorker.RunWorkerAsync(
    (int)this.decimalPlacesNumericUpDown.Value);
}
```

Here, we use the CancellationPending property of BackgroundWorker to find out whether we've already canceled the pi calculation, in which case we're stuck until the worker thread notices (more on that later).

If there's no cancellation pending, we check the IsBusy property to determine whether the BackgroundWorker is currently executing. If so, it means that the user has pressed the Cancel button. In that case, we disable the Cancel button to let the user know we're working on it, and we invoke CancelAsync to instruct BackgroundWorker to cancel executing.

Finally, if cancellation isn't pending and if BackgroundWorker isn't busy, it means that the user pressed the Calculate button, so we change the text to Cancel and start the calculation process.

When the calculation has started, CancelAsync is actually only a request, so the worker thread needs to watch for it by checking the BackgroundWorker component's CancellationPending property:

```
void CalcPi(int digits) {
  StringBuilder pi = new StringBuilder("3", digits + 2);

  // Report initial progress
  this.backgroundWorker.ReportProgress(0,
    new CalcPiUserState(pi.ToString(), digits, 0));

  if( digits > 0 ) {
    pi.Append(".");

    for( int i = 0; i < digits; i += 9 ) {
      int nineDigits = NineDigitsOfPi.StartingAt(i + 1);
      int digitCount = Math.Min(digits - i, 9);
      string ds = string.Format("{0:D9}", nineDigits);
      pi.Append(ds.Substring(0, digitCount));

      // Report continuing progress
      this.backgroundWorker.ReportProgress(0,
        new CalcPiUserState(pi.ToString(), digits, i + digitCount));

      // Check for cancellation
      if( this.backgroundWorker.CancellationPending ) return;
    }
  }
}
```

Although you can simply return if CancellationPending is true, you should also set DoWorkEventArg's Cancel property to true; in this way, you can detect whether the long-running operation was canceled from the RunWorkerComplete event handler by inspecting the Cancelled property exposed by RunWorkerCompletedEventArgs:

```
void backgroundWorker_DoWork(object sender, DoWorkEventArgs e) {
  ...
  CalcPi((int)e.Argument);

  // Indicate cancellation
  if( this.backgroundWorker.CancellationPending ) {
    e.Cancel = true;
  }
  ...
}
```

```
void backgroundWorker_RunWorkerCompleted(
  object sender, RunWorkerCompletedEventArgs e) {
  ...
  // Was the worker thread canceled?
  if( e.Cancelled ) {
    this.resultsTextBox.Text = "Canceled";
    return;
  }
  ...
}
```

BackgroundWorker Work Flow

DoWork, ProgressChanged, and RunWorkerCompleted comprise the three events you can handle for BackgroundWorker, with at least DoWork being fired when RunWorkerAsync is invoked from the UI thread. Figure 18.15 illustrates the overall work flow, including optional cancellation.

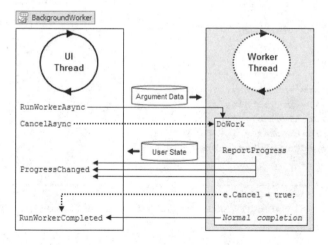

Figure 18.15   BackgroundWorker Work Flow

Shared Data

Thus far, we've been passing around data copies or data ownership. For example, consider the case where we pass the desired number of digits of pi into the worker thread. Because we pass an integer, the worker thread receives its own copy of that data. On the other hand, when we pass an instance of the CalcPiUserState object from the worker thread to the UI thread, we're passing *ownership* of that data; in other words, the worker thread creates the object but no longer touches it after passing it to the UI thread:

```
void CalcPi(int digits) {
  ...
  // Pass ownership of the CalcPiUserState from the worker to the UI
  this.backgroundWorker.ReportProgress(0,
    new CalcPiUserState(pi.ToString(), digits, i + digitCount));
  ...
}
```

By passing copies or ownership of data, we avoid a situation where multiple threads share simultaneous access to data. For example, suppose we decide that we prefer shared access to an object that holds state associated with the pi calculation:

```
class SharedCalcPiUserState {
  public string Pi;
  public int TotalDigits;
  public int DigitsSoFar;
}

SharedCalcPiUserState state = new SharedCalcPiUserState();

void CalcPi(int digits) {
  ...
  // Update state and notify UI
  this.state.Pi = pi.ToString();
  this.state.TotalDigits = digits;
  this.state.DigitsSoFar = i + digitCount;
  this.backgroundWorker.ReportProgress(0);
  ...
}
```

Here, the UI thread is free to access the shared state data while the worker thread continues its calculation:

```
void backgroundWorker_ProgressChanged(
    object sender, ProgressChangedEventArgs e) {

  // Show progress
  ShowProgress(
    this.state.Pi, this.state.TotalDigits, this.state.DigitsSoFar);
}
```

I hope that something inside you cringes when you look at this code.

If you're going to do multithreaded programming, you must watch out for situations where two threads have simultaneous access to the same data. Shared access to data between threads makes it very easy to get into *race conditions,* in which one thread is racing to read data that is only partially up-to-date before another thread has finished updating it. In this example, it's completely possible to be forming a call stack to the ShowProgress method on the UI thread while the worker thread continues to update the values in the background, causing you to pass values from the SharedCalcPiUserState class from as many as three different iterations of the worker thread.

For proper concurrent access to shared data, you must *synchronize* access to the data—that is, make sure that one thread waits patiently while another thread works on the data. To synchronize access to shared data, C# provides the *lock* block:

```
SharedCalcPiUserState state = new SharedCalcPiUserState();
object stateLock = new object();

void CalcPi(int digits) {
  ...
  // Synchronize access to shared data
  // on the worker thread
  lock( stateLock ) {
    this.state.Pi = pi.ToString();
    this.state.TotalDigits = digits;
    this.state.DigitsSoFar = i + digitCount;
    this.backgroundWorker.ReportProgress(0);
  }
  ...
}

void backgroundWorker_ProgressChanged(
  object sender, ProgressChangedEventArgs e) {

  // Synchronize access to shared data
  // on the UI thread
  lock( stateLock ) {
    ShowProgress(
      this.state.Pi, this.state.TotalDigits, this.state.DigitsSoFar);
  }
}
```

Now that your data has been properly protected against race conditions, you must watch out for another problem known as a deadlock. A *deadlock* occurs when each of two threads has locked a resource and both subsequently wait for the resource held by the other thread, causing each thread to stop dead, waiting forever. When two threads are deadlocked, each of them waits for the other to complete its work before continuing, thereby ensuring that neither actually progresses.

If all this talk of race conditions and deadlocks has caused you concern, that's good. Can you look at the CalcPi method and the ProgressChanged event handler and know for sure that we haven't introduced a deadlock, or even that we have solved our race condition properly?

Multithreaded programming with shared data is hard. By passing copies or ownership of data around, we ensure that no two threads need to share access to any one piece of data. If you don't have shared data, there's no need to synchronize access to it. But if you find that you need access to shared data—maybe because the overhead of copying the data is too great a burden in space or time—then you need to read up on multithreading and shared data synchronization, topics that are beyond the scope of this book.

Luckily, the vast majority of multithreading scenarios, especially as related to UI multithreading, seem to work best with the simple passing of copies or ownership of data, an approach we've employed in our CalcPi example.

Asynchronous Web Services

In addition to causing work to happen on another thread, you'll also want to cause work to happen on other machines, which is an ideal use of web services. Calling a web service is similar to passing a message between threads, except that web services messages travel between machines using standard protocols such as HTTP and XML.

Imagine a .NET web service that calculates digits of pi using a version of CalcPi that's been modified to handle web service disconnection mid-calculation:

```
// CalcPiService.cs
class CalcPiService : System.Web.Services.WebService {
  [WebMethod]
  public string CalcPi(int digits) {
    StringBuilder pi = new StringBuilder("3", digits + 2);

    if( digits > 0 ) {
      pi.Append(".");

      for( int i = 0; i < digits; i += 9 ) {
        // Calculate next i decimal places
        ...

        // End execution if client disconnects from web service
        if( !Context.Response.IsClientConnected )
          break;
      }
    }
    return pi.ToString();
  }
}
```

Now imagine a version of the CalcPi program that uses the web service instead of our slow client-side algorithm to calculate pi on giant machines with huge processors (or even better, databases with more digits of pi cached than anyone could ever want or need). The underlying protocol of web services is HTTP- and XML-based, and we could readily form a web service request to ask for the digits of pi we're after. Still, it's simpler to let VS05 generate a class to make the web services calls for you.

You do this in the Project menu using the Add Web Reference item. The Add Web Reference dialog, shown in Figure 18.16, allows you to enter the URL of the WSDL (Web Services Description Language) that describes the web service you'd like to call.

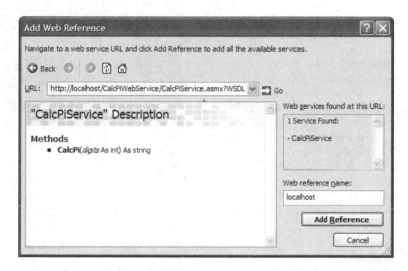

Figure 18.16　Adding a Web Reference to the CalcPiWebService WSDL

For example, after installing the web service sample you'll find at our web site, you can access the WSDL via the following URL:

```
http://localhost/CalcPiWebService/CalcPiService.asmx?WSDL
```

Accepting the WSDL in the Add Web Reference dialog generates a *client-side web services proxy class*, a helper class that turns your method calls into web services messages.[5] The generated proxy code for the CalcPi web service looks like this:

```
using System.ComponentModel;
using System.Web.Services;

namespace WebServiceCalcPiSample.CalcPiWebService {
   [WebServiceBinding(
```

[5] Internally, the generated proxy class stores the web service's URL as an application setting of the special type "(Web Service)". The naming convention conforms to the following: *namespace_webReferenceName_webServiceName*.

```
        Name = "CalcPiServiceSoap", Namespace = "http://tempuri.org/")]

    class CalcPiService : SoapHttpClientProtocol {

      // Properties
      public string Url { get; set; }
      public bool UseDefaultCredentials { get; set; }

      // Methods
      public CalcPiService();
        [SoapDocumentMethod(
        "http://tempuri.org/CalcPi",
        RequestNamespace="http://tempuri.org/",
        ResponseNamespace="http://tempuri.org/",
        Use=System.Web.Services.Description.SoapBindingUse.Literal,
        ParameterStyle=Protocols.SoapParameterStyle.Wrapped)]
      public string CalcPi(int digits);
      public void CalcPiAsync(int digits);
      public void CalcPiAsync(int digits, object userState);
      public void CancelAsync(object userState);

      // Events
      public event CalcPiCompletedEventHandler CalcPiCompleted;
    }

    // AsyncCompletedEventArgs is new in .NET 2.0
    class CalcPiCompletedEventArgs : AsyncCompletedEventArgs {
      // Properties
      public string Result { get; }
    }

    delegate void CalcPiCompletedEventHandler(
      object sender,
      CalcPiCompletedEventArgs e);
  }
```

Because web services make calls across machine (and often network) boundaries, you should assume they'll take a long time, and, if called synchronously, they'll block the UI thread. You can use the standard techniques discussed in this chapter to call web service methods asynchronously. But as you can tell in the generated proxy code, there's built-in support for asynchronous operations via the *MethodName*Async and CancelAsync methods, one for each method on the web service.

The first step in retrofitting the sample application to use the web service is to call the web service proxy's CalcPiAsync method:

```
// AsyncCalcPiForm.cs
partial class AsyncCalcPiForm : Form {

  bool isBusy = false;
  bool cancellationPending = false;
  ...
  void calcButton_Click(object sender, EventArgs e) {

    // Don't process if cancel request pending
    if( this.cancellationPending ) return;

    // Is web service currently executing?
    if( this.isBusy ) {
      // Cancel asynchronous pi calculations
      this.service.CancelAsync(null);
      this.cancellationPending = true;
    }
    else {
      // Start calculating pi asynchronously
      this.calcButton.Text = "Cancel";
      this.resultsTextBox.Text = "";
      this.isBusy = true;
      this.service.CalcPiAsync(
        (int)this.decimalPlacesNumericUpDown.Value);
    }
  }
  ...
}
```

Notice that this code looks similar to the CalcPi sample, which used BackgroundWorker. This is because the generated proxy is built on the same .NET-provided threading infrastructure that BackgroundWorker is. Unfortunately, it's not as advanced; you don't have properties that tell you whether the worker thread is busy, or whether a cancellation is pending. Because of the dynamic nature of the generated proxy class and web services in general, tackling this problem would be tricky. However, you can easily use your own state member variables to do so, as this sample does. To cancel a web method call, you simply call the CancelAsync method.

If you are interested in the web method's response, the next step is to register with an event implemented by the generated proxy that uses the *MethodName*Completed naming convention:

```
// AsyncCalcPiForm.cs
partial class AsyncCalcPiForm : Form {
  ...
  public AsyncCalcPiForm() {
```

```
      InitializeComponent();
      this.service.CalcPiCompleted += service_CalcPiCompleted;
    }

    void calcButton_Click(object sender, EventArgs e) {...}
    ...
  }
```

The handler you register also looks similar to the BackgroundWorker samples:

```
// AsyncCalcPiForm.cs
partial class AsyncCalcPiForm : Form {
  ...
  void service_CalcPiCompleted(
    object sender,
    CalcPiCompletedEventArgs e) {

    Debug.Assert(this.InvokeRequired == false);
    if( this.InvokeRequired == true ) throw new Exception("Doh!");

    // Reset UI state
    this.calcButton.Text = "Calculate";

    // We're not busy anymore
    this.isBusy = false;

    // Was there an error?
    if( e.Error != null ) {
      this.resultsTextBox.Text = e.Error.Message;
      return;
    }

    // Was the worker thread canceled?
    if( e.Cancelled ) {
      this.resultsTextBox.Text = "Canceled";
      // Allow calculations to start
      this.cancellationPending = false;
    }
  }
  ...
}
```

This code sets the state member variables—isBusy and cancellationPending—depending on how the web method call ended. The code also checks for exceptions, something that is particularly important given the less resilient nature of using the web. Figure 18.17 shows what happens when a connection to the web service is lost mid-call.

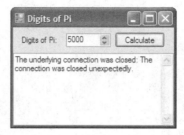

Figure 18.17   The Result of a Lost Connection Mid-Call

The code to operate web services turns out to be relatively lightweight, thanks to the generated proxy class added to your project when you add a web service reference.

Web Service Components

You can enjoy a slightly more Designer-driven experience by using the component that VS05 generates for each referenced web service, as shown in Figure 18.18.

Figure 18.18   A Web Service Component

As a component, a web service can be dragged and dropped right onto your form. The main benefit is that you gain full Properties window-driven configuration of the service, as shown in Figure 18.19.

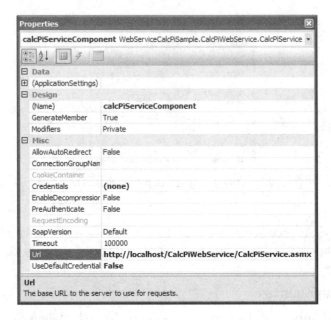

Figure 18.19   Configuring a Web Service Component

Additionally, each *MethodName*Completed event exposed by a web service component is available from the Properties window, as shown in Figure 18.20, thus allowing you to leverage the Windows Forms Designer's ability to automatically hook up those events for you.

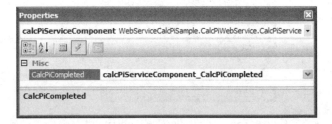

Figure 18.20   Hooking the *MethodName*Completed Events Automatically

Updating our asynchronous web service code to use the component directly produces the following result.

```csharp
// AsyncCalcPiForm.cs
partial class AsyncCalcPiForm : Form {

  bool isBusy = false;
  bool cancellationPending = false;

  public AsyncCalcPiForm() {
    InitializeComponent();
  }

  void calcButton_Click(object sender, EventArgs e) {

    // Don't process if cancel request pending
    if( this.cancellationPending ) return;

    // Is web service currently executing?
    if( isBusy ) {
      // Cancel asynchronous pi calculations
      this.calcPiServiceComponent.CancelAsync(null);
      this.cancellationPending = true;
    }
    else {
      // Start calculating pi asynchronously
      this.calcButton.Text = "Cancel";
      this.resultsTextBox.Text = "";
      this.isBusy = true;
      this.calcPiServiceComponent.CalcPiAsync(
        (int)this.decimalPlacesNumericUpDown.Value);
    }
  }

  void calcPiServiceComponent_CalcPiCompleted(
    object sender,
    CalcPiCompletedEventArgs e) {

    Debug.Assert(this.InvokeRequired == false);
    if( this.InvokeRequired == true ) throw new Exception("Doh!");

    // Reset UI state
    this.calcButton.Text = "Calculate";

    // We're not busy anymore
    this.isBusy = false;
```

```
    // Was there an error?
    if( e.Error != null ) {
      this.resultsTextBox.Text = e.Error.Message;
      return;
    }

    // Was the worker thread canceled?
    if( e.Cancelled ) {
      this.resultsTextBox.Text = "Canceled";
      // Allow calculations to start
      this.cancellationPending = false;
    }

    // Display result
    this.resultsTextBox.Text = e.Result;
  }
}
```

The code isn't dramatically smaller, although producing it is slightly faster. It also leaves open the possibility of performing further configurations via the Properties window, including binding web service properties to application and user settings.

Where Are We?

The pi calculator example demonstrates how to perform long-running operations while displaying a progress dialog and keeping the UI responsive to user interaction. You use the BackgroundWorker component to spawn worker threads and safely pass data between UI and worker threads. Although you could use shared data, it's better to use Background-Worker's implicit message-passing scheme between threads to avoid the complications of synchronization. A subset of the internals used by BackgroundWorker is also used to generate web services proxy classes, resulting in a familiar coding model for long-running web service calls. VS05 also turns web service references into components for easier design-time configuration and coding.

.NET has extensive threading support, so you can certainly use techniques other than message passing to achieve the same ends. Whatever method you choose, it's important to remember that a worker thread can neither call methods nor set properties on any control created on the UI thread; only the UI thread can do that. Of all the options, though, Back-groundWorker provides the lowest bar of entry for safely creating worker threads.

■ 19 ■
ClickOnce Deployment

S O FAR, THIS BOOK HAS FOCUSED ON THE development of Windows Forms applications. At some point, though, a Windows Forms application needs to be deployed. The traditional means for doing so is via a setup application or, more recently, a Microsoft Installer (MSI) file. Both vehicles are fine for packaging application installations, although the trick is to get them executed on the desired client machines and then keep them up-to-date.

Web applications, on the other hand, offer a more primitive application and control implementation framework, but a much simpler deployment model. All that's needed to keep a web client user up-to-date is to keep the files on the web server up-to-date. Additionally, users don't have to be administrators of a particular client machine to use web applications, in contrast to many Windows-based installations.

In Windows Forms 1.*x*, a web-style deployment model was incorporated into Windows Forms as a technology known as HREF-Exe or No-Touch Deployment, which allowed Windows Forms applications to be hosted on and deployed from a web site. This simple technology was later augmented by Microsoft with the richer Application Updater Block deployment framework.[1]

With Windows Forms 2.0, these technologies have evolved into *ClickOnce deployment* (a.k.a. ClickOnce), a comprehensive and secure deployment framework that's tightly integrated with Windows Forms 2.0 and VS05. ClickOnce marries the power of Windows Forms development with the simplicity of the web deployment model.[2]

new

---

[1] http://msdn.microsoft.com/library/default.asp?url=/library/en-us/dnpag2/html/updaterv2.asp (http://tinysells.com/43).

[2] ClickOnce really works only when Internet Explorer is the default browser, so users with other browsers will likely have problems.

A Day in the Life of ClickOnce Deployment

As a test of the ClickOnce deployment model for Windows Forms applications, I built the simple game shown in Figure 19.1.[3]

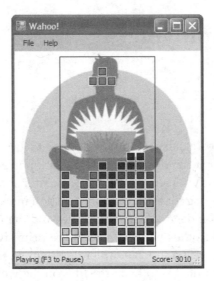

Figure 19.1　The Game of Wahoo!
(See Plate 20)

Wahoo is a standard Windows Forms application that allows users to start, pause, and resume games, with game play controlled from the keyboard. Additionally, Wahoo uses a web service to track the top 10 scores. When Wahoo can't use the web service, the top 10 scores for the current player are saved to the local file system.

Wahoo functionality is split across two assemblies: One assembly (WahooControl-Library.dll) encapsulates game play within a control and is hosted in the other assembly (Wahoo.exe), which provides the game UI.

Because Wahoo is fun for everyone, making it available over the Internet is ideal. The easiest way is to use ClickOnce, a technology that manages the delivery of a Windows Forms application from a development (or build) machine to a user's client machine over the Internet. As shown in Figure 19.2, delivery can be broadly categorized into two stages: publishing and launching.

---

[3] Any similarity to any other very popular game that you may already be familiar with is strictly intentional.

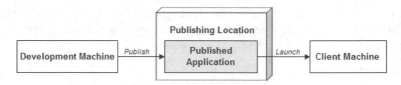

Figure 19.2 Application Delivery with ClickOnce Involving Publishing and Launching

Publishing is a developer-driven process that creates an application installation and makes it available to users from a suitably accessible *publish location*, the place to which developers copy the application files. *Launching* is a user-driven process that relies on ClickOnce to download an application from the publish location before installing and executing it.

Publishing an Application

To publish an application from VS05 for ClickOnce deployment, you first identify all the files needed to ensure that the application will execute on a client machine, before bundling the files into a logical installation package that is promoted to a publish location. At minimum, developers need to elect a publish location.

Designating the Publish Location

The easiest way to designate a publish location is to exploit the integration between Click-Once and VS05 and use the Publish Wizard. You open it by right-clicking your project in Solution Explorer and selecting Publish. On the first page of the Publish Wizard, shown in Figure 19.3, you specify a publish location.

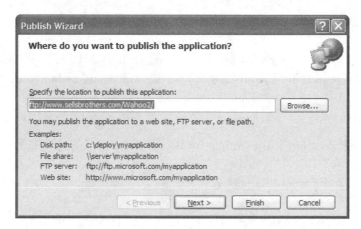

Figure 19.3 ClickOnce Publish Wizard: Choosing a Publish Location

As you can see, VS05 supports publishing an application to four types of locations: local disk paths, file shares, FTP sites, and web sites. For Wahoo, which is hosted by an Internet service provider (ISP), we can publish only to an FTP server:

```
ftp://www.sellsbrothers.com/Wahoo2
```

However, we want Wahoo users to be able to launch the application from a web site, so we need to pick a web location to launch from.

Designating the Launch Location

Users get an application from a *launch location*, which, in most cases, is the same as the publish location. However, ClickOnce doesn't support launching from FTP servers. If you specify an FTP site as the publish location, the Publish Wizard asks for an alternative launch location, as shown in Figure 19.4.[4]

Figure 19.4   ClickOnce Publish Wizard: Choosing a Launch Location

You can see that the launch location options are web sites, Universal Naming Convention (UNC) paths or file shares, and CDs or DVDs. Wahoo will be launched from the Sellsbrothers web site:

```
http:www.sellsbrothers.com/Wahoo2
```

With a publish location and a launch location, click Finish to publish the application.

[4] You can also manually configure publish and install locations via Project Property Pages | Publish.

Preparing an Installation Package for Publishing

Before an application is published, VS05 creates an installation package that comprises all the files needed to execute an application. For web site publish locations, the package is structured as shown in Figure 19.5.

Figure 19.5   Wahoo Installation Package Published to a Web Site

As you can see, VS05 has copied the Wahoo game assembly (Wahoo.exe), the dependent Wahoo game control assembly (WahooControlLibrary.dll), and the application settings file (Wahoo.exe.config) to a folder under the Wahoo web site. This folder is automatically created by VS05. Its name is a concatenation of the application's assembly name and publish version and is formatted this way:[5]

```
AssemblyName_MajorVersion_MinorVersion_BuildNumber_RevisionNumber
```

Notice that the names of the assembly files and the application settings file have been appended with ".deploy." VS05 does this by default for files published to web servers as a security measure: It is common for web server configurations to preclude them from hosting application files (.exes and .dlls).[6]

We know that the assembly and settings files comprise the files required to run this application, but our users don't know that and certainly should not be made to download them one at a time. Instead, ClickOnce takes on the burden in typical .NET fashion by using an *application manifest* to specify which files are required for an application to execute on a

---

[5] ClickOnce publish version numbers and versioning in general are discussed later in this chapter.

[6] Use of the .deploy extension is determined by the "Use .deploy file extension" check box of the Publish Options dialog, which you open from a project's property pages by selecting Publish | Options.

client machine. The manifest, as you can see in Figure 19.5, is created by VS05 during publishing using the following naming convention:

```
AssemblyName.exe.manifest
```

Because multiple versions of an application can be published, there could be one or more folders, delineated by a unique version number and application manifest. In the face of such a choice, there needs to be a way to advertise which is the latest downloadable version. And there is: the deployment manifest, as shown in Figure 19.6.

Figure 19.6   ClickOnce Deployment Manifest

The *deployment manifest* references the application manifest to obtain the current version of the application to download. VS05 creates two ways to launch an application by generating two deployment manifests in the publish location's root: one that's version-specific (*AssemblyName_PublishVersion*.application), and one for the version-to-install (*Assembly-Name*.application). Users should navigate to the version-to-install deployment manifest, which, for Wahoo, is found in the following location:

```
http://www.sellsbrothers.com/wahoo2/wahoo.application
```

As each version of an application is published, VS05 generates the version-specific folder and both the application and the deployment manifests, copying them to the appropriate locations. Additionally, VS05 updates the version-to-install deployment manifest, making it a copy of the latest published version-specific deployment manifest.

Because VS05 incorporates a layer of indirection between a single version-to-install deployment manifest and one or more version-specific manifests, application publishers can easily roll back a potentially bad new application version by manually replacing the version-to-install deployment manifest with one that refers to a previous, working version of the application.

Figure 19.7 illustrates the relationship between deployment and application manifests after several versions of an application have been published.

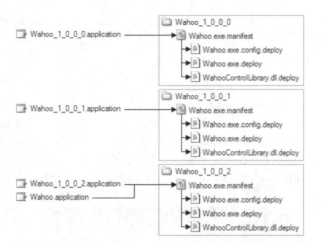

Figure 19.7   ClickOnce Deployment Manifest and Application Manifest Relationships

VS05 generates two additional files and adds them to the root: setup.exe and publish.htm. The setup.exe file is a standard installation application that downloads and executes the necessary prerequisites that a ClickOnce-deployed application needs in order to execute on the client machine, including .NET Framework 2.0. The publish.htm file, shown in Figure 19.8, is an HTML page that users can browse to launch an application.[7]

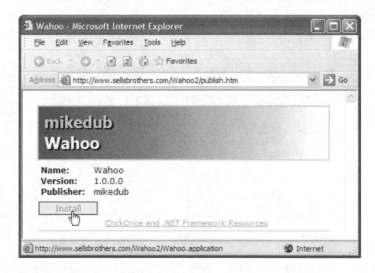

Figure 19.8   The publish.htm Page

[7] publish.htm is intended as an exemplar for application publishers to use as a model for their own installation web pages. If you prefer, you can prevent VS05 from generating publish.htm by unchecking "Automatically generated deployment web page after every publish" in the Publish Options dialog (project properties | Publish | Options).

The Install button is a link to the version-to-install deployment manifest, and clicking it initiates application launch.

Launching an Application

Whether a user launches an application indirectly from publish.htm or by navigating directly to a deployment manifest, the ClickOnce launch process is initiated and begins a process comprising several steps: downloading the manifests, verifying their signatures and file hashes, and using them to determine whether the application is already cached on the client machine. This process is reported visually to the user via the dialog shown in Figure 19.9.[8]

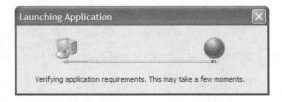

Figure 19.9　Verifying Application Requirements

If the result of checking application requirements is that ClickOnce can download the application, it performs a further analysis of the manifests, checking the application's publisher, security requirements, install files, and publish location. If some combination of these raises ClickOnce's hackles, the Security Warning dialog in Figure 19.10 is shown.

Figure 19.10　Security Warning

Users can open a more verbose description of the security concerns from the Security Warning dialog by clicking the More Information link label (Figure 19.10), which opens the dialog shown in Figure 19.11.

---

[8] An application can be launched only from a client machine on which .NET Framework 2.0 is installed. Ensuring that this is the case is discussed later in this chapter.

Application Install - More Information

🛡 **Publisher**
The publisher of this application cannot be verified. Only run applications from publishers that you trust.

🛡 **Machine Access**
This application will gain access to additional resources on your computer, such as your file system or your network connection. This may put your computer at risk. Do not approve unless you trust the application's publisher.

ⓘ **Installation**
This application will be installed on your computer. It will add a shortcut to your Start menu and will be added to the Add or Remove Programs list.

ⓘ **Location**
This application comes from the Internet. Only run applications from locations that you trust.

Close

Figure 19.11   Security Warning: More Information

In this example, ClickOnce has determined that the application's publisher is unknown to the client, and the application requires more access to the client than the client allows for applications launched from the Internet. Both requirements are considered critical, and they are marked as such with the appropriate icons. Less critical is the footprint the application will leave on the client machine and the location from which it's being launched.

If all factors are soothing, the Security Warning dialog is not shown at all. However, typically some factors are troubling, so users need to consider these warnings before deciding whether to continue downloading the application. If they are comfortable with the security concerns, they can click Install to download the actual application.[9] Obligingly, ClickOnce begins downloading the required application files, keeping the user updated of its progress by displaying the progress dialog shown in Figure 19.12.

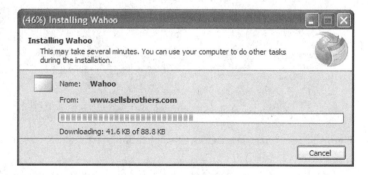

Figure 19.12   Download and Installation Progress

At the end of the download, ClickOnce begins installing the application.

---

[9] No application code is downloaded until the user chooses to, a practice that provides an added degree of security.

Application Installation

By default, a ClickOnce-deployed application's files are placed in a folder on the local disk in a nonroaming, per-user location (*%UserProfile%*\Local Setting\Apps on Windows XP). Additionally, the default behavior for ClickOnce-deployed applications is to provide a modest level of integration with the shell, beginning with the addition of an entry in the Add or Remove Programs control panel, as shown in Figure 19.13.

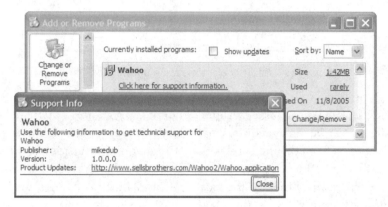

Figure 19.13   Integration with Add or Remove Programs Control Panel

Additionally, a Start menu item is created for your application, as shown in Figure 19.14, which the user can select to activate the application even if no longer connected to the network.

Figure 19.14   ClickOnce-Deployed Application Start Menu Shortcut

If the publish location can't be reached, ClickOnce instead executes the currently installed application.[10]

[10] The Start menu shortcut plays a pivotal role in application updates and versioning, as covered later in this chapter.

After installation or after users click the Start menu shortcut item, the ClickOnce launch process comes to an end and the application itself finally executes on the client, as shown in Figure 19.15. This is cause enough to shout Wahoo!

Figure 19.15   Wahoo in ClickOnce-Deployed Action

Because Wahoo is deployed from the Internet, information pertaining to security issues is displayed for users every time the application is run.

As the sun sets on a day in the life of a ClickOnce-deployed application, you'll fondly remember that even the simplest possible deployment configuration—choosing a publish location—causes the ClickOnce juggernaut to roll into action. It creates and publishes an installation package to a publish location and, when the application is launched, manages the secure download, installation, and execution of the application to a client machine.

All this relies on VS05 to make a lot of decisions about the deployment process on your behalf, including creating a custom setup.exe to install application prerequisites, assembling the application files, deciding whether to integrate with the shell, and allowing users to stay current with new application versions if the publish location can be reached. If these defaults are unsuitable, don't worry. You can easily configure virtually any aspect of a ClickOnce deployment from VS05, including those you've seen and a whole lot more.

ClickOnce Configuration

The Publish Wizard is a lightweight UI wrapper that provides a quick-fire publishing option. However, the Publish Wizard hides the rich support provided by ClickOnce from VS05 that allows developers to tailor application deployment to fit a wide range of scenarios. The place you start is the Publish tab of a project's property pages, as shown in Figure 19.16.

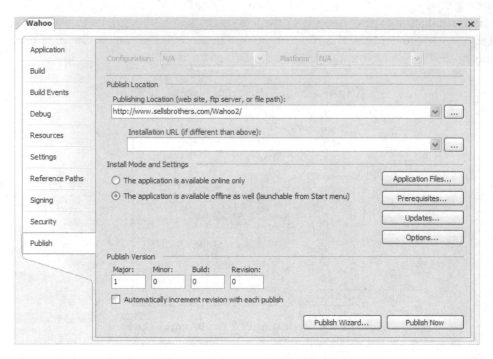

Figure 19.16   Configuring ClickOnce Deployment for Your Application from the Publish Tab

Now let's look at the configurations available from the Publish tab.

Bootstrapping

Before an application can be installed, the client machine must meet certain installation requirements. For Windows Forms 2.0 applications, this means that the client must have installed at least Windows 98 and the .NET Framework 2.0 in order to run both the application and ClickOnce. If an application has other prerequisites, the client machine must be bootstrapped with them. *Bootstrapping* is the process of determining the minimum set of prerequisites for executing an application, checking the client for those prerequisites, and installing any that are missing.

VS05 allows you to specify your application's prerequisite installation needs in the Prerequisites dialog shown in Figure 19.17. The Prerequisites dialog is available by clicking Properties | Prerequisites.

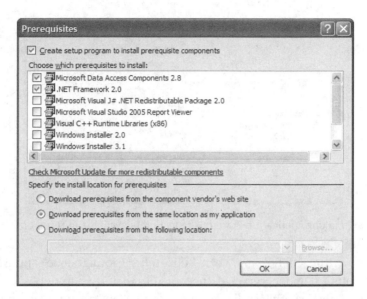

Figure 19.17   Configuring ClickOnce Published Application Prerequisites

.NET Framework 2.0 is checked as a prerequisite by default, and you can select or des-elect other prerequisites as dictated by your application's requirements and your expected client needs. Windows Installer 2.0 and 3.1 versions are included with the .NET Framework 2.0 redistributable, so you probably don't need to check those.

Additionally, VS05 does its best to anticipate your prerequisites; for example, if you include a SQL Server .mdf file in your application, the "SQL Server 2005 Express Edition" option listed in the Prerequisites dialog is automatically checked. If your prerequisites are not available from the list, you can click "Check Microsoft Update for more redistributable components" to find them.[11]

After you specify your prerequisites, you can also specify where the bootstrapper will get them—a component vendor's web site, your application's publish location, or some other location.

When an application is published, your prerequisite configurations are turned into the setup.exe that VS05 generates by default. When run on the client, setup.exe pulls down and executes the installer for each missing prerequisite. If you choose to have users download the installers from your application's publish location, VS05 ensures that the required installers are copied there, as shown in Figure 19.18.

---

[11] You have several more options for configuring this list and the bootstrapper in general, all of which are covered in a very good article by Seane Draine: http://msdn.microsoft.com/msdnmag/issues/04/10/ Bootstrapper/ (http://tinysells.com/44).

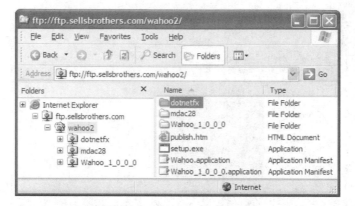

Figure 19.18   Making Application Prerequisite Installers Available in Your Publish Location

You can see that the .NET Framework 2.0 installer (dotnetfx.exe) and Microsoft Data Access Components 2.0 (mdac_typ.exe) are copied to their own folders.

The ability to detect whether .NET Framework 2.0 is installed on the client machine is built into publish.htm with JavaScript. If .NET Framework 2.0 is the only selected prerequisite and is installed, then publish.htm tailors itself to display a link directly to the deployment manifest, as you saw earlier. However, if .NET Framework 2.0 is not found, or if further prerequisites are required, publish.htm renders differently, as shown in Figure 19.19.

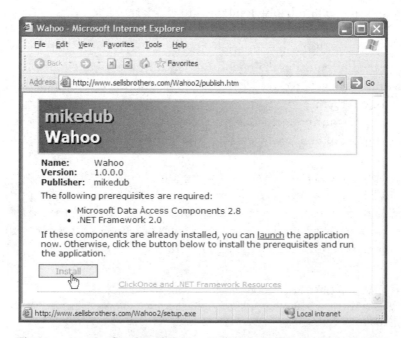

Figure 19.19   Configuring ClickOnce Published Application Prerequisites

You can see that all the prerequisites are listed, and clicking the Install button will download and execute setup.exe instead of the deployment manifest. If users think they have the appropriate prerequisites already installed, they can bypass the setup and run the application immediately by clicking the "launch" link.

After the setup application has completed execution, the version-to-install deployment manifest is automatically downloaded and processed to continue the application launch.

Application Files

Just as you need to make sure that a client machine contains the appropriate prerequisites, you also need to make sure that VS05 publishes the application and data files your application requires to execute, which can often be more than a single assembly. Fortunately, VS05 does a great job of identifying these files. You can view its selection in the Application Files dialog, shown in Figure 19.20, by clicking the Application Files button on the Properties tab.

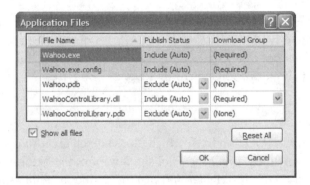

Figure 19.20 Configuring Mandatory ClickOnce Application Files

For Wahoo, VS05 has already identified both Wahoo.exe and Wahoo.exe.config and has marked them as mandatory (colored gray): They cannot be removed from this list. WahooControlLibrary.dll is also there and is required, although it can be excluded just as debug (.pdb) files are by default. You can change the publish status of the listed files from the drop-down in the Publish Status column, which supports the options shown in Figure 19.21.

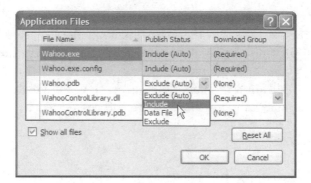

Figure 19.21   Changing the Default Publish Status

The default Publish Status of (Auto) specifies that VS05 decides based on file type.[12] Include and Exclude are self-explanatory. Data File specifies that files like Access .mdb files are stored in the data folder of the deployed application.[13] You can add files to this list by adding them to your project and setting their Build Action to Content, after which you can change their publish status as required.

The Application Files dialog also provides a context menu for each file in the list. In this menu, you can create download groups, reset the configuration of each file to its original value, and delete files removed from the project.[14] Whatever choices you make apply equally to all project configurations, including Debug and Release.

Publisher Details

Irrespective of the publish location from which users launch an application, they will probably want to know something about the publisher and product before they install it. ClickOnce allows you to configure publisher and product names as well as specify a web page users can visit for detailed product and support details. These options can be set from the Publish Options dialog, shown in Figure 19.22. It is accessible by clicking the Options button on the Publish tab.

[12] By default, .pdb files are excluded, and .mdf, .ldf, .mdb, and .xml files are set to a Data File publish status. Files marked with a Build Action of Content are marked with a publish status of Include.

[13] This location is the Data folder, which is found under %userprofile%\local settings\apps\data\hashed_path\data.

[14] *Download groups* are named sets of files that can be downloaded on demand, using the ClickOnce deployment framework, rather than with the initial application installation. The SDK is the place to start for more information.

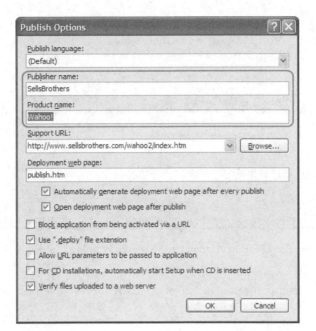

Figure 19.22   Configuring Publisher and Product Names

Applying these configurations changes publish.htm, as shown in Figure 19.23.

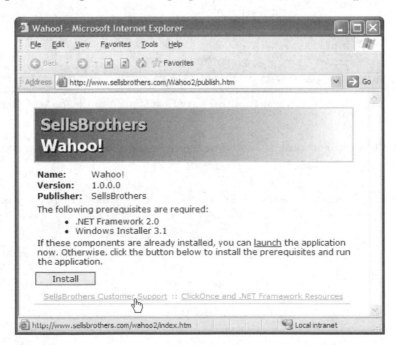

Figure 19.23   Product Name, Publisher Name, and Support URL on publish.htm

As you can see, the product name, publisher name, and support URL are all included on the publish.htm page. Additionally, the product name finds its way onto the Security Warning dialog, as shown in Figure 19.24.[15]

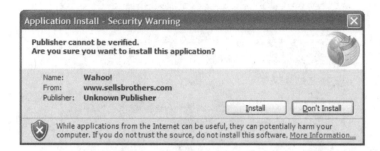

Figure 19.24   Product Name on the Security Warning Dialog

Publisher name, product name, and support URL are also used for Start menu integration, as shown in Figure 19.25.

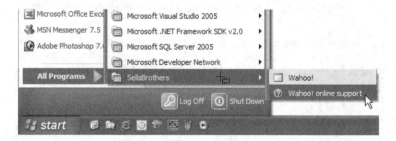

Figure 19.25   Product Name, Publisher Name, and Support URL in the Start Menu

Finally, all these details are available in the Add or Remove Programs control panel entry for the application, as shown in Figure 19.26.

[15] Note that the publisher in this case is not the publisher you configure via the Publish Options dialog. Instead, this refers to the publisher that digitally signed the application, which is discussed later in this chapter.

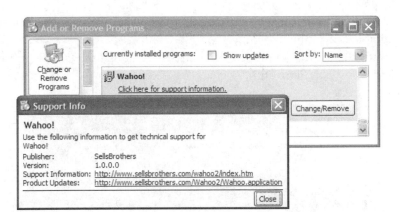

Figure 19.26   Product Name, Publisher Name, and Support URL in the Control Panel

Figures 19.25 and 19.26 illustrate the desire for ClickOnce to provide an informative user experience, including right in the Windows shell. Sometimes, however, ClickOnce-deployed applications may not require this level of integration with the shell; how much is determined by the install mode of a ClickOnce-deployed application.

Install Mode

ClickOnce weds Windows Forms development with web-style deployment, allowing clients to automatically stay keep their applications up-to-date. Additionally, ClickOnce offers a variety of version management features, all of which are dependent on a ClickOnce-deployed application's install mode.

The *install mode* specifies whether an application can be executed without a network connection. Consequently, there are two install modes: online/offline and online. *Online/Offline* install mode, the default, specifies that a ClickOnce-deployed application can execute without a network connection, which is a great option for standalone and smart client (semiconnected) applications.[16] For example, Wahoo makes a great candidate for online/offline mode, because game play does not depend on a network connection, although high scores can be sent to and retrieved from a scores web service when connected to a network.

For applications that require a network connection to execute, however, developers can prevent them from starting without one by choosing *online* install mode. Online applications

[16] The term *smart client* means many things to many people, although one might consider a key characteristic of smart client applications to be the ability to operate in a semiconnected fashion. Further information regarding smart clients can be found at http://msdn.microsoft.com/smartclient (http://tinysells.com/45).

typically need to be online because resources they depend on, such as web services and data-bases, are available only online.

You can configure the install mode from either the Publish tab (see Figure 19.15) or the Publish Wizard, shown in Figure 19.27.

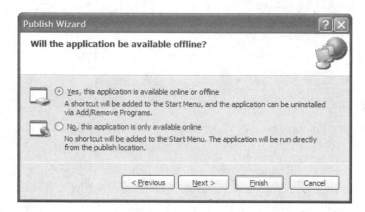

Figure 19.27   Configuring Install Mode via the Publish Wizard

For users, the difference between the two install modes is one of appearance: Online/Offline applications integrate with the shell to provide Start menu access to the application, and online applications don't. With the latter, users are forced to rerun the application from its original deployment location. In reality, though, ClickOnce-deployed applications are always downloaded to, installed on, and executed from the client machine.

Versioning

Whether an application's install mode is online or online/offline, users receive the latest version of the application when it is launched from the publish location. However, because the Start menu icons for online/offline applications load locally installed versions, we need to deploy a versioning policy with an application to instruct ClickOnce to check for and download a new application version when a network connection is available.

ClickOnce offers a variety of application update options that specify when and how updates are retrieved.

Publish Version

You can tell ClickOnce when and how to pick up new application versions, although they first need to be generated. This relies on managing an application's *publish version*, which is a ClickOnce-specific version number that can be configured from the Publish tab of a project's property pages, shown in Figure 19.28.

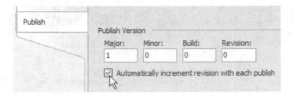

Figure 19.28   Configuring the Publish Version

The publish version comprises major, minor, build, and revision numbers; the same shape as the assembly and file version numbers you can specify via the AssemblyVersion and FileVersion attributes. However, assembly and file version numbers are independent of the publish number.[17] This means that you can publish one version of an application after one or more build versions have been produced.

You can increment the version number manually (for custom version-numbering policies), or you can let VS05 do it automatically for you by selecting the "Automatically increment revision with each publish" option. If you choose to autoincrement, the version number is updated *after* an application is published. Consequently, your application's first publish version will be 1.0.0.0. When the application is next published, a new version is uploaded to the publish location, as shown in Figure 19.29.[18]

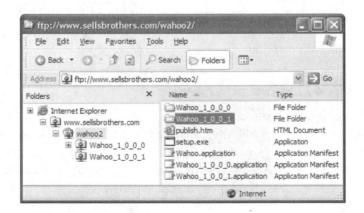

Figure 19.29   New Published Version of the Application

When and how this update is picked up on the client machine are determined by a variety of options available in the Application Updates dialog, shown in Figure 19.30. You open this dialog by clicking the Updates button on the Publish tab of your project's property pages.

---

[17] See Chapter 15: Settings for more information on the AssemblyVersion and FileVersion attributes.

[18] If you try to republish an application with a publish version that has already been used, VS05 provides an appropriate warning.

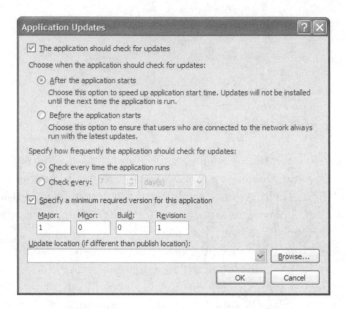

Figure 19.30   Configuring When and How a ClickOnce-Deployed Application Is Updated

You have a variety of options that include setting whether a ClickOnce-deployed application should even check for updates using the "The application should check for updates" check box. When checked, the update controls are enabled, allowing you to specify when and how often to check for updates.

Downloading a New Application Version

When an online/offline application is next launched in the presence of a network connection, ClickOnce compares the publish version number of the version installed on the client with the publish version number of the application referenced by the version-to-install deployment manifest. If the two values are different, it proceeds with an upgrade and displays the Update Available dialog, shown in Figure 19.31.

Figure 19.31   Informing the User of a New Application Version

Before users decide whether to download the new version, they can find more information about the update from the application's support web page, which they open by clicking the Name link.[19] If users are satisfied, they can get the new version by clicking OK, or they can click Skip to load their currently installed version.

If users click the Skip button, ClickOnce is instructed to wait seven days before again asking to update. However, if the dialog's Close button is clicked (X in the upper-right corner), users are asked to update the next time the application is launched.

Rollback

No matter how much testing you do, you may publish new application versions that contain bugs or whose behavior breaks existing functionality. For these situations, online/offline applications come with additional shell integration in the form of the Maintenance dialog. It's available from the Add or Remove Programs control panel, shown in Figure 19.32.

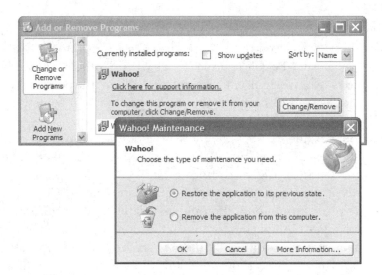

Figure 19.32   Restoring or Removing the Application

The Maintenance dialog is a safety net that supports rolling back a defective Click-Once-deployed application to the previous version, if installed. To reinstall earlier versions, users should be able to access the version-specific deployment manifests, as discussed earlier. If that doesn't do the trick, users can completely remove the application from their computer.

---

[19] This information is available only if you provide a support web page, something that is certainly recommended.

ClickOnce Security

ClickOnce, as you've seen, uses the manifests of the application it's about to download to analyze the application. If there are issues in one or more of four categories—publisher, machine access, installation, and location—those issues are flagged by ClickOnce, before displaying the Security Warning dialog. From this dialog, users can open the More Information dialog (shown earlier in Figure 19.10) to view precisely which of the security issues are flagged.

Of the four categories, there isn't much you can do about ensuring that location isn't flagged. Installation is dependent on how you configured the install mode for your application: If online/offline, this category is flagged. Ensuring that the publisher and machine access categories are not flagged requires you to dip your toes into code signing and .NET's code access security (CAS).

Code Signing

Because downloading code and executing it locally is akin to erecting a large neon sign saying, "Please destroy my computer!" users may feel uncomfortable about doing so. However, users also need to be able to do so. That's where Authenticode code signing technology comes into play.[20] Authenticode allows users to verify the publisher of the code they want to download, as well as hold the publisher accountable if something goes wrong, whether maliciously or accidentally.

The foundation of Authenticode is the *digital certificate,* which application publishers use to sign their code. In exactly the same way that Secure Sockets Layer (SSL) certificates are issued for secure web sites, digital certificates are issued to application publishers by trusted *certification authorities* (CAs), such as VeriSign and thawte. CAs have the power to accept or deny requests from application publishers for trust certificates. If a request is accepted, it means that a CA vouches for the application publisher, guaranteeing that the publisher is who it says it is. Additionally, the CA certifies that the application publisher is trusted to create and make claims about other keys. Either way, the resulting certificate lets downloaders know who it was that digitally signed published code. This allows users to find out exactly whom they might be downloading code from, as well as provides a mechanism by which users can deny or allow code to be downloaded.

ClickOnce relies heavily on the Authenticode code signing model to ensure that absolutely no application code is downloaded, let alone installed and executed, without the express permission of the user.

---

[20] See Microsoft's Authenticode FAQ for more information: http://msdn.microsoft.com/library/dcefault.asp?url=/library/en-us/dnauth/html/signfaq.asp (http://tinysells.com/46).

Digital Certificates

ClickOnce applications cannot be published unless they are digitally signed by an Authenticode certificate. You should absolutely acquire a digital certificate from a CA for your publicly published applications, but if you want users to trust and use them, you can temporarily get away without a CA-provided certificate for your development environment.

VS05 allows you to manually create a certificate from the Signing tab of a project's property pages by clicking the Create Test Certificate button, as shown in Figure 19.33.

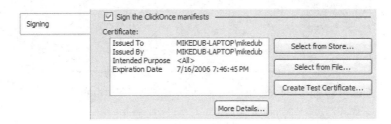

Figure 19.33 Viewing and Selecting Code Signing Certificates from VS05

When you create a test certificate, you are asked to password-protect it, which is obviously recommended. The resulting certificate is a .pfx file whose name conforms to the following format:

*ProjectName*_TemporaryKey.pfx

A .pfx file is a Personal Information Exchange certificate file (PKCS #12), which is a container for a digital certificate.[21] VS05 also adds this certificate to your computer's personal certificate store, as shown in Figure 19.34.[22]

---

[21] PKCS Standard #12 is described at http://www.rsasecurity.com/rsalabs/node.asp?id=2308 (http://tinysells.com/47).

[22] You can open the certificate store either by running certmgr.exe from the command line or by opening Internet Explorer and selecting Tools | Options | Content | Publishers.

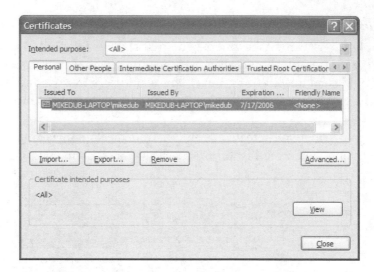

Figure 19.34   Managing Certificates on a Client Machine

As you can see, there are several certificate stores, although the Personal store is the library of certificates installed on your machine that are typically either for you or created by you. You gain two advantages by retaining personal certificates in the certificate store: Certificate sharing is simplified, and Windows take care of the complexities of key management. For example, applications like VS05 can ask Windows to sign code on their behalf, without their ever having to touch the private key. The advantage is that applications you may not trust with your key can still sign code for you.

You can proactively select a certificate from the Personal certificate store by clicking the Select from Store button shown in Figure 19.33.[23] Additionally, you can choose a certificate that's deployed with a personal certificate file outside your project. This action imports the .pfx file into your project and loads the certificate into the certificate store. Finally, if you haven't created a test certificate when you publish your application for the first time, VS05 creates one for you.

By default, a test certificate is untrusted, which is something you can determine by viewing detailed certificate information for the selected certificate in VS05. To do this, you click the More Details button in VS05 (see Figure 19.10 earlier) or the View button in the certificate manager (Figure 19.34), which opens the dialog shown in Figure 19.35.

---

[23] When you click the desired certificate in the list, you should also click the Advanced button to open the Advanced Options dialog and check that it is configured for code signing purposes.

Figure 19.35   Certificate for Untrusted Publisher as Created by VS05

You need to trust a certificate if you want to trust code signed by that certificate. Code signed by a certificate can become trusted only if the CA is listed in the certificate manager as a trust root certification authority; CAs like VeriSign and thawte already are listed there. Alternatively, you can manually add your test certificate to the Trust Root Certification Authorities list for the same effect. After you do, your certificate's details are updated to match, as shown in Figure 19.36.

Figure 19.36   Certificate for Trusted Publisher

Notice that the certificate is valid for only one year. Although VS05 arbitrarily chooses one year as the life span for test certificates, CAs like VeriSign and thawte always issue certificates with one-year life spans.[24] The reason? With mathematical certainty, digital certificates can be cracked. Additionally, private keys can be stolen or leaked, and certificate authorities have revocation lists for this purpose. Having certificates expire after one year prevents anyone with access to a few supercomputers from cracking them and, more importantly, protects someone who doesn't have an up-to-date revocation list.

However, it would be painful for users to have to download new versions of your application every year after a digital certificate is re-signed.

Time-Stamping

To avoid forcing users to re-download your application in the face of certificate expiration, a published application's digital signature can be time-stamped. This requires providing a hash of the code to a CA. Then, when the digital certificate expires, applications like Internet Explorer and ClickOnce can query a time-stamp server (typically operated by a CA) to confirm that the digital signature was created before the digital certificate expired.

VS05 allows you to specify a time-stamp server for your certificate by using the Signing tab, as shown in Figure 19.37.

Figure 19.37   Configure a Digital Certificate's Time-Stamp Server

You should check with your CA to determine the most appropriate time-stamp server to use.

Publishing Signed Code

The certificate you choose for digitally signing your application is not used by VS05 to sign the application files themselves. Instead, VS05 signs the application manifests, which control whether any actual application files are downloaded.[25] In other words, these files act as a barrier between users and actual application code; if users don't trust them, no application is downloaded.[26]

---

[24] .NET SDK tools like MakeCert and Mage create certificates that expire on the December 31, 2039, at 11:59:59 GMT (just in case you were wondering).

[25] The ClickOnce-generated setup application is also digitally signed and checked for tampering.

[26] Conceivably, particularly savvy users can discover the URL for and download actual application files. If they do, they are effectively shunning the protection provided by Authenticode.

Tamperproofing

Before the application manifest and setup files are even processed, a red flag is raised if they were tampered with after being published, in the form of the Application dialog that's shown in Figure 19.38.

Figure 19.38 Cannot Start Application Dialog

Clicking the Details button provides a summary of the reason. For tampering of a deployment manifest that looks like the following:

```
PLATFORM VERSION INFO
...
ERROR SUMMARY
  Below is a summary of the errors, details of these errors are listed
  later in the log.
* Activation of http://.../wahoo2/wahoo_1_0_0_16.application
  resulted in exception. Following failure messages were detected:
    + Exception reading manifest from
      http://.../wahoo2/wahoo_1_0_0_16.application:
      the manifest may not be valid or the file could not be opened.
    + Manifest XML signature is not valid.
    + The digital signature of the object did not verify.
...
```

When an application is published, each file listed in a manifest file is hashed, and then the entire manifest file itself is hashed. The hash of the manifest file is then signed with the private key contained in the certificate. On the client side, the hash is recomputed by Click-Once, and, if there is a mismatch, the XML signature in the downloaded manifest or setup files is considered invalid and the tampering exception is displayed.

Trusting a Signed Application

If the manifests are valid, users will see the dialog shown in Figure 19.39.

Figure 19.39   Downloading an Application from an Untrusted Publisher with ClickOnce

At this point, the application is confirmed to be untampered, although the publisher is still unknown. Clicking on the More Information link shows that the publisher as unverified, as with Figure 19.10 (presented earlier). If a user ignores this warning and clicks Install, the application is automatically trusted and is added to the list of Trusted Applications known to CAS.[27]

Subsequent downloads of the same application, via manifests signed with the same digital certificate, execute in true ClickOnce fashion, without the Security Warning dialog being shown. If you reuse the same .pfx file (and certificate) in a different application, users will need to trust the publisher again, because the application is different. To cause a client machine to trust a client certificate you have issued, you install it into the Trust Root Certification Authorities certificate store. If no other security warning categories are flagged, the Security Warning dialog is skipped during the launch process. If other security warnings are flagged, the Security Warning dialog is shown as in Figure 19.40.

Figure 19.40   Trusted Publisher with Other Security Warnings Flagged

---

[27] You can view the Trusted Applications list by opening the .NET Framework 2.0 Configuration application (Administrative Tools | .NET Framework 2.0 Configuration) and choosing .NET Framework 2.0 Configuration | My Computer | Runtime Security Policy | User | Trusted Applications.

This time around, the Publisher option in the More Information dialog is OK'd (as shown in Figure 19.41), because we've designated it as a Trust Root Certification Authority.

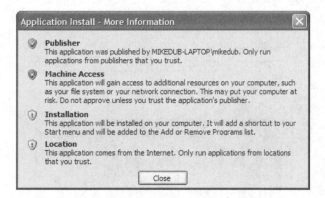

Figure 19.41   Configuring ClickOnce Application File Dependencies

So, the publisher is now known, but the client machine should know about a real publisher rather than the developer who built the application.

Code Signing with a Real Certificate

A real publisher is associated with a real certificate, which, as we've discussed, you need to purchase from a CA or obtain from your IT department. You then import this certificate into VS05, which requires a slightly different process from the one you use with a VS05 temporary certificate. Follow these steps (based on my thawte-issued certificate):

1. Install the certificate into the personal certificate store by right-clicking the certificate file and choosing Install to start the Certificate Import Wizard.
2. Click Next to specify the certificate file to import, which is automatically selected.
3. Click Next to enter the password for the certificate and to ensure that strong private key protection is enabled. This implies that the certificate password is asked for whenever the private key is used (I wasn't asked for the password during signing because VS05 didn't ask Windows for the private key).
4. Click Next to choose the certificate store in which to install the certificate, which should be the Personal certificate store because that's the only store VS05 looks at.
5. Click Next and then Finish to complete the wizard and install the certificate.

6. From VS05, open the Signing tab from the project's property pages.

7. Click the Select from Store button, which allows you to choose a certificate from the Personal certificate store.

8. Select the newly imported certificate.

When the certificate is imported into your project, you can publish as usual, although VS05 asks for permission to sign your application with the chosen certificate via the dialog shown in Figure 19.42.

Figure 19.42 Allowing VS05 to Sign an Application with a CA-Issued Digital Certificate

After you click OK, ClickOnce and VS05 publish the application as usual. Then, when the application is launched, the Security Warning dialog contains useful publisher information, as shown in Figure 19.43.

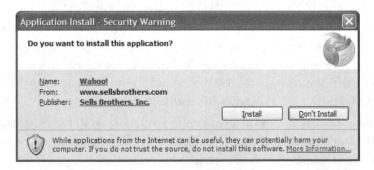

Figure 19.43 Certified Publisher Information in the Security Warning Dialog

Clicking the Publisher link opens the Certificate dialog shown in Figure 19.44.

Figure 19.44   Certified Publisher's Certificate Details

This allows users to discover more information about the publisher and helps them decide whether to continue downloading. The Publisher section of the More Information dialog, shown in Figure 19.45, also shows the updated publisher information.

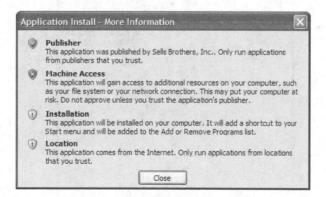

Figure 19.45   Certified Publisher Information in the More Information Dialog

With all this information in hand, users should feel much more comfortable about the origin of their application. But as you can see in Figure 19.45, users might not feel comfortable about what the application wants to do on their machine, as described by the Machine Access security warning. Understanding how an application should be configured to avoid this warning depends on code access security.

Code Access Security

All .NET assemblies execute within a security sandbox provided by the .NET Framework's code access security (CAS) technology. This sandbox controls the degree of access an assembly has to a computer's resources, which can include local disks, network connections, and the Registry. CAS provides different permissions based on evidence, which is most often a matter of where the application is launched from—the local machine, an intranet, or the Internet. Ensuring that your applications conform to these defaults is a key consideration for ClickOnce-deployed applications, because it enables you to advertise your applications as being safe, secure, and benign.

To access a computer's resources, an assembly needs an appropriate set of permissions that CAS grants based on where an application has come from. To view the current permission settings on your machine, use the Microsoft .NET Framework Configuration tool (available in your Administrative Tools menu). Drilling down into the Permission Sets for the machine's Runtime Security Policy reveals a number of entries, including FullTrust, LocalIntranet, and Internet. Figure 19.46 shows the set of default Internet permissions.

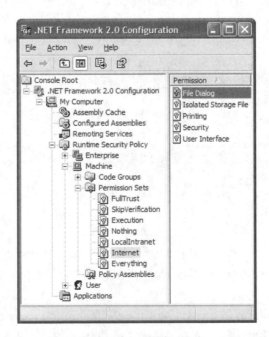

Figure 19.46   Drilling into a Machine's Permission Sets

Permission sets apply to every assembly that is loaded by the Common Language Runtime, whether they are user-run EXEs or DLLs loaded from other assemblies. Table 19.1 compares the LocalIntranet permission set to the Internet permission set.

Table 19.1   LocalIntranet Versus Internet Permission Sets

Permission	Level	LocalIntranet	Internet
Environment Variables	Read=USERNAME	Yes	No
File Dialog	Unrestricted	Yes	No
File Dialog	Access=Open	Yes	Yes
Isolated Storage File	Allow=AssemblyIsolationByUser	Yes	No
Reflection	Flags=ReflectionEmit	Yes	No
Security	Flags=Assertion	Yes	No
Security	Flags=Execution	Yes	Yes
UI	Unrestricted	Yes	No
UI	Clipboard=OwnClipboard	Yes	Yes
UI	Window=SafeTopLevelWindows	Yes	Yes
DNS	Permission=DNS	Yes	No
Web	Connect=http to Originating Site	Yes	Yes
Web	Connect=https to Originating Site	Yes	Yes
Printing	Level=DefaultPrinting	Yes	No
Printing	Level=SafePrinting	Yes	Yes

Assemblies are associated with a permission set in a number of ways, including the publisher, the site, the strong name, or the security zone. Most of the default code groups associate code with a zone. For example, the My_Computer_Zone is associated with the FullTrust permission set, the Local_Intranet_Zone with the LocalIntranet permission set, and the Internet_Zone with the Internet permission set.

The zone an assembly comes from is determined by that assembly's path, as configured in Internet Explorer via Tools | Options | Security (see Table 19.2).

Table 19.2 Determining the Zone an Assembly Is Deployed From

Path	Examples	Zone
Local file	c:\ foo\foo.exe	MyComputer
UNC Name or Nondotted Site URL	\\server\foo\foo.exe http://server/foo/foo.exe http://localhost/foo/foo.exe z:\foo\foo.exe (if z is mapped to a network share)	LocalIntranet
All-Numeric IP Address or Dotted Site URL	http://1115768663/foo/foo.exe http://www.sellsbrothers.com/foo/foo.exe http:// 64.85.21.138/foo/foo.exe http://127.0.0.1/foo/foo.exe	Internet

On the one hand, you've seen how CAS provides a default set of permissions to an assembly based on where it comes from. On the other hand, an assembly might require fewer, more, or different permissions from those provided by CAS. ClickOnce conveniently gives you a mechanism for requesting a custom set of permissions.

Requesting Permissions

An assembly needs a minimum set of permissions in order to execute; this set of permissions can be treated as unrelated to the set of permissions CAS grants to assemblies based on deployment location.

By default, a Windows Forms application is configured to support full trust, which is a way of saying that it needs all permissions awarded to users running the application as determined by their Windows user accounts. However, even though users can elevate permissions for such an application, it's your duty to ratchet down the required set of permissions by asking only for what you need to run. In this case, you need to consider configuring your assembly to support partially trusted execution.

You configure an assembly's trust level from the Security tab of the project's property pages, as shown in Figure 19.47.

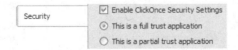

Figure 19.47   Managing the Security Settings of a ClickOnce-Deployed Application

By default, an assembly doesn't enable ClickOnce security settings until the first time you publish it, in which case VS05 automatically enables them for full trust; or you enable it manually yourself. The resulting selection is recorded in your published application's manifest:

```
// Wahoo.exe.manifest
<?xml version="1.0" encoding="utf-8"?>
<asmv1:assembly ... >
  ...
  <trustInfo>
    <security>
      <applicationRequestMinimum>
        <PermissionSet class="PermissionSet"
          version="1"
          Unrestricted="true"
          ID="Custom"
          SameSite="none" />
        <defaultAssemblyRequest permissionSetReference="Custom" />
      </applicationRequestMinimum>
    </security>
  </trustInfo>
  ...
</asmv1:assembly>
```

The applicationRequestMinimum tag contains all the information that ClickOnce needs on the client machine to determine which permissions are required by the application. For full trust applications, this means that the Unrestricted attribute of the PermissionSet tag is set to true.

When you elect to go with partial trust, VS05 provides the means to specify the subset of permissions that you need. It supports two preconfigured permission sets—LocalIntranet and Internet—or it lets you create your own, as shown in Figure 19.48.

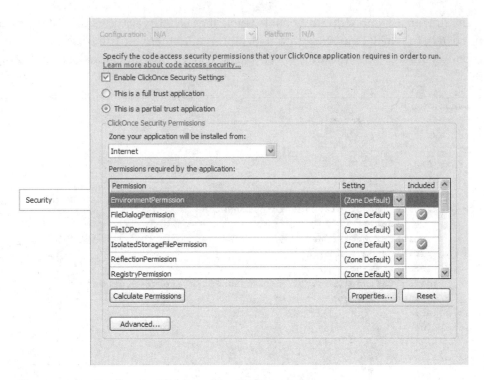

Figure 19.48   Configuring ClickOnce-Required Permissions

LocalIntranet and Internet correspond to the permissions provided by the Local-Intranet_Zone and Internet_Zone code groups you saw earlier. Wahoo, for example, will be deployed over the Internet, and hence the Internet zone selection. This has the effect of automatically including a request for the permissions from the Internet zone:

```
// Wahoo.exe.manifest
<?xml version="1.0" encoding="utf-8" ?>
<asmv1:assembly ...>
  ...
  <trustInfo>
    <security>
      <applicationRequestMinimum>
        <PermissionSet class="System.Security.PermissionSet"
          ID="Custom"
          SameSite="site">
          <IPermission
            class="FileDialogPermission
            Access="Open" ... />
```

```
          <IPermission
            class="IsolatedStorageFilePermission"
            Allowed="ApplicationIsolationByUser"
            UserQuota="512000" ... />
          <IPermission
            class="SecurityPermission"
            Flags="Execution" ... />
          <IPermission class="UIPermission"
            Window="SafeTopLevelWindows"
            Clipboard="OwnClipboard" ... />
          <IPermission
            class="PrintingPermission"
            Level="SafePrinting" ... />
        </PermissionSet>
        <defaultAssemblyRequest permissionSetReference="Custom" />
      </applicationRequestMinimum>
    </security>
  </trustInfo>
  ...
</asmv1:assembly>
```

As you can see, Wahoo is now configured to request the specified permissions, and only those permissions, for the security sandbox it runs in. But this also means that you must ensure that your application code doesn't require permissions beyond those specified to avoid run-time issues.

Permission Elevation

When the set of permissions required by your application exceeds those permitted by CAS for the zone, the Machine Access security warning category is flagged (see Figure 19.49), whether or not the client's machine has been configured to trust the publisher.

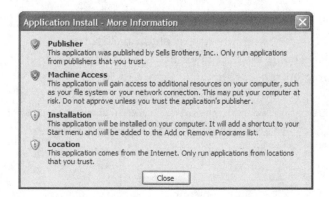

Figure 19.49 Trusted Publisher but Potentially Harmful Machine Access

At this point, the user can either cancel application launch or elect to grant the application the additional permissions it needs, a process known as *permission elevation*. When permission is granted, the permission set and application signature are added to the list of trusted applications managed by CAS. The application is then downloaded, installed, and executed within a CAS security sandbox that's configured to the permissions stored by CAS for the application. Partial trust applications don't appear under their own name in the Task Manager; the CLR uses applaunch.exe to launch partial trust applications, and it's applaunch.exe that you see in Task Manager.

After a publisher is trusted, permissions are granted as required and the application is executed. Users can subsequently execute and upgrade the same application as many times as they like. If users download a different application from the same publisher, however, they must go through the permission elevation process again if Machine Access is flagged. If the permissions required by an application are less than or equal to those allowed for a particular security zone, the Security Warning dialog gives the green light, provided that the publisher is trusted and the application is launched from a trusted location.

If subsequent versions of an application are deployed with increased permission requirements, users are prompted to elevate permissions again. Users are not prompted if subsequent versions either maintain or reduce the required permissions.[28]

Managing Permissions

ClickOnce doesn't force users to elevate permissions or to download an application, but you can avoid the issue altogether by programming specifically for partial trust. This involves detecting when your assemblies require more permissions than they advertise, refactoring your code to satisfy the advertised permissions, and, in some cases, enabling and disabling functionality to target a variety of deployment zones.

Determining Required Permissions

When you configure your assembly to execute in partial trust and you select the partial trust zone you are targeting, the list of permissions that you select is the default set of permissions for the targeted zone, as shown in Figure 19.50.

---

[28] Brian Noyes has written an article at http://msdn.microsoft.com/library/default.asp?url=/library/en-us/dnwinforms/html/clickoncetrustpub.asp (http://tinysells.com/48) that provides detailed insight into when prompting occurs, as well as the ability to alter it.

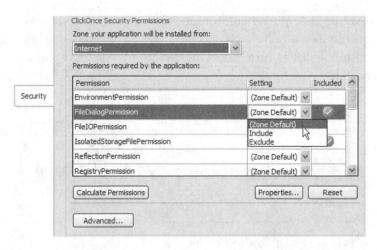

Figure 19.50   Green Ticks for the Default Internet Zone Partial Trust Permission Set

Each available permission is listed, along with a green tick indicating whether it's been included in the list of permissions required by the current application. Additionally, a Setting column allows you either to choose the zone default for each permission or to forcibly include or exclude a permission. If you want the set of requested permissions to revert to the zone default, you simply click the Reset button. If you're targeting a particular deployment zone, you should leave the setting as the zone default. If your application requires more permissions than those provided by the deployment zone, you can include them, although it will require users to elevate your application's permissions. The best practice, however, is to request only the permissions you need and no more; the more permissions you request, the more damage your application can be made to do if it is hijacked.

As you saw earlier in Table 19.1, each permission comes with one or more configurations. You can target these subpermissions by clicking the Properties button shown in Figure 19.50, which yields the dialog shown in Figure 19.51.

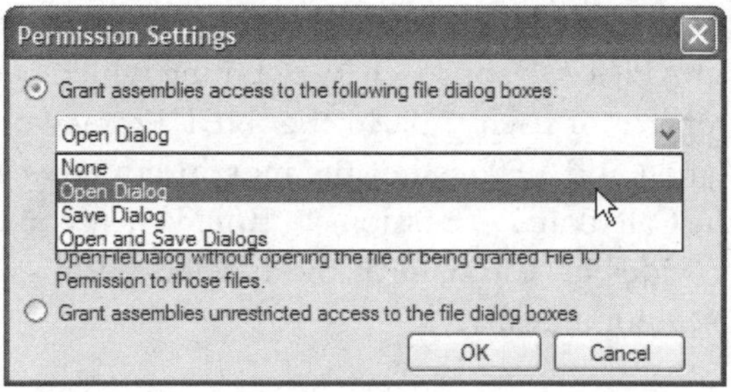

Figure 19.51   Configuring Permission Settings

Figure 19.51 shows the zone default for File IO permissions. If these were increased, to require access to the Save dialog or both Open and Save dialogs, it would result in an increased permission, which in turn causes the Security dialog to display a warning icon, as shown in Figure 19.52.

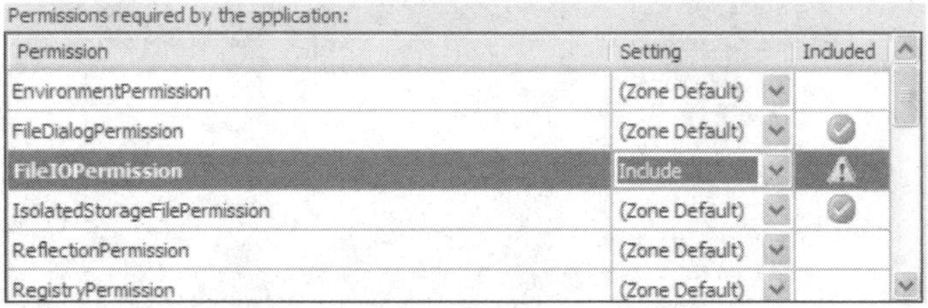

Figure 19.52   Permission Warning

Ascertaining Required Permissions

There is no relationship between the permissions your application requests and those that it actually requires. When you choose a permission set, you are simply saying that your application requires those permissions and no more. If your application code turns out to require more, CAS raises security exceptions like the one shown in Figure 19.53 whenever your application attempts to cross the security sandbox line.

Wahoo!

Unable to send high score: Request for the permission of type 'System.Net.WebPermission, System, Version=2.0.0.0, Culture=neutral, PublicKeyToken=b77a5c561934e089' failed.

OK

Figure 19.53   Security Exception

How do you determine exactly what permissions your application will require? The reference documentation provides one approach by detailing which permissions are required by each member or property of each type in the .NET Framework. Of course, flicking between the documentation and VS05 is not the most productive approach. Instead, the Security tab provides the Calculate Permissions button. When you click this button, VS05 analyzes your code, provides an estimate of the needed permissions, and updates the required permissions list automatically.[29]

---

[29] In VS05, permission calculation (performed by permcalc.exe for VS05) is not 100% accurate. Although it will be improved in later releases, for now it errs on the side of rounding up—estimating more permissions than you need.

When permission analysis reveals the need for extra permissions, again you have to consider whether to force permission elevation on the user. Alternatively, you can ratchet down the required permissions for the targeted zone and go about the business of updating your application code, with the help of the reference documentation, IntelliSense in Zone, partial trust zone debugging, and permission analysis, to ensure that it safely runs within the allowed permission set for that zone.[30] We now look at several things you have to consider and ways to handle them.

Considerations for Partially Trusted Assemblies

Both the Wahoo and the WahooControlLibrary assemblies are designed to work within the restricted set of Internet permissions; this meant that it was difficult to implement the complete set of functionality I wanted. I encountered the following challenges:

- Gathering assembly information
- Handling keystrokes
- Communicating via web services
- Reading and writing files
- Handling multiple partial trust deployment zones
- Debugging Partially-Trusted Applications

Gathering Assembly Information

One nice feature that comes with VS05 is the About Box form wizard, which generates a nice About box form for your Windows Forms project. I used this wizard to create a pretty

---

[30] IntelliSense in Zone is a Visual Basic feature for partial trust development. When it's enabled along with Auto List Members, all members that require more permissions than the partial trust zone you've selected for your project are grayed out as you enter code.

About box for Wahoo. This ran fine under full permission, of course, but it ran into trouble when executing the following code while running under partial trust:

```
// AboutBox.cs
partial class AboutBox : Form {
  public AboutBox() {
    ...
    this.labelVersion.Text =
      String.Format("Version {0}", AssemblyVersion);
  }
  ...
  public string AssemblyVersion {
    get {
      // Will throw a security exception under partial trust
      // (Internet Zone)
      return
        Assembly.GetExecutingAssembly().GetName().Version.ToString();
    }
  }
  ...
}
```

Internally, Assembly.GetName needs access to the file system to determine the assembly version, and this requires FileIOPermission. By default, the Internet zone does not provide FileIOPermission to applications, that explains the security exception that this code raises.

Fortunately, the workaround is relatively simple, requiring only that you find an alternative .NET Framework implementation that doesn't need FileIOPermission: the Application.ProductVersion property:

```
// AboutBox.cs
partial class AboutBox : Form {
  ...
  public string AssemblyVersion {
    get {
      // Will run under partial trust (Internet Zone)
      return Application.ProductVersion.ToString();
    }
  }
  ...
}
```

Application.ProductVersion has no permission requirements and executes without exception in any zone.

Handling Keystrokes

Safely discovering an assembly's product version is straightforward, but handling keystrokes may be less so. If the user input goes to one of the standard Windows Forms controls, that's not a problem from partially trusted code. However, if a control needs to handle special keys—WahooControlLibrary, for example, needs to handle arrow keys—then it must take special measures.

Arrow keys, Tab, and Shift+Tab are special keys because of their use in moving between controls in a form. This means that a rogue assembly that is allowed to consume the arrow keys could easily hijack an entire form. For that reason, a control is not allowed to override ProcessDialogKey or IsInputKey, either of which would allow such an activity. The .NET runtime throws a security exception whenever it attempts to compile a method that contains code that creates an instance of a type that overrides these or similar methods, protecting users from a form-jacking. Unfortunately, this means that you can't use these methods to have WahooControlLibrary handle the arrow keys.

Another way to handle the arrow keys is to let the parent form retrieve the keys in its own implementation of OnKeyDown (an action that's allowed) and pass them to the control for processing. For a form to handle keystrokes, such as the arrow keys, that can be handled by a child control, the form can set its own KeyPreview property to true.

For Wahoo, all this worked fine until experimentation showed that some of the current Windows Forms controls, such as MenuStrip and Button, don't actually let the parent form access these special keys when other controls that allow special keys, such as TextBox, aren't on the form. Because the main Wahoo form contains only a custom control, a MenuStrip, and a StatusStrip, this becomes an issue. As a workaround, the main Wahoo form creates an invisible TextBox and adds it to the list of controls that the form hosts:

```
// MainForm.cs
partial class MainForm : Form {
  ...
  public MainForm() {
    ...
    // HACK: Add a text box so that we can get the arrow keys
    Controls.Add(new TextBox());
  }
  ...
}
```

I'm not proud of this technique, but it lets the arrow keys through in a partially trusted environment, and one does what one must to work around issues in the platform.

Communicating via Web Services

Communicating with the user is not the only job of a ClickOnce application; often, it must also communicate with the outside world. In the partially trusted zones, this communication is limited to talking back only to the originating site and only via web services, as long as you have checked the "Grant the application access to its site of origin" check box located on the Advanced Security Settings dialog (Project Property Pages | Security | Advanced). Luckily, the originating site is often what we want to talk to anyway, and web services are flexible enough to handle most of our communication needs.

Generating the client-side proxy code necessary to talk to a web service is as easy as adding a web reference to your project. You do this by pointing VS05 at the URL for the web service's WSDL (as discussed in Chapter 18: Multithreaded User Interfaces).

After the web reference is added, the web service is exposed as a component and is hosted on the Toolbox, enabling you to drag and drop it onto your form and code against it:

```csharp
// MainForm.Designer.cs
partial class MainForm {
  ...
  private void InitializeComponent() {
    this.scoresService = new WahooScoresService();
    ...
    // scoresService
    this.scoresService.Url =
      "http://localhost/WahooScores/WahooScores.asmx";
    ...
  }
  ...
  WahooScoresService scoresService;
}

// MainForm.cs
partial class MainForm : Form {
  ...
  void GetHighScores() {
    ...
    // Get high scores
    scores = this.scoresService.GetScores();

    // Show high scores
    ...
  }
  void SendHighScore(int score) {
    // Send high score
    this.scoresService.RegisterScore(dlg.PlayerName, score);
    ...
  }
  ...
}
```

Because partially trusted code is only allowed to make web service calls back to the originating server, it's up to you to make sure that the web service URL points to the originating server. You can do this by replacing the URL that's hard-coded into the web service component (often pointing at http://localhost/...) with the site that you discover dynamically using the ClickOnce deployment framework.

First, you acquire the site from which your application was launched. This information is available from the UpdateLocation property, which is exposed by the deployment framework's ApplicationDeployment class:

```
using System.Deployment.Application;
...
Uri serverUri =
  ApplicationDeployment.CurrentDeployment.UpdateLocation;
```

Because update location is dependent on the application having been launched from ClickOnce (rather than by a double-click on application .exe), UpdateLocation has a value only when the application is opened using a deployment manifest (when opened from the Start menu or publish.htm). This means that we need to wrap the property inspection with some ClickOnce detection:

```
// UrlJiggler.cs
using System.Deployment.Application;
...
public static class UrlJiggler {
  public static Uri UpdateLocation {
    get {
      // If launched via ClickOnce, return the update location
      if( ApplicationDeployment.IsNetworkDeployed ) {
        return ApplicationDeployment.CurrentDeployment.UpdateLocation;
      }
      return null;
    }
  }
}
```

After we get the update location URL, we extract the web site from it and jiggle the web service component's URL to redirect it to point to the web service located on the same site as the web site:

```
// UrlJiggler.cs
using System.Deployment.Application;
using System.Security.Policy;
...
public static class UrlJiggler {
  ...
```

```
public static Uri UpdateLocation {
  get {...}
}

public static string JiggleUrl(string url) {
  // Get update location
  Uri updateLocation = UpdateLocation;

  // Bail if not launched via ClickOnce
  if( updateLocation == null ) return url;

  // Extract the site from the update location
  string site = Site.CreateFromUrl(updateLocation.AbsoluteUri).Name;

  // Jiggle URL
  UriBuilder jiggledUrl = new UriBuilder(url);
  jiggledUrl.Host = site;
  return jiggledUrl.ToString();
}
}
```

Now the client simply calls JiggleUrl:

```
// MainForm.cs
public partial class MainForm : Form {
  public MainForm() {
    InitializeComponent();
    ...
    // Redirect web service component URL to base site
    // from which application is being launched
    this.scoresService.Url =
      UrlJiggler.JiggleUrl(this.scoresService.Url);
  }
  ...
}
```

This code enables an application to dynamically adapt to the originating site in Debug mode, when run from VS05, and in Release mode, when run from either an intranet or the Internet. Fundamentally, this code also relies on the deployment framework, which is located in the System.Deployment.Application namespace, as you saw. Although it is beyond the scope of this book, you should know that the deployment framework gives you a fair degree of manual control over the deployment and versioning of an application, particularly when your versioning policies are more complex than those provided by the default ClickOnce configurations available from VS05.[31]

[31] See the book *Smart Client Deployment with ClickOnce™* by Duncan Mackenzie and Brian Noyes (Addison-Wesley).

Reading and Writing Files

After I got the current high scores via the web service, I found that I wanted to cache them for later access (to savor the brief moment when I was at the top). .NET makes it easy to read and write files and to show the File Save and File Open dialogs. Unfortunately, only a limited subset of that functionality is available in partial trust. In Table 19.1, notice that the Local Intranet zone has unrestricted file dialog permissions but no file I/O permissions. This means that files can be read and written, but not without user interaction.

Unrestricted access to the file system is, of course, a security hole on par with buffer overflows and fake password dialogs. To avoid this problem but still allow an application to read and write files, a file can be opened only via the File Save or File Open dialog. Instead of using these dialogs to obtain a file name from the user, we use the dialogs themselves to open the file:

```
// MainForm.cs
partial class MainForm : Form {
  ...
  void GetHighScores() {
    ...
    SaveFileDialog dlg = new SaveFileDialog();
    dlg.DefaultExt = ".txt";
    dlg.Filter = "Text Files (*.txt)|*.txt|All files (*.*)|*.*";

    if( dlg.ShowDialog() == DialogResult.OK ) {
      // NOTE: Not allowed to get dlg.FileName
      using( Stream stream = dlg.OpenFile() )
      using( StreamWriter writer = new StreamWriter(stream) ) {
        writer.Write(sb.ToString());
      }
    }
    ...
  }
  ...
}
```

Instead of opening a stream using the SaveFileDialog.FileName property after the user has chosen a file, we call the OpenFile method directly. This lets partially trusted code read from a file, but only with user intervention and provided that the code has no knowledge of the file system.

Handling Multiple Partial Trust Deployment Zones

In the preceding example, using the SaveFileDialog's helper methods is fine when you aren't executing in the Internet partial trust zone, which, by default, allows use only of OpenFile-Dialog. This code causes a security exception to be thrown when it attempts to execute.

Rather than remove this code altogether—and the ability to save files along with it—you can refactor the code to selectively execute this code only when the application has the required permissions, which you can detect via the following helper:

```
using System.Security;
...
// Check permission
static bool HavePermission(IPermission perm) {
  try { perm.Demand(); }
  catch( SecurityException ) { return false; }
  return true;
}
```

You can use this method from code:

```
// MainForm.cs
partial class MainForm : Form {
  ...
  // Check permission
  static bool HavePermission(IPermission perm) {...}
  ...
  void GetHighScores() {
    ...
    // Check for permissions to do this
    // (By default, won't have this permission in the Internet Zone)
    if( !HavePermission(
      new FileDialogPermission(FileDialogPermissionAccess.Save)) ) {
      string s =
        "This application does not have permission to save files ...";
      MessageBox.Show(s, "Wahoo!");
      return;
    }

    SaveFileDialog dlg = new SaveFileDialog();
    dlg.DefaultExt = ".txt";
    dlg.Filter = "Text Files (*.txt)|*.txt|All files (*.*)|*.*";

    if( dlg.ShowDialog() == DialogResult.OK ) {
      // NOTE: Not allowed to call dlg.FileName
      using( Stream stream = dlg.OpenFile() )
      using( StreamWriter writer = new StreamWriter(stream) ) {
        writer.Write(sb.ToString());
      }
    }
    ...
  }
  ...
}
```

Debugging Partially Trusted Applications

Whichever permission configuration you end up using, you can test how your code executes within the specified permission as you debug your application in VS05. You open the Advanced Security Settings dialog, shown in Figure 19.54, by clicking the Advanced button on the Security tab.

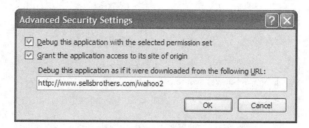

Figure 19.54   Configuring Partial Trust Debugging

Additionally, you can grant your application access to the site it was deployed from, as well as specify a real-world URL to simulate any URL-dependent functionality.

When you find code that requires permissions that exceed those specified, exceptions are raised and the debugger breaks on the defective code. Consequently, you can either increase the permission requirements for your application in the hope that users will elevate, or you can update the code to cope, using techniques you've just seen.

Processing Command Line Arguments

One other feature you need to support in a programmatic way is command line processing. In a normal application, command line parameters are available from the string array passed to Main:

```
static void Main(string[] args) {
  foreach( string arg in args ) {
    MessageBox.Show(arg);
  }
  ...
}
```

Similarly, URLs have a well-known syntax for passing arguments:

```
http://www.sellsbrothers.com/wahoo2/wahoo.application?columns=10&rows=20
```

The combination of the two makes it seem natural to pass command line arguments to ClickOnce applications using the special URL syntax. And it is.

First, you activate support by checking the "Allow URL parameters to be passed to an application" check box in VS05, which is available from your project's property pages | Publish | Publish Options, as shown in Figure 19.55.

Figure 19.55   Configuring Support for URL Parameter Passing to ClickOnce-Deployed Applications

ClickOnce makes sure that command line arguments are passed to the application for harvesting, although they are not passed to your application's entry point Main method, as per standard command line arguments. Instead, they are available from the application's activation URL in a query string format, which we need to parse appropriately:

```
// Program.cs
using System.Collections.Specialized;
using System.Deployment.Application;
...
static class Program {
  [STAThread]
  static void Main(string[] args) {

    Application.EnableVisualStyles();

    int columns = 10;
    int rows = 20;
```

```
    // Query string or command line args??
    if( ApplicationDeployment.IsNetworkDeployed ) {
      string activationUri =
      ApplicationDeployment.CurrentDeployment.ActivationUri.AbsoluteUri;

      if( !string.IsNullOrEmpty(activationUri) ) {
        Uri uri = new Uri(activationUri);
        if( !string.IsNullOrEmpty(uri.Query) ) {
          // Parse (expecting format: "?columns=Xxx&rows=Xxx")
          string query = uri.Query.ToLower();
          GetQueryArg(query, "columns", ref columns);
          GetQueryArg(query, "rows", ref rows);
        }
      }
    }
    else {
      // Process command line args as usual
      ...
    }
    Application.Run(new MainForm(columns, rows));
  }

  // A query string extraction helper
  static bool GetQueryArg<T>(string query, string arg, ref T value) {
    Regex regex = new Regex(arg + "=(?<value>[^&]*)");
    Match match = regex.Match(query);
    if( match == null ) { return false; }

    string s = match.Groups["value"].Value;
    if( string.IsNullOrEmpty(s) ) { return false; }

    TypeConverter converter = TypeDescriptor.GetConverter(typeof(T));
    if( !converter.CanConvertFrom(typeof(string)) ) { return false; }
    value = (T)converter.ConvertFrom(s);
    return true;
  }
}
```

Command line arguments for a URL are available only if the application was launched from a server, and this state is reflected by ApplicationDeployment.IsNetworkDeployed.[32] If this property is true, we retrieve and parse the query string using the GetQueryArg helper function I whipped up. If ApplicationDeployment.IsNetworkDeployed returns false, we check for normal command line arguments and process as usual.

---

[32] Remember, online/offline applications can be launched from the local machine via the Start menu shortcut.

Where Are We?

ClickOnce deployment allows you to deploy Windows Forms applications using the same model you might be accustomed to with web applications. But more than that, ClickOnce is a highly configurable framework for packaging, publishing, and launching your applications. It is built on a trustworthy computing model that incorporates Authenticode digital signatures for secure publishing and CAS for secure execution. Additionally, ClickOnce factors in other considerations such as file and installation dependencies, versioning, and alternative delivery methods. All in all, ClickOnce is a remarkably powerful tool that should make it a lot easier to take the Windows Forms route and enjoy all the benefits of the web development model.

▌APPENDIX A ▪
What's New in Windows Forms 2.0

T HIS BOOK HAS GROWN IN SIZE since the first edition, but it's not because two authors are now involved (at least, it's not *just* that two authors are now involved). Instead, it's due to the sheer mass of new functionality exposed by .NET, VS05, and—our favorite cross-section of both of those—Windows Forms 2.0. This appendix summarizes how Windows Forms 2.0 has evolved.

A Few Words About Windows Forms

When .NET 1.0 was released, way back in February 2002, the hype surrounding the technology was focused on its web-oriented capabilities. However, the inevitable trade-off of walking down the web path was to relinquish the simplified and rich development model provided by Windows Forms 1.0. The capabilities afforded by the new Windows Forms technology—which leveraged not only the benefits of managed code execution but also the rich library of functionality exposed by the .NET Framework—created a platform for developing more capable Windows Forms applications more quickly than anything that had come before. Even so, the inability to deploy Windows Forms applications with the same ease as web applications has always been a source of consternation for developers, who often need to take the web route to simplify their deployment lives.

With .NET 2.0, we find Windows Forms 2.0 richer still than Windows Forms 1.*x*. If you've already browsed this book, you'll agree that Windows Forms 2.0 is as far from Windows Forms 1.1 as Whidbey is from Everett.[1] If you haven't read the book, or if you

---

[1] The code names for .NET 1.1 (Everett) and .NET 2.0 (Whidbey) come from locations in the Washington state area of the United States of America. The name implies a location that's a certain distance from Redmond (where Microsoft is headquartered), with the proportions of the distance from each other being roughly analogous to the amount of new capability in each successive build.

simply enjoy statistics, here's a breakdown of changes to the System.Windows.Forms namespace, from a purely *public* implementation perspective:

- 329 new types
- 139 updated types
- 14,323 new members
- 104 new enumerations
- 8 updated enumerations
- 803 new values

This list is impressive, especially when you consider that all the supporting technologies relied on by Windows Forms have gone through as many improvements as Windows Forms itself. The most significant improvements across the board for Windows Forms developers include improved form handling and layout; updated drawing and printing; new and improved components, controls, and design-time integration; significantly simplified resources and settings management; application-focused features; more highly capable data binding; simplified multithreading; and last, but not least, web-quality application deployment.

Windows Forms 2.0 Enhancements

Although there are many more enhancements and additions in Windows Forms 2.0 than we can talk about, we have covered the most significant ones appropriately in this book. These are summarized in Table A.1.

Table A.1   Windows Forms 2.0 Enhancements

Feature	Improvements
Forms	Form class enhancements Richer control validation New form project wizards
Layout	SnapLines layout mode Margin and padding support on all controls and forms for automatic positioning Specialized layout controls for web-style flow and table layout, and splitting Automatic resizing of forms and controls Form and control autoscaling across screen dpi settings
Drawing	Native support for screen dumping TextRenderer for high-performance text drawing Enhanced automatic and manual double buffering Theme-based custom control drawing helpers

Table A.1   Continued

Printing	Improved printing support across the gamut of printing-specific events, event arguments, enumerations, dialogs, and general printing classes
Components and Controls	A host of new components and controls: • Office 2003-style draggable tool strip control suite (MenuStrip, ToolStrip, StatusStrip, and ContextMenuStrip) • MaskedTextBox control (masked text entry) • WebBrowser control (enables HTML browsing from Windows Forms applications) • SoundPlayer component (playing audio with asynchronous support) • Smart tag support on most controls and components for rapid configuration within VS05 • Improvements to almost all existing Windows Forms 1.¥ controls and components based on user feedback
Design-Time Integration	Several new design-time attributes Updated support for design-time component initialization Smart tag development capabilities for custom design-time components
Resources	Ability to either embed or link resources to an application Exposure of application resources via strongly typed wrapper classes Default projectwide resource support for Windows Forms projects Full right-to-left rendering support that can be internationalized
Applications	A variety of updates to System.Windows.Forms.Application Inclusion of native single-instance support
Settings	Complete overhaul of the settings system Exposure of settings via strongly typed wrapper classes Rich programmatic support for loading, updating, saving, rolling back, and migrating settings Safe settings persistence (for ClickOnce) VS05 and Windows Forms Designer enhancements Settings persistence to multiple data stores via settings providers
Data Binding	Unification of heterogeneous data sources via BindingSource Richer design-time configuration DataGridView control with greater binding and UI capabilities BindingNavigator for tool strip-style navigation of data sources Tighter integration with form validation

(Continued)

Table A.1   Continued

Multithreaded User Interfaces	Simplified multithreading via the BackgroundWorker component Improved support for asynchronous invocation of web services methods
ClickOnce Deployment	Automatic publishing, delivery, and installation Tight VS05 integration and configuration Trustworthy deployment Support for smart clients

Windows Forms 2.0: The Improvements

One of the key goals of Windows Forms 2.0 was to improve developer productivity. This goal manifests itself in the framework as a swath of tweaks and additions in your favorite programming languages, with enhancements like generics for C# and VS05 and an explosion of designer support. Additionally, there have been wholesale improvements to the key technology subsets, including settings, resources, data binding, and ClickOnce deployment. The following sections list some of the most significant.

Forms

As you would expect, System.Windows.Forms.Form—the heart and soul of Windows Forms development—has undergone a variety of enhancements as part of the Windows Forms evolution. In addition to a host of new properties, methods, and events for general form use, several sets of new members enable some of the more interesting advances, which we discuss next. Alternatively, you can dive straight into Chapter 2: Forms and Chapter 4: Layout for in-depth discussion of most of these.

Richer Control Validation

Windows Forms 1.*x* did provide a validation framework to support both control-by-control and formwide validation. However, it didn't provide a framework that allowed you to easily implement validation to let users freely navigate controls irrespective of the correctness of entered data. Instead, you had to write additional code both to avoid retaining focus on invalid controls and to make sure that all controls are validated when an OK button is clicked.

Windows Forms 2.0 improves the situation by allowing you to write the minimum validation code required for each control, and by letting you choose whether to retain focus on an invalid control. Additionally, formwide validation has been encapsulated in a way that allows you to validate either all the controls hosted by a form, or one of several subsets of those controls, including those that can be tabbed to, are selectable, or are visible. Chapter 3: Dialogs provides a complete discussion of Windows Forms 2.0 validation.

New Form Project Item Templates

VS05 offers two new form project item templates for Windows Forms 2.0. The first, covered in Chapter 2, allows you to create an MDI parent form implementation, complete with the basic UI elements and the functionality to make it all work. Although basic MDI parent forms are generally consistent enough to be supported by template generation, the uniqueness of an MDI application lies in the MDI child forms, which you need to build yourself. Luckily, the generated MDI parent form makes it easy to integrate the MDI child form.

The second template produces a stock standard, functional About box that you can use directly or easily tailor to your needs.

SnapLines Layout Mode

Although grid-style layout helps you position and size your controls on the UI, it enforces a rigid model. Grid-style layout is retained in Windows Forms 2.0, but a more useful and flexible layout style, SnapLines, is also included. SnapLines layout is more free-form, allowing you to drag your controls around a form and automatically snapping them into positions determined by horizontal or vertical alignment with other controls. The same thing applies when you resize your controls after they're hosted on a form. As explained in Chapter 4, SnapLines-style layout is powerful and simple, and it more easily supports your specific layout approach than does grid-style layout.

Margins and Padding

Just as SnapLines-style layout affords a more free-form and no less accurate layout experience than grid-style layout, the new Margin and Padding properties for forms and controls give you a free-form mechanism for specifying explicit margins between controls and between the form and other controls, as well as explicit padding within each control. Both properties are also used by SnapLines layout to snap controls to positions based on proximity to other controls, form edges, and contained text. See Chapter 4 for details.

Specialized Layout Controls

Sometimes, layout requirements are more complex than those you can easily or quickly establish using fundamentals like margins and padding. To aid you in several complex layout scenarios, Windows Forms 2.0 has introduced three new controls. SplitContainer basically evolves the Splitter control of Windows Forms 1.*x* fame into a full-fledged container control with a splitter bar and two adjacent panels to host child controls. More complex, web-style layout scenarios are enabled by the other two new controls: Flow-LayoutPanel and TableLayoutPanel. FlowLayoutPanel is a container control that collapses and expands child controls in similar fashion to HTML web pages. Similarly, Table-LayoutPanel supports web-style table layout, complete with margins, columns, and spanning, as well as fixed and proportional sizing. These layout tools are covered in Chapter 4 and Chapter 10: Controls.

Automatic Form Resizing

No matter how much layout support you have, you still need to expend a little effort in the Windows Forms Designer to adjust, fiddle, and tweak the form and hosted controls until they fit nicely together. Sometimes, this means expanding the form's client area to contain more, bigger, or taller controls. Sometimes, it means shrinking the form's client area when the reverse is true. All the time, you can configure a form to automatically grow and shrink in either situation and save yourself some effort, all thanks to the new AutoSize and Auto-SizeMode properties, which are explored in Chapter 4.

Drawing

Although drawing, in general, enjoys only modest enhancements, a few specific features are not only worth calling out but also getting to know, including support for screen dumping, high-performance text rendering, and enhanced double buffering.

Native Screen Dumping Support

When you explore Windows Forms 2.0 and .NET 2.0, you'll find a wide variety of new types and members that simplify your life by encapsulating functionality whose implementation required an inordinate amount of time in Windows Forms 1.*x* and .NET 1.*x*. The ability to provide screen captures is one example. It's enabled with a single method, it's a lot of fun, and it's covered in Chapter 5: Drawing Basics.

TextRenderer: GDI-Based Text Drawing

As in .NET 1.*x*, System.Drawing still provides a managed wrapper around the GDI+ API. GDI+ has all kinds of wonderful features (covered in Chapter 5: Drawing Basics, Chapter 6: Drawing Text, and Chapter 7: Advanced Drawing), but for the most accurate character set support for internationalization, and for output that looks just like the shell, you need the more seasoned GDI API. Although parts of the API haven't been wrapped, for text rendering, GDI is provided by the TextRenderer class in the System.Windows.Forms namespace. For more information about TextRenderer and the pros and cons of using it, see Chapter 6.

Enhanced Double Buffering

Double buffering is a technique by which you force one or more paint operations to take place in memory before blatting the results to the screen in one fell swoop. This technique has the advantage of producing markedly fewer flickers (ideally, none). Double buffering existed in Windows Forms 1.x, but you had to switch it on from code and it was somewhat more complicated than it needed to be. Now, double buffering can be triggered from a single form property, DoubleBuffered. Further, if you prefer more control of the way double buffering is used in your application, you can have it by using a suite of new types in the System.Drawing namespace. Double buffering is discussed in Chapter 7: Advanced Drawing.

Printing

A variety of tweaks across the existing System.Drawing.Printing namespace have enhanced printing support for Windows Forms applications. One example is the ability to determine whether users are printing to a printer, a file, or simply to a preview, all integrated with the existing print dialogs. Another example is the provision of more robust and more accurate output device measurements. Chapter 8: Printing explains this and many more improvements.

Components and Controls

Apart from a host of updates to the existing set of intrinsic Windows Forms components and controls, Windows Forms 2.0 includes several key new components and controls and additional Windows Forms Designer support for using them.

Office 2003-Style Tool Strip Controls

Arguably one of the most sought after features of any Windows Forms development platform is the ability to create UIs that look and feel like contemporary Microsoft applications such as Word, Excel, and Outlook. Central to this theme are the most common of all form adornments: menu strips, tool strips, status strips, and context menus. All these are exposed from Windows Forms 2.0 as a set of tool strip controls that provides the same appearance and functionality you expect from contemporary Microsoft applications such as Office 2003.

The tool strip suite is so important to Windows Forms that it's covered here in several chapters. Their frequent use on forms is covered in Chapter 2, along with MDI menu merging. When added to forms, tool strips are susceptible to being dragged around and resized, and Chapter 4 shows you how they capably cope with copious amounts of dynamic layout issues.

You can also dynamically update tool strip UIs using specialized customization enabled by theme-sensitive custom renderers, as discussed in Chapter 10. Tool strips can be dragged around the edges of a form, and that requires that they remember where they were and how big they were from one application session to the next. You can easily accomplish this using Windows Forms settings, as covered in Chapter 15: Settings. Finally, the tool strip suite is readily extensible, a case in point being BindingNavigator, which is discussed in Chapter 16: Data Binding Basics.

The DataGridView Control

Data presentation and manipulation are a major focus of Windows Forms applications. One of the most common ways to do this is to use a grid control. Although the DataGrid control from Windows Forms 1.*x* provided a solid, basic grid control implementation, it didn't go far enough to meet the demands of developers.

Microsoft responded to customer feedback and developed DataGridView, a wholly new grid control that offers a significantly more functional, configurable, and customizable grid experience than its predecessor. As you would expect, DataGridView is equally happy in bound and unbound scenarios, as well as offering virtualization. Unfortunately (or fortunately, depending on how you look at it), DataGridView is too powerful to be comprehensively covered in this book.[2] However, this book provides an overview in Chapter 10 and demonstrates its data binding capabilities in Chapter 16 and Chapter 17: Applied Data Binding.

The MaskedTextBox Control

Another long-sought-after control in Windows Forms provides masked text entry to display detailed information to users about what sort of data needs to be entered *before* they enter it. The new Windows Forms 2.0 MaskedTextBox control natively provides this support. An overview of MaskedTextBox is provided in Chapter 3.

The WebBrowser Control

As ironic as it sounds, there is a demand for displaying web pages from Windows Forms applications, particularly when it comes to rich content that's persisted as HTML. This was certainly possible with Windows Forms 1.*x*, but it required on interop with native Internet Explorer APIs. This technique is more complex than simply using a native .NET control, which Windows Forms 2.0 now includes. A brief exposé is provided in Appendix D: Component and Control Survey.

---

[2] Brian Noyes covers it nicely in *Data Binding with Windows Forms 2.0: Programming Smart Client Data Applications with .NET* (Addison-Wesley, 2006).

Smart Tag Design-Time Configuration

Components and controls have been configurable from a Properties window for a lot longer than .NET has been around. However, using the Properties window is not always the most efficient way to configure components and controls, particularly when you need to wade through tens or hundreds of properties to find the few you most often adjust. Rather than bring you to the mountain, Microsoft brings the mountain to you in the form of smart tags. The Windows Forms Designer uses smart tags to present the most common configurations for a control or component right next to it in the design surface, ultimately reducing the time you spend configuring.

Design-Time Integration

Design-Time integration may not be the most approachable of technologies, but it is certainly one you need to become familiar with to produce high-quality custom controls and components. Fortunately, the .NET and VS05 design-time infrastructure is nothing if not rich, and it is certainly richer with Windows Forms 2.0.

New Design-Time Attributes

Attributes provide the easiest path to influencing design-time integration of custom components and controls. There are several new attributes in Windows Forms 2.0, such as the DisplayName attribute, which allows you to change a property's text label in the Properties window from the raw property name. All new attributes are detailed in Chapter 11: Design-Time Integration: The Properties Window.

Granular Control of Form Initialization

Design-time components implement the popular ISupportInitialize interface for scenarios where the initialization of one or more properties is dependent on one more properties exposed by the same design-time component. However, sometimes one design-time component can't be initialized until another design-time component that it depends on has been initialized. ISupportInitialize doesn't cater to this situation, but the new ISupportInitializeNotification interface does, and it is described in Chapter 11.

Custom Smart Tag Support

Just as the intrinsic Windows Forms 2.0 components and controls employ smart tags to enhance the design-time configuration experience, your custom design-time components can leverage the same infrastructure to provide their own smart tag support. The infrastructure is rich enough that its coverage takes a chapter, Chapter 12: Design-Time Integration: Designers and Smart Tags. Smart tags are a must if you want to produce highly polished and usable custom design-time components.

Resources

Resource support in VS05, .NET, and Windows Forms 2.0 has undergone a host of improvements that ultimately make it easier for you to configure, manage, and code with resources. Take a look at Chapter 13: Resources for the good oil on resources.

Visual Resource Editor in Visual Studio 2005

Visual Studio .NET 200*x* and Windows Forms 1.*x* included an editor for managing resources, but it lacked luster, particularly because it was text-based, whereas many resources used by applications (images, icons, audio files, and text files) are visual and aural. Visual Studio 2005 and Windows Forms 2.0 provide a brand new, visual resource editor that simplifies the management of resources in a way that allows you to see or hear those resources as users will experience them at run-time.

Linked and Embedded Resources

Before Windows Forms 2.0, resources were managed by VS05. In the real world, applications may require resources that are not under the domain of either developers or VS05, and commercial-grade graphics applications are vastly superior to those that VS05 can provide. Graphical content is probably the most well known of these sorts of resources, and often it is produced, not by developers, but by a different group of people in a different location.

To facilitate this working arrangement, Windows Forms 2.0 allows you to link resources from VS05 at design time and embed them only at compile time. This loose coupling between resources and code allows graphics specialists to freely manipulate graphics during development independently of developers.

Strongly Typed Resources

.NET 1.*x* provided a variety of types to use in acquiring resources from code at run time, although using them required a nontrivial amount of code and they were type safe only insofar as they differentiated between string and object resources. Windows Forms 2.0 solves these problems by encapsulating both your application resources and the code to access them via a Designer-generated class that exposes each resource as a strongly typed property. Not only does this technique reduce the amount of the needed code to one line, but it also means that you can pick up resource coding errors at compile time, thanks to strong typing.

Full Right-to-Left Internationalization Support

Right-to-left support for Windows Forms 1.*x* applications was available, although not 100% consistent. However, with Windows Forms 2.0, creating right-to-left-oriented applications is not only 100% consistent but also integrated with internationalization support. That is really handy when half the world reads right-to-left. This feature is important when you want to make lots of money selling your application around the world.

Applications

There are many styles of Windows Forms applications, including single-document interface (SDI) and multiple-document interface (MDI). Variations of these, such as multi-SDI and single-MDI applications, rely on single instancing to enforce their unique models. Single instancing is possible for Windows Forms 1.*x* applications if you use a complex arrangement of code built on remoting. Windows Forms 2.0 applications can simply leverage the beauty of .NET and hijack new Visual Basic classes for single instancing. Chapter 14: Applications covers the gamut of scenarios that depend on single instancing.

Settings

The Windows Forms 1.*x* settings system has undergone an almost complete overhaul to produce a rich, Windows Forms Designer-integrated infrastructure for creating, managing, and deploying application, user, and roaming-user settings to one or more data stores. The settings system is discussed in its entirety in Chapter 15.

Visual Studio 2005 and Windows Forms Designer Enhancements

VS05 includes a Settings Editor that allows you to easily create, manage, and configure application, user, and roaming-user settings for all simple types and a wide variety of complex types. Additionally, you can bind control properties to settings via the Properties window, which has built-in support for doing so. Either way, you don't have to write code to create or load settings, and you need only a single line of code to save updated settings. The minimalist coding requirements and sweet designers alone are substantial improvements over the settings support found in Windows Forms 1.*x*. But wait, there's more.

Strongly Typed Settings

As with resources, accessing settings before Windows Forms 2.0 required extensive coding and a distinct lack of type safety. Also, Windows Forms 2.0 automatically encapsulates the mechanics of dealing with settings from a single Designer-generated wrapper class that exposes settings as strongly typed properties. Significant code reduction, readability, and maintainability are the benefits.

Rich Programmatic Support

The problem with settings is that they change; they can change not only from one installation to the next but also from one version to the next and even from one session to the next. These scenarios can work well only with support for loading, updating, saving, rolling back, and migrating settings. Fortunately, Windows Forms 2.0 and .NET 2.0 provide comprehensive programmatic support for all of them.

Safe Settings Persistence

In Windows Forms 1.*x*, an application that was fully trusted by the client machine it was executing on had complete access to all system resources, including memory, local hard drives, and the Registry. However, partially trusted applications might not have the same luxury. In particular, if an application needed to load and save application and user settings, you had to write special code to use isolated storage. Unfortunately, this turned out to be a lot of work. What's nice about Windows Forms 2.0 is that the settings system is equally safe and requires only one line of code to save any changed user settings. Even better, the same model is used for partial and full trust execution, making it compatible with Click-Once. This deployment technology is covered in Chapter 19: ClickOnce Deployment.

Settings Provider Model

By default, the settings system persists settings to the local file system. However, settings are often available from a variety of data stores, such as web services and the Registry. To give Windows Forms applications the freedom to choose where their settings will be persisted to, the settings system is built on the idea of settings providers. A settings provider is a special implementation that knows how to load and save settings located in a specific data store. They all implement the same interface to allow them to plug in to the settings system as required. The default is LocalFileSettingsProvider, although you can create your own, as described in the .NET Framework 2.0 SDK.

Data Binding

Data binding is about making it easier to build UIs that operate over data. In Windows Forms 2.0, data binding is more full featured because of the new BindingSource component. BindingSource's primary role is to act as a data-binding-savvy data source for types that aren't data binding savvy. This simple ability facilitates the creation of a single-client code model to operate over data sources independent of the type from which a data source is instantiated. Coupled with increased data binding integration into the Windows Forms code base, Windows Forms 2.0 data binding provides a big hook on which VS05 and the Windows Forms Designer hang the most extensive set of design-time features yet devised for creating and managing data-bound UIs.

Unification of Heterogeneous Data Sources

When you think "data source," you are likely to think of the most popular type: the typed data set. However, data sources come in many shapes and sizes, including relational, hierarchical, and object. All these could be bound to in Windows Forms 1.x, but each provided a different level of data binding integration. This had the effect of forcing developers to employ different coding models to suit, or potentially to spend a nontrivial amount of time building extra support for their data sources, such as implementing IBindingList, to achieve higher levels of data binding integration.

Windows Forms 2.0 addresses this problem with the BindingSource component, which is fundamentally capable of consuming any of these data sources and re-exposing them via a single, unified implementation to provide a consistent client coding model. Additionally, any data sources that have less than IBindingList levels of implementation are automatically "upgraded" to support IBindingList. This means that you can write a simple class as an item data source and use BindingSource to automatically convert it into a full list data source, with no extra code.

Richer Design-Time Configuration Support

If you like the idea of writing less code, then you'll love the addition of several new Windows Forms Designer features. The first of these is the Data Sources window, which allows you to either create or locate data sources to bind to. After the data source is acquired, you can drag it from the Data Sources window onto your form, and the Windows Forms Designer automatically creates either a details or a grid view style of UI for you. That is a major time-saver, especially when you consider that the Windows Forms Designer not only creates the controls and binds them as necessary, but also creates decent names for all controls involved. This works for any data source that can be consumed by the BindingSource component, so all your data sources can enjoy this feature.

Tool Strip-Style Data Source Navigation

The BindingSource component also incorporates currency management, thereby saving you the effort of finding, inspecting, and using one yourself, a common endeavor in Windows Forms 1.x to support data source navigation and editing. Although you could write code to leverage BindingSource's currency implementation, you would be better served by dropping a BindingNavigator onto a form and binding it to BindingSource. BindingNavigator has specific knowledge of BindingSource that allows it to automatically expose VCR-style navigation, along with various kinds of editing support. Further, the Windows Forms Designer automatically adds a BindingNavigator to a form when a data source is dropped onto it from the Data Sources window.

Tighter Integration with Form Validation

Windows Forms 1.*x* data binding provided a variety of hooks by which you could integrate with and influence the data binding process, but there were some areas that didn't, particularly those involved with validation of bound controls. When the value of a bound control was changed, data binding would automatically update the bound value in the data source, whether or not the data was valid. Additionally, any change was rolled back if the data could not be converted to the type of value on the data source. This made it difficult to support free-form UI data entry, which is the nominal user experience for Windows Forms applications.

Windows Forms 2.0 allows you to control exactly when the data source is updated after a bound control's value changes, including immediately, after it is successfully validated, or never. Thus, you can enjoy the freedom granted by Windows Forms 2.0's updated validation model and integrate nicely with data binding after a simple configuration.

Multithreaded User Interfaces

Long-running operations are common in Windows Forms applications, and they can cause your UIs to lock up if you don't use multithreading techniques to create additional worker threads. Achieving safe multithreading was a bother in Windows Forms 1.*x*. As is common with Windows Forms 2.0, you'll find multithreading greatly simplified. Chapter 18: Multithreaded User Interfaces has more details.

The BackgroundWorker Component

Previously, if you wanted to create a safe multithreading implementation to asynchronously spin off long-running operations onto worker threads, you had to make a serious coding investment that depended on an extensive knowledge of delegates and message passing. Now, BackgroundWorker encapsulates the communication complexities to provide a vastly simplified framework for spinning off worker threads, safely monitoring progress and completion, and easily incorporating cancellation.

Improved Support for Asynchronous Invocation of Web Service Methods

BackgroundWorker allows you to call web services asynchronously if you like, but the same underlying technology that BackgroundWorker depends on has been factored into the base class used to implement your web service client proxy classes. This lets you drop a web service component onto your form, allowing you to call them synchronously or asynchronously as you choose. And how do web services get into your Toolbox? They're added automatically whenever you create a new web reference.

ClickOnce Deployment

Web deployment for applications was available for Windows Forms 1.*x* developers via No-Touch Deployment (NTD), and it paved the way for a deployment experience that was fundamentally as easy as that for web applications. However, NTD fell far short in ease of use, configuration, and debugging (so much so that it's been disabled in Windows Forms 2.0 for Internet deployment). In Windows Forms 2.0, NTD has been replaced by the eminently more secure and configurable ClickOnce deployment. ClickOnce is a strategic technology that will support applications well into the future, although you can enjoy it right now by reading Chapter 19: ClickOnce Deployment.

Automatic Publishing, Delivery, and Installation

At the heart of ClickOnce is a simple deployment model that automatically takes care of publishing your Windows Forms application from VS05 to one of several publish locations, such as web sites or network file shares. Additionally, ClickOnce downloads and installs published applications (if permitted by the user). Users need only select the appropriate deployment manifest, a task that, for web sites, requires navigating to an appropriate web page (which ClickOnce generates for you) and clicking on the appropriate link.

Tight Visual Studio 2005 Integration and Configuration

An application's ClickOnce Deployment settings can be wholly configured from VS05. This support includes the ability to specify both installation prerequisites (such as .NET 2.0) and file dependencies, as well as to publish location and versioning requirements and specify alternative publishing and upgrade locations.

Trustworthy Deployment

Because deployment of Windows Forms applications with ClickOnce will occur most often from a web site, security needs to be involved. ClickOnce employs two key security models: Authenticode and code access security (CAS). Authenticode, a technology for trusting publishers, requires that a publisher's applications be digitally signed, with certificates issued by trusted certification authorities such as VeriSign. All ClickOnce-deployed Windows Forms applications must be digitally signed and, when requested by a user, display information about the publisher. This lets the user decide whether to actually download and install the application, and it provides recourse in the event that the code is dodgy. When downloaded and installed, an application executes within a CAS-managed security sandbox that allows only a predefined set of permissions, depending on the zone from which the application is deployed (the Internet, a local intranet, or the current machine). If the permissions required by an application exceed those provided by a particular zone, users are given the option to cancel the download or to grant the needed permissions.

◼ APPENDIX B
Moving from MFC

C HANCES ARE THAT if you're a C++ programmer with experience in Windows and an interest in client-side applications, you've been an MFC programmer. And whether or not you found that experience wholly pleasurable, you probably expect quite a few things from your client-tier application framework. This appendix briefly explains which of your expectations will be fulfilled (and then some), and which are going to cause you "issues."

A Few Words About MFC

In 1992, Microsoft released Microsoft Foundation Classes (MFC) 1.0 as part of the Programmer's Workbench. MFC was a set of approximately 60 classes targeted mainly at wrapping the windowing and drawing parts of the 16-bit Windows API. Its goal was to wrap the implicit and inconsistent object models inherent in the operating system with an explicit, consistent C++ object model, and it did as good a job as could be expected given the state of Microsoft's C++ compiler at the time.[1]

In 2002, Microsoft released MFC 7.0 as part of Visual Studio .NET 2002. MFC had grown to more than 200 classes, and, along the way, its goal had expanded: to provide a complete C++ object model replacement of the Win32 API. As of version 7.0, MFC grew to be the most feature-rich way to build commercial-quality client-tier applications in Windows.[2] Here's a list of the major features that MFC programmers have grown to rely on:

* Support for dialog-based, SDI, multi-SDI, and MDI applications
* Document-View Architecture

---

[1] At the time, Microsoft's C++ compiler was far behind the pack in the implementation of things such as templates, exceptions, and runtime type identification (RTTI). This tardiness caused ripples in the design of MFC, and in the Windows C++ programmer community, that can be felt to this day.

[2] It also grew on the server side, but MFC has always been firmly grounded on the client.

- Printing, print setup, and print preview
- Floating tool strips, status strips, and dialog bars
- Context-sensitive help
- Object Linking and Embedding (both client and server)
- OLE Automation
- COM control hosting
- Active Document servers
- Full integration into VS05, including four of the most comprehensive wizards that the IDE provides
- Dynamic Data Exchange and Validation
- Command routing
- Command UI updating
- Windows logo compliance
- Shell integration (icons, drag and drop, DDE, and command line parsing)
- Wrappers for a large percentage of the Win32 API, including windowing, drawing, databases, sockets, Registry access, the file system, threading, and more
- Auto-upgrade from 16 bits to 32 bits[3]
- Tons of third-party and community support

If you've read the rest of this book, you'll notice that MFC provides some features that I didn't discuss. If you're starting with this appendix as an MFC programmer wondering what Windows Forms does and doesn't offer, you may be disappointed to discover that I haven't covered all the features in this list (although I have covered a number of them). Either way, the hard, cold truth is that MFC provides more features than Windows Forms does for building stand-alone, document-based applications.

For example, if you want to build a text editor, you can do that in MFC by running a wizard, choosing the right options, and writing only a few lines of code. By running the wizard, you get an application to start with that includes a status strip, a tool strip (floating), all the File, Edit, and Help menu items implemented (including a most-recently-used-file list, printing, and context-sensitive help), all in a fully logo-compliant SDI, multi-SDI, or MDI application, based on your whim that day. As a document-based application framework, MFC has no peer.

However, in recent years, the world seems to have moved away from document-based applications. Relatively few folks seem interested in building text editors or word processors or spreadsheets. Instead, the bulk of the applications are either completely

---

[3] This isn't important now, but man oh man, it was a big deal when we were all busy porting our 16-bit applications to 32 bits.

HTML-based or are n-tier client applications talking to network, database, or Web services back ends. It's for this use that .NET as a whole and Windows Forms specifically have been tailored.

That's not to say that Windows Forms can't be used to build darn nice document-based applications. In fact, because Windows Forms is only a small piece of the huge number of public classes provided in .NET, if what you're looking for isn't in Windows Forms, it's probably found elsewhere in .NET. For example, Windows Forms itself (the System.Windows.Forms namespace) doesn't provide any custom drawing support at all. Instead, GDI+ (in the System.Drawing namespace) supplies that functionality.

And this is the chief difference between MFC and Windows Forms. MFC was meant as a replacement for the underlying Win32 API, but that didn't stop the Win32 API from growing. In fact, as much as MFC has grown over the years, the functionality of the underlying OS has increased at least tenfold. Windows Forms, on the other hand, is meant to be a replacement only for the windowing part of Win32. It's the rest of the .NET Framework classes that are meant to replace the rest of Win32. Of course, .NET will never replace the entire Win32 API, but because much more functionality has been added to Windows Forms 2.0 and .NET Framework 2.0, it's clear that placing your eggs in the .NET basket is a wise investment, particularly as we move toward the next-generation Windows Presentation Framework.

MFC Versus Windows Forms

Some folks do need to build document-based applications, and even though Windows Forms isn't designed to support that as well as MFC is, it's not very hard to build complete document-based applications if you're armed with the knowledge of what Windows Forms does and doesn't provide as compared with MFC. Table B.1 shows a feature-based summary focused on building document-based applications.

Table B.1   MFC Versus Windows Forms and .NET

Feature	MFC	Windows Forms and .NET
Application Wizards	Four MFC wizards	Two Windows Forms project templates
IDE Integration	Yes	Yes
Dialog, SDI, MDI Applications	Yes	Yes
Multiple-SDI Applications	Yes	Yes
UI Layout	Yes (dialogs only)	Yes

(Continued)

Table B.1 Continued

Docking and Splitting	Yes (simple)	Yes
Anchoring	No	Yes
Tool Strips and the Like	Yes	Yes
Printing, Preview, Setup	Yes	Yes
OLE, Active Documents	Yes	Yes (via the WebBrowser control)
COM Control Hosting	Yes	Yes
Automation	Yes	Yes (remoting)
F1 Help	Yes	Yes
DDX, DDV	Yes	Yes (DDX not needed)
Win32 Wrappers	Yes	Yes
Data Binding	Yes (very simple)	Yes
Cross-Language	No	Yes
Cross-Platform	No	Yes
Cross-Bitness	16, 32	32, 64
Web Deployment	No	Yes
Third-Party Support	Yes	Yes
Document-View	Yes	No
Document Management	Yes	Yes (via components in this book)
Shell Integration	Yes	Yes (via components in this book)
Command Unification	Yes	No
UI Updating	Yes	No
Command Routing	Yes	No
Source Code	Yes	No
Managed Environment	No	Yes

The Differences

The features shared by MFC and Windows Forms/.NET are often implemented differently in the two worlds, so the following is a short discussion of each of the features.

Application Wizards

VS05 provides MFC wizards to build applications, DLLs, COM controls, and Internet Server API (ISAPI) extensions. VS05 provides Windows Forms wizards to build applications and controls for each of the four languages that are supported (C#, VB.NET, C++, and J#). VS05 also gives you wizards (called "project templates") for producing class library and ASP.NET server-side applications and libraries. Although this book is littered with discussions of the Windows Forms project templates, Chapter 1: Hello, Windows Forms, Chapter 10: Controls, and Chapter 14: Applications are good places to start.

IDE Integration

VS05 provides direct IDE integration for developing MFC and Windows Forms applications and controls. The Windows Forms integration is more extensive, mainly because of the strong UI layout environment and data binding, which are discussed throughout this book.

Dialog, SDI, and MDI Applications

Both MFC and Windows Forms provide complete support for dialog-based, SDI, and MDI applications. However, although MFC comes with a wizard that provides a great deal of functionality to help you get started when you're building SDI and MDI applications, most of the Windows Forms wizards produce empty *forms,* which can serve as dialogs or MFC-style view windows depending on how they're used. This means that, in most cases, you must add the standard UI and all the features every time you need an SDI application in Windows Forms, although you can use the MDI Parent Form project item template to get a head start on MDI applications, as discussed in Chapter 2: Forms. Most of the body of this book is about how to develop applications that include the kinds of features you'd expect to find in an MFC application, including document management features (see Appendix F: Document Management, with the specifics of MDI applications covered in Chapter 2 and Chapter 14).

Multiple-SDI Applications

Multiple-SDI applications—applications that have a single instance but multiple top-level windows—are fully supported in MFC. Although Windows Forms doesn't come with a complete out-of-the-box solution to support multiple-SDI applications, Chapter 14 fully explains how to leverage some .NET Framework elements to build them.

UI Layout

Drag-and-drop design and layout of user interfaces are supported in MFC only for dialogs. Normal views must be laid out in code. Windows Forms, on the other hand, treats all windows in a unified manner, so the same drag-and-drop designer works for any kind of window. Which kind of window it is—modal or modeless, dialog or view—depends on how it's used, not on how it's designed.

Something else that's a bit different in Windows Forms is that the UI design environment reads and writes code instead of keeping control type and position information in a separate resource file. That code is relegated to a single method, but it is definitely mixed in with the rest of the code of the window (although divided between different files). For MFC dialogs in .NET 2.0, that is very different from the way MFC dialogs are built. Each scheme has its pros and cons, but MFC programmers will notice the difference right away (and then may let it make them unhappy before letting it grow on them).

The Windows Forms Designer is discussed throughout the book.

Docking and Splitting

Windows Forms lets you dock controls to the edges of a window as well as designate a control to take up the window's remaining space. You can dock controls within split containers so that as a splitter is moved, it resizes the appropriate controls. All this is available in the design environment so that you can see what the docking and splitting will look like at design time.

MFC, on the other hand, does docking and splitting in code only. The dialog editor doesn't support this feature. Also, splitting in MFC requires separate window classes, whereas in Windows Forms all the docked and split controls are easily accessible from within the single container. Docking and splitting are discussed in Chapter 4: Layout.

Anchoring

When a window is resized in MFC, any controls that need to change size with the size of the containing window must be resized by hand in the WM_SIZE message handler. In contrast, Windows Forms anchoring (combined with docking) allows a control to be resized automatically as the container resizes. Anchoring is discussed in Chapter 4.

Tool Strips and the Like

MFC excels in providing not only industrial-strength window adornments (such as tool strips, status strips, and dialog bars) for building full-featured applications, but also great IDE integration for editing them and a wizard to place initial versions for you. The same is true for Windows Forms with the use of its tool strip control suite, although these controls support dragging but not floating. However, the MFC tool strips are looking a little dated when compared with those found in modern applications, whereas the Windows Forms tool strips just got a major boost into the present with this release.

Printing, Preview, and Setup

Both MFC and Windows Forms provide similar complete support for printing, print preview, print settings, and page settings.

OLE and Active Documents

Object Linking and Embedding is a technology for exposing and consuming data and the UI from one application into another. MFC provides complete support for this technology. Windows Forms supports only enough OLE to host COM controls.

Active Documents, another COM-based technology, is rather like a cross between OLE and controls, but it has never really gained any traction. MFC supports it directly, but Windows Forms does not. However, you can host the WebBrowser control and use it as an Active Document host by navigating to a file from an application (such as Microsoft Word) that provides Active Document support.

COM Control Hosting

Both MFC and Windows Forms provide complete support for hosting COM controls, and both do it using wrappers that provide an API appropriate to their respective environments. Unfortunately, neither gives you seamless integration. See Chapter 10 for a discussion of the way Windows Forms hosts COM controls.

Automation

Both MFC and Windows Forms provide complete support for both consuming and producing COM objects for use in application automation. In addition, .NET gives you another way to access objects between processes. Called .NET remoting, this technology can be used as a means of application automation.

F1 Help

Both MFC and Windows Forms support integrating help into an application, although only MFC provides a wizard to get you started. The Windows Forms support for integrated help is discussed in Chapter 3: Dialogs.

DDX and DDV

Because MFC was developed before Microsoft's C++ compiler supported exceptions, MFC has a two-stage construction model for windows. This means that the C++ object comes into existence before the underlying OS object or any of the contained child controls. Because of this, MFC dialogs need to move data back and forth between member variables to allow clients to provide initial child control data before the child control is created, and to make the final child control data available after the child controls have been destroyed. The mechanism to make this happen is called Dynamic Data Exchange (DDX). Similarly, validating the data as it moves is called Dynamic Data Validation (DDV). Whereas DDX is necessary because of the design of the library, DDV is always necessary.

The Windows Forms data exchange model is different. Each Windows object is created as an object and is shown when necessary without forcing the developer to be concerned about whether the underlying OS handle has been created. This means that child control properties can always be accessed directly at any time during their lifetime. In other words, the DDX is handled transparently by the controls themselves, eliminating the need for developers to think about in it Windows Forms.

Data validation is still necessary, of course, and is fully supported in Windows Forms as discussed in Chapter 3.

Win32 Wrappers

Because both MFC and .NET are meant as replacements for the underlying Win32 API, it makes sense that both of them have a large number of wrapper classes to hide that API. And although .NET has MFC beat by about an order of magnitude in terms of APIs wrapped, MFC has the edge in that it's much easier to access unwrapped Win32 APIs in native C++ than it is in managed code.

Data Binding

MFC has only token support for data binding. The Windows Forms data binding support takes its cue from Visual Basic 6 and provides extensive data binding support and data provider integration with the IDE. Chapter 16: Data Binding Basics and Chapter 17: Applied Data Binding provide an introduction to this huge topic.

Cross-Language

MFC is a class library for C++ programmers only. Windows Forms (and the rest of .NET) is available to Microsoft-provided languages such as Managed C++, Jscript.NET, Visual Basic, and J#, as well as dozens of third-party languages (although only Managed C++, J#, C#, and Visual Basic .NET have Windows Forms Designer support).

Cross-Platform

MFC is supported across all versions of Windows and is supported across some UNIX variants by third parties. Windows Forms is supported under the desktop versions of Windows starting with Windows 98, and the latest version of Windows CE (although VS05 is required for Windows CE support).

Cross-Bitness

MFC was originally built to support 16-bit Windows and, because of the degree of isolation from the underlying OS, made porting to 32 bits largely a recompile in many cases. Windows Forms supports both 32 and 64 bits with no recompile necessary.

Web Deployment

MFC applications must be installed or copied to a machine before they can be run (with the exception of executing an application from a network share). Windows Forms applications support this mode of deployment, of course, but they also support ClickOnce deployment, which allows a Windows Forms application to be launched via an URL, downloaded automatically, and executed without an explicit copy or install, in a trustworthy fashion. This model, covered in depth in Chapter 19: ClickOnce Deployment, combines the richness of Windows applications with the deployment of Web applications.

Third-Party Support

MFC programmers have years worth of books, articles, sample code, FAQs, archives, third-party tools, and general community knowledge at their disposal, although this support has dropped dramatically since the initial release of the .NET Framework. Windows Forms has at least as much support in the community as MFC ever had, if not more.

Document-View

MFC 2.0 introduced Document-View, a simplified version of Model-View-Controller that separates a document's data from the view of that data. This model so permeates MFC that it wasn't until later versions of the IDE that the wizards supported generating non-Document-View code. The central idea of Document-View is a good one, but the MFC specifics of document management, such as serialization and dirty bit management, made it difficult for nondocument-based applications to fit the model.

Windows Forms went the other way. Instead of imposing an application framework model on all applications, Windows Forms provides only a windowing framework. However, the central idea of separating the data from the view is still a good one and needs no real support beyond what's provided by the .NET runtime itself.

Document Management

Beyond the idea of separating data from view, the major productivity enhancement of Document-View was the document management piece, including dirty bit management, file dialog management, most-recently-used-file lists, change notification, and so on. Those enhancements are sorely missed in .NET when it comes to building document-based applications. Luckily, building that support is not very hard, and, indeed, an appendix in this book is dedicated to this topic: Appendix F: Document Management.

Shell Integration

Another part of the document-based piece provided by MFC is the automatic registration of file extensions with the shell and the handling of file open request operations from the shell. Windows Forms provides direct support for neither of these operations, but both are discussed in Appendix F.

Command Unification

MFC unifies interaction for multiple kinds of controls to commands that can be handled singly. For example, to the user, choosing File | Open from a menu is the same as clicking on the Open File tool strip button. These activities are unified at the class and IDE level, letting the developer easily handle all ways of invoking the same command in a single spot. Windows Forms provides no such facility at the class or designer level. Only manual coding can reduce the duplication (although, to be fair, it's only a couple of lines of code).

UI Updating

Another benefit of command unification in MFC is the ability to enable or disable a command as needed without the explicit need to disable a menu item or a tool strip button separately. Windows Forms requires that UI elements be enabled or disabled explicitly.

Command Routing

MFC supports routing commands to any interested subscriber. .NET supports this same idea with delegates, as described in Appendix C: Delegates and Events.

Source Code

MFC provides full source code that can be read and stepped through in the debugger. The .NET Framework source code is not provided and cannot be stepped through in the debugger. Reading the source code for the .NET Framework requires a disassembler tool.[4]

---

[4] Easily the most robust and most popular .NET disassembler is Lutz Roeder's most excellent Reflector tool, which some people actually prefer to the source. See http://www.aisto.com/roeder/dotnet/ to download Reflector (http://tinysells.com/32).

Managed Environment

MFC is a *native* environment in the sense that memory and security must be handled by the developer explicitly. The .NET runtime provides automatic handling of both memory and security, making .NET a *managed* environment. A managed environment can sometimes cause a degradation in performance (although it's surprising how rare that is), but it always results in a more robust application, especially given how hard it is to track down and deal with memory and security problems. My experience is that even given a lack of some application framework features, I'm much more productive in .NET than I ever was in C++ or MFC.

Strategy

If you're moving from MFC as a programmer, this book will help you understand the new Windows Forms model, especially as focused by the discussion so far in this appendix. The basics are similar, so a typical MFC programmer won't have much difficulty picking up Windows Forms. However, Windows Forms is only a piece. I recommend spending some time with the C# language itself as well as the rest of the .NET Framework to fill in what you'll need outside Windows Forms.

If you're moving MFC code to .NET, you need some careful planning. Here are some considerations:

- If you can afford to start over from scratch, that will yield the most maintainable code base, but it will take the longest.
- If the bulk of your MFC code is in COM controls (or can be moved to COM controls), then you can use Windows Forms as a host for those controls and write new code in .NET.
- Alternatively, you can go the other way and host Windows Forms controls, user controls, and forms in your MFC applications, something that may be useful when you want to leverage the MFC libraries to hold together a UI constructed in Windows Forms.[5]
- If you need to bring the MFC application itself forward, you can flip the Use Managed Extensions bit on your MFC project and gain the ability to host Windows Forms controls from your MFC 7.1 code. This also lets you write new code in .NET.
- If the new code you'd like to integrate into your existing MFC code is not a control, you can use COM to interoperate with the .NET code while still keeping your MFC code unmanaged.

---

[5] Hosting Windows Forms controls, user controls, and forms in MFC applications is discussed in http://msdn2.microsoft.com/library/ahdd1h97(en-us,vs.80).aspx (http://tinysells.com/33) and later in this chapter.

Which options apply to you depend on your specific circumstances, but in general, I recommend a strategy that lets you write the bulk of your new code in .NET, even if it means building some of the features for Windows Forms that you're missing from MFC.

MFC and Windows Forms Interop

If you're going to mix your MFC and Windows Forms code, there are two things you'll most likely want to do: host MFC COM controls in Windows Forms, and host your Windows Forms controls in MFC.

Hosting MFC COM Controls in Windows Forms

The first step to hosting a COM control in your Windows Forms application is to get a COM control onto the Toolbox. You do this by right-clicking on the Toolbox, selecting Choose Items, clicking on the COM Components tab, clicking on the check box next to your COM control's name, and clicking the OK button. Figure B.1 shows a sample MFC COM control being added in this way.

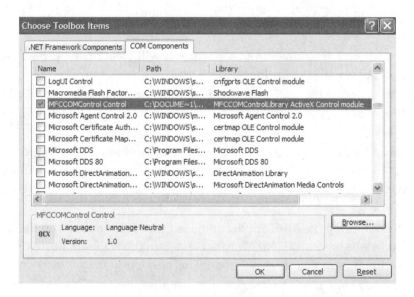

Figure B.1   Adding a COM Control to the Windows Forms Toolbox

After the control is added to the Toolbox, you can drop it onto your forms or user controls at will, as shown in Figure B.2.

Figure B.2   Hosting a COM Control on a Form

When dropped, you can set the control's properties and handle events using the Properties window, as shown in Figures B.3 and B.4.

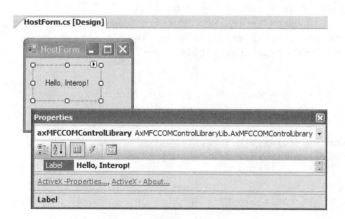

Figure B.3   Setting a COM Control Property in the Properties Window

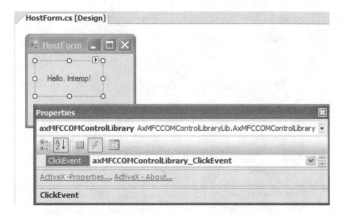

Figure B.4   Handling a COM Control Property in the Properties Window

The generated code works almost as you'd expect:

```
partial class HostForm {
  ...
  void InitializeComponent() {
    ...
    // axMFCCOMControlLibrary
    this.axMFCCOMControlLibrary.OcxState =
      ((System.Windows.Forms.AxHost.State)
        (resources.GetObject("axMFCCOMControlLibrary.OcxState")));
    this.axMFCCOMControlLibrary.ClickEvent +=
      this.axMFCCOMControlLibrary_ClickEvent;
    ...
    }

    #endregion

    AxMFCCOMControlLibraryLib.AxMFCCOMControlLibrary
      axMFCCOMControlLibrary;
    }
  ...
  void axMFCCOMControlLibrary_ClickEvent(object sender, EventArgs e) {
    ...
    }
  }
```

Notice that the Click event handler is established using normal .NET means, whereas the setting for the custom Label property is nowhere to be found. That's because COM controls prefer to be initialized in a big chunk via a COM *property bag,* which is a set of name/value pairs that the Properties window tucks into the form's .resx resource file (discussed in Chapter 13: Resources). The controls are then set via the OcxState property. If you want to get or set properties or call methods on a COM control programmatically, you should feel free to do so:

```
partial class HostForm : Form {
  ...
  void axMFCCOMControlLibrary_ClickEvent(object sender, EventArgs e) {
    // Set a COM property
    this.axMFCCOMControlLibrary.Label = "Ain't interop grand?";

    // Call a COM method
    this.axMFCCOMControlLibrary.AboutBox();
  }
}
```

The interop between Windows Forms and COM controls isn't perfect, but it should be good enough for you to leverage your existing investment in MFC controls without having to rewrite your working MFC control code.

Hosting Windows Forms Controls in MFC

If you'd like to avoid porting your MFC application code but extend it by hosting Windows Forms code, you can do that, too. The built-in support for hosting a Windows Forms control in an MFC 8 application relies first and foremost on the MFC application being compiled as a managed application—that is, an application managed by the Microsoft Common Language Runtime (CLR).

Because MFC has been around as a native application development platform that has direct access to the Win32 API, you might think that turning your MFC application into a managed one would be a big deal. Au contraire, mon frère. The C++ compiler writers at Microsoft have worked long and hard to make sure that you can flip the managed application switch on your MFC applications and compile them without change.[6] To build your MFC application as managed, giving you access to all the .NET types including your Windows Forms controls, open your MFC project's properties and set Configuration Properties | General | Project Defaults | Common Language Runtime support to "Common Language Runtime Support (/clr)," as shown in Figure B.5.

---

[6] Of course, that doesn't always happen, but it's amazing how often it does happen.

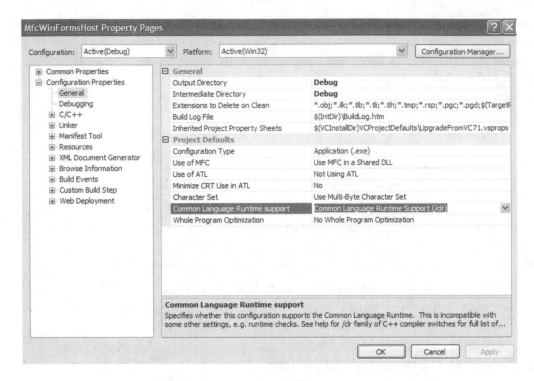

Figure B.5 Compiling Your Native MFC Project as a Managed .NET Project

At this point, compiling and executing your MFC application as managed should look and feel exactly the same. To host a Windows Forms control, you create a wrapper around it that MFC can talk to using COM control interfaces. For this, you need the CWindowsFormsControl MFC class, which is defined in the afxwinforms.h header file. This file is usually included at the bottom of your stdafx.h file:

```
// stdafx.h : include file for standard system include files,
// or project-specific include files that are used frequently
// but are changed infrequently
...
#include <afxwinforms.h>
```

With this header included, you can create an instance of the class in your MFC dialog class:

```
class CMfcWindowsFormsHostDlg : public CDialog {
...
private:
  // A wrapper for a Windows Forms control
  CWindowsFormsControl<System::Windows::Forms::MonthCalendar>
    m_wndWindowsFormsCalendar;
};
```

The CWindowsFormsControl template class is parameterized with the type of the Windows Forms control so that MFC can create the control at dialog initialization time. In this example, I'm using the built-in Windows Forms MonthCalendar control, but if you'd like to bring in your own custom Windows Forms controls, you can do so by right-clicking on your project in Solution Explorer, choosing References, and adding your assembly, as shown in Figure B.6.

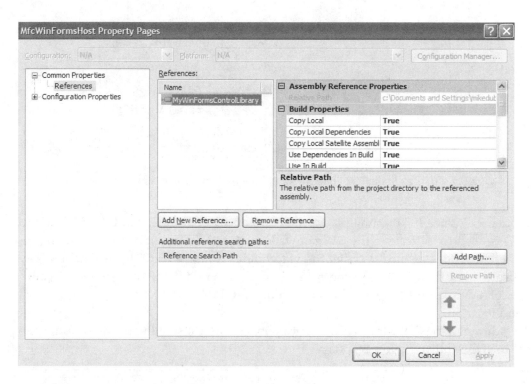

Figure B.6   Adding a Custom Windows Forms Assembly to an MFC Project

After you've created the wrapper type using the CWindowsFormsControl template class, you need a place to put your control after it's created. The CWindowsFormsControl class is designed to take the ID of an existing control on your dialog resource and use the size and location for its own size and location. This isn't anything like the designability that you've come to know and love from Windows Forms, but if you put a dummy placeholder control on your dialog, you can replace it at run time with your Windows Forms control. The easiest control to use for your placeholder is the Static Text control, as shown in Figure B.7.

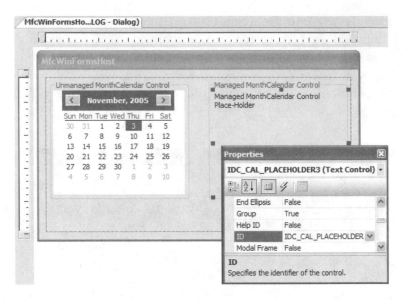

Figure B.7   Using a Static Text Control as a Placeholder for a Windows Forms Control

Notice in Figure B.7 that the placeholder has an ID of IDC_CAL_PLACEHOLDER. This ID is used to indicate to the CWindowsFormsControl at run time where the placeholder control goes. Notice also that the placeholder contains text. This is a handy way to indicate what that Static Text control is doing in the middle of your dialog. Because the placeholder control will be hidden at run time, it doesn't matter what's in it, only its size and location.

To indicate to the CWindowsFormsControl object where it should go requires only one line in the DoDataExchange method:

```
void CMfcWindowsFormsHostDlg::DoDataExchange(CDataExchange* pDX) {
    CDialog::DoDataExchange(pDX);
    DDX_ManagedControl(pDX, IDC_CAL_PLACEHOLDER, m_wndWindows FormsCalendar);
}
```

However, if you happen to be hosting the Windows Forms control in a groupbox or some other kind of container, as I do in Figure B.7, it's possible that your Windows Forms control will be obscured by the control that's supposed to be hosting it, even if the Static Text control shows itself in front of the hosting control at design time. To avoid this, I like to stick a BringWindowsToTop call in OnInitDialog:

```
BOOL CMfcWindowsFormsHostDlg::OnInitDialog() {
    CDialog::OnInitDialog();
    ...
```

```
// Make sure your control is showing
m_wndWindows FormsCalendar.BringWindowToTop();

return TRUE;  // return TRUE unless you set the focus to a control
}
```

Figure B.8 shows a dialog that hosts the unmanaged and managed MonthCalendar controls side by side on the same MFC dialog.

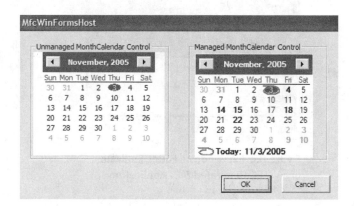

Figure B.8   Hosting a Windows Forms Control on an MFC Dialog

In addition to merely hosting a Windows Forms control in your MFC dialogs, you'll want to call methods, set properties, and handle events. You may also want to host your Windows Forms controls in a view instead of a dialog or even show a Windows Forms form, modally or modelessly. All these things are possible, and they're described very nicely in the VS05 product documentation.[7]

Windows Forms as a Better MFC

One of the big features provided by MFC is the ability to automatically generate basic application frameworks out of the box, including both SDI and MDI applications. However, Windows Forms 2.0 has evolved well beyond Windows Forms 1.x to provide more of the fundamental elements you need to match the default MFC-generated output from a functional point of view. Additionally, several components covered in this book make it that much easier.

---

[7] "Using a Windows Form User Control in MFC," http://msdn2.microsoft.com/en-us/library/ahdd1h97(en-us,vs.80).aspx (http://tinysells.com/34).

To compare Windows Forms with MFC, I set out to create a Windows Forms equivalent of a vanilla MFC wizard-generated MDI text editor application, using what was available in .NET, Windows Forms, and this book. The result is shown in Figure B.9.

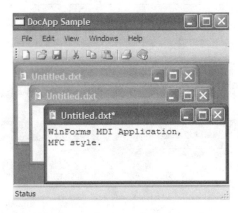

Figure B.9   A Windows Forms Equivalent of an MFC-Generated MDI Application

To create this application, I drew on the following pieces provided by Windows Forms, .NET, and this book:

- VS05 to create a new Windows Forms project
- MDI parent form (generated by VS05)
- A blank form as the basis for the MDI child form (generated by VS05)
- About box (generated by VS05)
- FileDocument component (from Appendix F)
- MRUMenuManager component (from Appendix F)
- Tool strip, menu strip, and text box controls (from .NET)
- DragAndDropFileComponent component (from Appendix F)
- WindowsFormsApplicationBase for single instancing (from .NET)
- Help compiler and System.Windows.Forms.Help (from vendor and .NET)
- Application and user settings system (from .NET)
- NTCOPYRES and a C++ .DLL project to generate and incorporate additional document icon resources into the application (from Chapter 13)
- PrintDialog, PrintPreviewDialog, PageSetupDialog, PrintDocument, and PageCountPrintController (from both .NET and Chapter 8: Printing)

To pull these pieces together, I had to provide additional configurations and custom code:

- Writing code to integrate form navigation
- Configuring user settings to remember MDI parent form size and location from one application session to the next
- Removing document-specific tool strip and menu strip controls from the generated MDI parent form and adding them to the MDI child form
- Configuring menu and tool strip merging for MDI
- Writing code to operate all printing components and to print a basic text document
- Configuring FileDocument, MRUMenuManager, and DragAndDropFile Component
- Creating and integrating help
- Configuring C++ resource project, including importing appropriate icon resources and writing two lines of script in the post-build event of the DocApp sample to inject additional icon resources into the DocApp executable from the C++ resource DLL using NTCOPYRES
- Writing code to support single-MDI application requirements (from Chapter 14: Applications)

Overall, I wrote just over 200 lines of code and 2 lines of post-build event script, to make it all work. Although MFC wins on the no-code front, if you start with the samples provided with this book, you should be off and running when starting your SDI or MDI document-based Windows Forms applications.

Also, when I was finished with the Windows Forms version of my MFC-like application, I gained access to several orders of magnitude more functionality in the .NET Framework Class Libraries than was ever provided in MFC.

APPENDIX C
Delegates and Events

T HE FOLLOWING STORY is adapted from a story on sellsbrothers.com as a more thorough, although less reverent, explanation of delegates and events than appears elsewhere in the book. The characters in this story are fictional and any similarity to real persons or events is unintentional.

Delegates

Once upon a time, in a strange land south of here, there was a worker named Peter. He was a diligent worker who would readily accept requests from his boss. However, his boss was a mean, untrusting man who insisted on steady progress reports. Because Peter did not want his boss standing in his office looking over his shoulder, Peter promised to notify his boss whenever his work progressed. Peter implemented this promise by periodically calling his boss back via a typed reference like so:

```
class Worker {
  Boss boss;

  public void Advise(Boss boss) {
    this.boss = boss;
  }

  public void DoWork() {
    Console.WriteLine("Worker: work started");
    if( this.boss != null ) this.boss.WorkStarted();

    Console.WriteLine("Worker: work progressing");
    if( this.boss != null ) this.boss.WorkProgressing();

    Console.WriteLine("Worker: work completed");
    if( this.boss != null ) {
```

```
      int grade = this.boss.WorkCompleted();
      Console.WriteLine("Worker grade= {0}", grade);
    }
  }
}

class Boss {
  public void WorkStarted() {
    // Boss doesn't care
  }
  public void WorkProgressing() {
    // Boss doesn't care
  }
  public int WorkCompleted() {
    Console.WriteLine("It's about time!");
    return 2; // out of 10
  }
}

class Universe {
  static void Main() {
    Worker peter = new Worker();
    Boss boss = new Boss();
    peter.Advise(boss);
    peter.DoWork();

    Console.WriteLine("Main: worker completed work");
    Console.ReadLine();
  }
}
```

Interfaces

Now Peter was a special person. Not only was he able to put up with his mean-spirited boss, but he also had a deep connection with the universe around him. So much so that he felt that the universe was interested in his progress. Unfortunately, there was no way for Peter to advise the universe of his progress unless he added a special Advise method and special callbacks just for the universe, in addition to keeping his boss informed. What Peter really wanted to do was to separate the list of potential notifications from the implementation of those notification methods. And so he decided to split the methods into an interface:

```
interface IWorkerEvents {
  void WorkStarted();
  void WorkProgressing();
  int WorkCompleted();
}

class Worker {
  IWorkerEvents events;

  public void Advise(IWorkerEvents events) {
    this.events = events;
  }

  public void DoWork() {
    Console.WriteLine("Worker: work started");
    if( this.events != null ) this.events.WorkStarted();

    Console.WriteLine("Worker: work progressing");
    if( this.events != null ) this.events.WorkProgressing();

    Console.WriteLine("Worker: work completed");
    if( this.events!= null ) {
      int grade = this.events.WorkCompleted();
      Console.WriteLine("Worker grade= {0}", grade);
    }
  }
}

class Boss : IWorkerEvents {
  public void WorkStarted() {
    // Boss doesn't care
  }
  public void WorkProgressing() {
    // Boss doesn't care
  }
  public int WorkCompleted() {
    Console.WriteLine("It's about time!");
    return 3; // out of 10
  }
}
```

Delegates

Unfortunately, Peter was so busy talking his boss into implementing this interface that he didn't get around to notifying the universe, but he knew he would soon. At least, he'd abstract the reference of his boss far away from him so that others who implemented the IWorkerEvents interface could be notified of his work progress.

Still, his boss complained bitterly. "Peter!" his boss fumed. "Why are you bothering to notify me when you start your work or when your work is progressing?!? I don't care about those events. Not only do you force me to implement those methods, but you're wasting valuable work time waiting for me to return from the event, which is further expanded when I am far away! Can't you figure out a way to stop bothering me?"

And so, Peter decided that while interfaces were useful for many things, when it came to events, their granularity was not fine enough. He wished to be able to notify interested parties only of the events that matched their hearts' desires. So, he decided to break the methods out of the interface into separate delegate functions, each of which acted as a tiny interface of one method:

```
delegate void WorkStarted();
delegate void WorkProgressing();
delegate int WorkCompleted();

class Worker {
  public WorkStarted Started;
  public WorkProgressing Progressing;
  public WorkCompleted Completed;

  public void DoWork() {
    Console.WriteLine("Worker: work started");
    if( this.Started != null ) this.Started();

    Console.WriteLine("Worker: work progressing");
    if( this.Progressing != null ) this.Progressing();

    Console.WriteLine("Worker: work completed");
    if( this.Completed != null ) {
      int grade = this.Completed();
      Console.WriteLine("Worker grade= {0}", grade);
    }
  }
}

class Boss {
  public int WorkCompleted() {
    Console.WriteLine("It's about time!");
    return 4; // out of 10
  }
}

class Universe {
  static void Main() {
    Worker peter = new Worker();
    Boss boss = new Boss();
```

```
        // NOTE: We've replaced the Advise method with the assignment operation
        peter.Completed = new WorkCompleted(boss.WorkCompleted);
        peter.DoWork();

        Console.WriteLine("Main: worker completed work");
        Console.ReadLine();
    }
}
```

And, because Peter was under so much pressure, he decided to take advantage of the shorthand notation for assigning delegates provided by C# 2.0:

```
class Universe {
    static void Main() {
        ...
        peter.Completed = boss.WorkCompleted;
        ...
    }
}
```

Static Listeners

Delegates accomplished the goal of not bothering Peter's boss with events that he didn't want, but still Peter had not managed to get the universe on his list of listeners. Because the universe is an all-encompassing entity, it didn't seem right to hook delegates to instance members (imagine how many resources multiple instances of the universe would need . . .). Instead, Peter needed to hook delegates to static members, which delegates supported fully:

```
class Universe {
    static void WorkerStartedWork() {
        Console.WriteLine("Universe notices worker starting work");
    }

    static int WorkerCompletedWork() {
        Console.WriteLine("Universe pleased with worker's work");
        return 7;
    }

    static void Main() {
        Worker peter = new Worker();
        Boss boss = new Boss();

        peter.Completed = boss.WorkCompleted;
        peter.Started = Universe.WorkerStartedWork;
```

```
    peter.Completed = Universe.WorkerCompletedWork; // Oops!
    peter.DoWork();

    Console.WriteLine("Main: worker completed work");
    Console.ReadLine();
  }
}
```

Events

Unfortunately, the universe, being very busy and unaccustomed to paying attention to individuals, had managed to replace Peter's boss's delegate with its own. This was an unintended side effect of making the delegate fields public in Peter's Worker class. Likewise, if Peter's boss got impatient, he could decide to fire Peter's delegates himself (which was just the kind of rude thing that Peter's boss was apt to do):

```
// Peter's boss taking matters into his own hands
if( peter.Completed != null ) peter.Completed();
```

Peter wanted to make sure that neither of these things could happen. He realized that he needed to add registration and unregistration functions for each delegate so that listeners could add or remove themselves but couldn't clear the entire list or fire Peter's events. Instead of implementing these functions himself, Peter used the event keyword to make the C# compiler build these methods for him:

```
class Worker {
  public event WorkStarted Started;
  public event WorkProgressing Progressing;
  public event WorkCompleted Completed;
  ...
}
```

Peter knew that the event keyword erected a property around a delegate, allowing only clients to add or remove themselves (using the += and −= operators in C#), forcing his boss and the universe to play nicely:

```
class Universe {
  ...
  static void Main() {
    Worker peter = new Worker();
    Boss boss = new Boss();
```

```
        peter.Completed = boss.WorkCompleted; // ERR!
        peter.Completed += boss.WorkCompleted; // OK
        peter.Started += Universe.WorkerStartedWork; // OK
        peter.Completed += Universe.WorkerCompletedWork; // OK

        peter.DoWork();

        Console.WriteLine("Main: worker completed work");
        Console.ReadLine();
    }
}
```

Harvesting All Results

At this point, Peter breathed a sigh of relief. He had managed to satisfy the requirements of all his listeners without having to be closely coupled with the specific implementations. But then he noticed that even though both his boss and the universe provided grades of his work, he was receiving only one of the grades. In the face of multiple listeners, he really wanted to harvest all of their results. So, he reached into his delegate and pulled out the list of listeners so to call each of them manually:

```
class Worker {
  ...
  public void DoWork() {
    ...
    Console.WriteLine("Worker: work completed");

    if( this.Completed != null ) {
      foreach( WorkCompleted wc in this.Completed.GetInvocationList() ) {
        int grade = wc();
        Console.WriteLine("Worker grade= {0}", grade);
      }
    }
  }
}
```

Asynchronous Notification: Fire and Forget

In the meantime, his boss and the universe had been distracted by other things, and this meant that the time it took them to grade Peter's work was greatly expanded:

```
class Boss {
  public int WorkCompleted() {
    System.Threading.Thread.Sleep(5000);
```

```
      Console.WriteLine("Better...");
      return 4; // out of 10
    }
  }

class Universe {
    ...
  static int WorkerCompletedWork() {
    System.Threading.Thread.Sleep(1000000);
    Console.WriteLine("Universe pleased with worker's work");
    return 7;
  }
    ...
  }
```

Unfortunately, since Peter was notifying each listener one at a time, waiting for each to grade him, these notifications now took up quite a bit of his time when he should have been working. So, he decided to forget the grade and just fire the event asynchronously:

```
class Worker {
    ...
  public void DoWork() {
    ...
    Console.WriteLine("Worker: work completed");
    if( this.Completed != null ) {
      foreach( WorkCompleted wc in this.Completed.GetInvocationList() ) {
        wc.BeginInvoke(null, null); // EndInvoke call required by .NET
      }
    }
  }
}
```

Asynchronous Notification: Polling

The call to BeginInvoke allowed Peter to notify the listeners while letting Peter get back to work immediately, letting the process thread pool invoke the delegate. Over time, however, Peter found that he missed the feedback on his work. He knew that he did a good job and appreciated the praise of the universe as a whole (if not his boss specifically). Plus, he was afraid that he was leaking .NET resources acquired by calling BeginInvoke without calling the corresponding EndInvoke method. So, he fired the event asynchronously but polled periodically, looking for the grade to be available:

```
class Worker {
  ...
  public void DoWork() {
    ...
    Console.WriteLine("Worker: work completed");
    if( this.Completed != null ) {
      foreach( WorkCompleted wc in this.Completed.GetInvocationList() ) {
        IAsyncResult result = wc.BeginInvoke(null, null);
        while( !result.IsCompleted ) System.Threading.Thread.Sleep(1);
        int grade = wc.EndInvoke(result);
        Console.WriteLine("Worker grade= {0}", grade);
      }
    }
  }
}
```

Asynchronous Notification: Delegates

Unfortunately, Peter was back to what he wanted his boss to avoid with him in the beginning: looking over the shoulder of the entity doing the work. So, Peter decided to employ his own delegate as a means of notification when the asynchronous work has completed, allowing him to get back to work immediately but still be notified when his work had been graded:

```
class Worker {
  ...
  public void DoWork() {
    ...
    Console.WriteLine("Worker: work completed");
    if( this.Completed != null ) {
      foreach( WorkCompleted wc in this.Completed.GetInvocationList() ) {
        wc.BeginInvoke(this.WorkGraded, wc);
      }
    }
  }

  void WorkGraded(IAsyncResult result) {
    WorkCompleted wc = (WorkCompleted)result.AsyncState;
    int grade = wc.EndInvoke(result);
    Console.WriteLine("Worker grade= {0}" + grade);
  }
}
```

Anonymous Delegates

At this point, Peter was using delegates to notify interested parties in the process of his work and using delegates to get notified when grades were available on the work he had completed. The delegates provided by his boss and the universe were provided by separate entities, so it made sense that they were encapsulated in methods on those entities. However, in the case of the WorkGraded method, there was really no good reason for this to be a separate method except the syntactic requirements of C# 1.0. As of C# 2.0, Peter could drop the code required to handle the processing of his work grade into an *anonymous delegate:*

```
class Worker {
  ...
  public void DoWork() {
    ...
    Console.WriteLine("Worker: work completed");
    if( this.Completed != null ) {
      foreach( WorkCompleted wc in this.Completed.GetInvocationList() ) {
        wc.BeginInvoke(delegate(IAsyncResult result) {
          WorkCompleted wc2 = (WorkCompleted)result.AsyncState;
          int grade = wc2.EndInvoke(result);
          Console.WriteLine("Worker grade= {0}", grade);
        },
        wc);
      }
    }
  }
}
```

Here, instead of passing in the name of a method to call when his work had been graded, he was passing in the body of the method itself as designated with a different use of the delegate keyword to create a method with no name (and therefore "anonymous"). The body of the method was fundamentally the same in that Peter still passed the Work-Completed delegate as a parameter to BeginInvoke and then pulled it out of AsyncState for use in extracting the result. However, Peter knew that one of the benefits of anonymous delegates was that he could make use of the variables in the surrounding context from within the anonymous delegate body, and so he rewrote his code thusly:

```
class Worker {
  ...
  public void DoWork() {
    ...
    Console.WriteLine("Worker: work completed");
    if( this.Completed != null ) {
      foreach( WorkCompleted wc in this.Completed.GetInvocationList() ) {
```

```
    wc.BeginInvoke(delegate(IAsyncResult result) {
      // Use wc variable from surrounding context (ERR!)
      int grade = wc.EndInvoke(result);
      Console.WriteLine("Worker grade= {0}", grade);
    },
    null);
  }
 }
 }
}
```

This code compiled just fine, but when it was run, it caused the following exception to be thrown:

```
System.InvalidOperationException:
  The IAsyncResult object provided does not match this delegate.
```

The problem was that although the wc variable was allowed to be used in the anonymous delegate, it was still being used by the for-each statement. As soon as the asynchronous invocation began, the wc variable changed, and the delegate used to start things (wc) no longer matched the async result passed as an argument to the anonymous delegate. Peter slapped his forehead and created a hybrid solution:

```
class Worker {
  ...
  public void DoWork() {
    ...
    Console.WriteLine("Worker: work completed");
    if( this.Completed != null ) {
      foreach( WorkCompleted wc in this.Completed.GetInvocationList() ) {
        // Create an unchanging variable referencing the current delegate
        WorkCompleted wc2 = wc;
        wc.BeginInvoke(delegate(IAsyncResult result) {
          // Use wc2 variable from surrounding context
          int grade = wc2.EndInvoke(result);
          Console.WriteLine("Worker grade= {0}", grade);
        },
        null);
      }
    }
  }
}
```

Happiness in the Universe

Peter, his boss, and the universe were finally satisfied. Peter's boss and the universe were allowed to be notified of the events that interested them, reducing the burden of implementation and the cost of unnecessary round-trips. Peter could notify each of them, ignoring how long it took them to return from their target methods, while still getting his results asynchronously and handling them using anonymous delegates, resulting in the following complete solution:

```
delegate void WorkStarted();
delegate void WorkProgressing();
delegate int WorkCompleted();

class Worker {
  public event WorkStarted Started;
  public event WorkProgressing Progressing;
  public event WorkCompleted Completed;

  public void DoWork() {
    Console.WriteLine("Worker: work started");
    if( this.Started != null )
      this.Started();

    Console.WriteLine("Worker: work progressing");
    if( this.Progressing != null )
      this.Progressing();

    Console.WriteLine("Worker: work completed");
    if( this.Completed != null ) {
      foreach( WorkCompleted wc in this.Completed.GetInvocationList() ) {
        WorkCompleted wc2 = wc;
        wc.BeginInvoke(delegate(IAsyncResult result) {
          int grade = wc2.EndInvoke(result);
          Console.WriteLine("Worker grade= {0}", grade);
        },
        null);
      }
    }
  }
}

class Boss {
  public int WorkCompleted() {
    System.Threading.Thread.Sleep(3000);
    Console.WriteLine("Better...");
    return 5; // out of 10
  }
}
```

```
class Universe {
  static void WorkerStartedWork() {
    Console.WriteLine("Universe notices worker starting work");
  }

  static int WorkerCompletedWork() {
    System.Threading.Thread.Sleep(4000);
    Console.WriteLine("Universe pleased with worker's work");
    return 7;
  }

  static void Main() {
    Worker peter = new Worker();
    Boss boss = new Boss();
    peter.Completed += boss.WorkCompleted;
    peter.Started += Universe.WorkerStartedWork;
    peter.Completed += Universe.WorkerCompletedWork;
    peter.DoWork();

    Console.WriteLine("Main: worker completed work");
  }
}
```

Peter knew that getting results asynchronously came with issues, because as soon as he fired events asynchronously, the target methods were likely to be executed on another thread, as was Peter's notification of when the target method had completed. However, Peter was familiar with Chapter 18: Multithreaded User Interfaces, so he understood how to manage such issues when building Windows Forms applications.

And so they all lived happily ever after.

The end.

■ APPENDIX D
Component and Control Survey

H ERE, WE LIST ALL COMPONENTS AND CONTROLS that appear on the Toolbox by default, in alphabetic order.[1] Some components and controls are discussed in detail throughout the book, and, where they are, a reference to the appropriate chapter is provided. The remaining components and controls are given brief coverage in this appendix.

Components

What follows is a brief survey of the standard Windows Forms 2.0 components, listed in alphabetical order.

BackgroundWorker

See Chapter 18: Multithreaded User Interfaces.

new

BindingNavigator

See Chapter 16: Data Binding Basics and Chapter 17: Applied Data Binding.

new

BindingSource

See Chapter 16 and Chapter 17.

new

ColorDialog

See Chapter 3: Dialogs.

---

[1] Except for those that are outside the core Windows Forms experience: ReportViewer, DirectoryEntry, DirectorySearcher, EventLog, FileSystemWatcher, MessageQueue, PerformanceCounter, Process, SerialPort, and ServiceController.

ErrorProvider

See Chapter 3.

FolderBrowserDialog

See Chapter 3.

FontDialog

See Chapter 3.

HelpProvider

See Chapter 3.

ImageList

Controls like TreeView and ListView contain tree nodes and list-view items whose images come from an ImageList component. ImageList manages a collection of images of the same size, color depth, and transparency color (as determined by the Size, ColorDepth, and TransparencyColor properties). The images themselves are stored in the Images collection and can contain any number of Image objects. You can edit the Images collection directly using the Images Collection Editor, as shown in Figure D.1.

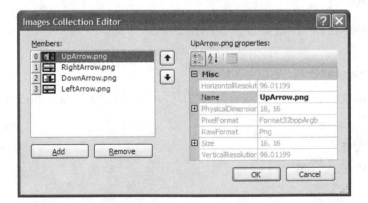

Figure D.1　　Images Collection Editor

To use ImageList after the images have been populated in the editor, you pull them by index from the Images collection property:

```
int imageIndex = -1;

void timer_Tick(object sender, EventArgs e) {
  ++this.imageIndex;
  if( this.imageIndex == 4 ) this.imageIndex = 0;
  this.BackgroundImage = this.imageList.Images[this.imageIndex];
}
```

What's nice about this code is that all the related images come from a single place. However, the ImageList component has some limitations:

- You can't edit an image after it's been added; you must remove the old image and add the edited image.
- The image can have only a fixed size of up to 256 pixels in either dimension.
- The Images Collection Editor is difficult to use for images larger than 16 pixels in either direction, because it shows images only as 16 ¥ 16 pixels and squeezes larger images to fit.
- You must set ColorDepth and Transparency before adding images for them to be applied.
- Images are available only as type Image and not directly as type Icon, so if you need the Icon type you must convert it from Image.

NotifyIcon

See Chapter 2: Forms.

OpenFileDialog

See Chapter 3.

PageSetupDialog

See Chapter 8: Printing.

PrintDialog

See Chapter 8.

PrintDocument

See Chapter 8.

PrintPreviewDialog

See Chapter 8.

SaveFileDialog

See Chapter 3.

SoundPlayer

SoundPlayer is an enigma: Located in System.Media, SoundPlayer is a class that cannot be added to the Toolbox and, consequently, can't be dropped onto a form in VS05 at design time. However, it is a very useful class that happens to make it easy to play sound files:[2]

```
using System.Media;
...
void soundPlayerButton_Click(object sender, EventArgs e) {
  SoundPlayer soundPlayer =
    new SoundPlayer(@"C:\WINDOWS\Media\tada.wav");
  soundPlayer.Load();
  soundPlayer.Play();
}
```

SoundPlayer also provides support for loading sound files from streams and URLs both synchronously and asynchronously, and for looping playback. Additionally, System.Media offers shortcuts for playing common system sounds using the SystemSounds class:

```
System.Media.SystemSounds.Exclamation.Play();
```

System sounds include Asterisk, Beep, Exclamation, Hand, and Question.

Timer

See Chapter 18.

Tool Tip

See Chapter 3.

Controls

What follows is a brief survey of the standard Windows Forms 2.0 controls, listed in alphabetical order.

---

[2] Be aware, though, that SoundPlayer is geared to play only .wav files encoded with pulse-code modulation (PCM).

Button

Buttons, such as the one in Figure D.2, are used to trigger actions on forms.

Figure D.2   A Button Control in Action

When a button is pressed, the Click event is triggered:

```
void button1_Click(object sender, System.EventArgs e) {
   MessageBox.Show("Ouch!");
}
```

In addition, buttons can be designated as a form's *AcceptButton* or *CancelButton*. These designations specify that the button is automatically clicked when the user presses the Enter key (AcceptButton) or the Esc key (CancelButton).

CheckBox

CheckBox objects, shown in Figure D.3, are most often used to indicate the answer to a yes/no question.

Figure D.3   A CheckBox Control in Action

Check boxes normally have two states: checked or unchecked. Testing the state of the check box is as simple as retrieving the value of the Checked property:

```
if( this.checkBox.Checked ) MessageBox.Show("Check box checked!");
```

Check boxes also support a mode in which they have three states: checked, unchecked, and indeterminate. You enable this mode by setting the ThreeState Boolean property to true, which causes CheckBox to start in an indeterminate state and, as a user clicks it, toggle between the checked, unchecked, and indeterminate states.

CheckedListBox

A CheckedListBox, shown in Figure D.4, is an extension of the ListBox that allows users to choose multiple items in the list by checking boxes.

Figure D.4   A CheckedListBox Control in Action

You can detect when an item is either checked or unchecked by handling the ItemCheck event:

```
void checkedListBox_ItemCheck(object sender, ItemCheckEventArgs e) {
  MessageBox.Show("Item checked: " + e.CurrentValue.ToString());
}
```

When multiple list item selection is common, checking one or more check boxes is easier, and more intuitive, to the user than Ctrl+Shift+left-clicking. In all other ways, the checked list box is identical to the standard list box.

ComboBox

The ComboBox control, shown in Figure D.5, is a hybrid of a list box and a text box.

Figure D.5   A ComboBox Control in Action

The text box part of the control allows users to enter data directly into the control. When the user clicks on the down button, a list of items is shown that users can pick from. Like a TextBox, a ComboBox can be configured to allow free-form entry of information or to allow users to select only items that are in the list of items within the control. Because the control is part TextBox and part ListBox, it's not surprising that it can do a little of both. As with text-oriented controls, the most common task is usually retrieving the text:

```
MessageBox.Show(this.comboBox.Text);
```

As with the list box, you can handle the event when the selected index changes:

```
void comboBox_SelectedIndexChanged(object sender, EventArgs e) {
  MessageBox.Show(
    "Selected Item: " + this.comboBox.SelectedItem.ToString());
}
```

ContextMenuStrip

See Chapter 2 and Chapter 4: Layout.

DataGridView

See Chapter 16 and Chapter 17.

DateTimePicker

The purpose of the DateTimePicker control, shown in Figure D.6, is to display a user-editable date or time or both.

Figure D.6   A DateTimePicker Control in Action

To help control the dates and times that are displayed, the control allows users to specify a minimum and maximum date and time. To specify whether to show either the date or the time portion of the current date/time, you can choose a format for the text in the control:

```
this.dateTimePicker.Format = DateTimePickerFormat.Short;
```

Short and Long specify different date formats, and Time specifies a time format. Usually, if you are using the control for times, you will want to enable the up and down buttons by specifying true for ShowUpDown, as shown in Figure D.7.

Figure D.7   A DateTimePicker with ShowUpDown Enabled

To retrieve the date or time from the control, you get the Value of the control:

```
MessageBox.Show(this.dateTimePicker.Value.ToShortDateString());
```

DomainUpDown

The DomainUpDown control, shown in Figure D.8, allows users to select from an item in a list and use arrow buttons to navigate between the items.

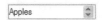

Figure D.8   A DomainUpDown Control in Action

Retrieving data from the control is identical to retrieving data from a TextBox:

```
MessageBox.Show(this.domainUpDown.Text);
```

FlowLayoutPanel

See Chapter 4.

GroupBox

Chapter 4.

HScrollBar

The HScrollBar control, shown in Figure D.9, is a horizontal scroll bar.

Figure D.9   An HScrollBar Control in Action

Most controls that use a scroll bar do so automatically, but you can use this control manually to specify a scroll bar for subtle uses such as specifying a range of large values. You can specify the minimum and maximum range using the Minimum and Maximum properties:

```
this.hScrollBar.Minimum = 0;
this.hScrollBar.Maximum = 10;
```

The ValueChanged event communicates when the value has changed, and the Value property exposes the current scroll value:

```
void hScrollBar_ValueChanged(object sender, EventArgs e) {
   MessageBox.Show("HScroll value: " + this.hScrollBar.Value.ToString());
}
```

Label

The Label control holds literal text that is meant to be informative to the user. For example, in a typical application, labels are displayed near other controls to guide users in their use, as shown in Figure D.10.

Figure D.10   A Label Control in Action

Although Labels can display images, they always display whatever string value is stored in their Text property. Labels automatically size to fit their contents by default, but you can prevent this by setting the AutoSize property to false. When you do, text inside a label wraps to the width of the label. You can align the text to any side or corner of the Label control, or its center, by using the TextAlign property:

```
this.label.AutoSize = false;
this.label.Text = "This is information for the user...";
this.label.TextAlign = ContentAlignment.TopCenter;
```

LinkLabel

LinkLabel objects, shown in Figure D.11, are just like labels but allow for one or more hyperlinks to be embedded in the displayed text.

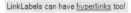

Figure D.11   A LinkLabel Control in Action

These links are clickable elements that trigger events, typically to allow users to navigate to help and support web sites from Windows Forms applications. You can add text to the link label in the same way as any other label. To specify a portion of the text value to be a link, you use the LinkArea property:

```
// Will automatically parse common URLs
this.linkLabel.Text = "Take me to Microsoft.";
this.linkLabel.LinkArea = new LinkArea(11, 9);
```

The link area is displayed as a hyperlink that, when clicked, fires the LinkLabel's Clicked event:

```
void linkLabel_Click(object sender, EventArgs e) {
   System.Diagnostics.Process.Start("http://www.microsoft.com");
}
```

You can add two or more links to the LinkLabel, where each link is a portion of the text in the Text property. To do so, you add Link items to the LinkLabel's Links collection:

```
// Will automatically parse common URLs
this.linkLabel.Text = "Take me to Microsoft or MSDN Online.";
this.linkLabel.Links.Add(
  new LinkLabel.Link(11, 9, "http://www.microsoft.com"));
this.linkLabel.Links.Add(
  new LinkLabel.Link(24, 11, "http://msdn.microsoft.com"));
```

To work out which link was clicked, you handle LinkClicked, which passes a Link-LabelLinkClickedEventArgs that contains the text value stored in the Link object:

```
void linkLabel_LinkClicked(
    object sender, LinkLabelLinkClickedEventArgs e) {
    // Start IE with the URL
    System.Diagnostics.Process.Start((string)e.Link.LinkData);
}
```

ListBox

ListBox, shown in Figure D.12, holds multiple text items that can be selected by a user.

Figure D.12   A ListBox Control in Action

The items in a ListBox are contained within a collection exposed by the Items property. A ListBox supports selection of one or more items in the list by the traditional Ctrl+clicking of items. You can find out the selected item by using the SelectedItem property:

```
MessageBox.Show(
   "Selected Item: " + this.listBox.SelectedItem.ToString());
```

In addition, you can handle the SelectedIndexChanged event whenever the selection changes:

```
void listBox_SelectedIndexChanged(object sender, EventArgs e) {
  MessageBox.Show(
    "Selected Item: " + this.listBox.SelectedItem.ToString());
}
```

To specify how many list items can be selected, you use the SelectionMode property, which can be any of the SelectionMode enumeration values:

```
namespace System.Windows.Forms {
  enum SelectionMode {
    None = 0, // No items can be selected
    One = 1, // One item can be selected at a time (default)
    MultiSimple = 2, // One or more items can be selected at a time
    MultiExtended = 3, // One or more items can be selected at a time,
                       // with the additional use of the Shift, Ctrl,
                       // and arrow keys
  }
}
```

ListView

The ListView control, shown in Figure D.13, is similar to the list box in that it shows multiple items that can be selected either individually or as multiple selections.

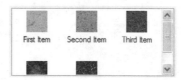

Figure D.13   A ListView Control in Action

The chief difference is that the ListView supports views much like Windows Explorer's view of files, including a large icon view, a small icon view, a list view, a details view, or a tiled view. The following code shows how to re-create Figure D.13.

```
// Show ListView in Large Icons mode
this.listView.View = View.LargeIcon;

// Associate with ImageList
this.listView.LargeImageList = this.listViewImageList;
```

```
// Add new list-view items to ListView
this.listView.Items.AddRange(
  new System.Windows.Forms.ListViewItem[] {
    new ListViewItem("First Item", 0),
    new ListViewItem("Second Item", 1),
    new ListViewItem("Third Item", 2),
    new ListViewItem("Fourth Item", 3),
    new ListViewItem("Fifth Item", 4)
  }
);
```

In this code, you can see that you associate images to list-view items using an ImageList, just as the TreeView does. You do this by setting either the LargeImageList or the Small-ImageList property, the former being used for large icon and tiled views, and the latter being used for small icon view.

If you choose details view, you need to create at least one column, using code like the following:

```
// Show ListView in Details mode
this.listView.View = View.Details;

// Create column
this.listView.Columns.Add("First Column");
...
```

This code yields Figure D.14.

Figure D.14   A ListView Control in Details View

As with the ListBox, you can trap the change in the selected index:

```
void listView_SelectedIndexChanged(object sender, EventArgs e) {
  // Show the first of the selected items
  MessageBox.Show(
  "Selected Item: " + this.listView.SelectedItems[0].ToString());
}
```

 MaskedTextBox

See Chapter 3.

MenuStrip

See Chapter 2 and Chapter 4.

MonthCalendar

The MonthCalendar control, shown in Figure D.15, is used to show or select specific dates.

Figure D.15   A MonthCalendar Control in Action

You can retrieve the selected date this way:

```
// Get all the Dates chosen
// SelectionStart is beginning Date
// SelectionEnd is last date
// SelectionRange will return all the dates
MessageBox.Show(
  string.Format("Date(s): {0} - {1}",
  this.monthCalendar.SelectionStart.ToShortDateString(),
  this.monthCalendar.SelectionEnd.ToShortDateString()));
```

You can change the look and feel of the calendar to blend in with your application's UI. In addition, you can show multiple months simultaneously by specifying the Calendar-Dimensions of the control. You can also add boldface to an array of specific dates or yearly dates on the calendar. The user can select multiple dates or a range of dates, although the maximum number of days selected is limited by the MaxSelectionCount property.

NumericUpDown

Functionally, the NumericUpDown control is much like the DomainUpDown control, but the intention of this control is to allow the user to specify a numeric value, as shown in Figure D.16.

Figure D.16   A NumericUpDown Control in Action

The control shown in Figure D.16 supports a minimum value, a maximum value, and the unit by which a clicked up or down button will increment or decrement the value. Unlike the other controls we've discussed that expose Minimum, Maximum, and Value properties as integers, NumericUpDown exposes them as decimals for fine-grained numeric incrementing:

```
this.numericUpDown.Maximum = 1.00;
this.numericUpDown.Minimum = 2.00;
this.numericUpDown.Increment = 0.5;
```

You can select the numeric value of the control using the Value property:

```
MessageBox.Show(this.numericUpDown.Value.ToString());
```

Panel

See Chapter 4.

PictureBox

The PictureBox control's only function is to display images to the user, as shown in Figure D.17.

Figure D.17   A PictureBox Control in Action

PictureBox supports most bitmap formats (.bmp, .jpg, .gif, and so on) and some vector formats (.emf and .wmf). You can set PictureBox's image via the Image property:

```
this.pictureBox.Image = new Bitmap(@"c:\windows\zapotec.bmp");
```

PrintPreviewControl

See Chapter 8.

ProgressBar

The ProgressBar control, shown in Figure D.18, is often used to provide visual feedback on the progress of a long-running operation.

Figure D.18   A ProgressBar Control in Action

A ProgressBar's progress is measured by its current value, as specified by the Value property. Value ranges between the Minimum and Maximum property values—usually 1 and 100, respectively—to display progress as a percentage of completion:

```
// Set the progress bar minimum, maximum, and current values
this.progressBar.Minimum = 1;
this.progressBar.Maximum = 100;
this.progressBar.Value = 60;
```

You create the appearance of progress by incrementing the Value property, starting at Minimum and finishing when Maximum is reached. To do this, you increment the Value property directly or call the Increment method:

```
// Increment progress bar
this.progressBar.Value += 1000000; // No range protection
this.progressBar.Increment(1000000); // Range protection
```

If you increment Value directly, you need to write additional code to make sure that Value does not extend beyond the range specified by the Minimum and Maximum properties; otherwise, an exception is generated. Alternatively, you can call Increment and feel secure in the knowledge that Value will be capped to the Maximum or Minimum property values if the increment value takes it beyond the range of either.

RadioButton

RadioButton controls, shown in Figure D.19, are similar to CheckBoxes in that they have checked and unchecked states, but RadioButton controls are typically used in a series to indicate a choice of one of a range of mutually exclusive values.

Figure D.19   RadioButton Controls in Action

When more than one radio button is placed in a container (a form or one of the container controls listed later), the radio buttons allow only one button at a time to be selected. You can test radio buttons in the same way you check CheckBoxes:

```
if( this.option1RadioButton.Checked ) MessageBox.Show("Option 1");
```

RichTextBox

Extending on the TextBox control, RichTextBox, shown in Figure D.20, is used for both editing and formatting text.

This is a rich text box. This format was
created by Microsoft
(http://www.microsoft.com).

Figure D.20　A RichTextBox Control in Action

Specifically, the control lets you set ranges of text with various fonts, colors, and sizes. You can save the document in the rich text edit control using the SaveFile method:

```
// Save the file
richTextBox.SaveFile("myRTFFile.rtf", RichTextBoxStreamType.RichText);
```

SplitContainer

See Chapter 4.

StatusStrip

See Chapter 2 and Chapter 4.

TabControl

See Chapter 4.

TableLayoutPanel

See Chapter 4.

TextBox

TextBox controls, shown in Figure D.21, are used to display user-editable text.

This is a text box.

Figure D.21　A TextBox Control in Action

The text box allows for both single- and multiple-line text editing and display. The most common thing you'll do with a text box is retrieve the text within it:

```
MessageBox.Show(this.textBox.Text);
```

ToolStrip

See Chapter 2 and Chapter 4.

ToolStripContainer

See Chapter 4.

TrackBar

The TrackBar, shown in Figure D.22, allows the user to specify a numeric value with a maximum and a minimum value.

Figure D.22   A TrackBar Control in Action

You specify the range using the Minimum and Maximum properties:

```
this.trackBar.Maximum = 90;
this.trackBar.Minimum = 10;
```

The control captures the arrow, Page Up, and Page Down keys to control how the values are moved on the track bar. You can specify the number of positions in the bar, the number of values between each visible tick, and the number of ticks to move on an arrow key move or on the Page Up and Page Down key moves. When the TrackBar value changes, you catch the ValueChanged event to handle it:

```
void trackBar_ValueChanged(object sender, EventArgs e) {
    MessageBox.Show(this.trackBar.Value.ToString());
}
```

TreeView

The TreeView control, shown in Figure D.23, is used to show hierarchies.

Figure D.23   A TreeView Control in Action

The tree is made up of nodes. Each node can contain a nested list as exposed via the Nodes property collection, which is what provides the hierarchy. To create nodes in the tree view, you use code such as this:

```
// Create top tree node
TreeNode topNode = this.treeView.Nodes.Add("Top Node");

// Add child nodes in the top node
topNode.Nodes.Add("Child Node");
topNode.Nodes.Add("Another Child Node");
```

If you want to specify images for each of the nodes, you need to associate an ImageList with your TreeView via the latter's ImageList property. Then, you set the TreeView's ImageIndex and SelectedImageIndex properties to specify the default icon for each node when unselected and selected, respectively:

```
// Associate with ImageList
this.treeView.ImageList = this.treeViewImageList;
this.treeView.ImageIndex = 0;
this.treeView.SelectedImageIndex = 1;

// Create top tree node
TreeNode topNode = this.treeView.Nodes.Add("Top Node");

// Add child nodes in the top node
topNode.Nodes.Add("Child Node");
topNode.Nodes.Add("Another Child Node");
```

TreeNode also has both an ImageIndex and a SelectedImageIndex property, which you use to specify images on a node-by-node basis. You can configure all this from the Properties window, too.

Finally, the TreeView control supports additional events for expanding and collapsing nodes, something that allows you to lazily load it as the user looks down the hierarchy.

VScrollBar

The VScrollBar control, shown in Figure D.24, is a vertical scroll bar. It is just like the HScrollBar but is drawn vertically instead of horizontally.

Figure D.24   A VScrollBar Control in Action

In general, you'll find that ScrollableControl is robust and will save you from most situations when you otherwise might have needed to implement scrolling support using the HScrollBar and VScrollBar building blocks.

WebBrowser

The WebBrowser control lets you display web page content, as shown in Figure D.25.

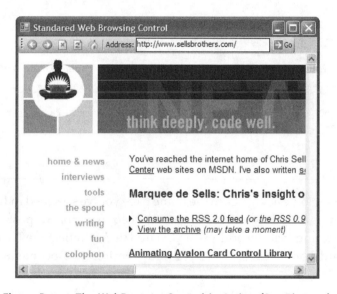

Figure D.25   The WebBrowser Control in Action (See Plate 21)

WebBrowser navigates to a web page when its Navigate method is invoked and passed the URL to navigate to:

```
// MainForm.cs
partial class MainForm : Form {
  ...
  void goToolStripButton_Click(object sender, EventArgs e) {
    // Navigate to url
```

```
      this.webBrowser.Navigate(this.addressToolStripTextBox.Text);
    }
    ...
  }
```

Additionally, WebBrowser provides methods to handle the other navigation options you would expect to find in any browser, including back, forward, stop, refresh, and home:

```
// MainForm.cs
partial class MainForm : Form {
  ...
  void backToolStripButton_Click(object sender, EventArgs e) {
    this.webBrowser.GoBack();
  }
  void forwardToolStripButton_Click(object sender, EventArgs e) {
    this.webBrowser.GoForward();
  }
  void stopToolStripButton_Click(object sender, EventArgs e) {
    this.webBrowser.Stop();
  }
  void refreshToolStripButton_Click(object sender, EventArgs e) {
    this.webBrowser.Refresh();
  }
  void homeToolStripButton_Click(object sender, EventArgs e) {
    this.webBrowser.GoHome();
  }
  ...
}
```

WebBrowser.GoHome navigates to the home page you've specified in Internet Explorer. When a document is fully downloaded, you may need to perform a post-navigation operation, such as ensuring that the address text is updated to reflect the URL resulting from navigating forward, backward, or home. WebBrowser fires the DocumentCompleted event for this purpose:

```
// MainForm.cs
partial class MainForm : Form {
  ...
  void webBrowser_DocumentCompleted(
    object sender, WebBrowserDocumentCompletedEventArgs e) {
    // When finished navigating, make sure Address text matches
    // the URL that we navigated to
    this.urlToolStripTextBox.Text = this.webBrowser.Url.ToString();
  }
}
```

█ APPENDIX E
Drag and Drop

N O MATTER WHAT KIND OF CONTROLS you're using or building, you often want to allow users to drag data from one and drop it on another. The communication protocol that supports this, known as *drag and drop*, has long been standardized and is fully supported in Windows Forms for both drag sources and drop targets. Additional support exposed by the TreeView and ListView controls provides a solid platform for building applications that exhibit behavior consistent with Windows Explorer.

Enabling Drag and Drop

Drag and Drop operations involve two elements: the drag source and the drop target.

The Drag Source

You initiate a drag-and-drop operation from a *drag source*, the control that contains the source data. This requires using the DoDragDrop method of the Control class. DoDragDrop is almost always placed in the handler for a MouseDown event:[1]

```
// MainForm.cs
partial class MainForm : Form {
  void dragSourceLabel_MouseDown(object sender, MouseEventArgs e) {
    // Start a drag and drop operation
    this.DoDragDrop(this.dragSourceLabel.Text, DragDropEffects.Copy);
  }
}
```

The DoDragDrop method's first parameter is the data, which can be any object. The second parameter is a combination of the drag-and-drop effects that the source supports.

---

[1] As you'll see later, ListView exposes a special ItemDrag event specifically for drag and drop.

The Drop Target

With the drag source in place, you now establish the *drop target*, a control that supports having things dragged and dropped onto it. A drop target can be any control on a form, or the form itself. You designate your drop target by setting its AllowDrop property to true:

```
// MainForm.cs
partial class MainForm : Form {
  void MainForm_Load(object sender, EventArgs e) {
    // Enable drop target
    this.dropTargetTextBox.AllowDrop = true;
  }
  ...
}
```

Next, you subscribe the drop target to one or more of the drag-and-drop events:

- DragEnter is fired when the mouse enters the area of a control containing drag-and-drop data. It is used by the target to indicate whether it can accept the data.
- DragOver is called as the user hovers the mouse over the target.
- DragLeave is called when the mouse leaves the area of a control containing the drag-and-drop data.
- DragDrop is called when the user drops the data onto the target.

All target controls must handle the DragEnter event, or else they can't accept any dropped data. The DragEnter event comes with an instance of the DragEventArgs class, which gives the source information about the data:

```
namespace System.Windows.Forms {
  class DragEventArgs : EventArgs {
    // Properties
    public DragDropEffects AllowedEffect { get; }
    public IDataObject Data { get; }
    public DragDropEffects Effect { get; set; }
    public int KeyState { get; }
    public int X { get; }
    public int Y { get; }
  }
}
```

A target control's DragEnter event handler checks the Data property to see whether it can be accepted when dropped. The object returned from the Data property implements IDataObject to make that determination possible:

```
namespace System.Windows.Forms {
  interface IDataObject {
    // Methods
    public virtual object GetData(string format, bool autoConvert);
    public virtual object GetData(string format);
    public virtual object GetData(Type format);

    public virtual void
      SetData(string format, bool autoConvert, object data);
    public virtual void SetData(string format, object data);
    public virtual void SetData(Type format, object data);
    public virtual void SetData(object data);

    public virtual bool GetDataPresent(string format, bool autoConvert);
    public virtual bool GetDataPresent(string format);
    public virtual bool GetDataPresent(Type format);

    public virtual string[] GetFormats(bool autoConvert);
    public virtual string[] GetFormats();
  }
}
```

The IDataObject interface is actually defined from its Component Object Model (COM) cousin, where drag and drop was born. Windows Forms continues to work with the COM-based protocol so that managed and unmanaged applications can participate in drag-and-drop operations between each other.

Furthermore, the COM-based protocol itself is based on the Windows convention for the way the Clipboard works. All data passed around using drag and drop is represented in Clipboard formats. Some Clipboard formats are customized for your own application, and others are well known to allow Clipboard and drag-and-drop operations between applications. The format strings used to specify the well-known formats are predefined as static fields of the DataFormats class:

```
namespace System.Windows.Forms {
  class DataFormats {
    // Fields
    public static readonly string Bitmap;
    public static readonly string CommaSeparatedValue;
    public static readonly string Dib;
    public static readonly string Dif;
    public static readonly string EnhancedMetafile;
    public static readonly string FileDrop;
    public static readonly string Html;
    public static readonly string Locale;
    public static readonly string MetafilePict;
```

```
      public static readonly string OemText;
      public static readonly string Palette;
      public static readonly string PenData;
      public static readonly string Riff;
      public static readonly string Rtf;
      public static readonly string Serializable;
      public static readonly string StringFormat;
      public static readonly string SymbolicLink;
      public static readonly string Text;
      public static readonly string Tiff;
      public static readonly string UnicodeText;
      public static readonly string WaveAudio;

      // Methods
      public static DataFormats.Format GetFormat(string format);
      public static DataFormats.Format GetFormat(int id);
    }
  }
```

In addition to supporting well-known data formats, .NET provides a conversion from some .NET types, such as String, to the compatible formats, such as DataFormats.Text and DataFormats.UnicodeText. Using the GetDataPresent method of the IDataObject, the target determines whether the type of data being dragged is acceptable for a drop:

```
// MainForm.cs
partial class MainForm : Form {
  ...
  void dropTargetTextBox_DragEnter(object sender, DragEventArgs e) {
    // Could check against DataFormats.Text as well
    if (e.Data.GetDataPresent(typeof(string))) {
      e.Effect = DragDropEffects.Copy;
    }
    else {
      e.Effect = DragDropEffects.None;
    }
  }
}
```

GetDataPresent checks the format of the data to see whether it matches the Clipboard format (or a .NET type converted to a Clipboard format). To find out whether the data is in a convertible format, you call the GetFormats method, which returns an array of formats. Calling any of the IDataObject methods with the autoConvert parameter set to false disables anything except a direct match of data types.

If the data is acceptable, the DragEnter event handler must set the Effect property of the DragEventArgs object to one or more flags indicating what the control is willing to do with the data if it's dropped, as determined by the flags in DragDropEffects:

```
namespace System.Windows.Forms {
  enum DragDropEffects {
    Scroll = -2147483648, // Scrolling is happening in the target
    All = -2147483645, // Data is copied and removed from the drag
                       // source, and scrolls in the drop target
    None = 0, // Reject the data
    Copy = 1, // Take a copy of the data
    Move = 2, // Take ownership of the data
    Link = 4, // Link to the data
  }
  ...
}
```

If a drop is allowed and it happens while the mouse is over the target, the target control receives the DragDrop event. You handle this event to retrieve the dragged data and to process the drop onto the target according to the chosen DragDropEffects:

```
// MainForm.cs
partial class MainForm : Form {
  ...
  void dropTargetTextBox_DragDrop(object sender, DragEventArgs e) {
    // Handles both DragDropEffect.Move and DragDropEffect.Copy

    // Retrieve drag data and drop it onto target
    string dragData = (string)e.Data.GetData(typeof(string));
    this.dropTargetTextBox.Text = dragData;
  }
}
```

When you implement the DragDrop handler, the Effect property of DragEventArgs is one of the effects that the source and target agreed on. Retrieving the data is a matter of calling GetData—using either a DataFormat format string or a .NET Type object—and casting the result.

Drop Targets and COM

When you enable a control as a target, you open yourself up to the possibility that the user will receive the cryptic message shown in Figure E.1.

```
static void Main() {
  Application.EnableVisualStyles();
  Application.SetCompatibleTextRenderingDefault(false);
  Application.Run(new MainForm());
}
```

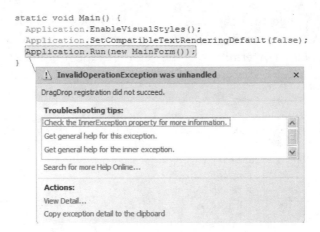

Figure E.1   Cryptic Drag-and-Drop Error Message

Because drag and drop is a feature provided using COM, COM must be initialized on the UI thread for drag and drop to work. Although .NET is smart enough to lazily initialize COM on the running thread as needed, for reasons of efficiency it picks the UI-hostile Multi-Threaded Apartment (MTA) for the thread to join unless told to do otherwise. Unfortunately, for drag and drop to work, the UI thread must join a Single-Threaded Apartment (STA). To ensure that that's the case, always double-check that the Main entry-point method on all your Windows Forms applications is marked with the STAThread attribute:

```
// Program.cs
static class Program {
  [STAThread]
  static void Main() {
    Application.EnableVisualStyles();
    Application.SetCompatibleTextRenderingDefault(false);
    Application.Run(new MainForm());
  }
}
```

By default, all VS05-generated code contains this attribute on the Main function (even Console applications), but just in case it somehow goes missing or you aren't using VS05, this is the first thing to check when you see the exception dialog shown in Figure E.1.

Drag and Drop in Operation

With a drag source and drop target in place, let's look at how a drag-and-drop operation takes place. Drag and drop is initiated when a user presses and holds the left mouse button over the drag source, at which point DoDragDrop is called. Figure E.2 illustrates a drag-and-drop operation initiated from the source Label.

Figure E.2   Initiating a Drag-and-Drop Operation

Because the drag source Label is not a drop target, the drag-and-drop effect is None, which explains the special mouse cursor shown in Figure E.2. As the drag-and-drop operation progresses, the DoDragDrop method tracks the mouse as it moves over controls, looking to see whether they are potential drop targets (as set with the AllowDrop property) and firing the DragEnter event to see whether potential targets can accept the data. Depending on whether the target can accept the data, DoDragDrop sets the cursor based on the current effect indicated by the target, thereby communicating to users what would happen if they were to drop at any point. Notice in Figure E.2 that the label itself is not a drop target, so the cursor indicates that a drop on the button would have no effect.

On the other hand, when the data is dragged over a text box that is enabled to accept string data, the DragEnter event is fired, and the control indicates the effect that it will support. This causes the cursor to be updated appropriately, as shown in Figure E.3.

Figure E.3   Drop Target Indicating the Copy Effect

When the user releases the mouse button, dropping the data, the DragDrop event is fired on the target, and the target accepts the data, as shown in Figure E.4.

Figure E.4   Completed Drag-and-Drop Copy Operation

When the drag and drop is completed, the DoDragDrop method returns with the effect that was performed, something that can be useful when you need to support multiple drag effects, such as the standard Copy and Move.

Adding Support for Multiple Drag-and-Drop Effects

Adding support for multiple drag-and-drop effects requires additional updates to both the drag source and the drop target controls.

Adding Multiple Drag-and-Drop Effects to the Drag Source

On the drag source, you must specify which effects are allowed and check the resulting effect after the DoDragDrop method returns:

```
// MainForm.cs
partial class MainForm : Form {
  ...
  void dragSourceLabel_MouseDown(object sender, MouseEventArgs e) {
    // Start a drag and drop operation
    DragDropEffects supportedEffects = DragDropEffects.Copy |
                                       DragDropEffects.Move;
    string dragData = this.dragSourceLabel.Text;
    DragDropEffects dragEffect =
      DoDragDrop(dragData, supportedEffects);

    // If the effect was move, remove the text of the button
    // If the effect was a copy, we don't have anything to do
    if (dragEffect == DragDropEffects.Move) {
      this.dragSourceLabel.Text = "";
    }
  }
}
```

This code examines the drag-and-drop effect returned by DoDragDrop and responds appropriately. In this case, that simply requires checking whether a Move operation occurred and, if so, enacting it.

Adding Multiple Drag-and-Drop Effects to the Drop Target

The DragDropEffects value returned by DoDragDrop is actually provided by the drop target. You need to establish which keys were pressed while the drag-and-drop operation took place, and to do that you examine the KeyState property of the DragEventArgs class. KeyState is a set of flags that determines which keys are being pressed. By Windows convention, the lack of modifier keys indicates a Move, the Ctrl modifier indicates a Copy, and the Ctrl+Shift modifier indicates a Link (which your application may or may not support).

Unfortunately, the KeyState property is an integer, and Windows Forms provides no data type for checking the flags. So, you need to write your own, such as this KeyState enumeration:[2]

```
// KeyState Values (not available in Windows Forms)
[Flags]
enum KeyState {
  LeftMouse = 1,
  RightMouse = 2,
  ShiftKey = 4,
  CtrlKey = 8,
  MiddleMouse = 16,
  AltKey = 32,
}
```

Because users may change the keys they're pressing at any time to get the effect they're looking for, you should specify the drop effect for the drag operation they are trying to do. To do this, you check the DragEnter and DragOver events:

```
// MainForm.cs
partial class MainForm : Form {
  ...
  void dropTargetTextBox_DragEnter(object sender, DragEventArgs e) {
    SetDropEffect(e);
  }

  void dropTargetTextBox_DragOver(object sender, DragEventArgs e) {
    SetDropEffect(e);
  }

  void SetDropEffect(DragEventArgs e) {

    KeyState keyState = (KeyState)e.KeyState;

    // If the data is a string, we can handle it
    if (e.Data.GetDataPresent(typeof(string))) {
      // If only Ctrl is pressed, copy it
      if ((keyState & KeyState.CtrlKey) == KeyState.CtrlKey) {
        e.Effect = DragDropEffects.Copy;
      }
      else { // Else, move it
        e.Effect = DragDropEffects.Move;
      }
    }
```

---

[2] The Flags attribute makes instances of the KeyState enumeration show up in a friendlier manner, such as "LeftMouse, CtrlKey" instead of "9," and supports bitwise operators like "|" and "&."

```
        // We don't like the data, so do not allow anything
        // e.Effect = DragDropEffects.None by default
    }
}
```

The SetDropEffect method makes sure that the data is a string because that is all we are expecting. If it finds a string, it tests to see whether the Ctrl key is pressed. If it is, it specifies that the operation is a copy; otherwise, it specifies that it will do a move.

Figure E.5 shows what the drag operation now looks like over the text box without the Ctrl key pressed, indicating a move effect.

Figure E.5   Dragging *Without* Ctrl, Causing a Move

Figure E.6 shows the same operation with the Ctrl key pressed, indicating a copy effect.

Figure E.6   Dragging *with* Ctrl, Causing a Copy

In our sample, a move is indicated when the user drops the data with no modifiers, and the text is removed from the drag source label when it drops the text to the text box, as shown in Figure E.7.

Figure E.7   After a Drag-and-Drop Move Operation

Drag and drop is a great way to allow your mouse-oriented users to directly manipulate the data that your application presents without an undue development burden on you.

Customizing Drag and Drop

A large part of avoiding undue development work is our dependence on the underlying drag-and-drop infrastructure to provide a consistent experience by default, something it does well. Although they are uncommon, some situations call for your applications to support a more specialized experience. The drag-and-drop infrastructure supports this by allowing you to customize the types of mouse cursors used for drag and drop. It also lets you control when a drag-and-drop operation completes and in what state it does so.

Using Custom Cursors

Some applications may have a special need for cursors other than the default system-provided drag-and-drop cursors. Such applications might include those that promote a highly stylized look and feel or those that, for contextual reasons, need to display dragging and dropping within a document in a different way from dragging and dropping across documents. In any case, Windows Forms provides the GiveFeedback event, which you handle within the scope of your drag operation. GiveFeedback is fired to the control or form on which DoDragDrop was called and allows you to detect the current drag-and-drop effect and change the cursor as appropriate:

```
// MainForm.cs
using System.IO; // For MemoryStream
...
partial class MainForm : Form {
  static Cursor CustomMoveCursor =
    new Cursor(new MemoryStream(Properties.Resources.CustomMove));
  static Cursor CustomCopyCursor =
    new Cursor(new MemoryStream(Properties.Resources.CustomCopy));

  void dragSourceLabel_GiveFeedback(
    object sender, GiveFeedbackEventArgs e) {
    // Is a drag and drop move in effect?
    if (e.Effect == DragDropEffects.Move) {
      // Use the custom move cursor
      e.UseDefaultCursors = false;
      this.Cursor = MainForm.CustomMoveCursor;
      return;
    }

    // Is a drag and drop copy in effect?
    if (e.Effect == DragDropEffects.Copy) {
      // Use the custom copy cursor
      e.UseDefaultCursors = false;
      this.Cursor = MainForm.CustomCopyCursor;
      return;
    }
```

```
    // Use default cursors for any other drag and drop effect
    // e.UseDefaultCursors = true by default
  }
  ...
}
```

When you provide a custom cursor, you need to let the underlying drag-and-drop operation know.[3] You do this by setting the UseDefaultCursors property exposed by Give-FeedbackEventArgs to false. If you don't, your cursor change is overridden by the system.

Also, make sure you set your cursor back to the default cursor if a custom cursor isn't required. Otherwise, the last cursor change is retained, incorrectly reporting the current drag-and-drop operation, if any:

```
// MainForm.cs
partial class MainForm : Form {
  ...
  void dragSourceLabel_MouseDown(object sender, MouseEventArgs e) {
    ...
    this.Cursor = Cursors.Default;
  }
}
```

Figure E.8 shows the effect of this code during a drag-and-drop move operation.

Figure E.8   Using a Custom Drag-and-Drop Move Cursor

Figure E.9 shows the same for a drag-and-drop copy operation.

Figure E.9   Using a Custom Drag-and-Drop Copy Cursor

---

[3] See Chapter 13: Resources for information about adding resources like cursors to your application.

Being able to change the default drag-and-drop cursors is essential when your drag-and-drop operations need more contextually relevant imagery. However, users are most familiar with the default cursors, so you should have a good reason to provide your own, and to require your users to become familiar with them.

Controlling Drag-and-Drop Completion

Just as you need a good reason to replace the system-provided drag-and-drop cursors with your own custom versions, you need a good reason to alter the default drag-and-drop completion behavior, which is to support dragging within and across applications. However, suppose your application uses highly sensitive data and you need to conform to security policy, which prevents data from being taken outside the application. As part of that policy, you might try to prevent data from being dragged anywhere except within the application.

In this case, you handle the QueryContinueDrag event, which, like GiveFeedback, is fired to the drop source. Handling QueryContinueDrag allows you to check for and, if necessary, cancel the drag-and-drop operation. You implement cancellation by setting the Action property on the QueryContinueDragEventArgs passed to QueryContinueDrag:

```
// MainForm.cs
partial class MainForm : Form {
  ...
  void dragSourceLabel_QueryContinueDrag(
    object sender, QueryContinueDragEventArgs e) {
    // Get the current cursor position, relative to the form
    Point cursorPosition = this.PointToClient(Cursor.Position);
    // Cancel the drag and drop operation if the cursor
    // is dragged outside the form
    if (!this.ClientRectangle.Contains(cursorPosition)) {
      e.Action = DragAction.Cancel;
    }
  }
}
```

Figure E.10 shows the result of cancellation when the mouse moves beyond the host form.

Figure E.10   A Canceled Drag-and-Drop Operation

The QueryContinueDragEventArgs.Action property that was used to cancel the drag-and-drop operation can be a value determined by the DragAction enumeration:

```
namespace System.Windows.Forms {
  enum DragAction {
    Continue = 0, // Continues the drag-and-drop operation (default)
    Drop = 1 // Forces the drag data to be dropped
    Cancel = 2, // Cancels the drag-and-drop operation
  }
}
```

QueryContinueDragEventArgs also provides KeyState information, just as DragEventArgs does, which may be useful when you need more granular information about the state of the drag-and-drop operation before you change the action.

Drag and Drop of Multiple Data Items

From a drag-and-drop perspective, our examples so far have discussed controls that allow selection of single data items and, therefore, provide only a single piece of data for a drag-and-drop operation. For example, text box controls allow you to select only a single piece of text, whether a string or substring. However, several controls do allow selection of multiple data items and, consequently, allow multiple items to participate in a single drag-and-drop operation.

TreeView and ListView are examples of such controls, and they are usually used in tandem for Explorer-style UIs. In these cases, a tree view is used to represent one or more arbitrary data containers, known as *tree nodes,* and a list view is used to display one or more arbitrary data items, known as *listview items,* that reside within each tree node. Moving and copying listview items around tree nodes is a common feature of Explorer-style UIs and is heavily dependent on drag and drop.

As you might imagine, implementing drag and drop to support multiple items is a little more involved than the drag-and-drop scenarios you've seen. However, TreeView and ListView come with extra support, and we'll spend the rest of this topic exploring it.

Dragging Multiple ListView Items

An Explorer-style UI is a great example for showing the most common multiple-data-item drag-and-drop operation: selecting and dragging one or more listview items from one tree node to another, as demonstrated in Figure E.11.

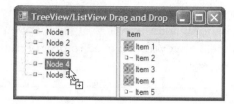

Figure E.11   An Explorer-Style Move Drag-and-Drop Operation in Action

This operation requires a solution that conforms to the following minimum set of behaviors:

- Multiple selection of listview items for drag and drop
- Support for switching between move and copy mid-drag
- Application of highlighting to tree nodes as the cursor moves over them to illustrate where the listview items will be moved or copied

However, before we can tackle this flavor of drag and drop, we need to get the basics working.

Pieces of an Explorer-Style UI

From a control and component point of view, there are four essential UI pieces to an Explorer-style UI: a vertically oriented SplitContainer control, a TreeView control in the SplitContainer's left panel, a ListView control in the SplitContainer's right panel, and an ImageList component to provide images for tree nodes and listview items. This configuration is shown in Figure E.12.

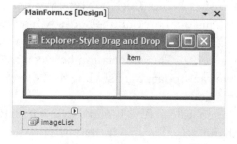

Figure E.12   The Four Basic UI Pieces of an Explorer-Style Application

When the ImageList contains the images, you can specify image list indices for tree nodes from the Properties window for a TreeView, if you happen to know what the nodes are going to be at design time. However, you need to programmatically specify an image list index for each listview item:

```csharp
// MainForm.cs
partial class MainForm : Form {

  public MainForm() {
    InitializeComponent();

    #region Create test data
    // Create some test listview items, passing name and image index
    this.listView.Items.AddRange(
      new ListViewItem[] {
        new ListViewItem("Item 1", 1),
        new ListViewItem("Item 2", 1),
        new ListViewItem("Item 3", 1),
        new ListViewItem("Item 4", 1),
        new ListViewItem("Item 5", 1)
      }
    );
    ...
    #endregion

    // Select first node
    this.treeView.Focus();
  }
}
```

In this code, we use the ListViewItem's constructor overload that accepts a string item name and an integer image index.

We could add tree nodes using .NET's TreeNode type (from the System.Windows.Forms namespace), but we need to consider how our tree nodes will be used. Fundamentally, they are containers for listview items; and consequently, we need to store which listview items are contained by which tree nodes. This association between tree nodes and the listview items is necessary so that we can update the list view to show only those items contained by the currently selected tree node.

Although we could use a separate tree node and listview item data structure to store this information in tandem with our actual tree nodes and listview items, it's easier to store containment information directly in the tree node. One approach is to derive from TreeNode and add a publicly accessible listview item data store:

```csharp
// ItemHolderTreeNode.cs
class ItemHolderTreeNode : TreeNode {
  List<ListViewItem> listViewItems = new List<ListViewItem>();
```

```
public ItemHolderTreeNode(
  string text, List<ListViewItem> listViewItems) {

  this.Text = text;
  if( listViewItems != null ) {
    this.listViewItems.AddRange(
      (IEnumerable<ListViewItem>)listViewItems);
  }
}

public List<ListViewItem> ListViewItems {
  get { return this.listViewItems; }
  set { this.listViewItems = value; }
}
}
```

As you can see, ItemHolderTreeNode stores a collection of listview items in a generic List<T> that's exposed by the ListViewItems property of the same type. ItemHolder-TreeNode's constructor accepts a string node name and the initial collection of listview items to contain. Now, we add our containment-supporting tree nodes and seed the first one with the initial collection of listview items:

```
// MainForm.Designer.cs
partial class MainForm {
  ...
  void InitializeComponent() {
    ...
    // treeView
    this.treeView.ImageIndex = 0;
    ...
  }
  ...
}

// MainForm.cs
partial class MainForm : Form {

  public MainForm() {
    InitializeComponent();

    #region Create test list view and tree view items
    // Create some test listview items
    List<ListViewItem> listViewItems = new List<ListViewItem>();
    listViewItems.Add(new ListViewItem("Item 1", 1));
    listViewItems.Add(new ListViewItem("Item 2", 1));
    listViewItems.Add(new ListViewItem("Item 3", 1));
    listViewItems.Add(new ListViewItem("Item 4", 1));
    listViewItems.Add(new ListViewItem("Item 5", 1));
```

```
       // Create some test treeview items, adding
       // listview items to first node
       ItemHolderTreeNode node1 =
         new ItemHolderTreeNode("Node 1", listViewItems);
       node1.Nodes.AddRange(
         new System.Windows.Forms.TreeNode[] {
           new ItemHolderTreeNode("Node 1", null),
           new ItemHolderTreeNode("Node 1", null),
           new ItemHolderTreeNode("Node 1", null),
           new ItemHolderTreeNode("Node 1", null),
           new ItemHolderTreeNode("Node 1", null)});
       this.treeView.Nodes.Add(node1);
       ...
       #endregion

       // Select first node
       this.treeView.Focus();
    }
  }
```

As tree nodes are selected by the user, we update the ListView control to show the list-view items contained by the currently selected tree node, and this means leaning on the ItemHolderTreeNode's ListViewItems property. The best place to handle this is after a tree node is selected, at which point the TreeView fires the AfterSelect event:

```
// MainForm.cs
partial class MainForm : Form {
  ...
  void treeView_AfterSelect(object sender, TreeViewEventArgs e) {
    // Refresh selected tree node to display list item(s)
    RefreshSelectedTreeNode((ItemHolderTreeNode)e.Node);
  }

  void RefreshSelectedTreeNode(ItemHolderTreeNode treeNode) {
    if( treeNode == null ) return;

    // Remove current listview items
    this.listView.Items.Clear();

    // Add selected tree node's listview items
    this.listView.Items.AddRange(treeNode.ListViewItems.ToArray());
  }
  ...
}
```

AfterSelect is passed a TreeViewEventArgs object that contains the selected node. This code casts that node to get the ItemHolderTreeNode to access its ListViewItems property.

The ListView's Items property is a ListViewItemCollection object that can be filled en masse via a call to its AddRange method. However, AddRange accepts only an array of ListViewItem objects, hence the ToArray call.

Figure E.13 shows the initial UI state of the application at run time based on our work so far.

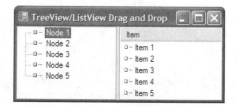

Figure E.13   The Basic Explorer-Style Application

This provides the minimum functionality we need to implement drag-and-drop for list-view items that support both move and copy operations.

Initiating a Drag Operation

We initiate a drag-and-drop operation in a similar fashion as we did earlier, although from a different event handler. When users drag a Label control's Text property data, the data is the Label control's UI. However, the area from which a listview item can be dragged is a combination of the width and height of its image and text content, as illustrated in Figure E.14.

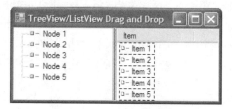

Figure E.14   ListView Item Drag Source UI Real Estate

When a listview item is dragged, the list view detects that the user would like to drag something and fires the ItemDrag event so that you can handle initiation of a drag operation. ItemDrag is also implemented by TreeView for the same reason. Therefore, to initiate a move-and-copy drag operation for a listview item, we handle ListView's ItemDrag event using familiar code:

```
// MainForm.cs
partial class MainForm : Form {
  ...
  void listView_ItemDrag(object sender, ItemDragEventArgs e) {
    // Don't drag unless left mouse button is down
    if( (e.Button != MouseButtons.Left) ) return;

    // Get drag data
    ListView.SelectedListViewItemCollection dragData =
      this.listView.SelectedItems;

    // Set supported drag effects
    DragDropEffects supportedEffects = DragDropEffects.Copy |
                                       DragDropEffects.Move;

    // Start a drag-and-drop operation
    DragDropEffects dragEffect =
      this.listView.DoDragDrop(dragData, supportedEffects);
    ...
  }
  ...
}
```

The ItemDragEventArgs object passed to the ItemDrag event handler references the last selected listview item. To support drag and drop of multiple listview items, though we must specify the drag data to be all selected items, and this is why we use the SelectedItems property on our ListView object.

Drag in Action

After a drag operation has begun, users need to know what will happen if they drop at any moment during an operation. First and foremost, we need to let them know whether they're going to get a move, a copy, a link, or no action. For this, we make sure that the cursor represents the appropriate icon. The best place to do this, as we discussed earlier, is in the DragOver event handler for our treeview drop target:

```
// MainForm.cs
partial class MainForm : Form {
  ...
  // KeyState Values (not available in Windows Forms)
  [Flags]
  enum KeyState {...}

  void treeView_DragOver(object sender, DragEventArgs e) {
    // Can't drop unknown data types
    if( !e.Data.GetDataPresent(
        typeof(ListView.SelectedListViewItemCollection)) ) {
```

```
      e.Effect = DragDropEffects.None;
      return;
    }

    // Can't drop outside of tree node
    if( !IsTreeNodeAtCursor(e.X, e.Y) ) {
      e.Effect = DragDropEffects.None;
      return;
    }

    // Show copy or move cursor
    KeyState keyState = (KeyState)e.KeyState;
    if( ((keyState & KeyState.CtrlKey) == KeyState.CtrlKey) ) {
      e.Effect = DragDropEffects.Copy;
    }
    else {
      e.Effect = DragDropEffects.Move;
    }
  }

  bool IsTreeNodeAtCursor(int x, int y) {
    return GetTreeNodeAtCursor(x, y) != null;
  }

  TreeNode GetTreeNodeAtCursor(int x, int y) {
    Point pt = this.treeView.PointToClient(new Point(x, y));
    TreeViewHitTestInfo hti = this.treeView.HitTest(pt);
    return hti.Node;
  }
  ...
}
```

If the cursor isn't over a tree node or isn't a collection of items from a list view, the drag effect is set to None. To determine whether the mouse cursor is currently over a tree node, the DragOver handler code relies on a couple of helper methods: IsTreeNodeAtCursor and GetTreeNodeAtCursor. These helpers use the tree view's definition of the area of a node, which comprises the maximum height of the image and text content, and the width from the start of the node content to the edge of the treeview control, as shown in Figure E.15.

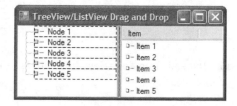

Figure E.15 Tree Node Drop Target UI Real Estate

If the tree view knows the type of data it's going to get and if it's in the area of a node, we look at the Ctrl key state to determine whether we should show the Copy or the Move drag effect.

In addition to keeping the mouse cursor showing the current operation, we want to highlight the target tree node to let users know where their drop operation will happen. To do this, we handle the GiveFeedback event for the drop source to detect whether we are over a tree node and, if we are, to select it:

```csharp
// MainForm.cs
partial class MainForm : Form {
  ...
  void listView_GiveFeedback(object sender, GiveFeedbackEventArgs e) {
    // Select tree node if dragging over one
    Point pt = Cursor.Position;
    TreeNode node = this.GetTreeNodeAtCursor(pt.X, pt.Y);
    if( node != null ) {
      this.treeView.SelectedNode = node;
    }

    // Focus() forces the selection UI to be rendered
    this.treeView.Focus();
  }

  bool IsTreeNodeAtCursor(int x, int y) {
    ...
  }

  TreeNode GetTreeNodeAtCursor(int x, int y) {
    ...
  }
}
```

Figure E.16 shows this code in action.

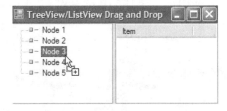

Figure E.16   Dynamic Tree Node Selection and User-Driven Drag Effect Changes

One problem you may have noticed is that you can't see the listview items contained by the tree node being dragged from. This is because the code in the AfterSelect event updates the list view for each selected tree node as the drag data is dragged over a tree node. To view the drag source list view during a drag operation, we need to disable the tree view's selection-handling code until after the drop:

```
// MainForm.cs
partial class MainForm : Form {
  ...
  bool dragging = false;

  void listView_ItemDrag(object sender, ItemDragEventArgs e) {
    ...
    // Start a drag-and-drop operation
    this.dragging = true;
    DragDropEffects dragEffect =
      this.DoDragDrop(dragData, supportedEffects);
    this.dragging = false;
    ...
  }

  void treeView_AfterSelect(object sender, TreeViewEventArgs e) {
    // Refresh listview control only if not dragging
    if( this.dragging ) return;

    // Refresh selected tree node to display dropped item(s)
    RefreshSelectedTreeNode((ItemHolderTreeNode)e.Node);
  }
  ...
}
```

If users don't cancel the drag operation mid-drag by pressing the Esc key (behavior intrinsically supported by the drag-and-drop infrastructure), they'll drop their data on a tree node, and this will require some processing on your part.

Completing a Drag Operation

Drag-and-drop completion needs to be handled by both the drop target and the drop source. For our drop target, this means handling the TreeView control's DragDrop event, capturing the drag data, and adding it to the drop target tree node. We also need to ensure that the list view is updated to show the new set of listview items contained by that node. The following code encompasses this logic:

```
// MainForm.cs
partial class MainForm : Form {
  ...
  void treeView_DragDrop(object sender, DragEventArgs e) {
    // Don't drop if attempting to drop at a nondroppable location
    if( !this.IsTreeNodeAtCursor(e.X, e.Y) ) return;

    // Get drag data
    ListView.SelectedListViewItemCollection dragData =
      (ListView.SelectedListViewItemCollection)e.Data.GetData(
        typeof(ListView.SelectedListViewItemCollection));

    // Move or copy listview item(s) to the drop target tree node
    ItemHolderTreeNode targetNode =
      (ItemHolderTreeNode)this.GetTreeNodeAtCursor(e.X, e.Y);
    foreach( ListViewItem item in dragData ) {
      targetNode.ListViewItems.Add(item);
    }
  }
  ...
}
```

We implement both copy and move operations for our tree view by adding the dragged listview items to the drop target tree node's ListViewItems collections.

For our list view, handling completion on the drop source means removing data from the drag source tree node for a move operation, and refreshing the currently selected tree node to display the dragged listview items:

```
// MainForm.cs
partial class MainForm : Form {
  ...
  void listView_ItemDrag(object sender, ItemDragEventArgs e) {
    ...
    // Remember source tree node
    TreeNode dragSourceTreeNode = this.treeView.SelectedNode;
    ...
    // Start a drag-and-drop operation
    this.dragging = true;
    DragDropEffects dragEffect =
      this.listView.DoDragDrop(dragData, supportedEffects);
    this.dragging = false;

    // Move if required
    if( dragEffect == DragDropEffects.Move ) {
      foreach( ListViewItem item in this.listView.SelectedItems ) {
        ((ItemHolderTreeNode)dragSourceTreeNode).ListViewItems.Remove(
          item);
      }
    }
```

```
      dragSourceTreeNode = null;

      // Refresh drop target tree node to display dropped item(s)
      RefreshSelectedTreeNode(
        (ItemHolderTreeNode)this.treeView.SelectedNode);
    }
    ...
  }
```

This completes the functionality required to provide the minimal solution for dragging multiple listview items and dropping them onto tree nodes. For a full-blown Explorer-style UI, we'd also like to show the items being dragged during a drag operation. The implementation of that functionality is beyond the scope of this book, but I recommend an article by Chris Sano titled, "Custom Windows Forms Controls: ColorPicker.NET" (*MSDN Online*, March 2005) for the GDI+ magic required to show what the user is dragging.[4]

File Drag and Drop

Another common use for drag and drop is to allow dragging files from Explorer onto an application that can process them. Because support for this kind of drag and drop has nothing to do with the Control class's DoDragDrop method, and because this feature is something that document-style applications such as Word and Excel need to support, a solution is provided in Appendix F: Document Management.

[4] http://msdn.microsoft.com/library/default.asp?url=/library/en-us/dnwinforms/html/colorpicker.asp (http://tinysells.com/36).

APPENDIX F
Document Management

C ONSIDER THE RATES OF RETURN application shown in Figure F.1, an application used to calculate both average and annualized rates of return.

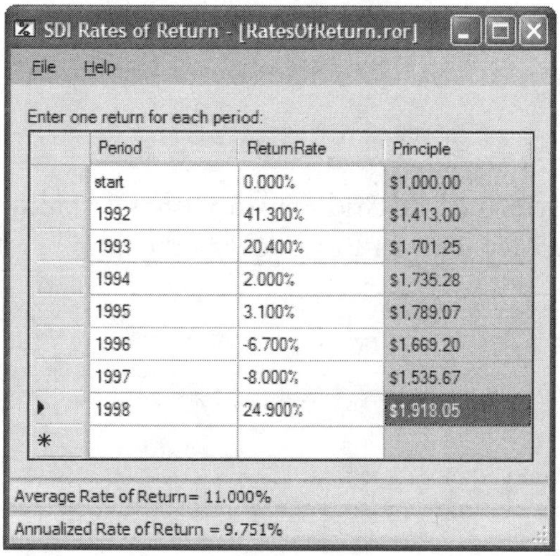

Figure F.1   The Rates of Return Application

Each row represents a single period of return that's encapsulated by the PeriodReturn type:

```
// PeriodReturn.cs
class PeriodReturn {
    string period;
    decimal returnRate;
    decimal principal;
```

```
public PeriodReturn() {}

public PeriodReturn(
  string period, decimal returnRate, decimal principal) {
  this.period = period;
  this.returnRate = returnRate;
  this.principal = principal;
}

public string Period {
  get { return this.period; }
  set { this.period = value; }
}

public decimal ReturnRate {
  get { return this.returnRate; }
  set { this.returnRate = value; }
}

public decimal Principal {
  get { return this.principal; }
  set { this.principal = value; }
}
}
```

The following code binds the DataGridView to a list of PeriodReturn objects and detects changes to the data source list in order to recalculate the rates of return:[1]

```
// RatesOfReturnForm.Designer.cs
partial class RatesOfReturnForm {
  ...
  void InitializeComponent() {
    ...
    this.PeriodReturnBindingSource =
      new BindingSource(this.components);
    ...
    // PeriodReturnBindingSource
    this.PeriodReturnBindingSource.DataSource =
      typeof(SDIRatesOfReturn.PeriodReturn);
    this.PeriodReturnBindingSource.ListChanged +=
      this.PeriodReturnBindingSource_ListChanged;
```

[1] Data binding and the BindingSource component are covered in Chapter 16: Data Binding Basics and Chapter 17: Applied Data Binding. We haven't implemented INotifyPropertyChanged on PeriodReturn because this application doesn't need item change notifications; for example, we don't ever change the PeriodReturn objects programmatically, only through the grid. See Chapter 16 for the what, why, and how.

```
   ...
   // dataGridView
   this.dataGridView.DataSource = this.PeriodReturnBindingSource;
   ...
   }
   ...
   BindingSource PeriodReturnBindingSource;
   DataGridView dataGridView;
}
```

To complete our simple app, we prepopulate the data source with an initial row and handle the data source's ListChanged event to implement the average and annual rates of return calculations:

```
// RatesOfReturnForm.cs
partial class RatesOfReturnForm : Form {
  ...
  void RatesOfReturnForm_Load(object sender, System.EventArgs e) {
    // Add starting principal
    this.PeriodReturnBindingSource.List.Add(
      new PeriodReturn("start", 0M, 1000M));
  }

  void PeriodReturnBindingSource_ListChanged(
    object sender, ListChangedEventArgs e) {
    // Calculate average and annual returns
    ...
  }
}
```

Thanks to data binding, the development experience was quite enjoyable, until I realized that I needed to save our newly entered rates of return data to disk for later use. Windows Forms and VS05 provide all kinds of support for easily writing data-bound applications, but neither provides any real support for the staple of MFC programmers everywhere: document-based applications.[2]

Oh, it's easy enough to lay out the File menu and to show the file dialogs. It's even easy to dump the contents of the data source to the disk using the run-time serialization stack in .NET:[3]

```
// RatesOfReturnForm.cs
...
using System.IO;
using System.Runtime.Serialization;
```

[2] See Appendix B: Moving from MFC for more information regarding Microsoft Foundation Classes.

[3] The various kinds of serialization stacks provided in .NET are beyond the scope of this book. However, I can recommend Jeffrey Richter's "Run-time Serialization" piece (*MSDN Magazine*, April 2002), found at http://msdn.microsoft.com/msdnmag/issues/02/04/net/ (http://tinysells.com/39).

```
using System.Runtime.Serialization.Formatters;
using System.Runtime.Serialization.Formatters.Binary;

[Serializable]
class PeriodReturn {...}

partial class RatesOfReturnForm : Form {
  ...
  void saveToolStripMenuItem_Click(object sender, EventArgs e) {
    if( this.saveFileDialog.ShowDialog(this) != DialogResult.OK ) {
      return;
    }

    string filename = this.saveFileDialog.FileName;
    using( Stream stream =
      new FileStream(filename, FileMode.Create, FileAccess.Write) ) {
      // Serialize object in binary format
      IFormatter formatter = new BinaryFormatter();
      formatter.Serialize(stream, this.periodReturns);
    }
  }
  ...
}
```

However, document-based applications require a lot more than just showing a file dialog and dumping an object's contents into a file. To satisfy a Windows user's basic expectations, both SDI and MDI applications are required to support a specific set of document-related features.

A minimal document-based application needs to support the following document management behavior:

- Show the file name of the currently loaded document in the form's caption (for example, Stuff.txt).
- Prompt users to save a changed document when they attempt to close it without saving.
- Let users save changes to the current document without providing the file name for each subsequent save. This is the difference between File | Save after the first save and File | Save As.
- Create new documents, clearing any currently active document.

For completeness, it should also support the following features:

- Show the user that a document has changed from its last saved state, commonly with an asterisk next to the file name (Stuff.txt*).
- Register custom file extensions with the shell so that double-clicking a file opens the appropriate application, with the chosen file loaded.

- Associate the icon for the document type and the application itself.
- Add opened and saved files to the Start | My Documents menu.
- Open previously saved files via a most-recently-used (MRU) menu.
- Handle drag and drop of files from the shell to open the file.

Although Windows Forms provides no implementation of these document-related features, we of the ex-MFC brethren (and sistren) shouldn't let that stop us.

The FileDocument Component

The FileDocument component comes with the source code for this book and was built specifically to provide MFC-style document management to your Windows Forms SDI and MDI applications. When it is added to the Toolbox, you can drag it onto a form and use the Properties window to set the properties as appropriate, as shown for the SDI Rates of Return application in Figure F.2.

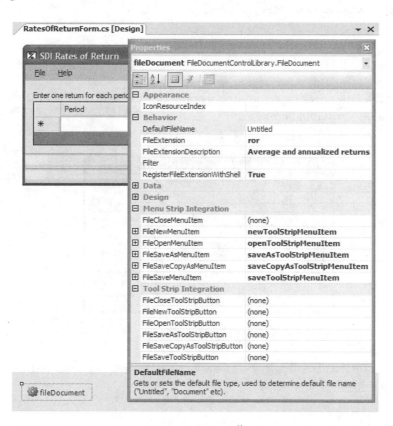

Figure F.2   Managing a FileDocument Component in the Properties Window

As you can see, a wide variety of document management and shell integration support can be configured from the Properties window. Let's see how it works.

Dirty Bit Management

Noticing when the document has changed is an application-specific task, but storing whether it's been changed is application-generic, typically stored in a Boolean called the *dirty bit*. In our sample, we track when the data has changed in the data source's ListChanged event and set the FileDocument component's dirty bit:

```
// RatesOfReturnForm.cs
partial class RatesOfReturnForm : Form {
  ...
  void PeriodReturnBindingSource_ListChanged(
    object sender, ListChangedEventArgs e) {
    ...
    // Update the dirty bit
    this.fileDocument.Dirty = true;
    ...
  }
  ...
}
```

The FileDocument component updates the caption text for the hosting form to reflect the dirty bit, as shown in Figure F.3.[4]

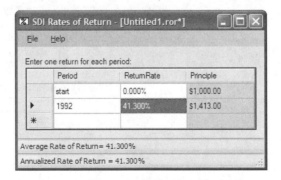

Figure F.3　Dirty SDI Application Data

---

[4] The FileDocument component knows about the hosting form via techniques described in Chapter 11: Design-Time Integration: The Properties Window.

Of course, if you want to let users know that their data is dirty, you need to provide enough file management support to allow them to save their dirty data to disk and to reload it.

File Management

To provide file management support, the FileDocument component provides a Default-FileName property to specify a default file name; FileExtension and FileExtensionDescription properties to set the file dialog properties appropriately for custom file extensions; and a RegisterFileExtensionWithShell property to register the extension so that double-clicking a custom application file launches the application from the shell.

After your application has been run once, thereby allowing the FileDocument component to register your file extension with the shell, double-clicking one of your application's document files will launch a new instance of the application and open the desired file.[5] To manage that, our sample handles retrieving a file name from the command line arguments:

```
// Program.cs
[STAThread]
static void Main(string[] args) {
  Application.EnableVisualStyles();

  // Load main form, taking command line into account
  RatesOfReturnForm form = new RatesOfReturnForm();
  if( args.Length == 1 ) {
    form.OpenDocument(Path.GetFullPath(args[0]));
  }

  Application.Run(form);
}
```

The main form implementation of the OpenDocument method passes the file name to the FileDocument component:

```
// RatesOfReturnForm.cs
partial class RatesOfReturnForm : Form {
  ...
  // For opening document from command line arguments
  public bool OpenDocument(string filename) {
    return this.fileDocument.Open(filename);
  }
  ...
}
```

---

[5] To limit your application to a single instance, see the discussion in Chapter 14: Applications.

When the FileDocument object is first created or cleared through the New method (as an implementation of the File | New menu item would do), FileDocument fires the New-Document event, which we use to set the initial seed data on our form:

```
class RatesOfReturnForm : Form {
  ...
  void fileDocument_NewDocument(object sender, EventArgs e) {
    // Reset list
    this.periodReturns.Clear();
    this.periodReturns.Add(new PeriodReturn("start", 0M, 1000M));
  }
  ...
}
```

On the other hand, if a file is passed through the command line or if we call the Open method on the FileDocument (as we would when implementing the File | Open menu strip item), the FileDocument fires the ReadDocument event, which is an excellent place to deserialize the contents of a file:

```
// RatesOfReturnForm.cs
partial class RatesOfReturnForm : Form {
  ...
  void fileDocument_ReadDocument(
    object sender, SerializeDocumentEventArgs e) {
    // Deserialize object
    IFormatter formatter = new BinaryFormatter();
    this.periodReturns =
      (BindingList<PeriodReturn>)formatter.Deserialize(e.Stream);
    this.PeriodReturnBindingSource.DataSource = this.periodReturns;
  }
  ...
}
```

The ReadDocument event passes an object of the custom type SerializeDocument-EventArgs, which contains the file name of the document to be read and a stream already opened on that file. When you ask the FileDocument to open, it checks the dirty bit to see whether the current document needs to be saved first, prompts the user, saves the document as necessary, uses the FileExtension to show the file open dialog, gets the file name, updates the hosting form's caption with the new file name, and even puts the newly opened file into the shell's Start | Documents menu. The FileDocument component asks us to do only the small application-specific part (reading the data from the stream) by firing the ReadDocument event at the right stage in the process.

In the same way, saving is a matter of handling the WriteDocument event:

```
// RatesOfReturnForm.cs
partial class RatesOfReturnForm : Form {
  ...
  void fileDocument_WriteDocument(
    object sender, SerializeDocumentEventArgs e) {
    // Serialize object
    IFormatter formatter = new BinaryFormatter();
    formatter.Serialize(e.Stream, this.periodReturns);
  }
  ...
}
```

Just like Open, the FileDocument component handles all the chores of the Save family of operations, including the slightly different semantics of Save, Save As, and Save Copy As. The component also makes sure to change the current file and the dirty bit as appropriate, asking the application to do only the application-specific serialization.

Handling the File Menu Items

The NewDocument, ReadDocument, and WriteDocument events are called as part of the implementation of the File menu strip items. You could handle the menu strip item clicks by calling the corresponding FileDocument methods:

```
// RatesOfReturnForm.cs
partial class RatesOfReturnForm : Form {
  ...
  void newToolStripMenuItem_Click(object sender, EventArgs e) {
    // You really don't need to do this...
    this.fileDocument.New();
  }

  void openToolStripMenuItem_Click(object sender, EventArgs e) {
    // or this...
    this.fileDocument.Open();
  }

  void saveToolStripMenuItem_Click(object sender, EventArgs e) {
    // or this...
    this.fileDocument.Save();
  }

  void saveAsToolStripMenuItem_Click(object sender, EventArgs e) {
    // or this...
    this.fileDocument.SaveAs();
  }
```

```
    void saveCopyAsToolStripMenuItem_Click(object sender, EventArgs e) {
      // or even this...
      this.fileDocument.SaveCopyAs();
    }
    ...
  }
```

Because FileDocument knows that this is the kind of thing you're likely to do, it lets you select the appropriate menu strip item in the Properties window from a drop-down list, as shown in Figure F.4, handling the menu items for you.

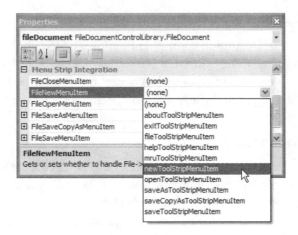

Figure F.4　Letting the FileDocument Handle the File Menu Strip Items

The FileDocument component also provides equivalent tool strip integration for associating FileDocument actions with tool strip buttons.

Notice that File | Exit isn't on the menu integration list (nor is it on the tool strip integration list). It is up to the form to implement Exit:

```
// RatesOfReturnForm.cs
partial class RatesOfReturnForm : Form {
  ...
  void exitToolStripMenuItem_Click(object sender, EventArgs e) {
    // Let FileDocument component decide whether this is OK
    this.Close();
  }
  ...
}
```

All the main form has to do to implement File | Exit is to do what it normally would in any application: close itself. Because FileDocument knows which form is hosting it, it can handle the main form's Closing event and let it close or not based on the dirty bit and users' preferences for saving their data; you don't need to write any special code to make this happen.

MDI and the FileDocument Component

The MDI use of the FileDocument component is nearly identical to the SDI case, except that the File menu options are split between the child and the parent.[6] The MDI parent implements File | New, File | Open, and File | Exit, and the MDI child form provides the File | Save family of menu items and the File | Close menu item. The File | Save menu items are implemented in the MDI child exactly as they'd be implemented in an SDI form hosting a FileDocument component, whereas the File | Close menu item is implemented by hooking up the FileCloseMenuItem property, as shown in Figure F.5.

Figure F.5   FileDocument Configuration for an MDI Child Form

---

[6] The construction of MDI applications in Windows Forms, including menu merging, is discussed in Chapter 2: Forms.

Except for the code generated by the Designer, our complete MDI child form document management implementation looks like this:

```
// RatesOfReturnForm.cs (MDI Child Form)
partial class RatesOfReturnForm : Form {

  BindingList<PeriodReturn> periodReturns;

  public RatesOfReturnForm() {
    InitializeComponent();

    periodReturns = new BindingList<PeriodReturn>();
    this.PeriodReturnBindingSource.DataSource = this.periodReturns;
  }

  // For opening document from command line arguments
  public bool OpenDocument(string filename) {
    return this.fileDocument.Open(filename);
  }

  void fileDocument_NewDocument(object sender, EventArgs e) {
    // Reset list
    this.periodReturns.Clear();
    this.periodReturns.Add(new PeriodReturn("start", 0M, 1000M));
  }

  void fileDocument_ReadDocument(
    object sender, SerializeDocumentEventArgs e) {

    // Deserialize object
    IFormatter formatter == new BinaryFormatter();
    this.periodReturns =
      (BindingList<PeriodReturn>)formatter.Deserialize(e.Stream);
    this.PeriodReturnBindingSource.DataSource = this.periodReturns;

    // Calculate returns on reload
    ...
  }

  void fileDocument_WriteDocument(
    object sender, SerializeDocumentEventArgs e) {

    // Serialize object
    IFormatter formatter = new BinaryFormatter();
    formatter.Serialize(e.Stream, this.periodReturns);
  }
```

```
void PeriodReturnBindingSource_ListChanged(
  object sender, ListChangedEventArgs e) {
  // Recalculate returns
  ...

  // Update the dirty bit
  this.fileDocument.Dirty = true;
  ...
}


void CalculateReturns(int periods) {
  // Calculate average and annual returns
  ...
}
}
```

The MDI parent form doesn't have an instance of the FileDocument but instead implements File | New and File | Open by creating new instances of the MDI child form, passing the file name from the command line if it gets one:

```
// MdiParentForm.cs
partial class MdiParentForm : Form {

  // For use by Main in processing a file passed via the command line
  public void OpenDocument(string fileName) {
    // Let child do the opening
    RatesOfReturnForm child = new RatesOfReturnForm();
    if( child.OpenDocument(fileName) ) {
      child.MdiParent = this;
      child.Show();
    }
    else {
      child.Close();
    }
  }


  void newToolStripMenuItem_Click(object sender, EventArgs e) {
    // Create and show a new child
    RatesOfReturnForm child = new RatesOfReturnForm();
    child.MdiParent = this;
    child.Show();
  }


  void openToolStripMenuItem_Click(object sender, EventArgs e) {
    this.OpenDocument(null);
  }
```

```
void exitToolStripMenuItem_Click(object sender, EventArgs e) {
    // Children will decide whether or not this is allowed
    this.Close();
}
}
```

You implement File | Exit in the MDI parent by closing the form and letting the FileDocument component judge whether the MDI children can be closed based on the dirty bit and the user's input.

The results of hosting a FileDocument component in each MDI child and wiring it up (including the addition of the MDI features described in Chapter 2) are shown in Figure F.6.

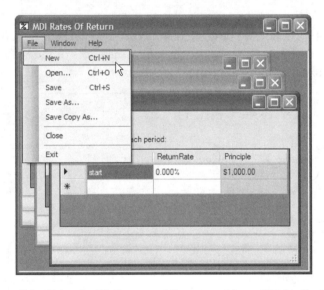

Figure F.6　Using the FileDocument Component in an MDI Application

Shell Integration

Because both SDI and MDI versions of the Rates of Return application use a file with a custom extension (.ror) and support opening such files from the command line, we've got the fundamentals in place to support full shell integration.

Integrating with the Shell

The shell we're interested in integrating with is the Explorer shell where users keep track of their documents (although the command line shell picks up some integration here, too). The simplest kind of shell integration for a document-based application is to make sure that the application's documents are associated with the application so that double-clicking on one of the documents opens the application with the document loaded. The trick is to place the correct entries in the Registry to map a custom file extension—such as .ror to a ProgID (programmatic identifier)—and then to register one or more commands under the ProgID (mapping Open to launch SDIClient.exe or MDIClient.exe).

To add a custom extension, we need a new key under the HKEY_CLASSES_ROOT Registry hive for the extension that maps to the ProgID. To add a new ProgID, we also need a new key under HKEY_CLASSES_ROOT, along with a subkey for the Open command. The goal, as shown in the Registry Editor (regedit.exe), looks like Figure F.7 (for the custom extension) and Figure F.8 (for the associated open command).

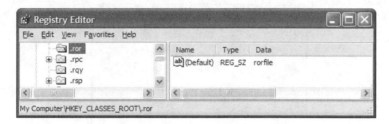

Figure F.7   Mapping a Custom File Extension to a Custom ProgID

Figure F.8   Registering an Open Command with a Custom ProgID

Notice the use of the quoted %L argument in Figure F.8 as part of the full path to our custom application's .exe file. When the user double-clicks on a .ror file or right-clicks and chooses Open from the context menu, the command in the Registry is executed, replacing %L with the long name of the chosen file. The use of the double quotes surrounding %L ensures that even a file name with spaces will come through as a single argument.

Although .NET provides a set of classes for Registry manipulations in the Microsoft.Win32 namespace, when the FileDocument component is created (and the RegisterFileExtensionWithShell property is set to true), it handles the registration of your custom file extension for you.[7] After the registration of the file extension, when the user double-clicks a file with that extension, the application is executed with the arguments passed in the string array to the Main method. Consequently, when the application opens, a file is loaded as a document.

Document Icons

In addition, after the Open command is registered under Microsoft Windows XP, the shell replaces the unregistered extension icon (shown in Figure F.9) with an icon composed of a miniature icon from the application itself (shown in Figure F.10).

Figure F.9   Document File Without an Extension Association

Figure F.10   Shell-Created Document Icon Based on the Application's Icon (16 × 16)

If you prefer a custom icon for your document types, you can set the DefaultIcon key under the ProgID in the Registry. The key is the name of the Windows EXE or DLL containing native icons, followed by an icon indicator. If the indicator is negative, it's

---

[7] Permission to write to the Registry is not available to ClickOnce applications unless they are awarded full trust or custom permissions that allow writing to the Registry. See Chapter 19 for details.

interpreted as a resource ID (after the minus sign is dropped). If the indicator is positive, it's interpreted as an offset into the list of native icons bundled into the EXE or DLL. For example, Figure F.11 shows the DefaultIcon key using an icon from the shell32.dll that comes with current versions of Windows.

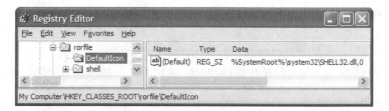

Figure F.11   DefaultIcon Key

Notice the use of the %SystemRoot% variable in the key value. Like %L, this variable is expanded by the shell. Unfortunately, you can't use the DefaultIcon key to pull managed icon resources out of .NET assemblies, because the shell supports only native icon resources. To use a custom document icon, you must either bundle a separate DLL containing a native icon resource or use a tool to bundle the native icon resources into your application's assembly. The .NET command line compilers support bundling native resources, but VS05 does not (except for one special "application icon" that can be set in the project properties for your application).

The easiest way to distribute an icon resource with your application is to embed it into your EXE. Using ntrescopy.exe, which is discussed in Chapter 13: Resources, you can create a C++ DLL project to package your resources. Then, ntrescopy can copy icons from a .dll file you create into the target assembly, which can be either MDIClient.exe or SDIClient.exe. The samples for this chapter illustrate how to do this with the aid of post-build events in both the MDIClient and SDIClient projects. That sample, which you'll find at our web site (http://www.sellsbrothers.com/writing/wfbook), includes support for using the IconResourceIndex property of FileDocument to specify the index of the resource icon you want as the document icon. FileDocument then registers the icon when it registers the Open command.

The update of the DefaultIcon Registry key now forces the document icon to be loaded from the index in your application's assembly, resulting in the icons used in Figure F.12.

Figure F.12   Custom Resource Document Icon (32 × 32) and Application Icon

In addition to seeing their files in the Explorer, users are accustomed to seeing their most recently accessed documents in the Start | Documents menu.

Start | Documents

Ever since Windows 95, opened and saved files go into a systemwide MRU that's managed by the shell and is available from the documents item in the Start menu.[8] To add files to this list, you call the Win32 function SHAddToRecentDocs, which is exposed from shell32.dll. Unfortunately, there's no .NET wrapper for that function, so you have to use a bit of Win32 interop to gain access to it.[9]

Luckily, because the FileDocument component is in charge of when files are opened and saved, it can add the files to the documents menu for you. Because our custom extension has been registered with an icon, that icon is displayed in the list, as shown in Figure F.13.

Figure F.13   Custom Document Added to Start | Documents

[8] Depending on whether you're showing recent documents from the Start menu, and whether you're showing the "classic" Start menu, the documents item is labeled "Documents" or "My Recent Documents" under Windows XP.

[9] Check out Adam Nathan's most excellent site at http://pinvoke.net (http://tinysells.com/7) to look up the P/Invoke signature for this Win32 API and most others. The following shows SHAddToRecentDocs and a sample usage: http://www.pinvoke.net/default.aspx/shell32/SHAddToRecentDocs.html (http://tinysells.com/40).

Further, because we've already provided an Open command for our custom .ror extension in the shell, an instance of our application is loaded whenever a document from the documents menu is selected.

The MruMenuManager Component

Applications focused on document management often employ a special UI feature to provide quick access to documents currently receiving high rotation. This set of documents comprises the most recently used (MRU) and are typically made available as a menu item located in the File menu.

An MRU menu typically exhibits the following characteristics:

- It provides access to the last n most recently used documents, where n is a predefined number that's provided a default at application installation. Users can change this number.
- Each document is represented as a single menu strip item that contains the document's file name as the text value and a numeric menu access key that represents the file's position in the list of most recently used from most recent to least recent—that is, 1 to n.
- When an MRU menu strip item is clicked, its corresponding file should be opened.
- When a file is opened or saved, a menu strip item for it should be added to the MRU menu in the most recent position, with the remaining menu strip items repositioned accordingly.
- When an MRU menu strip item is clicked, it should be moved to the most recent position, with the remaining menu strip items repositioned accordingly.
- If the file name is too long to display within the available width of a menu, it should be shortened by replacing the removed text with an ellipsis. The removed text usually contains one or more folder names in sequence.
- The total number of MRU menu strip items displayed is the lesser of the number of files loaded and n.
- If a user changes n and n is now less than the total number of MRU menu strip items currently displayed, all superfluous MRU menu strip items should be removed from the MRU menu.
- The MRU menu should work equally from SDI and MDI applications.
- If the MRU menu doesn't contain any items, it should be disabled.
- Users should have the option to remove an item from the MRU menu if the file doesn't exist.

- The set of items in an MRU menu can be displayed either within an existing menu or within a submenu. Microsoft Word favors the former, and VS05 is partial to the latter.

- An MRU menu should remember the most recently used files from one application session to the next.

That's a lot of work for such a small feature. If the idea of building this functionality yourself doesn't get you up for the big game, you can use the reusable MRU component, MruMenuManager, which you'll find with the samples for this chapter. This component addresses each of our criteria for MRU menus.

Getting an MRU Menu

The MruMenuManager component can be dropped onto a form like any other component. After it's there, MruMenuManager first needs a reference to a menu item, which it will use as a placeholder to add and remove MRU menu items on your behalf. The MRU menu typically resides beneath a top-level menu item, so you need to create a placeholder menu item specially, as shown in Figure F.14.

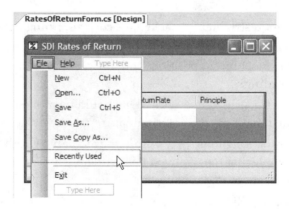

Figure F.14   Creating a Placeholder Menu Item for the MRU

After you have the placeholder menu item, you simply reference it from the Mru-MenuManager component's MruListMenu property, shown in Figure F.15.

Figure F.15   Pointing the MruMenuManager at the MRU Placeholder Menu Item

With that in place, MruMenuManager has the basic piece of information needed to provide its services. The first of those is configuring how your MRU menu will look.

Configuring the MRU Menu Appearance

MruMenuManager offers three main configurations: menu display style, the maximum number of items displayed, and the maximum text width.

Classically, there are two types of display styles for MRU menus: in menu and in submenu. *In-menu* MRU menus display zero or more most recently used menu items within the submenu of a top-level menu item. *In-submenu* MRU menus, on the other hand, display their menu items from a cascading submenu of a top-level menu item. Figure F.16 illustrates an in-menu MRU menu, and Figure F.17 shows an in-submenu MRU menu.

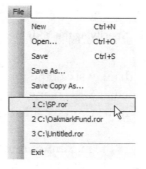

Figure F.16   In-Menu MRU Style

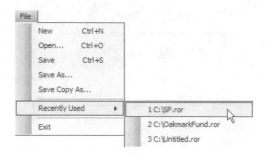

Figure F.17   In-Submenu MRU Style

MruMenuManager allows you to choose either style via its DisplayStyle property, which can be one of the two MruListDisplayStyle enumeration values:

```
enum MruListDisplayStyle {
    InMenu,
    InSubMenu
}
```

This property is most easily set from the Properties window, as shown in Figure F.18.

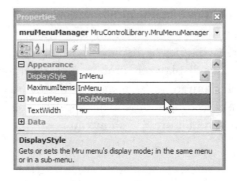

Figure F.18   Specifying the MRU Menu's Display Style

When you choose the InMenu display style, the menu item that you specified as the MruListMenu is replaced with the actual MRU menu items. If you choose InSubMenu, the MruListMenu remains visible with the text you specified for it, although it is disabled when there are no MRU menu items.

The next option you can specify is the maximum number of items the MRU menu will contain. MruMenuManager has a default value of 10 items, but most applications typically allow users to specify their own number from the Tools | Options menu. This value is captured by MruMenuManager's MaximumItems property.

The final option is to specify the maximum display width of your MRU menu items. The norm for an MRU menu is to display an entire file path, unless the file path is too long, like the one in Figure F.19.

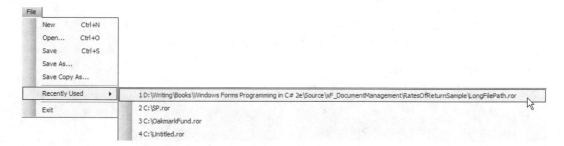

Figure F.19   A Very Wide MRU Menu Item

You use the TextWidth property to limit the number of characters to display. If a file path's length exceeds the value stored in TextWidth, MruMenuManager truncates the file path by replacing one or more folder elements with an ellipsis, as shown in Figure F.20.

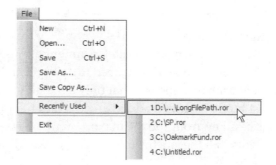

Figure F.20   Truncating Very Wide MRU Menu Items

With the appearance taken care of, we start adding menu items to MruMenuManager so that it can display them.

Adding a File to the MRU Menu

To add files to MruMenuManager, you invoke the Add method, which accepts a single file path string argument. You need to write the code to call this method, typically from wherever you open or save documents. For example, here's where they would go in the SDI Rates of Return application:

```
// RatesOfReturnForm.cs
partial class RatesOfReturnForm : Form {
  ...
  void fileDocument_ReadDocument(
    object sender, SerializeDocumentEventArgs e) {
    ...
    // Add to MRU menu
    this.mruMenuManager.Add(e.Filename);
  }

  void fileDocument_WriteDocument(
    object sender, SerializeDocumentEventArgs e) {
    ...
    // Add to MRU menu
    this.mruMenuManager.Add(e.Filename);

    // Let file document take care of saving
    e.Handled = false;
  }
  ...
}
```

As you can see, MruMenuManager.Add works very nicely from handlers for the File-Document component's ReadDocument and WriteDocument events.

As it turns out, that's the minimum work you need to do to get an MRU menu to display MRU menu items. MruMenuManager ensures that only a maximum number of characters are displayed; that the last menu item you added is moved to the top of the list; and that each item has a number access key, from 1 to the maximum number of allowable items. But displaying menu items is only half the job; the other half is to handle user selection of those items to open the corresponding files.

Opening an MRU File

For users to open a file from the MRU menu, MruMenuManager needs a file path, and it needs to know when an MRU menu item is clicked so that it can notify the client application, which implements the deserialization logic to open a file. To manage this, MruMenu-Manager uses a custom tool strip menu item both to store the file path and to hook its Click event. When the custom tool strip menu item is clicked, it extracts the associated file path and fires the MruMenuItemClick event, to which it passes the file path via an MruMenu-ItemClickEventArgs. Your application should handle MruMenuItemClick by calling the appropriate file open method:

```
// RatesOfReturnForm.cs
partial class RatesOfReturnForm : Form {
  ...
  void mruMenuManager_MruMenuItemClick(
    object sender, MruMenuItemClickEventArgs e) {

    this.fileDocument.Open(e.Filename);
  }
  ...
}
```

In some cases, the file pointed to by an MRU menu item may have been deleted or moved, thereby breaking the MRU menu item. In these cases, MruMenuManager fires the MruMenuItemFileMissing event, passing an MruMenuItemFileMissingEventArgs object. This object includes the path to the missing file and an option to have MruMenuManager remove the file from the MRU menu or keep it there. Consequently, you can allow the user to decide what to do when a file goes walkabout:

```
// RatesOfReturnForm.cs
partial class RatesOfReturnForm : Form {
  ...
  void mruMenuManager_MruMenuItemFileMissing(
    object sender, MruMenuItemFileMissingEventArgs e) {

    DialogResult res =
      MessageBox.Show(
        "Remove " + e.Filename + "?",
        "Remove?",
        MessageBoxButtons.YesNo);
    if( res == DialogResult.Yes ) {
      e.RemoveFromMru = true;
    }
  }
  ...
}
```

When you set RemoveFromMru to true, MruMenuManager removes the related item from the MRU menu, never to be seen again.

Persisting the MRU Menu across Application Sessions

One thing you do want to be seen again is the MRU menu, with menu items, the next time users open your application. Because the files that make up the MRU Menu are dictated by the current user of the current application, it makes sense to leverage Windows Forms settings support to store MRU files on a per-user basis.[10] MruMenuManager does this via two properties: UseSettings and SettingsKey.

UseSettings is a Boolean that allows you to choose whether your MRU menu items are automatically stored as user settings; by default, it is true. SettingsKey is the string key value that MruMenuManager uses to distinguish its settings in the user.config file. By default, the SettingsKey value is set to MruMenuManager.MruItems, although you can change it as necessary. So, by default, your items are persisted to user.config:

```xml
<?xml version="1.0" encoding="utf-8"?>
<configuration>
  ...
  <userSettings>
    <MruControlLibrary.MruMenuManagerSettings.MruMenuManager.MruItems>
      <setting name="MruListItems" serializeAs="Xml">
        <value>
          <ArrayOfString xmlns:xsi="http://www.w3.org/..."
                         xmlns:xsd="http://www.w3.org/...">
            <string>C:\...\Desktop\S&P.ror</string>
            <string>C:\...\OakmarkFund.ror</string>
          </ArrayOfString>
        </value>
      </setting>
    </MruControlLibrary.MruMenuManagerSettings.MruMenuManager.MruItems>
  </userSettings>
</configuration>
```

If you prefer to control when settings are loaded and saved, you can eschew the default behavior by setting UseSettings to false and calling MruMenuManager.Load-Settings and MruMenuManager.SaveSettings directly. Alternatively, you can retrieve the list of file paths stored via MruMenuManager.FileNames and persist them somewhere beyond the domain of MruMenuManager. In most cases, the default, automatic option should do the trick.

MruMenuManager and MDI Applications

MruMenuManager requires a little more effort when used by MDI applications. Even though the MDI parent form handles File | Open, it's the FileDocument component on the MDI child form that does the work of reading the actual document. Furthermore, the MDI child form handles File | Save, using its FileDocument to write the document. The MDI parent form needs to detect when both reading and writing occurs to update its MRU menu appropriately. Consequently, the MDI parent form must handle the ReadDocument and

---

[10] See Chapter 15: Settings for the lowdown on application and user settings.

WriteDocument events that are raised by the MDI child form's FileDocument Component. First, this means exposing the FileDocument component from the MDI child form:

```
// RatesOfReturnForm.cs
partial class RatesOfReturnForm : Form {
  ...
  public FileDocument FileDocument {
    get { return this.fileDocument; }
  }
  ...
}
```

This allows the MDI parent form to hook the appropriate events:

```
// MdiParentForm.cs
partial class MdiParentForm : Form {
  ...
  void newToolStripMenuItem_Click(object sender, EventArgs e) {
    // Create and show a new child
    RatesOfReturnForm child = new RatesOfReturnForm();
    HookMDIChildFileDocument(child);
    child.MdiParent = this;
    child.Show();
  }
  ...
  void HookMDIChildFileDocument(RatesOfReturnForm mdiChild) {
    mdiChild.FileDocument.ReadDocument +=
      MDIChildFileDocument_ReadDocument;

    mdiChild.FileDocument.WriteDocument +=
      MDIChildFileDocument_WriteDocument;

    mdiChild.FormClosing +=
      MDIChild_FormClosing;
  }

  void UnhookMDIChildFileDocument(RatesOfReturnForm mdiChild) {
    mdiChild.FileDocument.ReadDocument -=
      MDIChildFileDocument_ReadDocument;

    mdiChild.FileDocument.WriteDocument -=
      MDIChildFileDocument_WriteDocument;

    mdiChild.FormClosing -=
      MDIChild_FormClosing;
  }
```

```
    . . .
    void MDIChildFileDocument_ReadDocument(
      object sender, SerializeDocumentEventArgs e) {
      // Add to MRU menu
      this.mruMenuManager.Add(e.Filename);
    }

    void MDIChildFileDocument_WriteDocument(
      object sender, SerializeDocumentEventArgs e) {
      // Add to MRU menu
      this.mruMenuManager.Add(e.Filename);

      // Let file document take care of saving
      e.Handled = false;
    }

    void MDIChild_FormClosing(object sender, FormClosingEventArgs e) {
      UnhookMDIChildFileDocument((RatesOfReturnForm)sender);
    }
  }
```

As you can see, even though you have to spread the code over two forms, it isn't much different with the MDI child Rates of Return form from what it is with the SDI Rates of Return form.

Opening Files Dragged and Dropped from the Shell

SDI and MDI applications currently provide two mechanisms for opening files: the File | Open menu or double-clicking a file in the shell. However, there's a common file open mechanism that's missing: allowing users to drag files from the shell and drop them onto the application.

To detect when a file is dropped onto an application's main form, the application needs to filter its Windows message queue for the message that's sent whenever one or more files are dropped. To do that, your application registers an IMessageFilter (from System.Windows.Forms) implementation and broadcasts its ability to accept dropped files by calling the DragAcceptFiles function from the shell32.dll.

When the IMessageFilter implementation detects the dropped-files message, it calls the DragQueryFile function to determine how many files are being dropped; then it gets the file name of each one by again calling DragQueryFile, this time passing an index to the required file. When processing is complete, the IMessageFilter implementation must call DragFinish to release memory allocated by the system for this operation. After the set of file names is retrieved, it is passed to the client for processing.

Assembling this code, although fun, isn't necessary, because you'll find a component with the book's samples at our web site (http://www.sellsbrothers.com/writing/wfbook) a component, DragAndDropFileComponent, that you can drop onto a form to provide this support.[11]

When this component is on the form, you can configure DragAndDropFileComponent's FileDropped event, as shown in Figure F.21, to detect when files are dropped onto your application so that they can be processed as the application sees fit.

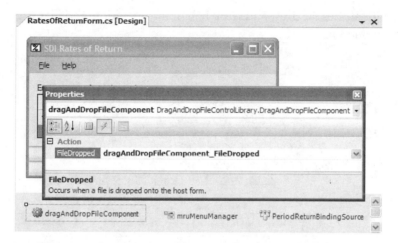

Figure F.21   Handling the DragAndDropFileComponent's FileDropped Event from the Properties Window

When DragAndDropFileComponent is hosted on a form, it fires the FileDropped event whenever one or more files are dragged from the shell onto the host form at any one time. The FileDropped event handler is passed a FileDroppedEventArgs from which you determine the files that were dropped (it could be more than one) and use this information to open it:

```csharp
partial class RatesOfReturnForm : Form {
  ...
  void dragAndDropFileComponent_FileDropped(
    object sender, FileDroppedEventArgs e) {

    // Process each file
    foreach( string filename in e.Filenames ) {
      // Only open files with the appropriate extension
      string extension = Path.GetExtension(filename);
```

[11] This component relies on P/Invoke with shell32.dll to do its magic, and it was inspired by a nice VB.NET sample provided by Matthew Day, at http://www.codeproject.com/vb/net/vbnetdragdrop.asp (http://tinysells.com/41).

```
      if( extension == ".ror" ) {
        OpenDocument(filename);
      }
      else {
        MessageBox.Show("Can't open files of type " + extension);
      }
    }
  }
}
```

Figure F.22 illustrates the drag-and-drop half of the operation, and Figure F.23 shows the consequently opened file.

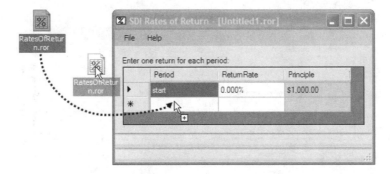

Figure F.22   Dragging and Dropping a File from the Shell onto an Application

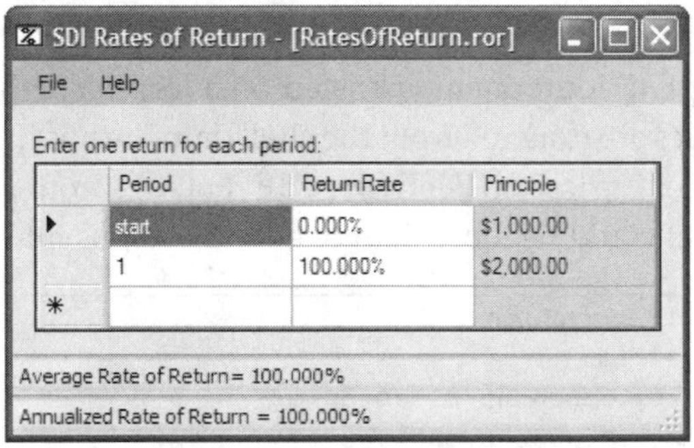

Figure F.23   The Dropped File Is Opened

Note that for MDI applications, DragAndDropFileComponent must be dropped onto the MDI parent form, because this is the form that is exposed to the shell. However, when the component is dropped, the code to handle the FileDropped event on an MDI parent is the same as for SDI applications.

Bibliography

The following resources either were used to prepare this book or are good resources for more information.

Ballard, Paul. "Give Your Everyday Custom Collections a Design-Time Makeover." *MSDN Magazine*, August 2005.

Box, Don, with Chris Sells. *Essential .NET, Volume 1: The Common Language Runtime*. Boston: Addison-Wesley, 2003.

Brumme, Chris. "Asynchronous Operations, Pinning." *Chris Brumme's WebLog*, http://blogs.msdn.com/cbrumme/archive/2003/05/06/51385.aspx, May 2005.

Calvo, Alex. "Timers: Comparing the Timer Classes in the .NET Framework Class Library." *MSDN Magazine*, February 2004.

Celko, Joe. *Instant SQL Programming*. Birmingham, UK: Wrox Press, 1995.

Chiu, Peter. ntcopyres.exe. http://www.codeguru.com/cpp_mfc/rsrc-simple.html, October 2001.

Draine, Sean. "Bootstrapper: Use the Visual Studio 2005 Bootstrapper to Kick-Start Your Installation." *MSDN Magazine*, October 2004.

Foley, James D., Andries Van Dam, and Steven K. Feiner. *Introduction to Computer Graphics*. Reading, MA: Addison-Wesley, 1993.

Fosler, Jessica. "Creating Applications with NotifyIcon in Windows Forms." *Windows Forms .NET*, http://www.windowsforms.net/articles/notifyiconapplications.aspx, March 2004.

Fosler, Jessica. "Suggestions for Making your managed Dialogs Snappier." *JFo's Coding*, http://blogs.msdn.com/jfoscoding/archive/2005/03/04/385625.aspx, March 2005.

Griffiths, Ian. "Opening Component Classes in Code view in Visual Studio .NET." *IanG on Tap*, http://www.interact-sw.co.uk/iangblog/2004/06/10/codeviewinvs, October 2004.

Harsh, Mike. "DesignModeDialog Sample." *Mike Harsh's Blog*, http://blogs.msdn.com/mharsh/archive/2005/03/14/395304.aspx, March 2005.

Lacouture-Amaya, Miguel. "Text Rendering: Support Complex Scripts in Windows Forms Controls to Build World-Ready Applications." *MSDN Magazine*, March 2006.

Lhotka, Rockford. "Windows Forms Data Binding." *MSDN Online*, February 2003.

Mackenzie, Duncan, with Noyes, Brian. *Smart Client Deployment with ClickOnce*. Boston: Addison-Wesley, 2006.

Microsoft Developer Network. http://msdn.microsoft.com.

Noyes, Brian. "Configuring ClickOnce Trusted Publishers." *MSDN Online*, April 2005.

Noyes, Brian. *Data Binding with Windows Forms 2.0*. Boston: Addison-Wesley, January 2006.

Onion, Fritz. *Essential ASP.NET*. Boston: Addison-Wesley, 2003.

PInvoke .NET. http://www.pinvoke.net.

Rammer, Ingo. *Advanced .NET Remoting*. Berkeley, CA: APress, 2002.

Richter, Jeffrey. *Applied Microsoft .NET Framework Programming*. Redmond, WA: Microsoft Press, 2002.

Richter, Jeffrey. "Run-time Serialization." *MSDN Magazine*, April 2002.

Sano, Chris. "Custom Windows Forms Controls: ColorPicker.NET." *MSDN Online*, http://msdn.microsoft.com/library/default.asp?url=/library/en-us/dnwinforms/html/colorpicker.asp, March 2005.

Sells, Chris. ".NET Delegates: A C# Bedtime Story." http://www.sellsbrothers.com/writing/delegates.htm, 2001.

Sells, Chris. "Safe, Simple Multithreading in Windows Forms." *MSDN Online*, June 2002.

Sells, Chris. "Components Are Not Just For GUIs." *Windows Developer Magazine Online*, http://www.windevnet.com/documents/s=7481/win1027981809543/, July 2002.

Sells, Chris. "A Second Look at Windows Forms Multithreading." *MSDN Online*, September 2002.

Sells, Chris. "Resources and WinForms." *Windows Developer Magazine Online*, http://www.sellsbrothers.com/writing/ResourcesAndWinForms.htm, September 2002.

Sells, Chris. "Safe, Simple Multithreading in Windows Forms, Part 2." *MSDN Online*, September 2002.

Sells, Chris. "Creating Non-Rectangular Windows." *Windows Developer Magazine Online*, http://www.windevnet.com/documents/s=7535/win1034118484572/1003cso.html, October 2002.

Sells, Chris. "Increasing Permissions for Web-Deployed WinForms Applications." *MSDN Online*, November 2002.

Sells, Chris. ".NET Image Re-Coloring." *Windows Developer Magazine Online*, http://www.sellsbrothers.com/writing/DotNetImageReColoring.htm, November 2002.

Sells, Chris. "WinForms Auto-Scaling." *Windows Developer Magazine Online*, http://www.sellsbrothers.com/writing/winformsAutoScaling.htm, November 2002.

Sells, Chris. "WinForms Data Validation." *Windows Developer Magazine Online*, http://www.sellsbrothers.com/writing/winformsDataValidation.htm, November 2002.

Sells, Chris. "Windows Forms Layout." *MSDN Online*, December 2002.

Sells, Chris. "Safe, Simple Multithreading in Windows Forms, Part 3." *MSDN Online*, January 2003.

Sells, Chris. "Microsoft .NET Framework Resource Basics." *MSDN Online*, February 2003.

Sells, Chris. "Serialization Basics, Part 1." *Windows Developer Magazine Online*, http://www.windevnet.com/documents/s=7481/win1044571786904/, February 2003.

Sells, Chris. "Serialization Basics, Part 2." *Windows Developer Magazine Online*, http://www.windevnet.com/documents/s=7481/win1045093344162/, February 2003.

Sells, Chris. "Printer Margins, Part 1." *Windows Developer Magazine Online*, http://www.windevnet.com/documents/s=7481/win1048094898724/, March 2003.

Sells, Chris. "Serialization Basics, Part 3." *Windows Developer Magazine Online*, http://www.windevnet.com/documents/s=7481/win1046801931106/, March 2003.

Sells, Chris. "Windows Forms: .NET Framework 1.1 Provides Expanded Namespace, Security, and Language Support for Your Projects." *MSDN Magazine*, March 2003.

Sells, Chris. "Printer Margins, Part 2." *Windows Developer Magazine Online*, http://www.windevnet.com/documents/s=7481/win1049396577703/, April 2003.

Sells, Chris. "Creating Document-Centric Applications in Windows Forms, Part 1." *MSDN Online*, September 2003.

Sells, Chris. "Creating Document-Centric Applications in Windows Forms, Part 2." *MSDN Online*, October 2003.

Sells, Chris. "Creating Document-Centric Applications in Windows Forms, Part 3." *MSDN Online*, November 2003.

Sells, Chris. Genghis class library. http://www.genghisgroup.com.

Skinner, Morgan. DebugIEHost Registry setting. http://discuss.develop.com/archives/wa.exe?A2=ind0109A&L=DOTNET&P=R9256&I=-3, September 2001.

Weinhardt, Michael. "Smart Tags: Simplify UI Development with Custom Designer Actions in Visual Studio." *MSDN Magazine*, July 2005.

Weinhardt, Michael, and Chris Sells. "Regular Expressions in .NET." *Windows Developer Magazine*, http://www.wd-mag.com/documents/s=7547/win0212d/, November 2002.

Weinhardt, Michael, and Chris Sells. "Building Windows Forms Controls and Components with Rich Design-Time Features, Part 1." *MSDN Magazine*, April 2003.

Weinhardt, Michael, and Chris Sells. "Building Windows Forms Controls and Components with Rich Design-Time Features, Part 2." *MSDN Magazine*, May 2003.

Weinhardt, Michael, and Chris Sells. ".NET Framework 2.0: Craft a Rich UI for your .NET App with Enhanced Windows Forms Support." *MSDN Magazine*, May 2004.

Weinhardt, Michael, and Chris Sells. "Draft a Rich UI: Ground Rules for Building Enhanced Windows Forms Support into Your .NET App." *MSDN Magazine*, May 2005.

Weinhardt, Michael, and Chris Sells. "Smart Clients: Draft a Rich UI For Your .NET App With Enhanced Windows Forms Support." *MSDN Magazine, Special Edition*, March 2006.

Windows Forms .NET. http://www.windowsforms.net.

The material from the following *MSDN Magazine* articles served as the basis for various topics throughout the book:

Weinhardt, Michael, and Chris Sells. ".NET Framework 2.0: Craft a Rich UI for your .NET App with Enhanced Windows Forms Support." *MSDN Magazine*, May 2004.

Weinhardt, Michael, and Chris Sells. "Draft a Rich UI: Ground Rules for Building Enhanced Windows Forms Support into Your .NET App." *MSDN Magazine*, May 2005.

Weinhardt, Michael, and Chris Sells. "Smart Clients: Craft a Rich UI For Your .NET App With Enhanced Windows Forms Support." *MSDN Magazine, Special Edition*, March 2006.

The material from the following *MSDN Magazine* articles served as the basis for Chapter 11: Design-Time Integration: The Properties Window, and Chapter 12: Design-Time Integration: Designers and Smart Tags:

Weinhardt, Michael, and Chris Sells. "Building Windows Forms Controls and Components with Rich Design-Time Features, Part 1." *MSDN Magazine*, April 2003.

Weinhardt, Michael, and Chris Sells. "Building Windows Forms Controls and Components with Rich Design-Time Features, Part 2." *MSDN Magazine*, May 2003.

Weinhardt, Michael. "Smart Tags: Simplify UI Development with Custom Designer Actions in Visual Studio." *MSDN Magazine*, July 2005.

Index

S

safety, multithreading, 743–746, 748–750
Sano, Chris, 925
Save dialog, 816
SaveFileDialog component, 101, 328, 823
saving
    application settings, 611
    graphics settings, 205–207
scaling
    controls, automatic scaling, 163–166
    fonts, 271–272
    images, 212–214
    transforms, 270–272
scope settings, 20, 590, 593
screen, drawing to, 180–183
screen captures, 834
Screen class, 586–587
screen copying images, 222–223
scripts, 257
ScrollableControl base class, 391
scrolling, 284
    custom controls, 390–392
SDI (Single Document Interface), 839
    applications, 549
    multiple-SDI application, 563–572
    windows, 1
SDK command line compilers, 506
searches, Help, 133
searching data, 711, 714–716
Secure Sockets Layer (SSL) certificates, 798
security, ClickOnce deployment, 798
    CAS (code access security), 808–814
    code signing, 798–807
Security dialog, 816
security exceptions, CAS, 816
Security Warning dialog, 782–783, 792,
    806–807
Sells, Chris, xxxiii, xxxvi, 2
Sells, John, xxxvii
Sells, Melissa, xxxvii
Sells, Tom, xxxvii
Sellsbrothers.com, 867
Send/Receive Progress dialog (Outlook), 99
SetDigitSubstitution( ) method, 247–248
SetPropertyName( ) method, 424–426
SetTabStops( ) method, 245–246
settings
    applications, 20–23, 579, 590
        alternative storage, 625–628
        Application settings, 19, 589–603

compile-time settings, 579–582
configuration files, 596–597
Configuration Manager, 599–601
designer settings, 617–625
editing, 592–595
environment, 579–589
loading and inspecting, 607–609
managing, 591
migrating, 613–614, 616
roaming-user settings, 589–603
rolling back, 611–613
run-time settings, 582–589
saving, 611
scope, 590
settings files, 590–591
strongly typed settings, 604–614, 616
types, 590
updating, 609–610
user configuration files, 601–603
User settings, 19, 589–603
    printers, 308–315
    Windows Forms 2.0, improvements to,
        839–840
settings class, 606–607
Settings Designer, 617–625
Settings Editor, 591
settings files, 590–591
settings providers, 608
SettingsSingleFileGenerator custom tool, 604
shapes, drawing, 203
    curves, 203–205
    graphics settings, 205–207
    smoothing modes, 205
shaping (BindingSource), 653
shared data, multithreading user interfaces,
    763–766
shearing transforms, 275–278
ShearTransform( ) method, 278
shell integration, 940–945
    MFC, 854
shells
    dragged and dropped files, opening,
        954–956
    Windows, 256–257
Shibata, Hodaka, xxxvi
ShouldSerializePropertyName( ) method,
    440, 442
Show( ) method, 2–3
ShowDialog( ) method, 3, 27, 42
ShowHelp property, 308
ShowIcon property, 65

Microsoft .NET Development Series

.NET Framework Standard Library Annotated Reference
Volume 1: Base Class Library and Extended Numerics Library

Brad Abrams

0321154894

.NET Framework Standard Library Annotated Reference
Volume 2: Networking Library, Reflection Library and XML Library

Brad Abrams
Tamara Abrams

0321194454

.NET Web Services
Architecture and Implementation

Keith Ballinger

0321113594

A First Look at SQL Server 2005 for Developers

Bob Beauchemin
Niels Berglund
Dan Sullivan

0321180593

Visual Studio Tools for Office
Using C# with Excel, Word, Outlook, and InfoPath

Eric Carter
Eric Lippert

0321334884

Visual Studio Tools for Office
Using Visual Basic 2005 with Excel, Word, Outlook, and InfoPath

Eric Carter
Eric Lippert

0321411757

Graphics Programming with GDI+

Mahesh Chand

0321160770

Framework Design Guidelines
Conventions, Idioms, and Patterns for Reusable .NET Libraries

Krzysztof Cwalina
Brad Abrams

0321246756

Enterprise Services with the .NET Framework
Developing Distributed Business Solutions with .NET Enterprise Services

Christian Nagel

032124673X

Data Binding with Windows Forms 2.0
Programming Smart Client Data Applications with .NET

Brian Noyes

032126892X

Essential ASP.NET with Examples in C#

Fritz Onion

0201760401

Windows Forms Programming in Visual Basic .NET

Chris Sells
Justin Gehtland

0321125193

The Visual Basic .NET Programming Language

Paul Vick

0321169514

THIS BOOK IS SAFARI ENABLED

INCLUDES FREE 45-DAY ACCESS TO THE ONLINE EDITION

The Safari® Enabled icon on the cover of your favorite technology book means the book is available through Safari Bookshelf. When you buy this book, you get free access to the online edition for 45 days.

Safari Bookshelf is an electronic reference library that lets you easily search thousands of technical books, find code samples, download chapters, and access technical information whenever and wherever you need it.

TO GAIN 45-DAY SAFARI ENABLED ACCESS TO THIS BOOK:

- Go to **http://www.awprofessional.com/safarienabled**

- Complete the brief registration form

- Enter the coupon code found in the front of this book on the "Copyright" page

Addison
Wesley